ALSO BY LARRY DIAMOND

Squandered Victory:
The American Occupation and the
Bungled Effort to Bring Democracy to Iraq

THE SPIRIT OF DEMOCRACY

THE SPIRIT OF DEMOCRACY

THE STRUGGLE TO BUILD FREE SOCIETIES
THROUGHOUT THE WORLD

LARRY DIAMOND

TIMES BOOKS

HENRY HOLT AND COMPANY   NEW YORK

Times Books
Henry Holt and Company, LLC
Publishers since 1866
175 Fifth Avenue
New York, New York 10010
www.henryholt.com

Henry Holt® is a registered trademark of
Henry Holt and Company, LLC.

Library of Congress Cataloging-in-Publication Data
Diamond, Larry Jay.
The spirit of democracy : the struggle to build free societies
throughout the world / Larry Diamond.
    p. cm.
Includes bibliographical references and index.
ISBN-13: 978-0-8050-7869-5
ISBN-10: 0-8050-7869-X
1. Democracy. 2. Democratization. I. Title.
JC423.D56 2008
321.8—dc22   2007037199

Henry Holt books are available for special promotions and
premiums. For details contact: Director, Special Markets.

First Edition 2008

Designed by Kelly S. Too

Printed in the United States of America
1   3   5   7   9   10   8   6   4   2

To Mahatma Gandhi, Václav Havel, and Aung San Suu Kyi,
and to all of those who have devoted their lives
to the struggle for freedom

The spirit of democracy cannot be imposed from without. It has to come from within.

The spirit of democracy is not a mechanical thing to be adjusted by abolition of forms. It requires change of the heart.

The true democrat is he who with purely nonviolent means defends his liberty and, therefore, his country's and ultimately that of the whole of mankind.

—MAHATMA GANDHI

CONTENTS

THE SPIRIT OF DEMOCRACY

INTRODUCTION

AT THE DAWN OF THE DEMOCRATIC ERA

I am a child of the Cold War, and this book has its genesis in that titanic struggle.

This may seem a strange way to begin a book about the prospects for universal democracy. The Cold War did not unite the world; it divided and bloodied it. Indeed, in October 1962, it came very close to destroying much of it. In the name of fighting global communism and "defending freedom," the United States often betrayed and undermined its own democratic values during that four-decade global contest, supporting the overthrow of democratically elected governments in Iran in 1953, in Guatemala in 1954, and in Chile in 1973 (among other covert interventions), while backing a host of right-wing military and monarchical dictatorships that took "our side." If this Cold War "realism" of advancing the national interest, no matter how unsavory the dictator we had to embrace, could be described in a phrase, one could hardly outdo Franklin Roosevelt's purported characterization of the Nicaraguan dictator Anastasio Somoza: "He may be a son of a bitch, but he's our son of a bitch."

Yet there was another more principled side to America's posture in the Cold War. In his 1961 inaugural address, President John F. Kennedy expressed it when he promised to "pay any price, bear any burden, meet any hardship, support any friend, oppose any foe, in order to assure the survival and the success of liberty." If these words could be interpreted as more of the same "realism," embracing any ally against the Communists,

Kennedy promised more. The United States would support the new post-colonial states in their struggle for real freedom, even while not always expecting them "to support our view." His America would help people around the world to help themselves "to break the bonds of mass misery." In the Americas, he would launch "an alliance for progress" to eliminate poverty and launch a "peaceful revolution of hope."

Kennedy's idealism was largely crushed by his perception of the imperatives in the battle against Communist expansion, drawing him (and the country) deeper and deeper into a disastrous engagement in Vietnam, and draining the military might, economic resources, diplomatic energy, and moral authority that might have been brought to bear to truly defend and expand freedom in the world. His assassination cut short what might have been a change in course, and led to two of the most cynical and coldly realist presidencies (in international terms) of our time, those of Lyndon Johnson and Richard Nixon. But the democratic and idealist impulse in the American national spirit—that we must stand *for* something in the world, and that something must involve our core founding faith in freedom—could not be extinguished. It returned first in President Jimmy Carter's initiative to promote and defend human rights, and then in Ronald Reagan's far more ambitious policy of promoting democracy, which established a number of institutions, principles, and initiatives that his presidential successors sustained. Still, throughout these various presidencies, the tension between two divergent visions of America's role in the world—realist and idealist—has endured.

My own engagement with the global quest for freedom began with Kennedy's inaugural address and his bold appeal to the country and the world. As a nine-year-old boy, I was deeply and (as it would turn out, enduringly) moved by his call "to bear the burden of a long twilight struggle, year in and year out, 'rejoicing in hope, patient in tribulation'— a struggle against the common enemies of man: tyranny, poverty, disease, and war itself." I could not possibly understand then what it all meant, but I believed that communism was evil, that dictatorship in all forms could not be tolerated, that people everywhere deserved to live in freedom and dignity. Kennedy's call inspired me to read about the world. I became fascinated with the new political leaders of what was then called the *Third World* and with the march to freedom of a vast number of countries in Asia and Africa that were then breaking the bonds of European colonial domination. I became captivated by the personal stories of Third World leaders like Jawaharlal Nehru, Sukarno, and Kwame Nkrumah.

My college years were dominated by the war in Vietnam and the growing mass movement against it on campuses throughout the United States. I came to see how a noble quest to stop the spread of communism had become blinded to the forces of nationalism and anticolonialism and obsessed with preserving an image of American steadfastness, at tragic cost. The result was a moral, humanitarian, and geopolitical disaster. As I watched the United States backing one dictatorship to stave off another, destroying villages in order to save them, I began to question other aspects of our foreign policy, and to criticize the distorted calculus of national interest that had led us to embrace—and even to usher into power—so many "friendly" dictatorships around the world. I believed we had to press for democracy and responsible governance among our own allies if we were going to be credible and effective in challenging our Communist enemies. Then, during my senior year in college, in one of the low points of a long sad history of American engagement in Latin America, the Chilean armed forces brutally overthrew the elected government of the Socialist president, Salvador Allende, and, it soon became clear, with backing from the Nixon administration. The clarion call of Kennedy's inaugural address had become a cruel joke, and my own alienation from what my government was doing around the world deepened.

Although I had been engaged, morally and politically, with world events, I had not yet actually seen the world. When I graduated in June 1974, I was determined to do that, and planned a six-month trip through some of the countries that had captured my attention. I began in late October of that year in Portugal, which six months before had just had a military revolution to overthrow a quasi-fascist dictatorship that had stood for half a century. The country was then locked in a fateful struggle between Communist and other radical leftist forces that sought to establish a new form of dictatorship and a diverse array of parties committed to a democratic future. From there I traveled to Nigeria as it was experiencing the first full flush of an oil boom and was supposed to be returning to democratic rule—only to have the military dictator, Yakubu Gowon, postpone the transition shortly before my arrival in December 1974. I continued on to Egypt and Israel as they were each emerging from the drama of the 1973 war, to Thailand as its new democracy was trying to find its footing (which it would ultimately fail to do), and then to Taiwan, one of the key authoritarian states in the East Asian miracle.

My month in Portugal in November 1974 marked the real beginning of my journey to understand what constitutes and sustains the spirit of democracy. There I observed for the first time a live political struggle for democracy. Having recently been an elected student body leader at a time when American universities and society were in upheaval, and having struggled against intolerant, Marxist revolutionary currents within the antiwar movement on my own college campus, I found familiar echoes in the political atmosphere of Lisbon.

However, in the United States during the late 1960s and early 1970s, the stakes had been limited: to end our enervating involvement in a misguided war, to terminate the military draft, to create a more just society, and to open up power and the full possibilities of American life to racial minorities and women. Beyond that, "the revolution" was never more than a fantasy; it had the potential to disrupt the academy, to discredit the quest for peaceful change, and to polarize the country. But it never seriously threatened our democratic institutions.

In Lisbon, I found familiar revolutionary slogans and zeal, and the same struggle between closed and open minds, between two types of quests for justice and social progress: through a ruthless ideological certainty or through a flexible, tolerant politics of dialogue, persuasion, and coalition building. There, however, a country's whole political future was at stake. Democracy hung in the balance.

I could not know what the outcome would be. But as I watched and interviewed for a month, two things struck me most. One was not just the differences in program and ideology, but the contrast in *spirit* between the drab, dogmatic, unquestioning atmosphere of the Communist Party, with its grim visages of Lenin and Stalin bearing down, and the life and color, the spontaneity and openness, the idealism and pragmatism, the faith in freedom and intellectual skepticism, as well as the turbulent creativity that infused the offices, meetings, and rallies of the principal democratic parties, the Socialist Party, the Popular Democratic Party, and the Social Democratic Center. The second was the commitment, talent, and nerve of the people I had met in the democratic parties and their obvious passion for freedom.

If nothing else, that experience taught me what much subsequent research, reading, travel, and reflection has reinforced: that the fate of democracy is not simply driven by abstract historical and structural forces. It is a consequence of struggle, strategy, ingenuity, vision, courage, conviction, compromise, and choices by human actors—of *politics* in the best sense of the word. This is some of what I mean by the *democratic spirit*. In the end, the democrats won in Portugal, in part because of the tenacity, courage, and skill of democrats like Mário Soares, leader of the Socialist Party, who would later become prime minister and then president, and in part because of the heavy investment Western democracies made in support of the democratic parties. That international solidarity to advance freedom was the harbinger of a much greater effort to come and the manifestation of another dimension of the democratic spirit.

I drew from the Portuguese experience, and from my experiences in Thailand and Nigeria, where democracy was so clearly and hopefully struggling to take root, a strong sense of democratic possibilities and an instinctive skepticism about the academic theories that would dismiss them out of hand for a whole class of countries. This led me, in graduate school, to make a choice that was then easily ridiculed among the rising ranks of my chosen discipline, sociology. Rather than studying the processes of economic development, state building, or revolution, or the forces of "international dependency" (and by frequent extension, international capitalist "exploitation") that were inhibiting autonomous development, I wanted to study democracy itself. I did not accept that democracy was a facade that did not matter to people, or that we had to give up hope for democracy in poor countries. If India could survive as a democracy for decades (with only a brief interruption), why not Nigeria? They were both poor, intensely divided along ethnic lines, and with British colonial traditions. Why did Nigeria's democracy break down in the mid-1960s, and with the traumatic fallout of a civil war? In my doctoral dissertation, I attempted to answer that question, and in doing so, I sought to identify the cultural, economic, political, and international factors that might foster and sustain democracy, even in the poorest countries. In the discipline of sociology in the late 1970s, my effort seemed to many quixotic and naive, if not absurd. Frequently my work was dismissed with the derisive declaration that the challenge was not to explain why democracy would fail in a place like Nigeria, but why it should be present anywhere outside the West, with its high levels of development and Judeo-Christian cultural traditions. I did not accept this way of looking at the world, intellectually or morally, and fortunately so. For the world was going to change during the next two decades in ways that neither my critics nor—frankly—I could possibly imagine.

As I document in the first part of this book, democracy would boom during the quarter century after the Portuguese revolution. That boom—what Samuel P. Huntington calls the *third wave* of global democratic expansion[1]—began slowly and imperceptibly with the transitions to democracy in Portugal, Spain, and Greece, then spread to Latin America, and then far and wide beyond. By the mid-1980s, about two in every five states were democratic. By the mid-1990s, after the Berlin Wall had fallen and the Soviet Union collapsed, about three in every five states were. The 1980s and '90s expressed the spirit of democracy in a third sense. During these two decades, democracy became a zeitgeist, literally (from the German) "the spirit of the time." While the term encompasses the entire cultural and intellectual climate of an era, it denotes politically "a feeling shared across national boundaries that a particular [form of political] system is the most desirable," typically reinforced by the perceived dynamism of powerful states "that are successful with a particular type of regime."[2] Just as the zeitgeist of the interwar period seemed to be fascism, that of the twentieth century's last two decades was democracy.

While the overall number of democracies more or less stabilized after 1995, the birth of more than ninety democracies in this period represents the greatest transformation of the way states are governed in the history of the world. By the mid-1990s, it had become clear to me, as it had to many of my colleagues involved in the global struggle for democracy, that if some three-fifths of the world's states (many of them poor and non-Western) could become democracies, there was no intrinsic reason why the rest of the world could not do so as well. But if this transformation is to be completed, we have to identify the historical and structural obstacles to democracy around the world and the conditions not only for getting to democracy but for sustaining it and making it work. That, in essence, is what this book aims to do. To begin, it is useful to recall what the world looked like in the mid-1970s and why the prospect of a democratic world seemed, so recently in historical time, such an illusion.

THE WORLD IN 1974

When the Movement of the Armed Forces overthrew the nearly fifty-year-old dictatorship in Portugal on April 25, 1974, there was no reason for anyone to expect that it would mean very much for the future of democracy. It was a grim time for freedom in the world. Just the previous October, the Chilean military had overthrown the Allende government in a bloody, traumatic coup, with the encouragement of an American administration obsessed with the Cold War struggle against Communist expansion. In the deadliest front of that struggle, the United States was in the process of disengaging from a war in Vietnam that had cost the lives of over fifty-eight thousand Americans and several million Vietnamese. U.S. efforts to shore up a corrupt and repressive South Vietnamese government were failing; by April 1975 Saigon would fall to the combined Communist forces of the Vietcong and the North Vietnamese Army, necessitating a hasty and humiliating American evacuation from the city and completing the first American military defeat in a major war. Worldwide, Soviet (and Chinese) power and self-confidence were waxing, as the Communist powers backed one after another Marxist and nationalist insurgency in Asia, Africa, and Latin America. As South Vietnam fell to Communist rule, so did Laos and Cambodia, empowering in the latter case one of the most murderous regimes of the twentieth century, the Khmer Rouge, believed responsible for the deaths of at least a million Cambodians (out of an original population of about 7 million). In the Soviet Union and its East European satellite states, totalitarian rule seemed secure for decades to come. Less than six years earlier, Alexander Dubček's effort to temper and reform Czechoslovakia's Communist system by granting more freedom and creating "socialism with a human face" had been crushed by Soviet tanks. Back home, American democracy was mired in the depths of the Watergate scandal, as President Nixon obstructed justice and abused his constitutional authority in a desperate bid to cling to power, before finally resigning in August 1974.

In April 1974, dictatorship, not democracy, was the way of the world. Barely a quarter of independent states chose their governments through competitive, free, and fair elections. Most of those were the wealthy capitalist countries of the "West" plus a number of small island states with British colonial legacies. Save for Costa Rica, Venezuela, and Colombia, Latin America was under repressive military rule or abusive civilian governments with heavy military influence. Brazil had been under military rule for a decade, and many were hailing a "miracle" of development under its modernizing autocrats, as investment poured in. The previous year, Argentina's former populist dictator, Juan Perón, had returned to Buenos Aires after eighteen years of exile to take the helm of an elected left-wing government with his wife, Isabel, as his vice president. Barely two months after the April revolution in Portugal, Perón died, and his hapless wife assumed office amid mounting corruption, left-wing guerrilla action, and right-wing terrorism, which brought the military back to power in 1976.

Meanwhile, East Asia (save for Japan) was being transformed economically by authoritarian, not democratic, states. South Korea, Taiwan, and

Singapore were recording spectacular rates of economic growth under authoritarian regimes that seemed to many scholars and observers to have the formula for rapid development: concentrate state power to generate high savings, steer investment to critical industries, repress labor unions, keep wages low, ensure political "stability," and so attract high levels of foreign investment. In the mid-1960s, Indonesia followed suit under General Suharto's "New Order" regime. After an exceptionally bloody campaign to liquidate non-Communist Asia's largest Communist movement, claiming perhaps several hundred thousand lives, Suharto's dictatorship quickly "produced a new surge of orderly development in what had been Southeast Asia's most obvious case of arrested development."[3] The Thai military also sought to refashion itself, or portray itself, in this efficient, "bureaucratic authoritarian" mold. The model was profoundly alluring not only to Asian societies hungry for development but to American policy makers desperate for pro-American success stories that could stand up to the Communist threat. Thus, when Philippine president Ferdinand Marcos (having failed to amend the constitution to remain in office beyond his second and final elected term) declared martial law in September 1972—overthrowing the 1935 constitution, assuming dictatorial powers, and locking up thirty thousand members of the opposition—his alliance with the United States drew even closer. But it was not just America's cynical connivance that enabled the demise of Philippine democracy. "What Marcos in 1972 was reflecting was an almost pan–Southeast Asian disgust with the outcomes produced by democratic politics."[4] With a similar type of claim to be defending civil order and economic development, Indian prime minister Indira Gandhi overturned the world's largest democracy in June 1975, suspending democratic elections and civil liberties under a state of emergency in order to neutralize a Supreme Court ruling that would have invalidated her own election and removed her from office. In less than two years, Gandhi would go down to a crushing defeat in elections she had overconfidently called, but the ease with which India's democratic institutions seemed to be swept aside was a further sobering blow to the democratic prospect at mid-decade.

In Africa, where the retreat of European colonial rule was less than two decades old, the picture was much grimmer still. Of the (then) thirty-eight states of sub-Saharan Africa, only three were democracies, and each of them—Botswana, Gambia, and Mauritius—had a million people or less. During the 1960s, Africa's biggest and most promising democracy,

Nigeria, had broken down amid debilitating ethnic strife, leading to a civil war in which as many as one million people may have died. South Africa was firmly in the grip of a racist, apartheid state. Mobutu Sese Seko had established in Zaire (the former Congo) one of the world's most savagely kleptocratic states, with the generous support of Western democracies eager for access to the country's vast mineral wealth. Most of the opposition—political and intellectual—to African dictatorships bore sympathy for socialism and a deep wariness of the capitalist West. Western intellectuals themselves were infatuated with Tanzania, the one-party socialist state of Julius Nyerere, taking little note of the way in which his agrarian socialist economic principles were running the country's economy into the ground. Wars of liberation were in the process of driving out the last European colonial presence, Portugal, but in countries like Mozambique and Angola the movements that were winning were Marxist and authoritarian, not democratic. As the new Portuguese military government withdrew its forces from Angola and Mozambique in 1975, these countries became independent under Marxist parties that were fighting civil wars against American-backed ethnic and ideological challengers. In September 1974, radical young military officers, also influenced by Marxist ideology and soon to ally with the Soviet Union, deposed Ethiopia's longtime pro-Western emperor, Haile Selassie, after a devastating drought and famine, ending his more than four decades of rule.

By the time Haile Selassie fell, almost all of sub-Saharan Africa was under military or one-party rule. So was the Arab world, where Lebanon was the only democracy, and one that would soon expire as the country descended into civil war. More broadly in the Middle East, there were democracies as well in Israel and Turkey, but Israel was considered a Western country in its culture and level of development. Turkey was a more encouraging case of a modernizing and secular Muslim country, but its democracy had significant military influence. And the Turkish model would be shaken during the second half of the 1970s by a slide into polarization, violence, and terrorism, which claimed more than five thousand lives until the September 1980 military coup.[5]

TRANSCENDING INTELLECTUAL PESSIMISM

In the mid-1970s, you had to be a crank or a romantic to believe that the bulk of the world's countries would become democratic over the next quarter century. In the academy, the comparative study of democracy had declined, and the most important work on democracy in the second half of the 1970s was on the breakdown of democratic regimes.[6] Only a few years before, in his classic work, *Polyarchy* (published in 1971), the esteemed Yale political scientist and democratic theorist Robert Dahl reached a pessimistic conclusion about the prospects for anything more than incremental progress toward *polyarchy,* by which he meant a reasonably democratic political system. Emphasizing the importance for democratic development of some history of political competition and "a tradition of toleration toward political oppositions," Dahl observed:

> It is unrealistic to suppose, then, that there will be any dramatic change in the number of polyarchies within a generation or two. . . . As with a great many things, the safest bet about a country's regime a generation from now is that it will be different, but not radically different, from what it is today.[7]

In 1984, even as a new, still unnamed wave of democratization was gathering steam, Samuel P. Huntington proffered a similar assessment. In a famous article—"Will More Countries Become Democratic?"— Huntington answered, in essence, not many.[8] Reviewing the economic, social, and cultural conditions that favor democratization, he predicted transitions only in a few of the more developed countries in Latin America and perhaps East Asia.

> The substantial power of anti-democratic governments (particularly the Soviet Union), the unreceptivity to democracy of several major cultural traditions, the difficulties of eliminating poverty in large parts of the world, and the prevalence of high levels of polarization and violence in many societies all suggest that, with a few exceptions, the limits of democratic development in the world may well have been reached.[9]

Just seven years later, Huntington would publish his book naming and tracing the stunning "third wave" of global democratic transformation.

The pessimism of the time was driven in part by the preeminence of *modernization* theory, which found a powerful correlation between democracy and the level of economic development. Most of the world's democracies in the early 1970s were the advanced industrial countries of the West. They sustained democracy, so the theory went, because they had high levels of education and personal income, and a large middle class. These features of development, in turn, bred among the general public the political knowledge and participation, the toleration of dissent and opposition, the inclination to political moderation and restraint, the desire for freedom and accountability, and the propensity to form and join independent organizations that made democracy possible. Such a broad political culture of democracy constitutes a key dimension of the *democratic spirit.* The famous political sociologist Seymour Martin Lipset termed these economic, social, and cultural factors the *social requisites of democracy,*[10] and while he did not intend for them to be, strictly, *pre*requisites, they were largely taken as such by scholars and policy makers during the 1960s and '70s. To be a democracy, a country first had to develop economically. So the logic was to side with and invest in modernizing authoritarian rulers—Chiang Kai-shek in Taiwan, Park Chung Hee in South Korea, Lee Kuan Yew in Singapore, Suharto in Indonesia, Ferdinand Marcos in the Philippines, the generals in Brazil and Chile, the shah of Iran—and eventually, with development, democracy would follow. Driving the logic in policy terms was the convenient fact that all these dictators were allies of the United States and the West in the Cold War. Siding with these dictatorships could even be justified in terms of our democratic values: they were transitional regimes, not permanent ones, and partial dictatorships, not total ones like the Communist movements that threatened them, and that they came to power to eliminate.[11] So to defend and advance freedom, we violated the spirit of democracy.

There was during this period a deeper form of pessimism, culturally based. It was no accident, so the argument went, that democracy had emerged largely in the West, with its Judeo-Christian and Enlightenment cultural traditions. The non-Western democracies of this period were mainly in countries that had been infused with the liberal cultural norms of the West, such as the former British colonies of India, Sri Lanka, and Jamaica, or Japan, which had been conquered and occupied by the United States after World War II. Elsewhere, the prospects were deemed thin. Writing in the mid-1960s, one prominent U.S. scholar of Latin America declared, "The social and cultural matrix within which Latin America's leaders operate at present is such that effective and representative popular democracy is, with really few exceptions, not a feasible alternative."[12] For another, the Catholic countries of Spain, Portugal, and especially Latin America were "probably ill-suited" to Western-style democracy, either because they were influenced by the hierarchical and authoritarian traditions of the Catholic Church or because their conception of democracy was of a Rousseauan tradition that feared excessive pluralism and viewed participation more in "organic, corporate, and group terms" than through the individualistic forms that have triumphed in the West.[13] Others argued that Asian culture, or Islamic culture, was not likely to be compatible with democracy because of its emphasis on order over freedom, consensus over competition, and the community over the individual.[14]

How did a world that seemed so naturally and even ineluctably authoritarian in 1975 become predominantly democratic by 1995? How could so many social science and foreign policy experts have been so wrong? That is the story of several of the early chapters of this book. But it is, unfortunately, not the whole story, or even really the story of the current moment.

As this book is written, the democratic boom has given way to recession. Its start, I argue, may be traced to the 1999 military coup in Pakistan, which symbolized the failure of many of the new democracies to perform decently in delivering development, social peace, and good governance. Since then, there have been setbacks to democracy in highly influential states such as Russia, Venezuela, Nigeria, and Thailand, and democracy is seriously deteriorating in other big, important countries like the Philippines and Bangladesh. China's rapidly rising power has heightened the authoritarian trend, giving many autocracies around the world a new strategic sponsor and apologist, eager for their natural resources and markets. The bold campaign by President George W. Bush to transform the Middle East by first overthrowing Saddam Hussein and transforming Iraq from dictatorship to democracy has backfired badly, leaving that country in chaos. With Islamists gaining political and frequently electoral ground throughout the region, even the Bush administration has pulled back from its own democracy agenda, and Arab democrats feel betrayed. Around the world, a backlash has gathered against international democracy promotion efforts, led by Russia and China, and such regional petropowers as Iran and Venezuela.

Many observers see in this downturn the natural limits of democratic possibilities. Out of the ashes of America's imperial overreach in Iraq, a new current of realist thinking is gathering that once again admonishes the United States to mind its own business and deal with the world as it is, not as we would like it to be. As the American interventions in Iraq and quite possibly Afghanistan become more embattled, this neorealism will likely gain ground.

There are genuine grounds for concern, sobriety, modesty, and reassessment—but not for democratic despair. As I show in this book, there remains considerable underlying momentum and potential for democratic progress in the world. Increasingly, democratic values and aspirations are becoming universal—even in the supposedly unfriendly Middle East and Muslim world more broadly. And these global democratic norms are reflected in regional and international institutions and agreements as never before. If we look at the causes of democratic expansion in the world, both domestic and international, we see that the factors that gave rise to the democratic boom are still very much alive. The central challenges are whether the new democracies can deliver what their peoples expect in terms of development and decent, lawful governance, and whether the rich, established democracies can summon the will and wisdom to refashion and sustain their efforts to promote democracy.

The second part of this book looks at the challenges of democratic development and consolidation in each of the regions where democracy has yet to take deep root: Latin America, postcommunist Europe, Asia, Africa, and the Middle East. These chapters show wide variation in democratic progress and prospects, but also the urgent need to combat corruption and strengthen the ability of states to provide a rule of law and an enabling environment for economic growth. Yet, where there are threats to democracy, there are also opportunities. Even countries like Iran and China, which now seem so immune to the global democratic trend, stand a very good chance of becoming democratic in the next two to three decades. And if China can democratize, why not the entire world?

In the end, I maintain, it is the policies and the collective will of the established democracies that could make the crucial difference. The last three decades have unleashed unprecedented hopes and expectations for democratic development, even quite remarkably in poor countries. Now, democracy is really the only broadly legitimate form of government in the world. The enemies of democracy—such as the global jihadist movement of radical Islam—can win only if democrats defeat themselves through arrogance, intransigence, ineptitude, and greed. History has seen no shortage of those features of human nature, which have played a large role in previous breakdowns of democracy. But human progress follows from the capacity to learn from and transcend our failings. The underlying dynamics of global economic and political development, and the broad trends in world culture and institutions, remain quite favorable to democracy in the long run. Shrewd and visionary policies emanating from the established democracies—led, but in a far more collegial fashion, by the United States—could reignite and sustain global democratic momentum. Then the horizon of the long run might draw considerably nearer to the point where, some few decades hence, the whole world could capture the spirit of democracy.

PART ONE

A WORLD PARTIALLY TRANSFORMED

1

THE UNIVERSAL VALUE

Since the American and French revolutions, two views of liberty have contested. One is that these revolutions expressed universal rights and values. The American Declaration of Independence did not assert a peculiarly American right to "life, liberty and the pursuit of happiness." It declared that "all men are created equal, that they are endowed by their Creator with certain unalienable Rights." It asserted, as a general rule under "the Laws of Nature and of Nature's God," "That to secure these rights, Governments are instituted among Men, deriving their just powers from the consent of the governed." Although many of the founding fathers of American democracy doubted how far freedom could really travel, implicit in their language, and in much of America's engagement with the world since then, has been a belief in the universal promise and possibility of democracy.

The second view of liberty has been that if people are in some sense created equal, they are nevertheless not imbued with the same values and expectations of government. Freedom and democracy are not universal values but rather Western concepts. Culture limits how far they can travel. One of the most famous advocates of this position has been the longtime prime minister of Singapore, Lee Kuan Yew, who, in trumpeting the Asian values of order, family, and community, has made it his "business to tell people not to foist their system indiscriminately on societies in which it will not work."[1] In a 2001 interview on the PBS show *Commanding Heights,* he observed:

> I do not believe you can impose on other countries standards which are alien and totally disconnected with their past. So to ask China to become a democracy, when in its 5,000 years of recorded history it never counted heads; all rulers ruled by right of being the emperor, and if you disagree, you chop off heads, not count heads. . . .
>
> The agenda must include human rights. But I don't think you can impose on them how they should govern themselves, whether they should have one man, one vote to elect a president, or whether they should be governed in some other way. I don't think . . . it's wise or practical to ask other societies to follow your system of government. They may not be ready for it.[2]

Lee's skepticism has been matched by a significant body of academic analysis arguing that there are distinct Asian values, and that they do not fit well with Western liberal notions of democracy. In an influential 1985 book, one of America's most distinguished scholars of Asia, the MIT political scientist Lucian Pye, argued that Asian societies generally lack the individualism and suspicion of authority that have made for successful democracy in the West. Asian societies, he argued, stress loyalty to the family and group over individual freedom and needs, defer to authority in order to "answer deep psychological cravings for the security of dependency," and value order over conflict. To the extent that democracy exists at all, he explained, it is the kind of shallow or illiberal democracy that mutes criticism of authority, scraps checks and balances, and concentrates political power in individual leaders.[3]

In a variety of ways, this cultural skepticism has also been applied to Latin America as well as the Middle East. Particularly prior to the late 1970s, prominent scholars of Latin America saw the region as steeped in "absolutist, elitist, hierarchical, corporatist, and authoritarian" cultural traditions, "inherited from Spain," that were "not conducive to democratic rule."[4] Jeanne Kirkpatrick, President Ronald Reagan's ambassador to the United Nations, once said, "The Arab world is the only part of the world where I've been shaken in my conviction that if you let the people decide, they will make fundamentally rational decisions. But there, they don't make rational decisions, they make fundamentalist ones."[5]

This view continues to shape the way the West thinks about the possibilities for Arab democracy. In 1992, the late conservative British historian Elie Kedourie penned this sweeping dismissal.

> There is nothing in the political traditions of the Arab world—which are the political traditions of Islam—which might make familiar, or indeed intelligible, the organizing ideas of constitutional and representative government. The notion . . . of a popular sovereignty as the foundation of governmental legitimacy, the idea of representation, of elections, of popular suffrage, of political institutions being regulated by laws laid down by a parliamentary assembly, of these laws being guarded and upheld by an independent judiciary, the ideas of the secularity of the state, of society being composed of a multitude of self-activating autonomous groups and associations—all these are profoundly alien to the Muslim political tradition.[6]

Instead, Kedourie argued, that tradition was one of highly centralized, absolute rule by a religious caliph over a community "not defined by any permanent territorial frontiers" and thus inclined to war to expand those frontiers. Attempts at democracy in the Arab world had "uniformly failed," first and foremost because these countries "had been accustomed to . . . autocracy and passive obedience."[7]

In the midst of the staggering failure of the George W. Bush administration's project to bring democracy to Iraq, many foreign policy thinkers and commentators once again trumpet a general pointlessness or danger in trying to promote democracy in the Arab world. It is not difficult to see in the Iraq calamity striking confirmation of Samuel P. Huntington's thesis of a "clash of civilizations" and of his warning that "those who do not recognize fundamental [civilizational] divides are doomed to be frustrated by them."[8] In 1996, Huntington wrote with pessimism about the global prospects for liberal democracy.

> The West differs from other civilizations . . . in the distinctive character of its values and institutions. These include most notably its Christianity, pluralism, individualism, and rule of law. . . . In their ensemble these characteristics are peculiar to the West.

He agreed with Arthur M. Schlesinger Jr. that Europe was "the source— the *unique* source" of the "ideas of individual liberty, political democracy, rule of law, human rights, and cultural freedom." In Huntington's words,

"They make Western civilization unique, and Western civilization is valuable not because it is universal but because it *is* unique."[9]

Not only are the liberal democratic values of the West not universal, but in addition, Huntington warned—in what some skeptics might now view as a prophetic insight—the effort to diffuse them across cultural divides would require force. "Imperialism is the necessary logical consequence of universalism." Therefore, the United States and Europe should "recognize that Western intervention in the affairs of other civilizations is probably the single most dangerous source of instability and potential global conflict in a multicivilizational world."[10] In the wake of the Iraq debacle, Huntington's cynicism is seductive. Cultural arguments about the limits to democracy are fashionable again. But are they right?

My purpose in writing this book is to answer this audacious question: can the whole world become democratic? Is it really possible to build free and democratic societies throughout the world? Doing so must involve more than the creation of new political structures; it requires the generation of new *norms,* as Gandhi put it, "change of the heart." Democratic structures will be mere facades unless people come to value the essential principles of democracy: popular sovereignty, accountability of rulers, freedom, and the rule of law. And without those essential principles in place, those seeming democracies will eventually give way to tyranny, whether in civilian or military guise. But is the spirit of democracy largely confined to Western culture, or is it a universal norm and aspiration?

Quite apart from whether one finds them offensive or alluring, notions of the inherent cultural limits to freedom do not stand up to logic or evidence. Not only is there a powerful range of philosophical and religious argument against them, much of it from *non*-Western thinkers and leaders, but the view of democracy as particular to Western culture does not square with the growing body of public opinion survey data, which shows considerable support for democracy around the world. Neither does it fit with the trends in international law and treaties. All of these suggest that some universal values are beginning to emerge in the world, and two of them are liberty and democracy.

WHAT IS THE DEMOCRATIC VALUE?

It is useful at this point to pause and consider a bit more closely what is necessary for a country to be termed a *democracy.* To many Americans, and to many others who live or believe they live in a democracy, the term is so intuitive it seems straightforward. In a democracy, people have the right to choose their leaders in regular, free, and fair elections. But how many "people" are we talking about? Is a political system democratic if some of its citizens are denied the right to vote and run for office? What if a lot of people just don't care and drop out? Elections must be openly competitive to be free. That means allowing multiple parties to compete. But must the electoral arena be open to any party, no matter its creed or values? What about personal freedom? Isn't democracy also about the individual freedoms embedded in the American Bill of Rights, the Universal Declaration of Human Rights, and so many national and international charters and covenants dating back decades and in fact centuries? Can a country be a democracy if it does not grant its people the basic civil freedoms of speech, press, association, and assembly? Don't citizens have the right to "redress their grievances" in between elections, through petition and protest? And what about other personal freedoms: the right to practice one's religion, to live where one wants, to travel freely, to own and dispose of private property, and to conduct commerce? How can a system be called a democracy if it abuses and disenfranchises ethnic, racial, or religious minorities? Can a political system really be called a democracy if it does not ensure a rule of law, in which all citizens are equal before the law, no one is above the law, and the laws themselves are known in advance and administered by an impartial judiciary?

A country cannot be a democracy if there is no freedom of speech and association and no rule of law. But is this because elections themselves cannot be free and fair under such circumstances, or because free and fair elections are not enough for a country to be a democracy?

Among political scientists, there is no consensus answer to these questions. Neither does one exist among democratic policy makers, or think tank analysts, or human rights activists, or even ordinary citizens. Defining *democracy* is a bit like interpreting the Talmud (or any religious text): ask a room of ten rabbis (or political scientists) for the meaning, and you are likely to get at least eleven different answers. In the case of democracy, however, these answers tend to group into "thin" and "thick" conceptions. On the thin side, in a minimal sense, democracy is defined as the Austrian economist Joseph Schumpeter outlined it in the 1940s: a system "for arriving at political decisions in which individuals acquire the power to decide by means of a competitive struggle for the people's vote."[11] Or to put it in modern terms, by means of regular, "free and fair" elections. On the thick side, a system is not a democracy unless it also ensures the following attributes:

- Substantial individual freedom of belief, opinion, discussion, speech, publication, broadcast, assembly, demonstration, petition, and (why not) the Internet.
- Freedom of ethnic, religious, racial, and other minority groups (as well as historically excluded majorities) to practice their religion and culture and to participate equally in political and social life.
- The right of all adult citizens to vote and to run for office (if they meet certain minimum age and competency requirements).
- Genuine openness and competition in the electoral arena, enabling any group that adheres to constitutional principles to form a party and contest for office.
- Legal equality of all citizens under a rule of law, in which the laws are "clear, publicly known, universal, stable, and nonretroactive."[12]
- An independent judiciary to neutrally and consistently apply the law and protect individual and group rights.
- Thus, due process of law and freedom of individuals from torture, terror, and unjustified detention, exile, or interference in their personal lives— by the state or nonstate actors.
- Institutional checks on the power of elected officials, by an independent legislature, court system, and other autonomous agencies.
- Real pluralism in sources of information and forms of organization independent of the state; and thus, a vibrant "civil society."
- Control over the military and state security apparatus by civilians who are ultimately accountable to the people through elections.

How do we sort through these many reasonable expectations of democracy? There cannot be any one "right" answer to the question of what democracy is; we can only be transparent, and logical and consistent, in whatever standard we adopt. My own decision—in this book and in a long career as a political scientist and activist struggling over this conceptual terrain—has been to view democracy as a political system that varies in depth and may exist above two distinct thresholds.

At the minimal level, if a people can choose and replace their leaders in regular, free, and fair elections, there is an *electoral democracy.* Calling a political system a democracy doesn't mean it is a good or admirable system, or that we needn't worry much about improving it further. It simply means that if a majority of the people want a change in leaders and policies and are able to organize effectively within the rules, they can get change.

But electoral democracies vary enormously in their quality. Competitive and uncertain elections, even frequent alternation of parties in power, can coexist with serious abuses of human rights, significant constraints on freedom in many areas of life, discrimination against minorities, a weak rule of law, a compromised or ineffectual judiciary, rampant corruption, gerrymandered electoral districts, unresponsive government, state domination of the mass media, and widespread crime and violence. Genuine competition to determine who rules does not ensure high levels of freedom, equality, transparency, social justice, or other liberal values. Electoral democracy helps to make these other values more achievable, but it does not by any means ensure them.

When we speak of democracy, then, we should aspire to its realization at a higher plane, to the achievement of the ten "thick" dimensions. When these exist in substantial measure, we can call a system a *liberal democracy*.[13] To the extent that these are greatly diminished, democracy— if it exists at all—is *illiberal*. If there are regular, multiparty elections and other formal institutions of democracy like a national assembly, court system, constitution, and so on, but the people are not able to vote their leaders out of power because the system is, in effect, rigged, then the country has what I call *pseudodemocracy*.[14]

If this distinction seems neat and manageable, it is not. First, if elections are to be considered democratic, they must be meaningful in the sense of bestowing real power to govern on those who are elected. Even if elections were free and fair today in Iran (which they are not), the country could hardly be considered a democracy when the ultimate power to decide rests with a religious "supreme leader" who is not accountable to the people. The same could be said for Morocco or Jordan, where the ultimate power remains with the monarchy, or for some Central American countries in the 1970s and '80s, when the ultimate power rested with the military, despite elections. All these systems are or were pseudodemocracies, or what is sometimes called *electoral authoritarian regimes*.

A similar problem applies when the state is so thinly present, or so dominated by foreign powers, that the elected government is a hollow shell, with little effective authority. When civil war rages with little or very limited effective authority for elected government officials, as in Sierra Leone recently and Afghanistan today, the mere fact of competitive, reasonably fair elections does not create a democracy.

Many other regimes in the world are only pseudodemocracies because the realities and rules of the political game really do not make it possible, except through extraordinary means, to evict the ruling party, coalition, or cabal from power. The standard of "free and fair" is in fact a fairly demanding one. Elections are "free" when the legal barriers to entry into the political arena are low, when competing candidates, parties, and their supporters are free to campaign, and when people can vote for whom they want without fear and intimidation.

Freedom to campaign requires some considerable freedom of speech, movement, assembly, and association in political life, if not more broadly in civil society. However, it is hard to separate these two spheres. How many opposition candidates and supporters must be killed or arrested before one discerns a blatantly undemocratic pattern? Perhaps it is more than one, but certainly it is less than the twenty-one political killings, mainly of opposition supporters, in the two months prior to Cambodia's 1998 elections.[15] Yet in India, election-related killings have a long history and have in recent years risen to an alarming degree. No major observer denies that India is a democracy, but particularly in states like Bihar, where corruption, criminality, murder, and kidnapping have heavily penetrated the electoral process, it is an illiberal and degraded one.

Assessing electoral fairness can be similarly complicated. The political scientists Steven Levitsky and Lucan Way argue that political systems descend into *competitive authoritarianism* when violations of the "minimum criteria" for democracy are so serious that they create "an uneven playing field between government and opposition."[16] Yet even among the liberal and established democracies, there is rarely a truly level playing field. Most governing parties or executives enjoy advantages of incumbency: readier access to the media, an easier time raising money from business, and the ability (strictly legal or not) to use government transport and staff while campaigning. It is a virtually intrinsic feature of incumbency that the ruling party can (to one degree or another) steer government spending and benefits to swing districts and voters. In the United States, electoral competition has become so disfigured by the scientific gerrymandering of electoral districts that only about a tenth of the seats in the House of Representatives are competitive. In the European Union, political corruption and favoritism remain so entrenched in the process of government contracting that one new study labels it "the best system money can buy."[17] If we demand a fully level playing field as the test of electoral fairness, few if any political systems will qualify. In the real world, every elected government tries to draw some electoral advantage from its incumbency, every system is vulnerable to abuse, and maintaining democratic quality requires constant vigilance. Scattered violations of the rules, or the fact that the ruling party has some competitive advantages, do not make elections undemocratic, so long as it is still possible for the voters to "throw the bums out" through normal political means.

There is by now a rather well-evolved set of criteria for electoral fairness. Elections are fair when they are administered by a neutral authority; when the electoral administration is sufficiently competent and resourceful to take specific precautions against fraud; when the police, military, and courts treat competing candidates and parties impartially; when contenders all have access to the public media; when electoral districts and rules do not grossly handicap the opposition; when independent monitoring of the voting and vote counting is allowed; when the secrecy of the ballot is protected; when virtually all adults can vote; when the procedures for organizing and counting the vote are widely known; and when there are transparent and impartial procedures for resolving election complaints and disputes.[18] Serious efforts to compromise the freedom and fairness of elections form a visible pattern, beginning well before election day. The biases and misdeeds are there for international observers to see if those observers have the time, experience, courage, resources, and expertise in the country's politics to do so.[19]

Unfortunately, however, international observers are typically reluctant to denounce a superficially competitive election as rigged beyond redemption. Over and over, from Armenia to Nigeria to Venezuela, the instinct is for international observer missions to declare that even if there was extensive fraud the election broadly reflected "the will of the voters"— as if foreign observers could clearly discern that in the absence of a decent election! The fact that the voting results more or less match reasonably accurate preelection opinion polls does not make an election democratic, for elections are a process that involves much more than merely casting votes on election day and counting them fairly. As Miriam Kornblith, an independent member of Venezuela's National Electoral Council who watched the country's president gradually subvert democracy after his initial election in 1998, warns, "Elections can serve to express the collective will and consolidate democracy only when the voting and all that surrounds it are free and fair. Elections that deviate significantly from such standards can serve different ends—including the consolidation of an autocracy that disdains the very democratic mechanisms it loosely and instrumentally follows."[20]

Since the elements of electoral constraint and unfairness span the continuum from isolated to systematic, it is hard to know where precisely to draw the line between democratic and not. Some countries, such as Venezuela, Nigeria, Tanzania, Armenia, and Kyrgyzstan, occupy an ambiguous or disputed space between democracy and overt authoritarianism. They have a multiparty electoral system, with significant opposition. They have some space for civil society and intellectual dissent. However, individual and associational freedoms are under such mounting pressure, or elections are so riddled with fraud, or the arenas of political opposition and competition are so constrained and intimidated by the domineering power of the incumbent, that it is difficult to call the systems democratic, even in the minimal sense. I therefore classify them all, as well as Malaysia, Singapore, and Iran, as electoral authoritarian.[21] There are many such regimes in the Middle East and Africa, including monarchies (like Morocco and Jordan) and one-party hegemonic systems (like Cameroon and Ethiopia), which have multiparty elections but are not democracies either because the winning parties do not have real and full power to rule, or because the political opposition does not have a realistic and fair chance of winning. In none of these cases do voters have an adequate chance to hold their rulers accountable.

Although there remains an extensive international system for observing elections, there is also a growing tendency to take democratic elections for granted, as something that, once achieved, becomes easily consolidated. This is a pity, because while free and fair elections are only one component of democracy, they are the most indispensable one, and they are one that ruling parties and presidents have a strong incentive to manipulate and degrade.

IS DEMOCRACY A LUXURY?

Forty years ago, Seymour Martin Lipset argued that the richer the country, the greater the chance that it would sustain democracy.[22] Since then, Lipset's argument has become conventional wisdom, and researchers have sought to solidify the argument in statistics.

In one innovative and rigorous study, Adam Przeworski and his colleagues found that there was in fact a striking relationship between development level and the probability of sustaining democracy between 1950 and 1990. With every step up in a country's level of economic development, the life expectancy of a democratic regime increases. In upper-middle-income countries (specifically, those richer than Argentina was in 1975), democracy never breaks down, whereas in the very poorest countries, democracy has a 12 percent chance of dying in any particular year, with an average life expectancy of eight years.[23]

Yet, since 1990, several democracies in the lowest income category have outlived that expected life span, including Benin, Mali, and Malawi.[24] Among the bottom third of countries in terms of human development, democracy has been in place for over four decades in Botswana, for over half a century in India (with only a brief interruption), for almost two decades in Namibia. Over the past three decades, an unprecedented number of very poor countries have embraced democratic forms of government. Of the thirty-six countries that the United Nations Development Program ranks at the bottom, with "low human development," about a third of these (thirteen) are democracies. If one takes the bottom third of countries in terms of human development (a broad index that takes into account a nation's average life expectancy, education, and per capita income), the proportion of democracies rises to 42 percent (twenty-five of fifty-nine). And of the poorest half of states, almost half of them are democracies. If democracy is the distinctive cultural attribute of the rich, mainly Western, countries of the world, why has it spread so far to the poor and the non-Western?

Of course, it is possible to dismiss this as a fad, a product of superficial diffusion, or a temporary concession to international pressure. From this perspective, democracy can spread anywhere, but it cannot take root and be sustained anywhere. Where it is not really valued by the people, it either won't emerge or won't last.

To be sure, democracy is weak and is in serious difficulty in many poor and even some middle-income countries. But in most of these countries, the problems of democracy have more to do with the shortcomings and betrayals of elites than the apathy or authoritarian sentiments of the population. If democracy can emerge and persist for more than fifteen years in a destitute, landlocked, overwhelmingly Muslim country like Mali—in which the vast majority of adults are illiterate and live in absolute poverty, and the life expectancy is forty-eight years—then there would seem to be no intrinsic reason why democracy cannot develop in every poor country, and indeed every country.

In fact, a strong case has been made that democracy is not an extravagance for the poor but a necessity. Amartya Sen won the Nobel Prize for Economics in 1998 in part for showing that democracies do not have famines. This is because the relatively free flows of information in a democracy raise the flag on food (and other) emergencies, while the mechanisms of political accountability give politicians a powerful incentive to be responsive. Beyond this, however, Sen argues that people cannot even properly conceive their economic needs until they have some sense of what is feasible—until they determine, through free discussion and information, which types of deprivations are preventable and what can be done about them. Thus, "people in economic need also need a political voice. Democracy is not a luxury that can await the arrival of general prosperity [and] there is very little evidence that poor people, given the choice, prefer to reject democracy."[25] Sen notes the vigor with which Indians defended their freedom and democracy in the 1977 election, tossing from office the prime minister, Indira Gandhi, who had suspended political and civil rights. But there have been countless other instances—from Burma and Bangladesh to Kenya and South Africa—where poor people have mobilized passionately for (and in defense of) democratic change. The fact that they have sometimes, as in Burma, been crushed by sheer force, while a timid world watched and protested ineffectually, does not negate the overwhelming expression of their sentiment. Neither do the pervasive abuses of power and theft of public resources by elites who have been given (or have claimed) the power to rule.

Sen argues that the mark of a universal value is not that it has the consent of everyone, but that "people anywhere may have reason to see it as valuable."[26] By this measure, there is growing evidence of all kinds, as we shall see, that democracy is becoming a truly universal value.

IS DEMOCRACY A WESTERN CONCEPT?

Cultural skeptics argue that since democracy is an intellectual and political product of the West and the European enlightenment tradition, and since the thinking and practice of modern democracy cannot be traced back to any non-Western sources, we must conclude that democracy is culturally unique to the West, not universal. But as Amartya Sen writes, "The championing of democracy and political freedom in the modern sense cannot be found in the pre-enlightenment tradition in any part of the world, West or East. What we have to investigate, instead, are the constituents, the components, of this compound idea." And in this regard, Sen, and many other Asian thinkers and scholars, find a "powerful presence" of many of these elements.[27]

Take the Confucian tradition. Neither Sen nor any of the experts on Confucianism would insist that this magisterial philosophical and moral tradition is essentially democratic. It is elitist to the core and offers no justification for such fundamentals of democracy as popular sovereignty and competition for power. But, Sen writes, "Confucius did not recommend blind allegiance to the state. When Zilu asks him 'how to serve a prince,' Confucius replies, 'Tell him the truth even if it offends him.'" And there is also, Sen notes, the Confucian admonition to oppose a bad government.[28]

Writing in reply to Lee Kuan Yew in 1994, the South Korean dissident Kim Dae Jung (who would three years later be elected president) celebrated Asia's "rich heritage of democracy-oriented philosophies and traditions." These include the works of the Chinese philosopher Meng-tzu, who identified a right of the people to overthrow a king "in the name of heaven" if he did not provide good government, and the Korean religion of Tonghak, whose "ideas inspired and motivated nearly half a million peasants in 1894 to revolt against exploitation by feudalistic government internally and imperialistic forces externally."[29] In fact, Kim asserted, when Europe was wallowing in feudalism, China and Korea enjoyed centuries of enlightened rule that valued freedom of speech, practiced a rule of law, recruited to the civil service on merit, and enabled scholars and civil servants to check the abuse of power. To be sure, this was still a system of monarchy, explains Hahm Chaibong, a leading Korean scholar of Confucianism. But it generated a tradition of "opposition to despotism" and "suspicion of state power" that was a precursor to liberalism if not democracy.[30] Although Confucianism lacks a philosophy or historical experience of democracy per se, the irony for Hahm is that liberal democracy in contemporary East Asian countries like Japan, South Korea, and Taiwan has "opened up a free space . . . in which the Confucian tradition of serious thought and ethical reflection . . . can truly come into its own for the first time ever."[31]

Sen demonstrates that there are strong roots for respecting pluralism,

tolerance, diversity, and independence of mind in the diverse cultural traditions of India. For one thing, "it is difficult to out-do the Indian traditions
in arguing endlessly and elaborately."[32] The third-century BC emperor
Ashoka championed "egalitarian and universal tolerance," a theme that
runs prominently through many subsequent writings, including dramas
and edicts. The Mogul emperor Akbar, who reigned for the last half of the
sixteenth century, promoted tolerance and freedom of worship and religious practice when "the Inquisition was in full throttle in Europe."[33]
Many other Mogul emperors of India also practiced tolerance and respect
for differences to a degree far beyond what was known in Europe at that
time.

The Indian experience of religious tolerance under a Muslim empire is
but one example of a long historical tradition of tolerance and progress
within the Islamic societies of the Middle East. The problem that Islamic
culture presents for democracy, a large and growing body of liberal Muslim thinkers maintain, does not emanate from Islam as a religion, or from
its cultural roots, but rather from a series of social and political transformations in the region dating to the nineteenth century, when, to quote
the esteemed Moroccan scholar Abdou Filali-Ansary, "some modern
Muslims . . . elevated the actual conditions and rules under which their
medieval forefathers lived to the status of a norm," or religious and cultural obligation.[34] What was broadly instructive became a literal guide.
Now, Filali-Ansary and many other Muslim liberals argue that Islam can
and must be reconciled with democracy.[35]

Of course, it would strain credibility to suggest that any liberal reinter-
pretation of Islam (or for that matter Confucianism or Christianity) could
convincingly establish it as an essentially democratic religion. What
these reconsiderations do, however, is contradict claims of a fundamental
incompatibility between religion and democracy. As with other religions,
so "one can find within Islamic doctrine and Muslim traditions both elements that are and elements that are not congenial to democracy; and
this in turn means that the influence of the religion depends, to a very
considerable extent, on how and by whom it is interpreted."[36]

In recent years, not only liberal Islamic thinkers but a wide range of
Arab scholars, professionals, and civil society activists have been challenging the democracy and freedom deficit that pervades the Arab world. The
Arab authors of the first *Arab Human Development Report*—an extraordinary
document published by the United Nations Development Program in
2002—recognized that democratization had "barely reached the Arab

states. This freedom deficit undermines human development and is one of the most painful manifestations of lagging political development."[37] They continued (in a vein that would be repeated in subsequent reports):

> There can be no real prospects for reforming the system of governance, or for truly liberating human capabilities, in the absence of comprehensive political representation in effective legislatures based on free, honest, efficient and regular elections. If the people's preferences are to be properly expressed and their interests properly protected, governance must become truly representative and fully accountable.[38]

Finally, it is worth noting that the most prominent advocates of the cultural limits to democracy, from within the non-Western countries that are presented as having authoritarian values, are the authoritarian leaders of these very same countries and their spokesmen. While Lee Kuan Yew and other Singaporean leaders figure prominently here, African autocrats like Uganda's Yoweri Museveni and Zimbabwe's Robert Mugabe, as well as Arab, Burmese, and Chinese leaders, have pressed similar lines of defense. There is in their protestations a striking coincidence of political interest and argument that renders the whole claim, as Kim Dae Jung said with respect to Lee, "self-serving."[39] How can an autocrat who has not been freely elected claim to be the unique and true voice of his or her society and culture? Government leaders and ministers "do not have a monopoly in interpreting local culture and values," Sen writes. "It is important to listen to the voices of dissent in each society. Aung San Suu Kyi has no less legitimacy—indeed clearly has more—in interpreting what the Burmese want than have the military rulers of Myanmar, whose candidates she had defeated in open elections before she was jailed."[40]

THE SPIRIT OF THE PEOPLE

Fortunately, a growing body of data from public opinion surveys is telling us what ordinary people in diverse regions really think about democracy. One way to gauge whether democracy is a universal value is to ask people around the world whether they think democracy is the best form of government. Another way is to see to what extent people living in democracies would approve of some authoritarian form of government instead. Globally, answers to these and related questions show surprisingly high levels of democratic commitment in non-Western societies. Moreover, while regions or cultural groupings (and certainly countries) differ in their levels of commitment to democratic values, those differences are not always in the direction that cultural theories expect.

The most eye-opening public opinion data come from two sources. One is the World Values Survey, a comprehensive survey of attitudes concerning everything from politics to national goals to gender roles. It is conducted about every decade, and the most recent survey (1999–2001) spans eighty countries, from very rich to very poor, that account for approximately 85 percent of the world's population.[41] While the survey contains only a few questions on democracy, its advantage is that the questions are worded the same in every country.[42] Since the mid- to late 1990s, a second (and for these purposes, richer) source of data has emerged in the form of regional barometers that periodically assess how citizens feel about democracy, authority, and the performance of their government. The barometers more deeply cover regions with a history of democratic struggle or uncertainty: Latin America, Africa, East Asia, South Asia, postcommunist Europe, and soon (with the Arab Barometer now in formation) the Middle East. However, since they represent several distinct survey projects rather than a single global one, the questions asked are less standardized. This makes comparison more difficult. Nevertheless, these regional barometers of public opinion are increasingly using identical questions, on which we can compare how people from widely divergent cultures and development levels view democracy.

Three questions from the World Values Survey provide a good initial picture of democratic inclinations. First, to what extent do people support democracy, by agreeing with the statement "Democracy may have its problems, but it's better than any other form of government"? Second, to what extent do people reveal an authoritarian temptation, by approving the idea of "having a strong leader who does not have to bother with parliament and elections"? Third, to what extent do people say it would be "a good thing" if there were "greater respect for authority"—a signal of less liberal values?[43] As can be seen in table 1.1, the belief that democracy is (at least in principle) the best system is overwhelming and universal. While there is a slightly higher preference among the Western industrialized countries, in every region—even the former Soviet Union—no less than 80 percent of people on average say democracy is the best system. When the question about democratic preference is worded a little differently, however, people are often much more willing to give a nondemocratic answer, even when concrete regime alternatives are posed. So, for

TABLE 1.1 DEMOCRATIC ORIENTATIONS, BY REGION			
Region (and number of countries)	Percent agree: "Democracy may have its problems, but it's better than any other form of government"	Percent endorse: "Strong leader who does not have to bother with parliament and elections"	Percent agree: "Greater respect for authority" would be a "good thing"
West (22)	92	24	54
Eastern Europe (16)	88	33	53
Former Soviet Union (7)	81	48	63
Latin America (9)	88	45	73
Asia (11)	85	39	52
Muslim Middle East (6)	88	36	78

example, the idea of a "strong leader" who would override mechanisms of democratic accountability appeals to nearly half of those in the former Soviet Union (and as we will see in chapter 9, an even larger percentage in Russia), an average of 45 percent of respondents in nine Latin American states, about two in five people on average from eleven Asian states (including China and India), and a little over a third of the public in six Middle Eastern Muslim states. This compares to only a quarter of citizens in twenty-two Western countries and a third in the sixteen countries of Central and Eastern Europe. Finally, majorities in every region would like to see greater respect for authority. But while there is no difference between the slight majorities favoring more respect in the West, Asia, and Eastern Europe, it is clearly desired in the former Soviet Union, and especially in Latin America and the Muslim Middle East.

What do we learn from these regional comparisons, partial though they are in coverage of some of the countries? One lesson, which we will see evidenced dramatically in the more detailed discussions of the data in part II of this book, is to be wary of the stereotypes and assumptions of culturally based theories. There is a broad desire for democracy in the world, stretching across regions. Even in Africa, the poorest region of the world, there is a surprisingly strong commitment to democracy, with three in five citizens, on average, saying that democracy is preferable to any other form of government—a proportion exceeding that in Latin America and that in the former Soviet Union.[44] Yes, outside the West, there is a stronger authoritarian temptation, but in no region does it reach a majority preference on average. And if some non-Western societies may tend toward a less liberal (or illiberal) form of democracy compared to the West, others may approach more closely the Western commitment to liberal values, even in East Asia, as we will see shortly.

IS ISLAM THE PROBLEM?

Another nagging question addressed in the surveys is whether Islam is the obstacle to democratic values. Although much has been made of the "clash of civilizations," especially since September 11, 2001, Afrobarometer survey evidence indicates that "Muslims are as supportive of democracy as non-Muslims." In four African countries with substantial Muslim populations (Mali, Nigeria, Tanzania, and Uganda), the barometer found that large majorities of Muslims as well as non-Muslims support democracy, and any hesitancy in supporting democracy among African Muslims "is due more to deficits of formal education and other attributes of modernization than to religious attachments."[45]

In the Arab world, the survey evidence collected to date suggests that "Islamic orientations and attachments have, at most, a very limited impact on views about democracy."[46] In particular, the University of Michigan professor Mark Tessler finds that the degree of personal Islamic religiosity does not seem to be related to support for democracy in any country. After weighing the statistical evidence, he concludes, "Islam is not incompatible with democracy and does not discourage the emergence of attitudes favorable to democracy."[47]

A similar pattern holds in Central Asia. In Kazakhstan and Kyrgyzstan, Richard Rose, an American political scientist who has done the most wide-ranging surveys of attitudes and values in the postcommunist world, finds that there is little difference among religious groups in support for democracy. "The most observant Muslims are almost as democratic as those who are nonobservant." In each country, majorities of all religious groups—Muslim and Orthodox, observant and nonobservant, as well as those with no religion—believe "democracy is better than any other form of government."[48]

The most systematic test of the "clash of civilizations" thesis with respect to Islam and democracy has been administered by Pippa Norris and Ronald Inglehart, using public opinion data in nine predominantly Muslim countries and twenty-two Western, predominantly Christian countries gathered through the World Values Survey. Their results are striking. Across several questionnaire items, the two groups of countries (or in Samuel Huntington's conception, *civilizations*) are virtually identical in their average levels of support for democratic ideals (86 percent), approval of democratic performance (68 percent), and disapproval of nondemocratic forms of decision making (61 percent). On each of these political dimensions, the two groups of countries are at least somewhat more democratic than most other cultural groups. However, when it comes to social issues—approval of gender equality, homosexuality, abortion, divorce, and disapproval of having religious standards for political leadership—there is a staggering difference. Western societies are far more liberal on these issues (typically by margins of 25 percentage points or more) than are Muslim countries, which have the most socially conservative value leanings of any of the nine "civilizations" identified by Huntington. Thus, Norris and Inglehart conclude, "support for democracy is surprisingly widespread among Islamic publics, even among those that live in authoritarian societies. The most basic cultural fault line between the West and Islam involves issues of gender equality and sexual liberalization."[49] Those issues, in turn, affect the content and depth of democracy, but they do not necessarily bear on the vigor or viability of it.

A similar pattern is evident when comparing Muslims and Christians (or in India, Muslims and Hindus) within nine developing and postcommunist countries. On social issues, Muslims tend to be less liberal and tolerant. On questions of democratic culture, such as political tolerance, participation, support for free speech, and disapproval of nondemocratic alternatives, Muslims usually do not differ significantly from non-Muslims, and when they do it is not in a predictable direction. Thus, it is "not possible . . . to say that the Islamic culture is either less or more supportive of a democratic system of government" than Christian or other cultures.[50]

If what matters is not a fixed doctrine but continually evolving and contesting interpretations of Islam, there is some encouraging news. Across the Arab world and Iran, as well as in Europe and the United States, we see a renaissance of what Filali-Ansary calls "enlightened Islamic thought," dating back to the early twentieth century. Based on pluralism, tolerance, and critical reasoning, its sensibilities are either explicitly democratic or quite compatible with democracy.[51] Throughout the last century, however, it has had to contest with "a rising number of Muslim thinkers" who have sought "to produce religious arguments against democracy and in favor of more 'authentic' Islamic models," like the Egyptian founder of the Muslim Brotherhood, Sayyid Qutb, and the founder of the Islamic

Republic of Iran, Ayatollah Ruhollah Khomeini.[52] These radical and fundamentally antidemocratic Islamic doctrines have had the benefit of much more effective (and ruthless) political organization, while Islamic liberals in the Arab world have had to struggle against both the fundamentalists and the secular authoritarian state. The latter has used the Islamic threat to demonize all challengers, including the liberal Islamists and their natural allies, the secular democrats.

Now, Muslim liberals like Filali-Ansary are advancing an agenda for reconciling Islamist religious thought with democratic practice. This will require, he writes, the "updating of religious conceptions" (as happened with Christianity and Judaism) so that most of the faithful "give religious dogmas a symbolic truth-value" that render them "amenable to rational understanding and scientific scrutiny." In this process (which some hail as an Islamic Reformation but Filali-Ansary prefers to call a more "general evolution"), the literal meaning of sacred terms and symbols fades while commitment to Islam's larger moral teachings is entrenched—and joined to universal values like the rule of law.[53]

THE "ASIAN VALUES" THESIS

The public opinion data also sound a rebuttal to the idea, long held by Asian autocrats but also by many in the West, that Asians, and more specifically East Asians, manifest more authoritarian, communitarian, and illiberal political values than others. Asians prefer democracy as a political regime at levels very close to those in the West. Russell Dalton and Doh Chull Shin constructed an index of commitment to democratic rule by identifying four broader beliefs: that having a democratic political system is good and that having rule by a strong leader, by the army, or by "experts" is bad. While the four "Western" countries of the Pacific Rim (New Zealand, Canada, Australia, and the United States—in that order) score highest on this scale, the differences with Asian countries were on the whole "quite modest," and in the case of Japan, Singapore, South Korea, and Hong Kong, negligible.[54]

On a similar scale asking how democracy works—whether it causes problems of order, indecision, or bad economic performance—it is even more difficult to distinguish between West and East. While Western citizens are remarkably positive about democracy, so are East Asians, even those (in China and Vietnam) who live in extremely authoritarian countries. In particular, "given the presumed emphasis on agreement and aversion to conflict in Asian societies, it is striking that large majorities reject the view that democracy is not good at maintaining order."[55] Moreover, Dalton and Shin cite a 2002 Pew survey indicating that two-thirds of Vietnamese even favor "democracy as it exists in the United States"!

If arguments about "East Asian values" have any validity, East Asians should support democracy of a distinctly illiberal type, privileging order over freedom, the community over the individual, and the leader over the law. But this assumption also holds up poorly against the public opinion data. Asians do not seek "greater respect for authority" any more frequently than do Western citizens. In fact, when Dalton and Nhu-Ngoc T. Ong looked at authority in the family and other social realms, they found that people in Canada, Australia, and the United States were more likely to rank highly on it (65 percent on average) than people in East Asia (49 percent on average, across eight countries).[56]

The East Asia Barometer posed a number of more political value statements to individuals in six East Asian democracies.[57] On average, six in ten disagreed that "the most important thing for a political leader is to accomplish his goals even if he has to ignore the established procedures," and the same proportion rejected the idea that a leader with majority support could "disregard the views of the minority."[58] Only a third said it is okay for the government to disregard the law when "facing a difficult situation," and over half stood up against state censorship and for judicial independence. Indeed, when looking at one of the purest expressions of the presumed "Asian values"—"Government leaders are like the head of a family; we should all follow their decisions"—the survey found that 53 percent rejected the principle. While the proportion in China was only a little over a third, in Hong Kong it was two-thirds.

On each of these indicators of liberal values, the economically developed Asian countries—Japan, South Korea, and Taiwan (and also Hong Kong)—regularly exhibit a much stronger commitment to liberal values and the rule of law than the less developed countries (Thailand, the Philippines, and Mongolia). In addition, in Taiwan—where some of these survey questions have been administered since 1984—there is a striking (though not uniform) trend of continuing growth in liberal value orientations, including tolerance for pluralism and an unwillingness to defer blindly to government authority.[59] All of this suggests that Asian values are eroding with economic development and the practice of democracy itself. Rather than representing a barrier to democracy, these traditional values, to the extent that they are suspicious of freedom and democratic pluralism, tend to give way as people become wealthier, more educated, and more experienced with democracy. Yet less-developed Asian countries can be surprisingly insistent on democratic principles. When Indonesians were interviewed (for the first time) for the Asian Barometer in 2006, 64 percent said democracy is always preferable (one of the highest levels in the survey) and over 80 percent (equal to the proportion in Taiwan) disagreed that political leaders should ignore established procedures if necessary to achieve their goals.[60] When we look closely at the poorer and more authoritarian Asian countries, the political values of their people do not well fit the Asian values thesis. According to Dalton and Shin, "Instead of the hesitancy (or outright opposition) to liberal democracy that some previous scholarship had suggested, contemporary public opinion surveys are finding a breadth of support for democracy as a regime and the working of the democratic process across most nations in East Asia."[61]

Of course, it is not only beliefs and values that have changed dramatically in the last three decades. This cultural shift reflects and has also partly driven the breathtaking expansion of democratic governance in the world, which I document in the next chapter.

2

THE DEMOCRATIC BOOM

Shortly after midnight on April 25, 1974, young left-wing officers of the Movimento das Forcas Armadas (MFA) overthrew Portugal's forty-eight-year-old nationalist dictatorship, the Estado Novo. The swift, efficient, nearly bloodless military coup elicited an effusion of popular relief and celebration. Despite appeals from military rebels for the public to stay home, thousands poured into the streets of Lisbon, cheered the soldiers, and, wielding nothing more deadly than red carnations, persuaded the regime defenders not to resist. In images that were televised worldwide, the rebels let civilians place the carnations in the barrels of their rifles. Thus, the uprising that toppled Europe's oldest remaining dictatorship came to be known as "the Carnation Revolution."

For more than a decade, Portugal had been mired in hopeless, debilitating wars in an attempt to hang on to its African colonies of Angola, Mozambique, and Portuguese Guinea. As with the United States in Vietnam, casualties and costs were mounting, with no prospect of victory. Unlike in the United States, however, there was no political mechanism to express the anger and frustration that were swelling within both the armed forces and the public at large. Portuguese settlers and soldiers were returning home from the colonies bitter and disillusioned. Portugal itself was falling further and further behind the democracies of Western Europe, which had come together in a common market, the European Economic Community, that required as a condition for membership a democratic regime with a rule of law. Isolated from its neighbors and obsessed with a fear of social upheaval at the hands of the powerful underground Communist Party, the country was stagnating politically and economically. Seeing no future, hundreds of thousands were emigrating. When the founding dictator, António Salazar, died in 1970, the Estado Novo lost its coherence and self-confidence. The new autocrat Marcello Caetano tried to modernize and liberalize the regime, but without success.

When the dictatorship fell to the Carnation Revolution, it was far from clear that Portugal would become a democracy. It had never been one before. It had just been through half a century of quasi-fascist rule. The ailing Spanish dictator, Francisco Franco, clung to power over the border. Both countries were steeped in a Latin, Catholic culture that was dismissed by many political scientists and commentators as being unsuited to democracy, a logic that was used to explain the virtual absence of democracy in Latin America at the time. Quickly, the Portuguese armed forces fractured into ideological factions, and the country fell into a period of intense political mobilization, intrigue, and peril. As Samuel Huntington summarized it:

> For eighteen months after the April coup, Portugal was in turmoil. The MFA officers split into competing conservative, moderate, and Marxist factions. The political parties covered an equally wide spectrum, from the hard-line Communist party on the left to fascist groups on the right. Six provisional governments succeeded each other, each exercising less authority than its predecessor. Coups and countercoups were attempted. Workers and peasants struck, demonstrated, and seized factories, farms, and media. Moderate parties won the national elections on the anniversary of the coup in 1975, but by the fall of that year civil war appeared possible between the conservative north and the radical south.[1]

For a time, it looked as though the Communists would take over in Portugal. In September 1974, Secretary of State Henry Kissinger warned Mário Soares, leader of the moderate Socialist Party (PS), that he would wind up like Alexander Kerensky in Russia—swallowed by the Bolsheviks.[2] But the West bet heavily on a democratic outcome and channeled aid to democratic parties and movements, including the PS. The April 1975 constituent assembly elections indicated a clear preference for the democratic center. When radical military units tried to seize power in

1975, they were crushed by "a taciturn prodemocracy colonel," António Ramalho Eanes.[3] A constitutional compromise was reached in April 1976 and a democratic government elected shortly thereafter.

THE THIRD WAVE OF DEMOCRATIZATION

The triumph of democracy in Portugal was the beginning of a political boom for democracy in the world. In his highly influential book, Huntington termed this the *third wave* of democratic expansion in the world.[4] He dates the first long wave of democratization to 1828, with the expansion of democratic suffrage in the United States, through the early 1920s, with the ascendance of Mussolini in Italy and the *first reverse wave*. A second, shorter, democratic wave began with the Allied victory in World War II, incorporating a number of Latin American and newly independent (primarily former British) colonies. But by 1962, a *second reverse wave* had begun, bringing widespread military and one-party rule and leaving only two states in South America democratic.

With the overthrow of the dictatorship in Portugal in 1974, the third wave of democratization began. At that time, there were only about forty democracies in the world, mainly in the advanced industrial countries (and including a dozen microstates with populations of less than one million). Among countries with more than one million people, Huntington counts only thirty democracies in the world at the end of 1973, slightly less than a quarter of all states.[5] Scattered through Africa, Asia, and Latin America were a few other democracies: India, Sri Lanka, Botswana, Costa Rica, Venezuela. But military, one-party, or one-man dictatorships dominated most of Latin America, Asia, Africa, and the Middle East. All of Eastern Europe and the Soviet Union were under Communist rule.

Since then, democracy has expanded dramatically. For some time following the Portuguese revolution, however, there was only a modest and gradual trend, giving no sign of the global transformation to come. Three months after the Portuguese revolution, the seven-year-old Greek military dictatorship fractured following its military defeat by Turkey in Cyprus. Humiliated and in disarray, the Greek military was forced to call on civilians to form a caretaker government, which led to parliamentary elections in November 1974 and a restoration of civilian constitutional rule.

The following year, the Spanish dictator Francisco Franco, in power nearly four decades since his alliance with Fascist Italy and Nazi Germany during the Spanish Civil War, became terminally ill, and Prince Juan Carlos, who had previously been designated as heir to the Spanish throne, assumed provisional powers in October. When Franco died the next month, Juan Carlos became king, and pressure for democratic transition escalated dramatically with the young king's tacit support. In July 1976, Franco's last prime minister was replaced by a shrewd and able young reformist conservative, Adolfo Suárez. He deftly shepherded a transition by negotiating compromise "pacts" with opposition forces and keeping the military and the conservative elements involved. Suárez held control of government for the conservatives in the June 1977 parliamentary elections and forged an agreement with the Socialist and Communist parties on social and economic reforms in October (the famous Pact of Moncloa). A year later, the parliament overwhelmingly approved a new constitution, completing the transition to democracy in late 1978. The Spanish model of a "pacted" transition, in which the old authoritarian establishment and the rising democratic opposition negotiate a series of mutual guarantees and restraints, would become a model for many future democratic transitions in Latin America, Eastern Europe, and Africa—in particular, South Africa.

This democratization in Portugal and Spain influenced the scene in Latin America, which was under pressure from increasingly assertive popular movements and from the United States, where a new foreign policy emphasis on human rights had been introduced by President Jimmy Carter. In 1978, the authoritarian strongman of the Dominican Republic, Joaquin Balaguer, was defeated and left office, marking the first real electoral alternation of government in Dominican history. That same year, a constituent assembly was elected in Peru to draft a new constitution, and in May 1980, a democratically elected government assumed power. In 1979, a transition back to elected civilian rule occurred in Ecuador.

In a seminal event for the region, the brutal Argentine military dictatorship imploded in 1982 following its ill-considered invasion of the Falkland Islands and its humiliating defeat at the hands of the British military. Led by Raúl Alfonsín, democratic forces independent of both the military and the long-dominant party of the populist demagogue Juan Perón scored a decisive victory in the October 1983 elections and began to revive respect for human rights and the rule of law. At the same time, Brazil experienced an extended process of *abertura* (opening) from two decades of military rule to civilian leadership. Brazil's political decompression was completed in January 1985, when the opposition leader Tancredo Neves won the presidency in the electoral college, despite procedures favoring the military party. Although Neves died tragically soon thereafter, the liberalization process continued with the adoption of a new constitution in October 1988.

Despite these important changes in Europe and the Americas, the global democratic trend remained quite limited. By 1980, the proportion of democracies in the world had only increased to a third of all states, from a little over a quarter in 1973. Moreover, significant reversals were occurring. Democracy had given way to the military in Turkey and to civil war in Lebanon, and three prominent new democracies—Bangladesh, Ghana, and Nigeria—broke down within a few years. Between 1973 and 1980, the number of democracies increased from forty to fifty-four, but more than a third (nineteen) were in microstates with fewer than one million people. Seven of the new democracies of the 1970s were in tiny Caribbean and Pacific island states that had recently become independent. By 1984, the proportion of democracies among states with over one million population (29 percent) was less than half that among the microstates (62 percent).

A decade into the third wave, the world remained predominantly authoritarian, unaware that an unprecedented global transformation was under way. Western Europe was now entirely democratic, as was about half of Latin America. But Communist regimes appeared firmly entrenched, and Japan remained the only East Asian democracy. Africa was still untouched by the changes in Europe and Latin America. In fact, the military had just seized power in the continent's largest and most dynamic country, Nigeria, after grotesque electoral fraud returned the venal ruling party to power by a huge margin.

Then, in 1986, a "miracle" happened. In the first of what would be a number of "people power revolutions" during the third wave, the Philippine opposition mobilized society with tactics of nonviolent resistance to split the regime and bring down the dictator.[6] In November 1985, President Ferdinand Marcos, under growing domestic and international pressure for looting the country and suppressing dissent for two decades, sought to shore up his sagging legitimacy by calling an early presidential election. The opposition had been inflamed since August 1983, when the charismatic democratic leader Benigno Aquino was assassinated on the tarmac of the Manila airport upon his return from exile in the United States. A government commission of inquiry placed responsibility for the murder with the armed forces chief of staff, General Fabian Ver (a one-time chauffeur and bodyguard to Marcos), but he was acquitted by a biased court and reinstated to his job, intensifying the unrest. Thinking he could win a quick test of his popularity, Marcos announced a "snap election" in order to "restore confidence" in his rule. But, under moral pressure from the esteemed Catholic archbishop Jaime Cardinal Sin, the normally fractious opposition united around Aquino's widow, Corazón. And when Marcos brazenly rigged the election, the fraud was documented by an unprecedented citizen vote-monitoring effort, the National Citizens' Movement for Free Elections (NAMFREL), as well as by foreign observers. Heading President Reagan's official U.S. delegation of election observers, Senator Richard Lugar endorsed the NAMFREL vote count, as did the Catholic Church. With Marcos and Aquino both claiming victory, Aquino called for civil disobedience, boycotts, and other forms of peaceful protest to "bring down the usurper," and reform-minded military leaders defected from Marcos and recognized Aquino as the legitimately elected president. At the urging of Cardinal Sin, hundreds of thousands of Filipinos then poured into the highway in Manila (EDSA) that connected the two military rebel bases and prayed on their knees. In what came to be known as the "miracle at EDSA," crowds linking arms and nuns holding rosaries stopped tanks and troops loyal to Marcos in their tracks. Support for Marcos evaporated, and he fled into exile.

The spirit of democracy was spreading to East Asia. The next year it was the turn of South Korea. When the military dictator, President Chun Doo Hwan, suspended all consideration of constitutional reforms necessary for meaningful democratization, mass protests erupted in April 1987, drawing the middle classes that had swelled in size over two decades of economic growth. With the mobilization of a more moderate opposition and the Olympics due to be held in Seoul the following summer, the United States warned Chun not to use force to suppress the demonstrations. In the face of intense domestic and international pressure, Chun's designated successor, Roh Tae Woo, felt compelled to yield to the opposition's demands for constitutional reform and the release of political prisoners. Although the opposition ultimately divided between Kim Dae Jung and Kim Young Sam, enabling Roh to win the December 1987 presidential election with a plurality, nearly three decades of authoritarian military rule came to an end.

By then, a transition to democracy had begun in another East Asian "tiger," Taiwan. In October 1986, President Chiang Ching-kuo lifted martial law and decided to allow opposition parties to organize (as one had already boldly done the previous month). Chiang, the son of the nationalist

Chinese dictator Chiang Kai-shek, was heir to a reign of one-party domination stretching back more than half a century to the Chinese mainland. But Communist China was beginning to boom and his own health was poor, and he could see the need for change. Even in the absence of formal party opposition, increasingly competitive elections had been occurring for decades, and (as in Korea, but with less radicalism) economic development was giving rise to a growing array of vocal civil society organizations. When Chiang died in January 1988, power passed for the first time to a member of the native, Taiwan-born majority, Lee Teng-hui. Over the next eight years, Lee led a series of sweeping constitutional, legal, and electoral reforms that dismantled the authoritarian structures, separated the ruling party from the state, and culminated with his own landslide win in the country's first direct presidential election in 1996.

By the late 1980s, the winds of democratic change were blowing vigorously in Asia, though not always with successful outcomes. In August 1988, Thailand crossed the murky line from a military-dominated semi-democracy to an electoral democracy when Chatichai Choonhavan became the first elected member of parliament to become prime minister since the breakdown of the country's previous democratic experiment, in 1976. Chatichai's effort to assert greater civilian control over the military motivated two generals to seize power in 1991. However, when they tried to restore "democracy" through the old superficial guise of military-backed parties and an unelected prime minister, it set off massive demonstrations and a return to genuine democracy.

Affected by the democratic change sweeping the region, thousands of students and intellectuals came to Beijing's Tiananmen Square in April 1989 to mourn the sudden death of the reformist general secretary of the Communist Party, Hu Yaobang. As their numbers swelled, their concerns broadened to include demands for press freedom and for a dialogue on democratic reforms between elected student representatives and regime officials. The students staged a mass hunger strike, supported by hundreds of thousands of other students, intellectuals, and workers in Beijing. Millions joined the protests as they spread to cities around China. It looked as though the Chinese regime might agree to significant reforms or even unravel, but hard-liners crushed the demonstrations in a deadly military assault on June 4.

Around this time, most of the remaining Latin American dictatorships were giving way as well. In Chile, the once polarized democratic parties united with other civic forces in a vigorous campaign in 1988 to defeat a plebiscite that would have given the military dictator, General Augusto Pinochet, another eight years in power. The next year, the democratic coalition decisively defeated the regime's favored candidate. In February 1989, Alfredo Stroessner's thirty-five-year dictatorship in nearby Paraguay was overthrown, and the country began a rocky transition through free (if not fair) elections. In December 1989, the Panamanian dictator Manuel Noriega was ousted by American troops, enabling the legitimate victor in the presidential elections to be inaugurated. Two months later, the violent conflict in Nicaragua ended with democratic elections that dealt a stunning defeat to the authoritarian Sandinista regime. In January 1992, a negotiated settlement peacefully ended El Salvador's civil war, permitting a more inclusive and meaningful democracy to emerge.

Meanwhile, in South Asia, democracy was also being restored. The Pakistani military's effort to manipulate elections and thwart popular pressure for a return to genuine democracy lost steam when the dictator, General Zia ul-Haq, died in a plane crash in August 1988. Three months later, national parliamentary elections led to the appointment as prime minister of Benazir Bhutto, the daughter of a former civilian prime minister and an eloquent campaigner for democracy. In Bangladesh, the military strongman General Hossain Ershad maneuvered for years to find a formula to extend his hold on power, converting his status into that of an "elected" president, but he never succeeded in taming the unruly political parties or civil society. When opposition demonstrations snowballed into nationwide (and increasingly violent) strikes, Ershad's support collapsed, and in October 1990, he resigned; an elected civilian government was restored in early 1991. Around the same time, Nepal was moving from a more or less absolute monarchy (with a feckless array of parties and elected bodies) to a constitutional monarchy with a freely elected government. Widespread popular protests forced the autocrat to yield.

THE SECOND BURST OF THE THIRD WAVE

When Nepal's bitterly divided parties came together into the new Movement for the Restoration of Democracy in February 1990, they drew inspiration from the dramatic images of democratic change in other countries. But the source of their encouragement was not Pakistan, or Bangladesh, or any other Asian country, so much as it was the stunning events of the preceding six months in Eastern Europe.

The dividing line between the two phases of the third wave is marked by the events of 1989. Indeed, the changes wrought by the downfall of East European communism were so profound that some scholars have dubbed the subsequent period of democratization a *fourth wave*.[7] At the end of 1988, only two of every five governments in the world were democratic; the global democratic trend had spread from Western Europe to Latin America and then to Asia, but not beyond. With sudden and startling force, that shifted. By 1994, another 20 percent of the world's states had become democratic, even as new states were being created with the breakup of Yugoslavia and the Soviet empire. In barely half a decade, forty countries made transitions to democracy at a dizzying speed.

The cascade began unexpectedly in August 1989, when Communist Hungary opened its border with Austria, and over thirteen thousand East German tourists escaped to freedom. Crucial also were the Soviet leader Mikhail Gorbachev's "perestroika" reforms, which appeared to remove the specter of military intervention from the east, as had happened with the crushing of the Hungarian uprising in 1956 and the Prague Spring in 1968. Anti-Communist demonstrations, inspired by the moral leadership and vision of courageous democratic dissidents like Czech playwright Václav Havel, swept through Eastern Europe, and Communist regimes toppled. On October 18, 1989, the aging but still ruthless East German party boss, Erich Honecker, who had predicted that the Berlin Wall would stand for a "hundred more years," resigned in the face of massive demonstrations and flights from the country, and soon thereafter his desperate successors began dismantling the wall. A year later, the two Germanys were united as one democracy.

Democratization swept rapidly through the other Communist regimes of Eastern Europe. Most of these countries had long been socially and culturally ready for democracy and had offered courageous resistance to Communist dictatorship. Dissident intellectuals, journalists, clerics, students, trade unionists, and other activists were well established. Hungary had been evolving toward a softer, more pluralistic, and economically mixed form of Communist rule for decades, and during the 1980s political change had been pressed forward in Poland by the best known of the resistance movements, the independent trade union movement, Solidarity. After a decade of strikes, protests, negotiations, and ineffectual repression, the regime accepted a series of groundbreaking (if still partial) democratizing reforms with the still-outlawed Solidarity in April 1989, several months before the Berlin Wall came down. But change was not everywhere delivered with such relative tranquillity and mutuality. In mid-December 1989, the most Stalinist and seemingly impervious East European dictatorship, that of Nicolae Ceauşescu in Romania, collapsed like a house of cards. Antigovernment demonstrations spread across the nation, army units rebelled, fighting ensued, and the hated dictator and his wife were captured and executed on December 25.

By early 1991, Poland had elected its first democratic head of state in more than sixty years; Hungary and Czechoslovakia were struggling to restructure and consolidate formal democratic institutions; Bulgaria was moving toward radical economic reform and full democratization under a noncommunist parliamentary government; and large demonstrations in Belgrade were demanding the ouster of a Serbian government that remained Communist in everything but name. Communists had lost power in four of the six Yugoslavian republics before intense nationalist mobilization led to violent ethnic conflict between Serbia and Croatia and then between Serbia and Bosnia-Herzegovina.

In the Soviet Union, the most artificial and ethnically complex of the former Communist states, President Gorbachev had failed to grasp that his liberalization policies, rather than revitalizing the Communist system, would open the space for its disintegration. After the Berlin Wall fell, nationalist mobilization merged with democratic sentiment to dissolve the power of the Soviet Union's central government. Governing authority rapidly shifted to the governments in the republics, many of them elected through a competitive, quasi-democratic process with some popular legitimacy (most visibly to Boris Yeltsin's government in Russia). In August 1991, a group of Communist hard-liners attempted to grab power from Gorbachev; on December 25, he resigned. The sudden demise of central authority left a daunting triple challenge for the Soviet Union: hastening the transition to a market economy, crafting and institutionalizing new democratic structures in the republics, and working out a new system of economic and political interaction among the republics. Many of the new republics, particularly in Central Asia and the Caucasus, quickly came under new forms of hegemony, as party bosses and repressive structures simply dropped the Communist label in favor of nationalist identities. But the three Baltic republics of Estonia, Latvia, and Lithuania quickly became democratic, and Russia itself emerged as a struggling new democracy, the most pluralistic of the other former Soviet republics.

The stunning changes in Eastern Europe and the Soviet Union had an immediate impact in Africa. In February 1990, two events launched a tide of popular movements that came to be known as the *second liberation*. In Benin, a coalition of forces in civil society declared itself "sovereign," seized governing power from the military Marxist who had ruled for eighteen years, and launched a transition to democracy. The dictator, Mathieu Kérékou, was defeated at the polls in 1991 and simply left office, to return in the next election, five years later. That same month, now freed from the specter of a Communist takeover and feeling the pain of international sanctions, South Africa's new president, F. W. de Klerk, took a bold decision to release Nelson Mandela after twenty-nine years of imprisonment and to legalize opposition parties, including Mandela's African National Congress. This began an extended process of dialogue and reconciliation, yielding the most complex, perilous, intricately negotiated and phased democratic transition in Africa. After more than two years of talks, ultimately involving twenty-six parties from across the political spectrum, and extensive ethnic and right-wing violence, a transitional government and constitution were agreed upon in late 1993, dismantling the last vestiges of the apartheid system. In April 1994, the ANC won a massive victory in the country's first multiracial, democratic elections, and Nelson Mandela became president at the helm of a five-year, transitional power-sharing government that included de Klerk as second deputy president.

Inspired by these changes and disgusted with the oppression, corruption, and economic and moral bankruptcy of one-party rule, the rest of the continent was swept by a wave of regime openings and broad-based demands for multiparty democracy. Under heavy pressure from international donors as well as their own peoples, most African states at least legalized opposition parties and allowed civil society greater freedom. Dictators-for-life who had ruled without challenge, such as Félix Houphouët-Boigny in the Ivory Coast, Omar Bongo in Gabon, and Kenneth Kaunda in Zambia, were forced to accept multiparty electoral competition. Kaunda's landslide electoral defeat in October 1991 and his graceful exit after twenty-seven years in power marked an important turning point in Africa's postindependence politics. Influenced by the events in Benin, other Francophone authoritarian regimes in the Congo, Togo, Niger, and Madagascar were obliged—after considerable resistance—to accept the same formula of a sovereign national conference. In early 1991, the island nations of Cape Verde and São Tomé y Principe voted out long-ruling single-party regimes in competitive elections that marked transitions to democracy. Passionate public opposition also compelled

Zimbabwean president Robert Mugabe to abandon his dream of a one-party state (but not his hold on power), and President Abdou Diouf of Senegal brought opposition parties into his government. Even Africa's Marxist regimes were shaken by the rapid breakdown of Communist rule abroad and their own abysmal economic failures at home. Ethiopia's regime finally collapsed after years of civil war, while Mozambique and Angola negotiated ends to their civil wars, dismantled socialism, and opened their economic and political systems. By the end of 1991, roughly twenty-six countries, or about half of all the states on the continent, could be "classified as either democratic or moderately or strongly committed to democratic change."[8]

Denouncing democratic demands as foreign-inspired, stubborn opponents of political pluralism and liberty, such as Kenya's president Daniel arap Moi, Cameroon's Paul Biya, and Malawi's Hastings Banda, appeared increasingly isolated. Yet even the Moi regime, heavily dependent on international aid, had to legalize competing parties in 1992 and jettison some of its most corrupt ministers. In May 1994, the ailing, octogenarian Banda was defeated decisively in the country's first democratic presidential election. By the mid-1990s, a continent that had mainly known military, one-party, and personal dictatorships suddenly witnessed a fluorescence of democratic politics.

Across Africa, opposition parties were legalized, personal and press freedoms widened, and new constitutions took effect. Many of these openings, however, were largely a facade, marred by continued repression and blatant vote rigging, as in Cameroon. In Kenya, the opposition was its own worst enemy, dividing into so many ethnic and personal factions that Moi was able to cling to power with a thin plurality of the vote, though the elections were riddled with fraud and violence. Nevertheless, by 1997 almost all African states had held some kind of multiparty elections,[9] and the number of democracies had grown to well over a dozen. Globally, the third wave had by then crested and stabilized with about 117 democracies (see appendix, table 2).

One last spurt of democratic change in the postcommunist world dramatized again the courage, ingenuity, and commitment of popular movements mobilizing Gandhian-style nonviolent power during the third wave.[10] A sequence of massive popular mobilizations (reminiscent of what had occurred in the Philippines in 1986) defeated ruling parties in elections and then, when regimes attempted to nonetheless declare themselves the winners, turned out hundreds of thousands of citizens to peacefully protest and ultimately reverse the fraud. On October 5, 2000, two weeks of disciplined protests—culminating in a million-person march on Belgrade—forced the resignation of Serbian president Slobodan Milošević. According to the Stanford University political scientist Michael McFaul, "Similarly dramatic events unfolded in Georgia after [President Eduard] Shevardnadze tried to steal the November 2003 parliamentary elections, leading to his resignation as president and a landslide victory for opposition leader Mikhail Saakashvili."[11] The popular uprising in Georgia came to be known as the Rose Revolution when opposition forces, led by Saakashvili, marched with roses in their hands and peacefully took control of parliament while Shevardnadze was speaking. In the autumn of 2004, the democratic opposition in Ukraine consciously adopted the tactics of the Serbian and Georgian revolutions (with assistance from Serbian and Western democratic NGOs) in order to reverse the regime's claimed victory for its chosen presidential candidate and compel the recognition of democracy advocate Viktor Yuschenko as the legitimately elected president. They wore the color orange, giving the revolution its name: the Orange Revolution.

The three revolutions bore remarkable similarities, McFaul observes. Each used the limited space provided in a semiautocratic regime to challenge an unpopular incumbent and rally disparate opposition forces. Each mounted extensive, well-trained, citizen vote-monitoring efforts "to provide an accurate and independent tally of the actual vote quickly after the polls had closed," and thus to convincingly cry foul when results were falsified. Each deftly utilized a "modicum of independent media" to report the vote fraud and "to publicize mounting popular protests." In each, newly formed student organizations worked with other NGOs and the principal opposition parties to mobilize tens and ultimately hundreds of thousands of citizens for "coordinated, well organized, and massive" protests against the fraud. And each was able to prevail in part because splits among the security forces discouraged or rendered ineffective the use of repression to end the demonstrations and save the regime.[12]

HOW THE THIRD WAVE HAPPENED

While these heroic tales of the democratic boom are inspiring, their similarities and phases are instructive. As Huntington observes, the early transitions were mainly triggered by internal grievances and events: defeat in war (for Greece and Argentina), the death of a dictator (in Spain), the murder of an opposition leader (in the Philippines), and the emotional visit of Pope John Paul II (to his native Poland in June 1979). But later transitions became increasingly stimulated by earlier ones. Huntington labels the dynamic *snowballing,* a process by which earlier transitions gave momentum to later ones.[13] The demonstration effects were particularly potent within regions or among culturally similar countries: the Philippine example of "people power" helped ignite and inspire the mass Korean protests the next year and the Tiananmen protests in 1989, while the mass mobilization in Poland and then East Germany emboldened democratic movements in other East European countries. Specific models of democratic change, from the strategy of forging compromise pacts to the particular tactics of popular mobilization and protest, also moved across national borders. By the late 1980s and 1990s, there was an increasingly *global* quality to the processes of democratic change. This globalization was manifested not only in the scope of change but in the accelerating interactions among democratic politicians and civic movements from disparate parts of the globe and the gradual forging of ties of regional and international solidarity, partly facilitated by the networking efforts of the American organization the National Endowment for Democracy (NED). In South Africa, the ANC made a systematic and deliberate effort to learn from other democratic transitions and constitutional systems, sending teams of experts to countries on several continents.

A second noteworthy feature of these transitions was their frequently negotiated character.[14] To be sure, not all were "pacted" in the classic manner of the Spanish, Latin American, or later the South African transitions. Some systems simply collapsed in the face of military defeat or mass demonstrations; in other cases (Taiwan and Brazil, for example), the transition was largely steered from above (what Huntington calls *transformation*). But a large number involved negotiated agreements between regimes and oppositions that had some equivalence of power. This required each side to moderate its demands and to make painful concessions while protecting its fundamental interests. Typically, leftist oppositions were not able to effect the social and economic transformation of society they had once dreamed of. Often it meant that the perpetrators of terrible human rights abuses (on all sides) walked away free or, as in South Africa's Truth and Reconciliation process, had the opportunity to do so if they publicly confessed and apologized for their actions.

Third, in most transitions—even the ones that were supposedly led and managed from above—civil society played a crucial role in mobilizing and articulating the public pressure for democratic change. For much of the third wave, the dominant view among scholars and policy makers was that democratic transitions happened largely as a result of elite calculations and negotiations, between leaders of the regime and the opposition political parties. One influential theory went so far as to argue that "there is no transition whose beginning is not the consequence—direct or indirect—of divisions within the authoritarian regime itself," principally between "hard-liners" and "soft-liners."[15] But that theory itself stressed the importance of the "resurrection of civil society." As more transitions happened and more scholarship accumulated, it became clear that authoritarian elites (even the "soft-liners") became willing to deal, or convinced of the need to plan for their exits, in large part because mounting protests, strikes, demonstrations, and other acts of resistance were hurting the economy, destabilizing the authoritarian order, and robbing the regime of its legitimacy. The mix and weight of civil society actors varied widely across transitions, but typically they included some substantial combination of trade unions, student organizations, churches, professional associations, women's groups, human rights organizations, ethnic associations, underground (or even legal) mass media, and assorted groupings of intellectuals, journalists, merchants, and peasants.[16] Sometimes they were drawn together into broad pro-democracy fronts.

Fourth, a crucial vehicle for bringing about democratic change was the electoral process. In one sense, of course, this was true by definition: democracy is a system that confers power via elections. But as Huntington notes in a perceptive analysis, a stunning feature of democratic transitions in this period was the regularity with which authoritarian leaders blithely overestimated their prospects of victory at the polls.[17] Over and over again—in Peru, the Philippines, South Korea, Burma, Chile, Nicaragua, Poland, Zambia, Malawi, and later Serbia, Ukraine, and Georgia—autocrats held plebiscites and elections thinking their constitutional project or political party would win, only to find that the people were not with them. In a number of cases, beginning with the Philippines, authoritarian regimes had counted on a final safety valve of electoral fraud to deliver them from peril, to find that combinations of domestic monitors and international observer teams were able to document and frustrate the rigging. In retrospect, it appears that elections also had another somewhat surprising effect. Repeated competitive elections in Africa tended to bring about marked improvements in freedom, even when they were not (or at least, not initially) free and fair. Staffan Lindberg speculates that competitive elections raised the democratic consciousness of citizens, made people more politically active and demanding, forced even autocratic regimes to be more accountable and responsive, built up the skills and capacity of civic organizations, enhanced the inclination of courts to defend citizen rights, and opened greater space for the mass media.[18] This thesis would seem to be borne out not only by the rising levels of freedom in countries with regular elections but by the surprising number of countries that held rigged or heavily constrained elections—in some cases, as in Taiwan, Senegal, Mexico, and Kenya, for decades—and then made transitions to democracy through the process of these elections.

To appreciate the depth and breadth of the third wave of democratization, consider that of the 110 nondemocratic states in 1974, 63 (57 percent) subsequently made a transition to democracy. This included all of Central Europe, most of Latin America, and much of Africa and Asia. Outside the Middle East, it included virtually all of the largest states under authoritarian rule—Brazil, Mexico, the Philippines, Indonesia, Pakistan, Bangladesh, Nigeria, South Africa, and Russia—with one massive exception, China. Moreover, most of the 63 states that made democratic transitions remained democracies.

The third wave of democracy also gathered momentum with the birth of many new states. Since 1974, 27 states have become independent from colonial rule, and 21 of these have become democracies (though 19 were states with less than a million population). Of the 19 new states created by the breakup of Yugoslavia and the Soviet Union, 11 (58 percent) became democracies. Overall, of the 46 new states created since the third wave began, 32 (over two-thirds) have become democracies, though in the case of the former Soviet Union, some of them (such as Ukraine and Georgia) have been only weakly and uncertainly democratic.

As democracy spread within each continent, it grew into a *global* phenomenon. Today about three-fifths of all the world's states are democracies. Not only are all of the rich Western countries democracies, but so are 90 percent of Latin American and Caribbean states, almost two-thirds of the former Communist countries, and two-fifths or more of Asia and Africa. The only region of the world that does not have a critical mass of democracies is the Middle East, and among the major cultural blocs in the world, only the Arab world lacks a single democracy (see appendix, tables 4 and 5 and figure 1).[19] Moreover, there has been a steady and impressive expansion of freedom in the world, and thus a dramatic improvement as well in the number of liberal democracies.[20] Regionally, freedom's gains were especially visible in the postcommunist states, Latin America, and Africa. By the mid-2000s, most of the East European democracies and about half of those in Latin America and the Caribbean could be considered liberal (based on their ratings on political rights and civil liberties from the nonprofit monitoring group Freedom House), and there was some significant presence of liberal democracy in Asia and Africa as well. (See appendix, figure 2.) Again, the only region that has seen virtually no lasting change in its overall levels of freedom has been the Middle East.

Some (perhaps as many as a dozen) of the countries rated by Freedom House as democracies would, by a stricter standard, be classified as "electoral authoritarian." Taking a tough stand on the ambiguous cases diminishes the number of democracies and the momentum of democratic expansion, but only somewhat. Neither they nor the more blatant dictatorships pose an ideological or normative challenge to democracy in the world today. As has been the case since around 1990, there are no global rivals to democracy as a broad model of government. Communism is dead. Military rule lacks appeal everywhere, and if it is tolerated anywhere, it is only as a temporary expedient to restoring order or purging corrupt rulers. One-party states have largely disappeared, for what single party—in this day and age—can credibly claim the wisdom and moral righteousness to rule indefinitely and without criticism or challenge? Only the vague model of an Islamic state has any moral and ideological appeal as an alternative form of government—and then only for a small portion of the world's societies. Moreover, the only actual example of such an Islamic state is the increasingly corrupt, discredited, and illegitimate "Islamic Republic" in Iran, whose own people overwhelmingly desire to see it replaced by a truly democratic form of government.

From this perspective, the broad arc of history since 1974 looks extraordinarily positive. The world has gone from dictatorship to democracy as the modal system—from democracy limited to one part of the world to democracy widespread in most parts of the world. But in the past few years, beneath the headlines of continuing democratic progress, a new and sinister trend has been gathering: a democratic recession.

3

THE DEMOCRATIC RECESSION

On the night of October 12, 1999, the Pakistani military overthrew the country's constitutional democracy after a decade of deepening political corruption, confrontation, and violence. The trigger for the coup—the fourth military overthrow of civilian government in the country's fifty-year history—was the ill-considered attempt by Prime Minister Nawaz Sharif to replace the armed forces chief of staff, General Pervez Musharraf, with a close family friend, the head of Pakistan's intelligence service. Just one year earlier, Sharif had forced out Musharraf's predecessor "after he, like Musharraf, had criticized the poor performance of Sharif's government."[1] A crafty political operator, Sharif acted while Musharraf was attending a conference in Sri Lanka. But this time, "the army moved quickly to defend its chief and preserve the unity of the most powerful institution in the country." Upset at the prime minister's increasing interference with the military, Musharraf's army loyalists alerted him, and he flew back to Pakistan on a commercial flight. Sharif, informed of the maneuver, ordered that Musharraf's plane be denied permission to land at the Karachi airport. With that, the military quickly moved in to secure the airport—and the country. Sharif and his cabinet were arrested, along with some two hundred other politicians and senior bureaucrats. Early the next morning, "General Musharraf told the nation in a televised address that Sharif 'had played around with state institutions and destroyed the economy' and had tried to 'destabilize, politicize, and divide the armed forces.'" Musharraf proclaimed a state of emergency, suspended the constitution, removed the leaders of all of the country's democratic institutions, and named himself the "chief executive" of the country, while decreeing that the courts could not consider the constitutionality of the military seizure of power. The military, he vowed, would rule Pakistan through a national security council and a cabinet of technocrats "until the army could return the country from the present 'sham' democracy to a 'true' democracy."

If Western democracies were unsettled by this abrupt dispatch of constitutional government in what had been the world's fifth most populous democracy, the Pakistani people did not seem to share the distress. As Ahmed Rashid, one of the country's best political journalists, subsequently reported:

> The bloodless coup met with overwhelming public support. Leaders across the political spectrum hailed the army for "saving" Pakistan. Not a single member of Sharif's Pakistan Muslim League (PML) condemned the coup or supported Sharif, demonstrating how isolated the prime minister had become from public opinion and from his own party.

For several reasons, the Pakistani coup was the single most serious reversal of democracy up to that point during the third wave. Pakistan was the largest country (over 130 million people) to have suffered a breakdown of democracy since 1974. Other big and strategic countries—Turkey, Thailand, Nigeria, and Sudan—had suffered military coups during the third wave, but in the former two cases, the military had quickly withdrawn, and the Nigerian and Sudanese coups occurred during the 1980s, after only a few brief years of democratic functioning and before the third wave hit the African continent. Pakistan was also the most powerful, *strategically influential* country to have suffered a democratic breakdown since the Turkish coup in 1980. Not only did it have nuclear weapons, but it also had become a major source of terrorist training and finance and of Islamic militancy. And while Pakistan's democracy was vigorous in at least the minimal electoral sense—despite rampant corruption and a weak rule of law, the two major political parties regularly exchanged power in highly competitive elections—it did not figure to follow Turkey's or Thailand's path of rapid democratic restoration. Successive authoritarian regimes and then eleven years of venal misrule under Benazir Bhutto and Nawaz Sharif had greatly damaged the country's democratic institutions and norms. Many in Pakistan appeared grateful to the military for interrupting what they feared was the country's descent toward a failed state.

The immediate precipitant for General Musharraf's seizure of power involved personal and institutional interests. However, Pakistan's democratic breakdown had more fundamental causes, each of which eroded the legitimacy of the civilian constitutional regime and left it incapable of managing political conflict peacefully.[2]

First, the justice system and the rule of law had deteriorated. Never very strong or autonomous, Pakistan's judicial system was corrupt and pliable under the seesawing administrations of Bhutto and Sharif. Executive power was personalized, and criminal prosecutions were politicized, as relations between ruling and opposition parties fell victim to "a depressing cycle of persecution and resistance."[3] Under the second administration of Prime Minister Sharif, who swept into office in February 1997 determined to consolidate his grip on power, the judiciary was set upon Bhutto and her People's Party of Pakistan; press freedoms were curbed. In the name of fighting terrorism, civil liberties were flagrantly abused and summary military courts were established to try acts of political violence in Sind Province. Ironically, Sharif increasingly relied on the military to maintain order and administer the country, including the huge water and power utility. But there was less and less order to maintain, as political and sectarian violence mushroomed.

Second, Pakistan was increasingly polarized along ethnic and religious lines. Diverse groups felt they were being (or could soon be) marginalized, and Bhutto and Sharif each relied upon a dominant political base in different provinces (Bhutto in Sind and Sharif in Punjab). Minority regions felt increasingly alienated, and ethnic political parties as well as extremist religious movements turned to violence and thuggery. These brutal tactics, "in the view of many Pakistanis, legitimized the use of violence by the state to curb their demands."[4] State repression in turn further radicalized them. Sectarian violence between militant Shia and Sunni Muslim groups (each with external backers) dealt an additional double-blow to political stability, escalating violence, terrorism, and insecurity while rejecting the legitimacy of democracy.

Third, the mounting problems of lawlessness, abuse of power, and ethnic and religious conflict were fed and compounded by economic failure and injustice. Under civilian rule, Pakistan was unable to achieve the economic growth necessary to reduce widespread poverty; with life expectancy of only sixty years and an adult literacy rate of only 43 percent, Pakistan ranked 138 of 173 countries in "human development."[5] During the 1990s, its human development indicators improved only slightly, and modest annual economic growth of 4 percent barely kept ahead of population growth (2.8 percent).[6] Unable to tax its major sources of national income (licit and illicit), the government had been borrowing to the point where it was spending 40 percent of its budget on debt servicing. With another quarter going annually to the military and more leaking out in corruption, "little . . . remain[ed] for development."[7] The successive civilian administrations were unable to implement the necessary reforms—controlling corruption and smuggling, taxing agriculture (and thus the feudal landlords) while rationalizing tax burdens, and liberalizing state controls—to build confidence among investors. Capital fled, unemployment rose, and legitimate economic activity increasingly gave way to the smuggling of drugs, weapons, and consumer goods, and to other forms of predatory profiteering, from kickbacks on state contracts to milking the increasingly depleted banking system.

Pakistan's travails of governance viciously reinforced one another. Deepening poverty heightened the tensions between different ethnic and religious groups. Violent ethnic and religious strife deterred investment. Corruption, capital flight, smuggling, gunrunning, drug trafficking, and the evaporation of international donor and investor confidence, in turn, all undermined state capacity, quickening Pakistan's descent into generalized state failure. In retrospect, the military coup seemed almost inevitable.

THIRD WAVE REVERSALS

One of the defining features of the third wave has been the small number of breakdowns of democracy. Until 1999, there had been relatively few democratic breakdowns, and many of the ones that occurred came within a decade of the 1974 Portuguese revolution: Lebanon in 1975, India in 1975, Turkey in 1980, Ghana in 1981, Nigeria in 1983. Subsequently, military coups toppled democracy in Fiji in 1987, Sudan in 1988, Thailand in 1991, and the Gambia and Lesotho in 1994, while elected presidents eviscerated democracy with Alberto Fujimori's *autogolpe* (self-coup) in Peru in 1992 and Frederick Chiluba's desecration of the electoral process during his 1996 "reelection" in Zambia. However, emergency rule in India lasted less than two years, and Turkey and Thailand returned to democracy after similarly brief periods of military rule. Ghana and Nigeria both returned to democracy around 2000, and Lesotho in 2002. Peru and Zambia returned to democracy with new presidential elections in 2001. If Fiji and the Gambia still festered in a pseudodemocratic state, they were at least small countries.

The coup in Pakistan was the harbinger of something different. It was not likely to be—and indeed it has not been—an instance of a brief, "corrective" military stay in power. It took place when the third wave of democratization was seemingly at its peak. And it reflected deep-seated problems of governance with which many other new and fragile democracies were also struggling. Since then, democracy has been extinguished by the undemocratic actions of elected presidents in Russia and Venezuela, by a royal coup in Nepal, by massive electoral fraud in Nigeria in 2003, and by the military (again) in Thailand in 2006. While Nepal is, at this writing, in the process of returning to democracy, and Thailand will likely do so before long as well, the authoritarian strongmen in Russia and Venezuela, with the aid of massive windfalls of oil revenue, have been consolidating their dominance of power. Russia and Venezuela are prominent among the reversals of democracy that have not yet turned back to democracy, and that threaten to be longer lasting (table 3.1).

In none of these countries have the United States or the other main Western democracies been able to mobilize much in the way of effective pressure for a return to democracy. In fact, they could not even do so in the Gambia—one of the world's smallest and weakest states, with an annual national income barely 10 percent of the yearly operating budget of Stanford University. The Gambia's erstwhile military strongman (a twenty-nine-year-old lieutenant when he seized power in 1994) has been able to domineer the country for more than a decade with little to fear from the democratic "West."

As we will see, these breakdowns of democracy are far from the only worrisome trends. Some other democracies, notably Bangladesh, are functioning very poorly and could be veering toward collapse. Several countries that have had democratic revolutions—the Philippines, Ukraine, Georgia, and Kenya—are in danger of squandering them in a downward spiral of factional infighting and bad governance. What seemed like the beginnings of a democratic revolution in the Arab world—in Iraq, Lebanon, and Palestine—have been melting into chaos and looming civil war. Elsewhere, as in Taiwan and Mexico, controversies over close elections and corruption scandals have generated crises that have slowed progress

TABLE 3.1 **BREAKDOWNS OF DEMOCRACY DURING THE THIRD WAVE**
(1974 through 2006)

Type of breakdown	Number of breakdowns	Percent of all democracies[a] during third wave	Countries with dates of democratic breakdown (and renewal)
Breakdown with subsequent return to democracy	8	5.7	India, 1975 (1977) Turkey, 1980 (1983) Ghana, 1981 (2000) Nigeria, 1983 (1999)[b] Thailand, 1991 (1993)[c] Peru, 1992 (2001) Lesotho, 1994 (2002) Zambia, 1996 (2001)
Breakdown with no return to democracy by 2007	12	8.5	Lebanon, 1975 Fiji, 1987 Sudan, 1989 the Gambia, 1994 Pakistan, 1999 Kyrgyzstan, 2000 Russia, 2000 Nepal, 2002 Nigeria, 2003[b] Venezuela, 2005 Thailand, 2006[c] Solomon Islands, 2006
Total	20	14.2	

[a] This counts all 141 democratic regimes that existed between April 1974 (the beginning of the third wave) and January 2007, as follows: 40 democracies already existed; 95 countries made transitions to democracy; and 6 of those 135 countries suffered a breakdown and then a return to democracy (and are thus counted twice).

[b] Nigeria had two democratic reversals in this period: the military coup of 1983 and the massively rigged elections of 2003.

[c] Thailand had two democratic breakdowns in this period: the military coup in 1991, leading to a return to democracy in 1993, and the military coup in 2006, with military rule still in place at the time of publication.

toward consolidation. And several powerful authoritarian countries—such as China, Belarus, Uzbekistan, and Egypt—have been narrowing the space for dissent and opposition and closing down channels of international assistance in order to preempt any democratizing pressures.

When one looks at all the states in the world, the trends of the last few years have continued to appear quite positive. Globally, even as the number of democracies has held constant or increased only slightly in recent years, average levels of freedom have continued to improve, and the number of countries raising their overall levels of freedom has usually outstripped by a considerable margin the number of countries with diminishing freedom. From 1991 through 2005, gains in freedom outpaced losses in twelve of the fifteen years, and usually by a margin of at least two to one. This occurred consistently and dramatically during the period 2002 through 2005, prompting Freedom House in its annual assessments to hail "significant gains for freedom around the world" in the preceding year,[8] "the lowest number of Not Free societies identified by the survey in more than a decade,"[9] and "a new watermark in the number and proportion of democratically elected governments."[10] All of these assessments were fair and encouraging, if all countries are weighted equally. But if we look at the countries that matter most outside the firmly democratic West, we see a different story. And that story became more globally apparent in 2006, when setbacks for freedom offset the gains for the first time in five years (figure 3.1), and Freedom House noted in its annual report "a series of worrisome trends that together present potentially serious threats to the stability of new democracies."[11]

One way to assess the global democratic trend over the past decade is to look at what I call the *strategic swing states*. Beyond the obvious candidates, like China and India, any such list inevitably involves judgment and is therefore open to dispute. I offer what I think is a defensible list: the twenty-one states outside the industrialized West that either have populations over 80 million people or have gross national incomes over

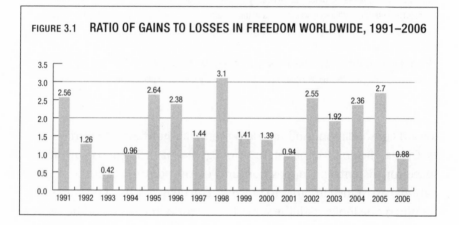

FIGURE 3.1   RATIO OF GAINS TO LOSSES IN FREEDOM WORLDWIDE, 1991–2006

$130 billion. To the list, I add Ukraine, the most important post-Soviet state aside from Russia (and a "swing" state between East and West if ever there was one), as well as Egypt, the most populous and politically influential Arab state. These twenty-three countries expose a decidedly mixed picture of democratic progress in the last decade (table 3.2). Eleven have made democratic progress, either by achieving transitions to democracy (as in Mexico, Indonesia, and Ukraine) or by improving the quality of democracy, as in Brazil, Turkey, Poland, and Taiwan. But Taiwan and Mexico have slipped recently, and the other twelve states have either

TABLE 3.2 **THE STRATEGIC "SWING" STATES**

Country	Gross national income, 2005 (billions of U.S.$)	Population, 2005 (in millions)	Average freedom score, 2007	Regime type	Ten-year democracy trend
China	2,263.8	1,305	6.5	Authoritarian	⇔
India	793.0	1,095	2.5	Democracy	⇑
South Korea	764.7	48	1.5	Liberal democracy	⇑
Mexico	753.4	103	2.5	Democracy	⇑
Brazil	644.1	186	2.0	Liberal democracy	⇑
Russia	639.1	143	5.5	Electoral authoritarian	⇓
Turkey	342.2	73	3.0	Democracy	⇑
Taiwan	304.0	23	1.5	Liberal democracy	⇑
Saudi Arabia	289.2	25	6.5	Authoritarian	⇔
Indonesia	282.2	221	2.5	Democracy	⇑
Poland	271.4	38	1.0	Liberal democracy	⇑
South Africa	224.1	45	2.0	Liberal democracy	⇓
Iran	187.4	68	6.0	Electoral authoritarian	⇓
Thailand	176.0	64	5.5	Authoritarian	⇓
Argentina	173.0	39	2.0	Liberal democracy	⇑
Venezuela	127.8	27	4.0	Electoral authoritarian	⇓
Philippines	108.3	83	3.0	Democracy	⇓
Pakistan	107.3	156	5.5	Authoritarian	⇓
Egypt	92.9	74	5.5	Authoritarian	⇔
Nigeria	74.2	132	4.0	Electoral authoritarian	⇓
Ukraine	71.4	47	2.5	Democracy	⇑
Bangladesh	66.2	142	4.0	Democracy (suspended)	⇓
Vietnam	51.7	83	6.0	Authoritarian	⇔

Sources: World Bank, World Development Report, 2007 (New York: Oxford University Press, 2006), and Freedom House, 2007 Survey of Freedom in the World, www.freedomhouse.org/template.cfm?page=15. The Taiwan figure is calculated from Freedom House, Freedom in the World, 2006.

remained firmly authoritarian (China, Vietnam, Saudi Arabia, Egypt) or degenerated politically. In Pakistan and Thailand, the military has over-thrown democracy. In the key states of Russia, Venezuela, and Nigeria, elected presidents or party politicians have subverted it. Iran has regressed from a somewhat pluralistic political state under President Mohammad Khatami to a more extreme and repressive dictatorship under Mahmoud Ahmadinejad. Bangladesh's democracy is at risk of collapsing; the Philip-pines is seriously deteriorating. Aside from the military coups in Pakistan and Thailand, the three most important reversals of democracy in recent years have been in Russia, Venezuela, and Nigeria. It is probably no coin-cidence that each of these three countries derives most of its government revenue from oil exports. In each case, democracy has been subverted from within while its outer institutional shell of legitimacy has been superficially preserved.

That half of the most important states outside the securely democratic West are authoritarian regimes or slipping away from democracy testifies to a worrisome turn in the global democratic trend. So does the growing backlash against international efforts to promote democracy. We have entered a period of global democratic recession, with the swing states as harbingers of a possible broader downturn.

TURNING BACK DEMOCRACY IN RUSSIA

Nowhere has the regression away from democracy been more strategi-cally significant than in Russia. The meteoric rise of Vladimir Putin from an obscure former KGB agent to deputy mayor of St. Petersburg in 1994, and then within a few years, key aide to Boris Yelstin's presidency, head of the Federal Security Service (the successor institution to the KGB), appointed prime minister, elected president, and finally a postmodern czar parallels the gradual constriction of freedom and strangulation of democracy in the country. To be sure, Russian democracy under Yeltsin was in many ways superficial and chaotic, plagued by weak political par-ties, the constitutional concentration of power in the presidency, "a dis-engaged civil society, the lack of an independent judiciary, and declining popular support for democracy."[12] The mid-1998 crash of the ruble brought down the liberal reformers in Yeltsin's government and increased his dependence on illiberal actors. Some even trace the demise of democ-racy to the manipulation behind Yeltsin's 1996 reelection.[13]

As Yeltsin's physical health and political abilities declined precipitously in his second term, Russian democracy drifted into near paralysis, while the politically connected business "oligarchs" grew fabulously rich. Official corruption and collusion in the privatization process reached such a monumental scale that one American scholar called it the "feudalization of the state."[14] As Yeltsin's second term was drawing toward the end of its constitutional mandate in 2000, the increasingly detached leader seemed mainly concerned to protect his family assets and security. After testing a string of prime ministers as possible successors, Yeltsin settled on the wily Putin, appointing him prime minister in August 1999 before resigning on December 31.

Yeltsin's move allowed Putin to run as the incumbent in an early election that saw the campaign period cut in half. Aided by nationalist sentiment bred by the Russian war in Chechnya and by mysterious apartment building explosions in Moscow and Volgodonsk—which the government attributed to Chechen terrorists—Putin won a resounding first-round victory in March 2000, with 53 percent of the vote (to 29 percent for his nearest rival, the Communist Party leader).[15] International observers deemed the election marred by serious irregularities, and a leading independent newspaper concluded that absent fraud, Putin would have faced a runoff election against his Communist rival.[16] Yet few analysts doubted that Putin would have won in any case: "after years of revolutionary turmoil, the Russian people clearly want[ed] a strong hand [promising] to build a stronger state."[17]

With his electoral mandate secure, Putin moved deftly and with ruthless efficiency to centralize power in the Kremlin, rout the badly fragmented liberal opposition, and gradually vanquish every independent source of power and accountability. An early priority was the ravaging of Russian federalism, a key foundation for political pluralism and check on central power. With a firm pro-government majority in the Duma, the lower house of parliament, Putin subjugated the upper house, the Federation Council, by removing from that body the country's eighty-nine independently elected regional governors and the elected heads of regional legislatures. He replaced them with his own appointees, turning the upper house "into a rubber stamp."[18] He then superimposed a layer of seven "super regions," again headed by his appointees, who controlled vast accesses to resources. Over time, he stacked these executive authorities, as well as his own cabinet and Kremlin staff, with former state security and military officials (the *siloviki*) who were staunchly loyal to him and hostile to democratic pluralism.

One by one, Putin also turned on the business oligarchs who would not bow down before the new party of power. The billionaires who owned independent mass media, Vladimir Gusinsky and Boris Berezovsky, were early targets. Through politicized corruption investigations and tax assessments, these politically independent tycoons were stripped of their media assets and persecuted into exile; others got the message. In June 2003, "the last independent television network, TVS, was seized by the government, allegedly to settle the company's debts," and since then "all Russian national television networks have been controlled by the government or by economic interests that support the government and uniformly praise the president."[19] In October 2003, Putin unleashed his prosecutors on the country's richest businessman, Mikhail Khodorkovsky, the dynamic forty-year-old owner of the Yukos petroleum company. Khodorkovsky, who was rumored to be preparing a political challenge to Putin, was indicted for tax evasion, detained, and beaten, and his business empire was dismantled even before his conviction. Khordorkovsky's fate—he was sentenced to nine years in prison (in May 2005)—silenced Russia's political and financial leaders, the last major source of resistance to Putin's hegemony.

The fear intensified in October 2006 with the murder of Russia's most courageous and outspoken independent journalist, Anna Politkovskaya. "The 13th Russian journalist to be targeted in a contract-style murder since President Vladimir Putin came to power in 2000," Politkovskaya had reported fearlessly on atrocities in the Chechen war and was "preparing an exposé on torture and disappearances in Chechnya carried out by [pro-Moscow] security forces . . . when she was killed." In the wake of her murder, one human rights activist termed the climate of Russia today *fascism*.[20] While investigating her death the next month, the former KGB agent Alexander Litvinenko was murdered in exile in London by poisoning with highly radioactive polonium. On his deathbed, he accused President Putin of killing him.[21]

With big business cowed or co-opted and the mass media almost entirely consumed or silenced, Putin was poised to win overwhelming victories in the Duma in December 2003 and for president in March 2004. As opposition parties struggled to project their message through government-controlled airwaves, the Kremlin-controlled Unity Party and its right-wing and nationalist allies captured over two-thirds of the Duma.[22] Among real opposition parties, only the Communists captured more than a handful of seats. The principal liberal parties fell just short of the 5 percent vote threshold required for proportional representation— "despite exit polls that showed they had passed it"—raising questions of fraud.[23] "The national broadcast media and most print media [were] uniformly favorable to incumbent President Putin," making the presidential election the following March a farce. Putin won 71 percent of the vote; his nearest rival, again the Communist candidate, mustered 14 percent.[24] Nestled into power for another term, Putin directed the parliament to abolish popular election of governors in Russia's eighty-nine regions, further "hardening authoritarianism."[25]

In my view, Russia ceased to be a democracy in 2000, when Putin moved vigorously to eliminate the checks and balances in the creaky constitutional system. Already by the end of 2000, Freedom House had downgraded Russia to a 5 on the seven-point scales of political rights and civil liberties (during most of the Yeltsin years, the scores were 3 and 4 respectively). Yet many observers (including Freedom House) had continued to consider Russia as a kind of rough, illiberal democracy until Putin's 2004 election, which cemented four years of subversion, intimidation, and repression. By the end of 2004, Freedom House classified Russia as authoritarian and downgraded it from "partly free" to "not free" status for the first time since the breakup of the Soviet Union.[26]

VENEZUELA'S PSEUDODEMOCRACY

Like Russia, Venezuela has seen a steady constriction of freedom and competition by an authoritarian strongman who was initially elected president in a competitive election. Indeed, the noted Bulgarian liberal Ivan Krastev counts Venezuelan president Hugo Chávez and Russian president Putin as the quintessential modern despots, one revolutionary, the other antirevolutionary, each using the language and formal institutions of democracy to rule an autocracy.[27]

Venezuela's long sad political descent had its seeds in the early period of domination by two powerful, factionalized parties that constrained political competition and divided up the oil income. Still, the inter-party pacts and expanding oil revenues sustained Venezuelan democracy through difficult times for Latin America in the 1960s and '70s. However, as global oil prices weakened in the 1980s, the economy contracted and living standards declined while public corruption continued at high levels and crime soared. The rapidly growing and increasingly impoverished underclass became fed up with its exclusion, and the country tired of the stranglehold on power held by the two dominant political parties.[28] Twice in 1992, then lieutenant colonel Chávez tried to overthrow the democratic system in bloody and nearly successful coup attempts (for which he served two years in prison before being pardoned). Six years later, in December 1998, he was elected president on a radical populist platform, pledging to lay the foundations of a new "Bolivarian" republic.[29] The new president wasted no time in delivering his revolution. "At his swearing in, he unilaterally altered the oath of office, declaring the 1961 constitution 'moribund.' He then proceeded—with the blessing of the Supreme Court—to violate it by holding elections for an assembly endowed with supra-constitutional powers to write a new constitution."[30]

With his supporters dominating the constituent assembly and the public disenchanted with the old parties, Chávez quickly obtained a new constitution that greatly strengthened the powers of the presidency, lengthened its term and allowed reelection, weakened the national legislature, and dismissed the existing Congress and Supreme Court. The new constitution, overwhelmingly approved in a December 1999 referendum, also created a new "Citizen Power" branch of government (consisting of the ombudsman, comptroller-general, and public prosecutor) to expose and prevent the abuse of power. But Chávez and his ruling party controlled these institutions, as they did the courts, the electoral commission, and the intelligence services.

After Chávez was elected in July 2000 to a six-year term under the new constitution, his power grew. The assembly gave him authority to rule by decree for a year, which he used forty-nine times. Unrest with his authoritarian lurch intensified, and in April 2002, hundreds of thousands took to the streets in Caracas in support of a general strike. Violence erupted, nineteen people were killed, and shortly thereafter "dissident military officers attempted to remove him from office with backing from some of the country's leading business groups."[31] In a huge and costly miscalculation for democracy, some anti-Chávez civil society groups also appeared to back the coup; the United States, for its part, was slow to condemn it. When the new provisional government reversed all of Chávez's policies, suspended the constitution, and dismissed the National Assembly, a countercoup rallied military and popular support and restored Chávez to power after only two days.

Intense protests continued, and the country's polarization deepened. In October 2002, an estimated one million marchers demanded that Chávez call early elections or a referendum on his rule, then launched a sixty-two-day general strike. When that failed, the opposition began to organize for a recall vote (constitutionally permissible during the second half of a presidential term). In an effort to mediate the crisis, former U.S. president Jimmy Carter proposed an internationally monitored recall vote for August 19, 2003—the first allowable date.[32] The two sides agreed on circulating recall petitions, but not on when the vote should be held if enough petitions were signed. With oil prices declining, Chávez's public support was hemorrhaging, and he scuttled the recall vote through his control of various government bodies. The names of recall petition signers were leaked and published on the Internet; many were harassed and victimized. "Public workers and contractors were fired, members of the military were forced to resign, and signers had their national-identification cards and passports revoked."[33] Validation of signatures was tortuously stingy and slow. Official obstacles to the referendum "continued to multiply" while 2 million new voters were hurriedly registered, many under dubious circumstances.[34]

The opposition finally prevailed, and the vote was held in August 2004, amid widespread malpractices, long delays in voting, and "significant limits" placed on both international observers and domestic vote-monitoring groups. Miriam Kornblith, a respected democratic scholar and a member of the minority opposition faction of the electoral commission, concluded that "the government made a largely successful attempt to commit institutional fraud" and that "this was the worst run election in Venezuela's long and varied experience, and the most ominous in terms of voters' rights."[35] But with opinion polls showing Chávez with a solid majority—generated by a massive infusion of government spending[36]—the Organization of American States (OAS) and the Carter Center blessed the election as reflecting the will of the electorate.[37] The opposition was deflated. In the October 2004 regional elections, Chávez captured twenty-one of the twenty-three state governments and more than 90 percent of municipalities.

After his defeat of the recall, Chávez completed the transformation of Venezuela into a pseudodemocracy. The institutions meant to check and scrutinize power were stacked with his loyalists. The armed forces were relentlessly purged of "opposition sympathizers—suspected or real" and converted into a "praetorian guard."[38] A new "Organic Law of the Supreme Court allowed Chávez to limit the tribunal's independence," expand it, and pack it with his supporters,[39] "putting the whole of the judiciary at the service of the revolution."[40] Another law gave the government control over radio and television programs. In typical Orwellian fashion, Chávez hailed it as an instrument for the Venezuelan people "to free themselves from . . . the dictatorship of the private media."[41] The "McCarthyite" use of data from the recall petitions and elections reached the point where "millions of government opponents" were excluded "from jobs, contracts, credits, and access to public services."[42] Concerns rose over the secrecy of the ballot in the December 2005 parliamentary elections. As Chávez tightened his grip, the opposition boycotted the elections, giving Chávez all of the seats, though no more than a quarter of the electorate voted. With that triumph, the "Bolivarian" president vitiated the last potential check on his authority. The next year, he coasted to reelection, with the opposition hounded and in disarray.

Going into the elections, Chávez's government enjoyed "a virtual stranglehold on the economy,"[43] lavishly funding populist programs and directing resources to his support groups at fiscally unsustainable rates out of oil-boom profits. Corruption, job discrimination, and media domination cemented ambivalent groups to his side.[44] Two months after the presidential election in February 2007, the reelected president announced a new eighteen-month period of rule by presidential decree.

In early 2006, Phil Gunson, a Caracas-based foreign correspondent, observed, "[Chávez] openly talks of staying in power until 2030, and his supporters have plans to change the constitution to allow this, on the grounds that the 'will of the people' should not be frustrated."[45] The only thing that seemed poised to slow Chávez was the fact that, even with a fivefold increase in oil prices in three years, his reckless spending was driving the economy into serious fiscal deficits and inflation.

MONEY AND DEMOCRATIC PROSPECTS IN NIGERIA

As in Venezuela, but with much greater chaos, violence, and repression (and even greater corruption), oil wealth has spoiled democracy in Nigeria. In Africa's most populous country, the promise of democratic reform was squandered in the early 2000s by a combination of gross electoral fraud, rising levels of political violence and criminal penetration of politics, and a relentless effort by President Olusegun Obasanjo and his supporters to amend the constitution to permit him to run for a third term. To be sure, political corruption, fraud, and violence have plagued Nigeria since the days of the First Republic (after Nigeria became independent in 1960), and massive electoral rigging figured prominently in the breakdown of both the First Republic in 1966 and the Second Republic in 1983.[46] One could argue that the 1999 inaugural elections for Nigeria's Fourth Republic (the third was aborted by the military in the early 1990s) were too corrupt to be considered democratic, but they did yield a pluralistic and largely credible set of outcomes.

As in 1983, electoral fraud in the country's 2003 elections disfigured results, most of all at the vitally important state level at which Nigeria's governors wielded enormous power and financial resources. As in 1983, the irregularities were pervasive and legendary, running from stuffing (or snatching) ballot boxes to forgery, often with the collusion of the police. The widespread fraud generated a "gap in credibility so vast that the victors writ large [could] hardly claim to hold the legitimate mandate of the Nigerian people."[47] Presidential delays in funding led (perhaps deliberately) to a hasty, inept, and chaotic voter registration exercise, in which "as many as 10 million voter cards [were] fraudulently issued" while many opposition voters were denied registration.[48] In addition, "the president effectively prevented local government elections" from taking place, as constitutionally mandated, in 2002, arranging instead for the thirty-six governors (the majority from his party) to appoint caretaker local committees, packed with their loyalists.[49] As the elections neared, political chieftains became warlords, raising private militias to do electoral battle. Individual candidates were assassinated, and communal violence flared. In the end, scores, perhaps hundreds, of Nigerians died in election-related violence, and many voters simply gave up from fear, confusion, or exhaustion. One asked, "Why should I risk my life trying to vote in an election whose outcome is already rigged?"[50]

The best independent academic assessment, by the political scientist Darren Kew (who was an international election observer in 2003), judged that in a third of the thirty-six states, serious irregularities occurred but they probably "did not significantly alter what would have been the outcome in genuine elections." In another third of the states, ruling party "leaders did not even attempt to erect a façade of validity."[51] Kew, who personally witnessed "widespread ballot stuffing for the PDP" (the ruling People's Democratic Party), recounts the election as follows:

> Ballot boxes were brazenly stuffed in the presence of observers . . . and returns were altered at higher levels. In some cases, polls never opened, and in others voters were intimidated and kept away.
>
> Reports of wholesale rigging came in particular from across the oil-rich Niger Delta and the Igbo-dominated southeast, where many polling booths did not open. . . . [In one state] entire ballot booklets were tossed

into the [ballot] box after being marked, and the boxes were dropped directly at [local government] headquarters, which never bothered to count them regardless. No count was necessary because the PDP had already circumvented the process.[52]

The losing presidential candidate, Muhammadu Buhari—who, like Obasanjo, was a former military ruler—pressed an outraged legal challenge to the results, but to no effect. Despite a fairly candid and in places scathing report from EU observers, Western governments congratulated the "reelected" president, assuming that he would have won even without the extensive fraud. As in 1983, the rigging led to a ruling-party landslide in the National Assembly—where the PDP won two-thirds of the Senate seats and 60 percent of the House seats—and at the state level, where it won dominance in twenty-eight of the thirty-six states. When Buhari's protest campaign fizzled and international attention moved on, the ruling party became bolder still. "Several PDP members of the House of Representatives from Anambra (state) who won reelection but who had voted to impeach Obasanjo in 2002 found that their names had been replaced with another list of PDP candidates" sent to the electoral commission.[53]

If there were reassuring elements to the 2003 fiasco, they lay in the widespread mobilization of civil society for the vote-monitoring effort, the credibility of elections in at least some of the states, the high turnover rate (roughly 80 percent) of National Assembly incumbents, and the practical acceptance of the results by a Nigerian public that did not want a return to military rule and so was willing "to suffer a bit longer with a massively imperfect system."[54] In addition, there continued to be extensive freedom of speech and the press, and in fact burgeoning pluralism in the electronic mass media. Most encouraging of all was the prospect that a second term would free President Obasanjo to pursue real reform of Nigeria's endemically venal system of government.

In fact, Obasanjo did take unprecedented steps in his second term to accelerate economic reform and to fight corruption through the new Economic and Financial Crimes Commission. But as the drumbeat for a constitutional amendment to allow a third term intensified, the countercorruption apparatus zeroed in on the president's foes. As the fateful National Assembly vote approached in 2006, legislators were reportedly offered four hundred thousand dollars each to vote with the president to amend the constitution, and some were threatened with prosecution if they did not accept the offer. A few legislators were even photographed carting away huge bags of cash from the bank as they cashed their checks, but the presidential bazaar continued while the anticorruption authorities seemed not to notice.[55] Despite the lucrative inducements, and heavy pressure from many governors—who would also have been given a chance at a third term—the Senate rejected the proposed package of constitutional amendments in May 2006. Obasanjo magnanimously hailed the vote as a "victory for democracy," but fears persisted that he would try to extend his term by more extraordinary means: starving the electoral commission of funding so that elections could not be held on time, or seizing on the various ethnic clashes and local insurgencies to declare a state of emergency.[56] By the end of 2006, Nigerian democracy was sinking deeper into chaos. Five state governors had been impeached and removed from office, and most of the rest were under federal criminal investigation for corruption.[57] (One of the worst offenders temporarily escaped to London dressed as a woman.) Some of the impeachments were engineered by political "godfathers" (bosses) who had made the governors and then been spurned. Officeholders were discovered to have criminal records, and were absconding with most of the country's windfall oil revenue, little of which was visible to the voters through improvements in public services or economic opportunity. State-level power struggles became increasingly violent; in two states, armed thugs of the alienated godfathers terrorized and shot up government buildings but failed to assassinate the governors.[58] In other states, militias waged ethnic separatist campaigns, attacked rival communities, intimidated opposing candidates, and engaged in organized crime. In the Niger Delta, ethnic militias attacked oil installations, illegally tapped into oil production, kidnapped oil officials, and fought one another for dominance in battles that claimed hundreds of lives.

Despite much trepidation—and astonishingly (but it seems deliberately) poor preparation—the 2007 national elections took place in April. Fraud was even more pervasive and outrageous than in 2003. Not only did Obasanjo's handpicked successor, Governor Umaru Musa Yar'Adua, win a landslide against two strong competitors, but the ruling PDP won huge majorities of the National Assembly seats and the thirty-six governorships. While the PDP, with its incumbency advantages, might have been returned to power nationally and in many states, the margins were simply beyond credibility, generated by flagrant and often quite open malpractices. The leader of the international election observer team, former

U.S. secretary of state Madeleine Albright, termed the elections "a failed process," and the normally mild-mannered EU issued a blistering and detailed indictment of the "lack of essential transparency, widespread procedural irregularities, . . . voter disenfranchisement," fraud, violence, and lack of a fair playing field.[59] The defeated parties and candidates demanded new elections. So did the country's broad coalition of independent election-monitoring groups, which—after fielding fifty thousand Nigerian monitors around the country—denounced the elections as "a charade" and called for their cancellation.[60] The only saving grace was that power had rotated from a southern Christian president to a northern Muslim, and in fact one who did not have a reputation for corruption. To signal his concern for transparency, Yar'Adua publicly declared his personal assets soon after taking office.

The democratic spirit survived in Nigerian society, but it was sorely disillusioned, and it lacked a democratic state and political class to give it room to grow. Severe disenchantment with the state of Nigeria's politics was already apparent during the 2005 Afrobarometer survey, which recorded sharp declines in a number of key indicators. The percentage of Nigerians saying they were satisfied with the way democracy was working in their country declined from a euphoric 84 percent in 2000, not long after the end of sixteen years of military rule, to 57 percent in 2001, 35 percent in 2003, and 25 percent in 2005. This paralleled a similar steady decline in public approval of President Obasanjo's performance (from 72 percent in 2001 to 32 percent in 2005) and of the National Assembly's performance (from 58 to 23 percent). By 2005, two-thirds of Nigerians felt that their elections did not enable voters to remove their leaders, and the percentage saying their country was not a democracy had climbed from 1 percent in 2000 to 19 percent. While two-thirds or more of Nigerians continued to profess faith in democracy and to reject authoritarian alternatives, erosion was evident, and the percentage of people willing to give democracy "more time to deal with inherited problems" declined from 79 to 55 percent.[61]

THE EXCEPTIONAL CURSE OF OIL

There is one striking fact about the twenty-three countries whose economies are most dominated by oil today: not a single one of them is a democracy. Venezuela and Nigeria were democracies until a few years ago, but democracy declined as oil revenues surged. A similar story prevailed in Putin's Russia, though the decline began earlier. Seven of the non-democratic states whose economies are dominated by oil are located in the Persian Gulf; together, they produce over a quarter of the world's oil. In the sixteen other states, oil (and in some cases gas) revenues account for the bulk of export earnings (70 to 90 percent or more) and generally half or more of government revenue and a third or more of the overall economy. Some of these countries, including Venezuela and Nigeria as well as Algeria, Angola, and Libya, suffer from an extreme and long-standing dependence on oil. Others are just beginning to develop extreme levels of oil dependence, as surging production and skyrocketing revenues transform their economies (table 3.3).

Statistical analysis shows that "oil does greater damage to democracy in poor countries than in rich ones" and when oil exports become a major revenue source for the first time—particularly bad omens for newly developing oil states like Chad, Sudan, and Kazakhstan.[62] Interestingly (and hopefully), it is also the case that where oil declines as a factor in a developing economy, democracy may finally flower. This has been the case since the late 1990s in Mexico and Indonesia, where oil was once dominant but now accounts for less than a third of exports.[63] When oil is a country's dominant export, huge amounts of revenue flow from outside the country directly into the coffers of the state ("external rents"). The state then becomes the most powerful economic actor, and its people become clients, not real citizens. Hence, oil economies become distorted, and the greater the dependence on oil, the greater the social and political distortion of development. When oil dominates, a middle class emerges, but it is not an entrepreneurial class with independent means and men-talities; rather, it works for the state and is dependent on it. In addition, individuals get rich—some, unimaginably rich—but not as a result of independent initiative and enterprise. Domestic business elites feed off state largesse and concentrate heavily in services connected to or enabled by the oil industry.

With the main source of national income controlled by the state, one of two things happens: either a more or less unified elite gets control of the national oil revenue and divides it up consensually (as in Saudi Arabia and the other oil monarchies of the Gulf), or elites fracture and contest in a no-holds-barred struggle for power and wealth (as in Nigeria, as well as Venezuela and Russia, until Chávez and Putin won the game). Either way, that classic driver of Western democratization—the bourgeoisie, or inde-pendent capitalist class—does not emerge. The business class is co-opted

TABLE 3.3 OIL AND AUTHORITARIAN REGIMES

All of the oil-rich countries of the world remained under or returned to authoritarian rule after 1974 and the third wave of democratization.

Country	Estimated percent of export earnings from oil (and gas)	GDP per capita rank minus HDI rank[a]
Middle East and North Africa		
Algeria	97	−19
Bahrain	60	−10
Iran	80–90	−24
Iraq	90+	n.a.
Kuwait	90–95	2
Libya	90+	7
Oman	75	−14
Qatar	85	−14
Saudi Arabia	90	−31
Syria	80+	8
United Arab Emirates	70	−25
Yemen	90+	18
Sub-Saharan Africa		
Angola	90	−32
Chad	90+	−39
Congo, Republic (Brazzaville)	94	25
Equatorial Guinea	97	−90
Gabon	80	−43
Nigeria	90–95	−1
Sudan	70	−2
Other Regions		
Azerbaijan	90	12
Brunei	90	2
Russia	65+[b]	−6
Venezuela	75+	17

[a] The GDP (gross domestic product) is calculated in PPP (purchasing power parity) U.S. dollars. HDI stands for the Human Development Index. Figures are for 2005.

[b] Includes exports of metals.

Sources: Energy Information Administration, "Country Analysis Briefs," http://www.eia.doe.gov/emeu/cabs/contents.html; *The World Factbook* (CIA), http://www.cia.gov/cia/publications/factbook/index.html; Heritage Foundation, *2006 Index of Economic Freedom*, http://www.heritage.org/research/features/index/index.cfm; U.S. Department of State, Country Notes, http://www.state.gov.

by the rulers, or the political and business classes are intermingled. If the population is small enough relative to the revenues, as in tiny oil-rich states like Kuwait and Brunei, the whole country can, in a sense, be continuously bought off with cash payments and lavish services from the state. In larger countries, if the authoritarian state gets into political trouble, it just spreads around more cash, buying up support and undermining civil society—as Chávez has done so extravagantly with Venezuela's swelling oil revenues.

But this ability to buy authoritarian control depends on high international prices for oil. Because oil prices (like those of many primary commodities) fluctuate wildly, regimes that rely on oil are doubly vulnerable: to revenue shortfalls when prices plunge and to popular revulsion at the grotesque corruption and waste that accompany booms. Where regimes boosted by oil must attend to large populations—as in Venezuela, Nigeria, Iran, and Algeria—the need to embrace spending spurts and populism impairs economic development and imperils political stability.[64]

Oil curses developing countries in additional ways, especially when the state itself owns and controls the oil. One is that oil states have more resources to build and maintain repressive apparatuses—to train and equip the police, military, intelligence, and other internal security services to monitor and punish opposition. Those resources can be used to undermine the autonomy and vigor of organizations that might otherwise constitute an independent civil society.

A second effect is cancerous corruption. When there is so much money flowing into the state directly and effortlessly, without mediating mechanisms or scrutiny, the temptations are staggering. Oil wealth is a kind of magical bounty, a true windfall. No one had to sweat for it, and so it is all too easy for state officials to rationalize that no one will really miss it. The oil states of Nigeria, Angola, and Iraq have become virtually synonymous with the terms *bribery* and *corruption*. Every year, Transparency International, a Berlin-based NGO, compiles a "Corruption Perceptions Index" by polling businesspeople and country risk analysts. Most of the African oil states score in the worst 20 percent on government corruption. To some extent, this is because they are poor, and poverty and venality tend to go together (with weak governmental institutions). But oil states are more corrupt than we would expect from their development levels. This becomes evident when we compare country rankings (in percentiles) on the UN Development Program's Human Development Index with their rankings on the Corruption Perceptions Index. Venezuela, for example, is in the forty-first percentile in development (with the first being highest), but the eighty-fifth percentile in controlling corruption—a 44-percentage-point gap. Russia boasts a 37-percentage-point gap, Kazakhstan 23, Libya 28, Sudan 16, and Iran 10.[65]

Such swollen state sectors and extensive corruption give rise to other devastating effects. With massive corruption comes massive inequality, as a small, politically connected elite corners the lion's share of a country's wealth. Where the population is large relative to the oil income, as in Nigeria, most of the people realize few if any of its benefits. That situation is made worse by the fact that the oil boom has drawn large numbers of Nigerians off the land into the cities, but without generating the jobs in the industrial and service sectors that would appear in a more balanced economy. And because the oil and gas industries are notoriously capital-intensive, unemployment mushrooms for want of investment in agriculture and industry.

As different parties, ethnic groups, and movements struggle for control of the bounty, internal conflict escalates. Natural resource wealth of all kinds—not just oil—is associated with a greater likelihood of civil war.[66] Most profoundly, oil states are deceptively weak and fragile states, highly centralized structures floating atop a distant, alienated populace.

With the huge, easy inflows of revenue, "state officials become habituated to [substituting] public spending for statecraft."[67] In particular, oil states lack the connective tissues to society that induce political accountability. When states derive the bulk of their revenue from oil exports (either through direct production or from taxing companies), they do not need to tax their own people. Consequently, neither do they feel any great need to respond to the demands and grievances of their own people. By the same token, when people surrender little or nothing in taxation, they may feel little or no stake in what happens in the political arena. If there is an inherent tendency for citizens to proclaim, as Americans did at the founding of their republic, "No taxation without representation," there is, so Samuel Huntington suggests, also "no representation without taxation."[68]

Finally, oil-rich states are not as rich as they seem. Or to put it differently, they are rich in money but not in human capital. Income gushes when oil prices rise, but productivity lags. In fact, the really rich oil states rank much worse (among all states in the world) on the overall Human Development Index (including education and health) than they do on per capita income alone. Saudi Arabia ranks 31 places lower, United Arab

Emirates 25, Iran 24, Oman and Qatar 14 places lower (table 3.3). On average, the oil states fall 10 places lower on human development than they do on the dollar measure of economic development. Oil states underinvest in health and education, so as their extreme concentrations of wealth and power prevent people from achieving the high levels of personal autonomy that typically come with development, the states do not experience the cultural transformation or civil society boom that states with "normal" development patterns do. "Hence, the liberating effects that modernization produces are largely absent in the oil-exporting countries, contributing only weakly to emancipative values and democratic institutions."[69] The richer the oil state—as in the Gulf—the more severe the imbalance between the monetary indicators of development and the underlying human development that breeds personal autonomy and a demand for freedom.

While the difficulty of building democracy in oil states is sobering, there is a hopeful corollary. Economic development fosters democracy only to the extent that it changes political values, class structure, and civil society. If dependence on oil can impede these conditions for democracy, other factors can generate them in advance of economic development (as they have done in India, Costa Rica, Botswana, and perhaps now Mali). Countries do not have to be rich to be democratic (as we will see), but they do have to cultivate the spirit of democracy.

THAILAND'S DEMOCRATIC AGONIES

As the most economically advanced and dynamic region of the developing world, East Asia has generated reasonable grounds for optimism about its democratic progress. By the late 1990s, the region had more of the social and economic conditions favorable to democracy, and its richest country had been a democracy for five decades. Taiwan and South Korea had made largely peaceful transitions to democracy, and the Philippines was completing a relatively stable and successful presidential term under Fidel Ramos, one of the leaders of the military rebellion that helped to topple Ferdinand Marcos. Thailand had recently adopted a highly innovative constitution to strengthen democratic checks and balances, and after several years of stable democratic functioning, the military appeared to have retreated to the barracks for good.

But as the millennium turned, the Philippines, Taiwan, and Thailand each fell into prolonged periods of democratic difficulty, and in September

2006 the military returned to power in Thailand. As several Asian presidents began to concentrate power and stifle democracy in the late 1990s,
Prime Minister Thaksin Shinawatra was doing so in Thailand, with an
eye on long-term political domination. Thaksin, a former police official
from a provincial business family who made a fortune from "a string
of government-granted, oligopolistic telecommunications concessions,"
made no secret of his admiration for Singapore's system of one-party hegemony.[70] It seemed that Thaksin's political dominance, unconstrained in a
parliamentary system by term limits, might last indefinitely. But Thailand
had three things that proved Thaksin's undoing: a strong monarchy, a
unified military, and a history of successful military coups. When Thaksin
was elected prime minister at the helm of a new party in 2001, he was
already a billionaire and one of the country's richest men. The country
had just experienced its most liberal government in history, following the
adoption in 1997 of a new democratic constitution with extensive, innovative mechanisms for checking and balancing power. But it was also
still reeling economically from the effects of the 1997 East Asian financial crash, and Thaksin's populist campaign—promising, for example,
low-cost health care and a moratorium on rural debt—won over the countryside in particular. There was just one problem: the National Counter-
Corruption Commission, created by the 1997 constitution, ruled that he
had falsified his mandatory wealth-disclosure declaration as a minister in
1997 and was therefore legally banned from serving in parliament or as
prime minister for five years. Thaksin fought back in populist style, prevailing in the Constitutional Court by a single vote. Suspicions abounded
that the margin of decision had been purchased, and "some of the judges
admitted that they had [acquitted him] on the grounds that removing
such a popular figure would risk disorder."[71] Portraying himself as a man
of the people arrayed against the old political class, Thaksin set about
delivering to his constituencies "while his approval rating soared to
70 percent."[72]

In many respects, Thaksin was an efficient and responsive prime
minister—but with a dark side. He did not tolerate criticism or opposition, or even the ponderous constraints of the rule of law, and he set
about systematically trying to eliminate them. "Critics of his policies [were]
attacked as unpatriotic or 'stupid.' [The] Anti-Money Laundering Office,
set up to investigate major crimes, began investigating journalists and
other government critics."[73] In early 2003, he launched a war on drugs that

appeared to give police license to kill. "In three months, 2,500 alleged drug dealers died," most of them, it appears, "petty users or low-level sellers."[74] Dismissing the high death toll, Thaksin said, "Bad people deserve to die."[75] He responded with similar ruthlessness to violent unrest among the country's minority Muslims in the far south, which claimed more than one thousand lives during 2004 and 2005. At the same time, he instructed the government media (accounting for four TV stations and all the radio stations) to limit their broadcasts to "positive" news and pressured privately owned channels (knocking two of them off the air). The once vibrant print press was attacked and subdued "through political intimidation, libel suits, and the threat of lost corporate and government advertising revenues."[76] NGOs that criticized the government faced "petty bureaucratic harassment or even criminal investigation."[77]

In February 2005, Thaksin faced the voters as the first elected prime minister to complete a full four-year term. What would have been a reelection turned into a rout after the Indian Ocean tsunami devastated Thai shores on December 26. The prime minister took "center stage in the televised drama of Thailand's crisis response,"[78] supervising the relief and cleanup efforts and hastening aid to the needy with a dispatch that the Bush administration could hardly fathom in the wake of Hurricane Katrina. Thaksin's popularity skyrocketed. Two months later, his party swept three-quarters of the seats in a country that had never before given one party a parliamentary majority in an election.

After his reelection, the polarization between Thaksin supporters, largely based in the countryside, and his sworn enemies among the urban middle class deepened. Opposition turned to moral and nationalist outrage when it was revealed that Thaksin had sold his entire family stake in his giant Shin Corporation (which included the principal satellite linkage in Southeast Asia and much of the country's cell phone market) to a Singaporean firm for nearly $2 billion while paying no tax on the proceeds. As in the Philippines in the 1980s, civil society groups took to the streets, mobilizing tens of thousands of demonstrators and demanding the elected leader's resignation or impeachment. Pro-Thaksin rallies countered with even greater numbers. To disarm his critics, Thaksin suddenly dissolved the parliament in February 2006, barely a year after his landslide reelection, and called snap elections for April 2. The opposition parties, crying foul, boycotted and kept a number of unopposed ruling party candidates from getting the minimum number of votes necessary for election. A constitutional crisis ensued, since parliament was forbidden to open until all seats were filled. The Supreme Court declared the election invalid, leaving Thaksin in power for six months as caretaker prime minister, awaiting new elections on October 15. Further complicating the crisis, the Attorney General's Office, investigating electoral wrongdoing by Thaksin's party, recommended to the Constitutional Court in June that it dissolve not just the ruling party but the principal opposition party and three others as well, and Thaksin hinted that the October election might have to be postponed, even though the country was without a parliament.

Through the summer of 2006, Thailand drifted in grave political limbo, with Thaksin warning of a plot to overthrow him by unconstitutional means. One of his few remaining media critics, the *Nation* newspaper, accused him of making "preposterous" charges and "paranoid claims,"[79] but on September 19 the military realized Thaksin's worst fears and seized power while he was attending the UN General Assembly meeting in New York, to the cheers of Bangkok's embittered middle class.

Many theories have been advanced for the military coup, Thailand's eighteenth since the end of the absolute monarchy in 1932. As with the coup in Pakistan, the military was not short of justifications, including the predictable allegations of corruption, abuse of power, and human rights violations. These were all valid. More or less like Sharif in Pakistan, Chávez in Venezuela, Obasanjo in Nigeria, and Putin in Russia, Thaksin was undermining the rule of law, dismantling constitutional checks and balances, stifling dissent, delegitimizing opposition, and polarizing the country. Strikingly, in each of these cases, a once popular elected ruler attempted to diminish or eliminate all countervailing sources of power in a bid to remain in power indefinitely. The postcoup analysis by the Thai historian Thongchai Winichakul, a professor of history at the University of Wisconsin, merits careful reflection.

> Thaksin's opponents wanted a quick fix by any means possible. They believed that democracy no longer worked under Thaksin. They did not accept elections. They campaigned for such undemocratic solutions as a royally appointed government. Now they have enthusiastically greeted the coup. It is, they say, a necessary evil, the only solution to the crisis that is Thaksin. . . . For them the end goal of deposing Thaksin justifies the means.[80]

Like several other analysts (not all of whom are willing to say so explicitly in a country that retains strong lèse-majesté laws), Thongchai explained the coup as "without doubt a royalist plot," in which forces loyal to the widely revered king, Bhumibol Adulyadej, removed a prime minister who was degrading democracy and subverting established institutions.[81]

The inspiration if not the architect of the coup was widely presumed to be General Prem Tinsulanonda, the retired army chief and former (unelected) prime minister who heads the king's Privy Council. As the military settled into power with a Prem ally and former military chief as interim prime minister, the generals seemed intent on reshaping the constitution and the political landscape to their liking. While Thais' still-passionate commitment to democracy made prolonged military rule unlikely, the enormous liberal democratic promise of the 1997 constitution has suffered serious and possibly lasting damage.

THE AUTHORITARIAN BACKLASH

Broad dissatisfaction with democracy is not a sign of its expiration, nor is political satisfaction necessarily a sign of democracy. The fact that a ruler has considerable popular support does not make him or her democratic. In 2005, the Latinobarometer found 65 percent of Venezuelans approved of the Chávez administration, a proportion exceeded in only three of eighteen Latin American countries surveyed, yet only 49 percent thought elections were clean. The results are paradoxical, because while they seem to suggest public tolerance for Venezuela's democratic regression, they also show comparatively high levels of support for democracy, rejection of military rule, and recognition of the need for political parties and a Congress to have a democracy.[82] This implies that Chávez's ambition to entrench himself in power for decades will eventually meet growing popular resistance.

Alongside the erosion of democracy in a number of strategic states, in recent years there has been a consolidation of dictatorship in authoritarian regimes. Opposition parties and civil society forces have been subjected to heightened repression and intimidation at the same time as international assistance to democratic movements has been disrupted or terminated. In their obsession with survival, authoritarian regimes have carefully observed nearby democratic transitions and derived lessons for preventing their replication at home.

An instructive example has been Belarus, a retrograde post-Soviet state that has been under the increasingly thorough domination of Alyaksandr Lukashenka since he was elected to the presidency in 1994. Alarmed at the possibility that the Orange Revolution in neighboring Ukraine and the other postcommunist "color revolutions" might spread to Belarus, Lukashenka—along with other post-Soviet autocrats, including Putin in Russia—spurred "efforts to destroy the opposition's organizational capabilities, silence independent media, undermine independent nongovernmental organizations (NGOs), and create surrogate institutions that make faking democracy and manipulating political processes less risky."[83]

In a 2006 article in the *Journal of Democracy,* the young Belarusian political scientist Vitali Silitski dissected the regime's preemptive assault on democracy. Lukashenka, who had pushed through a constitutional amendment in 1996 extending his presidential term and broadening his powers, first arranged yet another constitutional referendum—this time to remove presidential term limits. Next, the regime denounced the color revolutions while state security organs gathered information on how regime change might unfold in Belarus—and how they could prevent it. Third, security forces were given more leeway to disperse demonstrators with force. Fourth, the government harassed opposition leaders and rewrote housing codes to close the nearly three hundred local political party offices that had operated out of residences. Last, and to Silitski, most important, "the regime launched a frontal attack on civil society." This included an April 2005 court order that "shut down the country's largest independent polling agency." Public opinion surveys were required to have a license or face criminal prosecution. In December 2005, new laws were enacted that established jail terms of up to three years for running an unregistered NGO, training people in (color revolution–style) techniques for mass protest, "or 'defaming' the Belarusian republic in the international arena" (which the Belarusian academic could be accused of doing merely by having written this article).[84] Many civil society and opposition activists were arrested. Leaving nothing to chance, Lukashenka moved the date of the presidential election from July to March 2006 to cut short the opposition's campaign and to force the opposition to stage any protests in much colder weather, which would depress turnout.

Despite these daunting conditions, two opposition candidates for the presidency and their supporters collected the necessary signatures for nomination and then campaigned loudly on democracy and human rights. They had no chance of winning the election; Lukashenka totally controlled the mass media, the state treasury, the laws, the police, the Central Election Committee—and thus the results. One candidate was badly beaten; neither was able to deliver his final campaign message. The entire opposition movement was demonized as a treasonous plot. Nevertheless, and amid "KGB threats to charge protesters with terrorism and press for the death penalty," some twenty thousand defied fear and cold in several days of postelection protests.[85]

Lukashenka had majority support in the election (though not the 83 percent reported), and there had been no signs of broad disaffection with his rule before he cracked down. But the logic of preemptive authoritarianism does not allow space for a democratic "accident" that might destabilize even an established, popular (and seemingly impregnable) dictatorship.

Authoritarian crackdowns have had another common feature: a fanatical crusade to sever ties between indigenous democratic actors and international sources of financial, technical, and moral support. Many of the remaining authoritarian regimes perceive international democracy assistance to civic organizations and popular movements (like the color revolutions) as an existential threat to their survival. As Ivan Krastev, Bulgaria's most important liberal thinker, argues, "Ukraine's Orange Revolution was Russia's 9/11," transforming Russian foreign policy thinking into viewing the EU as "Russia's major rival."[86] The trend extends beyond the infamous cases in Russia and other post-Soviet authoritarian states to Egypt, which has traditionally allowed some space for civil society, and China, which had begun in recent years to loosen state control. This "resistance to democracy programs" cuts off grants and aid to NGOs, think tanks, media, and political parties. Legal and regulatory obstacles impede work and shut down institutions. Representatives of international democracy assistance organizations have been expelled, while their civil society partners have been denounced, physically attacked, and imprisoned.[87]

As dictatorships try to draw lessons from the successful democratic revolutions of their neighbors, they also draw aid and comfort from one another. Formed in 2001 as "a confidence-building mechanism to resolve border disputes," the Shanghai Cooperation Organization—grouping China, Russia, Kazakhstan, Tajikistan, Kyrgyzstan, and Uzbekistan—has moved beyond issues of regional security and trade. Recently it has become a vehicle for Russia and China to contain the U.S. military and political presence in Central Asia, and for the members to collectively rebuff international criticism of their human rights practices.[88] Pledging "non-interference in the internal affairs of sovereign states" and the pursuit of "a new international political and economic order," the SCO seeks to thwart efforts to promote democracy in the region. Vladimir Putin and China's president, Hu Jintao, said as much before the 2005 SCO summit when together they denounced attempts to "ignore objective processes of social development of sovereign states and impose on them alien models of social and political development."[89] With Russia and China holding joint military maneuvers for the first time in 2005, with Russia beginning to promote its own version of "Moscow-coloured" democracy,[90] and with China aggressively reaching out to befriend dictators, including Lukashenka in Belarus and Robert Mugabe in Zimbabwe, it appears that there is an emerging global alliance for supporting authoritarian backlash. Techniques and strategies for repression are shared among these authoritarian states. "Lukashenka reportedly acquired China's latest internet monitoring and control technology while in Beijing in December 2005."[91]

So far, the United States and the European Union have not been able to do much to reverse these developments. In egregious cases of regression, as in Belarus and Zimbabwe, they have imposed targeted sanctions, such as travel bans and asset freezes on regime leaders, but these have had little effect. Elsewhere, new military regimes, such as in Pakistan and Thailand, have encountered relatively little Western outrage or hard pressure to transfer governing authority expeditiously back to civilians.

Democratic change does not happen merely as a consequence of specific efforts, domestic and international. It also takes place in a larger political, strategic, and moral context. Since September 11, 2001, and the declaration of a global war on terrorism, democracy promotion has been buffeted by two conflicting trends. One has been the resurgence of Cold War–style "realist" imperatives to do business with despotic but strategically important leaders and regimes: Putin in Russia, Pervez Musharraf in Pakistan, Hosni Mubarak in Egypt, Nursultan Nazarbayev in Kazakhstan, and—until the West simply could not ignore an atrocity as great as the massacre in Andijon—Islam Karimov in Uzbekistan. The other has been an unprecedented emphasis on democracy promotion *as a strategic imperative* by U.S. president George W. Bush. The emphasis and the rhetoric have been lofty and inspiring. But in overreaching while undercommitting in Afghanistan and Iraq, and in failing catastrophically to stabilize, much less democratize, post-Saddam Iraq, the Bush administration generated a new geopolitical context: drastically diminished American power and moral stature, and eroded international consensus around the legitimacy of democracy promotion. In this context, democracy has been sliding backward in hugely important countries even while America's rhetorical commitment to advancing it has never been greater.

4

WHAT DRIVES DEMOCRACY:
THE INTERNAL FACTORS

We have seen in previous chapters how democratic transitions were made possible by a crisis of legitimacy among authoritarian regimes. A regime is legitimate when its people believe it is the most appropriate form of government for their country—better than any alternative they can imagine—and therefore that it has the moral right to make laws, collect taxes, direct resources, and command obedience.[1] In some cases (the Philippines, Argentina, Eastern Europe, and Africa), authoritarian failures to deliver development, control corruption, co-opt society, or maintain order crystallized a broad sense that the regime had forfeited its legitimacy, or what the late political sociologist Seymour Martin Lipset often called the *moral title to rule*. In others (Spain, South Korea, and Taiwan), the developmental successes of authoritarian rule created a more educated and politically demanding public with new ideas on what constituted a moral title to rule. In either case, changing international circumstances heightened the sense that the regime lacked legitimacy not only among its people but among other powerful states and global public opinion.

By the same token, however, democracies have been undone—either by power-hungry executives like Vladimir Putin in Russia and Hugo Chávez in Venezuela or by the military, as in Pakistan—when they lost or failed to build legitimacy. Typically, where democracy has collapsed, the breakdown has been facilitated by a dramatic loss of public faith, if not in democracy in general then at least in the institutions that constituted the country's democratic regime. It is one thing to lose faith in a particular government—the leader and his or her ruling party or coalition can be replaced in the next election. But when the general public comes to believe the *system* of government lacks the moral authority to rule, that system is threatened, particularly if it is a democracy.

All regimes—even the established democracies of the West—depend on some mix of legitimacy and force. There is probably no country of any significant size where every single citizen regards the system of government as legitimate; sometimes, force or the threat of force is necessary to compel compliance and punish behavior directed against the system. By the same token, no regime, no matter how brutal and totalitarian, relies purely on force to survive. Someone has to apply the force; someone has to believe in the regime. Even if most citizens privately detest the system, as in Burma, there is always some set of regime loyalists and true believers who regard the regime as legitimate and who are devoted to its defense and maintenance. If they are ruthless and efficient enough in controlling the state and its security apparatus, and in subduing the population through terror and fear, this base of regime loyalists may be as small as one or a few percent of the population.

But the less total and terrifying a dictatorship, and the more it gives some space for opposition and dissent, then the more it depends for survival on some degree of voluntary popular acceptance. Part of this acceptance may be active legitimacy. Part of it may be pragmatic coexistence or co-optation. Part of it may be resignation or apathy. What a dictatorship cannot tolerate, however, is a large pool of organized, confident citizens who actively reject the legitimacy of the regime. In a democracy, when the opposition organizes and wins over a majority of the public, it brings about a change in the governing party or coalition. In a dictatorship, when the opposition organizes and mobilizes a majority of the public, it brings about a change in regime.

Much more than dictatorships, democracies depend for their stability on legitimacy and voluntary compliance. For one thing, a democracy is, by nature, a system of popular consent. For another, there is a limit to how much force can be used while still calling a regime a democracy. The smaller the proportion of citizens who believe a democracy is legitimate, the more vulnerable the system is to breakdown, by a military overthrow, an executive seizure of power, a disintegration of political order, or a collapse of the state. Legitimacy is the lifeblood of democracy, and would-be dictators are like sharks in the water. When they smell legitimacy bleeding away, they sense vulnerability and they attack.

As rulers, dictators also face legitimacy dilemmas. For although they depend less on legitimacy for their political survival, they also have more difficulty establishing and maintaining legitimacy. As the prevailing ideas about what constitutes a legitimate form of rule have over the past few decades increasingly become democratic ideas, it has become ever more difficult to maintain straightforward authoritarian rule. As a result, dictatorships are today limited in their efforts to establish or sustain legitimacy, which was not the case in previous eras when rule by one man, family, clique, party, or military unit was viewed as a natural form of government, a divine right, or a means to justifiable revolutionary ends. It has become harder and harder to claim that authoritarian rule is *intrinsically* good.

Today, authoritarian regimes—with the exception of a few remaining traditional monarchies, like Saudi Arabia, or the one remaining totalitarian regime, North Korea—have to justify themselves in large measure based on their performance. To do so, any dictatorship faces an intrinsic dilemma, a classic catch-22. If it does not deliver what the people expect in exchange for tolerating authoritarian rule—order and economic development—it forfeits its only basis of legitimacy. But if it does succeed in solving the problems that ushered it into power—often economic crisis, social polarization, political violence, or insurgency—its harsh measures are no longer needed. And if a dictatorship produces sustained economic development, over time it transform its society in ways that makes authoritarian rule even more dispensable—and longed to be dispensed with—in favor of democratic rule.

AUTHORITARIAN DIVISIONS

An essential insight into the causes of a democratic transition looks at "fractures" in authoritarian regimes. In a seminal comparative study of transitions from authoritarian rule in Southern Europe and Latin America, Guillermo O'Donnell and Philippe Schmitter flatly concluded, "There is no transition whose beginning is not the consequence—direct or indirect—of important divisions within the authoritarian regime itself," principally "between hard-liners and soft-liners."[2] A review of cases in Asia and Africa supports their thesis, as well. Divisions within the leadership or the support base of the regime constitute a central factor in democratic transition.

Of course, such an argument emphasizes the role of elites, and as I hinted in chapter 2, broad mobilization in civil society often plays a decisive role in bringing down authoritarian rule. Still, the choices of a relatively small number of leaders in a regime and its opposition—their calculations, blunders, rivalries, conflicts, coalitions, and agreements—can determine whether, how, and at what pace democracy can be effected.[3] In every instance of democratic transition (save by foreign conquest or revolutionary upheaval), the dictatorship loses its will, its cohesion, or its base before it loses its power. But why do some of the dictatorship's leaders (or supporters) come to believe that the regime must liberalize and then ultimately even surrender power?

A crucial reason is that authoritarian regimes lose domestic legitimacy when they fulfill their self-proclaimed missions and become redundant— or when they completely fail to do so and clearly cannot deliver. But when a dictatorship fails to perform, the catalyst for change lies in its failures rather than in internal divisions. A number of third wave transitions were driven by such failure: the dictatorships in Greece, Argentina, Uruguay, the Philippines, Eastern Europe, Benin, Zambia, Indonesia, and the color revolutions in Serbia, Georgia, and Ukraine. These were not mainly negotiated agreements for exit but dramatic ruptures generated by bad economic or political performances. In Greece, Argentina, and Portugal, the democracy movements were hastened by stunning military setbacks, either wars recklessly initiated by the regime or the mounting costs of fighting colonial insurgencies (in the case of Portugal).[4] By the late 1980s, even the Communist Party elites in Eastern Europe no longer believed in the efficacy of their system, which kept falling behind their Western neighbors. Fear and Soviet power had sustained these dictatorships, and when the Soviets withdrew, the way to democracy was opened. In the Philippines, Serbia, Georgia, and Ukraine, an effort to rig national elections and deny peaceful political change signaled the regime's political failure.

In Indonesia, three decades of breathtaking development and sure-handed economic management imploded in just a matter of months under the strain of the 1997 East Asian financial crisis, exposing the extreme cronyism within President Suharto's "New Order." Until then, Indonesia had been an authoritarian success story: "From 1975 to 1997, no country in the world that began the period with a low [level on the

UNDP's Human Development Index] improved more than Indonesia."[5] In the quarter century preceding the crash, per capita income in Indonesia tripled.[6] Suharto capitalized on the nation's material progress (along with the judicious use of bribes and force) to stir up fears that the disarray of the Sukarno regime would return with civilian democracy and "to fend off demands for political accountability. . . . But the longer Suharto's experiment lasted, the fewer Indonesians there were who had personally experienced the 'bad old days' of life under Sukarno."[7] When Suharto clumsily turned to thuggery to shove a popular challenger, the late Sukarno's daughter, Megawati, out of the 1997 presidential election, he undermined his standing. Stories began to surface of colossal corruption and monopolistic practices on the part of the president's children and associates. Then, when the Indonesian rupiah came under selling pressure in late 1997, the aging dictator "responded . . . with inconsistency and vacillation," refusing to close ailing and corrupt banks.[8] Months of uncharacteristic indecision turned a financial emergency into a crisis. In May 1998, when the government announced cuts in fuel and electricity subsidies, there were widespread riots, during which security forces shot several students. With the New Order literally unraveling on the streets, Suharto was forced to resign and the transition to democracy began.

The staggering failure of authoritarian rule figured most prominently in the regime transitions that began in Africa in early 1990. Three decades of independence had produced miserable development across the continent. Per capita incomes in sub-Saharan Africa had increased only 22 percent in real terms during the period, compared to 60 percent in Latin America,[9] and during the 1980s, per capita incomes in sub-Saharan Africa *declined* an average of 1.1 percent annually.[10] Most African countries were crippled by massive external debts. Between 1982 and 1989, total external debt for sub-Saharan Africa had doubled—to a level equal to these countries' gross domestic product, and almost four times their annual export earnings. Servicing the debt cost on average about half of annual export earnings, leaving little in the government budget for delivering basic services. Dependence on foreign aid, already heavy, steadily increased, but despite an annual aid inflow of $15 billion, standards of life had actually declined in many countries since they had gained independence. As a result, twenty-five of the thirty lowest countries in human development in 1989 were African.[11] Ten percent of infants died before age one. Well over half of adult populations, on average (and in some countries, two-thirds or more of adults), remained illiterate. Throughout the continent, the physical infrastructure built up during the late colonial and early postcolonial periods was breaking down. Clinics were without drugs and doctors, schools without books, paper, or chalk. With governments lacking the foreign exchange to purchase spare parts, public transportation was collapsing to the point where people were trekking hours each day on foot to and from work. In some countries, civil servants went unpaid for months in a row because the state was essentially bankrupt.

These failures of performance were not just economic but political as well. As dictatorship deepened in African countries, and the idealism of the early postindependence years waned, one-party rule became increasingly arbitrary and oppressive, and the rulers, many of whom had started off as socialists, became brazenly rich. Political and bureaucratic corruption became so common that it was in fact the main *way* to get rich. Rulers ate away their countries' capital, their social compact, and what remained of their own political legitimacy as their bases of support narrowed to a clique of party loyalists, personal cronies, and ethnic kin.

As the authoritarian states became too broke to buy off their oppositions and too exhausted to repress them, protests escalated. Michael Bratton and Nicholas van de Walle's account of the Benin dictator Mathieu Kérékou's demise is indicative of the failures that stretched across the continent.

> In January 1989, students marched out of classes at the national university. . . . They demanded that the government immediately disburse long-delayed scholarships and restore guarantees of public sector employment for university graduates. By July, civil servants and schoolteachers also took to the streets with threats of a general strike to protest having gone without salaries for months.
>
> The government of Benin could not respond to these demands because it was bankrupt. Tax revenues had been slumping for years, capital flight was increasing, and top public officials were embroiled in embarrassing financial scandals.[12]

His power crumbling, Kérékou invited reformers into the government's cabinet and released two hundred political prisoners. The partial concessions did not assuage the protestors, who "escalated their demands to include an end to ill treatment of political detainees and a clampdown on corruption." By December, Kérékou felt compelled to terminate one-party rule and appoint a broad "national reconciliation conference," and "perhaps sensing the leader's weakness, key elements in the ruling coalition began to defect." The army and the trade unionists declared their independence from the regime, and by the end of 1989, demonstrations paralyzed the capital. When the national conference met in early February 1990, it declared itself sovereign, stripped Kérékou of power, and launched a transition to democracy.[13]

Yet, authoritarian regimes do not collapse merely because they become rotten and fail to address the needs and aspirations of their people. The Communist regimes of Eastern Europe persisted for four decades amid manifest signs of a superficial, cynical base of "legitimacy." Many despised dictatorships stagger on for years, even decades, because they have the resources to buy off support from the military and a network of party elites, top bureaucrats, trade union leaders, and businessmen. But the resources to co-opt must come from somewhere, and when the state performs so miserably that it cannot collect taxes from its people, it must find alternate sources or fail. If the regime is lucky enough to control a territory that produces oil, diamonds, copper, or other mineral wealth, that may be enough—in the case of oil, more than enough, as we saw in chapter 3—to sustain the regime. Otherwise, the dictatorship depends on foreign aid and is vulnerable when, as with Kérékou and other African rulers in the late 1980s and early 1990s, the donors finally pull the plug in response to the regime's failure to implement economic and governance reforms.

AUTHORITARIAN DEVELOPMENT

A complementary driver of democratic transition over the past three decades has been delivered in the form of authoritarian success in producing economic development. In South Korea, Taiwan, Brazil, Chile, and Spain, standards of living rose briskly or even boomed under dictatorship. Over the course of two different military dictatorships in Korea between 1960 and 1987, per capita income (measured in 2004 purchasing power parity dollars) increased more than fivefold; by 1987, per capita income had reached about $8,500, making Korea an upper-middle-income country. By that time, Taiwan had reached an even higher level of per capita income; per capita income levels grew after 1964 at an astonishing annual rate of over 7 percent, with economic growth averaging over 9 percent.[14] In Latin America, democratic transitions were also pushed by economic success. Brazil's per capita income neared $7,000 at the time of its move to democracy in 1985, having doubled over two decades of military dictatorship, and Chile's was only a little lower when it turned democratic in 1989. At the time of their transitions, South Korea, Taiwan, Brazil, and Chile were all at the higher end of what Huntington identified as a developmental *zone of transition*.[15] Between 1960 and the death of Francisco Franco in 1975, Spain's real per capita income (adjusted for inflation) more than doubled, as well. Its per capita income in 1975 was over $13,000 (again in 2004 dollars), putting it in the ranks of developed countries—almost all of which were by then already democracies.[16]

These five countries were exceptional, but in a number of other countries, authoritarian rule raised levels of personal income, education, access to information, and awareness of the world in ways that jumpstarted democratization. One of Taiwan's leading political scientists, Tunjen Cheng, succinctly documented the role of economic development in transforming political landscapes.

> Rapid growth . . . had liberalizing consequences that the [ruling party, Kuomintang (KMT)] had not fully anticipated. With the economy taking off, Taiwan displayed the features common to all growing capitalist societies: the literacy rate increased; mass communication intensified; per capita income rose; and a differentiated urban sector—including labor, a professional middle class, and a business entrepreneurial class—came into being. The business class was remarkable for its independence. Although individual enterprises were small and unorganized, they were beyond the capture of the party-state. To prevent the formation of big capital, the KMT had avoided organizing business or picking out "national champions." As a result, small and medium enterprises dominated industrial production and exports. As major employers and foreign exchange earners, these small and medium businesses were quite independent of the KMT.[17]

Democratization in Taiwan was particularly advanced by "the newly emerging middle-class intellectuals who had come of age during the period of rapid economic growth." These leading thinkers were connected through family and social ties to the new business class and had been trained abroad in law and the social sciences, which heavily disposed them to "Western democratic ideals."[18]

Over the last half century, the notion that there is a strong association between a country's level of economic development and its likelihood of being a democracy has been one of the most prominent theories of the social sciences, and one of the best sustained by the evidence. Since 1959, when Seymour Martin Lipset published his famous essay, "Some Social Requisites of Democracy," one study after another, using a variety of statistical methods, has documented the powerful relationship between economic development and democracy.[19] As I explained in chapter 1, that relationship, however, has eroded in recent years, as a surprising number of poor countries have adopted democratic systems. Yet, among richer states, the correlation remains almost unassailable. The United Nations Development Program annually ranks 177 countries on its Human Development Index, which takes into account per capita national income, life expectancy at birth, and average levels of knowledge (mainly, the adult literacy rate).[20] Of the 25 independent countries with the highest level of "human development," only Singapore is not a democracy. Of the 40 most developed countries, only three small oil-rich monarchies, Kuwait, Bahrain, and Brunei, join the list of nondemocracies. In the 50 most prosperous countries, there are only two more authoritarian exceptions, Qatar and the United Arab Emirates, which are also small, oil-rich states.[21]

The association between economic development and freedom—political rights and civil liberties, as measured annually by Freedom House—is no less striking.[22] In fact, the 44 democracies among the world's 50 most developed states are all liberal democracies, save for the tiny island country of Seychelles. Most of them (38 of the 44) have the highest freedom ratings granted by Freedom House on both political rights and civil liberties. Illiberal democracies now only emerge at lower levels of economic development.

There is debate about the grounds for this association between development and democracy, and between development and freedom. Some social scientists have suggested that democracies produce more rapid economic development, but the evidence is murky. For a time, there was a vogue for the argument that it was because democracy had emerged in the West, and the West, with its Protestant, capitalist, and liberal traditions, was better poised for development; thus, development followed or coincided with democracy. That causal just-so story turned out to be untenable when a number of poorer countries in Asia and Latin America developed and then became democracies. Clearly, countries could develop economically and then transition to democracy, regardless of their region and history: an authoritarian regime could lift the country into middle- or upper-middle-income status and then give way to democracy. Indeed, outside the West, the relationship between democracy and development is very strong. The Stanford economist Henry Rowen found in 1990 that the positive association between economic development and freedom remains powerful even when the rich Western democracies are excluded. In fact, the strong correlation between economic development and freedom levels holds as well *within* all but one of the major cultural groupings of countries that Huntington labeled *civilizations*. The exception: the Islamic civilization, and there the exceptional group is not all Muslim-majority countries but the Arab world. Rowen concluded, "These results support the interpretation that the wealth-democracy nexus is more than just a Western phenomenon."[23]

Of course, this still leaves open two possibilities. One is that development makes transitions to democracy more likely. The other—Lipset's original argument—is that development sustains democracy whenever it emerges. Both appear to be true. A comprehensive study of regime change between 1850 and 1990 found that per capita income levels have a strong positive effect on transitions to democracy. This was especially true before World War II, but the effect remains strong today at lower to moderate levels of development. "More development always increases the probability that a transition to democracy will occur."[24]

Studying the narrower period of 1950 to 1990, Adam Przeworski and his colleagues showed that economic development powerfully maintains democracy—the poorer the country, the greater the likelihood of a breakdown of democracy. In the poorest countries, democracy had a 12 percent chance of collapsing in any given year (yielding a democratic regime "life expectancy" of eight years). At the next level of income, the expected duration increased to eighteen years, and so on, up to the level of per capita income Argentina had in 1975, about $9,300,[25] and no democracy above that level broke down during the four decades (and since then, none ever has).[26] If one examines the fifty-eight countries in the world today that lie above that income level, a striking rule emerges. Aside from the eight countries that derive the bulk of their national income from oil[27]—which distorts politics, social structure, and development in ways I examined in chapter 3—there are only two nondemocratic countries in the world richer than Argentina was in 1975: Singapore and Malaysia, the principal challengers to any thesis about the kinship of economic development and democracy, which are discussed in depth in chapter 10, "The Asian Exception?"

FREE VALUES

Economic development transforms a society in several ways that make it more difficult to sustain the concentration of power in one man, one party, or a narrow, unaccountable elite. First, it alters a country's social and economic structure, widely dispersing power and resources. Second, it profoundly shifts attitudes and values in a democratic direction.

On the structural side, economic development enlarges the middle class and raises levels of education and information among the general public. After a country attains a middling level of development and national income, inequality tends to fall, reducing the social distance, and political polarization, between classes. For Lipset, well before the democratic boom of the third wave, this was a crucial factor in making democracy feasible: "Economic development, producing increased income, greater economic security, and widespread higher education, largely determines the form of the 'class struggle' by permitting those in the lower strata to develop longer time perspectives and more complex and gradualist views of politics."[28] In recent years, the Princeton University political scientist Carles Boix has shown that this is not just theory. As countries develop, incomes do become more equally distributed, which diminishes the threat of excessive taxation and intense class conflict and enables the wealthy to tolerate the uncertainties of dispensing with authoritarian rule—and the less well off to be patient for change. Hence, greater equality increases the chances both for a transition to democracy and then for its survival.[29]

Often, economic development also realigns interest coalitions, as shrewder or more visionary elites realize that the withering of extremist threats renders a dictator obsolete; that uneven development under authoritarian rule—as in Brazil and South Africa—must be mitigated to preserve the state's stability; or that newly assertive social groups must be incorporated into the political system. In large part, this may be because as more people join the middle class, the power of populist labor and peasant organizations declines. In such populations flushed with economic development, middle-class groups "bec[o]me increasingly confident of their ability to advance their interests through electoral politics."[30]

This newly emerging middle class may embrace what the late social scientist Daniel Lerner calls *psychic mobility*.[31] As people leave the countryside for the cities, cutting their ties to traditional oligarchs, bosses, or *caciques,* they also adopt new political attitudes and beliefs, transformed by rising education levels and expanding, and increasingly global, communication. With development, the quantity and variety of information available explodes, and more important, control over it is dispersed. Radios, satellite television dishes, computers, Internet access, cell phones, text messaging, and other technology become physically and financially accessible to a much wider range of people. With recent technological revolutions, the ability to generate information and opinion has been radically decentralized through low-cost FM radio, cable television stations, and Web-based blogs and international news sources, all of which are more difficult for authoritarian regimes to control than past mass media. As people acquire more income and information, they become more politically aware and confident, more inclined to participate in politics, to think for themselves, and thus to break free of traditional patron-client ties.

With these sweeping social and psychological changes, people in growing numbers form and join organizations—including professional and student associations, trade unions, human rights and civic groups—to service their interests and needs. As these independent organizations grow in number, resources, and sophistication, they become more assertive and more capable of checking and challenging the state, generating the foundations for a vibrant civil society. So as a country gets richer, the balance of power shifts from the state to the society.

Most striking, however, is the wealth of data that has accumulated to show that as people's lives are transformed by economic development, they increasingly espouse democratic values: the higher the levels of education, income, mass media exposure, and occupational status, the more democratic the people's attitudes, values, and behavior. In particular, more educated people tend to be more tolerant of differences and opposition, more respectful of minority rights, more valuing of freedom, and more trustful of other people. They are more inclined to participate in politics and to join organizations and more confident of their capacities to influence government.[32] Some of these democratic values—trust, tolerance, antiauthoritarianism, and confidence in one's ability to influence politics—even appear to be fostered simply by living in a more developed country, independent of the individual's socioeconomic status.[33]

The most recent, comprehensive, and ambitious analysis of the relationship between development, value change, and democracy comes from Ronald Inglehart of the University of Michigan, the founder of the World Values Survey, who has been analyzing global trends in basic value orientations for over thirty years. Inglehart began in the 1970s with a simple thesis, based on the psychologist Abraham Maslow's theory of a hierarchy of human needs. According to Maslow, the "lower order" needs for safety, security, and sustenance take precedence until they are met, after which people will give priority to such "higher order" needs as belonging, esteem, and self-expression. Through an ingenious research design, Inglehart showed, initially across a number of Western societies, that people who grew up in periods of economic prosperity and security tended to have "postmaterialist" values, emphasizing (for example) freedom and the environment, while those who grew up and had their values formed in periods of economic insecurity and stress tended to have "materialist" values (emphasizing economic and physical security). With economic development and generational change, there was a marked shift over time from materialist to postmaterialist values.[34]

As the World Values Survey expanded to include eighty-one countries in every major region of the world, Inglehart and the German political scientist Christian Welzel dug into four waves of surveys conducted between 1981 and 2001 to assess what impact this value distinction might have on democracy. Their results are stunning. Adding to the materialist/postmaterialist distinction, they analyzed survey questions measuring trust, tolerance of diversity, and willingness to protest, which together yield an assessment of a society's "survival values" versus "self-expression values," which emphasize "human autonomy and choice."[35] Societies tend to cluster in consistent ways around these value orientations. The post-Soviet states and low-income developing countries veer strongly toward survival values (and toward more culturally traditional and religious values), while Western, high-income countries bunch around self-expression values (and "secular-rational" values). Middle- and upper-middle-income developing countries in Latin America and Asia tend to be in the middle—in what seems a transition toward self-expression values that is quite visible in Korea and Taiwan, despite the supposed "Asian" emphasis on order, authority, and community. Self-expression values flower fully in postindustrial countries, where the service economy dominates and values are shaped by the reality of prosperity and pluralism. Thus, Ingelhart and Welzel write, "socioeconomic development tends to propel societies in a common direction"—toward self-expression values and "emancipation from authority"—"regardless of their cultural heritage."[36] Consequently, there is an extremely high correlation between a country's level of development and its level of self-expression values.[37]

This cultural shift toward tolerance, trust in others, suspicion of authority, and valuing of freedom has profound political consequences. For one thing, it generates higher levels of peaceful protest activities (such as petitions, demonstrations, and consumer boycotts) that challenge ruling elites. This effect holds for both old and new democracies, and in the latter case, even well after the surge of mass mobilization to bring down dictatorship has subsided.[38] And as people come to embrace self-expression values, and so to challenge authority, they come to demand democracy—and not just any democracy but the institutions to protect individual freedom and choice that encompass liberal democracy. The extent of self-expression values in a society, Inglehart and Welzel find, is highly correlated with the extent of democracy, even stronger when measured against the status of liberal democracy (based on Freedom House rankings), and astonishingly so when indexed against the level of "effective democracy" (which also factors in the World Bank's anticorruption index).[39] In fact, "without exception, any society in which more than half the population emphasizes self-expression values scores at least 90 percent of the maximum score on liberal democracy."[40] Moreover, their statistical analysis shows, this is not just an association. Rather, the growth of self-expression values has "a strong causal impact" on the emergence of electoral democracy and effective, liberal democracy, in part because these values generate the associations and civic actions that compel rulers to be more honest, accountable, and respectful of the law.[41]

From this extraordinary work, we see economic development as an integrated and powerful process unleashing individual choice and autonomy. As people's income, education, access to information, and occupational status rise, they become more independent financially and intellectually. At the same time, they become more socially independent and capable, and thus they more easily form and join organizations and come together to protest. "As growing socioeconomic resources broaden the range of activities that people can choose, self-expression values broaden the range of activities to which they aspire." Sooner or later, people who have become "materially, intellectually, and socially more independent" also want political independence. Thus they are led to give "liberty priority over discipline, diversity over conformity, and autonomy over authority"— and therefore "to seek the civil and political rights that define liberal democracy."[42] These value transformations are so ineluctable that Inglehart and Welzel predict that China and Vietnam, with their booming economic growth, will experience transitions to democracy within twenty years, and that Singapore, already developed, will achieve full democracy within ten years. In chapter 10, I will consider more closely the prospect for democracy in Asia, and why I think Inglehart and Welzel are likely to be correct, if off by a few years.

THE RISE OF CIVIL SOCIETY

Inglehart and Welzel are leading "structuralists," part of the group of democracy scholars who identify broad changes in social structure, driven by economic development and social change, as the key drivers of democracy. Structuralists criticize the "parochialism" of theories that emphasize the elite's choices and institutional designs: "The very essence of democracy is that it reflects people power and not simply the constitutional choice of enlightened elites."[43]

Another camp considers a primarily "elite-centered" provocation for democratic transitions. Yet, while Guillermo O'Donnell and Philippe Schmitter recognize the importance of ferment in civil society, their "elite-centered" argument remains inadequate in explaining the democratic trend throughout the world. The first shortcoming of O'Donnell and Schmitter's theory is the image of civil society they present, one of resurrection, resurgence, and restructuring—a return to open expression and free associations that is largely accurate for Europe and Latin America but woefully inaccurate for most new democracies since 1974. Missing is the process of economic development that creates organizations and capacities that never existed before.

Second, they isolate the critical contribution of civil society into the period *after* the authoritarian regime has split, when ascendant "soft-liners" begin to liberalize the regime. At this point, in their view, an "upsurge" of popular mobilization pushes the transition forward. O'Donnell and Schmitter do acknowledge that what turns some of the old hard-liners into emerging soft-liners "is their increasing recognition that the regime they helped to implant . . . will have to make use, in the foreseeable future, of some degree or some form of electoral legitimation," and thus will have to begin by introducing certain freedoms.[44] But most "visionary" regime liberalizers undertake democratic reform not out of any intrinsic commitment or conversion to democratic norms, but for hardheaded, calculating, strategic reasons. They foresee that they cannot hold on to power indefinitely. And the reason they cannot is often the real origin of democratic transitions: the changes and mobilization in civil society. While some regimes dissolve because they never intended to remain in power, most authoritarian rulers only abandon power because society will not let them hold it indefinitely without costs the elites do not wish to pay.

Any one of several changes may explain why civil society will no longer condone the continuation of authoritarian rule. For one, political values may have shifted in a democratic direction. Economic development, as we have seen, is a potent cause of this shift, but it is not the only cause. In much of Latin America during the 1970s and early 1980s, the experience of brutal repression transformed the values of influential groups, triggering a "revalorization" of democracy, especially on the left.[45] A similar process occurred in Africa, as people from all walks of life realized the false promises and brutal failings of the one-party state. As the public comes to place a higher value on political freedom and civil liberties—in and for themselves—more people speak out, demonstrate, and organize, beginning with the denunciation of human rights abuses.

A second change may come in the alignment of interests in society. An important turning point in the transition to democracy comes when the privileged—landowners, industrialists, merchants, and bankers— "come to the conclusion that the authoritarian regime is dispensable," again either because it has succeeded or because it has failed, and its continuation might risk damage to their long-run interests.[46] Such large-scale shifts were crucial in bringing about democratic transitions in the Philippines and Indonesia, and they mattered (albeit more incrementally) in Thailand and Taiwan as well. They were a major factor pressing for democratic transition in South Africa, where the major white industrial and banking interests emerged as leading critics of apartheid, once they saw it as inconsistent with the long-term security of a capitalist system increasingly dependent on skilled black labor.

A third, profound change arises with the growth of formal and informal organizations in civil society, and in their capacities, resources, autonomy, and initiative, all of which can radically alter the balance of power. An authoritarian regime that could once easily dominate and control gets thrown on the defensive. Students march in the streets demanding change. Workers paralyze industries with strikes. Lawyers refuse to cooperate in judicial charades. Alternative sources of information shatter the illusion of legitimacy and the veil of secrecy and disinformation. Local development groups break the dependence of peasants on landlords or the state, and generate alternative sources of political power and activity. Informal networks of production and exchange emerge that deny resources to the state. Not all of these developments are necessarily positive in their implications for democratic development, but they all contribute in a cumulative way to the erosion of authoritarian control.

In much of the world, it is this increase in independent organizational capacity and density that represents the real, indigenous origins of democracies. And this is not a new development; it was a critical dimension in the spread of democracy in the United States two centuries ago,[47] and in the mobilization for and subsequent success of democracy in India before and after independence.[48] In Eastern Europe, the Soviet Union, and China, the growth of autonomous organizational, cultural, and intellectual life, surreptitiously at first, has provided the cutting edge of democracy movements.[49] In Taiwan, democratic change during the 1980s was stimulated and advanced by a host of social movements—of consumers, workers, women, aborigines, farmers, students, teachers, and the environmentally concerned—breaking free of traditional deference or state intimidation and control to seek specific demands and long-range goals.[50] In Thailand, similar developments during the 1990s led to the reform of the constitution and the deepening of democracy, and in Indonesia, the growth of opposition helped to enable the country's democratic opening.

In the Philippines under Ferdinand Marcos, Nigeria under the military, Kenya under Daniel arap Moi, and Latin America under various military regimes, associations of all kinds—initially of students, intellectuals, lawyers, and human rights workers, and then of trade unions, businesspeople, manufacturers, women, doctors, teachers, and peasants—kept democratic aspirations alive, protested authoritarian abuses, and then pressed for democratization.[51] In Spain, Peru, and Argentina, labor protests and strikes "were crucial in destabilizing authoritarianism and paving the way for democratization," by engendering divisions within the dictatorships and pressing them to surrender power before they were ready.[52] Throughout Africa, the growth of informal organizations and movements, and of political participation in them, sustained pressure for democracy until a more favorable juncture for transition came in 1990.[53] In a great many countries—notably, Brazil, Chile, El Salvador, Nicaragua, the Philippines, South Korea, Poland, Haiti, South Africa, and Kenya—religious institutions (especially the Catholic Church) played prominent roles in the movements to oppose, denounce, frustrate, and remove authoritarian regimes.[54] Without the broad mobilization of civil society, first in well-prepared efforts to monitor elections and then in massive and well-coordinated street protests, the democratic color revolutions would not have happened in Serbia, Georgia, and Ukraine.[55] Finally, where the press was allowed some autonomy under authoritarian rule or an underground press functioned—as in the Philippines, South Africa, Nigeria, and Poland—its exposure of abuses and airing of liberal viewpoints made an important contribution to the momentum for democracy.[56]

Much depends on the ability of civil society forces to unite across competing political parties and disparate social classes into a broad front or movement, and that requires not just societal wealth in the form of economic development, but some dispersal of resources outside state control. As we have seen, many of the remaining autocracies of the world—not only in the Middle East but among African states such as Angola, Gabon, and Republic of Congo—derive their power and resources from the control of expensive local commodities like oil. Given the political pressures that build when a dictator delivers broad-based economic development, an authoritarian ruler with an eye to longevity does better by monopolizing the income from mineral exports and using that revenue to co-opt some opposition and repress the rest. The principal other source of external rents today is foreign aid—which for many poor countries has functioned like oil in sustaining authoritarian rule. When aid is suspended, a dictatorship may face crisis or collapse, as in the case of Benin. During the third wave, more than ever before, the external environment has had a potent impact in obstructing or facilitating democratic change, as we will see in the next chapter.

5

WHAT DRIVES DEMOCRACY:
THE EXTERNAL FACTORS

In addition to its breathtaking scope, one other feature has distinguished the third wave of democratic change: the impact of international influences and pressures in fostering democratic change. But except where democracy emerged out of foreign military intervention—as in Grenada in 1983 and Panama in 1989—external factors were not the decisive ones. And even in those cases where international force was used, democracy could not long survive in the absence of domestic support for it, as was revealed in Haiti in 1994, when an impending U.S. intervention helped oust the military regime, only to have the country revert to its authoritarian practices.

Over the past two decades, however, traditional notions of sovereignty—of "nonintervention" in the internal affairs of other countries—have fallen out of favor, while deliberate efforts to promote democracy have flourished. In a number of instances, international interventions tipped the political balance against besieged authoritarian regimes, making democratic transitions possible where they would otherwise not have taken place—or at least not so soon and so free of violence. In other instances, international interventions helped to deter the overthrows of democratic regimes, to pressure for restoration of democracy, and to deepen and consolidate emerging democratic institutions.

External drivers of democratization have run the gamut from the subtle to the incremental to the blunt and overwhelming. But the most significant, or at least measurable, effects have come from specific, intentional efforts of international assistance and pressure. By the late 1980s and '90s, these external drivers helped establish the impressively global quality to democratic change, which manifested itself not only in the reach of democracy but in the accelerating interactions among democratic politicians and civic movements from disparate parts of the globe, and the gradual forging of ties of regional and international solidarity.

DIFFUSION AND DEMONSTRATION EFFECTS

An isolated event at the edge of world attention offers a telling example of how democracy and the means of its promotion have traveled across vast distances, culturally and geographically. In June 1999, the National Democratic Institute (NDI)—one of the four "core institutes" of the flagship U.S. democracy promotion organization, the National Endowment for Democracy—organized an international meeting of political, civic, and economic leaders from some of the smaller, more isolated, and more neglected new democracies. The conference took place in the ancient capital of Yemen, Sanaa, and as I prepared to attend, I worried about the message of hosting the event in a pseudodemocracy like Yemen, whose president had been in power two decades, and of inviting other faux democracies, like Morocco and Georgia, to attend. But the conference, called the "Emerging Democracies Forum," provided a chance for countries like Benin, Ghana, Namibia, Bolivia, El Salvador, Mongolia, and Macedonia to get some attention—and learn from one another.

Like most such international meetings, this one ended with a flourish of goodwill and a unanimous declaration committing the participants to a far-reaching set of democracy-building guidelines. Yet, something smaller, quieter, and more important also happened. One of the participants was the president of Mali, Alpha Oumar Konaré, a dedicated democrat who had supervised a remarkable growth of constitutionalism in one of the world's poorest countries in the wake of more than thirty years of dictatorship. While he was at the Sanaa meeting, Konaré learned from his Latin American colleagues about statutes created by the Organization of American States to provide for the collective, regional defense of democracy in the case of challenges to or interruptions of the constitutional order.

[He then] instructed the Malian embassy in Washington to seek out a hard copy of the provisions, and had it sent to him by Federal Express. This served as the basis for Konare's proposal that the OAU [Organization of African Unity] adopt its own similar policy. On his initiative, the 1999 OAU summit in Algiers took a strong stance against non-democratic governments, stating that any leader who comes to power through undemocratic means would not receive recognition.[1]

During the third wave, ideas and models of democratic change flowed freely across national borders. The early transitions to democracy were mainly triggered by internal grievances and events in Southern Europe and Latin America that led to popular protests, authoritarian divisions, military rebellions, and so on. But over time, transitions became increasingly stimulated, and instructed, by what had taken place in earlier democratic waves. This dynamic *snowballing* effect of earlier transitions, as Huntington says, allows for the "stimulating and providing models for subsequent efforts at democratization."[2]

These demonstration effects—showing *that* democratic change could happen, *how* it could happen, and what mistakes to avoid—were particularly potent within regions or among culturally similar countries.[3] The Philippine example of "people power" inspired the mass Korean protests the next year and the Tiananmen protests in China in 1989. "A month after Cardinal Sin played a central role in the regime change in the Philippines, Cardinal Kim for the first time called for constitutional change and democracy in Korea," and a month after that (in April 1986), Korean opposition leader Kim Dae Jung declared, with specific reference to the Philippines, "This is the time of people's power in the developing countries of Asia. We have never been so sure before."[4] By the same token, processes of democratic change in Poland, driven from below by the courageous mobilization of civil society, spread to its Eastern European neighbors, and their collective transformation had great impact on the Soviet Union. This was evident in the manner and timing of Communist parties' surrender of their legal monopoly on power.

Thus, in January 1989 the Solidarity movement was legalized in Poland, at about the same time that the Hungarian Party decided to abandon its leading role, and accept multiparty elections. Then, in the June 1989 [Polish] elections, Solidarity scored an overwhelming victory. . . . In October, the Hungarian [Communist] Party changed its name to the

Hungarian Socialist Party and explicitly abandoned its Leninism. Then in November 1989 the Czech and German parties respectively lost their political monopolies through mass protests. Finally, in February 1990 the [Soviet Communist Party] abolished clause 6 of the Soviet Constitution, which has for so long formally guaranteed the party's leading role in Soviet society.[5]

A decade later, the model of mass peaceful mobilization to reverse electoral fraud and effect a democratic revolution spread from Serbia in 2000 to Georgia in 2003 and Ukraine in 2004. The scale and discipline of demonstrations in Ukraine's Orange Revolution then ignited the civil society movement in Romania, which was struggling with a Communist hangover of corruption, criminality, and authoritarianism. In the 2004 Romanian elections, these civic efforts helped to bring to power "a new generation of young, pro-European democrats" vowing a sharp break with the sleazy, semiauthoritarian practices of the former Communists, who had ruled for most of the period since 1990.[6]

Perhaps nowhere was the snowballing more robust than in Africa after the seminal shifts in South Africa and Benin in 1990. The pressure for liberal democracy in South Africa had been spurred by changes elsewhere in the region, as the withdrawal of Cuban troops from Angola relieved the perceived threat from Marxist forces while Namibia's passage to independence under black-majority rule in 1989 intensified South Africa's isolation.

The South African democratic transition, however, laid bare the divergence between what African leaders were demanding for that country and what they were doing to oppress their own peoples. By 1990, Africans themselves were exposing the hypocrisy of demanding liberties in South Africa that were routinely trampled elsewhere in sub-Saharan Africa. In condemning the repression of Samuel Doe's regime in Liberia, a prominent Nigerian newspaper editorialized, "The very same reprehensible practices, which the world has persistently condemned in South Africa, are being daily replicated by the government of an independent African country."[7] Declared Roger Chongwe, chairman of the African Bar Association, "All Africa demands: if South Africa is to have one man, one vote, why not us?"[8] African leaders finally conceded at the OAU summit in July 1990 that they would need "to democratise further our societies and consolidate democratic institutions."[9]

Significantly, their statement on the need for human rights, political accountability, and the rule of law was titled "The Political and Socio-Economic Situation in Africa *and the Fundamental Changes Taking Place in the World*."[10] Africans displayed an acute responsiveness to the democratic wave sweeping through Eastern Europe and across the globe. As Nigeria's UN ambassador, and political scientist, Ibrahim Gambari observed, Africans "listen to the BBC, the Voice of America, Radio Moscow, sometimes in their local language. They're fully aware [of what's been happening in Eastern Europe] and they ask, 'Why not here?'"[11] Indeed, "Many young African protesters, inspired by television images showing Eastern European crowds demonstrating against communism, [were] seeking to emulate the success of Poles, Hungarians, East Germans, Czechoslovakians, Bulgarians and Romanians in throwing off unpopular one-party governments and demanding multiparty democracy."[12] Even one of the architects of the African one-party state, Tanzania's Julius Nyerere, said that his country could learn a "lesson or two" from Eastern Europe.[13]

The impact of Eastern Europe's democratic changes on Africa shows that snowballing rolled far beyond the confines of individual regions. The Spanish and Portuguese transitions had a profound impact on their former colonies in the Americas, which then turned to democracy as well. By the 1980s, civil society struggles for democratic change were linked across the globe. "Solidarity's struggle in Poland and Marcos's downfall in the Philippines had a resonance in Chile, that would have been unlikely in earlier decades."[14] Virtually all of the democratic countries in Asia, Africa, and the Caribbean had been British colonies, and in the early 1990s, many movements against authoritarian regimes in Africa drew from a common reservoir of historical values and linkages from the colonial past.

Methods and techniques of democratic change also began to spread widely across borders, through passive observation and direct transfer of skills, from the strategy of forging compromise pacts to the tactics of popular mobilization and protest. The model of peaceful nonviolent resistance that brought down the dictator Slobodan Milošević spread to Georgia and Ukraine, partly through the efforts of the very activists from the student group Otpor who had spawned the democratic revolution in Serbia. In the early 1990s, the African National Congress (ANC) made what may have been the most systematic and deliberate effort to learn from other democratic transitions and constitutional systems, sending teams of experts to study models in a number of different countries on several continents.

The relative success of democratic countries, the deepening failure of various types of authoritarian regimes, the consequent exhaustion of authoritarian ideologies, and the absence of alternative visions of regime legitimacy also helped diffuse democratic values. As news spread of nearly universal authoritarian dysfunction and corruption, people living under an authoritarian regime placed their national experiences within a wider context. They "could and did ask the relevance for themselves of political events in far-off countries."[15] Authoritarianism was failing as a system, not because of the perversion of an individual or an experiment gone wrong. With the end of the Cold War, communism was as thoroughly discredited as fascism had been by its defeat in World War II.

Diffusion effects are also, by their nature, long-term, involving a gradual swing toward the values of personal liberty, pluralism, and political voice and a preference for market competition. In Taiwan, the leaders of the democratic movement that emerged in the 1970s were mainly educated abroad in law and the social sciences. They returned "ready to apply at home" the "ideas and institutions of a reference society" in the West. "They adopted Western democratic ideals as well as democratic procedures, institutional design, political techniques, and legal frameworks."[16] Through overseas study, economic exchange, and the explosive growth of international communications, democratic, antiauthoritarian norms and ways of life have seeped into many countries. While the points of contact have initially been through elites, the diffusion of Western news, opinion, music, and entertainment has influenced the reception of democratic movements.[17] Together, these dense international connections fed an unprecedented global democratic zeitgeist.

PEACEFUL PRESSURE

Since the mid-1970s, the established democracies—in particular, the United States—have used peaceful forms of pressure against authoritarian states to advance human rights and democracy. Initially, under President Jimmy Carter, this pressure was limited to the goal of diminishing repression and saving its victims. Under President Ronald Reagan, pressure increasingly focused on promoting and sustaining democratic regime change, a goal that Reagan's successors in the presidency embraced.

During the late Cold War and post–Cold War periods, Western pressure for political liberalization of authoritarian regimes had a significant impact—in certain conditions. Steven Levitsky and Lucan Way demonstrate that *leverage* and *linkage* determine the potential for exercising effective peaceful pressure for democratic change.[18] Generally, the impact has depended not only on the resolve of the states or coalitions applying the pressure, and to some extent on their unity, but also on the leverage that Western democracies have had over autocratic states, and on the degree to which those states have been linked socially, culturally, and economically to the West. Linkages that render authoritarian states vulnerable to Western pressure include conventional economic ties (trade, investment, and credit), security ties (treaties and guarantees), and social ties (tourism, immigration, overseas education, elite exchanges, international NGO and church networks, and Western media penetration). Strong linkages forge cultural bonds that help rally democratic societies and parliaments to lobby for the defense of human rights and democracy, as seen with pressure on the Clinton administration to move against the Haitian military dictatorship in 1994 and the "extensive Hungarian lobbying" of the European Union to press Romania and Slovakia to improve the treatment of their Hungarian minorities.[19]

At the same time, international linkages can make critical social and political constituencies within authoritarian countries either more committed to democracy or more sensitive to Western pressures. Ties to the West induced elites both "to reform authoritarian parties from within (as in Croatia, Mexico, and Taiwan)" and "to defect to the opposition (as in Slovakia and, to a lesser extent, in Romania during the mid-1990s)."[20] After Western countries "forced severance of [Taiwan's] formal ties" and revoked Taiwan's UN membership in order to warm relations with mainland China, Taiwan's elites saw that democratic reform might provide a means to renew the sympathy and support of the American public and other Western democracies.[21] The desire to be accepted as a partner among industrial nations also contributed to the democratic transitions in South Korea as it prepared to host and risked losing the 1988 Olympics and in Chile as it prepared for the 1988 referendum on whether to extend Pinochet's dictatorship. In these contexts, international criticism of authoritarian rule bred a sense of isolation and a desire to be regarded with respect by the industrialized democracies.[22] But where ties are less intimate, for example, in the former Soviet Union and much of the rest of Africa, Western pressure to democratize has been less consequential.

Leverage, too, depends on the power of the authoritarian state, and thus, mighty states like China and the Soviet Union (and subsequently Russia) have largely been immune. The realization that trade sanctions just were not going to move a country as big and powerful as China to liberalize politically persuaded the Clinton administration to lift its conditioning of "Most Favored Nation" trading status on human rights in 1994. In the cases of Iran, the Arab Gulf states, Nigeria, and more recently Azerbaijan and Venezuela (under Hugo Chávez), Western dependence on their vast oil revenues greatly diminishes the leverage of the rich democracies.

Alternately, support from an external authoritarian power can insulate a dictatorship that might otherwise be susceptible to Western leverage, as with China's role in sustaining dictatorships in Burma and North Korea against extensive Western sanctions and Russia's obstruction of democratic pressures on regimes in Belarus, Armenia, and Central Asia. But for many regions, including Central Europe and the Americas, "no alternative regional power exists, leaving the EU and the United States as 'the only game in town.'"[23] It can, of course, be a democracy that provides a lifeline for authoritarian survival, as with France's renewed backing for authoritarian strongman Paul Biya in Cameroon and the sometimes fluid American stances toward authoritarian states.

Indeed, leverage is reduced when other policy interests compete with the concern to promote democracy and human rights. Sometimes these interests are economic, as when the Clinton administration balked at applying vigorous sanctions against the Nigerian military dictatorship after the regime aborted a democratic transition in 1993 and then in 1995 executed the widely admired Niger Delta human rights leader Ken Saro-Wiwa, along with eight other activists. U.S. officials at the time told me (and others who lobbied for pressure) that they worried a tough stance might prompt the Nigerian military to take away the lucrative concessions of American oil companies and give them to French and other European companies. More often, though, competing interests have been strategic. For most of the Cold War, the United States readily supported right-wing, anti-Communist dictatorships as part of its containment of the Soviet power bloc. Until Jimmy Carter elevated human rights in U.S. foreign policy, America maintained warm relations with the dictatorships in South Korea, Taiwan, the Philippines, Indonesia, Pakistan, Brazil, Chile, Iran, Saudi Arabia, Zaire, and Kenya because they were firm allies in the Cold War. Indeed, several of these autocratic regimes came to power with the active or at least tacit support of the United States.

The strategic imperative subsided with the end of the Cold War but resumed again after the September 11, 2001, terrorist attacks, when a new group of authoritarian "frontline" states in the war on terror—Pakistan, Egypt, Saudi Arabia, Kazakhstan, Kyrgyzstan, and Uzbekistan—assumed much greater importance to American security, and thus relative immunity from pressure to democratize. Even before September 11, "Pakistan's status as a nuclear power hostile to India, with ties to the Taliban regime in Afghanistan and fundamentalist factions gaining ground at home," led the Clinton administration to temper its response to the October 1999 military coup.[24] In recognition of Peruvian president Alberto Fujimori's support for the war on drugs, the Clinton administration maintained military cooperation and attended his third-term inauguration despite describing Fujimori's fraud-ridden 2000 election as "invalid." For its part, the Bush administration initially welcomed the attempted April 2002 coup against Venezuelan president Hugo Chávez, because of his leftist and anti-American policies, and only endorsed an OAS resolution condemning it after most major Latin American leaders denounced the unconstitutional seizure of power.[25] Then, in the fall of 2005, Bush refused to meet with opposition forces in oil-rich Azerbaijan. "This sent a clear signal that the United States would tolerate a tainted parliamentary election there in November 2005," and six months later, President Ilham Aliyev was granted an official White House visit.[26]

Peaceful pressure to democratize generally takes three intentional forms: diplomacy, the conditioning of aid, and sanctions. Often these converge or overlap. Diplomacy may be more effective in encouraging democratic change when it offers to sustain or initiate positive inducements (various forms of aid) in exchange for democratic reforms, and when it threatens to impose costs (sanctions) for authoritarian defiance. But where diplomacy advances democracy, it usually happens in a fairly narrow time frame, during a period of political crisis when an authoritarian regime that is on the defensive must decide whether to repress or reform. Conditionality and sanctions, in turn, may seek to have an impact over a much longer period of time.

Diplomatic pressure pushed a number of countries toward democracy during the late 1970s and 1980s. The initial wedge of change was President Carter's campaign against human rights abuses in Latin America. By documenting and publicly denouncing abuses in countries like Argentina and Uruguay, and coupling these denunciations with reductions in aid—in the case of Argentina, entirely eliminating military aid and voting against most of its international loan applications—the new policy "helped to limit direct human rights abuses." In addition, by reducing symbolic and material support the policy helped "to isolate military regimes from a traditional ally," which in turn undermined their legitimacy and strengthened soft-liners.[27] In a classic instance of diplomatic intervention to tilt the balance in a crisis, Carter directly contributed to the Dominican Republic's turn to democracy in 1978. When the country's military stopped the presidential election vote count in the face of an apparent opposition victory, the administration led a chorus of vigorous warnings from international actors, including President Carter, U.S. secretary of state Cyrus Vance, American embassy staff and military attachés, and the commander in chief of the U.S. Southern Command. These pressures persuaded the Dominican military to allow the opposition candidate to take office, inaugurating a nascent, if troubled, period of democracy.[28] The defeated incumbent, Joaquin Balaguer, returned to power in 1986 and ruled the country until 1996, when he was legally removed from office in the wake of electoral fraud, under pressure from the United States and through mediation by the OAS.[29] Regional diplomacy also helped to broker agreement on constitutional and legal reforms of the electoral process.

On the Reagan administration's diplomatic watch, the Philippine dictator Ferdinand Marcos was induced in late 1985 to call a presidential "snap election" that independent election observers judged he lost to Corazón Aquino. In the tense days following the February 7, 1986, vote, Marcos's bid to retain power through massive electoral fraud was frustrated by a U.S. policy, led by Secretary of State George P. Shultz, to "accelerate the succession." The United States warned Marcos against suppressing the independent poll-watching group NAMFREL; vigorously challenged the election's credibility; threatened to cut off military aid if Marcos used force against a pro-democratic army rebellion; and finally—with the prospect of mass bloodshed—told Marcos it was time to resign.[30] The Reagan administration also deterred Chun Doo Hwan's dictatorship in South Korea from forcibly suppressing pro-democracy demonstrations in 1987 and prevented military coups in El Salvador, Honduras, Bolivia, and Peru by warning of a sharp downturn in relations with the United States.[31] In the second Reagan term, Shultz began laying a strategy to encourage democratic change in Chile, beginning with the dispatch of a new ambassador instructed to press for human rights and a return to democracy.[32] In each of these cases, the private messages and public actions of the United States pressured the dictator to hold elections and grant civic freedoms that ultimately brought him down. "However, international support for democracy *reinforced* domestic groups and sectors of the military opposed to military intervention."[33] Moreover, throughout the Reagan years, the goals of promoting democracy and fighting communism struggled for preeminence in American foreign policy. Although the former increasingly prevailed, military assistance to El Salvador, Guatemala, and Honduras did much to undermine the ability of embattled democratic forces to wrench control from abusive militaries.[34]

Sometimes diplomacy has worked hand in hand with coercion. The combination of diplomatic pressure, the promise of aid, and support for the Contra military resistance figured prominently in the decision of the Sandanistas to hold early and free elections.[35] When Haiti's president Jean-Bertrand Aristide was deposed by the military in 1991 after just eight months in office, the Clinton administration, working through the OAS and then the United Nations, imposed a trade and oil embargo. Only after sanctions failed to oust the regime did the United States threaten force (successfully). In Serbia, it was a combination of sanctions, force, diplomatic pressure, and assistance to the democratic opposition that brought down the authoritarian regime of President Slobodan Milošević in the October 2000 election. After years of Western sanctions against the regime's aggression and "ethnic cleansing" in Croatia, Bosnia, and Kosovo, NATO launched a devastating seventy-eight-day bombing campaign in the spring of 1999 to force Milošević to accept the terms of the international agreement to bring peace and stability to Kosovo. The sanctions badly damaged the dysfunctional Serbian economy, but the bombing "crippled the entire civilian infrastructure of Yugoslavia." Milošević was forced to call elections before the winter months "because he was running out of money and the country's infrastructure was collapsing." At the polls, his traditional support base defected in response to the "falling wages, rising prices and crime statistics, empty store shelves, energy shortages, and too much corruption by officials high and low."[36]

THE LIMITS OF SANCTIONS AND AID CONDITIONALITY

Given the logic of linkage and leverage, it is not surprising that sanctions often fail to bring about democratic reform. For one thing, by isolating regimes, sanctions diminish the linkages that generate leverage. To the extent that sanctions are applied against regimes that are heavily linked to Western democracies, they may have a positive cumulative effect.

But where they isolate regimes—as in Cuba, North Korea, Burma, and Zimbabwe—with which the democratic West has few linkages and little leverage, they typically do little to bring about regime change.

Still, South Africa in the last decade of apartheid provides an instructive counterexample. When years of stiffening economic sanctions and disinvestment by Western powers—"as much a psychological as a financial blow"—were joined by a decline in gold prices and domestic debt and inflation, the result was a "protracted recession, capital flight, and a profound sense of isolation. . . . Whites began to realize that unless they came to terms with the political demands of the black population, the economic noose would not loosen."[37] Country-specific sanctions can work when major powers cooperate, when there is extensive linkage, and when domestic pressures converge.

Economic sanctions played an important role in Africa's "second liberation," in part because South Africa's democratic transition had a snowballing effect across Africa. The release of Nelson Mandela and unbanning of the ANC in February 1990 coincided with a sharp turnabout in the aid and diplomatic policies of the United States, Britain, and France, with each announcing that aid would be tied to political and economic liberalization. Other aid donors—the Netherlands, Norway, Sweden, Canada, and to some extent Germany and Japan—were also moving toward some degree of conditionality or consideration for human rights and democracy conditions in the allocation of aid.[38] The French embrace of conditionality (albeit temporary) was the most dramatic in its departure from a previous cynical, neocolonial posture, and it quickly contributed to the downfall of Mathieu Kérékou's regime in Benin, as discussed in chapter 4, as well as the initiation of democratic transitions in Mali, Niger, and Madagascar and more limited (and ultimately unsuccessful) political openings in Chad, the Congo, Ivory Coast, Cameroon, and the Gambia.[39]

In Kenya, the U.S. ambassador's appeals for democratic reform, which had become a thorn in the side of Daniel arap Moi's regime, were followed by a decision in November 1991 among the country's international aid donors to adopt "explicit political conditions for assistance, making Kenya a precedent for the rest of Africa."[40] New aid was suspended for six months, pending "the early implementation of political reform."[41] The regime was forced to immediately repeal its ban on opposition parties[42] and to hold multiparty elections within a year. That could have led to a democratic transition—if the political opposition (with

Machiavellian help from the regime) had not fractured along ethnic lines. A similar step in May 1992 to freeze $74 million in aid to Malawi following the first mass protest demonstrations there in twenty-eight years compelled the iron-fisted regime of Hastings Banda to liberalize. It then badly lost a national referendum on multiparty competition in June 1993, and the next year the ruling party was crushed in elections.

However, sanctions, like other forms of peaceful pressure, typically fail when they lack sufficient leverage over the authoritarian state or ruler, and when they do not gain the backing of powerful neighboring states. Following President Robert Mugabe's "reelection" in a rigged process that inflicted brutal violence on the opposition, the United States and European Union imposed travel sanctions on the regime's leaders and a ban on arms sales, while the British Commonwealth suspended Zimbabwe's membership. But South African president Thabo Mbeki refused to cooperate, and Mugabe remained in power. Similarly in Belarus, following the massive rigging of the 2001 presidential election that returned Alyaksandr Lukashenka to power, "the U.S. adopted a policy of 'selective engagement,' conditioning the bilateral relationship solely upon the regime's behavior" on such issues as free elections.[43]

The logic of conditioning economic assistance on democracy (or progress toward it) is relatively recent. While aid conditionality had been applied to some countries, prior to 2000 these instances were much more often linked—by negotiating teams from the World Bank and International Monetary Fund (IMF)—to a country's economic reform policies, and typically were linked to promises of future reforms rather than offered as rewards for prior behavior. With the initiation in 2002 of a new development assistance vehicle, the Millennium Challenge Account (MCA), the Bush administration brought the principle of conditionality to a new level. The MCA rewards developing countries for demonstrated performance in democratic governance, basic health and education, and economic freedom and entrepreneurship, ranking countries on a set of sixteen indicators. Countries that rank highly qualify for substantial new grants of aid, which must be negotiated with the Millennium Challenge Corporation in contracts for specific developmental programs. While the MCA has only been funded at a fraction of its promise ($2 billion for 2007, instead of the $5 billion projected), the bigger unsolved problem, as we will see in chapter 14, is the rigor of the criteria for selection.

Despite such innovations, limits to economic leverage remain. Nowhere was there greater potential for aid pressure than in Africa, particularly during the 1990s, when one country after another experienced vigorous domestic mobilization for democratic change. Yet many African transitions were aborted, overthrown, or reduced to pseudodemocracy. If international actors had so much relative power in Africa, why was there not more democratic progress? There was relatively weak social linkage of African societies to the West, as Levitsky and Way note, but in aggregate terms, there was very high leverage in terms of aid dependence.[44] Disastrous divisions among regime opponents (some with questionable commitments to democracy themselves) heavily contributed to setbacks in most of these instances, as did equivocation on the part of the international community. Although the United States imposed some sanctions on the Nigerian military regime following the annulment of the June 1993 presidential election, France, Germany, and Japan held back, and Britain later backed down from its tough stance. When the military regime executed the nine Ogoni activists in November 1995, the United States and EU states withdrew their ambassadors, the British Commonwealth suspended Nigeria from membership, and the European Union imposed travel and visa restrictions. But "a Clinton administration proposal to prohibit new investments and freeze the overseas assets of Nigeria's rulers collapsed owing to a lack of international support and U.S. reluctance to act unilaterally."[45]

Particularly damaging was the French retreat from democratic conditionality in the 1990s. Indeed, France really never adhered to President François Mitterrand's commitment in June 1990 to explicitly link the provision of financial assistance to the initiation of democratic reforms. Instead, it continued to give paramount weight to its perceived economic and political interests in Francophone Africa, and, depressingly, states undergoing democratic transitions received a smaller proportion of French development assistance than did steadfast authoritarian states or ones that aborted democratic transitions, such as Cameroon, Togo, and Zaire.[46] Indeed, only six days after a 1992 summit at which Mitterrand diluted France's "pro-democracy" policy, troops loyal to the Togolese dictator Gnassingbé Eyadéma launched a coup in Lomé to derail the democratic transition.[47] The French turnabout also encouraged authoritarian leaders to consolidate power through electoral fraud: despite ample evidence of fraud in Cameroon's 1992 elections, France endorsed the results and granted $110 million in new loans, enabling the country to reschedule its debts to the IMF and World Bank before a default would have halted all new aid.[48] In the Congo (Brazzaville), France threw its support in 1993 to the opposition to the democratically elected president, Pascal Lissouba, after he signed an oil-purchase agreement with U.S.-based Occidental Petroleum Corporation that would have undercut the French multinational Elf-Aquitaine's long-standing monopoly in the region.[49] In Cameroon and Nigeria as well, France competed with the United States for control of African oil resources, while providing aid to autocrats throughout its former colonies.

While utility of sanctions is often viewed with skepticism, the reality is more complicated. For years, critics of sanctions against the apartheid regime in South Africa insisted they were having and would have no effect—until F. W. de Klerk stunned the world in 1990 by launching a transition. The same was true in terms of Western pressure against Milošević in Serbia and the more limited Western sanctions against the Nigerian military. In each of these cases, sanctions wore down and weakened the regime while generating divisions within its ranks. In Serbia, economic pressure made it difficult for Milošević to impose the total dictatorship that might have sustained his power. In Nigeria, it is widely believed that the military dictator, Sani Abacha, did not die in June 1998 of a heart attack, as reported, but rather by poisoning at the hands of senior military colleagues, who had grown weary of the country's isolation and who dissolved the Abacha government, freed political prisoners, and launched a transition to democracy within weeks of assuming power.

DEMOCRACY ASSISTANCE

Recent democratization has been distinctive not only for the scope of international influence but also for the introduction of a new channel of influence: assistance to strengthen democratic institutions, reform governance, empower civil society, build democratic culture, monitor democratic elections, and, in authoritarian circumstances, assist forces in government, in civil society, and (in the worst cases) in exile working for democratic change. When the third wave began in 1974, efforts to assist democratic development were confined to the German party-building programs and a few other efforts, like judicial assistance, in the aid agencies. Mainly, these efforts were modest, indirect, or, in the case of Western efforts to aid Portuguese democrats in the mid-1970s, episodic and often undercover. As democratic possibilities and ambitions widened in the early 1980s, it became clear that dedicated instruments were needed to provide material, technical, and moral support to democratic forces.

A turning point came in 1983 with the establishment of the National Endowment for Democracy (NED). Although it drew inspiration from the German political party foundations, which received annual government appropriations for assistance to like-minded parties and civic efforts abroad, the NED blazed trails in several respects. It was the first congressionally funded but nongovernmental systematic effort to promote democracy abroad. It also functioned as a consortium, with the NED supporting democratic civil society organizations while other democratic actors were supported by four core grantees: the international institutes of the two U.S. political parties (NDI and IRI, the International Republican Institute), the Center for International Private Enterprise (CIPE), and the Free Trade Union Institute (now the Solidarity Center). By bringing together the classic constituent elements of American politics—Republicans and Democrats, business and labor, and NGOs—the NED provided enormous range and flexibility to support democratic movements and transitions worldwide.

Although it began with very small annual budgets (under $20 million—a fraction of the German foundations collectively),[50] the NED gave critical aid to democratic movements in Poland, Nicaragua, and Chile. Probably its greatest success story was in Poland, where the Free Trade Union Institute transferred substantial assistance to the Solidarity trade union to support its education, publishing, and human rights projects. Throughout Eastern Europe, NED helped to build the civic infrastructure that undermined communism in the late 1980s. In Nicaragua, NED helped the independent daily, *La Prensa,* to purchase printing supplies, enabling the newspaper to publish during the harshest period of Sandinista intimidation. NED support played a significant role in helping Chile's democratic parties, think tanks, trade unions, cooperatives, and other organizations to educate voters, stimulate political participation, and ignite the historic "Campaign for the No" that defeated General Pinochet's bid to extend his rule in the 1988 plebiscite. NED and its affiliates also contributed to peaceful democratic transitions in the Philippines, Namibia, Haiti, Zambia, and South Africa, in part by funding election-monitoring efforts and helping to organize international election-observing teams.

In these various efforts to support democratic change, it is easy in retrospect to regard the demise of authoritarian rule as inevitable. At the time, however, it was anything but that. Authoritarian rule was defeated at the polls through heroic levels of civic mobilization. In Chile in 1988, the Crusade for Citizen Participation, as it was known, had to find a way to overcome a climate of pervasive fear and resignation bred by "the military's continuous fifteen-year disinformation aimed at delegitimizing political parties."[51] In South Africa in the late 1980s, the demands of popular resistance against a brutally unjust order had to be balanced against the imperatives of constructing a multiracial coalition. In Serbia in 2000 and Ukraine in 2004, disparate and bitterly divided opposition forces had to unite against a regime known for its ability to mobilize both massive fraud and murderous violence.

Neither is it easy to assess just what contribution external assistance—and the specific contributions of organizations like NED—made to the eventual successes. But by tracing the impact of specific actors for whom external assistance was crucial—such as Poland's Solidarity, which received massive Western assistance (reaching $2.5 million from NED alone in 1989)—one can get a clue. Years of NED and other Western support enabled the Serbian independent radio station, B-92, to purchase vital equipment to provide a beacon of hope and a source of opposition to Milošević. The "unsparing professional coverage" provided by B-92 and its related independent media exposed "Milošević's wars, his economic policies, and his government's violent arrests and abuses of young protestors," and thereby "helped to undermine his support" among the Serbian people.[52] An indispensable player in Serbia's revolution was the student organization Otpor (Resistance), "whose members were trained in neighboring countries in the techniques of grassroots political organizing by Western non-governmental organizations," like NDI and IRI. One Otpor leader reflected after the revolution, "Without American support, it would have been much more difficult. There would have been a revolution anyway, but the assistance helped us avoid bloodshed."[53] A key player in Ukraine's Orange Revolution, the youth group Pora (It's Time), in turn "received training from Serbia's Otpor, and many Western NGOs and civil society groups provided key assistance to their Ukrainian counterparts." In addition, Western support for Ukrainian independent media "helped to spread the opposition's message throughout the country."[54]

In most cases, national elections were the vehicle by which authoritarianism was successfully challenged or the means to inaugurate new democracies. Thus, elections became a natural focal point for democracy assistance, from technical and financial aid to the official administration where new democracies were emerging; to financial support and training for civil society groups to educate and mobilize voters and monitor the vote; and to international election observation teams to help scrutinize the conduct of elections and detect and deter fraud.[55] No form of international aid has had a more dramatic and immediate effect, nor wider and more legitimate participation.[56]

During the 1980s and '90s, an expanding architecture of technical advice and support became available from the United Nations, regional organizations, official aid agencies, and such nongovernmental groups as the International Foundation for Election Systems (IFES), a U.S.-based NGO that is mainly publicly funded, and the International Institute for Democracy and Electoral Assistance (IDEA), a Stockholm-based consortium of smaller European and developing country democracies. IDEA facilitated and supported networking among election administrators and the dissemination of information, experience, and technology. It also developed the detailed Code of Conduct for Electoral Management around principles of independence, neutrality, transparency, accuracy, respect for law, and service to the voters. In sensitive moments of regime transition, from Nicaragua to Mozambique, expert, independent recommendations for reforming electoral codes and reorganizing electoral procedures broke deadlocks and won the public's confidence.

In a number of crucial founding elections, the international community invested enormously in the electoral architecture of both public administration and civil society. For its 1994 elections, South Africa ultimately received more than one thousand UN-organized international observers (augmenting many thousands of domestic monitors) and millions of dollars in assistance in public and private assistance for voter education and electoral administration. Similarly huge investments have accompanied UN-led political reconstruction missions in countries from Cambodia to East Timor.

Over the past two decades, international electoral observation has become an extraordinarily widespread practice, involving most regional and international organizations and a wide range of parties, NGOs, and foundations.[57] When such efforts deployed sufficient numbers of observers, carefully assessed the entire course of the electoral process, and worked in coordination with a much larger number of well-trained domestic monitors, it proved possible, with international will, to deter, thwart, or at least expose efforts to rig the vote.[58] A key instrument was the parallel vote tabulation, or "quick count," by which domestic monitors report the results from a random sample of polling stations (or even all or most of them) to a nonpartisan watch group, which then collates and announces its own count.[59] Aided by international observers, parallel vote tabulations have made the difference between a disputed election and one that was broadly accepted in countries including Panama, Nicaragua, Bulgaria, Haiti, Guyana, Paraguay, and the Dominican Republic.[60] Elsewhere, as in the Philippines in 1986 and the color revolutions in Serbia, Georgia, and Ukraine, these independent vote tallies exposed authoritarian efforts to steal the elections and helped to bring down the regimes.[61] The revolution that toppled Milošević from power began on the evening after the September 24, 2000, voting, when the opposition's parallel vote tabulation "made it clear that the challenger had defeated the incumbent in the first round." Two days later, an estimated three hundred thousand opposition supporters poured into the streets of Belgrade to celebrate their victory, and the popular mobilization for democracy became unstoppable.[62]

At a minimum, international observers helped to verify election results so as to enhance the credibility and legitimacy of the declared victor in a polarized, democratic contest, as in South Korea in 1987, Bulgaria in 1990, and Ghana and the Dominican Republic in 1996. In some countries, their presence deterred an authoritarian or incumbent government from forging or canceling the result, as with the December 1991 elections in Zambia that defeated President Kenneth Kaunda after twenty-seven years of rule and the 1994 founding elections in South Africa and Malawi, where long-ruling parties went down to peaceful defeat. When fraud did occur, observers were able to help document it and deny it legitimacy. And when changes in the rules rigged the electoral game, international observers withdrew cooperation to highlight the illegitimacy of the process, a tactic used by NDI in 1996 to challenge undemocratic constitutional amendments in Zambia. At times, international observers went much further, helping bitterly opposed sides to negotiate mutually acceptable terms and even mediating the implementation of a broader process of national reconciliation and democratization, as in Nicaragua, El Salvador, Albania, and Cambodia. Many times, this proved truly indispensable, since mediation and observing of elections requires impartial arbiters whom all sides can trust.[63] The political scientist Jennifer McCoy (a veteran of the Carter Center's election-monitoring efforts) found that between 1988 and 1995, almost all the successful elections in Latin America and the Caribbean involved international observers and mediators as well as strong support from international donors.[64]

Like other forms of political assistance, international election observation missions also failed on many occasions. Sometimes this owed to a lack of adequate engagement with the process, sometimes to a profusion of poorly coordinated groups creating a "zoo-like atmosphere," as in the 1996 Nicaragua election.[65] Often missing was the political will on the part of the international community to hold a particular regime to rigorous democratic standards, and to impose sanctions if it did not meet them. Sometimes the potential impact was vitiated by international divisions, as in the 1992 presidential elections in Cameroon and Kenya. While NDI's observer mission found widespread irregularities in Cameroon's elections and the United States imposed sanctions, France ignored the evidence of fraud and embraced the regime. In Kenya, NDI was excluded from the international observing process altogether, and its efforts to aid civic organizations to develop a nonpartisan election-monitoring program were hindered.[66] This left the international responsibility to 160 observers, from IRI and the British Commonwealth, who were less aggressive and more inclined to declare the voting itself largely "free and fair," in contrast to the Kenyan monitors, who detailed numerous irregularities. As a result, the Moi regime squeaked through to reelection with some remnant of legitimacy and international tolerance.[67] In Haiti, the official U.S. delegation delivered a sympathetic verdict on the elections (affirming Clinton administration policies), while the IRI delegation, "affiliated with a political party harshly critical" of administration policy, "found much to condemn in the process."[68]

Geopolitical interests can also squelch international efforts. The strategically located, cooperative, and oil-rich regime in Azerbaijan stole yet another election in November 2005 despite the deployment by the Organization for Security and Cooperation in Europe (OSCE) of 1,600 foreign observers supporting 17,000 domestic monitors, who documented numerous gross abuses of campaign freedom and vote integrity.[69] However, President Ilham Aliyev correctly judged that he could get away with repressing opposition demonstrations while his Constitutional Court confirmed the falsified results. "After the U.S. State Department expressed satisfaction with the manner in which the Constitutional Court had handled election-related complaints, the Azerbaijani opposition blamed the United States for having a double standard and failing to be serious about assertively promoting democracy in Azerbaijan."[70] Similarly in oil-rich Nigeria—the fifth-largest supplier of oil to the United States—EU and NDI international observer teams reported blatant malpractices and fraud in the 2003 national elections, throughout many of the country's thirty-six states, but the finding had no real impact on the country's relations with Europe and the United States.[71]

One of the most important functions of international electoral assistance has been to help prepare and finance the scope of domestic election monitoring needed to deter and detect fraud, a task requiring thousands of trained monitors: 3,500 in Zambia in 1991, 4,000 in Nicaragua and in Ghana in 1996, 8,000 in Georgia in 2003, 20,000 in Mexico in the 1994 presidential elections and 36,000 six years later (when the opposition finally won), 25,000 in Bangladesh in 1996, some 40,000 in Nigeria in 2003, and an extraordinary 500,000 in the Philippines for the February 1986 election. Financial grants from NED, the U.S. Agency for International Development (USAID), and other international donors have helped indigenous NGOs like Mexico's Civic Alliance, Nigeria's Transitioning Monitoring Group (TMG), Ghana's Network of Domestic Election Observers (NEDEO), and Bangladesh's Fair Election Monitoring Alliance (FEMA) to construct the volunteer organization, training programs, communication network, and media strategy necessary to monitor national elections.[72] According to one of Ghana's leading civil society activists, E. Gyimah-Boadi:

> Civic groups in Ghana are enthusiastic but beset by organizational and financial shortcomings. They depend heavily on external agencies for funding, sometimes for moral or political support. Domestic election-observation groups, for instance, depended almost completely on foreign donors. NEDEO had a strong human-resource base, but little money of its own, slender material resources, and no experience in something as massive and complex as monitoring an election. NEDEO could not have trained and deployed its monitors, or collated reports on the election, without the generous funding it received from the U.S. Agency for International Development and the National Democratic Institute.[73]

But international democratic assistance has focused on much more than elections. Support has flowed from a wide range of Western donors and aid agencies to improve the capacity of political parties, elected parliaments and local councils, judicial systems and human rights protection, public administration and corruption control systems, civil society organizations, civic education programs, and the independent mass media. Assistance programs have sought to overcome the pervasive image of emerging democratic parties as corrupt, self-interested, shallow, petty, personalistic, and unresponsive. They have offered training and advice on how to develop and utilize membership bases, volunteer networks, campaign organizations, local branches, fund-raising, public opinion polling, policy platforms, media messages, constituency relations, and democratic methods of choosing their leaders and candidates and involving members. Some of this has come during election campaigns, but much of it is ongoing organization building, helping parties to govern and legislate, to recruit and campaign, and to involve women and youth.[74]

Civil society assistance has also involved instruction in the tasks of organizational development, but most of all it has given crucial financial support to independent groups focused on a range of causes: human rights, anticorruption, political reform, voter education, election monitoring, environmental defense, community development, consumer protection, and the rights of women, youth, minorities, and the disabled. Aid has also gone to more traditional interest groups—such as trade unions and business chambers—to help them represent their interests and democratically pursue economic and social reforms. It has supported independent media and information networks, creating more informed and pluralistic societies. And it has increasingly focused on the intellectual and analytic foundations of democratic change, by supporting think tanks that research issues of democracy, governance, and development and that advocate for political reforms such as limiting presidential terms, making electoral systems fairer, and tightening ethics laws.[75] Such aid can tap into and support internal shifts toward democratic values. It also helps to generate a pool of future governmental leaders, often drawn from civil society roles. And it promotes a host of reforms—of judicial systems, banking systems, parliament, electoral systems, campaign finance, and corporate structures—that make emerging democracies more inclusive, transparent, efficient, lawful, fair, and economically productive.[76]

Total U.S. spending on these types of democratic assistance exploded from $100 million in the late 1980s to over $700 million in 2000, and to over $1.5 billion during the second term of George W. Bush.[77] Most of these funds were allocated by USAID, but significantly increased congressional funding for democracy promotion went to NED and to other NGOs like IFES, Freedom House, the Asia Foundation, and the Eurasia Foundation. In addition, in 2002, the Bush administration established the Middle East Partnership Initiative (MEPI), which has as one of its four principal aims the support of democratic electoral processes, political parties, judicial institutions, and mass media in the region. In the subsequent four years, it allocated almost $300 million to those programs and others for economic reform, educational development, and women's empowerment. Many European states—including not only Britain and Germany but also smaller states like Sweden and the Netherlands—gave significant portions of their foreign aid budgets to democracy and governance programs, with well over a billion dollars a year coming from the combined public and private efforts of Europe. What qualifies as democratic assistance, however, is a matter of difficult (and disputed) interpretation, and one study finds that the European Commission "has remained wedded to a focus within which democracy promotion was secondary to loosely-defined governance initiatives and traditional conflict resolution activities."[78] Private foundations like the Ford, Hewlett, Mott, and MacArthur foundations also invested in projects to develop democratic institutions and practices, especially in civil society. The most ambitious by far has been the Open Society Institute, "a network of 31 fairly autonomous country-specific foundations financed by the American philanthropist George Soros." Over the past decade and a half, Soros has donated an astonishing half a billion dollars *a year* of his own funds to these democracy-building efforts.[79] And multilateral organizations also dramatically expanded their efforts. By 2005, the United Nations Development Program was devoting about $1.4 billion per year to democratic governance programs in over 130 countries, which included support for "one in three parliaments in the developing world."[80] Current plans call for democratic governance programs to receive nearly half of the entire UNDP budget in coming years.

A glimpse at NED's grants in 2005 in three countries conveys some of the flavor of its efforts to aid democratic civil society. In Argentina, NED supports NGOs working in the Buenos Aires shantytowns to stimulate participation in local government and offer legal assistance. Other grants enable Argentine NGOs to monitor and publish on the Internet how legislators vote and how the president uses his emergency decree powers; to strengthen provincial human rights organizations and enable them to report on abuses in the sprawling interior; to improve debate on the budget and fiscal policies; and to strengthen the political participation of neighborhood associations. In Nigeria, one NED grant is helping the

Constitutional Rights Project to track the budget process and train National Assembly staff in tasks including how to formulate a public budget and make the process transparent. Another enables the League of Democratic Women to train women in northern Nigeria in political advocacy and paralegal skills. Several grants support efforts to educate citizens about their legal rights and civic responsibilities, and to train local party officials and youth leaders, while others are helping community groups in areas plagued by violence, particularly the oil-rich Niger Delta, to mediate conflicts between ethnic communities, train youth activists in conflict management, lobby for environmental protection, and document human rights abuses. Following the Orange Revolution, NED bet heavily on democratic change in Ukraine, making more than thirty grants to democratic forces in 2005. One, to Pora, the student group that played a leading role in the revolution, facilitates its work to develop student unions and to encourage students to participate in the national elections. Others support human rights research and monitoring, human rights training and curriculum development for secondary school teachers, posting information on regional government procedures to fight corruption, civic education and election monitoring in rural regions, scrutinizing the activities of elected representatives, assessments of Ukrainian media, debates on public policy issues, and research on and analysis of pro-democratic legislative initiatives. Other grants for Ukraine are building the capacity and democratic commitment of trade unions and helping business associations to participate in the economic reform process.[81]

Since 1999, the NED has added an important connective tissue to these grants by drawing its grantees and other democracy activists together into a "network of democracy networks," the World Movement for Democracy.[82] The movement, which held World Assemblies in New Delhi in 1999, in São Paulo in 2000, in Durban in 2004, and in Istanbul in 2006, has spawned diverse associations that link democracy advocates and civil society representatives in regional networks and functional exchanges. One connects more than sixty think tanks around the globe in the Network of Democracy Research Institutes, through which they can exchange research findings and cooperate in the search for reforms to deepen democracy. The World Assemblies, drawing as many as six hundred delegates, have been hothouses for the diffusion of democratic techniques and strategies, and sources of hope and inspiration for democrats in dire straits.

If there is a common thread that runs through these initiatives, it is empowerment. Indeed, one longtime NED grantee in Argentina is named Poder Ciudadano (Citizen Power). If democracy is to work at more than a superficial level—if democratically elected governments are to be reasonably honest, responsive, fair, effective, and respectful of the law and the constitution—then citizens must know their rights and responsibilities and have the capacity to act on them. The work of democracy is arduous and not very glorious. It is also decentralized, truly involving "a thousand points of light." Not every grant works with equal effect. Not every donor organization is equally serious and successful in evaluating what and whom to support. But over time, in many countries, international assistance to civil society is helping to build the civic architecture of free and pluralistic society.

In some countries, democratic possibilities appear to be crushed, extinct, or at best fragmentary. But one can never know when the death of a dictator, a natural disaster, an economic crisis, or a sudden turn in geopolitics will create an opening for democratic change. Part of the strategy of some democracy assistance organizations, like NED, is therefore to "keep hope alive" within these circumstances. In the most thoroughly closed circumstances—such as China, its autonomous region of Tibet, Burma, Vietnam, North Korea, Cuba, and Iran—this must be done in large measure or entirely through support to groups in exile that are monitoring human rights conditions, tracking individual political prisoners, analyzing internal political conditions, hosting dissident Web sites, conducting historical analysis, translating democratic works, developing democratic ideas, and broadcasting news and information back to those countries via satellite television and shortwave radio. Sometimes, exile groups and NGOs can channel democratic assistance innovatively into closed societies through porous borders, albeit at great risk. Sometimes, opportunities emerge to conduct respectful and incremental programs inside in the country, as with U.S. assistance to village elections, the National People's Congress, and judicial reform in China. In countries that are sliding backward to authoritarianism, fragments of autonomous civil society may persist and be able to make use of international support, as with the NED grant to the Cambodian Human Rights Action Committee, a coalition of eighteen human rights groups that investigates violations, provides legal assistance, and advocates for better conditions.[83]

As we have seen above, there have been many instances where external democratic assistance made a critical difference to democratic breakthroughs, and others where the effects were either modest or faint.

Whatever the impact, however, such aid always plays a supporting role behind larger structural and historical factors, internal and external, that erode the viability of an authoritarian regime and drive a democratic transition. Democracy assistance can enhance these factors and "support democratic activists, but it is not a substitute for [indigenous] democracy groups' own courage, energy, skills, and legitimacy."[84] Not surprisingly, as Thomas Carothers notes in one of the most carefully researched and balanced assessments of U.S. efforts, international democracy assistance appears to have the most visible positive effects where there are already modestly favorable conditions, such as indigenous support for democracy, weak and divided authoritarian rulers, previous historical experience with democratic institutions, "a peaceful regional setting in which democracy is spread," and some degree of economic and educational development.[85] If, as in South Korea and Taiwan, conditions are highly favorable, democratic assistance is unlikely to add much benefit (and in any case, generally does not flow to prosperous countries). If, as in Cambodia and Haiti, the conditions are quite unfavorable, even large amounts of international democracy aid may not prevent the consolidation of authoritarian rule or the descent back into chaos.

Overall, Carothers wisely appeals for restrained expectations of what democracy assistance programs can deliver, and how fast.

> The effects of democracy programs are usually modestly positive, sometimes negligible, and occasionally negative. In countries where democratization is advancing, democracy aid can, if properly designed and implemented, help broaden and deepen democratic reforms in both the governmental and nongovernmental sectors. In countries where an attempted democratic transition has stalled or regressed, democracy programs can help actors keep some independent political and civic activity going and, over the long term, help build civic awareness and civic organizations at the local level. In countries that have not experienced a democratic opening, democracy programs may help democracy activists survive and gradually expand their work and may increase the flow of political information not controlled by the government.[86]

One reason to maintain modest expectations is that most democracy assistance programs are only modestly funded. Critics have complained about the "exorbitant cost" of donor-financed transitional elections, utilizing technologies that poor countries cannot afford to sustain; the overly expensive models of party organization and finance exported by the West; and the tendency for Western donors to support "only a narrow range" of "democracy NGOs" that are "elitist" and detached from deeper bases of societal tradition and support.[87] While such criticisms are not entirely unfounded, they miss the fact that these more extensive expenditures to secure transparent, free, and fair elections in many cases achieved impressive results, facilitating wide participation and broad acceptance of the results.[88] As for the civil society recipients, they are overwhelmingly drawn from the educated middle class, and some are merely opportunists, even shysters who construct "briefcase NGOs" to milk the international community. But around the world, I have seen a great many of these internationally funded NGOs working courageously—often at great personal risk and sacrifice and with manifest levels of grassroots support—to defend human rights, expose government corruption, broaden popular participation, disseminate democratic values and skills, and deepen democracy. As Gyimah-Boadi writes, "Professionally run NGOs and watchdog groups are indispensable to sustained democratic change because they are typically more 'civic-minded' and are relatively resistant to government cooptation and repression." With their educated talent and international resources and standards, these groups have brought "energy, dynamism, and professionalism into a sector whose effectiveness has often been hampered by amateurism and apathy."[89]

Further, once a formal transition occurs, the impact of democracy assistance programs will be gradual and incremental, hopefully cumulating in a deepening consolidation of democracy. According to Carothers, "The country must be not too large (so that the aid is not spread too thin), the aid must be extensive and varied, and the political system must be populated with enough reform-oriented actors to take advantage of the aid."[90] When this assessment was made almost a decade ago, the countries meeting these conditions were mainly in Latin America and Eastern Europe, and Romania was a striking example, because "in almost every area where positive change seems to be taking place, external aid is present." In his visits to the country, Carothers found that an "extremely high" percentage of Romanians active in politics and civil society had received significant Western training or exposure. He concluded: "Romania's democratic progress since 1989 is primarily the work of Romanians. Yet Western aid, taken together, has been a substantial partner."[91] That judgment is even more apt for Romania (and Bulgaria) in 2007 but also applies to countries like Ghana, Mali, and Mongolia that are making democratic progress against historical odds.

And while overall, general levels of foreign aid appear to make no difference in the strength of democracy, the higher the level of USAID expenditures on democracy and governance in a country, the greater the level of
democratic progress, as measured, for example, by the annual Freedom
House survey. When they were assessed recently by a team of social scientists, the effects were "consistent and clear" but modest because individual
country levels of assistance amounted on average to only about $2 million
per country per year between 1990 and 2003 (rising to about $3.7 million
on average in 2003). Larger levels of democracy assistance yield larger
impacts. Each additional million dollars of democracy assistance increases
the "normal" rate of improvement in democracy by 50 percent, "or in
other words, ten million additional dollars would produce—by itself—
about a five-fold increase in the amount of democratic change that the
average country would be expected to achieve, ceteris paribus, in any
given year."[92] Among the "toughest" regions, two of the three (Asia and
Africa, but not the Middle East) showed the largest effects as the levels of
democracy assistance increased. The findings—unprecedented for their
empirical depth and statistical precision and sophistication—fully justify
the authors' conclusions that overall levels of democracy assistance should
be increased, and that democracy assistance should be sustained in countries even after they have reached what has heretofore been considered a
"satisfactory" stage of democratic development.

DEMOCRATIZATION BY FORCE

When all else fails, the last resort open to international actors is the use or
threat of force to impose or restore democracy. However, the record of
accomplishment of democratization by international coercion is not very
encouraging—as evidenced by the disaster of the American invasion and
occupation of Iraq and the difficulties in postwar Afghanistan. There are
of course the oft-cited success stories of post–World War II Germany and
Japan (as well as Italy), but those transitions came in a different era, when
the Axis powers had been totally defeated in war and the American occu-
pations had broad international legitimacy. Three examples from the
Americas provide more recent guidance about the potential for success,
and for failure, of forcing democracy.

In October 1983, U.S. forces invaded Grenada—with the endorsement
of the Organization of Eastern Caribbean States and after Grenada's governor general appealed to that body for help—restoring a parliamentary

democracy that had been toppled by a left-wing insurgency four years previously. In December 1989, American forces invaded Panama, arrested the military strongman Manuel Noriega on drug-trafficking charges, and enabled the winner of the May presidential election, Guillermo Endara, to assume office. Both of those democracies endured.

Yet, those successes offered few transferable lessons when it came time to use force for the sake of democracy in Haiti. In July 1994, after almost three years of escalating sanctions through the United Nations and OAS, the Haitian military regime retained power while the elected president, Jean-Bertrand Aristide, waited in exile to return to office. The UN Security Council was enjoined to vote on an authorization for member states "to use all necessary means to facilitate the departure from Haiti of the military leadership" and "the prompt return of the legitimately elected President."[93] The ensuing 12–0 Security Council vote was historic—the first time that the United Nations authorized the use of force to restore a democratically elected government. And it did so explicitly under chapter 7 of the UN Charter, thereby linking the humanitarian crisis, "the illegal de facto regime," and the "systematic violations of civil liberties" to that chapter's justification of force "to maintain or restore international peace and security." It was an unprecedented show of muscular international support for democracy.

Although a number of Latin American states criticized the vote, it had its intended effect. As President Clinton readied twenty-one thousand American troops for invasion in September 1994, the Haitian generals blinked. They accepted an eleventh-hour mission to Port-au-Prince, during which "former president Jimmy Carter, Senator Sam Nunn, and General Colin Powell negotiated an agreement that returned Aristide to power without a violent invasion."[94]

But while the threat of military intervention could restore an elected president to power, it could not make him govern democratically; nor could it build a culture of tolerance and nonviolence overnight. Haiti lapsed into a new version of its previous woes, as political forces fragmented and fought one another and successive elections were marred by fraud and boycotts that robbed them of legitimacy. Some years later, in Iraq, the United States would learn the limits of democracy by force much more bitterly.

6

WHAT DRIVES DEMOCRACY:
THE REGIONAL INFLUENCE

To solve the mystery of democratic progress in the world, it is sometimes necessary to examine, as Sherlock Holmes did in *Silver Blaze,* the dog that did not bark. On April 22, 1996, the dog did not bark in Paraguay. In this, one of Latin America's most physically isolated and politically and economically backward countries—the last South American country to democratize—the military did not seize power in a constitutional crisis, as it was so accustomed to doing. The army commander, General Lino César Oviedo, tried and—amazingly—failed.

The crisis began when the power-hungry Oviedo refused to comply with an order to resign from Paraguay's newly elected and weak president, Juan Carlos Wasmosy. After Wasmosy's election in 1993 and what passed, rather superficially, for a democratic transition, General Oviedo remained (and considered himself rightfully to be) the most powerful man in the country. But by 1996, Wasmosy, other branches of the armed forces, and most of the rest of the country had had enough of the army chief's domineering. When Oviedo rejected the president's order, demanding instead that Wasmosy resign, the country girded itself for yet another coup.

But this time, the inter-American community rallied to the president's, and Paraguay's, defense. The United States was joined by Brazil, Argentina, and Uruguay—Paraguay's partners in the Southern Cone Common Market (MERCOSUR)—in condemning Oviedo's defiance as "a direct challenge to the constitutional order in Paraguay" and contrary "to the democratic norms accepted by the countries of the hemisphere."[1] The Organization of American States (OAS) called an emergency meeting of its Permanent Council under the terms of Resolution 1080, providing for the collective defense of democracy in the region. Other democracies in the region followed suit. "As dawn approached, support for the president from the international community swelled into a torrent," bucking up the wavering president and mobilizing significant sectors of the Paraguayan population in defense of the constitutional order. With the swift and unconditional support of Paraguay's neighbors, the OAS, the United States, and many European democracies, Wasmosy found "the resolve to stand firm in the face of military insubordination," and Oviedo was forced to resign, preserving Paraguay's fragile democratic experiment.[2]

The defense of democracy in unlikely Paraguay was indicative of something powerful that had been emerging in the Americas, and around the world. As we saw in chapters 1 and 5, democracy has increasingly become an international norm, and international actors are increasingly inclined to promote and defend it, laying aside long-standing purist conceptions of national sovereignty. But the actions and norms that have driven this trend are not only at the level of the international community as a whole, or at the discretion of individual democracies, particularly the United States. With rising frequency and vigor, groupings of states have embraced democracy as an important regional norm, incumbent on all member states, and have created mechanisms and taken actions to advance it. The regional promotion of democracy has been boldest in postcommunist Europe and, as in Paraguay, has begun to have a decisive effect in Latin America. In other parts of the world, it has proceeded more meekly or, as in the case of Southeast Asia and the Middle East, not at all. And in Africa—which was, until recently, not to be undone in its jealous defense of the absolute sovereignty of its member states—regional resolve is on the rise.

THE EUROPEAN LEAD

No regional organization or influence has had a more powerful impact on democratization in its own neighborhood than the European Union (EU). The European Community (now the European Union) was the first regional body to take democracy seriously. In 1962, it set as a condition for membership that states "guarantee on their territories truly democratic practices and respect for fundamental rights and freedoms."[3] And this conditionality provided an important incentive for the early consolidation of democracy in Spain, Portugal, and Greece in the 1970s. In the 1992 Maastricht Treaty establishing the European Union, the condition was heartily reaffirmed, with EU membership opened to any European state that respects the principles of "liberty, democracy, respect for human rights and fundamental freedoms, and the rule of law."[4] The following year, the new Copenhagen Criteria for EU admission required that candidate countries demonstrate "stability of institutions guaranteeing" the Maastricht attributes of liberal democracy.[5] These membership requirements were then elaborated in overpowering detail in the *acquis communautaire,* which mandates laws, norms, and standards across a sweeping set of political, economic, bureaucratic, and technical issues, stretching to thirty-one chapters and some eighty thousand pages.[6]

The highly conditional process of European enlargement, particularly following the adoption of the Maastricht Treaty, has constituted the most compelling set of external peaceful pressures for reform of governance (and economic structure) in the history of the modern nation-state. After communism collapsed, the European Union exerted a magnetic gravitational pull on the postcommunist states of Central and Eastern Europe. Not only would admission bring tangible economic benefits of integration and aid; it would also "mean 'a return to the West'—something that many East European politicians often described as their most important goal" and that East European publics wanted passionately.[7] The return involved more than cultural identification; it had an expressly political motive as well: the hope "that the European Union could do for the Poles, the Czechs, and the Hungarians what it had done successfully for democratic consolidation in Spain, Portugal, and Greece."[8] Democratic politicians, civil society activists, and intellectual leaders in the region knew that if their countries became embedded in European institutions, defection from democracy would become unthinkable.

The EU's postcommunist enlargement was repeatedly postponed, however, as prospective members struggled to meet the political, legal, bureaucratic, and economic conditions for entry. After Poland, Hungary, the Czech Republic, Slovenia, and Estonia were approved for the accession process in July 1997, "each candidate country had to enter into extensive negotiations with EU officials in order to prove that it would be able to meet EU standards and conform itself to the *acquis.*"[9] (As other postcommunist candidate states were admitted to the negotiation stage, the same process applied to them.) Annually the European Commission closely monitored and reported on the implementation of the necessary reforms in each candidate's state, which culminated after seven years with the entry into the European Union of eight postcommunist states (along with Cyprus and Malta) on May 1, 2004.

Often the commission reports cited specific deficiencies in the quality of democracy and market institutions, thereby inducing states to adopt specific remedies. Thus, thanks in part to EU pressure, "the Czech Republic, Slovakia, and Latvia all gradually cleaned up and stabilized their banking systems."[10] Poland, Slovakia, and the Czech Republic decentralized state administration to bring it closer to the people. The Baltic states changed laws and practices that discriminated against their Russian-speaking minorities. The Czech Republic, Slovakia, and Hungary adopted measures to improve the treatment of their Roma (Gypsy) minorities. "All candidates received numerous EU requests to speed up judicial reforms" by removing tainted judges and prosecutors and enhancing efficiency; they also were put under pressure to depoliticize the civil services.[11] And every EU candidate had to agree to be bound by the treaties on which the European Union was founded, legally committing them to a host of human rights standards. Throughout the region, the accession process forced candidate countries to rein in the cronyism, corruption, fraud, and insider speculation that had accompanied the first phase of market reforms after the fall of the Communist system.

These pressures had similarly potent effects on Bulgaria and Romania, which had to overcome the legacy of more rigid and unreformed rule, and with less of a liberal past to draw upon than some of the Central European states. Even after they were finally admitted to the European Union on January 1, 2007, doubts persisted about the stability of reforms in Romania and Bulgaria. Hence, they were made "subject to unprecedented safeguards devised to keep them from backtracking." These gave the European Commission the power to suspend economic aid and some other benefits of EU membership if democratic reforms faltered.[12]

Nowhere was the impact of EU conditionality more dramatic than in Slovakia, which alone among the initial postcommunist candidate countries had failed to meet the EU's democratic criteria for accession negotiations. Shocked by the European Union's July 1997 decision to exclude the country from the first wave of negotiations, Slovak voters booted the authoritarian premier Vladimír Mečiar out of power in 1998 in favor of a political coalition committed to EU and NATO integration. Subsequently, "on issues ranging from respect for the rule of law to the new language law accommodating the aspirations of the Hungarian minority, Slovakia's desire to catch up with its Central European neighbors on the road to Europe [exerted] a powerful incentive for democratic reforms."[13]

More incrementally, the desire to join the European Union has had a notable liberalizing effect in Turkey. When Turkey first applied for EU admission in 1987, it was one of the most illiberal states in the world that could conceivably be called a democracy. Only after military influence had significantly receded was Turkey granted official candidate status in late 1999. Even then, heavy abridgments of freedom, due process, and minority rights persisted until the moderately Islamist but pro-European AK Party won a stunning victory in the November 2002 elections. Turkey then steered itself toward meeting the sweeping requirements for EU accession. The EU's decision to authorize the start of formal accession negotiations in October 2005 led to a host of further liberalizing reforms. These have loosened restrictions on demonstrations and expression, granted wider scope for the Kurdish minority to use its own language, increased civilian oversight of the military, abolished the death penalty and State Security Courts (notorious for human rights abuses), overhauled the penal code to bring it in line with European standards, reformed the banking industry, and generally enhanced individual freedoms and due process. Although Turkey is not yet a liberal democracy, and remains far from EU standards on many questions, it has traveled an impressive distance down the European road to reform. As one EU official responsible recently remarked, while reflecting on the historical, cultural, and ideological barriers that Turkish leaders have had to overcome, "What is most impressive is the scale, and pace, of Turkish reforms, and we owe this to the pressure placed upon Turkey from the EU."[14]

EU conditionality also had a discernible impact on public opinion. During the 1990s, high levels of authoritarian sentiment and communist nostalgia only gradually eroded, particularly in the two countries that lagged behind in qualifying for accession talks, Romania and Bulgaria. As in Slovakia, though, voters eventually turned away from more authoritarian and illiberal political options as the prospect of EU accession grew more real. In neighboring Moldova, by contrast, where there is no near-term prospect or process for EU accession, "backers of one-party rule still top 50 percent, and a city council has just voted to replant the statue of

Lenin in the central square. The moral should be clear: People learn faster when the right incentives are at hand."[15]

It is possible to argue that history was on the side of democracy in Eastern Europe, and that it would gradually have taken root with or without the close scrutiny and powerful draw of the European Union, but at a minimum, the process of entrenching democratic values and institutions would have taken much longer and gone less far.[16] Consider that although its charter committed NATO at its founding in 1949 to "safeguard the freedom" of the member states and their common principles of democracy and the rule of law, that did not stop the organization in its early decades from admitting or retaining nondemocratic states like Portugal, Greece, and Turkey.

Until the Cold War ended, NATO was preoccupied with containing and deterring the Soviet threat, not promoting or defending democracy by any political means. With that military threat lifted, however, NATO "firmly resolved to include democratic principles as both a mainstay of its new security concerns and a requirement for admission."[17] To facilitate democratic enlargement, it launched partnership programs to reach out to Eastern Europe's democratizing states and help to prepare them for membership, but scholars dispute whether NATO's democratic conditionality really amounted to much. To be sure, it lacked the EU's rigorous architecture of monitoring and enforcement, and for the postcommunist countries eager to become part of the West, it is difficult to disentangle the incentives generated by the European Union as opposed to NATO integration. For the West, consolidating democracy and ensuring the unity and peace of Europe were twinned objectives. For the East, though, a primary incentive of NATO membership continued to be a brand of Cold War security—specifically from future Russian encroachment—not necessarily democracy. But while NATO enlargement did not generate anything like the EU's compelling pressure to deepen democracy, it did enhance civilian control over the armed forces, the transparency of military budgets, and the military's professionalism and autonomy from politics. In these respects, "it is beyond question that the demands of NATO membership have had a strongly prodemocratic effect in Eastern Europe."[18]

At the peak of the Cold War, in 1975, another regional body, the Organization for Security and Cooperation in Europe (OSCE), was founded to reduce security tensions, particularly in Europe, through the adoption of the Helsinki Final Act. The agreement was denounced by the Right as conceding the legitimacy of Soviet bloc dictatorships by recognizing existing borders and treaties and by affirming (with the usual diplomatic language) each state's sovereign right to choose its own political and economic system and to "determine its laws and regulations." Indeed, in these respects, the Soviet Union considered that it had won a historic diplomatic victory. However, in mandating that all states "respect human rights and fundamental freedoms, including the freedom of thought, conscience, religion or belief," in getting all thirty-five signatory states, including the Soviet Union, to pledge to respect these individual rights and freedoms, and in affirming the "right of the individual to know and act upon his rights," the Helsinki Final Act changed the culture of communism and ultimately did much more to undermine than to reinforce the legitimacy of its dictatorships.[19] In 1990, a year after communism had collapsed in Eastern Europe, "all OSCE members" gathered and "recognized democracy as their common and sole system of government" in the Charter of Paris for a New Europe. The OSCE went on to codify its principles and expectations of governance and political performance in more than fifteen declarations and agreements affirming democracy and the rule of law.[20]

The OSCE's impact has been more ambiguous than the European Union's, but it is still significant. The landmark 1975 Helsinki agreement legitimized dissent and the monitoring of human rights. Over the course of the 1990s, the OSCE became more active and institutionalized, as it transformed from a forum for dialogue to a regional organization that reached from Vladivostok, Russia, through Europe to Vancouver, Canada. But the breadth of its membership—which includes a number of blatantly undemocratic post-Soviet states as well as a politically churlish Russia—more often obstructed forceful action to promote and defend democracy. The organization began assisting and observing elections, monitoring human rights, and assisting the development of both governmental and civil society elements of democracy in 1991, but when observer missions criticized questionable elections in Armenia and Azerbaijan in the mid- to late 1990s, Russia and other post-Soviet OSCE members objected to their "bias" and sought to dilute OSCE oversight. Subsequent OSCE election observation assessments in Belarus, Kazakhstan, and Russia, while disappointing some democracy advocates for not being blunt enough in rejecting unfair elections, drew increasingly strident protests from Russia and its authoritarian neighbors. Although the OSCE did succeed in suspending the Yugoslav government from participation until Slobodan Milošević left office and a legitimately elected leader was seated, it has generally suffered from a lack of means to enforce human rights commitments and impose punitive measures. Hence, it mainly serves to reinforce the pressures and expectations of the European Union and NATO. Countries on the political margin but with some chance to join these other bodies (like those in Southeastern Europe) thus have a "tremendous incentive to meet OSCE criteria," but for the post-Soviet states of the Caucasus and Central Asia, the incentive has been much weaker.[21]

THE INTERNAL AFFAIRS OF THE AMERICAS

When the Organization of American States (OAS) was formed in 1948, World War II had only recently ended and the region's dominant concerns centered on mutual security and defense. Thus, the first article of the charter pronounced that the member states created the OAS "to achieve an order of peace and justice, to promote their solidarity, to strengthen their collaboration, and to defend their sovereignty, their territorial integrity, and their independence." The preamble did speak of consolidating "within the framework of democratic institutions, a system of individual liberty and social justice," and "the effective exercise of representative democracy" was among the principles that states reaffirmed. But the original charter gave little further attention to democracy. Instead, its purposes were to prevent aggression, promote cooperation for development, and peacefully resolve disputes between states. To the extent it worried about how countries were governed, it was to assert the right of each state to "organize itself as it sees fit" and to be free from any form of external intervention.[22]

With the amendment of the charter in Buenos Aires, Argentina, in 1967, and with a series of subsequent resolutions and acts, the OAS has become much more firmly committed to democracy as, to quote the current charter preamble, "an indispensable condition for the stability, peace, and development of the region." Now, an explicit purpose of the organization is "to promote and consolidate representative democracy" (albeit "with due respect for the principle of nonintervention").[23] Since 1990, the OAS has gone much further to realize its stated purpose of promoting democracy. In June of that year, it established the Unit for the Promotion of Democracy to assist member states "in their efforts to renew, preserve, or strengthen democratic institutions."[24] Then it developed a substantial infrastructure for providing electoral observer missions, training, and creation and dissemination of knowledge and expertise. In 1991, in what came to be known as the "Santiago Commitment to Democracy," the OAS unanimously adopted Resolution 1080, establishing mechanisms of rapid and collective response to interruptions of or threats to democracy in the region. In 1992, the Protocol of Washington amended the OAS charter to give the body the right to suspend a member state when its democratically elected government is overthrown by force. The amendment was ratified in 1997.

At its Third Summit of the Americas in Quebec City, Canada, in 2001, the OAS adopted a still stronger democracy clause, excluding from participation in the summit process any state that has suffered "any unconstitutional alteration or interruption of the democratic order," whether by forcible overthrow or other means. This led to the crowning entrenchment of democratic norms in the Americas, the Inter-American Democratic Charter—the most sweeping affirmation of democratic principles and standards of any regional instrument outside Europe. Signed on September 11, 2001, the charter declared as its very first article, "The peoples of the Americas have a right to democracy and their governments have an obligation to promote and defend it." Incorporating a detailed list of democratic rights, it also inseparably linked vigorous multiparty electoral democracy and "the effective exercise of fundamental freedoms and human rights." And building on the language of the Quebec City clause, it ruled out the participation in any OAS bodies or activities of any state that has suffered an unconstitutional interruption of democracy *or* an "alteration of the constitutional regime that seriously impairs the democratic order."[25]

Of course, by the late 1980s, the Western Hemisphere was, for the first time in its history, composed almost entirely of democratically elected governments. This development, along with the accelerating pace of democracy transitions in Eastern Europe and worldwide, emboldened the OAS to take dramatic new steps to promote and defend democracy. When the Panamanian general Manuel Noriega annulled the presidential election in May 1989, the OAS held an emergency meeting of foreign ministers that condemned the military strongman and sent an OAS mediation team to try to negotiate a peaceful transfer of power to the democratically elected president. "The mediation failed but established an important precedent—that IGOs [intergovernmental organizations like the OAS] have a right to address internal political issues."[26]

Under Resolution 1080 and its "Santiago Commitment to Democracy," the OAS has grown increasingly active in the defense of democracy in the region. The first test came three months later, when a military coup overthrew Haiti's president Jean-Bertrand Aristide. The OAS imposed sanctions, but they only heightened the benighted country's humanitarian crisis. Ultimately, as discussed in the previous chapter, the United States had to step forward with its threat of military intervention.

The OAS responded more successfully to the April 1992 *autogolpe* (self-coup) of President Alberto Fujimori in Peru. After Fujimori shut down the country's congress and abrogated constitutional rule and civil freedoms, the OAS Permanent Council swiftly convened to demand that he "immediately reinstate democratic institutions" and convoked an ad hoc meeting of the foreign affairs ministers of all the OAS states. This OAS pressure helped rally international donors around a U.S. request that they suspend almost $3 billion in loans and assistance to Peru. Fujimori was forced to call new elections for a constituent congress and to restore a formal, constitutional order. Yet, the collective pressure did not prevent him from strengthening his powers under a new constitution and fashioning a pseudodemocratic system.[27]

A more rapid and decisive victory for democracy came the following year in Guatemala. An attempted *autogolpe* by the elected president, Jorge Serrano, unraveled in May 1993 when the Guatemalan military was dissuaded from backing him as the result of intense OAS and U.S. action. The United States threatened severe sanctions, and the OAS member states issued a unanimous, "unequivocal and immediate message . . . that Guatemala would face political isolation and economic sanctions if constitutional rule remained disrupted."[28] This paved the way for intervention in Paraguay by the OAS, which averted an almost certain military coup and preserved democracy there in 1996.

In 2000, the OAS got a second chance in Peru, and this time—with an extraordinary twist of luck—it did better. Violating a constitutional ban on a third term, President Fujimori ran for reelection again, and the electoral process—closely monitored by the OAS—fell into crisis when Fujimori was declared to have a near-victory after the first round of balloting. Amid signs of extensive procedural fraud and unfairness, the principal challenger, Alejandro Toledo, withdrew from the next round of the election and the OAS suspended its election observation mission. The United States, and much of Peruvian civil society, pushed for collective action under Resolution 1080, but the OAS declined in the absence of an overt interruption of democracy. Instead, it sent an official "High-Level Mission" to Peru, charged with "exploring . . . options and recommendations for strengthening democracy." The mission, led by OAS secretary-general César Gaviria and Canadian foreign minister Lloyd Axworthy, devised a twenty-nine-point agenda for strengthening Peruvian democracy, and most crucially, established a roundtable negotiating process, the *mesa de diálago,* where representatives from the Fujimori government, opposition parties, and civil society discussed ideas for political reform and reconciliation. As it proceeded from August to November 2000, the *mesa* did not produce a breakthrough, but by "fostering a sustained and detailed intra-elite discussion about the political future of Peru, the *mesa* undoubtedly helped to prevent a slide toward further state repression, a military coup, or even civil war."[29] During the process, a television station obtained and broadcast a videotape that showed Fujimori's dreaded intelligence chief, Vladimiro Montesinos, bribing an opposition congressman. This triggered the dismissal of Montesinos, his flight from Peru and theatrical return amid coup rumors, and finally Fujimori's resignation—by fax from a hastily assumed exile in Japan. A transition to democracy then ensued. While the OAS did not compel Peru's return to democracy, it did create a favorable climate by filling an institutional vacuum after the bitterly disputed 2000 elections and by providing a vehicle for decision making during the crisis leading to Fujimori's resignation.[30] At the least, it deterred the worst possibilities of brutal repression or a military coup, by showing "that the international community was watching political events in the country and would not tolerate a blatant dictatorship."[31]

Beyond these specific interventions, the OAS also developed institutions to assist the development of democracy, electoral administration, and the rule of law. The Inter-American Commission on Human Rights began in 1959 as a not very effectual body issuing reports on conditions in specific countries, but over time it has become more outspoken in exposing severe rights problems and promoting respect for human rights and democratic values. In the process, it "has helped to create the norms and environment" in which the region's commitment to democratic standards could become more explicit.[32] Electoral observation began quite tentatively in 1962 but accelerated dramatically in 1989 when OAS Resolution 991 explicitly authorized such missions upon the invitation of a host government. In 1990, the Unit for Democratic Development was established to promptly respond to OAS member requests for electoral observation or assistance with electoral administration. Since then, OAS missions have observed more than ninety elections in twenty countries in the region, sometimes in collaboration with nongovernmental international organizations like the ones profiled in chapter 5.[33] OAS observers have documented Nicaragua's 1990 elections, which opened the way to democracy, and 2006 elections, which brought the Sandanista leader Daniel Ortega back to the presidency; Haiti's 1991 elections, when opponents of the dynastic Duvalier dictatorships triumphed; and the Dominican Republic's 1994 elections (exposing fraud) and 1996 elections (deterring it).

The OAS has come a very long way since its days of obsession with national sovereignty and resistance to any intervention in the "internal affairs" of a member state. Since 1990, the growth of explicit democratic standards and means to extend and defend them has been impressive. Yet for democrats in the region, the organization continues to fall short. The Inter-American Democratic Charter attempted to fill the gaps in Resolution 1080 by defining the essential elements of democracy and legitimating OAS action against democracy's subversion, even by a democratically elected government. Yet, the body has not been able to use the charter to arrest the gradual suffocation of democracy in Venezuela by Hugo Chávez, despite an early laudable attempt in that regard by Secretary General Gaviria.[34] The more that challenges to democracy stem from murky use of competitive elections, the more difficult it is to identify the threshold for OAS action, even now that, under the Democratic Charter, only two-thirds of member states, rather than all, are required for political agreement. And in 2005, the United States unsuccessfully pushed a proposal that would have allowed NGOs to bring complaints about democratic backsliding by their governments before the OAS.[35]

AFRICAN DISUNITY?

As much as any regional organization in the world, the now defunct Organization of African Unity (OAU) reflected the determination of the Third World to defend its sovereignty and assert its independence from the superpowers. This meant independence not only from formal colonial rule but also from foreign interference in how the new states governed themselves internally. Moreover, until very recently, African states have also been loath to do anything at all to protect democracy or human rights in other African states—perhaps because they have virtually all been (until recently) overwhelmingly authoritarian. Regional efforts to promote democracy follow, to some extent, democratic change in the region. If the states of a region are less democratic, they will have a weaker commitment to serious regional mechanisms for monitoring and pressing for democracy. As the states of a region become more democratic, their collective resolve and institutional mechanisms will grow more vigorous, with the EU and OAS cases in point. With a broad but still limited wave of democratizing regime changes sweeping Africa after 1990, the principal regional organization could be expected to finally begin to pay attention to the nature of governance in member states, and it did.

Like their counterparts in the Americas, when the African heads of state put aside their Cold War divisions in Addis Ababa to adopt the OAU charter in 1963, advancing democracy was not among their purposes. Rather, their aims were to defend the sovereignty of their states and territories, to promote their own "unity and solidarity," to end colonialism, and to promote regional and international cooperation. Throughout the charter's thirty-two articles, the word *democracy* was striking for its complete and total absence. In contrast, when African heads of state convened almost forty years later to form a more perfect union, replacing the OAU, the normative environment was completely transformed. After four decades of developmental and state failure, African peoples were more concerned about their own individual rights than the rights of their states, and expectations for better governance had risen dramatically in the international community as well. African leaders were feeling the heat. Consequently, the Constitutive Act of the African Union (AU), signed in Lomé, Togo, in July 2000 by all fifty-three heads of state, is replete with references and commitments to democracy and human rights. In its preamble, the new union announced its determination "to promote and protect human and peoples' rights, consolidate democratic institutions and culture, and to ensure good governance and the rule of law." These goals were formally acknowledged as objectives of the AU, which also condemned (among its founding principles) "unconstitutional changes of government."[36]

To some extent, the ground had already been laid by the 1981 African Charter on Human and People's Rights. That document, which went into effect in 1986, affirmed a number of basic human rights, such as liberty, security of the person, equality before the law, due process of law, freedom of conscience and expression, and freedom of assembly and association. Still, the word *democracy* was not mentioned, only a weak and vague reference to the right "to participate freely in the government . . . in accordance with the provisions of the law."[37] In this respect, the explicit commitment of the new AU charter to "promote democratic principles and institutions" is historic, even revolutionary when one considers how many African dictators felt compelled to sign on to it. Moreover, the charter also took the bold step of banning from any AU participation governments that "come to power through unconstitutional means."[38] And the parallel "Declaration of Lomé," released simultaneously with the Constitutive Act, specified emergency mechanisms and sanctions, modeled on those of the OAS, for pressing the return of overthrown or interrupted constitutional governments. The documents go on to detail, to an unheard-of degree for the region, the necessary elements of constitutional democracy, including separation of powers, judicial independence, and a recognized role for opposition.[39] Since its formation, the African Union has launched several other initiatives to implement its new democratic commitments.

From the time of its founding in 1963 through the end of the Cold War, the OAU had also stood out among regional organizations for its unwillingness to criticize or act against the internal governance of member states, no matter how brutal and oppressive they were. It even elected as its chairman the Ugandan dictator Idi Amin at the height of his murderous reign. But as more and more democracies (and other civilian, elected governments) emerged in Africa during the 1990s, they began to exert greater influence within the OAU. "One [early] example of this was the reaction to the May 1997 military coup in Sierra Leone, which was unanimously condemned by OAU members, several of which went on to support using force to reverse the coup."[40] Subsequently, at its 2000 summit in Lomé, the OAU refused to seat military dictators who had recently taken power in Ivory Coast and the Comoros, contributing in the former case to the general's failure to legitimize and sustain his rule.

When the OAU converted itself into the explicitly democracy-minded AU, it did so with new institutional means for responding to unconstitutional changes in rule. The Lomé declaration specified several means of displacing elected government that would trigger official AU condemnation and a range of possible sanctions. When the military overthrew the president of Guinea-Bissau in 2003, AU president Joachim Chissano (the president of Mozambique) censured the coup as a violation. Under pressure from the AU and the international community, the military-backed government held elections and withdrew from power over the following two years. An even more rapid reversal followed forceful AU denunciations of a military coup in São Tomé and Principe in 2003. However, when the military sought to thwart a constitutional succession process in Togo in 2005, the AU (acting with the West African organization ECOWAS) achieved only partial success: it compelled the military-installed son of the deceased dictator, Gnassingbé Eyadéma, to resign and imposed sanctions on the regime, but the regional intervention did not keep the son from regaining the presidency in hasty and grossly fraudulent elections, which set off rioting and cost hundreds of lives.[41]

Hopes that the AU would become a much more significant promoter of democracy depend heavily on the new African Peer Review Mechanism (APRM), established in 2002 as part of the body's New Partnership for African Development (NEPAD) to meet the expectations of international aid donors for better governance. Under the process, when an African state agrees to participate (as half had done by 2007) the AU heads of state appoint a panel of "eminent persons" to conduct a peer review of the institutions and practices of democratic governance, economic management, corporate governance, and socioeconomic development. A comprehensive initial analysis is followed by periodic reviews every two to four years thereafter. But the process, still in its early stages, has yet to yield strong reproofs of authoritarianism or dramatic democratic pressures. In this respect, what supporters proclaim as the strength of the process—that its "non-confrontational, consensus-based" approach is more in tune with "African political and cultural realities"— may instead reflect its superficial and heavily symbolic intent.[42] Because the country peer review panels are appointed by the other African heads of state, there is a powerful norm of mutual restraint and reciprocity at work: "you scratch my back and I'll scratch yours." Because few if any African political leaders, no matter how democratic, want truly searching appraisal and frank criticism of their governance, the emphasis is on "consensus" rather than "review" and on voluntary commitment and sympathetic encouragement rather than serious pressure and conditionality. Further, a major shortcoming has been built into the process, as independent advocates of good governance in civil society, who would render more candid assessments and press for far-reaching reforms, have been given weak roles. Thus, the promise of the peer review process for promoting democracy in Africa seems likely to remain potential and, at best, incremental, for some years to come.

A SHARED COLONIAL HERITAGE

Though not constituting a purely regional organization, the fifty-four independent states that comprise the Commonwealth of Nations share a unique legacy of having once been part of the British Empire and having more or less imbibed its rule-of-law traditions.[43] It is therefore not surprising that its members have, over time, adopted statements that have increasingly amounted to a right to democracy. The 1971 Declaration of Commonwealth Principles affirmed a host of conventional rights as well as individuals' "inalienable right to participate by means of free and democratic political processes in framing the society in which they live."[44] The 1991 Harare Declaration reaffirmed these values and the commitment of member states to promote them, but the 1995 Millbrook Commonwealth Action Programme went much further by effectively requiring members to adhere to principles including democracy. In addition, "it established a Commonwealth Ministerial Action Group to deal with violations . . . especially the unconstitutional overthrow of a democratically elected government."[45]

Although membership in the British Commonwealth confers in and of itself no more than a symbolic benefit, it does represent a kind of international prestige that member states do not want to lose. And when member states are sanctioned by the commonwealth—through protests, suspension from participation in councils, or suspension from the entire body—it causes embarrassment and isolation and can embolden other international actors to take punishing steps.

On seven occasions since the mid-1980s, the commonwealth played a role in ostracizing member states for authoritarian practices. From 1984 until the end of apartheid in 1994, South Africa was forced to withdraw from membership over its racist policies. Fiji found itself excluded from commonwealth administrative councils for a decade, beginning with the military coup that overthrew the constitutional government in 1987. Under repressive military rule, Nigeria was suspended in 1995 after the execution of Ken Saro-Wiwa and his fellow Ogoni activists. Military coups or human rights violations also led to the suspension of Sierra Leone in 1997, Pakistan in 1994, Fiji (for a second time) in 2000, and Zimbabwe in 2002. The last, long-overdue action came only after the failure of lesser steps, repeated divisions and delays over Zimbabwe in the ranks of the commonwealth, and then grotesque malpractices in the 2002 elections. The organization's ability to exert pressure has been "limited by its own model of inclusivity and consensus."[46] Yet, as one official of the commonwealth secretariat observed in 2005, "Falling adrift of the Commonwealth consensus is a surprisingly powerful [threat]. There does seem to be a genuine fear of being dragged in front of other members, accused of violating collective democratic principles, and then ostracized, suspended, or even expelled."[47]

THE LIMITS OF REGIONAL DEMOCRATIZING NORMS

Just as the Arab world is the least democratic region of the world in terms of its regimes, so the long-standing Arab League is the weakest regional organization in terms of democratic norms and actions. Established in March 1945 to "strengthen relations among member-states" and to cooperate "to safeguard their independence and integrity," the Arab League is an anachronism.[48] Its charter, which has not been significantly amended in half a century, lacks any mention of democracy or individual rights. That huge lacuna is only modestly filled by the Arab League Charter on Human Rights, adopted in 1990, the motivation of which appears to be more the fight against "racism, zionism [sic], occupation, and foreign domination" than the battle to defend the individual rights of Arab citizens. To be sure, the charter mentions the standard civil liberties (absent any mention of democracy or free and fair elections), but even these freedoms can be restricted by law when "deemed necessary to protect the national security and economy, public order, health or morals or the rights and freedoms of others"—which is to say, any time the state so chooses.[49]

A similar problem plagues Southeast Asia and its more recent organization, the Association of Southeast Asian Nations (ASEAN). When the body was formed in 1967 by Indonesia, Malaysia, the Philippines, Singapore, and Thailand, only the Philippines could be said to be a democracy, and that democracy would not last long. In keeping with the prevailing ideologies of its most economically dynamic states, Singapore and Malaysia, ASEAN has mainly emphasized growth and aggressively guarded its claims to the inviolability of national sovereignty. While Thailand, under democratic governments in the 1990s, tried to push ASEAN to promote democracy and human rights through a policy called *constructive intervention,* the initiative had little impact. Instead, during the second half of the 1990s, ASEAN expanded to include four more extremely undemocratic states: Vietnam, Burma, Cambodia, and Laos.[50] The more its center of gravity shifted toward authoritarianism, the less likely it was to join with most of the rest of the world in requiring and promoting democratic values and practices among its members. The shadows cast by authoritarian China and booming India, along with the tempting threat of emerging markets in countries like Vietnam, also helped to keep any concern for democracy at bay.

In September 2007, it seemed that ASEAN and the Southeast Asian region might be awakening from a long authoritarian slumber. For more than a week, tens of thousands of Burmese citizens, led by the country's revered Buddhist monks, braved the wrath of the country's extremely repressive military dictatorship. What began on August 18 as limited protests over a fuel price hike escalated into a broad challenge to the regime's legitimacy, with many protestors shouting at soldiers, "Give us freedom, give us freedom!" When the regime finally responded in late September with brutal force, Burma's fellow ASEAN member states declared their "revulsion" at the killings in Rangoon and, in blunt language, demanded that the regime cease its violent crackdown on the peaceful protests.

The unprecedented protest might have helped induce the dictatorship to allow a UN special envoy to enter the country. But with China, India, and Thailand all hungry for Burma's natural resources and maneuvering for strategic advantage, the generals seemed to have enough money, guns, and international tolerance to stagger on with their predatory rule. While ASEAN issued its strongest statement against a member government in it forty-year history, the country's regional economic and strategic importance, and the organization's traditional emphasis on consensus, figured to neutralize calls for tough action. Ironically, at the time of the crisis, ASEAN was preparing to approve a new charter aimed at making it a more effective, rules-based body, but it still lacked leverage, as "a proposed clause to expel or suspend members was not included in the organisation's final charter draft agreed to in July."[51]

7

WHAT SUSTAINS DEMOCRACY

In June 1975, when a High Court ruling invalidated her election to parliament and banned her from office for six years, Indian prime minister Indira Gandhi suspended the constitutional democracy that her father, Jawaharlal Nehru, had nurtured and built from independence nearly three decades earlier. Rather than temporarily stepping aside from office and challenging the questionable ruling judicially, the imperious prime minister claimed a conspiracy to subvert social order and economic development in India, invoked emergency powers, and ruled by decree. Fear and submission reigned. The months following the June 16 declaration of national emergency were "marked by mass arrests, suppression of civil rights and all opposition voices, elaborate censorship of the media, and a carefully orchestrated campaign to celebrate the virtues of collective discipline promoted by the national leader, her increasingly powerful son Sanjay, and their nominees." In the face of the authoritarian onslaught, Mrs. Gandhi's two-thirds parliamentary majority meekly endorsed her bid to amend the constitution to emasculate the judiciary.[1]

It would not have been unreasonable to expect the dawn of emergency rule to mark the end of India's democratic experiment. At the time, many scholars and observers could not understand how India—one of the world's least developed countries—had been able to sustain a democracy for nearly three decades. Globally, democracy was flagging. In Asia, Indian democracy was an exception, a curiosity, and a system that was often compared unfavorably with the unity and energy that was said to be delivering a forced march to modernization in China. Neither was there significant international clamor for Mrs. Gandhi to restore democracy. For one thing, India was just too big to be pressured successfully. But in addition, the international norms and structures to defend democracy had barely even begun to take shape. And India's prime minister represented only the latest in a string of Asian emergency regimes, a "season of Caesars."[2] For well over a year, Mrs. Gandhi seemed secure. The world's biggest democracy, it seemed, had been reduced to a pseudodemocracy.

But neither India's civil society nor its opposition parties accepted such a fate. Despite widespread arrests, torture, and intimidation, democratic activists persisted in the shadows. While the media as a whole did little to resist censorship, "some newspapers expressed their dissent symbolically by leaving the editorial columns of the paper blank or framing the front page with a funereal black border."[3] A few state courts struck down egregious instances of censorship. When Mrs. Gandhi made the mistake of so many dictators—believing the assurances of her party and intelligence sycophants that the people loved and supported her—she was defeated overwhelmingly in elections she had called in March 1977 in her quest for a fresh parliamentary mandate.

What was it about Indian democracy that enabled it to rally so quickly to sweep an emerging autocrat from power? Why—with that one, nineteen-month exception—has democracy survived so heartily in such a poor and fragmented country? The remarkable history of India's decades-long struggle for self-rule and its independence since 1947 reveals surprisingly robust cultural, social, and political support for democracy. While these advantages tend to emerge naturally with economic development and a growing middle class, as I discussed in chapter 4, the seminal lesson of India's experience is that a country does not have to be rich, industrialized, urban, or even heavily literate in order to acquire the attributes that develop and sustain democracy.

POLITICAL CULTURE

Perhaps the most important reason why this desperately poor, rural, illiterate country—deeply divided by language, caste, and religion—was able to sustain democracy is that from the start, its political and societal elites as well as the population at large believed in it. As Amartya Sen has shown, Indian culture displays a readiness for democracy, stemming from traditions that value political and religious tolerance and extensive argument and debate.[4] Some of this may have owed as well to "the inherent pluralism of Hinduism" as a religion.[5] But nearly two centuries of British colonial rule exhibited paradoxical effects on the country's political culture. It transferred certain British rule-of-law norms and traditions but also an ugly, racist system of exploitation and domination that was intrinsic to the very nature of colonial rule. It forcibly imposed the British Crown, yet over the final several decades of that rule, it gradually introduced competitive elections to representative bodies at the provincial and national levels, stimulating the formation of political parties and movements and enfranchising millions of Indian voters. It opened space for Indian parties and associations, but it did so only reluctantly—thus prompting the political bodies to demand more, to seize the freedom they ultimately achieved while building (especially through the Congress Party) a national identity.

As we saw in chapter 1, no set of values is fully dominant in any society, but most societies have certain types of values, beliefs, and sentiments that shape how their people tend to think and act politically. A democratic political culture values democracy as the best form of government and thus affirms certain basic rights and obligations of citizenship, including the obligation to vote and to participate in politics. If people are going to bother to participate, they need to have some basis of information and knowledge, and some confidence that their own individual participation can make a difference, that it has "efficacy." Related to this is a certain healthy suspicion of authority. One of the paradoxes of democracy is that sustainable self-governance must be respectful of government authority yet also distrustful of it, "watchful" but not "blindly submissive."[6] The political philosopher Sidney Hook put it this way: "A positive requirement of a working democracy is an intelligent distrust of its leadership, a skepticism stubborn but not blind, of all demands for the enlargement of power, and an emphasis upon critical method in every phase of social life."[7]

A democratic culture also embraces moderation, accommodation, cooperation, and bargaining. In a vibrant democracy, people may have strong beliefs and preferences, but then they will have strong disagreements that they must somehow resolve. Democracy is a system of regular conflict between competing interests and ambitions, but it can only survive if it resolves these conflicts peacefully and lawfully. This implies the need for pragmatism and flexibility, an ability to transcend or even at times suspend ideological beliefs and ethnic solidarities. Finally, if people (and parties and interest groups) with sharply different goals and beliefs are going to be able to bargain and compromise, they have to respect one another. That requires tolerance of political, ethnic, racial, and other differences, and a shared commitment to democracy.

As democracy began to emerge under colonial rule, India was fortunate to see these democratic norms take root, first among the elite and then among the mass public. With some strange resemblance to the American colonies under British rule, Indian elites embraced liberal values, even when they favored more extreme methods to force the British to grant sovereignty and leave. With the formation in 1885 of the Indian National Congress (which became the long-ruling Congress Party), and then a series of constitutional reforms to grant limited political rights of elections, "a culture of political bargaining" emerged, nurtured by an infusion of lawyers into the ranks of elected representatives and the need for candidates to build broad coalitions in order to win in sizable constituencies.[8] The independence movement brought forth leaders with "a remarkably democratic temper."[9] In the last three decades of colonial rule, constitutional reforms greatly enhanced the powers of elected provincial councils and the scope of the franchise, gradually drawing new segments of the society into the political arena, as happened the previous century in Britain itself.

Founding leadership often plays a hugely important role in shaping the political culture of a new democracy. Just as George Washington legitimated the new American democracy with his personal charisma, affirming values of moderation, inclusion, and limited power,[10] so Nehru, during his long tenure as India's first prime minister (1947–64), made enormous contributions to the development of Indian democracy. "In schoolmasterly fashion, he encouraged parliamentary debate, maintained internal democracy within the Congress party, continued the British tradition of a politically neutral civil service, fostered judicial independence, encouraged press freedom, boosted secularism, and firmly entrenched civilian control over the military."[11]

But the democratic leadership of government and party politics exhibited by Nehru and fellow Congress Party leaders was only half the story. During the waning decades of the British raj, the more militant campaign for freedom also practiced, preached, and extended democratic norms. No Indian activist so epitomized these norms as Mahatma Gandhi, the British-trained lawyer who led the independence movement with his strategy of *satyagraha* (mass civil disobedience to resist tyranny). A life-long advocate of religious and social tolerance, Gandhi "emphasized the importance of a consensual resolution of conflict within Indian society in his essentially organic conception of the Indian social order."[12] His struggle for self-government in India was based on the philosophy of devotion to truth (one literal meaning of *satyagraha*), tolerance for difference, complete and total nonviolence, relentless but peaceful defiance of injustice, courage, humility, and personal responsibility and sacrifice that he had begun to fashion during his tenure fighting racial oppression in South Africa between 1893 and 1914. In affirming the equal worth and dignity of every individual and the possibilities for human empowerment through direct nonviolent action, Gandhi contributed immeasurably to the growth of democratic practice and culture (not only in India but worldwide, as Americans would discover when Martin Luther King Jr. adopted many of Gandhi's tactics).[13] He also transformed the early liberalism of Indian elites into an inclusive mass movement for self-governance, bringing the downtrodden and dispossessed into political consciousness and building "an important historical foundation for future democratic development."[14]

It is possible to argue, given the bloody trauma of partition at independence and the high levels of violence in recent decades, that Gandhi's philosophy of nonviolence had no lasting effect on his new nation. But India is a continental country of great diversity and ongoing democratic innovation. Gandhi's influence persists in the predominantly peaceful nature of Indian politics and public mobilization, in the continuing ability to forge political coalitions across a myriad of social divisions, in the steady incorporation of marginal groups into the politics, and in the extraordinary energy and pluralism of India's civil society.

CIVIL SOCIETY

Throughout its modern history, India's diversity has been both a threat and a salvation. To survive as a democracy, the country has had to learn to manage and accommodate its breathtaking ethnic, regional, religious, and caste divisions. At the same time, a tremendously rich civic life has been a major foundation of Indian democratic persistence. Over the last century, India's manifold professional associations, trade unions, grassroots groups, Gandhian social movements, and independent mass media have fueled a vibrant civil society that Alexis de Tocqueville would have admired.

India's civil society encompasses groups with widely divergent interests and values, and is itself a theater of political conflict. Moreover, not
all of the groups in civil society are necessarily committed to democratic
values and goals. Yet, the components of civil society do share, by definition, some crucial characteristics: they are independent of the state;
organized, even if very loosely and informally, *for* something that relates
to the public realm; and hold the ability to mobilize resources and act collectively. They may wish to defend and advance group interests, be they
economic, professional, or ethnic, or promote broader goals, such as
human rights, environmental quality, women's empowerment, social justice, and consumer protection.

A spirited civil society plays a vital role in checking and limiting the
potential abuse of state power, but it also sustains and enriches democracy. Civil society organizations provide channels, beyond political parties and election campaigns, for citizens to participate in politics and
governance, to air their grievances, and to secure their interests. At the
local level, autonomous organizations of landless laborers, indigenous
peoples, women, and the poor may challenge authoritarian bosses and
entrenched inequalities, transforming power relations. There lies a whole
realm of civil society activity devoted to personal development and self-
help. When civil society is effective in organizing communities to advance
their collective welfare, it takes some of the load off the state and enhances
the legitimacy of the overall system.

All of these functions (and more) have been visible in the extraordinary performance of civil society in democratic India. The brief bout with
authoritarianism during Indira Gandhi's emergency rule revived anti-
colonial norms of resistance to repression and gave particular momentum to human rights groups like the People's Union for Civil Liberties.
Indian grassroots movements in the past three decades have "targeted
various forms of injustice," such as "subordination on the basis of inherited caste status," wanton destruction of natural resources on which people
depend for their survival, and entrenched gender discrimination.[15] They
have defended poor and powerless Indians who were being displaced
from their homes by dams, mining ventures, and missile ranges, or who
were losing their livelihoods to illegal logging. During the 1980s and '90s,
the Narmada Bachao Andolan (Save the Narmada Movement) staged
protests by tens of thousands of poor people who were threatened by the
huge Narmada River Valley dam projects, which were "expected to sub-
merge thousands of villages, displace millions of mostly peasant and

'tribal' people, and destroy tens of thousands of hectares of forest lands."[16] Their dogged public advocacy, Gandhian-style protests (such as fasting, boycotts, and long marches), legal challenges, and international appeals built a transnational coalition and won an indefinite Supreme Court stay on the project's implementation.

India's remarkably pluralistic mass media have played a pivotal democratic role, as well, exposing corruption at high levels and despair and suicide among the indebted rural poor. The penchant for challenging wrongdoing goes back deep into the colonial era and was reawakened by the shame of capitulation to censorship during Mrs. Gandhi's emergency rule. "An increasingly feisty and sometimes irreverent journalism was born, characterized by an adversarial relationship with authority."[17] Since the emergency, "the Indian press has performed a yeoman watchdog role, exposing governmental corruption, taking recalcitrant civil servants to task, revealing governmental indifference to violence against minorities and lower-caste groups, and reporting on failures of governance in all parts of the country."[18] Investigative exposés of bribery and other scandals have brought down a prime minister, a defense minister, a communications minister, and the notorious chief minister of one of India's most crime-ridden states, Bihar. This renewed assertion of freedom by the press coincided with an explosion in the size of the mass media. By 2006, over sixty-thousand news publications, in 123 different languages and dialects, reached over 200 million readers, and the satellite television audience surged to an estimated 230 million viewers. While "the relentless corporate takeover of the Indian press" has diminished its civic content and contributions,[19] it remains a diverse arena outside government control and with the ability to check governmental misconduct.

Civil society groups have also pushed specific reforms to improve democracy. In India, as in other developing countries, a recent campaign has helped pass Right to Information acts (similar to the U.S. Freedom of Information law) in nine states and in the national parliament in 2005. The acts compel each government department to appoint a public information officer, who must respond within thirty days to requests from the public or the media. The campaign for transparency has created innovative methods of public scrutiny, such as the *jan sunwai* (people's hearing), during which "local officials and elected representatives are held to account by the people of the village, in the presence of invited intellectuals or distinguished public figures."[20] This "new type of anti-corruption activism" has sought to expose specific acts of corruption by "utilizing the investigative energies of ordinary people," and by focusing at the local level, "where theft of public resources was personal, and where citizens could [do] the most to expose the precise mechanisms by which corruption took place."[21] These grassroots efforts, which have frequently pulled together elite professionals, retired civil servants, and the lower-caste poor, have mobilized an army of "citizen auditors" to secure the wages, food, and government services to which people are entitled, and to combat illegal practices, such as police harassment and slum relocation, that thrive in a context of graft.

By one count, there were over a million NGOs in India by 2001.[22] The largest share of them were devoted to promoting development and delivering services in such fields as primary education, basic health care, water and sanitation, microcredit, and appropriate technology. Others addressed local community problems of traffic, crime, pollution, and recreation. While these do not directly enhance democracy, they help to address the social and economic problems that could threaten democracy if they were not relieved. Moreover, in fostering a culture of civic concern and grassroots initiative, these groups sustain the spirit of Mahatma Gandhi while also creating "social capital," the horizontal relations of trust, cooperation, and reciprocity that enable people to collaborate for the common good.[23] Still, not all NGOs are good for democracy. Some are illiberal and "uncivil," preaching ethnic and religious intolerance. Hindu chauvinist groups have organized violence against Muslims and Christians and have freely justified exclusion and discrimination. Even pro-democratic organizations are not always internally democratic or externally accountable. But "even if sections of civil society are themselves characterized by a democratic deficit . . . India's robust civil society has been a bulwark of its democracy."[24]

POLITICAL MANAGEMENT OF DIVERSITY

Democracy is not sustained by cultural and social factors alone. The nature and quality of political institutions may have a huge impact in determining whether democracy will be able to address social injustices and economic problems, and thus whether it will be able to generate and maintain public commitment to democracy.

As we saw in chapter 1, there is a growing amount of evidence to suggest that people are more likely to express support for democracy when they see it working to provide genuine political competition, including alternation in power, and when it has at least some effect in controlling corruption, limiting abuse of power, and ensuring a rule of law. One of the great blessings of Indian democracy has been its resilient political party system. Highly competitive elections have seen political power at the federal level transfer peacefully among parties or coalitions seven times since the end of Congress dominance in the mid-1970s, while voter turnout has risen to levels—above 60 percent—that exceed those in the United States. Electoral turnover has been no less vigorous at the consequential level of state government, as the former chief election officer, M. S. Gill, proudly observed: "Between 1993 and 1997. . . elections for all 25 of India's state legislatures saw the incumbent party go down to defeat on no fewer than 19 occasions. That works out to a 24 percent probability of a ruling party winning the next election."[25]

India's institutions have also managed to keep the country from tearing apart along any of its numerous divisions. Some of this impulse toward moderation lies in the very complexity of India's diversity, in which the ties of language, ethnicity, religion, class, region, state, and "most distinctively, caste . . . create multiple and cross-cutting cleavages."[26] Individuals shift between identities that vary in salience over time, and so hold a dampened sense of devotion to any single one.[27] Political institutions have chosen to enhance the gravitational pull toward the center rather than the extremes. A seminal influence was exerted by the nature of the Congress Party as "a grand coalition of the major political and social forces" in India, transcending ethnicity, region, and religion.[28] The electoral system also facilitated the success of such an expansive, diverse party against a host of much narrower challengers. By electing parliament through the British-style, "first past the post system" in single-member territorial districts (each of which now contains more than one million voters), competing candidates were forced to appeal to large and socially diverse constituencies. This distinct parliamentary system enabled a long, stable period of Congress dominance after independence, but did not permit complacency, as the Congress faced stiff competition in most districts. Once that dominance collapsed, the system compelled Congress's main rival, the right-wing Bharatiya Janata Party (BJP, or Indian People's Party) to attenuate its northern, Hindu chauvinist, and upper-caste leanings in order to attract the wider social and regional base needed to win a plurality of seats and assemble a governing coalition.[29]

Two other institutions have contained India's potential for destructive fragmentation and steered it toward pragmatism, bargaining, and a larger national commitment. The most crucial of these has been federalism, which has devolved considerable power and autonomy to state and local governments. Federalism is a particularly powerful tool of ethnic conflict management because it can provide many mechanisms for reducing conflict, including: dispersing conflict from the center by reducing the points of power, softening conflict between groups by generating conflicts within groups, creating incentives for interethnic cooperation, and encouraging alignments on interests other than ethnicity.[30] In a number of deeply divided democracies, such as India, Belgium, and Spain, federalism has been constitutionally embraced as a successful means for maintaining democratic stability.[31] In recent decades, the devolution of power away from the center has been one of the most powerful democratizing trends worldwide, especially in Africa and Latin America. When people in a region or locality, through their own elected governments, have some independent ability to raise and spend their own resources and to set their own development priorities, government is closer to the people, the people have more say, and political legitimacy is enhanced. This does not mean that decentralized governance will always be less corrupt and abusive, but in the long run it increases accountability and responsiveness to local concerns, stimulates citizen participation, widens the access to power of deprived groups, checks the potentially overbearing power of the central government, gives opposition parties a chance to govern at lower levels, and so broadens commitment to democracy.[32]

In fact, it is impossible to imagine how such a large and immensely varied country as India could be a democracy except through a system that guarantees constitutionally significant autonomy to elected governments at the state and local levels. Virtually all of the territorially expansive and heavily populated democracies—the United States, Australia, Germany, Brazil, Argentina, and Mexico—are federal systems. This is also why democracy has only been possible in Nigeria under federalism, Indonesia's democracy has been moving toward a federal system, Sudan needs federalism to establish democratic peace, and the demise of democracy in Russia has coincided with Putin's evisceration of the country's federal institutions and restraints.

In India, federalism has given the country's diverse linguistic communities an important element of cultural pride and political autonomy within a larger national identity. The scale of the challenge is staggering. "Twelve languages are spoken by more than 5 million people each, and another four languages by more than a million each." Since the reorganization of India's states along linguistic lines beginning in 1956, most of these widely used languages have had a state of their own, "which essentially means that the official language of each state is spoken by a majority of its inhabitants."[33] Yet, states still contain great cultural diversity, which discourages secessionist tendencies. As a result, the federal system in India tends to "quarantine" most identity conflicts at a primarily local level. State governments have also been foundries for economic and social reform. While autonomy means that some states, like Bihar and Uttar Pradesh, have lagged miserably behind because of bad, corrupt governance, others, like Tamil Nadu and Karnataka, have been able to improve human well-being much more rapidly.

Federalism in India has worked far from perfectly. It has not always prevented outbreaks of communal violence and separatism. But often these have come "from the failure to adhere to the norms of federalism and autonomy,"[34] while these norms in turn have led to accommodations for many of the most aggrieved and deprived areas. Federalist devolution of power has enabled serious, and in some states appalling, problems of corruption, misrule, and abuse of human rights to fester. Moreover, the center's constitutional prerogative to topple elected state governments and impose direct "president's rule" has been used—infamously by Indira Gandhi—to advance narrowly political objectives rather than good governance and the rule of law. In allowing state autonomy in developmental policies during the last twenty years of economic liberalization, it has facilitated a vast "chasm separating wealthy states like Gujarat, Maharashtra, and Punjab" from the poor states of the northern Hindi heartland.[35]

Yet the system has also been adaptable. Six small, culturally distinctive states were created between 1962 and 1987, and another three in 2000, from territorial communities that felt severely deprived within larger states.[36] Crucially, by creating many thousands of offices and points of political entry, federalism has given a wide range of people a stake in the political system. One of the leading scholars of Indian federalism, James Manor, captures it well: "Not only are there elections for the national and state legislative assemblies; there are also positions of influence available in three tiers of decentralized, elected councils, and in numerous quasi-official boards, cooperatives, associations, and the like. The existence of so many opportunities to capture at least some power persuades parties and politicians to remain engaged with elections and logrolling, even when they are defeated in some arenas."[37] In addition, regional parties have emerged to prominence within many of the linguistically distinct states, stimulating a fluid form of coalitional politics that has complicated the efforts for stable governance at the national level but also made Indian democracy much more inclusive.

It thus seems difficult to dispute the widespread academic assessment that India's federal system has been a foundation of its democratic stability. Two of the most distinguished American experts on India, Susanne and Lloyd Rudolph, recently concluded:

> Forty years ago, there seemed good reason to fear that Selig Harrison was right to warn that India's "fissiparous tendencies," particularly its linguistic differences, would soon lead to Balkanization or dictatorship. Today such worries seem unpersuasive. The federal system has helped India to live peacefully with its marked difference.[38]

A second mechanism for knitting India together politically has been the gradual attenuation of social and political inequalities through reserved quotas in political representation, public employment, and higher education for the lowest status groups: the "scheduled castes," or *dalits* (the former "untouchables," about 17 percent of the population), and the "scheduled tribes" (about 8 percent). More limited affirmative-action guarantees have since been provided to the "other backward castes" (accounting for about 44 percent of the population).[39] These extensive quotas have been cumbersome, inefficient, and controversial, guaranteeing roughly half of public-sector jobs and half the placements in higher education to these less privileged groups. However, they have helped to drive a social revolution that has dramatically accelerated social mobility and expanded political participation to the point where voter turnout among lower-caste groups is now higher than among the well-off. Poverty, malnutrition, illiteracy, and income inequality continue to blight the performance of Indian democracy, but as Amartya Sen argues, the country's free press and civil society have prevented the occurrence of any serious famine. And according to Sumit Ganguly, the country's social progress has been greater than the statistics reveal.

> Upper-caste dominance is steadily on the decline, progress has been made toward universal elementary education, [and] absentee landlordism

has been legally abolished. . . . Consequently, even fitful attempts to promote equality through public policies have had significant ameliorative effects that cannot be adequately measured through conventional statistical techniques."[40]

ACCOUNTABILITY AND THE RULE OF LAW

Few features of political life are more corrosive of public trust in government and support for democracy than corruption (and other forms of abuse of power). If nothing else, citizens expect that democratically elected officials will be held to the same standards as the people are, and that violators will be punished. When politicians become a class unto themselves, feeding shamelessly and lawlessly at the public trough, they generate an open invitation for citizens to reject democracy.

Sustaining and consolidating democracy therefore entails making it more accountable to the people and more respectful of the law. Stable democracy requires a rule of law, in which the constitution is supreme, all citizens are equal before the law, no one is above the law, corruption is minimized and punished, state authorities respect the rights of citizens, and citizens have effective access to the courts to defend their rights. A democratic rule of law requires a judiciary that is, at every level, neutral, independent from political influence, and reasonably competent and resourceful. Most of all, it requires a constitutional court willing to constrain the power of the mighty and defend the rights of the meek.[41] An independent judiciary, however, is only one type of democratic institution to constrain the abuse of power. A good democracy requires a dense web of institutions that check and balance the executive (and one another), as I explain in chapter 13.

India has not been free of serious problems of electoral violence and banditry, but for such a big and poor country, it has managed to institutionalize an exceptional degree of administrative integrity and competence in the holding of elections and the counting of votes. Regularly every few years, an electorate of over 600 million voters comes to the polls in sizable percentages (well over 50 percent). A decade ago, the chief of India's election commission, M. S. Gill, described the Herculean administrative challenges: "Holding a general election involves establishing no fewer than 900,000 polling stations from the high Himalayas to the desert of Rajasthan, including areas that can only be reached on the back of an elephant. Yet such is the miracle of our functioning anarchy in India that never has a single polling station failed the test."[42] One reason the process works well, and with growing credibility and integrity over the past two decades, is because of the career professionalism and total independence of the election commission, which in the period before an election commands 4.5 million staffers from throughout the government. As a result of this capacity and competence, elections in India have been broadly credible, intensely competitive, and largely free and fair.

The single most important institution for upholding accountability and the rule of law in India has been the judicial system. In what will likely remain its darkest moment, the Supreme Court overturned nine High Court decisions that declared Mrs. Gandhi's state of emergency unconstitutional.[43] However, once the emergency ended, the Supreme Court "embarked on an unprecedented burst of judicial activism" that dramatically expanded access to justice. "To this end, the Court introduced a system of public-interest litigation that enabled bonded laborers, disenfranchised tribal people, indigent women, the homeless, and other formerly powerless citizens to approach the bench in search of justice." Journalists and civil society activists also used this mechanism (roughly equivalent to the class action lawsuit in the United States) "to enforce existing environmental laws, to prevent the maltreatment of inmates in state prisons, and to expose corruption in high places."[44] As corruption mounted in the 1990s, the Supreme Court moved to strengthen the independence of another institution of accountability, the Central Bureau of Investigation, by overturning a requirement that the bureau needed "government concurrence" and consultation with a suspected ministry before it could investigate the ministry or its head. This removed an important constraint on the investigation of government corruption. Supreme Court rulings shut down over two hundred companies polluting along the Ganges while bolstering enforcement of clean air and water laws in the heavily polluted capital.[45] At lower levels, the courts remain horribly slow and inefficient, carrying a backlog of 20 million cases.[46] And as Pratap Mehta argues, the expansion of judicial power raises valid questions about the proper limits of unelected authority in a democracy (and has motivated constitutional amendments to renew limits on judicial power).[47] But at the same time, higher-level judicial actions have not only strengthened the rule of law, they have also served as a main front for deepening the responsiveness of Indian democracy, and hence its popular esteem.

SUSTAINING DEMOCRACY IN A DEVELOPING COUNTRY

The persistence of democracy in developed countries presents no real mystery. As we saw in chapter 4, economic development naturally brings about transformations in individual values and social structure that press societies toward democracy and make it difficult to sustain nondemocratic government. Indeed, there has never been a case of democratic breakdown—ever—in a rich country. This is not an invitation to apathy. There is a natural human tendency to want to corner power and monopolize resources, and thus democracy remains continually vulnerable. For rich countries, the success of reform determines the quality and scope of democracy. For poor countries, the survival of democracy is at stake.

We have seen in this chapter what has allowed India to sustain sixty years of nearly uninterrupted democracy—and that, potentially, *any* country, rich or poor, can follow its path. Despite its recent economic growth, India has not boasted high levels of national wealth or education, a feverish miracle of development, or a revolution in its governance. Incremental improvements may be good enough—but they must occur.

At the most general level, two things have sustained democracy in India: the decent functioning and gradual deepening of democracy and a rising hope for a better life. Over time, Indian democracy has worked substantially to provide electoral choice, rotation of power, checks on ruling elites, exposure of abuse of power, and legal and political redress of grievances. The gains have been uneven, but at critical historical moments, change has been achieved and justice has been won. Aggrieved groups have seen that the constitutional system can be made to work for them—and for everyone. Citizens have come to know that democracy means more than occasional elections, that it provides an ongoing means for achieving accountability and responsiveness, and for making the political leadership more broadly representative—"an accomplishment of which many Indians are rightly proud."[48]

At the same time, democracy in India has worked in another political sense, with huge implications for other divided societies in Asia, Africa, the Middle East, and parts of Europe and Latin America. Democracy has provided peaceful means to manage and accommodate deep differences. Again, these have progressed without serious setbacks, but constitutional and legal instruments have prevented or contained large-scale violent conflict while deepening groups' stakes in the democratic system. India's federal structure, its electoral and party systems, and its rules for empow-erment of minorities have worked because they fit the country's particu-lar circumstances and because they have been able to adapt to changing circumstances over time.

Finally, Indian democracy has been powerfully sustained by the steady expansion of the public's hope in it. Until the last decade or so, India's economic development was unnecessarily—really, tragically—retarded by a long-lingering ideological devotion to socialist principles of state intervention and economic autarky. Since the liberalization and opening of the Indian economy began in 1991, economic growth rates have risen well beyond the tortoiselike "Hindu rate of growth" of the country's first four decades, and transformation is finally under way. But even during those several decades of underperformance, the lives of Indians did improve. Between 1970 and 1992, life expectancy rose from fifty to sixty-one years, infant mortality fell by almost half, and adult literacy rose from 34 to 50 percent.[49] Moreover, "the economy registered a fairly steady, although unspectacular, rate of growth, experienced partial reno-vation of agricultural production leading to self-sufficiency in food, developed a structure of industrialization that produces most of what the country basically needs, expanded the supply of educated and sophisti-cated technical workers, consistently held down the level of inflation to one of the lowest in the world, and in the process ensured a level of self-reliance and payment ability that sheltered it from major debt crises."[50] It was a record that almost any African country would have been glad to have. If it did not lift nearly enough people out of poverty, it did at least make progress and gave people hope for a better life and an increased sense of group dignity and national pride. Weighed against the chal-lenges the country faced at independence and the developmental failures of many of its neighbors, these are no small achievements.

With a better understanding of the kinds of economic policies that promote development and of the technical means to fight disease, increase crop yields, and improve human capacity, most developing countries today have the potential to grow faster than India did during its first four decades. But the lesson of India's remarkable experience is that even modest but consistent economic development, combined with a decent functioning and gradual deepening of democratic institutions, can sustain a free political system just about anywhere.

PART TWO

THE PROSPECTS FOR GLOBAL DEMOCRACY

8

LATIN AMERICA'S UNEASY PROGRESS

Alejandro Toledo does not fit the image of a Latin American president. His skin is too dark; his nose is too prominent; his hair is too long. When he was elected president of Peru in 2001, he was the first member of the country's majority of indigenous descent to be democratically chosen for the post. And his story is in some ways a metaphor for the hopes and travails of democracy in Latin America.

Toledo was born in the Peruvian highlands, twelve thousand feet above sea level, the son a bricklayer and a maid and the eighth of sixteen children—seven of whom died in infancy or early childhood. The family had no access to medical care; as a boy of five, he cut the umbilical cord of his newborn brother (his father had left to find work in a mine). At that early age, while tending the family's sheep and pigs and sleeping in a room with fourteen people, he became "an Indian rebellious against poverty."[1] When the family moved to the fishing village of Chimbote, Alejandro took any job he could get, carrying bags at the train station, shining shoes, selling newspapers and lottery tickets. His father was egalitarian, determined that each of his children attend elementary school. But each had to work to support the family as the next child took a turn at school. Finding in Alejandro a student of prodigious intellect and ambition, his teachers urged the family to send him to high school. His father said no, the family needed him to work, but Toledo found a way to do both, attending school by day while shining shoes at night and selling shaved ice on the weekends.

In his third year of high school, at age fourteen, Toledo met and befriended two American Peace Corps volunteers who had arrived in Chimbote and were looking for housing. By then, the reality of his class and ethnic background was catching up with him. "I wanted to go to university, but I knew there was no possibility," he told me. "Concluding high school would be my maximal accomplishment academically." His goal was to go into a business, maybe as a mechanic, "to be a little higher than my father." Nevertheless, the Americans encouraged him, gave him philosophy books, and, in hours of conversations, helped him learn English. He soared academically and became president of his high school class. He won a writing contest and became the Chimbote political correspondent for *La Prensa,* the leading national newspaper. He was still shining shoes and selling lottery tickets when he experienced the first flush of pride at being published, and the humiliation of his place in life when the man whose shoes he was shining laughed at the thought that an Amerindian shoeshine boy could possibly have been the author of the newspaper article he was reading.

Then Toledo got another break. He won a Rotary Club scholarship for a year of study at the University of San Francisco (USF). It only covered tuition for one year, so again he had to struggle to support himself, while keeping up with college courses. Shortly after arriving in San Francisco, he took a job doing household work for a European family in exchange for housing. Never having seen electrical appliances, he burned the toast, botched the chores, and was berated for his incompetence. The family told the Peace Corps volunteers, who had helped him find the job, "You brought this person to satisfy your own ego. The best thing you can do is send him back to his tribe." It was not the only indignity he suffered. He was Hispanic. He was Indian. He wore his hair very long, falling down his back. People would ask, "Are you a Navajo? What reservation do you come from?" But Toledo was determined. He went to night school and pumped gas on the late-night shift. From 7:00 AM to noon he slept. From noon to 1:30 PM he washed dishes at school. From 2:00 to 5:00 PM he played soccer on a university scholarship that covered his tuition for his final three years. In this way, he earned a bachelor's degree in economics from USF in 1970 and won full funding to do a Ph.D. in international development at the Stanford School of Education. He went on to earn two master's degrees (one in economics) as well as a Ph.D.

When he left Stanford, Toledo took a number of positions and consultancies in international development, working for the United Nations and the World Bank among others. He interspersed these with periods in Peru chairing the board of economic advisers of the president of the central bank and teaching at Peru's leading business school. From 1991 to 1994, he served as a scholar in residence at the Harvard Institute for International Development and a guest professor at Waseda University in Tokyo. From abroad, he watched with alarm as President Alberto Fujimori seized power in his *autogolpe* in 1992, dissolving congress, decimating independent centers of power, and twisting Peru's institutions into a pseudodemocracy. Appalled by Fujimori's destruction of democracy, and frustrated that he was writing about poverty but having no impact on the lives of the poor, Toledo resolved to enter politics. In August 1994, he arrived in Peru and launched an independent candidacy to challenge Fujimori in the 1995 presidential election. With Fujimori at the peak of his popularity, Toledo was trounced, winning only 3 percent of the vote. Still, he persisted. Despite deepening authoritarianism and (by his own account) over a hundred death threats, he founded a new political party, Perú Posible, in 1999 and again challenged Fujimori in the 2000 election. Through relentless political effort, Toledo emerged as the principal challenger to Fujimori, who was seeking a third term in violation of the constitutional ban. When Fujimori massively tilted the playing field for the first round of voting, and then the count was riddled with charges of fraud, OAS monitors condemned the election and Toledo withdrew from the second round. Donning a headband, he led the opposition in protest, as hundreds of thousands of Peruvians came out in the streets to demand a return to genuine democracy. When Fujimori's corruption was exposed some months later and he was forced to resign, Toledo contested again and was elected president in 2001.

Toledo's five years as president were on balance a governance but not a political success. During his term, the Peruvian economy recorded its best performance in six decades, averaging 5 percent annual economic growth, one of the best rates in the entire region. "Inflation remained low and fiscal management was prudent."[2] The annual fiscal deficit shrank from 3.3 percent of the gross domestic product to almost nothing, and the rate of nonperforming loans in the banking sector fell by over 80 percent. By 2006, Peru had one of the lowest levels of country risk of any Latin American country, so foreign investment poured in, increasing 50 percent during Toledo's tenure. With expanded investment in the critical mining sector, Peru's export earnings tripled.[3] Yet, the core dilemma of development in Latin America—enormous poverty and massive inequality that ranks the region worst in distribution of income and wealth in the world—continued to frustrate the public and the president himself. "The benefits of growth were limited primarily to the top third of the income distribution and barely reached the poor, who make up 48 percent of the population. Unemployment remained stubbornly high. Real wages were stagnant, and job security provisions continued to erode."[4] To some extent, all countries that implement fiscal restraint and economic reform confront such difficulties in the face of globalization, with its intense mobility of capital and its downward pressure on wages. Toledo's efforts delivered some reductions in absolute poverty (by one-quarter) and infant and child mortality, as state expenditures in social programs and in basic health and education increased, but it was much less than his constituencies—particularly Peru's long-deprived indigenous people— were expecting.[5]

On the political side, Toledo sacked the country's top military chiefs and began to restructure the armed forces. In 2002, a reform of Peru's highly centralized system "gave new regional governments almost a quarter of the national budget and a range of powers that had long been the province of the central government."[6] But these changes threatened powerful interests, and Toledo had to contend with the daunting legacy of a decade of authoritarian rule under Fujimori and his intelligence chief, Vladimir Montesinos, who had systematically corrupted much of the Peruvian political, social, and corporate elite. As prosecutors sought to extradite the former president from his exile in Japan and prosecuted Montesinos and a number of other prominent Fujimori-era officials, the old guard fought back viciously. The Toledo government's investigation of some 1,500 people on corruption charges "threatened a significant swath of elites." Many powerful business and media magnates—dubbed "the Montesinos mafia"—"retaliated by scheming to bring about Toledo's downfall, hoping that a new government would approve an amnesty."[7] They did not succeed, but they did generate relentlessly negative and humiliating media coverage, ridiculing the president at every turn. And Toledo himself made mistakes, raising his salary in his first year, alienating some of his original cabinet members, and initially refusing to acknowledge paternity of an out-of-wedlock daughter. Although he governed with a degree of integrity and restraint that was rare in Peruvian history, the hostile media did its best to portray him as a high-living politician insensitive to the poor, part of a corrupt political class, while barely mentioning that "it was Fujimori's government that had stolen $1.8 billion from the state."[8] Consequently, Toledo's approval ratings plunged as low as 10 percent amid public cynicism about politicians as a class.

By the time he left office, Toledo had recovered considerably in public approval (to about 50 percent) as the scope of his policy achievements began to sink in.[9] "For the first time in its republican history, a presidential transition" was taking place in Peru "while its politics is democratic, social peace reigns, the economy grows apace, and world markets shine on Peruvian products."[10] But Toledo had learned some crucial lessons, with much wider implications for democracy in Latin America. His economic understanding, democratic commitment, and good intentions had not been enough. He had respected human rights, freedom of the press, and the independence of democratic institutions, garnering Peru its best freedom ratings in many years. He had instigated sorely needed economic reforms and overseen a skillful management of the national economy. But, he realized, economic reforms had to be coupled with "much earlier and deeper social projects targeted on the urban and rural extreme poor, those who live on less than one dollar a day." And, further, to be successful politically, a president must battle for public opinion. The problem, he is convinced, is not Peru's alone.

> If these levels of poverty are not reduced dramatically, if we don't deal with the social exclusion, then there will be much louder noises in the streets, from the unions, the coca cultivators, the indigenous people, and these noises will impede capital investment. You can't redistribute poverty, so we need sustained rates of economic growth. But to grow, we need investment, and for that we need economic, social, and legal stability. We can't get that stability with the levels of inequality and poverty we have in Latin America today. We need specific social projects targeted at the extreme poor, to go along side by side with longer-term investments in basic health and education. Without those short-term improvements, we may not have the time to respond to popular expectations and protests. Democracy in Latin America may not be at risk, but democratic governability is. With each new term, presidents have less time to respond.[11]

DEMOCRATIC HOPES IN THE AMERICAS

Peru is hardly the most challenged case of democracy in the Americas. Inequality is at least as great in Brazil, the exclusion of the indigenous majority (until very recently) has been even more severe in Bolivia, and in Ecuador, populist mobilization and poor governance have forced out one president after another. Since the mid-1980s, sixteen Latin American presidents have not completed their terms.[12] Nevertheless, the success of the democratic system in Latin America and the Caribbean has been nothing short of remarkable. If in 1975 someone had predicted that within a generation every military regime in the region would be dismantled and virtually the entire region would be democratic, that person would have been considered a wildly naive optimist. Yet, for more than a decade, that has been the case in Latin America. Cuba's Communist regime persists as the last overt dictatorship in the region. After a long period of democratic decline, Venezuela has descended into authoritarian strongman rule. And, since the fall of the Duvalier dynasty in the 1980s, Haiti has had competitive elections but not democracy. Apart from these three countries, however, the other thirty states of Latin America and the Caribbean are all, in the least, electoral democracies in which government leaders are selected and can be—and frequently *are*—replaced in regular, more or less free and fair elections.[13] Typically, these elections elicit high rates of participation on the national level and yield results that are widely viewed as legitimate.[14] In fact, Latin America has made great strides in institutionalizing the culture and the administrative infrastructure of multiparty electoral competition—an extraordinary achievement for a region with so much history of vote buying, electoral rigging, intimidation, and violent struggle for power. Moreover, when eleven Latin American countries elected new presidents in 2006, with the exception of the closely fought contest in Mexico, "all the losing candidates accepted defeat," and a growing respect for the electoral process and the independent institutions that oversee it was apparent.[15] Military influence over politics has steadily receded.

If the free and peaceful struggle for power through the ballot box is becoming entrenched in Latin America, other dimensions of democracy are not. For ethnic and racial minorities and the vast legions of poor, democracy has yet to bring full rights of citizenship. In much of the region, crime and violence are rampant, the police demand bribes and abuse individual rights, the state is corrupt and unresponsive, the judiciary is feeble and horribly backlogged, and justice is partial and agonizingly slow, if it comes at all. In short, democracy is real but shallow. Until it becomes deeper, more liberal, and more accountable, it will continue to be vulnerable to the temptations of authoritarian populism.

Despite the temptations of populist forces, Latin Americans still believe in the promise of democracy. A majority consistently (and by some measures, overwhelmingly) prefer democracy to any other form of government, though they are not happy with the way democracy is performing in their country. As measured by the annual Latinobarometer from 1995 through 2006, there was some early erosion in the belief that democracy is always preferable (declining from about 60 percent in the late 1990s to around 53 percent), but this support rebounded (to 58 percent in 2006). And the gains were greatest in precisely those countries where democratic support had previously been weak: Brazil, Paraguay, Guatemala, and Honduras.[16] In comparison, the percentage of Latin Americans preferring authoritarian rule has remained virtually constant, at only 15 percent, over the course of the decade.

When Latin Americans were asked in 2005 if they would "support a military government to replace the democratic government if the situation got very bad," 30 percent said yes—but a decisive majority, 62 percent, said no.[17] And when the preference for democracy is put in a more realistic tone—"Democracy may have problems, but it's the best system of government"—fully three-quarters of Latin Americans, on average, agree.[18] Two-thirds say democracy is the only way to become a developed country.[19] Moreover, across time and across most countries, a majority of Latin Americans recognize that democracy cannot exist without a congress (58 percent) and without political parties (55 percent).[20]

On the level of personal participation, 58 percent on average say that the way one votes "can change the way things will be in the future,"[21] yet they also perceive high levels of corruption (including in the electoral process) and low levels of regime responsiveness to their concerns. Further, 70 percent see little or no equality before their country's law. Over two-thirds think their government serves the interest of powerful groups rather than of all the people.[22] As a result, they have little confidence in their politicians or in most democratic institutions. Only about one in five trusts political parties, a quarter the congress, and a third the judiciary. Elected presidents fare somewhat better of late (47 percent in 2006), but this might signal a worrying trend toward trust in personalities over institutions.[23] Generally, the three most liberal and consolidated

democracies—Uruguay, Chile, and Costa Rica—do better on these measures, but even Costa Rica, the region's oldest continuous democracy, has
been gripped by presidential corruption scandals of late. While the percentage of Latin Americans satisfied with the way democracy works
improved noticeably in 2006—jumping by 14 percentage points or more
in Brazil, Argentina, Mexico, Bolivia, and Panama as popular presidents
delivered on some of their promises—the regional average was still a mere
38 percent, and that was the highest level in a decade.[24]

Latin America appears to consist of three regions rather than one.
There are the countries where democracy seems deeply rooted in norms
and expectations, and where people express substantial satisfaction with
democratic performance and trust in democratic institutions and leaders.
Among this group, Uruguay almost always ranks at the top, followed by
Costa Rica and Chile, and, of late, Argentina, Panama, and the Dominican Republic, where presidents have won public confidence by delivering
economic progress and avoiding massive scandals. Citizens are more optimistic, believing overwhelmingly (by two-thirds or more) that democracy
can bring development. In these countries, people more positively assess
the judiciary and the congress and have higher confidence in government in general (near or well above a majority). They perceive a rule of
law: that the state has some capacity to enforce the laws and to deliver
justice. And a higher percentage of the public (approaching 45 percent)
sees some progress in the battle against corruption (compared to a
regional average of just 30 percent). Venezuela also falls into this group of
more optimistic, pro-democratic countries—a seeming anomaly given
President Hugo Chávez's assault on democratic institutions, but perhaps
explained by his populist mobilization and massive social spending. In
all seven countries in this group, people perceive a higher quality of
democracy than in the rest of Latin America,[25] and half of the public (on
average) is satisfied with the way democracy works compared to just
27 percent in the other countries surveyed.[26]

Then there are the Latin American countries that have faced historic
democratic difficulties but now appear to be improving and stabilizing:
Mexico, Colombia, and Brazil, and on some measures Honduras and Bolivia.
These countries fall at about the regional average in their publics' perceptions of the extent of democracy in their country and in support for and
satisfaction with democracy. Recently, Brazilians and Colombians have
rated their judiciary and congress more positively than do Latin Americans overall. In both cases, popular presidents were solidly reelected on a

platform of delivering economic or security progress that has helped to raise democratic hope and satisfaction.

Finally, there are the region's weakest democracies, as judged both by external observers and by their own peoples. These countries generally have the lowest levels of democratic support and confidence and the biggest accumulated problems of poverty, social inequality, and political exclusion. They include the Central American countries (Guatemala, El Salvador, Nicaragua, and on some measures Honduras), the Andean countries (Ecuador, Bolivia, and Peru), and Paraguay. In these eight countries, only about a quarter of the population is satisfied with the way democracy works (in Paraguay, it is just 12 percent). People in Bolivia appear temporarily hopeful about the election to the presidency of Evo Morales, a member of the country's long-marginalized indigenous majority. In the other seven countries, however, pessimism persists. All told, only 42 percent in these countries express confidence in the ability of democracy to bring development (compared to 65 percent in the other countries surveyed). Citizens rate the economy as bad, and less than a quarter detect any recent improvements.[27] Similarly, only a quarter or less see progress in reducing corruption. People in these countries are the most skeptical of all Latin Americans about the capacity of their states to enforce laws; they see most officials as corrupt and their institutions as performing very poorly. Only 29 percent on average rate the work of their judicial system positively.

SLOW PROGRESS

The institutionalization of electoral democracy in Latin America stands as a momentous achievement of the last three decades. In most of the region's democracies, power has rotated between different political parties and social groups, often across considerable ideological distance. Since the late 1990s, left political parties and candidates have won power in Venezuela (1998), Chile (2000 and 2006), Brazil (2002 and 2006), Argentina (2003), Uruguay (2005), Bolivia (2006), Peru (2006), Ecuador (2006), and Nicaragua (2006). Often, these presidential candidates overcame long odds, triumphing in Brazil only after repeated defeats at the ballot box, in Ecuador against the political war chest of the country's wealthiest businessman, in Bolivia against nearly five centuries of political exclusion of the indigenous majority, and in Chile against powerful traditions of male dominance. These elections opened possibilities for real change, bringing to power a once-radical trade union leader in Brazil (Luiz Inácio Lula da Silva), an indigenous leader of the coca leaf-growing peasants in Bolivia (Morales), and "the first female head of state in the Americas to be elected without any connection to the political career of a male relative" in Chile (Michelle Bachelet).[28] Power has also rotated (as in Mexico in 2000), and no doubt will repeatedly again, to the right of the political spectrum. Increasingly, though not perfectly, electoral uncertainty and a significant degree of electoral fairness and transparency have become institutionalized—even, it appears, in Latin America's most illiberal democracy, Guatemala.[29] In some countries, such as Brazil and Mexico, parties and party systems are also maturing, and growing into effective mechanisms for representation and accountability.[30]

Many of the left-of-center presidents have governed pragmatically and reasonably effectively, implementing fiscal discipline and sound economic fundamentals while increasing social spending. This has been true not only of social democratic presidents like Toledo in Peru and Fernando Henrique Cardoso in Brazil, but of presidents representing nominally socialist or more historically leftist parties, such as Ricardo Lagos in Chile (2000–2006), Lula in Brazil, and Tabaré Vázquez in Uruguay (elected in 2005). Cardoso's eight years in Brazil—a democracy considered virtually ungovernable when he entered office in 1995—were historic, settling more than six hundred thousand landless peasants on homesteads (three times the number established in the preceding thirty years) and boosting enrollments in primary schools to encompass virtually all children (a 20 percent increase) while restraining inflation and corruption and beginning to consolidate the country's shaky democratic institutions.[31]

Some of this progress is the result of a fundamental reorientation of Latin America's leftist political parties and groups, which have become more moderate by jettisoning Marxist and revolutionary ideological doctrines and more democratic by embracing electoral politics and abandoning "violence, revolution, or other antisystemic approaches to resolving issues of social justice."[32] The transformation has been far from universal, as evidenced by Hugo Chávez's suffocation of democratic pluralism in Venezuela and Evo Morales's socialist economic policies (including nationalization of key industries) in Bolivia. But in most of the region, the Left has moved toward the center and governed more or less pragmatically.

By the same token, the political Right has also moderated. In Mexico,

Vicente Fox overcame the right-wing image of his National Action Party (PAN) by appointing a cabinet that included leftist intellectuals and then proceeded to govern with greater transparency than had been experienced in the authoritarian Mexico of the past. If Fox failed to record as much progress in fighting poverty, corruption, crime, and unemployment as the public demanded, he did generate enough economic growth and decent governance to make it possible (barely) for his party to recapture the presidency in 2006. In El Salvador, the once militantly right-wing Arena Party implemented the 1992 peace accords, increased social spending as a percent of the economy, and significantly reduced poverty. It also accepted the constraints of a democratic system in which the leftist party of the former guerrillas has controlled a plurality in the legislature and several municipal governments, including the capital.[33]

Democratic governments have also achieved significant reforms. Throughout Latin America, and particularly in the deeply divided polities of Central America and the Andean region, the political process has been opened to previously disenfranchised and even brutalized groups. Indigenous peoples—who represent a majority or nearly so in Bolivia, Guatemala, Peru, and Ecuador and sizable minorities in Mexico, Honduras, Chile, El Salvador, and Colombia—have raised group consciousness, organized social protests, and stimulated political participation. The expansion of freedom and invigoration of democracy have enabled indigenous peoples to win significant social and legal reforms, including increased access to bilingual education, official status for indigenous languages, protection of collective property rights, and legal recognition of indigenous customary law.[34] One of the factors facilitating the local empowerment of indigenous parties has been the gradual decentralization of government power, which, as in India, has created more elected governments at the municipal, state, and regional level. As indigenous parties have won control of local governments, they have sometimes brought with them "indigenous self-governing practices that emphasize consensus-seeking, community participation, leadership rotation, and reciprocity," leading to a higher quality of democracy.[35] Their mobilization has also generated other positive effects, as a growing number of political leaders and legislators from indigenous groups, particularly in Bolivia, have been elected on broader political party platforms.

Gradually, Latin American democracies have also made progress (after long periods of impunity) in imposing accountability for past human rights abuses. This has been a particular priority of Argentine president Néstor Kirchner since he took office in 2003. Argentina's congress annulled (in 2003) and the Supreme Court declared unconstitutional (in 2005) two amnesty laws passed in the late 1980s that had granted immunity to those responsible for torture, political killings, and disappearances under military rule. With Kirchner's strong support, prosecutions resumed after a nearly two-decade hiatus. In one important case, two police officials were convicted in 2006 for torture and disappearances and were sentenced to weighty terms. After a period of blockage, Chile moved vigorously to prosecute former military officials accused of grave human rights abuses under General Augusto Pinochet's dictatorship. As of October 2006, Chile's "courts had convicted 109 individuals [including former generals] for crimes including 'disappearances,' extrajudicial executions, and torture under military rule."[36] And in October 2006, new president Bachelet announced her intention to challenge a law that still provides amnesty for official abuses committed during the period 1973 to 1978.

No less important has been the gradual reduction in the political influence and role of the military in Latin America and its subjection to civilian control. The process has gone the furthest in the former military dictatorships of the Southern Cone—Argentina, Brazil, and Chile—but throughout the region, the autonomous power and special privileges of the military (including their involvements in the economy and internal security) have gradually been reined in. Military budgets and the overall size of the armed forces have also been scaled back in many countries. In Chile, the authoritarian constitutional enclaves secured by Pinochet were gradually removed, and in August 2005 a package of constitutional reforms—debated for more than a decade—came into effect, abolishing appointed senators and restoring the president's power to dismiss the commanders in chief of the armed forces and the police.[37] Reforms have also been achieved in Central America, the most military-dominated area of Latin America, and the one with the worst record of military abuse of human rights. Over the past decade, domestic and international pressures—the cumulative effect of democratic elections and the end of the Cold War and of armed leftist insurgencies—"have largely subordinated the military to civilian control and curbed its political influence" in El Salvador, Honduras, Nicaragua, and even Guatemala. There, and throughout Latin America, the OAS's vigilance in removing the coup option has narrowed the armed forces' ability to resist the reforms of elected civilian authorities. Yet, Central American militaries still enjoy (particularly in Guatemala) levels of institutional autonomy, freedom from democratic oversight, impunity for human rights abuses, and centrality in intelligence gathering that seriously diminish the quality and stability of democracy.[38]

THE WEAKNESSES OF LATIN AMERICAN DEMOCRACY

In Central America, there is a species of deadly ants—known as *marabunta*, or *maras*—that move in huge colonies and destroy everything in their path. The term now applies as well to the murderous youth gangs, "spawned in the ghettos of Los Angeles and other U.S. cities," that have spread like a fast-moving plague throughout Central America and up to Mexico and the United States.[39] Fed by the explosive growth of youth populations and the region's tenacious social ills, the gangs not only threaten democracy directly but serve as a powerful metaphor for the crisis of lawlessness in Latin America.

More than anything else, democracy in Latin America continues to be degraded and disfigured by a weak rule of law. To be sure, the region has come a long way from the days of brutal military dictatorships and even the tentative regime transitions. With the end of civil wars in Central America and the suppression of the Shining Path insurgency in Peru, gross human rights abuses such as massacres, death squads, and torture have been eliminated or at least sharply reduced. Yet, a vexing syndrome of violence, criminality, and abuse persists, driven by poverty, unemployment, inequality, and the weakness and corruption of state social services and criminal justice systems. This indictment from the Brazilian political scientist Paulo Sérgio Pinheiro (one of the region's leading authorities on violence and a member of the Inter-American Commission on Human Rights) remains all too apt though it was written in 1999.

Since the return of democratic rule to many countries in Latin America, relations between government and society, particularly the poor and marginalized members of society, have been characterized by the illegal and arbitrary use of power. . . .

Human rights abuses occur every day and the majority of the perpetrators are not punished or otherwise held accountable for their heinous crimes. . . . Growing criminality not only erodes democratic expectations (as many surveys in the continent have demonstrated) but also sanctions arbitrary violence, weakening the legitimacy of the political system. There are large portions of the territory, mainly in the rural areas, where the local ruling classes continue to manipulate state institutions, including the judiciary and the police. . . .

Despite significant advances in civil society and democratic governance, the poor continue to be the preferred victims of violence, criminality, and human rights violations. . . .

Police and other institutions of the criminal justice system tend to act as "border guards," protecting the elites from the poor. Police violence remains cloaked in impunity because it is largely directed against these "dangerous classes," and rarely affects the lives of the privileged. . . . Middle-class and elite crimes—such as corruption, financial scams, tax evasion, and the exploitation of child or slave labor—are not perceived as threats to the status quo. The same is generally true for the activities of organized crime, including drug trafficking, money laundering, contraband, and even the profitable arms trade. . . .

Torture under police investigation and the abominable conditions of prisons throughout most countries in Latin America are still pervasive even after the political transition. . . .

[In addition], summary executions of suspects and criminals are common practices in many countries. . . . The victims tend to be from the most vulnerable groups—the poor, the homeless, and the African descendants.[40]

Pinheiro maintains that today, "an *un-rule of law* continues to be a daily reality for millions of people across Latin America."[41] The region's crime rate is double the world's average, and "the Inter-American Development Bank estimates that Latin America's per capita gross domestic product would be 25 percent higher if the region's crime rates were equal to the world average."[42]

Over the past decade, the nexus of poverty, crime, violence, drug trafficking, and state abuse has intensified with the rise of the youth gangs, drawn primarily from the ranks of the unemployed and undereducated. Homicide rates have soared to the highest in the world, while corrupt and ill-equipped police struggle to cope. As organized crime networks sink roots in the still-burgeoning trade in illegal drugs, "the divide between youth gang violence and organized narco-crime is becoming increasingly blurred."[43] Latin American countries themselves must also grapple with rising drug addiction.

The strength of organized crime networks underscores that the most serious challenge for democracy—and governability—in Latin America is not the overpowering strength of states but rather their incapacity and lack of effective authority. In Brazil, "paramilitary gangsters control most of Rio's roughly 700 *favelas* [slums]. Drug bosses decide whether the electricity company installs a new power line or not; they decide when the pre-school closes and who can visit the priest. They've built a parallel government—like the ones in São Paulo prisons, the slums of Caracas and Medellín, and the streets of Acapulco and Mexico City."[44] In El Salvador, more than a dozen municipalities "are believed to be effectively ruled by the *maras*."[45] Even in the long-established democracies of the Caribbean, drug trafficking, "money laundering, and the inevitable, attendant corruption" are eating away at the quality of democracy.[46] In Mexico, the drug traffickers have, in the words of one state official, "replaced the local government" in some areas; they now pose such a fundamental challenge to the authority of the state that President Felipe Calderón has mobilized the country's armed forces to crack down on them.[47] Also feeding the vicious circle are the easy access to small arms and the spread of increasingly powerful automatic weaponry.

High levels of income inequality, joblessness, racial discrimination, and perceived exclusion from the benefits of globalization lead poor youth to "romanticize" crime.[48] As in the United States, it is mainly poor communities that are victimized. This feeds demands (or tolerance) for vigilante justice, and countervailing public and media pressure for get-tough policing guidelines that trample civil liberties and incarcerate growing numbers of troubled, deprived, and violent young people in dysfunctional and overcrowded prisons, the equivalent of "gangland finishing schools."[49] In prison, detainees face physical abuse, sexual assault, and torture. Moreover, police and prosecutors do a poor job of investigating crimes, as well as state abuses, and the state does an even worse job of giving the weak and the accused access to justice, including legal representation. Hence, according to Pinheiro, "the region continues to struggle with seemingly intractable problems in criminal justice: abusive use of lethal force by police forces, extrajudicial killings, lynching, torture, abominable prison conditions, and persistent corruption."[50] The problems appear particularly severe in Brazil, Mexico, Colombia, Venezuela, Central America, and Jamaica, but are evident elsewhere in the region.[51] And these are not just problems for Latin America. The Central American gang problem has spilled over with a vengeance into the United States. A single Salvadoran gang—MS-13 (Mara Salvatrucha), one of the region's largest and most brutal—is estimated to have as many as ten thousand members operating in thirty-one U.S. states (among a total international membership of fifty thousand).[52]

Two decades after the return of civilian rule, all of these challenges stand in stark relief in Guatemala. Human rights groups, peasant activists, and trade unions (as well as anyone seeking justice for past rights abuses) are the frequent targets of violent attacks, assassinations, and death threats.[53] Gang violence in and out of prison is rampant. The country has one of the worst murder rates in the Western Hemisphere, almost eight times the U.S. rate.[54] According to one comparative study, "one has to go back to fourteenth-century London, at a time prior to the establishment of regular police forces, to find historical homicide rates as high as found in contemporary Guatemala."[55] (Yet, in El Salvador and Honduras, experts fear the rate may now be higher.) The problem is compounded by the country's barely functioning judiciary, "plagued by corruption, inefficiency, capacity shortages, and violent intimidation of judges, prosecutors, and witnesses."[56] Due to the turgid pace of justice and weak protection for rights, "the Public Defenders Institute estimates that as many as 65 percent of all inmates have yet to be convicted of a crime."[57] During Guatemala's thirty-six-year-old civil war, which ended in 1996, some two hundred thousand people were killed, most by government forces. While the UN-sponsored Truth Commission could ascertain the scope of the bloodshed, efforts to establish legal accountability for it have been plagued by inefficiency, lack of resources, obstruction, and violent retaliation from "clandestine groups." Consequently, "of the 626 massacres documented by the truth commission, only two cases have been successfully prosecuted in the Guatemalan courts."[58] Impunity governs for more "common" crimes as well. "The Guatemalan Human Rights Ombudsman's Office estimates, for example, that arrests are only made in 3 percent of the cases involving murders of women and girls."[59] The weaknesses of the justice system allow dozens of public lynchings each year.

Persistent poverty, insecurity, and extreme inequality provide fertile soil for these political and institutional pathologies. On average, the top 10 percent of income earners in Latin America capture 40 percent of national income, while the bottom 20 percent take home less than 4 percent. By contrast, in India, Indonesia, and Ghana, the respective shares are about 30 percent of income for the top tenth and 6 to 9 percent for the bottom fifth. The average ratio of top tenth to bottom fifth income shares in Latin America stands at 11:1—and in Brazil, Chile, Colombia, and Panama, it is 15:1 or worse, comparable to South Africa, with its awful legacy of apartheid.[60] This compares to income-share ratios of less than 3:1 in Korea, Germany, and Slovenia, less than 4:1 in India and Indonesia, and less than 7:1 in Turkey and the Philippines, both of which are known for their inequality. When inequality is as extreme as it is in Latin America, it breeds "diffuse patterns of authoritarian relations between the privileged and the others."[61] The wealthy see themselves as entitled to power, while the poor are viewed as innately inferior and denied the means to exercise their citizenship rights. The problem is exacerbated by racial discrimination against indigenous peoples as well as those of African descent. In Guatemala, the poverty rate for the indigenous population (75 percent) is twice that for the ladino population; the rate of extreme poverty is almost four times as high; and the level of average educational attainment is barely half.[62]

With severe inequality comes massive poverty. In many Latin American countries, particularly in Central America and the Andean region, the percentage living in poverty is estimated at between 40 and 50 percent, or higher. In Ecuador, "official figures put the combined rate of underemployment and unemployment throughout the workforce at 58 percent," despite a recent boom in oil revenues.[63] Moreover, most Latin Americans consider themselves to be poor. When asked in 2005 to rank themselves on a ten-step ladder (with 1 representing the poorest people and 10 the wealthiest), citizens in thirteen of seventeen Latin American countries delivered an average ranking under 4. That same year, an average of 56 percent across the region said their income was not sufficient to meet their needs.[64] With the region experiencing its fourth consecutive year of growth in 2006, economic worries eased a bit, but unemployment was still most often mentioned as the biggest problem facing the country, and an astonishing two-thirds of Latin Americans said they were worried that they would be unemployed or left without work in the next twelve months.[65] But then, their anxieties were based in economic reality: in 2005, three of every five households in the typical Latin American country reported at least one adult unemployed in the previous twelve months.[66] On the bright side, since 2003, Latin Americans have actually been growing steadily more optimistic about their personal economic prospects; fully half, on average, expect improvement. And after a decade in which less than 10 percent of Latin Americans saw their country's economic situation as good or very good, the percentage rose to 18 percent in 2006. (Twice as many still see their country's economic situation as bad or very bad.) And while the percent who view their own family economic situation positively rose for three straight years starting in 2004, it was still only 30 percent in 2006.[67]

Poverty and inequality, like crime and violence, are reproduced in vicious cycles, and the two cycles reinforce each other. Wealthy elites evade paying taxes and distort government spending priorities, inhibiting the kinds of social investments that would alleviate poverty in the short term and, through spending on education and health, reduce it over the long run. The heavy weight of poverty, lawlessness, and violent crime discourage foreign investment and so retard economic growth— which is essential to lifting the poor out of poverty.

All of these problems are exacerbated by high levels of corruption, which undermines every dimension of governance. Corruption makes it more difficult to spend resources effectively on social needs. It reduces the efficiency of public investments. It distorts investment priorities and discourages investors from risking their capital in the face of rigged awards for contracts, pervasive demands for bribes, and uncertain legal protection for property rights. In the political arena, it can generate cynical deals between disparate parties to provide legal immunity for past wrongdoing, as in Nicaragua.[68]

The result is the widespread cynicism about parties and politicians that has taken hold in Latin America, a cynicism that in turn aggravates the fragmentation and volatility of the party system. The combination of an angry, disaffected public and a weak, personality-driven party system makes it exceedingly difficult to build the political coalitions necessary to enact bold reforms of the state and economy, and can bring down a presidency very quickly. Between 1985 and 2004, a dozen Latin American presidents had their terms ended prematurely by impeachment or mass demonstrations that forced their resignations.[69] Since then, presidents have again been "abruptly forced out of office" by mass street protests in Bolivia (for the third time in twenty years) and in Ecuador (for the third time in a decade).[70] When Néstor Kirchner took office in May 2003, he was the sixth Argentine president in eighteen months.[71] Many of these presidents were corrupt or incompetent and deserved to go, but a distinctly Latin American social and political dynamic has been at work contributing to the string of failed presidencies.

Parliamentary systems might work better to manage these tensions, mobilize legislative support for the executive, and foster smoother means of leadership succession in crisis, but Latin America is so steeped in the tradition of presidentialism that the most one can hope for is limited reforms to promote stability, such as concurrent legislative and executive elections (which would increase the prospects of presidential party support in the congress).[72]

SECURING DEMOCRACY IN THE AMERICAS

At a formal level, democracy has made remarkable progress in Latin America, but if we look at the way institutions actually function and how citizens evaluate them, much remains to be done before democracy can be considered secure. Creeping authoritarianism in Venezuela and the abuses of power under another left-wing populist in Bolivia show the vulnerability of democracy in the absence of economic growth, social freedom, and good governance.

If democracy is to be consolidated in Latin America, it must be deepened institutionally and deliver broadly distributed material progress. This implies a simultaneous agenda of what Alejandro Toledo calls "three parallel paths." First, democracies have to get the fundamentals of economic policy right, as Toledo did, as the leftist Brazilian president Lula da Silva did, and as successive governments in Chile have done, to generate sustained growth. Only that can provide a context for social reforms to reduce poverty and inequality. But second, those reforms cannot wait for longer-term investments to work their gradual effects. Targeted programs are needed to address extreme poverty, such as "micro-credit for micro-enterprise and the development of markets for the products of the very poor." Third, specific efforts are needed to strengthen democratic institutions of accountability and representation, including an independent judicial system, an effective apparatus to monitor and control corruption, a pluralistic and independent press, and elected regional and local government.[73] As we will see in subsequent chapters, these priorities in Latin America are not so different from those in other parts of the world.

9

THE POSTCOMMUNIST DIVIDE

With the collapse of the Soviet bloc—first, the fall of the Berlin Wall in 1989 and then, the demise of the Soviet Union in 1991—the former Communist states have moved in two dramatically different directions. On the one hand, the Central and East European countries (along with the three Baltic states of the former Soviet Union) quickly evolved into genuine and, in many respects, liberal democracies, though not without some serious defects. However, the other twelve states of the former Soviet Union—most prominently Russia—have mainly regressed from democratic possibilities or reestablished dictatorship without communism.

In Central and East Europe, countries turned to a long-eclipsed history of democratic or semidemocratic governance or were impelled by the powerful incentive of membership in NATO and the European Union. As early as 1992, Hungary, Poland, Czechoslovakia, and Slovenia emerged as somewhat liberal democracies, while Bulgaria, Romania, Albania, Croatia, and Macedonia were initially more tentative and illiberal. The three Baltic states of Estonia, Latvia, and Lithuania, which were annexed by the Soviet Union as a consequence of Stalin's pact with Hitler in 1940, embraced democracy by 1992, as well. Only Yugoslavia was undemocratic in 1992—just one year after its initial breakup.

By 1995, eight European postcommunist states had settled into liberal democracies in terms of their standing on political and civil liberties,[1] and over time, all have become increasingly free, open, and competitive politically. (The number of states in the region has grown to sixteen with the final disintegration of Yugoslavia and the separation of the Czech Republic and Slovakia.) By 2006, only Bosnia-Herzegovina (under international trusteeship) was not a democracy, and only Albania and the former Yugoslav republics of Serbia, Macedonia, and Montenegro were not fairly liberal democracies.

The remaining states of the former Soviet Union have met quite a different fate. Under Boris Yeltsin, Russia explored a pluralistic if rough democracy, but democratic freedom and competition rapidly receded under his successor, Vladimir Putin, as we saw in chapter 3. Georgia, Ukraine, Kyrgyzstan, and Belarus became increasingly authoritarian; though at various moments observers have disagreed as to how to classify them, by the late 1990s, none were democracies.[2] Of the twelve non-Baltic republics of the former Soviet Union, only Russia and Moldova had held on to the democratic mantle through the 1990s, and Russia soon thereafter succumbed to authoritarian drift.

The color revolutions pulled pseudodemocratic regimes into young democracies in Georgia in 2003 and Ukraine in 2004. In 2005, the spirit of democracy also brought down Kyrgyz president Askar Akayev, who had initially been hailed as a Central Asian democrat in a sea of despotisms but had grown increasingly autocratic. Yet, Kyrgyzstan, unlike Ukraine and Georgia, has not become a democracy, and an authoritarian backlash has settled over most of the region.[3]

A postcommunist divide thus runs starkly across the Soviet-European border of 1939. Fifteen of the sixteen states to the west of that historic boundary are democracies, and most are free and stable. Even the exception, Bosnia, displays many elements of democracy. But nine of the twelve post-Soviet states to the east of that boundary are authoritarian, and the three democracies—Georgia, Ukraine, and Moldova—are illiberal, even questionably democratic, and unstable.

It is tempting to attribute this blunt divide to the way the European Union drew the geographic boundary of its vision of enlargement. Of the eleven liberal postcommunist democracies, the Czech Republic, Slovakia, Hungary, Poland, Slovenia, Estonia, Latvia, and Lithuania were admitted to the EU in 2004, and Bulgaria and Romania were admitted in 2007. Croatia, the one liberal democracy that was not an EU member by 2007, is the next most likely future candidate for admission (along with Macedonia), and the other postcommunist Balkan states are now recognized at least as "potential candidate countries."[4] The post-Soviet states enjoy no such realistic prospect.

But perhaps more acutely, the divide reflects deep historical and cultural legacies that make the post-Soviet states much less hopeful prospects to satisfy the EU's membership conditions of democracy, good governance, and a rule of law. Nowhere is the striking divergence among the former Communist countries more apparent than in the attitudes and values of their people.[5] In 2004 and early 2005, the New Europe Barometer discovered that in most of the ten new EU members, the populace strongly rejects authoritarian regimes. When offered four alternatives to a democratic system—army rule, Communist rule, a dictator, or suspending parliament and elections in favor of "a strong leader who can decide everything quickly"—six in ten citizens rejected all four. The proportions rejecting all authoritarian options ranged from 72 percent of Hungarians to around 60 percent of Estonians, Slovenians, Lithuanians, and Czechs; to a little over 40 percent of Bulgarians and Poles. Since the mid-1990s, the percentage of the public in Central and Eastern Europe rejecting authoritarianism has been consistently high or has steadily increased. In recent years, these attitudes have weakened somewhat in the Czech Republic, Poland, and Bulgaria, because of corruption and political infighting, but they are still held by a significant portion of citizens.

By contrast, citizens surveyed in the former Soviet countries of Russia, Belarus, and Ukraine are much more welcoming of authoritarianism, with only a quarter of Russians and Belarusians rejecting all authoritarian options. Nearly half of Russians said they could support suspension of parliament and elections—and over 40 percent endorsed a return to Communist rule—while nearly two-thirds of Belarusians endorsed the option of a dictator. The three post-Soviet states also showed higher levels of approval for the previous Communist regime.[6] While Russians have been consistently amenable to authoritarianism, in the late 1990s Belarusians briefly moved against authoritarian options before slipping back to their current attitudes. Only in Ukraine, with the Orange Revolution, did the same low proportion rejecting authoritarianism finally rise significantly (to 44 percent) when the country was surveyed in February 2005.[7]

Further, in the ten new democracies of Eastern Europe, an average of 53 percent agreed that democracy is "always preferable" (a figure identical to that found in Latin America in 2005). While surveys in Belarus and Ukraine showed comparable support for democracy, only a quarter of people surveyed in Russia expressed a steadfast preference for democracy and 43 percent believed that sometimes "an authoritarian government can be preferable." Although only 37 percent of Poles said democracy is always preferable, it was not because of wide authoritarian sentiment. Only one in five Poles—the average for all of the new postcommunist EU members—supported that option. Rather, Poles appeared apathetic and alienated, with 43 percent choosing the third response option: "For people like me, it doesn't matter whether we have a democratic or a non-democratic regime."[8]

These surveys seem to indicate a weakness in the democratic spirit in the former Communist bloc. But in 1995, when Richard Rose, the political scientist who developed the New Europe Barometer, and his colleagues posed three authoritarian alternatives—army rule, Communist rule, and a "strong leader who can decide everything quickly"—67 percent of people in the seven newly born East European democracies rejected all three options.[9] Ten years later, an identical proportion of citizens in those seven democracies plus the three Baltic states rejected the same three authoritarian options.[10] East Europeans are clearly committed to democracy, despite skepticism and hostility in the former Soviet Union.

LIBERAL BUT TROUBLED DEMOCRACY

In less than a generation, the countries of Central and Eastern Europe have attained levels of political freedom, pluralism, and competition that were hard to imagine during the decades of Soviet domination. But the vigorous democracy in the region is accompanied by public cynicism about parties and political institutions—a hangover of Communist rule. In addition, new and persistent corruption and insider dealing have cemented this cynicism and created deep social divisions between the winners and losers of so-called market reforms. "Antiliberal" populist movements have risen on the right and the left and captured control of governments in recent elections.

On the positive side, in most of Central and Eastern Europe, there is intense electoral competition, with political parties alternating in power across a significant ideological spectrum. As new parties have risen, others have retreated into near oblivion or actual extinction, as with Poland's Solidarity Electoral Action, an alliance of center-right parties that came to power in 1997 but was so plagued by internal bickering that it disappeared from parliament after failing to clear the necessary electoral threshold in 2001.[11] Between the collapse of communism in 1989 and 2007, Poland seated thirteen prime ministers in a continual reshuffling of its political landscape. In other countries, electoral politics has settled along a familiar left-right opposition, with two or three parties dominating, as in Hungary, where the Hungarian Socialist Party and the conservative Fidesz-Hungarian Democratic Forum (Fidesz-Magyar Polgári Szövetség) are the main competitors, and in the Czech Republic, where the rightist Civic Democrats and the leftist Social Democrats captured between them two-thirds of the vote in the 2006 elections.

In most countries, the left of the spectrum is anchored (or at least was, for some time) by a successor to the former Communist ruling party. Many held strong support from the public, such as the Bulgarian Socialist Party, which won the country's first postcommunist elections in 1990 and then oscillated in and out of power.[12] In Poland and Hungary, the Communist successor parties were immediately democratic in character and social democratic in ideology (like their West European brethren). The Democratic Left Alliance in Poland ruled until 2005, when it was routed by the Right, which trained the public's diffuse desire for change on "a weak economy, high unemployment, and high budget deficits" as well as persistent allegations of corruption.[13] In Romania, however, the successor left party was a barely reconstructed Communist party that, under the former party functionary Ion Iliescu, ruled for ten of the first fourteen post-Soviet years, most of the time in a highly illiberal fashion and while fashioning "antimarket and xenophobic messages."[14]

Over time, the tensions, divisions, and disappointments of the postcommunist era have found expression in public support for authoritarian nationalist parties and candidates and a recurrent (and recently escalating) political mainstreaming or "legitimation of xenophobia."[15] The most infamous example is the ascendance in Serbia of Slobodan Milošević, who plunged the region into war by exploiting Serbian nationalist passions and fears. Yet Milošević was not unique. During three turns as prime minister, Vladimir Mečiar stunted the democratic development of Slovakia following its "velvet divorce" from the Czech Republic in 1993. The Greater Romania Party catapulted Vadim Tudor, an antidemocratic xenophobe, to runner-up in the country's presidential race in 2000.

Numerous smaller, more extreme, and explicitly racist parties have maneuvered their way into ruling coalitions. Xenophobic sentiments in Romania mobilized against ethnic minorities—most often the Roma

(Gypsies) but also ethnic Hungarians—and neighboring countries. In Poland and Slovakia, populist movements have happily pulled extremist parties into their governing coalitions.[16] The leader of the Slovak National Party—which entered the governing coalition after winning 12 percent of the vote in the June 2006 parliamentary election—"said he would not mind sending the leader of the Hungarian minority to Mars 'with a one-way ticket.'"[17] The second-place candidate in the 2006 Bulgarian presidential election, Videron Siderov of the "National Union Attack" Party, is "a proto-fascist who says he hates Turks, Gypsies and Jews."[18] He lost decisively to the ex-Communist incumbent president, but in the process he garnered a quarter of the second-round vote. In Poland, the new right-wing populist government appointed as its minister of education and deputy prime minister the thirty-five-year-old leader of the ultranationalist, anti-European, and extreme Catholic traditionalist League of Polish Families, Roman Giertych. "Asked about his intention to repudiate Darwinism from school curricula, [he] answered, 'We've managed without tolerance for long enough. And we shall manage without it even now.'"[19] The precise programs and political alignments of these populist parties and movements vary, but the one thing they have in common is intolerance: "Eastern Europe's populists do not act as if they face a political opponent (or ethnic, religious, or sexual minority) with whom they can negotiate, but rather an enemy they must destroy."[20] Sometimes this is also reflected in the extremely hierarchical (or authoritarian) internal governance of these parties.

As in Western Europe, party fragmentation is fostered by the electoral system of proportional representation, which gives seats in parliament in proportion to a party's share of the overall vote, if it clears an electoral threshold, typically of 3 to 5 percent. This system provides opportunities for niche parties that appeal to distinct social groups with populist messages of anger and protest. An example is the Polish party Samoobrona (Self-Defense), which began in 1992 as a union of small farmers but has reinvented itself as a Euro-skeptic, populist-nationalist party of rural and traditional values. Another is the League of Polish Families, which attracts the older generation in provincial towns and villages.[21] Following the 2005 Polish elections, both parties entered the government at the invitation of the socially conservative, center-right winner, the Law and Justice Party, which had been formed only four years before. To reformers, that populist coalition was a disheartening alternative to the expected coalition of Law and Justice with its main election rival, the centrist Civic

Platform, an advocate of continued market reforms which, like Law and Justice, could trace roots to the Solidarity movement of the 1980s.

The victory of the Law and Justice Party, which went from 44 parliamentary seats in 2001 to 152 in 2005 (out of 460 in Poland's lower house), illustrates the political volatility of Central and East European democracies. Throughout the region, free and fair electoral competition is now institutionalized, but the parties that wage this competition are not. Since 1989, parties not only have come and gone from power but have come and gone from the political scene altogether. The bare victory of Romania's center-right in the 2004 presidential elections came on the wings of a brand-new political party, the Alliance for Truth and Justice, which was able to overcome association with the fractious and ineffective center-right rule that followed the 1996 elections. A pattern has been set of a new political force debuting as the antithesis of corrupt, establishment politics, winning power amid anti-incumbent sentiment, and then squandering public favor through corruption and disappointing policy performance, especially on the economy. In 2001, Bulgaria's former child king, Simeon II, emerged out of nowhere to win half the parliamentary seats, thrusting aside both the socialists and the (then-ruling) right-of-center Union of Democratic Forces (UDF). By 2005, however, his coalition government "had lost popular support owing to economic difficulties and widespread corruption."[22] That year's June elections were emblematic of postcommunist party instability: the National Movement for Simeon II (which, in choosing the former king's name said something significant about its shallowness as a party) lost to the resurgent socialists but nevertheless formed a coalition government with the socialist prime minister and a smaller third party. Negotiations were complicated by the facts that neither of the two principal parties would join a coalition with the new radical nationalist party, Attack, which won 9 percent of the seats, and that the previously dominant UDF won barely 8 percent of the vote.

The situation was no less complicated and fractious in the Czech Republic, where coalitions led by President Vaclav Klaus's Civic Democratic Party and the leftist Social Democratic Party each won exactly half of the two hundred parliamentary seats, creating a stalemate that blocked formation of a viable government for half a year. Finally, the Civic Democrats were able to form a government in January 2007 when they persuaded two Social Democratic MPs to be absent from the chamber for a confirmation vote. But the public did not take favorably to that cynical bargain, and many in the Civic Democratic camp (including Klaus) also objected to the prominent role of the Green Party in the new government. For the Civic Democrats, the return to the leadership of government— which they had dominated through most of 1990s, until a privatization scandal caused the party to hemorrhage support—was bittersweet and likely, based on regional history, short-lived.

Postcommunist Europe thus presents a mixed picture of vigor and volatility. On the one hand, the new democracies of the East should not be held to higher standards than their West European counterparts, which have also been condemned—and frequently replaced—for sleaziness, influence peddling, cynical political maneuvers, and corruption. Unfortunately, some of this seems to come, invariably, with the terrain of democratic politics, and to become more of a problem as ruling parties stay longer in power. It is difficult from any calculus of democratic norms to complain when the public boots a ruling party or coalition from power out of dissatisfaction with its performance. But there is cause for concern when the practice becomes a habit, and when the habitual rejection of ruling parties reflects a protracted disillusionment with political institutions at large. Poland, Bulgaria, and Romania, for instance, appear mired in a ceaseless search for new and more morally worthy political forces. Even as vote totals shift back and forth, democracy requires some stability in the identity and support bases of its constituent political parties for effective governance—from tamping down budget deficits to forging a consensus on key national issues—to be within reach. That minimum party stability has not yet been achieved in a number of Central and East European democracies.

It is in this light that the rapid unraveling of public order in Hungary— one of the most stable, successful postcommunist democracies—must be pondered. On an audiotape leaked in September 2006, Hungary's reelected Socialist Party prime minister, Ferenc Gyurcsány, was captured admitting that the party had "lied in the morning and lied in the evening" about the state of the country's finances and had underestimated the budget deficit and made unwarranted promises of social welfare programs in order to win the April 2006 elections.[23] Tens of thousands poured into the streets and plazas of Budapest to protest following the revelation, and did so again in October on the fiftieth anniversary of Hungary's anti-Soviet uprising. Some of the protestors carried World War II–era Nazi Hungarian flags, which were even more visible at the rallies of the rightist opposition party, Fidesz. Opposition feeling was so intense that half a year later, massive steel barriers remained around Hungary's parliament building "to protect legislators from radical and potentially violent protestors."[24]

THE POSTCOMMUNIST STATE OF PLAY

Under pressure from the EU accession process, courts have become more independent and rule-of-law institutions have improved throughout postcommunist Europe. In Romania, for example, the new National Anticorruption Department charged 744 defendants, including high-ranking politicians and magistrates, in 2005 alone, after years of nonaction by a previous anticorruption office.[25] In Bulgaria, the national ombudsman has gained the right to hear complaints and investigate corruption allegations, while ethics laws have been tightened and monitoring strengthened through the National Audit Office.[26] But the reform process is almost everywhere (even in the most liberal democracies) partial and even tenuous—incremental steps in a long, protracted struggle against the entrenchment and reassertion of special privilege. Prime Minister Gyurcsány's confession of having lied during the campaign about the economy touched a nerve of resentment regarding the conduct of postcommunist reform. Corruption, a sense of legal and economic unfairness, and broad distrust in political institutions plague the postcommunist European democracies. And when it comes to these issues, the postcommunist divide fades somewhat.

In fact, all postcommunist publics are cynical and dissatisfied—it's just that the post-Soviet ones are more so. Among the ten new postcommunist members of the European Union, 72 percent think "more than half" or "almost all" their public officials are corrupt. Belarus matches that percentage, while in Russia and Ukraine the figures are 89 and 92 percent respectively. Similarly, an average of 71 percent among the ten EU entrants think their laws are enforced unfairly, while in Russia and Ukraine about 85 percent think so.[27] In these and other perceptions of the rule of law, the original eight postcommunist EU entrants are the least negative, with Bulgaria and Romania more negative, and Russia and Ukraine again so. Thus, an average of 57 percent of people in the 2004 EU entrants think their government has "some" or "a lot of" respect for human rights, but only about a third felt this in Romania, Bulgaria, and Russia, and only 27 percent in Ukraine. The pattern holds with regard to democratic satisfaction as well. In 2004, only a quarter of Ukrainians and one out of five

Russians were satisfied. In the ten EU entrants (or soon to be entrants), the average was 36 percent—significantly better, though still fairly low.[28]

There is also a generalized legacy of distrust of political institutions among postcommunist states that transcends the divide. Almost half the public in the first eight EU entrants, and well over half in Romania, Bulgaria, Ukraine, and Russia, distrust the courts. In all ten EU entrants, almost two-thirds do not trust the parliament and three-quarters do not trust political parties, quite similar to the averages for Russia and Ukraine (though the former is always more cynical).[29] In a more recent Gallup International survey, only one-third of the region's citizens said they trusted democracy, and just 22 percent felt that their "voice matters."[30]

Another reason for the low levels of democratic trust and satisfaction— and for the exceptionally high levels of electoral volatility, and the surge in illiberal populism—is that people in Eastern Europe still feel pressed economically, nearly two decades after the fall of the Berlin Wall. In 2003, the unemployment rate was 19 percent in Poland, 17 percent in Slovakia, 28 percent in Serbia and Montenegro, 44 percent in Bosnia, and over 10 percent in each of the three Baltic states.[31] In 2004, only about 30 percent of Central and East Europeans felt they were getting enough money from their main source of income "to buy what you really need." The figure was the same for Ukraine and Belarus; in Russia it was only 14 percent. Slightly over half of the public in the postcommunist EU ten even claimed that their household economic situation was better before the transition to the private market, and a similar percentage was unsatisfied with the current economic situation of their household.[32] The belief that corruption is widespread, and the particular disenchantment with its role in making many former Communists manifestly rich during the privatization process, inflames these feelings of economic hardship and stress. The current upsurge of illiberal, antielitist populist forces is poised to reassert state involvement in the economy while denouncing "external threats to sovereignty" and promoting skepticism about globalization and European integration. Consequently, "the assumption . . . that joining the European Union would cause Eastern European countries to consolidate their new democracies now seems to have been overly optimistic."[33] Yet, even Jacques Rupnik, the liberal French chronicler of East European illiberal populism, expresses some confidence that time and the constraints of the European Union "may be working against the populists."[34]

Moreover, if the principal challenge in Central and Eastern Europe is to strengthen democracy and make it more lawful, tolerant, accountable, and responsive, in most of the post-Soviet states the challenge is much cruder and more fundamental. The twelve post-Soviet states (leaving aside the democratic EU member states of Estonia, Latvia, and Lithuania) are mostly caught in varying forms of authoritarian rule or outright dictatorship. Georgia, Ukraine, and Moldova are tenuous democracies (at best). Armenia and Kyrgyzstan have some significant elements of civic space and electoral competition, but within a context that lacks the wider political freedom and electoral fairness of democracy. The other post-Soviet states are authoritarian—extremely so in the case of Uzbekistan and Turkmenistan (which have the worst possible scores on the Freedom House scales of political rights and civil liberties), and quite substantially in the case of Russia, Belarus, Azerbaijan, Kazakhstan, and Tajikistan. The progressive narrowing of the political arena and victimization of opposition parties, civic movements, and independent journalists have strangled democracy in Russia and made Belarus a dictatorship, as we saw in chapter 3. These repressive trends have beleaguered other post-Soviet states, though none of them began with the degree of political pluralism and democracy that Russia enjoyed in the early 1990s.

With their electoral revolutions in 2003 and 2004, Georgia and Ukraine have implemented institutional reforms that have made them more democratic and accountable. But in each case, significant impediments to democracy remain, far beyond those facing the new Central and East European democracies. In Ukraine since the Orange Revolution, freedom for civil society organizations and the media has increased and become more legally embedded.[35] Under a new constitution, the domineering power of the presidency has been diminished in favor of a more powerful elected parliament that holds independent authority to name the prime minister (as in the established democracies of postcommunist Europe). In the March 2006 elections for parliament, the opposition, pro-Russian Party of Regions, the authoritarian party that was defeated in the Orange Revolution, rebounded to win a plurality and formed a new government. But in large measure, severe internal divisions among democracy advocates opened the way for the Party of Regions, which only won a third of the vote in "the freest" election "in the country's fifteen years of independence."[36] The hero of the Orange Revolution, President Viktor Yushchenko, has proved a rather ineffectual leader, unable to govern with his principal rival, Prime Minister Yulia Tymoshenko, in the pro-reform coalition. In September 2005, a piqued Yushchenko dismissed the opposition government, and in an attempt to make up for his lack of support in parliament, fell to the temptation of trying to extend his presidential power beyond its formal limits. While some improvements have been made in the judiciary under Yushchenko, the system remains weak and heavily influenced by the executive, and governmental corruption remains widespread.

In Georgia, democratic progress has been threatened not by the divisions among the makers of the Rose Revolution but rather by the overwhelming scope of their victory. As a result, "there still is no credible opposition to the United National Movement," the ruling party of President Mikheil Saakashvili that came to power when voter fraud was thwarted in the November 2003 elections. Constitutional changes shortly after the elections "weakened the Parliament and moved Georgia in the direction of superpresidentialism."[37] Since coming to office, Saakashvili has used his enormous power to implement reforms to improve state efficiency, increase state salaries, enhance budgetary transparency, combat bureaucratic and political corruption (with numerous high-profile arrests), reduce tax evasion, decentralize government, increase judicial independence, and curb (and even prosecute) human rights abuses by the police and other agencies.[38] In early 2007, the president signed into law constitutional reforms to remove his own power to appoint and sack judges—thereby increasing the independence of the judiciary.[39] As a result, freedom, accountability, and the overall quality of governance have increased, even while the government has had to cope with two Russian-supported regional separatist movements in Abkhazia and South Ossetia. Georgia is now a democracy for the first time in its post-Soviet history. But with an overwhelming majority in parliament and a 90 percent election victory in the 2004 presidential election, Saakashvili's power is concentrated in his personal office to a degree that could well impede or reverse the country's democratic development. The distance still to travel is indicated partly by the fact that as recently as June 2006, half of the public in a national poll thought that Georgia was not a democracy, while only a quarter considered it one, and the parliament, the courts, and the government were each trusted by less than a fifth of the public, though the president had the trust of nearly half the population.[40]

In the remainder of Central Asia and the Caucasus region, varying forms of authoritarianism prevail. The striking thing about the region, in sharp contrast to the postcommunist states of Central and Eastern

Europe, has been the carryover of leadership and ruling elite structures from the Soviet era. A major reason for this continuity from Communist rule is that these regime transitions were not made from below by opposition forces (as in Russia or Czechoslovakia), or negotiated between the old order and the rising one (as in Hungary and Poland), but rather imposed from above (or fairly quickly hijacked) by the old Communist establishments, whose power dwarfed that of incipient democratic or pluralistic political forces. The "preponderance of power" in favor of the old dictators was especially strong in Central Asia.[41] "In three of the five Central Asian states, the same elites that ruled under Mikhail Gorbachev" when the Soviet Union collapsed were still in power a decade and a half later. In early 2007, Islam Karimov and Nursultan Nazarbayev remained, with no end in sight, the utterly dominant personal rulers of Uzbekistan and Kazakhstan, while in Turkmenistan it took a fatal heart attack at the end of 2006 to remove the absolutist and cultist "president for life," Saparmurat Niyazov (or as he called himself, Turkmenbashi, "the Father of All Turkmen"). Even in Kyrgyzstan and Tajikistan, "the current presidents held high office during communist rule."[42] In the Caucasus state of Azerbaijan, the former head of the region's Communist Party under Soviet rule, Heydar Aliyev, returned to power in a military coup in 1993 (overthrowing a freely elected president) and remained there until ill health led him to withdraw for his son, who in 2003 won a "landslide" victory for presidency in an election "marred by widespread fraud."[43] The president of Armenia, Robert Kocharian, assumed office in 1999, when much of the government leadership was assassinated inside the National Assembly. His return to power in 2003 in a deeply flawed election left the country bitterly divided and prompted the well-developed opposition to boycott the parliament in outrage. And until the Rose Revolution, Georgia had been ruled for eleven years by its former Soviet-era Communist Party boss (and Gorbachev's foreign minister), Eduard Shevardnadze.

At the more liberal end of the spectrum, Kyrgyzstan has opposition parties, movements, and even some significant opposition representation in parliament, as well as a measure of freedom and pluralism in civil society. In 2005, political pluralism and freedom improved following the ouster of the increasingly autocratic president, Askar Akayev, in the Tulip Revolution against rigged parliamentary elections. But in his first years in office, the new president, Kurmanbek Bakiyev, largely failed to deliver on his promises of democratic reform. A new constitution in 2006 raised the possibility of checking presidential power but was watered down when the parliament adopted it at the end of 2006. Still, the constitution did allow the parliament to approve the president's nominee for prime minister and even to reject him—as it did in early 2007. In contrast to their experience in more authoritarian Central Asian neighbors, political opposition and civil society activists in Kyrgyzstan do not generally meet fierce and murderous repression, and the U.S. State Department noted some improvements in human rights conditions during 2006.[44] Under Bakiyev, the country seems to have reverted to being a corrupt but somewhat pluralistic autocracy.

In most of the region, however, the movement has been in the direction of consolidating authoritarian rule, or in the case of Uzbekistan and Turkmenistan, outright tyranny. None of these regimes want the "mistake" of the color revolutions repeated on their soil, and so all have been cracking down vigorously at any sign of organized political challenge or threat. In advance of the December 2005 presidential election in Kazakhstan, the government stepped up harassment and attacks against opposition activists and independent journalists; used new repressive laws to constrict the activities of independent civil society organizations, mass media, religious groups, and political parties; and produced a reelection landslide for Nursultan Nazarbayev of 91 percent.[45] But more than in most post-Soviet states, the Kazakh regime has the money and the savvy to rely on more subtle means of domination. Since the fall of the Soviet Union, Kazakhstan has emerged as a major oil exporter. Ranked only fourteenth in the world in 2005 (at 1.1 million barrels a day), it is expected to be among the top five oil producers in the world by 2020 (with over 3 million barrels a day in production). With Western companies investing some $25 billion, the surge in oil wealth has driven economic growth rates to over 8 percent annually since 1999, enabling Nazarbayev to lavishly use corruption and patronage to buy off potential dissent. The result is that "pro-regime financial interests and political parties fully control the Parliament, which does not have a single opposition or independent deputy," while one of the two opposition parties has split into militant and more accommodating factions.[46] The president has also tapped into the oil windfall to co-opt much of civil society with government grants, hoping to reduce every other government institution—including the judiciary and local governments—to pawns of his centralized control as well as enrich a vast extended network of kin and cronies. The latter have "amassed enormous political power by creating or sponsoring political parties that control the parliament, while capturing the country's media market and pushing out independent media channels."[47] In fact, the president's increasingly omnipresent daughter and her husband "wield virtually unrivaled control and influence over the entire informational sphere."[48] Or at least they did until the son-in-law, Rakhat M. Aliyev, fell out of favor for publicly criticizing constitutional amendments to enable "Nazarbayev to become president for life." In exile in Vienna, Aliyev was summarily divorced from the president's daughter and indicted for kidnapping, while he hurled charges of dictatorship and massive electoral rigging at his former father-in-law.[49] The combination of burgeoning oil wealth, strategic importance, Western support, and political skill has made Nazarbayev so confident that he did not wait long after reelection to indicate that he planned to run for another seven-year term, despite the two-term limit in the constitution.

In contrast to the more selective repression of Nazarbayev, President Islam Karimov "has pursued a scorched earth strategy in Uzbekistan, seeking to destroy any and all opposition he confronts."[50] Such brutal, indiscriminate repression in turn radicalizes the Islamic opposition and makes the regime even more insecure. In May 2005, the Karimov government fired on and killed hundreds of (and possibly close to a thousand) largely unarmed civilians in the city of Andijan to suppress antigovernment protests, or what the government labeled an uprising of "radical Islamists and evil forces."[51] Then it turned on what remained of a battered civil society, closing down independent media and NGOs while expelling foreign media outlets and international democracy assistance efforts.[52] The human rights situation in Uzbekistan deteriorated so badly in 2005 that even the Bush administration—desperate for Central Asian allies in the war on terrorism—called for an independent investigation into the unrest in Andijan, prompting the Uzbek government to expel the U.S. military from a crucial air base it had been using since the 2001 invasion of Afghanistan. According to Human Rights Watch, internal efforts to document and protest the deteriorating situation in Uzbekistan have been met with "methods that range from intimidation, threats and harassment to physical attacks, imprisonment, and torture. Numerous civil society activists—including human rights defenders, independent journalists, and members of the political opposition—have been beaten by unknown assailants, threatened by local authorities, set upon by mobs, and placed under house arrest."[53] Some of them have been "held incommunicado for months at a time."[54]

The authoritarian regime in Uzbekistan is in many ways typical of

Central Asia, only more extreme. Government power is highly centralized, and corruption is pervasive and plundering, virtually obliterating the boundaries between public office and private interests. One man, with political roots in Soviet Communist rule, dominates the system, controls all branches and levels of government, and appears set to rule indefinitely. Family, clan, and crony interests radiate out from him and grow rich because of him. NGOs, human rights activists, independent media, and international media and aid efforts are all viewed with extreme suspicion as threats to state security. Behind the impenetrable walls of the state's monopoly control of information, President Karimov lives "a life of exceptional luxury," accumulating a fortune from state revenues and the seizure of successful private businesses while building—Saddam Hussein–style—a string of opulent residences in every significant regional city. One of those residences, in one of the poorest cities in Uzbekistan—which is the second poorest country in Central Asia—"contains a German-made glass elevator so the president need not trouble himself with stairs." When an American attorney and Freedom House consultant, Robert Freedman, toured the exterior, "workmen were installing new marble floors in the residence, because during the president's one and only night's stay, he expressed displeasure at the color of the original marble."[55]

The combination of severe repression, persistent poverty, and decadent corruption of a narrow ruling elite has bred in Uzbekistan the most serious challenge in the region from radical Islamist groups, which have gained more support as the government has grown more repressive and venal. In neighboring Tajikistan, where Communist apparatchik-turned-president Imomali Rakhmonov waged a bloody five-year civil war against militant Islamists that claimed an estimated fifty thousand lives, the regime learned a lesson about the limits of force. After five years of fighting, it signed a UN-mediated peace agreement in 1997 that brought the opposition into the government and has allowed for a degree of political contest and media pluralism within its authoritarian system. This modest pluralism "limits the attractiveness of extremist and revolutionary Islamist ideology."[56]

DEMOCRATIC PROSPECTS AFTER TOTALITARIANISM

The task of constructing truly liberal and stable democracies in Central and Eastern Europe has clearly not ended with the admission of ten of these countries into the European Union. Indeed, there are signs that the decision to finally admit a country, and with that lose a powerful form of political leverage, has produced a diminished concern for liberal norms among ruling elites and an anti-EU backlash among more rural and traditional segments in some countries, including Poland. If there is one thing that recent developments in the region counsel against, it is a kind of glib confidence that the story of democratic development in this region is now complete. Of course, it is not complete anywhere in the world. Even the more liberal of these postcommunist democracies have serious flaws, but they appear highly likely to remain democratic, and they also stand a good chance of becoming more liberal, accountable, and institutionally settled as their economies grow and new generations acquire more democratic experience.

In Georgia and Ukraine as well as Moldova, where the Communist Party maintained its majority in 2004 parliamentary elections that involved harassment of the political opposition, there is much further to go toward stabilizing democracy. Because they share a physical border with the European Union, Ukraine and Moldova are better positioned in simple geographic terms to progress politically than more distant Georgia. (This might change, however, if Georgia's southern neighbor, Turkey, is granted EU membership.) To the extent that these three countries continue to look to the West, toward NATO and the EU, they will be pressured to at least maintain the broad parameters of electoral democracy. Still, liberal forces in politics and civil society face a protracted struggle to institutionalize the political and economic reforms and norms that will make it possible to sustain democracy.

The remaining states of the former Soviet Union will likely linger in varying stages of authoritarian rule for some time to come. But the stability of these regimes, too, should not be taken for granted. If the Tulip Revolution did not bring electoral democracy to Kyrgyzstan, it did reaffirm certain norms about sustaining political pluralism and containing personal aggrandizement and abuses of power. That is something to build upon. In Kazakhstan, the trigger for change may be more gradual economic development and global integration of its booming oil economy. In Uzbekistan, President Islam Karimov has bet heavily on deepening repression and on his reliance on authoritarian sponsors in Russia and China.

This underscores a larger point: the extent to which the stability of authoritarian rule in the post-Soviet space depends on authoritarian stability and support at the core of the former Soviet Union, in Russia itself.

As Vladimir Putin's term draws to a close, with a Russian presidential election due in March 2008, a struggle for succession has been building that could once again throw open the political future of Russia itself. If the Russian regime ceased to be a democracy very early in Putin's reign, it has not become a consolidated dictatorship either. Neither is it a demonstrably better governed and less corrupt state than it was under Boris Yeltsin. It is just a richer state, an authoritarian beneficiary of the boom in oil and gas prices. If those prices decline, the privileged political, state security, and business interests that have become wealthy and dominant under Putin may come under serious challenge, regardless of how many "oligarchs" they take down and assets they seize.[57] While Putin has destroyed or co-opted much of the opposition, he remains unable to subdue all of it. The recent rise of a new pro-democracy movement under the leadership of the former world chess champion, Garry Kasparov, reflects the resilience of liberal forces and values in Russia. Kasparov "contends that Mr. Putin's control of all levers of power has obscured the fundamental weaknesses in the system: the corruption, the vast gap between rich and poor, the declining standards of health care, education and living conditions."[58] As we have seen, authoritarian regimes that rely on external resource flows become vulnerable when those resources diminish. If Russian democracy was weak and vulnerable under Yeltsin, so Russian authoritarianism is vulnerable today, and in that lies hope for renewed democratic development throughout the region. Michael McFaul's speculation of several years ago remains as apt today: "As Russia goes, so goes the region."[59]

10

THE ASIAN EXCEPTION?

No nondemocracy has ever been as rich and as successful as Singapore. When it gained independence from Malaysia in 1965, Singapore was a poor, racially volatile, and strategically vulnerable postcolonial city-state, a tiny dot on the map wedged between Malaysia and Indonesia. Since then, it has recorded one of the highest sustained rates of economic growth and amassed the largest foreign reserves per capita in the world. It is one of the twenty-five richest countries, one of most highly educated and efficiently run, and, in the view of the international business community, one of the least corrupt—all without democracy.[1] In the 2006 parliamentary elections, the ruling People's Action Party (PAP) won eighty-two of eighty-four seats.[2] Indeed, in every election since independence, the PAP has won at least 95 percent of parliament.

Singapore's leaders, beginning with its founding prime minister, Lee Kuan Yew, have attributed the PAP's dominance to the people's appreciation for its governance record. There is truth in that assessment. In its four decades, the party has crafted a subtle system of authoritarian rule that lends Singapore the outward appearance of an advanced, industrial state. The charismatic Lee serves as a "minister mentor" to the current prime minister, his son. Elections, contested by opposition parties, have been held at regular intervals, and no evidence has emerged of vote fraud. The country has become a popular site for international conferences, such as the World Bank and IMF (in 2006) and the International Bar Association (in 2007). For one prominent critic, the secret of the regime's durability is that it has "kept itself open and connected—to its mass base to which it remains highly responsive, to the elite whom it works hard to co-opt, and to global economic forces with which its policies are kept in tune."[3]

Beneath the impressive facade, however, the state is quick to suppress challengers and to discipline its insecure elite. Repression is highly selective, often covert, and carefully targeted—what the Singaporean journalist and academic Cherian George calls *calibrated coercion*—and therefore exerts its control largely out of public and international view.[4] Political prisoners in the classic sense are rare. More common are blocked professional opportunities, lawsuits, and even, some allege, institutionalization. "They put people in mental institutions all the time," said a foreign observer who has lived in Singapore for several years. "A person was discovered writing anti-Lee graffiti in an HDB [Housing Development Board] block, and he was put away."[5] With such a smooth but unshakable grip on power, Singapore has become a model pseudodemocracy for dictators around the globe to emulate.

It is no accident that the PAP has, in five of the last six elections, won almost all parliamentary seats with only about two-thirds of the votes. Through government-linked companies, the regime controls all television stations and almost all radio stations; "two companies own all of the newspapers in the city-state: one is government-controlled, and the other has close relations to the government."[6] Political films are banned, and in the 2006 elections, "political parties were not allowed to use the internet as a video platform" or to send e-mail chain letters, thus cementing the PAP's media dominance.[7] There are fears (unfounded but nevertheless consequential) that the vote—which is compulsory for all eligible citizens—is not secret because each ballot carries a serial number. The boundaries of voting districts are typically not delimited until shortly before an election, and most are "group representation constituencies" that award all six district seats to the party that wins a plurality. The government insists these multiseat districts ensure racial balance, since candidate slates must include at least one member of the Malay or Indian minorities, but the districts also greatly magnify the winner-take-all character of elections. Moreover, a majority of seats in three of the last four elections have been uncontested because of the high financial deposits required from candidates, a lack of access to the media, and the threat of ostracism or financial ruin.

Three outspoken opposition politicians, J. B. Jeyaretnam, Tang Liang

Hong, and Chee Soon Juan, have been sued into bankruptcy by PAP elites who claimed defamation for criticisms of Singapore's government and of them personally. Bankrupt individuals are not allowed to sit in parliament; this forced Jeyaretnam to surrender his seat and Chee to relinquish future runs for office.[8] They can also be barred from traveling internationally, as Chee was in 2006 when he tried to attend the World Movement for Democracy conference in Istanbul, Turkey. Tang felt compelled to go into exile after the 1997 elections, when he faced numerous defamation suits from PAP ministers and MPs after he called them liars for labeling him as dangerous, anti-Christian, and a Chinese chauvinist.[9]

Yet Chee—a neuropsychologist whose career was ended in his early thirties when the regime engineered his dismissal from National Singapore University—continues undaunted. With each arrest for speaking in public without a permit or handing out a party newspaper, he serves longer sentences, in worse conditions, following judicial proceedings that are (as he describes them) ever more peremptory and biased. "I am already bankrupt," he told me in a bare walk-up apartment that serves as his party headquarters. "I don't know how they can make me more bankrupt. Every time they move against me, it makes me more determined."[10] Like few other critics, Chee has gotten under Lee's skin. An astute observer of Singapore explained that Chee "is the type of person they would have recruited. He is articulate and focuses on issues they are vulnerable on, like income disparities."[11] In addition, Chee directly challenges the government's prized image of honesty and openness, urging Singaporeans to protest the Orwellian limits on public assembly and speech.

For Lee Kuan Yew, who won massive defamation suits against both Chee and Jeyaretnam, this is too much. "He is an opportunist. He is mad," the minister mentor told me in 2006. "If he is mad," I asked, "why bother with him?" Because, Lee said, "that is not the kind of opposition we want to encourage." But it became clear during our conversation that there was something more at issue—the way Chee repeatedly attacked the regime's ethics on managing public funds. Chee had compared the regime to the National Kidney Foundation, a charity that got embroiled in a 2005 scandal for its lack of transparency and misuse of donated funds. Mentioning the allegations, Lee said, with visible agitation, "He is a liar. . . . We guard our reputation as incorruptible people jealously. What is wrong with that?" Lee fondly recalled the days, after the PAP defeated the Right and the Communists in the mid-1960s, when "we got an opposition that behaved." He continued, "You behave like a first-world opposition and we will treat you like that. You try to destroy the system, and we will respond in kind."[12]

Lee's protective stance toward the system exposed the nature of Singapore's regime: an incestuous intertwining of party and state and a penetration of the state into nearly every corner of society. While Singapore is hailed as one of the world's freest economies, in reality, government-linked corporations control much of it. The National Trade Unions Congress (to which almost all unions are affiliated) is headed by a government minister. Although most Singaporeans own their apartments, they do so with levels of state assistance that establish what is effectively massive public housing—leveraging political dependence. Constituencies that reward the ruling party at election time are themselves rewarded with "housing upgrades." Civil society has been cowed and contained. Even some critics of the ruling party recognize that its communitarian ideology fits well with the predominant Confucian culture, while its responsiveness to social needs gives it legitimacy and staying power.[13] As a result, "the PAP is nowhere; the PAP is everywhere."[14] The party is the system.

In many ways, Singapore has become the face of Asian exceptionalism, the most confident and persistent advocate for a different path than "Western" liberal democracy. What happens in Singapore in the coming years as its founding leadership leaves the scene will have a powerful influence, out of all proportion to the country's size, on the future of democracy in Asia. Singapore's political stability could foreshadow a resilient form of capitalist-authoritarianism in China, Vietnam, and elsewhere in Asia. But the expected imminent passing of Singapore's founding generation has sown growing doubts that its authoritarian system can survive. And there is a larger question: does the developmental success of one pseudodemocracy in a small city-state offer a model for the world's biggest dictatorship, China?

THE TRUE ASIAN EXCEPTION

With the coming generational change in leadership and the visible reality of growing inequality, the Singapore model has begun to fray. The PAP's strategy has been to cater to the welfare of all citizens. As the regime recruits top talents and rewards them handsomely—some senior ministers earn salaries over one million dollars a year—the economy appears less fair, undermining Singapore's communitarian ethos.[15] Another growing issue is the government's lack of transparency. While it is considered one of the world's least corrupt governments, it is also one of its more opaque. As Chee Soon Juan stresses, scant information is available about how the regime invests its massive foreign reserves (more than $100 billion), how it manages the Central Provident Fund (its comprehensive pension savings system), and precisely what it pays its top officials.[16] And while the regime has forged a national consciousness across the Chinese/Malay/Indian divide, it also remains obsessed with racial fissures in a way that unwittingly perpetuates them. The promotion of Singaporean pride also exacerbates the alienation of the country's one million noncitizen residents, who mainly fill marginal jobs, including as maids and prostitutes. These support workers make up a quarter of Singapore's population and over time could equal or outnumber the indigenous population.

Overbearing state management and even subtle repression have their costs. There is significant desire among citizens for greater accountability and political pluralism of the parliamentary and party systems. About a third of Singaporeans can be classified as "pluralists" in this respect, while only a quarter are stout defenders of the system. Moreover, it is the highly educated who most want liberalizing change (nearly half of university graduates do), while the least educated and lowest in income and occupational status are most likely to support the status quo.[17] This suggests that as education and income levels continue to rise, pressure will mount to free the press, make the electoral system fairer and more competitive, and reform the authoritarian "mindset, ideology, and hierarchy" of the ruling party, which may constitute the most essential and most difficult reform of all.[18] This evolving range of sentiments among Singaporeans reflects a larger diversity, in attitudes, preferences, and behaviors, across the region.

Of course, no region of the world exhibits greater variation in regimes than does Asia. It contains the most populous democracy in the world (India) and the most populous dictatorship (China); two of the freest democracies of the former developing countries (Taiwan and South Korea); and the two most successful and self-confident pseudodemocracies (Singapore and Malaysia). The most economically dynamic dictatorships (China and Vietnam) are flanked by the most stagnant and isolated (Burma and North Korea). More than any other region, Asia will determine the global fate of democracy in the next two to three decades.

Unfortunately, democratic prospects seem to be receding in Asia, after an extended period of hope and progress. Democracy is institutionalized and stable in Japan and India, but even where democracy is most liberal, such as in Taiwan and Korea, it has come under stress. In the Philippines, democracy has descended into crisis. In Bangladesh, elections and elected government have been indefinitely suspended by a military-backed emergency government. In Sri Lanka, democracy has been seriously diminished and human rights badly abused by the twenty-year-long ethnic civil war that flared up in 2006 and has claimed over sixty-five thousand lives.[19] East Timor's fledgling democracy has struggled with the destabilizing legacy of "destruction, dispossession, and physical and socio-psychological trauma—and an associated sense of injustice—brought about by Indonesia's 1975 invasion and almost 25-year occupation."[20] Dramatically—and with great stakes for the West—the prospects for stabilization, not to mention democracy, have dimmed in Afghanistan, as security has deteriorated amid widespread corruption, state incapacity, obstructed development, warlordism, and the resurgence of the Taliban and the drug trade.[21] The country's decline underscores a lesson of all postconflict reconstruction: before there can be a democratic state, there must first be a state, with an effective monopoly over the means of violence.

This rather bleak picture holds across other countries, as well. More than seven years after the October 1999 coup, Pakistan continues to be dominated by General Pervez Musharraf, who refuses to yield his dual military and civilian leadership positions. In Thailand, the generals who in 2006 overthrew the elected government seem in no hurry to leave power, and a growing number of Thais have come to doubt the military's willingness to restore full democracy. In Singapore and Malaysia, authoritarian ruling parties continue to generate economic growth and maintain political stability—and secure their power. The dictator Hun Sen and his (former Communist) Cambodian People's Party appear equally entrenched, propped up by generous foreign aid despite extensive corruption and repression. Even more naked and repressive dictatorships seem unshakable in North Korea, Burma, Vietnam, Laos, and China.

But if this is a discouraging story, it is not the whole story. Democracy has taken hold in several surprising areas of Asia. In Indonesia, democracy is finally gaining ground, and it survives in a rather liberal form in Mongolia, one of Asia's poorest and most isolated countries. In Nepal, King Gyanendra's clumsy attempt in 2006 to reestablish monarchical rule in the form of a "guided democracy" collapsed amid massive street protests that sparked a peaceful nationwide uprising. Nepalese may even vote to terminate the monarchy altogether, and with an agreement between democratic parties and Maoist rebels to end the country's deepening civil war, the country has a real chance to get back to what was, during the heady days of the 1990s, an unlikely but promising democracy.[22] Civil society and opposition parties have mounted growing protests against the perpetuation of authoritarian rule in Pakistan, catalyzed anew in March 2007 when General Musharraf ousted the country's chief justice "out of fear that the judge would raise questions about what appears to be his ambition to be re-elected president while remaining army chief."[23] Four months later, in a stunning and widely popular rebuke to Musharraf, the Pakistani Supreme Court voted overwhelmingly to reinstate the chief justice. At the societal level, there are growing signs of readiness, if not yet demand, for political change in Singapore and China. Beneath the booming economy and self-confident leadership, the Chinese system is roiled by deep contradictions that I believe portend a turn to democracy within a generation.

Finally, the mass public in much of Asia expresses considerable support for democratic values, undermining the claim of Asian exceptionalism. A majority of Asian respondents—about six in ten both in East Asia (as surveyed in 2001–3) and in South Asia (2004)—think democracy is the best system of government. Asians have generally positive views of democracy and how it works. They are not more likely than citizens of Western democracies to demand respect for authority. Particularly in the more economically developed countries—Japan, Taiwan, and South Korea—they reject illiberal fears of pluralism and deference to authority that have been presumed to be core, distinct "Asian values."

To be sure, Asian public attitudes toward democracy are complex, changing, and vary across countries, sometimes in surprising ways. The most economically developed and Western-oriented of the new Asian democracies, Taiwan and South Korea, show ambivalence in their publics' commitments to democracy. Preference for democracy over any other kind of government has risen in Taiwan from 41 percent in 2001 to 48 percent in 2006, but this is still low compared to other Asian countries. In South Korea, the preference for democracy fell from 69 percent, just before the 1997 East Asian financial crisis, to 54 percent in 1998 and 45 percent in 2001, before rebounding to 58 percent in 2004.[24] Protracted political polarization also led to a drop in the preference for democracy in the Philippines (from 64 to 51 percent between 2001 and 2006) and Thailand (from 83 to 71 percent). In contrast, two-thirds of Japanese and 54 percent of respondents in China said democracy is always preferable.[25]

If we examine other dimensions of support, East Asians appear even more committed to democracy. Majorities in all the democracies of the region think democracy is "suitable" for their country. This sentiment has risen from 59 to 67 percent in Taiwan (2001 to 2006), from 64 to 79 percent in South Korea (1997 to 2007), and it has remained at or over 80 percent in Thailand and Mongolia through 2006.[26] Two-thirds of East Asians in the six democracies surveyed think democracy can effectively solve the problems of their society. In most of East Asia, large majorities reject the authoritarian alternatives of military rule, one-party rule, and getting rid of parliament and elections in favor of a strong leader.[27] In fact, during the first half of the 2000s, the proportion rejecting all three of these alternatives rose from 56 to 69 percent in Taiwan, from 71 to 77 percent in South Korea, and from 46 to 54 percent in Thailand.[28] In the 2005 and 2006 surveys, at least three-quarters in Taiwan, South Korea, and Japan and two-thirds in Thailand rejected an authoritarian strong leader.

In South Asia, public opinion toward democracy is somewhat different. While support for democracy in principle is strong, resistance to authoritarian rule is not. Only in India does a majority reject getting rid of parliament in favor of a strong leader—and then only 52 percent do. Surprisingly, almost half the public in Pakistan does so as well, but only a quarter or less in Bangladesh, Nepal, and Sri Lanka.[29] Large proportions in India as well as Sri Lanka and Nepal (both of which are struggling to resolve long and draining civil wars) oppose military rule, but only about two in five Pakistanis and Bangladeshis do. That proportion appears to be growing in Pakistan, however, as the public wearies of General Musharraf's rule.

The new democracies of Asia face challenges similar in many respects to those faced in Latin America and postcommunist Europe: they must find ways to govern better and improve the quality and capacity of their institutions. As we have seen, the leaders in Singapore have developed a highly effective authoritarian rival to democracy, one that is appealing to its public not because of unique Asian values but because of its ability to deliver, for example, booming development, political stability, low levels of corruption, affordable housing, and a secure pension system. That success poses one of the most interesting challenges for democracy in the world.

DEMOCRACY UNDER STRESS

Since their democratic transitions in the late 1980s and early 1990s, Taiwan and South Korea have made striking progress in expanding societal freedom, imposing civilian control over the military, and dismantling the national security state. Taiwan is now one of the most vigorous democracies in Asia and witnessed a historic transition of power with the presidential victory of the longtime opposition party in 2000. South Korean voters have alternated between political parties and factions, and in 1997 elected longtime dissident Kim Dae Jung to the presidency. Early in its adoption of democracy, South Korea increased governmental and banking transparency, purged the authoritarian military and intelligence cliques, expanded parliamentary oversight, decentralized power, and established direct election of provincial governors and city mayors.[30] In the wake of the 1997 financial crash, the country implemented significant reforms to increase competition and rein in crony capitalism, which resulted in rapid economic recovery and vigorous growth.

With their ties to the world economy and high standards of living, education, and civil society, a return to military or undemocratic rule is nearly unimaginable for either Taiwan or South Korea, despite their publics' skepticisms about the way democracy is working. Yet, both countries have suffered through political crises that stifled strong prospects for institutionalizing liberal democracy. Democratic institutions have underperformed in both countries, and turmoil in Taiwan has blunted the country's potential as a model and an inspiration for democratic change in mainland China.

When Taiwan's opposition candidate, Chen Shui-bian, won the presidency with a modest plurality in 2000, it opened the democratic system to challenges. The contest pitted Chen's Democratic Progressive Party (DPP), which favored moving toward independence and promoting the identity of the native Taiwanese majority, against the Kuomintang (KMT), which had ruled Taiwan since the party's founders fled the Communist revolution on the mainland in 1949. After the election, the KMT still controlled the parliament and insisted that Chen should set up a French-style "cohabitation" arrangement, in which KMT would gain the prime minister's chair. But Chen wanted his party to govern alone, even though it controlled less than a third of the seats. The KMT (along with its breakaway faction, the People's First Party, PFP) swung into adversarial mode. When Chen canceled a new nuclear power plant and pushed his party's pro-independence agenda, the opposition vowed to impeach him for governing unilaterally. In parliament, the opposition coalition "blocked nearly every major bill that the government introduced," the government frequently circumvented legislative constraints, and dispute after dispute wound up in the constitutional court without clear resolution.[31] Anxious to reverse decades of one-party domination and secure their own hold on power, Chen and his allies turned to "some of the mischievous old practices," such as intervention in trade union elections, "unlawful surveillance of political foes, selective prosecutions and tax audits to make KMT donors or precinct captains switch sides," and lavish fund-raising from big business in exchange for government contracts and loans.[32]

As the economy stagnated, polarization and distrust reached new depths. The March 2004 presidential campaign evolved into not only a referendum on Chen's performance and the opposition's obstruction but an intensely mobilized contest between two radically different visions of the country: as ethnically "Taiwanese" or "Chinese" and as a separate, independent state or an "entity" open to eventual unification with the mainland. "Each side fears the other seeks power in order to . . . make irreversible changes in cross-Strait relations and the way in which national identity is construed."[33] Chen's "green" ticket had been trailing the "pan-blue" ticket uniting the KMT and PFP, but a bizarre assassination attempt on the election's eve, in which both Chen and his vice president were wounded, enabled him to eke out reelection. The opposition candidates, Lien Chan and James Soong, alleged that the shooting was an elaborate hoax by Chen to gain sympathy votes. The challengers failed in the courts, but the scandal put the election's legitimacy into question. In one poll, less than half of respondents viewed the election as fair.[34]

When corruption charges led to the indictment of Chen's son-in-law for insider trading in the summer of 2006, one hundred thousand demonstrators (led by some of the president's former supporters) mobilized to demand Chen's resignation. In response, the ruling party rallied its loyalists, sometimes clashing with protestors in the streets. Chen survived that storm of demonstrations, but the deadlock deepened. Protests renewed when the First Lady was indicted for corruption that November and the prosecutor indicated he would indict the president as well, if the constitution could permit it.[35] There was a "widespread popular belief that corruption at the highest echelon" had "run amok on [Chen's] watch."[36] Chen refused to resign, even under pressure from his own party. At the same time, Taiwan's economy continued to drag, growing at a rate well below its East Asian peers, and when Chen discouraged economic integration with the Chinese mainland, investors shifted elsewhere. The crisis testified to the resilience of Taiwan's democracy, particularly "the independence and integrity of the judicial system." A disciplined civil society, crossing partisan lines, demanded accountability.[37]

In South Korea, democracy became embattled after a left-leaning political outsider, Roh Moo Hyun, won a narrow election to the presidency in December 2002. Like the three previous Korean presidents since democracy was restored to the country in 1987, Roh took office with broad public approval and then squandered it. Seeking to challenge the status quo, Roh reached beyond his "progressive" predecessor, Kim Dae Jung, by "bypassing institutionalized avenues of democratic politics and appealing directly and emotionally to the people."[38] As in Taiwan, the new president became embroiled in a debilitating confrontation with the conservative majority in parliament. To rescue his sinking political capital, Roh suggested, after just one year in office, holding a national referendum on his rule, for which there was no clear constitutional provision. In March 2004, following an electoral commission ruling that the president had violated the legal requirement that he remain neutral during midterm elections, Roh became the first president to be impeached by Korea's National Assembly. He survived only when the constitutional court chose to chastise rather than remove him—and then after his party, in a stunning rebuke to conservative forces, won a majority of the seats in the midterm elections. The court, however, subsequently ruled against Roh's plan to remove the nation's capital from Seoul. The president also came "under attack for trying to push through legislation that would restrict the circulation of conservative dailies."[39] Like the country's three previous democratically elected presidents, Roh fell into a weak lame-duck presidency, hemorrhaging public support. "Bruised by South Korea's cutthroat politics, bewildered by voters' rapidly changing concerns and battered mercilessly in the polls," Roh found himself in late 2006 "limping toward the last year of his term" with a public approval rating of 11 percent.[40]

Yet in other respects, Korea continued a remarkable transformation from developing to industrial to postindustrial society. It boasts a level of real per capita income higher than Portugal's and almost equal to Greece's, an economy moving rapidly into high-tech production and innovation, and levels of broadband Internet and cell phone usage that make it "one of the most wired nations in the world,"[41] yet also has soaring divorce and plummeting birth rates. Korea is now "the most rapidly aging society in the world," and as in other postindustrial societies, particularly in Europe, its democracy will have to manage the transition to an increasingly multiethnic society as it imports labor to make up for the growing shortage of young workers.[42]

DEMOCRACY EMERGING

Elsewhere in Asia, democracy has experienced halting progress. In one surprising turn, after sixty-five years of one-party Communist rule and widespread poverty, Mongolia negotiated a rapid transition to democracy beginning in 1990. Since then, it has maintained significant levels of political and civil freedom, civil society activity, and electoral competitiveness. However, further development has been slowed, and recently endangered, by the weak and highly factionalized state of political parties, mounting corruption, and controversies over "the pace and extent of economic reform."[43] But while Mongolia provides a window into the far-flung opportunities for democratic progress in Asia, it is unlikely to influence the larger region, especially in comparison to Indonesia, the world's fourth most populous nation and the most powerful of the ten members of the Association of Southeast Asian Nations (ASEAN). Straddling some six thousand inhabited islands with explosive ethnic divisions and secessionist pressures, Indonesia poses serious challenges to the viability of democracy.

Since the 1998 resignation of authoritarian president Suharto after thirty years in power, Indonesia has embarked on one of the most consequential democratic transitions in Asia since the third wave of democratization began. Over the past decade, the country has steadily implemented political reforms that have dismantled the intertwined hegemony of the Indonesian military and its ruling party, Golkar. In 1999, the country began to decentralize power and held open multiparty elections. In 2003, it established a constitutional court, which was given administrative oversight over the increasingly independent judiciary as well as the Corruption Eradication Commission.[44] In just five years, it saw the first free parliamentary elections in more than forty years (in 1999) and the first fully democratically elected parliament (with the termination of thirty-eight appointed seats for the military, in 2004), while the presidency became directly elected. The 2004 elections, in which seventeen parties won seats in the 550-member parliament with no single party capturing as much as a quarter of the congress, were judged free and fair by international observers.[45] In the presidential election, Susilo Bambang Yudhoyono, a retired general who had helped to ease the military out of politics, was vigorously challenged during his run-off election victory.

Under President Yudhoyono, the pace of reform accelerated. The former general has continued to diminish military influence in politics, though it persists at local levels of administration. In 2005, for the first time in its history, Indonesia democratically elected its local government executives (some 180 of them), and the government negotiated a peace settlement in oil-rich Aceh Province to end a secessionist movement that had provoked extensive violence and repression since 1976. Meanwhile, with global oil prices soaring and the country's production receding to the status of a net importer, the president took the essential but politically difficult and costly step of slashing fuel subsidies.[46]

To be sure, Indonesia remains a troubled democracy with an extremely weak rule of law. "Abuse of public office for private gain remains endemic. . . . [C]orrupt relationships between powerful private actors, government bureaucrats, politicians and security officials infuse the political system and undermine it from within."[47] As a result, "oligarchic business interests exercise a preponderant influence on parties, legislatures, and the executive."[48] Corruption seeps deep into many local administrations, often hand in hand with "egregious human rights abuses."[49] The offending security officials and gangsters routinely go free because the judiciary itself (along with the police) is riddled with "extreme corruption."[50] These are the classic ills, serious and threatening to long-term viability, of an illiberal democracy. Yet consider how far Indonesia has come in a decade, and the scope of calamities its government has reckoned with: massive forest fires, the 2004 tsunami that killed more than two hundred thousand Indonesians, a 2006 earthquake in central Java that left over a million homeless. The ability of the democratic regime to cope under pressure is striking and gives the country a decent chance to sustain its nascent institutions with the aid of gradual reforms.[51]

ILLIBERAL DEMOCRACY IN CRISIS

The hope that democracy can take root in Asia has been driven in part by transitions to democracy in countries much poorer than Taiwan and South Korea, such as the Philippines and Bangladesh. As these countries became democracies, in 1986 and 1991 respectively, prospects for democracy throughout Asia brightened, and Bangladesh was mentioned prominently as evidence of the viability of democracy in predominantly Muslim countries, as well. Yet democracy has had to struggle with entrenched political corruption, abuses of power, political violence, feckless policy performance, and paralyzing confrontations between government and the opposition. Democracy in Bangladesh is in doubt, and in the Philippines, bad governance has undermined security and development and eroded public confidence.

Since 1986, Philippine democracy has struggled with many of the ills that plagued it when Ferdinand Marcos forcefully took over in 1972: violence, bossism, and corruption—or what analysts often label "guns, goons, and gold."[52] A few dozen political families dominate national politics, now supplemented (and joined by marital ties) with movie stars, athletes, and other celebrities. As the *Economist* observes, since these "political clans have few goals beyond preserving and expanding their influence, they have little interest in policy-making," and their legislative activity has shriveled in the past two decades.[53] Locally, politics revolves around "a small number of tightly interconnected families," who control business and government positions as well as the means of official—and unofficial—violence.[54] Most political parties have no program or ideological basis but are merely elite coalitions for capturing state power and resources. Corruption so "pervades all levels of government" that it "has crippled the government's attempts to achieve fiscal stability" while leaving "a disconnected scattering of substandard and often half-finished [infrastructure] projects." Organized crime, "virtually always operating with some degree of official collusion," accounts for an estimated 10 to 20 percent of annual national income.[55] Social inequality and injustice feed a long-running Communist insurgency that commands over ten thousand fighters and over a million loyal voters. In the Muslim-minority southern islands, a brutal separatist insurgency and counterinsurgency rages into its fourth decade.

Viewed sociologically, the relatively honest and reform-minded presidencies of Corazón Aquino and Fidel Ramos appear as anomalies, and the 1998 presidential election of the jolly actor-turned-politician Joseph Estrada seems a natural recurrence. Although Estrada won the country's "cleanest and most decisive election" with a campaign appealing to the huge impoverished underclass, he quickly sank into corruption and favoritism.[56] The public became outraged as lurid stories surfaced of presidential decision making in the midst of drinking binges with a "mid-night cabinet" of cronies and "vast sums of grease money being poured into personal indulgences, including mansions occupied by Estrada's mistresses."[57] When evidence materialized that Estrada had personally received payoffs from illegal gambling syndicates, the House of Represen-tatives voted in November 2000 to impeach him. His supporters in the Senate barely managed to block Estrada's removal by preventing prosecu-tors from unsealing crucial records. The move catalyzed Filipino "people power" again. After huge street protests and the defection of his cabinet, military leaders declared that they no longer supported him, and the Supreme Court (from a highly dubious constitutional standpoint) declared the presidency vacant. In January 2001, Vice President Gloria Macapagal-Arroyo was inaugurated as president. "The process was hardly democratic, but it was accepted as necessary, at least among Manila's upper and middle classes."[58]

To Philippine and international good governance constituencies, the elevation of Macapagal-Arroyo—an economist, technocrat, and daughter of a former president—seemed a godsend. The new president renewed President Ramos's economic reform agenda from the mid-1990s and backed U.S. president George W. Bush's global war on terror, thereby securing a sharp increase in American aid. But she was stymied by the recalcitrant problems of Philippine democracy, and the elite-dominated Congress blocked her reforms. In May 2004, she sought a full six-year presidential term in her own right, facing another populist movie star, Fernando Poe Jr.[59] Immensely popular, poorly educated, erratic, and closely tied to the Estrada clique, "Poe was the worst nightmare of edu-cated Filipinos."[60] Campaigning as an underdog, Macapagal-Arroyo pulled out all the stops, spreading patronage, pouring government funds into short-term projects, and enrolling large numbers of poor people in gov-ernment health insurance. Violence, claiming 150 lives, widespread reports of fraud, and agonizing delays in the vote count marred the elec-tion, but six weeks later the incumbent president was declared the winner by 3.5 percentage points.[61] Poe died of a stroke a few months later, allow-ing Macapagal-Arroyo to refocus on the country's pressing economic and security challenges.

Things seemed to have returned to "normal" until June 2005, with the discovery of an audiotape documenting a conversation between the pres-ident and the election commissioner during the vote-counting process. The tape, the authenticity of which government officials could not deny, circumstantially "seemed to confirm allegations that the president had used her incumbent powers to rig the elections."[62] With that, Philippine civil society turned again to the streets, seeking what would have been the third eviction by protest from the last five presidencies. A large bloc of liberal cabinet ministers resigned, narrowing the president's coalition, and further allegations emerged that the president's husband and son were receiving payments from the same illegal gambling activities that had brought down Joseph Estrada. Former president Corazón Aquino joined the opposition movement, as did "a broad array of civil society groups," from the Manila business community to left-wing NGOs, "and 11 former members of the government."[63] Public confidence in Macapagal-Arroyo's leadership plummeted, "and for several days in mid-July, the end of [her] presidency seemed imminent."[64]

But the technocrat turned out to be a wily, tenacious, and unforgiving political combatant. High-ranking government officials and military officers were ordered not to testify before Congress without presidential clearance. When a marine general proceeded to do so, he faced court-martial proceedings. "People power fatigue" set in, and street protests fizzled. With the aid of presidential power and patronage, Macapagal-Arroyo twice blocked impeachment efforts while she stacked government appointments with her loyalists. Reports of her husband's deep implication in illegal logging, smuggling, and gambling rackets continued, but the infrastructure for investigating the corruption was stalled. She soon launched a campaign to transform the Philippines into a parliamentary system, which her critics alleged was an attempt to hold on to power indefinitely.[65] On February 24, 2006, she declared a state of emergency, canceling all permits to hold demonstrations (including for the twentieth anniversary of the EDSA revolution), claiming she had foiled a coup plot.[66] "Water cannons and truncheons were unleashed on protestors."[67] After three weeks, the state of emergency was lifted in the face of widespread opposition, and its officials' acts were later declared illegal by the Supreme Court.

Since that crisis, democracy in the Philippines has staggered in a bruised, weary, and disillusioned state, with President Macapagal-Arroyo "beholden to her generals" and a coalition of corrupt politicians.[68] There is "growing skepticism about the desirability—and long-term viability—of the elite democracy established after Marcos's fall."[69] Citizen belief in democracy, and satisfaction with the way it works in the Philippines, are in sharp decline.[70] With police often in cahoots with local political and crime bosses and the military deployed in what the government has declared an "all-out war" against Communist insurgents, human rights violations—including "disappearances, kidnappings, extrajudicial killings, and abuse of suspects and detainees"—have accelerated.[71] During 2006, "dozens of killings, many widely thought to be politically motivated," took place without any prosecution of suspects (despite a presidential pledge and commission). A September 2006 investigation by Human Rights Watch uncovered "deep public distrust in the government's investigative effort, widespread fear among witnesses and victims' families, and a climate of fear in areas where the killings occurred."[72] Around the time when the government's commission was due to report in October, the Catholic bishop Alberto Ramento was stabbed to death in his bed. The bishop, who had supported striking workers at a local plantation while vocally criticizing the Philippine security forces, joined "several hundred outspoken priests, activists, journalists, and other dissidents murdered since President Gloria Macapagal-Arroyo came to office in 2001."[73]

Among the liberal ministers who left Arroyo-Macapagal's cabinet was an undersecretary of education, Jose Luis "Chito" Gascon. A veteran of the first "people power" campaign, he had been the youngest person on the 1986 Constitutional Commission and the youngest member of the Philippines' first congress following the end of martial law. A lawyer and university professor, he is deeply worried about the state of Philippine democracy. "It is certainly not the same democracy that emerged after 1986," he told me. "We have an ersatz democracy. We have a constitution, laws, processes and rules, but they are all regularly violated. There is very low trust in these institutions—and in all political parties. The public mistrusts the president, but also the opposition." Consequently, he feels, there is no alternative but to press the democratic cause through electoral means. "People are worn out. They are tired of extralegal means."[74] According to the journalist Steven Rogers, who has lived in the Philippines for more than two decades, the architects of the electoral fraud that returned Macapagal-Arroyo to power in 2004 probably "honestly believed that they were performing a patriotic and necessary act. As in the downfall of Estrada, democracy was broken in order to save it. There is an uneasy feeling, though, that it may have been broken, even with the best of motives, so many times that it may be impossible to put back together."[75]

But how illiberal and dysfunctional can a democracy be before it begins to fail as a state? The paradigmatic, fragile case of Bangladesh offers one answer. Mirroring in many respects the democratic experience of Pakistan before the 1999 coup, control of Bangladesh's government has regularly alternated between two highly personalized parties that differ little on policy but nevertheless despise and distrust each other. One party, the Awami League (AL), is led by the daughter of a former prime minister who was murdered by the military, and the other, the Bangladesh National Party (BNP), has allied itself with smaller Islamist parties in a bid to consolidate power during its recent rule. The electoral process has been marred by growing levels of political violence; the October 2001 parliamentary election campaign claimed more than 140 lives.[76] Corruption is endemic, crime and lawlessness are mounting, political polarization and religious extremism are intensifying, and there are growing fears that the democratic state will fail.[77]

In many respects, the situation in Bangladesh has actually grown worse than in Pakistan before the coup. It is hard to match the personal enmity between the AL's Sheikh Hasina Wajed and BNP's Khaleda Zia—whose late husband was a military ruler "allegedly complicit" in the 1975 assassination of Sheikh Hasina's father, the founding prime minister of Bangladesh, Sheikh Mujibur Rahman.[78] Since the restoration of democracy in 1991, the two have bitterly contested the leadership, alternating in power. When in power, each has led a government that persecutes and totally excludes the other party. In 1994, Hasina inaugurated a tradition of obstruction and stalemate with a boycott of parliament to protest the alleged corruption of Zia's BNP government. Since then, each party has organized nationwide strikes, challenged the incumbent administration's legitimacy, and demanded its resignation. Increasingly, the independence of the courts and the civil service have been undermined, parliament has been sidelined—and anything goes. Thus, "the parties have resorted to often violent means to unseat governments. Boycotts, general strikes and mass protests have become the normal tools of politics, leading to immense disillusionment among the public with the political process."[79] A local NGO reported 526 people killed in political violence in 2004.

A turning point came on August 24, 2004, "when a series of grenades exploded at an AL rally in Dhaka, leaving 22 people dead and hundreds injured, including several top party leaders."[80] Sheikh Hasina was nearly killed. A year later, radicals calling for the imposition of Islamic law set off five hundred small bombs in government buildings and press clubs, yet the government was hesitant "to crack down on radical Islamist groups as well as the presence of Islamist parties within the ruling coalition."[81] It appeared that "the political breach between the two [dominant] parties [was] being filled primarily by Jamaat-e-Islami" and other radical Islamist parties.[82]

As Bangladesh headed toward parliamentary elections in January 2007, confrontation built around the AL's demand for reform of the system of "caretaker government," which replaces elected officials with a neutral, nonpartisan government for the three months in advance of an election. In fact, ever since the system was implemented, the party in opposition has unblinkingly challenged the composition of the caretaker government. In the run-up to the 2007 elections, the AL vowed a boycott, charging that the BNP was preparing to subvert the caretaker government's neutrality in order to manipulate the elections. The strikes escalated into violent clashes involving both political parties, riot police, and soldiers and paralyzed the capital, Dhaka. Finally, just eleven days before the elections, the caretaker president, Iajuddin Ahmed, with backing from the army, declared a state of emergency and postponed the vote, while a new, more neutral caretaker government was named. In the view of the *Economist* magazine, the delay "averted a possible bloodbath,"[83] but it also left behind "a de facto military-controlled state" with "the democratic life blood" of the country "seeping away."[84]

Under the indefinite state of emergency, the government banned political and trade union activities and limited public demonstrations. It replaced the election commission and launched an extensive crackdown on corruption and tax evasion, detaining in the first two months 160 high-level figures from both of the main parties (and many thousands more). The right for the accused to seek bail was suspended in March 2007.[85] Though the AL called for elections by that June, the interim government said it must first clean up the elections system, implement other governmental reforms, and put corrupt politicians on trial.

Like the Philippines, Bangladesh has some important democratic elements in place to constrain abuses of power and provide some stability beneath the chaos. These include decent economic growth, expanding education, "a lively free media," an active civil society, including the famous microlending Grameen Bank of the Nobel Peace Prize winner Muhammad Yunus, and "a sophisticated electorate and a deep-rooted tradition of liberal secularism."[86] But the spirit of democracy has been badly eroded by the blood feud between the two major parties and their readiness to use and condone "the corruption, criminality, and organized violence that have become an integral part of politics."[87] Democracy in Bangladesh is in very serious trouble.

PSEUDOCAPITALISM

If democracy is to triumph throughout Asia and the world, it will have to succeed where authoritarianism has been most successful. And while Singapore is unrivaled economically among the nondemocracies, China has been engaged in a long experiment to combine its sprawling political authoritarianism over the largest citizenry on the globe with economic development and growth at a pace like that which has helped Singapore's rulers to sustain long-term hegemony.

In 1986, on instructions from China's paramount leader, Deng Xiaoping, Premier Zhao Ziyang set up a task force to examine possibilities for political reform. Driving its work was a broad sense among China's Communist ruling elites that "economic reform could not move forward without complementary political reform" to address the sclerotic inefficiencies of an overcentralized state utterly dominated by the Party.[88] Deng himself was wary, viewing reform in strictly instrumental terms. In 1987, he forced out the head of the Communist Party, Hu Yaobang, after Hu proved to be too agreeable to liberal reform and too tolerant of student demonstrations. But Zhao, who succeeded Hu as general secretary, and his "trusted aide" Bao Tong also sympathized with the reformist cause. They convened a group of "liberal intellectuals and officials" to discuss ambitions for separating the party from the state, introducing some checks and balances, establishing democracy (including political competition and freedom of speech) within the Communist Party, and gradually building grassroots democracy (with more protection for civil liberties at the mass level). Zhao's thinking was bold; he even suggested holding competitive elections for the provincial People's Congresses, the equivalent of U.S. state legislatures, except that most Chinese provinces are more populous than most countries. His goal was not liberal *democracy* but a *liberalized Communist system*, in which the party would rule in a more responsible and transparent way.

A year later, the task force submitted its report, which discussed "the necessity and urgency of political reform."[89] But even though its recommendations were fairly general, Deng warned, "We cannot abandon our dictatorship. We must not accommodate the sentiments of democratization."[90] The party Central Committee approved the general outline of reforms in October 1987, and the climate for debate loosened in 1988. But then, in April 1989, the plan imploded. Chinese university students and others in Beijing gathered to mourn the death of Hu Yaobang and protest the lack of adequate state recognition of his passing. The students took advantage of the relaxed political atmosphere to stage wider demonstrations in Tiananmen Square, denouncing corruption and advocating freedoms formally guaranteed in China's constitution. Eventually they were joined by mass protests among students, intellectuals, and workers in "somewhere between one-third and two-thirds of China's then-434 cities."[91] The calls for democracy and the mobilization of over a hundred thousand demonstrators in Beijing alone panicked the Communist Party. On May 20, it declared martial law, and then on June 4, it cleared Tiananmen Square with a bloody military assault and crushed the pro-democracy movement. Zhao and other liberal reformers were purged from positions of power, and Bao Tong was imprisoned for seven years. Seared by "the near-death experience" of the Chinese Communist Party[92] and then by the collapse of communism in Eastern Europe and the Soviet Union, the country's ruling elite squelched all prospects for democratic reforms for the foreseeable future.

China today is a dramatically more open and pluralistic country than it was in most of the 1980s and the aftermath of Tiananmen. Gone are the days of frenzied ideological campaigns—indeed, of much of communist ideology itself. Wealthy capitalists have been welcomed into the ranks of the party, and lifelong Communists strategically placed in provincial governments or as managers of state companies have become very wealthy capitalists. The mass terror of Mao's era, the rigid controls on movement and control, have given way to a "refined strategy of 'selective repression' [that] targets only those who openly challenge . . . authority while leaving the general public alone. China is one of the few authoritarian states where homosexuality and cross-dressing are permitted, but political dissent is not."[93] The Communist state is still a brutal one, officially executing somewhere between five thousand and twelve thousand people each year, more than all other states in the world combined.[94] Journalists, lawyers, civil society activists, intellectuals, and others who challenge the system are liable to be arrested and imprisoned (or confined to house arrest). But China's dictatorship increasingly takes a sophisticated form, infiltrating organizations; co-opting businesspeople, professionals, intellectuals, and students; and deploying some thirty thousand trained "Internet police" to screen Web sites, home pages, and e-mail.

The ambitious goal of that latter effort is to purge the Web of "harmful information" that might be accessed by the estimated 140 million Chinese users (including some 34 million Chinese bloggers) and used "against the regime at times of national crisis."[95] China's Internet tools today block "subversive" strings of words and key words such as *democracy, human rights, Falun Gong* (the anticommunist religious movement), and *June 4* (the date of the government's 1989 crackdown at Tiananmen).[96] With its enormous market power, the regime has intimidated foreign companies like Google, Yahoo, and Microsoft into self-censorship. In helping to build the Chinese Internet in 1998, Cisco Systems has been "accused of helping the authorities to program its equipment to allow filtering and online surveillance."[97] Since 2004, China has reinforced its Internet censorship with increasingly aggressive filtering measures, while overseas activists wage a cyberstruggle to get around them.[98]

There are many reasons to believe that some form of authoritarian rule—probably still Communist in name, if not in substance—can endure in China for a very long time. For one, a generation of economic reform and the opening up of the world's biggest market have created a boom that shows no sign of ending. Economic growth rates remain in the range of 8 to 10 percent (and even topped 10 percent in 2006, according to official figures).[99] In the twenty-five years following Deng Xiaoping's accession to power in 1978, per capita income in China increased sevenfold, and some 250 million people were lifted out of poverty.[100] The number of newspaper copies tripled, and the number of book titles published increased elevenfold. Today there is more than one color TV set for every two households, where in 1978 only three homes in every thousand had a TV of any kind.[101] Between 1975 and 2004, China recorded a roughly 50 percent improvement in its overall human development score.[102] If most people no longer feel ideological attachment to the Communist state, they at least seem pleased with what the system is doing to improve their living standards. Yet, the people who have fared best are the ones best positioned to make trouble, the rising urban elites in business, the professions, and the universities.

There are also political reasons to foresee what the Columbia University political scientist Andrew Nathan, a leading China specialist and advocate for democracy, calls *authoritarian resilience.* In many respects, the system has outgrown the personalistic dominance of the Mao and even Deng eras and become more institutionalized. Procedural rules and norms define succession to leading positions, and terms are limited to ensure rotation in power. The influence of the military and retired party elders has greatly diminished. The leadership is better educated and trained, more meritocratic in recruitment, and less factionalized. And there are increased means for people to participate in and complain about decision making, from the competitive village elections (first instituted in 1987) to the several levels of people's congresses to the ability of citizens to file administrative lawsuits against government agencies.[103]

Since the early 1990s, other governance reforms have been implemented to streamline administration, reduce state ownership of enterprises, establish financial regulatory agencies, introduce competition into government procurement, improve tax collection, and—most recently— begin to clean up the perilously overstretched banking sector, with its huge burden of nonperforming loans, and imprison the most corrupt offenders. Dali Yang, a Chinese-born political scientist at the University of Chicago, argues that these reforms "have helped improve the efficiency, transparency, and fairness of the administrative state," and "the environment for business."[104] From the perspectives of Nathan, Yang, and others, the contemporary leadership of China is smart, competent, pragmatic, undemocratic—and here to stay for a long time to come.

THE AUTHORITARIAN TRANSITION

But how long is long? And how might China's Communist rulers exit the authoritarian stage? There are four possible scenarios.

Authoritarian rule could extend for decades, with a gradual transition from the current dictatorship to a "consultative rule of law" regime that adopts judicial independence, civic pluralism, and means of public input but not competitive elections or, more threatening, a surrender of the hegemonic role of the Communist Party.[105] In other words, China's system would gradually converge with its model neighbor, Singapore, becoming noncommunist and less bluntly repressive. But beyond the striking difference in scale between the two countries, corruption in China is now so pervasive it is hard to see how it can be contained unless people are given the right, democratically, to hold their leaders accountable. And if China really does move to a "consultative rule of law" state with genuine judicial independence and significantly greater space for independent media and for civic organization and dissent, mass movements—on a scale that Singapore's rulers could not even contemplate—will undoubtedly emerge to demand full democracy, as they historically have in China over the past century.[106] This is precisely why China's Communist leaders fear the kind of political reforms pursued by Mikhail Gorbachev in the Soviet Union. And China's own democrats agree. One leading intellectual told me not long ago, "China's reform process accumulates risks. China is like a speeding train with no brakes. It will keep moving, past the Singapore model."

A second scenario is a gradual transition to democracy driven by economic development—as happened in Taiwan and (less gradually) South Korea. By the estimate of the Hoover Institution economist Henry S. Rowen, a former chairman of the National Intelligence Council, China's per capita income will keep growing briskly, even if it slows slightly to, say, 7 percent annually. That level of growth would raise China's per capita income from the current $6,000 (in purchasing power parity) to $10,000 (in 2006 dollars) by 2015—about where Mexico and Malaysia are today and slightly higher than South Korea's per capita income at the time of its democratic transition in 1987. By 2015, Rowen projects, China would have become at least "partly free" (as judged by the Freedom House ratings of political rights and civil liberties). Assuming a slower annual growth of 5 percent for the following ten years, Rowen projects that by 2025 per capita income would rise to $14,000 (in 2006 dollars), matching Argentina and Poland today. By that time, Rowen predicts, China would have made a transition to democracy, driven by the internal forces discussed in chapter 4: expanding levels of education and information, and growing societal complexity and pluralism, will press the state to grant much more political freedom and competition in order to maintain legitimacy.[107]

Public opinion survey evidence lends intriguing support to Rowen's analysis. Between 1993 and 2002, levels of support for democratic values increased significantly in mainland China, even though they remained well below the levels in Hong Kong and Taiwan. For example, the percentage of Chinese agreeing with the statement "Government leaders are like the head of family, we should all follow their decisions" fell from 73 to 53 percent; those willing to let "morally upright leaders . . . decide everything" fell from 70 to 47 percent; those saying judges should accept instruction from the executive branch in deciding important cases fell from 64 to 45 percent—all in the space of just a decade. By 2002, these levels of rejection of authoritarian values were not much different from those in Taiwan in the mid-1980s, shortly before it began its democratic transition.[108] Moreover, the individual attribute most powerfully associated with support for democratic values in China is level of education. As the Chinese become more educated, they will continue to become more supportive of democratic values.[109]

The final two possibilities for China's transition to democracy assume that the system will not last, nor will it transform itself gradually as a result of its own success. It will fall, either to a new form of authoritarianism or to democracy. In these very different views, there is a gathering rot in the foundations of China's economic miracle, and the party-state, the political scientist Minxin Pei argues, will not be able to address it and reform it, because the party and the state lie at the core of the problem. Pei, a resident scholar at the Carnegie Endowment in Washington who (like Dali Yang) was born and raised in China and is now one of America's top China scholars, insists that China's dictatorship is no longer "developmental." Rather, it is a "decentralized predatory state" in which "the individual interests of its agents"—to cash in on the boom while it lasts and to get rich as quickly as possible by any means—are slowly dismantling political stability. The result is unsustainable economic growth, "achieved at the expense of rising inequality, underinvestment in human capital, damage to the environment, and pervasive official corruption." [110] Many cities and counties have seen organized crime gain control of business with such collusion and protection from the authorities that they have become "local mafia states."[111] Local rulers prey on poor peasants, levying illegal taxes and fees and then selling off their land for lucrative developments.[112] A 2006 government report "claimed that over 60 percent of recent land acquisitions for construction were illegal."[113] In September 2006, "the country's top auditor warned that looting and misuse of government-held property were wrecking the value of many assets and constituted the biggest threat facing the nation."[114] President Hu Jintao has launched some high-profile crackdowns, but these have been selective— to neutralize rivals—and fail to address the vast scale of the crisis. Pei and other critics predict that the system will be unable to correct itself in more than superficial ways; sooner or later it will succumb to "the self-destructive dynamics found in nearly all autocracies: low political accountability, unresponsiveness, collusion and corruption."[115]

Viewed this way, China is caught midway in its transition and lacks the institutional means or the will to complete it. Before long, these pathologies will inhibit economic growth, intensify popular discontent, and further grind down the legitimacy and capacity of the state. Pei does not anticipate the fall of communism any time soon. Rather, the system could remain "trapped in prolonged economic and political stagnation" before it ultimately collapses "in the political equivalent of a bank run" if it is not fundamentally reformed first.[116] Already, China is seeing one of the most telling signs of a regime losing faith in itself. In 2006, a well-connected Chinese intellectual told me that more and more Chinese Communist officials are sending their own personal wealth abroad. "We are pessimistic [about the regime's prospects]," he said. "They are more pessimistic."

Pei believes a regime collapse will be just as likely to bring a new form of authoritarianism (or state failure) as democracy. However, there is a more hopeful view of where this "corruption, misgovernance, injustice, instability, and repression" will lead: to democracy.[117] In his provocative book, *China's Democratic Future,* Bruce Gilley, a Canadian political scientist who spent nearly a decade reporting on China, lays out what I think is the most plausible transition scenario for China.

All authoritarian regimes are damned by their success and damned by their failure. If Rowen is correct in his extrapolations of future Chinese economic growth, by 2025 or some similar date on the horizon, the majority of Chinese will have to some degree entered the middle class. Having gotten much of the material base of a better life, they will want more: justice, dignity, accountability, voice. Even in a future punctuated by gradual reform efforts and better governance, this new middle class will inevitably hold grievances regarding local corruption, favoritism, and oppression, and the central government will not be able to address them in the absence of the democratic mechanisms that give voters at all levels of government the ability to replace leaders who do not perform. That's the optimistic version. In a more pessimistic scenario, if China reaches Rowen's predicted level of national income without attenuating inequality and poverty, "the radicalization of the poor" will reach truly explosive dimensions and political change will come in a different, more violent way.[118] In either scenario, Gilley argues, Chinese rulers would have to contend with a larger, more resourceful, and better networked civil society than what existed during the last democratic uprising, in 1989. This is the ineluctable consequence of the dizzying generation of market reform and expansion over the past decade.[119] With the boom in newspapers, books, televisions, and computers, "China is now awash with information that would have been considered seditious as recently as the early 1990s."[120] The number of NGOs officially registered with the government has risen from 4,500 in 1988 to over 300,000 in 2006, and some estimate the actual number at ten times that.[121]

To meet the expectations of this much more confident, informed, connected, and democratically demanding society, China's leaders will at least have to allow greater freedom to organize, speak, and assemble, and competitive elections to replace nonperforming leaders well above the tiny and fairly inconsequential level of the village. China's ruling elites know where this path of reform will lead—to democracy, and very probably the fall from power of the Communist Party—and this is why they have been resisting it. Indefinite resistance, however, could mean a convulsion of popular protest, as in 1989, but this time drawn from a broader, more engaged civil society that could topple the regime suddenly and, crucially, before the party leaders could secure their persons and their assets. So, there may come a time (as there did in South Korea and Taiwan) when the ruling elites judge that it is better to take a risk on losing power than a risk on losing everything. For if things deteriorate, they may well have advisers who remind them of the lessons of recent history: "Regimes that waited too long saw their rulers dragged from their offices and shot in the head."[122]

Still, there is no sign yet that the Chinese Communist leadership is willing to embrace gradual democratic reforms. As Pei shows, the modest reforms that were launched in the late 1980s have stalled. Competitive elections for villagers' committees have increasingly been manipulated by local party bosses and criminal elements. The National People's Congress has failed to attain serious law-making and oversight power; not a single bill proposed by its delegates has become law, and its annual meetings remain, as the *New York Times* recently observed in an editorial, "a choreographed show to put the stamp of legality on decisions already made."[123] The number of administrative lawsuits declined sharply as plaintiffs discovered they had only a one-in-five chance of success. Lawyers have increasingly been detained and abused by the authorities. The courts remain poorly staffed and highly politicized.[124] This conservative retrenchment on political reform is unlikely to be reversed because, as Gilley explains, the Communist Party "leaders are caught in a prison of their own making. They can refuse reforms and face protests, or grant reforms and lose their jobs."[125]

Popular anger and protest could arise not only from democratic impatience born of development, as in South Korea in the 1980s, but from authoritarian bankruptcy. Like previous Chinese dynasties, the Communist regime could lose its "mandate of heaven" as pathologies of bad governance reach critical mass. Crime, corruption, cronyism, bank fraud, local tyranny, national unresponsiveness, and a host of other ills threaten the regime, as Gilley and Pei emphasize. The dramatic rise in economic inequality, to levels that now "rival some of the most skewed countries in Latin America or Africa," could become a poisonous spur.[126] The gap is widening fast between income strata and between the cities and the countryside. With development lagging and unemployment soaring in the rural areas, young men have moved to the cities and constitute a huge pool of rootless migrants, ready to be mobilized in protest. "At any given moment, there are over 120 million rural migrant workers roaming the streets of Chinese cities looking for jobs."[127] Sustained underinvestment in health and education, which makes the country vulnerable to pandemics like AIDS and avian flu or outbreaks like the SARS crisis of 2003, have deprived the poor of even the limited access to health care they enjoyed under (real) communism. Chronic disease is exploding, with reported cases of HIV increasing by 30 percent in 2006; hepatitis affects 10 percent of the population.[128] A third of China's land is severely eroded; three-quarters of its lakes and half its length of rivers have been polluted; a third of China's thirty-three thousand dams (including one hundred large ones) "are deemed 'defective.'" The results are spreading deserts (to the edge of Beijing), crippling pollution, and devastating floods.[129] Then there is the state of road and workplace safety: over a hundred thousand road fatalities in 2002, a hundred thousand illnesses in a year from rat poison seeping into the human environment, a level of mining deaths thirteen times that of India.[130] Any one of these problems, not to mention the complex interaction of them, could explode into crisis in the coming decade—or what Gilley calls "metastatic crisis," when dysfunction spreads beyond its initial boundaries to affect other functions and the country as a whole.[131]

China's ruling elite—who are increasingly competent managers—might continue to cope, to a point. But the question is whether they can address the fundamental ills that are eating away at the foundations of stability. If they do not, then in the midst of declining political and economic performance, any kind of crisis—a stock market crash, an environmental disaster, or an epidemic badly managed—could unravel the regime. For purely pragmatic reasons, business owners, even those who have been loyal to the regime or have no particular commitment to democracy, could be among the first to defect. The same is true of the growing middle class, who see the government squandering taxes from their hard-earned money. Already, businesspeople in some regions are quietly funneling money to democratic activists and intellectuals.

No less potentially ominous for the stability of Communist rule is the growing religious underpinning of civil society. There is the overtly anti-Communist challenge of Falun Gong, a recent movement based on Buddhist and other traditional Chinese teachings and practices, which the government estimated to have some 70 million adherents inside China when it launched a brutal campaign to suppress it in 1999.[132] Though it is still banned, Falun Gong retains a potent underground following that distributes its publications, including its "nine criticisms" of Communist Party rule, clandestinely and widely in China. Christianity is also booming. When one adds to the estimated 35 million followers of state-sanctioned churches the much larger number who worship in unregistered or "house" churches, the number of Christians may be over 100 million—substantially more than the 70 million official members of the Communist Party.[133] What must worry the regime is that the Communist Party members have largely lost their faith, while Christianity and other organized religions are filling the moral vacuum. Indeed, it is no coincidence that many of the leaders and intellectuals behind the 1989 Tiananmen movement have become devout Christians, while others have joined Falun Gong. Few systems of belief have the power to motivate and unite people in common cause as religion does.

There is also the belief system of democracy itself, which can be quite compatible with, and even stimulated by, religion.[134] "China is arguably better endowed with liberal intellectual leaders than was the Soviet Union" at the time of its transition.[135] Liberal and democratic ideas and classic works are circulating in China, not just in the universities but in official schools and institutes of the government and even the Communist Party.[136] Libertarian condemnations of the overweening state (including those by the Austrian economist Friedrich Hayek) are also popular, and many democratic works are quietly being translated into Chinese. But Chinese democratic thinkers are also returning to the Confucian and Taoist classics of their own culture and reinterpreting them in light of contemporary, democratic imperatives. Along with artists and writers, these scholars are seeking to turn democratic "knowledge into culture," as one of them explained to me. China's underground democratic activists are also inventive, circulating banned books and reformist magazines and finding ways around Big Brother on the Internet, often using code words to evade the e-police. The virtual world of e-mail, blogs, cell phones, and text messaging is enabling them to connect with one another across vast distances and to keep in touch across a wide range of activities. For all these reasons, the national civic networking necessary for a mass democratic movement is slowly taking shape and may have a surprising capacity to shake the system when the next crisis comes.

In the range of scenarios that Bruce Gilley and other observers of China envision, the emergence of such a mass civic movement would split the senior leadership. Reformists and pragmatists in the party would opt to negotiate with moderates in the democratic opposition. As in Spain, Latin America, Poland, and elsewhere, the resulting pact would offer "some face-saving and interests-saving" concessions to conservative elites as well as the military, which could break from the party establishment early in the crisis by refusing to repeat its mistake of 1989.[137]

The question then is whether there is any organization in society that might offer a political alternative. Today, there is not—but neither was there in Russia in 1990. And my guess is that what happened in Russia will happen in China: a broad coalition of opposition forces will come together temporarily to oust the Communist regime, before going their separate ways. It is far from certain that China will be a viable and functioning democracy by 2025, but by then the Communist Party (if it is still in power) will have ruled China for seventy-six years—exceeding the seventy-year reigns of Russia's Communist Party and Mexico's Institutional Revolutionary Party. Thus, I may venture a prediction with some confidence: in 2025, India will have essentially the same political system that it has today, and China will not.

11

AFRICA, OVERCOMING PERSONAL RULE

My first trip to Nigeria, in December 1974, was very nearly my last. I arrived in Lagos on an early flight, exhilarated by the pulse of life, quickly drained by the heat, and unprepared for what would follow. I came in the heady days of the first oil boom. In the previous year, prices had quadrupled while the country's oil production had reached 2 million barrels per day—the status of a major oil exporter. Nigeria's oil revenues had tripled, and the government was spending and building furiously. Everyone was hoping for a rush of development and a transition from military rule back to democracy.

After clearing customs, I headed downtown in search of a hotel room. My taxi driver, a jovial and welcoming man named Johnny, was skeptical when he heard how little I could afford to spend. Dutifully, he took me from one cockroach-infested dive to another, until we found a compromise, pricier than I could afford, dingier than I could imagine. I thanked Johnny and asked him how much I owed him.

He laughed expansively and said, "Don't worry about money, I am just your friend. Now we have to help you change your dollars."

"I can just change my traveler's checks at the bank," I replied.

"No," he said with indignation, "the banks cheat you. I will help you get a better rate."

Jet-lagged, I reluctantly followed Johnny on foot through the alleys of Lagos Island. We found our way to the bar of a posh hotel, where we met a figure out of central casting: sinister smile, dark sunglasses, alcohol on the breath at ten in the morning. I thought, "I've got to get out of here." I indulged them in their desire for a morning beer, and we exchanged pleasantries. Then we started talking rates. The money changer made a proposal. I laughed nervously.

"That's below what I can get in the bank," I said. (In fact, it was well below the official rate.) "I don't want to trouble you; I'll just go to the bank."

But Johnny was insistent, "Look, the banks cheat you. They charge commissions. You're my friend. I love Americans. I will take care of you."

We continued until I managed to obtain a rate slightly better than the official exchange rate. I said okay and agreed to change some money— much less than they were hoping for. We circled to the alley in back of the hotel, completed the deal, and then Johnny and I walked back to the hotel. I thanked Johnny and asked how much I owed him.

"Don't worry about money," he said, "we're friends. Let's have another beer." Starved of sleep, I indulged him once more. Then I told Johnny I wanted to settle my account with him. He gave me an astronomical sum. "You're kidding," I said, now very nervously. His tone changed to a gathering belligerence. He had driven me all around looking for a hotel. He had helped me change my money. He had become my "friend," and friends should not dispute matters of money. He did not add, but did not need to, that I had also been too green to negotiate the price in advance. In a respectful tone, I thanked him and told him that his proposed fee was inconceivable. We went back and forth as he finished his beer and ordered another. Finally, I put quite a lot of naira on the bar—much more than I could have imagined paying for his "help," much less than he was demanding—and said, "This is what I am paying you." He became angry. "My brother is on the police force," he said coldly. "I don't want to have to tell him about your changing money on the black market." Oh no, I thought. He agreed to a "partial" payment but made it clear he would be back so that we could drink more beer and do more business.

Through the wise and generous assistance of an entry-level official at the U.S. embassy, David Lyon, who, like me, had just recently graduated college, I was able to evade Johnny's clutches and was persuaded to stay on for the month I had planned. The experience changed the way I looked at developing countries.

In Nigeria, I encountered a country in an economic and political fever. There was more than the sudden economic boom, and the distortion of values that quick, easy money brings. There was also massive corruption, not just the petty kind that had fallen upon me, but massive bribery and theft of public resources. Press reports and rumors were flying of federal ministers and military governors growing brazenly rich while ordinary people lived in squalor—in downtown Lagos, there were tin shacks, fetid open sewers, and children dressed in little more than rags. After officials ordered 16 million tons of cement, "far in excess of actual demand or port capacity," the main seaport became "clogged for weeks with hundreds of vessels which languished . . . as bulk cement hardened in their hulls."[1] Mysterious shortages of gasoline developed, forcing dawn-to-dusk queues at gas stations.

In the first five years after Nigeria's independence in 1960, violence and corruption had reigned. The First Republic was overthrown by a military coup in January 1966, and the next year, the southeastern provinces attemped to secede, triggering the Biafran civil war of 1967–70. By 1974, Nigeria's ruler, General Yakubu Gowon, who had helped to heal and unite the country after the war, was growing remote from the public. He had indefinitely postponed a promised transition back to democracy, and the press and civil society were growing outspoken against the government's corruption, waste, and authoritarian rule. Through strikes, boycotts, and demonstrations, university students in particular were demanding accountability and freedom. Military officers outside of lucrative government positions were concerned that Gowon was dragging the armed forces into disrepute. On July 29, 1975, they overthrew him in a bloodless coup, the country's third in nine years. The new military regime of General Murtala Muhammad launched investigations, cashiered over ten thousand civil servants for abuse of office or lack of productivity, and then announced a precise timetable for the restoration of democracy. And the regime delivered on it, despite General Muhammad's assassination in an abortive coup just six months after he assumed power.

The inauguration of Nigeria's Second Republic on October 1, 1979, was in many respects the high-water mark for freedom, prosperity, and developmental promise in the country. Despite a controversy surrounding the presidential election, profound ethnic tensions, and charges of electoral fraud, there was an unprecedented sense of hope. Following an extended constitutional debate involving input from both the public and the country's political scientists, Nigeria adopted an innovative presidential-style system, modeled on that of the United States, with checks and balances to contain abuses of power, an independent electoral commission, a countercorruption bureau, a supreme court, and a delicately engineered federal system to manage ethnic conflict and disperse power and resources. Five different parties each controlled at least two of the nineteen state governments, and the federal ruling party represented the most ethnically diverse party in Nigeria's history. Economically, the country was booming again as global oil prices surged after the 1979 Iranian revolution. Between 1978 and 1980, Nigeria's oil revenues (which accounted for almost all of its export earnings and well over 80 percent of government revenue) increased two and a half times. "Federal revenues totaled $12 billion in 1980," and Nigeria's international reserves quickly swelled to more than $10 billion.[2]

It was simply too much to resist. When I returned to Nigeria in the summer of 1981, the Second Republic was settling into waste and plunder on a breathtaking scale. The federal and state governments were spending with abandon. Particularly favored were construction projects that commanded huge initial "mobilization fees," a good portion of which were kicked back to the official awarding the contract. Many projects were abandoned quickly, as soon as the fat fees had been collected. As if the surge in oil revenues was not enough, state governments borrowed from abroad whatever the banks would give them. Fantastic corruption scandals surfaced, including "the mishandling of $2.5 billion in import licenses by the minister of commerce, the alleged acceptance by legislators of large bribes from a Swiss firm, the rumored apprehension in London of a Nigerian governor trying to smuggle millions of naira into Britain, and the revelation by a federal minister that the country was losing close to a billion dollars a year in payroll fraud."[3] Public disgust erupted early in 1983 when one of Lagos's tallest buildings, the headquarters of a government telecommunications company, was destroyed by a fire that appeared, as one newspaper editorialized, to be "a calculated act, planned and executed to cover up corruption and embezzlement in the company."[4]

But it was not just that the politicians were getting spectacularly rich; the people were visibly deprived. During 1982–83, when I taught at Bayero University in Kano, the largest city of the predominantly Muslim north, books for classes were not available in the library (not to mention the bookstore), and instructors had to find their own supplies, even at times paper and chalk. These were only mild symptoms of scarcity amid the booming wealth. Virtually every state was pocked by the skeletons of unfinished hospitals and schools, treacherous, ungraded roads, abandoned bulldozers, and rusting pumps beside undrilled boreholes in communities that had no source of clean drinking water. Even for someone who had studied the failure of the First Republic, the reckless greed of those Second Republic politicians came as a shock.

The consequences of the theft and squandering were devastating. When the second oil boom went bust in 1983, as all mineral booms eventually do, revenue declined from a peak of $24 billion in 1980 to $10 billion. Imports of industrial raw materials and commodities were severely disrupted, forcing widespread shortages and layoffs. Prices skyrocketed. Hoarding and profiteering, especially of rice, by politicians and their business cronies aggravated the scarcities. Drained of revenue, state governments became unable to pay teachers and civil servants or to purchase drugs for hospitals. Many services were shut down by strikes. The economy seemed on the edge of collapse. People were desperate for political change.

But when most of the opportunities for advancement in life are controlled by the state—and when those opportunities can mean the chance to get rich—it is difficult to get politicians to play by the rules of a democratic game. If they will lie, bribe, embezzle, smuggle, and misuse power to accumulate an illicit fortune, they will also stuff ballot boxes, steal votes, buy electoral officials, intimidate the opposition, and murder rivals in order to gain or hold on to power. Well ahead of the 1983 elections, violent clashes proliferated, killing scores of people. Ominously, a Lagos newspaper warned, "We are tired of celebrating politics as a rite of death. . . . If politics cannot inspire recognition and respect for fundamental human rights . . . we can ask to be saved from politicians and their notoriously bloody style of politicking."[5] Student protestors began to call for the return of military rule.

Nigeria's politicians did not heed these warning signs and proceeded to poison the elections with gross incompetence, fraud, and administrative bias. Millions of legitimate names went missing from an electoral register that was swollen to approximately twice the number of eligible voters. A new opposition alliance was prevented from running a presidential campaign. Over each of the five successive weeks of elections for different levels of office, electoral malpractices grew more breathtaking.

Electoral officials at every level were bribed to falsify returns. Whole communities were disenfranchised. [Ruling party] agents collaborated with electoral officials and police to prevent opposition party agents from observing the polling and vote counting. In the absence of this crucial check (guaranteed in the electoral law), unbelievable returns were reported and announced.[6]

President Shehu Shagari was reelected decisively. The following week, the ruling party nearly doubled its control of state governorships to a commanding majority, claiming states it could not have won lawfully, and then the next week it captured two-thirds of the National Assembly seats.

Taking eyewitness accounts, I was dumbfounded by the scale of electoral theft, the obvious overreach. Nearing the end of my year in Nigeria, I made my way to the U.S. embassy and, at the invitation of Ambassador Thomas Pickering, met with the entire top staff in a secure, windowless room. "There's a coup coming," I warned. The military attaché was dismissive. He knew all the top generals and was sure they were well "taken care of" by the civilian regime—meaning, they had been amply bought off. The political counselor noted that the president was upgrading his cabinet and policies, and calm had returned to the country. (To his credit, the one high official who took my warning seriously was Pickering himself, one of the most able and decorated American diplomats of the last half century.) Yet, it was clear to me that the elections were a farce, the country was seething with anger, and the legitimacy of the Second Republic was spent. People around the country wanted political change. And when the avenue of peaceful change, through the ballot box, was stolen from them, the only alternative left was force. Three months later, on December 31, 1983, the Nigerian military overthrew the government to widespread celebrations around the country. Hundreds of former politicians were detained, and huge sums of cash were seized from their homes.

The assumption of those who cheered the coup—and I must confess, my own initial expectation—was that military rule would be brief and corrective. Instead, it lasted a decade and a half under three different dictators, each one more repressive and corrupt than the last. For eight years, the second and by far wiliest dictator, Ibrahim Babangida, managed to stay atop the heap (while growing staggeringly rich) by promising and then choreographing an elaborate, staged transition to democracy under constant pressure from an impressively organized and courageous civil society. But Babangida kept shuffling, reshuffling, and rescheduling the process, banning parties and candidates while the shadowy "Association for a Better Nigeria" emerged to demand that he remain in power. When finally, despite Babangida's efforts, presidential elections went off and an independent-minded business magnate, Moshood K. O. Abiola, was voted into office, Babangida found a pretext to annul the election before the results could be officially announced. Violent protests erupted in Abiola's home region in the Yoruba southwest and Babangida was forced to resign, but military rule persisted under his top deputy, General Sani Abacha.

Abacha proved even more plundering, cynical, and ruthless. Civil society protested anew, repression mounted, and the country piled on foreign debt of $30 billion. Finally, in June 1998, top generals—alarmed at the deterioration of the country and the armed forces—allegedly arranged for Abacha to have a "heart attack" while in the arms of foreign prostitutes, and then organized a hurried transition to democracy.[7] The elections, held in early 1999, brought to office the implementer of the first military transition to civilian rule, General Olusegun Obasanjo.

Over the subsequent eight years, another ruinous cycle of promise and despair played out. As detailed in chapter 3, the 2003 elections were rigged in a grotesque parody that returned Obasanjo and his People's Democratic Party to power with commanding majorities. While Obasanjo implemented some economic reforms, he governed like a general and labored obsessively (while failing narrowly) to remove the constitutional ban on a third presidential term. The 2007 elections—fueled by another oil boom and resulting in a more ludicrously improbable landslide for the ruling party—were worse than those of 2003, leaving some two hundred dead and prompting the normally mild-mannered European Union to issue the most damning report it had ever delivered from an election observation mission.[8] Nigeria remained trapped in one of the most viciously destabilizing paradoxes in the world: its people would not stand for prolonged authoritarian rule, and its politicians would not permit genuine democracy.

THE DEVELOPMENTAL TRAP

Nigeria's size and oil wealth make it distinctive within Africa. No one really knows Nigeria's actual population count—every census since independence has had to be scrapped over intense ethnic disputes—but estimates suggest that nearly a fifth of the entire 700-million population of sub-Saharan Africa is Nigerian. Almost all African countries have much smaller publics to support (under 30 million). Only six others depend, like Nigeria, on oil for most of their government revenue (and like Nigeria, those six are all authoritarian regimes).

Despite Nigeria's enormous natural wealth, it trails the African averages for life expectancy, per capita income, and the Human Development Index (a composite measure that averages life expectancy, per capita income, and knowledge levels). Nevertheless, the overall developmental plight of sub-Saharan Africa remains abysmal.* The twenty-three poorest countries in the world in terms of human development are all in Africa.[9] Of the forty-eight African countries, only two have managed to escape falling in the bottom third of the UN Development Program's human development ratings, and both are small island states (Mauritius and Cape Verde). With the HIV/AIDS pandemic ravaging many countries, life expectancy in Africa has plunged to forty-six years (compared to the next worst region, South Asia, at sixty-four years). An estimated half of all Africans lack access to a decent source of drinking water (compared to 28 percent in South Asia). Thirty percent of Africans are undernourished (half as much again as South Asia). Ten percent of all African infants die before the age of one, and 17 percent do not live to see the age of five. In under-five child mortality, no other region does even half as badly as Africa. Given these grim survival figures, it is not surprising that Africa also has the world's highest birth rate, since families expect many of their children will die.[10]

The survival figures are not unrelated to another set of data: the quality of governance. Until recently, Africa has been a desert in terms of democracy and the rule of law, and it remains one of the most corrupt and badly governed regions of the world. In the last few years, the Argentine economist Daniel Kaufmann and his colleagues at the World Bank Institute have developed six measures to assess a country's quality of governance, one of which, voice and accountability (including freedom of expression and citizen participation in selecting the government) is a rough (if partial) surrogate for democracy. The others measure political stability (and the absence of violence), government effectiveness (of public services and public administration), the quality of government regulation (to "permit and promote private sector development"), the rule of law (including the quality of policing and the courts), and control of corruption. Africa does poorly on all of these measures. On average it ranks

* For the remainder of the chapter, I will simply refer to sub-Saharan Africa as "Africa."

in the thirtieth percentile—a little better on the political measures of accountability and stability, but slightly worse on the measures of rule of law, corruption control, regulatory quality, and government effectiveness. On these latter four measures, which I collect together as a gauge of "state quality," Africa's mean percentile ranking, twenty-eighth, trails well behind Eastern Europe (fifty-ninth), Latin America and East Asia (forty-seventh), the Middle East (forty-second), and even South Asia (thirty-sixth). (See figure 11.1.) Based on these World Bank indexes, Africa and the former Soviet Union are the most badly governed regions of the world. This may help to explain why Africa ranks dead last, and by a wide margin, in its average Human Development Index score.

The picture grows worse still if we look at the African countries with populations over 30 million. Save for South Africa, which looks much more like an East European country with an average percentile rank of sixty-four, the data are alarming. Five of Africa's seven biggest countries have worse governance than the continent as a whole, and three of them dismally so. Across all six measures, Nigeria ranks in the thirteenth percentile. On rule of law and corruption control and political stability/control of violence, only 5 percent of countries score worse. Ethiopia ranks in the eighteenth percentile, Sudan in the fifth, the Democratic Republic of Congo (the former Zaire) in the third. Kenya and Tanzania do better, at the twenty-sixth and thirty-sixth percentile respectively, but Kenya still scores below the African average.

There is also the tragedy of violent conflict in Africa. Roughly two-thirds of the countries to which the United Nations has sent peacekeeping operations between 1998 and 2007 were in Africa.[11] About 70 percent

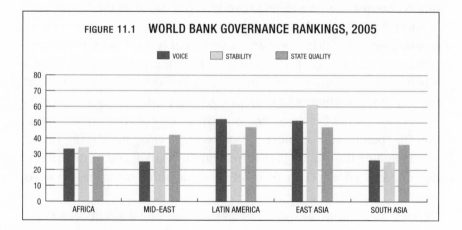

FIGURE 11.1   **WORLD BANK GOVERNANCE RANKINGS, 2005**

of the roughly seventy thousand UN peacekeeping troops deployed as of 2007 were in Africa. Since their independence, twenty-two African countries (almost half) have suffered civil wars—some of them claiming hundreds of thousands of lives, and several of them flaring up repeatedly.[12] By the end of 2005, Africa, which has only about a tenth of the world's population, had about 30 percent of the world's refugees—an estimated 2.5 million people.[13]

THE PATHOLOGY OF PERSONAL RULE

Why does Africa remain, half a century after the onset of decolonization, mired in poverty, stagnation, misery, violence, and disruption? A common assumption is a lack of resources. But that cannot explain why some of Africa's richest countries in natural resources—Nigeria, Angola, the Congo—stand among its most dysfunctional developmental failures. It cannot account for the fact that "Africa has received some $600 billion in foreign aid since 1960, yet most African nations are poorer today than they were then"[14] or that two-fifths of all official aid flows in 2004—a total of $26 billion—went to Africa.[15]

Oil and aid function in a similar fashion, since in many African countries, foreign aid accounts for half or more of the total government budget and a significant share of the total national economy—over a quarter in some cases. Both provide external rents that ruling elites can easily capture for themselves and their families and friends. In sufficient quantities, oil and aid revenues both enable economic irrationality and waste. Both fund the state apparatus of repression and patronage that sustains venal, unpopular governments. Both sever the bonds of accountability between rulers and ruled. And both feed the monster of African politics: corrupt, lawless, personal rule.[16]

For many years, social scientists have labeled this type of rule *neopatrimonialism,* drawing on the German sociologist Max Weber's notion that in small, traditional systems, highly personal and arbitrary rule converted ordinary people into clients of the ruler rather than citizens with rights. Postcolonial African states have been neopatrimonial because they combine the formal architecture of a modern bureaucratic state—constrained in theory by laws, constitutions, and other impersonal rules and standards—with the informal reality of personalized, unaccountable power and pervasive patron-client ties. These ties radiate down from the biggest "big man"—the autocratic president—to his lieutenants and allies, who in turn serve as patrons to lower-level power brokers, and down to the fragmented mass of ordinary citizens, who are trapped in relations of dependence on and support for their local political patrons.

In such systems, informal norms always trump formal rules and restraints. Thus, "the right to rule . . . is ascribed to a person rather than to an office."[17] Subordinates pay loyalty to their personal patrons, not to laws and institutions. Powerful presidents (and their subordinates) use state resources as a personal slush fund to maintain political dominance, giving their clients state offices, jobs, licenses, contracts, vehicles, bribes, and other access to illicit rents, while getting unconditional support in return.[18] State offices at every level become permits to loot, either for an individual or for a somewhat wider network of family, ethnic kin, political clients, and business cronies. Where the resources are greatest—in the oil states—the looting has been colossal. The head of Nigeria's Economic and Financial Crimes Commission estimated in 2006 that the country's civilian and military officials stole or wasted some $380 billion of the country's oil wealth during its first four decades of independence.[19]

The Northwestern University political scientist Richard Joseph, one of America's leading scholars of Nigeria and Africa, calls such entrenched corruption *prebendalism,* again building on Weber's work. For Weber, the *prebend* was an office of a feudal state, acquired through service to a lord or outright purchase and then used to generate income for its holder.[20] In prebendal systems, it is expected that state offices will be sought and then "utilized for the personal benefit of office holders" as well as their clients, and clients expect—and demand—their share of the spoils. Corruption, clientelism, and personal rule thus seep into the culture, making the system more tenacious. In Africa, contending patron-client networks organize along ethnic or subethnic lines, and the president judges his ethnic kin as the most reliable loyalists in struggles over power. This makes the system unstable, as identity, power, and resource conflicts mix in a volatile brew, prone to explosion.[21]

The fundamental purpose of neopatrimonial, prebendal governments is not to produce public goods—roads, bridges, markets, irrigation, education, health care, public sanitation, clean drinking water, effective legal systems—that increase productivity, improve human capital, stimulate investment, and generate development. Rather, it is to produce private goods for those who hold or have access to political power, as could be readily seen throughout Nigeria's troubled history. Contracts are let not on the basis of who can deliver the best service for the lowest price, but rather on who will pay the biggest bribe. Budgets are steered to projects that can readily generate bribes. Government funds mysteriously disappear into the overseas accounts of individual officeholders. Government payrolls are swollen with the ranks of phantom workers and soldiers. And staggering sums are spent to support the mansions, the transport, the cabinet, and the swollen retinue of the corrupter-in-chief, the president.

Consider Uganda. During the 1990s, the Clinton administration singled out President Yoweri Museveni as a leader among a "new generation" of African leaders who had turned their countries from socialism and war to democracy and the free market.[22] During both the Clinton and George W. Bush administrations, Uganda was showered with U.S. and other foreign aid—between 1987 and 2006, a total of $15 billion.[23] And it seemed to pay off. Uganda was an early leader in battling HIV/AIDS. It enthusiastically embraced economic reform. Between 1990 and 2004, it recorded a 3.5 percent annual rate of growth in per capita income (whereas Africa as a whole hardly grew at all).[24] But difficult questions lie under Uganda's apparent miracle. Between 2003 and 2006, the average annual growth rate in agriculture, on which most of the population depends, was anemic— under 1 percent. Fiscal deficits steadily widened, driving up interest rates.[25] Although two-thirds of Uganda's total foreign debt (of $3.2 billion) was written off in the late 1990s, the country rapidly accumulated new debt, bringing its total to almost $5 billion by early 2005—when the international community once again wrote off almost all Uganda's debt. Despite the brisk pace of economic growth, 92 percent of Ugandans still have no access to electricity, three-quarters live on earth floors, nearly 60 percent lack access to decent sanitation, and 40 percent to clean water, and life expectancy is under fifty years.[26]

Andrew Mwenda, the brilliant Ugandan journalist and editor, has been bold enough to ask, "Where has all the aid gone?" Here are some of his answers, culled from just one of Uganda's budgets (2006–7): $48 million for the residence and office of the president; $40 million for refurbishing the presidential residence; and $370 million on presidential appointments, including a cabinet of 69 ministers and 114 advisers, as well as "135 commissions and semi-autonomous government bodies, which are simply government patronage."[27] The annual bill for Museveni's presidential appointments alone exceeds by more than 50 percent average annual levels of U.S. aid to Uganda in recent years. And there is more, for example, $8 million to maintain the presidential jet—"enough to build 1,820 primary school classrooms . . . for Museveni's citizens who study under mango trees." Since the jet's purchase in 1998, Mwenda calculates that the total spent could have built 14,560 classrooms to accommodate nearly three-quarters of a million pupils. "Now it supports one man."[28]

Museveni assumed the presidency in 1986, when his insurgent National Resistance Army (NRA) forced out a repressive and ethnically divisive government, and has held power ever since. Although he agreed to allow multiparty electoral competition for the first time in 2006, it was only after he had secured a change to the constitution to allow unlimited terms. And once again, the election was rigged. With meaningful political accountability absent, rot has increasingly invaded the country's governance. An estimated one-fifth of Uganda's $200 million military budget, Mwenda reports, goes to pay ghost soldiers. Local governments (each with a prescribed number of jobs) have proliferated—from thirty-three districts in 1990 to eighty-one in 2005—to allow more clients of the ruling party to cash in on the foreign aid bounty. State funds have poured into "project monitoring units"—in theory a means of ensuring implementation of donor projects, in reality a means to maintain bureaucratic loyalty to Museveni by bestowing the staff with lavish salaries, allowances, four-wheel-drive vehicles, and overseas travel. In 2005–6, two-thirds of the project costs for agricultural development were eaten up in personnel expenses. Meanwhile, the Ministry of Health in the capital, Kampala, is flush with 3,000 vehicles (1,800 of them four-wheel drive) for its officials, while not a single one of the 961 sub-country dispensaries has an ambulance.[29]

All of this has come in a country considered—until very recently—to be one of the brightest stars of African development. Although he is a leading critic of Museveni, Mwenda acknowledges that many of Africa's leaders are worse. Compared to the plunder that has taken place in the most predatory states—Nigeria, Angola, and the Democratic Republic of Congo (Zaire)—Uganda's corruption seems run-of-the-mill. At least in Uganda, some services have been delivered. In Nigeria, the theft has been nearly total. In the richest of Nigeria's thirty-six states, Rivers State—the unofficial center of the country's oil industry in the Niger Delta—the 2006 state budget of about $1.3 billion was bigger than that of many African countries with larger populations, including nearby Niger and Mali. "But the state government has done little to alleviate poverty or improve the delivery of basic services, and has not lived up to its responsibilities under state law to rein in corrupt local government officials. At the same time, the governor of Rivers budgeted tens of millions of dollars that year alone on questionable priorities like foreign travel, 'gifts' and 'souvenirs' to unspecified recipients, and the purchase of jet aircraft and fleets of new cars for his office."[30] The amounts budgeted by the state for new cars ($11.5 million), two new helicopters ($40 million), and gifts and catering ($10 million) exceeded by almost three times the state's $22 million capital budget for health.[31] Yet, "one local government's primary health care coordinator told Human Rights Watch that many of his demoralized staff had simply given up, padlocking and abandoning their posts in rural areas because their salaries were in arrears and their clinics lacked any of the materials they needed to do their jobs. A school headmaster in another local government said that when he had complained about his school's lack of chalk, he was told the local government had no money for education."[32]

Still, Uganda's middling experience is instructive for considering the possibilities for development and democracy in Africa. If these are the realities in a country considered by the World Bank and Western donors to be a reformer, can most of the rest of the continent be much better? Uganda's tendency to devolve into political decay is paradigmatic of the cycle of neopatrimonial, personal rule, which is vulnerable to the mounting costs of maintaining support networks, co-opting and repressing opponents, and rewarding loyalty over competence. Such decay is most dramatic today in Zimbabwe, where a vengeful and increasingly absolute dictator, Robert Mugabe, has literally run his country into the ground, but Uganda is following the same trajectory. Unless it is sustained by external rents or gradually attenuated by the growth of formal institutions, neopatrimonial rule eventually collapses under economic irrationality: it is a system of consumption, not investment and production. Foreign aid simply delays the day of reckoning, subsidizing the clientelism and corruption of personal rulers and shielding them "from paying the price of their political folly."[33]

One thing that can arrest the decay and refresh the system is a change in leadership. But a key feature of the neopatrimonial system is the prolonged tenure in power of a single ruler. In 2005, President Museveni "openly bribed members of parliament, blackmailed and intimidated others to amend the constitution and remove term limits on the presidency so that he can run again, and again, and again."[34] In the run-up to the February 2006 presidential election, he stepped up his harassment and suppression of the independent media and those elements of civil society he had not already co-opted. Then he jailed the principal opposition presidential candidate, before finally claiming a highly suspect first-round victory through apparent manipulation of the vote count.[35]

Museveni's two decades in power hardly make him Africa's longest-serving president, however. That honor goes to Omar Bongo of oil-rich Gabon, who has ruled for nearly four decades. Mugabe's merciless reign has stretched past a quarter century. In Angola, Cameroon, and Guinea, presidents have also ruled for well over twenty years, and in Burkina Faso for nearly that. Sudan's Hassan al-Bashir has held power for eighteen years, and Meles Zenawi in Ethiopia and Yahya Jammeh in the Gambia for over a decade. None of them shows any sign of surrendering office. Prolonged personal regimes have held sway over much of postcolonial Africa's short history. Mobutu Sese Seko ruled Zaire for thirty-two years. Julius Nyerere in Tanzania, Kenneth Kaunda in Zambia, and Daniel arap Moi in Kenya each held the presidency for about a quarter century, and Abdou Diouf in Senegal for twenty years (after a similar stretch in power by his predecessor, Léopold Senghor). During each of these protracted reigns in power, their countries declined.

AFRICA'S (SOMEWHAT) NEW POLITICAL ERA

Personalization and concentration of government power remain stubborn realities in Africa. What is different today, however, is that the de facto "life presidency" is no longer the whole story of Africa. Since the "second liberation" of Africa in 1990, many long-serving presidents (including a number of those mentioned above) have been driven from power or defeated at the polls. Most countries have adopted presidential term limits, and a number have successfully resisted efforts by incumbents to lift them. Even where, as in Uganda and Zimbabwe, presidents are hanging on, it is with more societal resistance, political opposition, and moral outrage than was typically mobilized prior to 1990.

One factor containing the personalistic degradation of the state has been democracy itself, and the attendant growth of constitutionalism. Before 1990, there were never more than a few democracies on the continent, and those were mainly confined to very lightly populated countries like the Gambia, Mauritius, and Botswana. By the end of 2006, about twenty-three African states were democracies (see appendix, tables 4 and 5). Even if a few of these states are only dubiously democratic—with charges of electoral malfeasance, corruption, and ruling party domination of the state apparatus, civil society, and the press—the general transformation in the political character of the continent is extraordinary. Many of the electoral democracies that emerged after 1990—such as those in Benin, Mali, and South Africa—have persisted for more than a decade. Following two decades of rule under Jerry Rawlings (initially under his populist military regime, then under two terms as an elected civilian president), Ghana has emerged as one of Africa's most liberal and vibrant democracies, reclaiming a position of political leadership on the continent that was forged and squandered under independence leader Kwame Nkrumah. And the trend continues to be positive: between 2002 and 2006, Africa's average levels of freedom improved almost half a point on the Freedom House seven-point combined scale of political rights and civil liberties.

The positive trend is all the more remarkable when one looks at which African countries have become electoral democracies. They include the world's three poorest countries on the Human Development Index (Mali, Niger, and Sierra Leone) and several others in the bottom twenty (such as Burundi, Malawi, Mozambique, and Zambia). They include four countries (Burundi, Liberia, Mozambique, and Sierra Leone) where democratization was part of the efforts to end civil conflicts that left at least thousands (in the case of Burundi, two hundred thousand) dead. In Liberia, democracy came while the postwar country was still dependent on thirteen thousand UN peacekeeping troops. There is more political contestation and civil pluralism in Africa today than at any previous moment in its postindependence history. But democracy remains a faint and fragile flower.

For example, it would have been hard to imagine a more unlikely prospect for democratization in the early 1990s than Malawi. For nearly thirty years, the country was in the grip of a vain, eccentric dictator, Dr. Hastings Kamuzu Banda. Two years after independence in 1964, Malawi was officially declared a one-party state, and in 1971 Banda had himself named "president for life." Through the 1970s and '80s, no opposition of any kind was tolerated. The press was tightly controlled, and civil society was severely repressed. The public was bullied by the ruling party's paramilitary youth wing. All political activity outside the ruling party was deemed criminal. So paranoid was Banda that dissidents in exile were targeted for assassination or kidnapping.[36] Then in 1991, foreign aid donors pushed the ninety-year-old Banda to open up politically. Under protracted domestic and international pressure, he held a referendum in 1993 on whether Malawi should have a multiparty system and lost badly, with nearly two-thirds voting yes. The next year, the country's first multi-party elections brought a new party and a new leader, Bakili Muluzi, to power.

Muluzi's ten years in the presidency were not a great success. In his first five-year term, Muluzi released political prisoners, established basic freedoms, invested in health and education, and won the adoption of a new constitution enshrining multiparty democracy and limiting the president to two terms. However, regional and ethnic differences festered, and Muluzi won reelection only narrowly and over intense opposition protests. His second term "was marred by high inflation, low growth and widespread allegations of government corruption which led many donors to withhold promised funds, thereby worsening the economic crisis."[37] Moreover, Malawi's freedom ratings deteriorated as Muluzi grew consumed with trying to remain in power.[38] But domestic and international pressure again gathered on Malawi, and Muluzi was compelled to abandon his campaign to amend the constitution to allow him a third run for the presidency. At that point, he tapped an outsider, Bingu wa Mutharika, a seventy-year-old economist and international civil servant who had left Malawi out of opposition to Banda, to contend on his behalf. But when the new president (elected with only 35 percent of the vote) launched an aggressive anticorruption campaign—investigating the former president and several of his top associates—the ruling party split. President Mutharika was forced to form a new party, leaving him without majority support in parliament. Muluzi and his party tried (unsuccessfully) to impeach Mutharika, and the country was thrown into political turmoil. And while economic management improved under the technocratic Mutharika, the country struggled to come to grips with an HIV/AIDS pandemic that had infected an estimated one of every seven adults and lowered life expectancy to just forty years, while three-quarters of the population struggled to survive on less than two dollars a day.

For all its difficulty and uncertainty, there is a hopeful sign in Malawi's posttransition story. President Muluzi's effort to bend the constitution to his will failed. In contrast to what happened under Banda, the institutions won out over the ambitions of the ruler. And that is no longer a rare story in Africa; the formal constitutional rules on how leaders acquire and leave power are increasingly coming to matter. As the UCLA political scientists Daniel Posner and Daniel Young have shown, since 1990, Africa's politics have grown less violent and more institutionalized.[39] Between 1990 and 2005, six presidents, including Yoweri Museveni in Uganda, succeeded in eviscerating term limits, but these cases were the minority. Powerful rulers such as Jerry Rawlings in Ghana and Daniel arap Moi in Kenya, and ultimately ten others, were forced by term limits to step down from their presidencies. After more than two decades in power, Rawlings and Moi were tempted to hang on, but yielded to domestic and international pressure. Three African leaders—including President Olusegun Obasanjo in Nigeria—tried hard and failed to extend their presidencies. And even the leaders who scuttled term limits felt compelled to do so by amending the constitution incrementally rather than simply declaring themselves "president for life" (as was not uncommon immediately after independence). Further, in the 1960s, '70s, and '80s, more than two-thirds of African leaders left power violently—usually, as a result of a coup or assassination. During the 1990s, peaceful exits—principally, as a result of electoral defeat or voluntary resignation—became the norm, and between 2000 and 2005, roughly four in five African leaders were replaced this way. More decisive than the rise of democracy has been the end of the one-party state in Africa. Since the 1990s, elections have become increasingly regular and frequent, and almost all African elections have been contested. As has been the case in Nigeria—as well as in Ethiopia, the Gambia, Uganda, and most brutally, Zimbabwe, among others—many of these elections have been arbitrarily limited, manipulated, or blatantly rigged. But parties and leaders are beginning to lose elections. Whereas only one African president was defeated at the polls between 1960 and 1990, incumbent presidents lost one out of every seven times they contested between 1990 and 2005.[40] Moreover, electoral alternation has significant positive effects on public support for and confidence in democracy.[41] And even when elections have not been adequately free and fair, it appears that the repeated holding of competitive elections has produced gradual improvements in civil liberties by enhancing the democratic consciousness of citizens, strengthening civic organizations and mass media, and giving officeholders some incentive to service and maintain their bases of electoral support.[42]

Why do African presidents feel more constrained now? Posner and Young advance two intriguing explanations. One is that they feel more international pressure. The median level of foreign aid (as a percentage of the overall economy) in the countries where presidents did not attempt to secure third terms was almost twice as high as in those countries where the presidents did (and often succeeded). The other factor is public opinion. African publics are as awakened, attentive, and active now as they have never been before. Their expectations of government are higher, and their readiness and organizational abilities to challenge abuses of power are greater. The nine African presidents who felt constrained not to seek a third term had narrower electoral mandates than the nine who did, suggesting a greater sensitivity to public opinion.

This points to another positive trend in Africa, with potentially lasting consequences: the growth of civil society.[43] As a wide range of associations independent from the ruling party have begun to engage in political dialogue and advocacy, they have served as a great force for political accountability, challenging and at times even preempting a president's flirtation with staying in power. Some of these organizations date back to the colonial and immediate postindependence era—student associations, trade unions, religious bodies, and interest groups based on commercial, professional, and ethnic solidarities—but there is also a new generation of groups working explicitly for democracy and good governance: think tanks, bar associations, human rights organizations, women's and civic education groups, election-monitoring networks, and local and national-level development organizations. To a degree far beyond the early years of nationhood, the construction of democracy in Africa is a bottom-up phenomenon. Nongovernmental organizations are teaching people their rights and obligations as citizens, giving them the skills and confidence to demand accountability from their rulers, to expose and challenge corruption, to resolve conflicts peacefully, to promote accommodation among ethnic and religious groups, to monitor government budgets and spending, to promote community development, and to recruit and train new political leaders. Civic groups are also working at the national level to monitor elections, government budgets, and parliamentary deliberations; to expose waste, fraud, and abuses of power; and to lobby for legal reforms and institutional innovations to control corruption and improve the quality and transparency of governance (see chapter 13). These organizations draw strength not only from the funding and advice they receive from international foundations and donors, but more important, from their increasingly dense interactions with one another. Dozens of pro-democracy and good governance organizations in some thirty African countries are linked in the African Democracy Forum.[44] Some African civil society organizations, most notably the Institute for Democracy in South Africa (IDASA), have reached a point of institutional maturity where they are now assisting democratic development elsewhere on the continent.

THE BAROMETER OF DEMOCRACY

Coinciding with the flowering of civil society has been a visible public demand for and appreciation of democracy. When surveyed by the Afrobarometer in 2005–6, an average of 62 percent of the public in eighteen countries said that "democracy is preferable to any other kind of government" (as opposed to saying that "in some circumstances an authoritarian government can be preferable" or that "it doesn't matter").[45] Levels of support for democracy were as high as 75 percent in Ghana, Kenya, and Senegal, and at 65 percent or higher in ten of the countries surveyed. In fact, only a few African countries harbor much preference for any specific form of authoritarian rule, and never does it rise above a fifth of the population. Moreover, this is not just an abstract commitment to democracy in general. Four in every five Africans surveyed believe that "regular, open, and honest elections" are the only way to choose their country's leaders, and two-thirds agree that elected assemblies (not the president) should make the laws in the country, even if the president disagrees with them. About three-quarters of Africans are able to attach a meaning to "democracy," and among them, 75 percent say democracy is always preferable.[46]

Almost three-quarters of Africans also reject the option of military rule for their country. Most of the eighteen African publics surveyed reject military rule overwhelmingly (by margins of 80 percent or more in eight countries). Similarly, 71 percent reject one-party rule and 78 percent reject one-man rule, and these levels of resistance have held steady since the original Afrobarometer survey of twelve countries in 2000. On any one of these authoritarian options, only about one in six Africans, on average, expresses a positive preference. And a slight majority (52 percent) actively rejects all three authoritarian options.

Africans' support for democracy does not seem to be born out of a naive sense that democracy means or will necessarily quickly bring rapid economic progress. When asked to define what democracy means to them, "a majority of Africans interviewed (54 percent) regard it in procedural terms by referring to the protection of civil liberties, participation in decision making, voting in elections, and governance reforms."[47] Only about one in five said democracy means a substantive outcome, like economic development or social justice. And when asked whether they felt their system of electoral democracy "should be given more time to deal with inherited problems" or instead, if it "cannot produce results soon, we should try another form of government," 56 percent of Africans in 2005–6 chose to give democracy more time—and fully three-quarters in Mali, one of the world's poorest countries. This represents a significant increase in patience with democracy since 2000.

Moreover, the spirit of democracy survives in Africa despite the most brutal efforts to crush it. In Zimbabwe—by far the most repressive of the countries surveyed—nine in ten people reject the options of one-man rule and the one-party state, eight in ten say only the national assembly can make laws, and three-quarters agree that many parties are needed to give people political choice. On each of these items, Zimbabweans, who have the most raw and current experience of dictatorship, also express the strongest aspiration for democracy.

Michael Bratton, a political scientist at Michigan State University and one of the cofounders of the Afrobarometer, notes that while the demand for democracy is proving fairly resilient in Africa, the perceived supply is more questionable. For example, while 81 percent of Africans want free and fair elections that can remove leaders, only 47 percent think they are getting this in their country. Two-thirds of Africans want their president to be subject to the rule of law, but barely a third (36 percent) thinks he is. And while two-thirds want a representative parliament, only 46 percent think they have one that reflects "the views of voters."[48] The problem is not that Africans do not value and demand democracy but rather that African parties and politicians are not meeting their citizens' aspirations.

Consequently, some disillusionment is setting in. Between the surveys in 2000 and those in 2005, satisfaction with the way democracy works declined an average of 13 percentage points (from 58 to 45 percent). While satisfaction rose in a few well-functioning democracies like Ghana and South Africa, it declined in eight of the twelve countries surveyed both times. Nevertheless, even on the supply side there are cautious grounds for optimism. The perception that one's own country is a democracy has held constant at around 50 percent, and 54 percent think it is likely their country will remain a democracy.[49] Analyzing the early Afrobarometer surveys (from 2000 and 2002), Bratton and his survey cofounders, Robert Mattes and E. Gyimah-Boadi, found that the most powerful factors shaping the "supply of democracy" (a combination of satisfaction with democracy and the perceived extent of democracy) concerned the performance of the system. In keeping with the prevalence of neopatrimonial rule, evaluation of presidential performance had the most powerful impact on the supply of democracy, but whether citizens believed the last elections were free and fair was almost as strong a factor. Other factors included the government's overall performance on employment, education, and health; the perceived level of corruption; trust in state institutions; and the perceptions that political rights are being protected and that one's own ethnic group is being treated fairly.[50] Analyzing the 2005 data, Bratton found that perceiving the last elections to have been free and fair has become far and away the most powerful factor in shaping the extent of democracy citizens perceive. Thus, the ruler's performance is no longer enough to satisfy the public, and formal institutions are starting to matter more than informal ones.[51]

In determining the "demand for democracy," by contrast, individual attributes—understanding of democracy, political knowledge and awareness, formal education, and membership in the postcolonial generation—have the strongest effects. In fact, being among the generation "who achieved voting age between independence and the advent" of democratizing reforms "is the single best predictor of demand for democracy." Bratton and his colleagues consider this to be the case because the "postcolonial cohort bore the brunt of the oppression and deprivation meted out by" postindependence authoritarian regimes and thus "learned the hard way to reject authoritarian forms of government."[52]

CAN DEMOCRACY WORK IN AFRICA?

The challenges to the viability of democracy in Africa are not much different in nature than in other regions, only more pervasive and extreme. As in many parts of Latin America, the former Soviet Union, and Asia, democracy is being tested to see if it is capable of governing effectively. As elsewhere, no challenge is more profound than controlling corruption, because when public resources bleed profusely and officials serve their own ends rather than the public good, governance and development suffer, conflict intensifies, and citizens turn to alternative regimes.

There is also the challenge of developing democratic governance that allows opponents a fair chance to displace those in power. No region has more countries that straddle the divide between democracy and pseudodemocracy than Africa. Independent and effective electoral administration has become institutionalized in some African countries, such as South Africa and Ghana, and a few other democracies, such as Mali, are fairly liberal, but in most of Africa, civil liberties are constrained, opposition rights are tenuous, and elections are riddled with malpractices, to the point where it is fair to question whether some of these regimes are democratic in any sense.

In a number of countries, democracy is diminished by one-party dominance. In Botswana and South Africa, this occurs within a context of significant freedom and relatively effective governance. Still, the trends in South Africa have been negative in recent years, leading Freedom House to downgrade the country's freedom score. Rampant violent crime, producing one of the world's higher murder rates, retards investment and public confidence in South Africa, and numerous observers cite signs of "creeping corruption," particularly conflicts of interest, among government and ruling party officials. In 2005, a bribery scandal involving a contract for naval vessels led President Thabo Mbeki to dismiss his deputy president, Jacob Zuma, but it was attributed primarily to a power struggle between the two men. With the lack of vigorous investigations, "South Africa's young democracy is starting to look tawdry," in the words of one former ruling party MP who resigned in protest.[53] The lack of opposition to the African National Congress (ANC), the high degree of centralization and discipline within the ANC, and the parliament's lack of meaningful oversight on the executive branch produce a stultified democracy despite one of the world's most liberal constitutions and a strong constitutional court. And because the country's system of proportional representation has divorced members of parliament from geographic districts, virtually no South African knows who represents her in parliament (whereas in the average African country, about half of the public do). As a result, citizen detachment and disaffection have risen.[54] South Africans remain strong supporters of democracy and of liberal principles, and more satisfied than the average African with the way democracy works in their country.[55] But when surveyed in 2006, only about two in five said elections enable voters to remove leaders they do not want (compared to 47 percent of all Africans surveyed).[56]

In Mozambique, the ruling party allows less freedom. The legacy of the civil war that ended in 1992 still polarizes the competition between the ruling party, FRELIMO, and its principal challenger, RENAMO, and "independent monitors cited serious flaws in the voting and tabulation" during the 2004 election. The state controls "nearly all broadcast media" (and much of the print media as well).[57] Corruption is extensive, and efforts to investigate it can cost journalists their lives.

The political struggle in Africa remains very much a contest between the rule of law and the rule of the person. Yet, most African democracies also suffer to one degree or another from the concentration of power in the office of the president. When Senegal's longtime opposition leader, Abdoulaye Wade, won the presidency in 2000, ending four decades of Socialist Party rule, there were high hopes for a new era of democracy, built on some of the continent's oldest traditions of pluralism and liberal thought. But increasingly, the aging president Wade drew power and resources into his own hands and those of his family. In 2004, he dismissed his prime minister, Idrissa Seck, out of fear that Seck was rivaling him for control of the ruling party. Seck was first charged with embezzlement, then with treason, before the charges were dropped and he was released after several months of detention. Ultimately, Seck ran for president but officially won only 16 percent of the vote, enabling Wade, with a reported 56 percent, to avoid a runoff. In the years leading up to Wade's reelection in 2007, journalists, political activists, singers, and marabouts (Muslim spiritual leaders) who criticized Wade or supported the opposition were subjected to physical intimidation and violence.[58] Critics charge the election was marred by vote buying, multiple voting, and obstruction of opposition voting.

Despite a lackluster economic performance, Wade was able to mobilize support. According to one leading activist, his primary instrument has been corruption—co-opting religious figures, civil society leaders, local administrators, military officers, and opposition members of parliament with money, loans, diplomatic passports, and other favors. Now, it is alleged, the octogenarian president is preparing to hand power to his chosen successor—his son.[59] "He has destroyed all the institutions, including political parties. He has taken opposition with him and manipulated the parliament," the activist told me. "People are so poor and Wade controls everything. If you need something, you have to go with him." The reaction from Europe and the United States (without whose aid Wade's government could hardly function) has been muted. The activist lamented, "We expected more from the donors," referring to the defense of principles, not the gift of money.[60]

In Central and Eastern Europe, particularly among the new members of the European Union, there is a strong sense of inevitability to democracy: the costs of defecting from democracy would be too great to permit a return to authoritarian rule. African states, however, are far from this pragmatic level of democratic consolidation. The fact that military rule has virtually disappeared from the continent does not mean that new coups are unthinkable, or that once they seize power, new strongmen will not—as the young junior officer Yahya Jammeh did in the Gambia—"regularize" their status by exchanging the uniform for traditional dress and forming a domineering party. Thirteen years after the then-twenty-nine-year-old lieutenant seized power in a military putsch in 1994, Jammeh was reelected in 2006 amid massive fraud, with foreign aid still providing half the government budget. If international donors cannot get tough with a young punk autocrat in a tiny country of under 2 million people, can they do so anywhere?

Yet, if the continental picture looks fragile and discouraging, there are significant grounds for hope. Democracy endures—and with some of the highest levels of freedom on the continent—in landlocked and desperately poor Mali. To be sure, the challenges are legendary and may prove fatal: feckless political parties, a feeble judiciary, immense poverty, deepening inequality, spiraling corruption, and a "near-pathological dependence on foreign aid." But the country is fashioning a viable democratic culture based on pride in its heritage of tolerance; media pluralism is flourishing (with over 140 FM radio stations blanketing the country); Malian NGOs are compensating (albeit perhaps too much) for the state's limited ability to deliver services; and political decentralization is bringing government closer to the people while broadening the stakes in the democratic game.[61] One finds a similarly mixed but upbeat balance sheet for democracy in Ghana. Despite the relentless creep of corruption—with its swelling of the presidential cabinet, conflicts of interest, and generous patronage—Ghana has emerged as one of Africa's freest and most vibrant democracies and (aside from South Africa) its best hope for a takeoff to development. The judiciary has more independence and capability than in most of the continent, while better levels of education, infrastructure, and governance are beginning to attract foreign investment. Meanwhile, Ghana's energetic and independent press raises questions and seeks accountability, and civil society organizations like the Center for Democratic Development monitor the government and build coalitions for reform.

If Ghana and other African countries are to achieve sustainable development, democracy cannot stand still, and freedom alone will not be enough. Democratic institutions will have to work better to control corruption and constrain the exercise of power, so that the chief business of government becomes the delivery of public goods, not private ones.

12

CAN THE MIDDLE EAST DEMOCRATIZE?

In the aftermath of the American invasion of Iraq in March 2003, democracy seemed finally to be on the march in the Middle East. The worst tyrant in the most oppressive region of the world had been toppled by the world's most powerful democracy. Iraq's authoritarian neighbors were nervous, and the region appeared to enter political ferment. With the end of thirty-five years of Baath Party dictatorship in Iraq, Syria's Baathist regime wondered if it might be next, and Iran's clerical rulers sent a letter to the White House proposing broad negotiations.

President George W. Bush and members of his administration issued notice of a bold change in U.S. foreign policy toward the Middle East. Addressing the National Endowment for Democracy on November 6, 2003, President Bush declared a "forward strategy for freedom in the Middle East": "Sixty years of Western nations excusing and accommodating the lack of freedom in the Middle East did nothing to make us safe—because in the long run, stability cannot be purchased at the expense of liberty. As long as the Middle East remains a place where freedom does not flourish, it will remain a place of stagnation, resentment, and violence ready for export."[1] In his speech, Bush cited favorable political trends under way in Morocco, Bahrain, Qatar, Kuwait, Yemen, and Jordan but also made clear that it was time for Egypt to "show the way toward democracy in the Middle East."

The regime of Egyptian president Hosni Mubarak—which had held power for more than half a century, since Colonel Gamal Abdel Nasser had overthrown the monarchy in 1952—felt compelled to show some progress. Under mounting pressure from Western powers as well as its own society, and facing a gathering struggle over succession between the military establishment and supporters of his son, President Mubarak's government launched "a high profile effort to cast itself as a champion of reform."[2]

The years 2004 and 2005 carried real promise for liberalization in Egypt. During 2004, diverse strands of the opposition—Islamist, leftist, and liberal—converged in advocating systemic political reforms that would permit a freer and more open society and fairer and more neutrally administered elections. Their demands included a competitive presidential election, which had heretofore been a simple yes-or-no plebiscite to "reelect" the autocrat. By December 2004, some of the forces came together under the brash name Kifaya (Enough)—which summed up the country's mood—and called for an end to the indefinite reelections of President Mubarak and a renunciation of his effort to smooth the path for his son to succeed him.[3]

Despite harassment and security crackdowns, the Kifaya demonstrations persisted, and in 2005, after nearly a quarter century of domineering rule by Mubarak, "it suddenly became fashionable to publicly campaign for his ouster."[4] Needing American support and some measure of domestic legitimacy, the president steered a complicated course. In January, the most prominent opponent from the secular, liberal camp— Ghad Party chairman Ayman Nour—was arrested on highly questionable charges, but then released, as Mubarak attempted to hold court with the American administration, which continued to provide almost $1 billion a year in economic aid and $1.3 billion in military aid.[5] In September, Mubarak for the first time allowed (albeit with restrictions) a multicandidate presidential election. The regime permitted significant judicial monitoring of the vote and of the more open and competitive parliamentary elections that followed in November. Although formally banned, members of the Muslim Brotherhood were able to contest as independents, and for the first time in twenty years, the organization entered the parliamentary campaign with none of its members in government custody.[6]

At the same time that reform was bubbling in Egypt, Syrian domination of Lebanon—codified and entrenched by the Taif agreement that ended the Lebanese civil war in 1989—began to unravel. With Syria quietly trying to subvert the new political order in Iraq, the Bush administration "began openly criticizing the Syrian occupation of Lebanon, a policy reversal that inspired the opposition movement in Lebanon to reassert itself."[7] France and other European countries followed suit. Showing it would not be pushed around, Syria's forty-year-old regime reverted to strong-arm tactics, pressuring the Lebanese parliament to extend the presidential term of its faithful ally, Emile Lahoud, in September 2004. The next month, one of the key ministers to oppose that term extension was nearly assassinated, and three weeks later the popular prime minister Rafiq Hariri resigned in defiance of Syrian pressure. In February 2005, Hariri and some twenty others were killed by a car bomb in Beirut. With this attack, the Syrians seem to have overreached. A week later, tens of thousands of Lebanese demanded the withdrawal of Syrian troops and intelligence agents and accused Syria and Lahoud of Hariri's murder. The protests, which came to be known as "the Cedar Revolution," continued daily until Lebanon's pro-Syrian government resigned on February 28.[8] In mid-March, hundreds of thousands of Lebanese (by some accounts over a million) rallied in central Beirut for "Freedom, Sovereignty, Independence." With the political tides shifting dramatically, Syria was forced to withdraw from Lebanon in April 2005, and in elections at midyear, Hariri allies won control of the government. Shortly after Lebanon's Cedar Revolution, some fifty thousand Bahrainis—"one eighth of the country's population—rallied for constitutional reform."[9]

In Jordan, a limited but hopeful political opening was also forming. Following the outbreak of the second Palestinian intifada in September 2000, King Abdullah had dissolved parliament, suspended scheduled parliamentary elections, banned demonstrations, and cracked down on civil society in response to rising public sentiment against the peace treaty with Israel. But after Saddam's regime was toppled in 2003, the king, flush with increased economic aid from the United States and the Gulf oil states, liberalized. He relaxed restrictions on freedom of expression, held "reasonably free and transparent, though not fair, parliamentary and municipal elections," and struck a bargain with left and Islamist opposition groups, in which the latter reportedly agreed to restrain their mobilization against Jordan's pro-U.S. foreign policy in exchange for economic progress and more political space.[10]

In Palestine, the death of Yasser Arafat in November 2004—after several decades of his corrupt, inept political supremacy—pointed the way to a new era of pluralism, accountability, and possibly even democracy. With the election to the presidency in January 2005 of the more competent and open-minded Mahmoud Abbas, and then the complete withdrawal of Israel from Gaza in August after thirty-eight years of occupation, hopes rose for both internal and regional accommodation.

In Iraq itself, 2005 was a year of democratic possibilities, despite deepening violence and political polarization. Defying fears of chaos and massive bloodshed, nearly 12 million Iraqis turned out courageously to vote in the January elections for a transitional parliament to draft a new constitution. In October, they did so again in even larger numbers, adopting the new constitution in a national referendum. Then on December 15, they voted a third time for a new parliament under the permanent constitution.

It seemed the Arab Middle East—which alone lacked a single democracy—was catching up with the world. By the end of 2005, Freedom House recorded measurable improvements in political rights or civil liberties over the preceding three years in the Palestinian Authority and half of the region's sixteen Arab states: Morocco, Egypt, Jordan, Lebanon, Iraq, Qatar, Yemen, and even Saudi Arabia. In some of these countries, the change was very modest, leaving a highly authoritarian regime, particularly in Saudi Arabia. Nevertheless, the five-year trend was, in the opinion of Freedom House, "a positive regional trajectory," bestowing the Middle East as a whole with its best Freedom scores in the history of the survey.[11]

MONARCHY, POPULISM, AND ISLAM

Yet, just a year later, democratic prospects in the Arab Middle East looked much gloomier. The regimes and their external allies, the United States and Europe, struggled to come to grips with two alarming implications of the political openings: severe political polarization and dramatic gains by Islamist forces.

In Iraq, a constitutional stalemate, deepening civil war, and the unfortunate choice of proportional representation in a single nationwide district as the young democracy's electoral system transformed the January 30 elections into an identity referendum, with voters choosing on the basis of ethnic and sectarian loyalties. Sunni Arab parties boycotted the voting, fearing they would be underrepresented by lower voter turnout due to the greater violent unrest in their region. The Sunnis nursed a host of objections to the political order and the American occupation, but the boycott magnified their political marginalization. Interim prime minister

Ayad Allawi's "Iraqi List," the principal nonsectarian option, suffered a humiliating political rout as Shiite Islamists captured a commanding plurality of seats and, together with the Kurdish alliance, formed a transitional government.

With the Sunnis largely excluded from the parliament and from negotiations over a permanent constitution, the sectarian gulf widened. Under American pressure, fifteen Sunnis were ultimately added to the fifty-five-member constitutional drafting committee, but too late to produce a compromise before the August 15 deadline for completion of the draft—a deadline that the United States insisted on, despite Iraqi appeals for an extension under the terms of the interim constitution. The October 15 constitutional referendum thus became a second identity plebiscite, with the Kurds and Shia voting almost unanimously for the document and the Sunni Arabs overwhelmingly against it.

The same polarization held sway in the December 15 parliamentary elections under Iraq's new constitution. Parties and coalitions made "no-go" areas of their ethnic strongholds, and the secular and transethnic lists (particularly Allawi's) once again paid the heaviest price. In Baghdad and many other cities, the election was disfigured by bombings, assassinations, and other armed attacks. Although turnout increased to 77 percent of registered voters, ethnic and sectarian polarization hardened. "Any hopes that the electorate would vote to separate religion from politics or to transcend ethnic fissures were completely frustrated," as Allawi's Iraqi List wound up losing almost half the seats it had won in January and other independents were trounced.[12]

In the aftermath of the election, the violence in Iraq intensified and the political condition drifted under the hapless new prime minister, Nuri al-Maliki. Despite a prereferendum agreement in October 2005 to consider a broad package of amendments to the constitution within a few months of convening parliament, there was a deadlock over such basic issues as federalism, the structure of executive power, and the control of oil production and distribution of its revenue. Meanwhile, competing Shiite Islamist forces, including those loyal to the radical cleric Muqtada al-Sadr, tightened their grip over various parts of southern Iraq. Baghdad, Baquba, Kirkuk, Mosul, and other multiethnic cities in the center and north saw mounting terrorism, violence, and ethnic cleansing. By early 2007, something on the order of a hundred Iraqis were dying every day. An estimated 2 million or more Iraqis had fled the country, and at least another 1 million were internally displaced. One of every three Iraqis was unemployed, and electricity production was at only 60 percent of the target goal the American occupation had set for its June 2004 termination.[13] On every single indicator, a February–March 2007 public opinion poll showed dramatic deterioration in Iraqis' perceptions and hopes for the future. Sixty percent said their lives were going badly or very badly, compared to 29 percent in 2004 and 2005. Half said conditions in Iraq were worse than before the 2003 American invasion. Only a quarter of Iraqis said they felt safe in their neighborhoods (down from 63 percent in 2005); 88 percent said they had inadequate electricity (up from 54 percent in 2005); only 28 percent expected better electricity and 38 percent more jobs in the near future, compared to three-quarters who were hopeful in 2005.[14]

Arab autocrats seized upon the swelling turmoil in Iraq to dampen and rebuff public demands for democracy. In Egypt, Jordan, Algeria, and Yemen, regimes that had opened more political space for opposition and dissent firmly took it back. In essence, their message to their restive populations was, "You want democracy? Look at Iraq. You want that kind of chaos? Be grateful for what you have." In a private meeting with a long-serving "elected" president in the region, an Arab civil society activist warned brashly, "You had better allow democracy or you will face the fate of Saddam Hussein." But as chaos increasingly rolled over Iraq, the president campaigned in 2006 on the chilling rejoinder, in essence: "You had better vote for me or you will face the same 'democracy' as in Iraq."[15] Similarly, as the absolute monarchy in Saudi Arabia retreated from the modest atmosphere of reform that had accompanied the formal ascension of King Abdullah in 2005, political activists from the country's Shiite minority blamed the wars in Iraq and Lebanon for the new political freeze. "An oft-quoted phrase attributed to the late King Fahd has acquired new resonance, especially in the Eastern Province [where the Saudi Shia are concentrated]: 'Why start fires on the inside, when there are fires on the outside?' "[16]

Beyond the violence in Iraq, another force inhibited the tentative steps toward democratization of the Arab Middle East: Islamic fundamentalism. During the first round of Egypt's parliamentary elections in November 2005, the Muslim Brotherhood, contesting as independents, won more seats than the ruling National Democratic Party (NDP): eighty-eight seats, nearly 20 percent of the total. However, "authoritarian management" restored the hegemony of the NDP in subsequent rounds of voting.[17] In Palestine, the militant Islamist movement Hamas stunned the ruling Fatah Party by winning 56 percent of the seats in parliament (albeit with only a slim electoral plurality of 45 percent). In Iraq, Shiite and Sunni Islamist lists won a majority of votes and seats in 2005, and in Bahrain, they won a majority of the forty seats in the lower house of parliament in the 2006 elections. In Kuwait, Islamists won a third of parliamentary seats, the largest single bloc, in 2006.

Elsewhere in the region, including Jordan and other Gulf monarchies as well as Morocco, it became increasingly apparent that the principal political force that stood to benefit from electoral openings was the Islamists. All of these regimes were haunted by the specter of Algeria in 1991–92, when, following a "flowering of civil society" and the first "honest competitive elections" in the country's history, the Islamic Salvation Front (FIS) headed toward victory in parliamentary elections.[18] To avert that outcome, the army had intervened in January 1992 and canceled the second stage of voting. It then deposed the incumbent president, banned the FIS, and imprisoned its leaders, triggering a civil war that claimed around 150,000 lives.[19] With Iraq sinking into civil war, and with the United States and its European allies alarmed by the electoral gains of Islamist parties and candidates who were opposed to accommodation with Israel, Arab regimes saw an opportunity to reverse the tentative moves toward democracy and individual freedoms.

The reassertion of authoritarian hegemony was most sweeping in Egypt, the most populous and politically influential state in the Arab world. In the second and third rounds of the November 2005 parliamentary elections, the regime skillfully undermined the efforts of Egypt's surprisingly independent judges to oversee honest elections. The badly divided opposition and the underresourced civil society groups that were monitoring the vote were easily neutralized, and a variety of electoral malpractices—"from the arbitrary closing of polling stations to the use of thugs and outbursts of street violence to the cutting off of electricity during vote counting"—were mobilized to restore the dominance of the NDP.[20] As the principal association of the judges, the Judges Club, grew more outspoken in its criticism of the regime and electoral misconduct, it launched a public movement (with unprecedented street demonstrations) for legislation to enhance the fiscal and political independence of judges. But this vigorous activism fractured the judiciary, which the regime successfully exploited to push through a bill that substantially reconstituted executive control of the judicial branch.[21]

Following the NDP's ultimate victory and Mubarak's declared reelection landslide over Ayman Nour in September 2005, the NDP embarked on a campaign of constitutional "reform" to ensure against any political "accidents" in the future. Thirty-four constitutional amendments were rammed through the parliament on March 19, 2006, and approved one week later in a national referendum that was boycotted by the opposition—and by virtually the entire electorate as well.[22] A key purpose of the amendments was limiting the prospects for the Muslim Brotherhood to repeat its electoral gains. To ensure that the Brotherhood does not reconstitute itself as a party, the amendments ban any political party or activity that has a religious frame of reference. They also prevent the Brotherhood from winning seats through independent candidacies, as it did in 2005, by changing the electoral system "from a candidate-centered system to a mixed one that depends mostly on party lists."[23] To ensure that the elections do not again evade the regime's control, the amendments impose tighter controls on party funding and activities. More important, they nullify a 2000 ruling by the Supreme Constitutional Court requiring direct judicial oversight of elections, giving that responsibility instead to a new supervisory committee controlled by the presidency. While in theory the hand of the prime minister is strengthened, in fact the president and the security forces are given "unprecedented powers" to combat terrorism by carrying out searches, arrests, and wiretaps without warrants, and by referring suspects to military courts.[24]

By 2007, the Egyptian regime had established its hardened authoritarian grip. Municipal elections scheduled for 2006 were postponed for two years, and possibly longer. Ayman Nour remained in prison, amid faint American protests. The traditional liberal and leftist parties, with their scant few seats in parliament, remained co-opted and ineffectual— dependent on the regime for what little political space it allowed and fearful of the grassroots support for the Muslim Brotherhood, which remained the only near-term alternative to the regime.

The Brotherhood, in turn, was decimated by arrests of its leaders and financiers. Members of the Brotherhood were referred to trial by military courts—some after their cases were dismissed by a civilian criminal court—and human rights groups were denied requests to observe the trials.[25] In the weeks leading up to the baldly manipulated June 11, 2007, elections for Egypt's upper house, the Shura council, dozens of Brotherhood activists were arrested, mainly from districts where the group was fielding candidates. Overall, more than two hundred from the group were "imprisoned for attempting to exercise their rights to freedom of association and expression," marking the third time since Mubarak came to power in 1981 that he had launched a broad crackdown on the Brotherhood.[26] Some of the lesser-known Brotherhood detainees were reportedly tortured in government detention.[27]

The authoritarian wave also fell upon civil society in Egypt, as labor protests were suppressed, independent organizations were deprived of licenses, activists were arrested, and e-mail accounts were forcibly shut down when individuals appealed to the international community. There was greater political pluralism in the press, but also more intimidation and legal repression of critical publications, journalists, and bloggers.[28] An explicit, vigorous challenge from the United States and Europe—with the threat of consequential sanctions—could have stood as an effective counterweight to the authoritarian backsliding. But, panicked by Islamist gains, the rising tide of Iranian power, and political instability in the region, the Bush administration—not to mention the more wary European governments—determined that they needed Mubarak more than ever, and stood largely silent. It is not clear whether the dramatic Islamist electoral gains in 2005 flowed from authoritarian fatigue, miscalculation, or a shrewd move by Mubarak to engineer alarm in an American administration that had vowed to overturn sixty years of foreign policy. My suspicion is the latter.

A similar crackdown against dissidents, particularly Islamists, by Jordan's main intelligence agency gathered a claim to international legitimacy after the November 9, 2005, suicide bombings that killed sixty people in three hotels in Amman. Credible reports indicated beatings, harsh conditions, and in some cases torture of detainees—a common practice among regimes in the region.[29] In the case of Jordan, however, the retrenchment on the promise of political reform began years before. When King Abdullah succeeded to the throne in February 1999 upon the death of his father, King Hussein, hopes were high. In the preceding decade, martial law had been lifted, political parties had been legalized, parliamentary elections had been revived after a twenty-two-year hiatus, media freedom had increased, and economic reforms had begun. But before his death, it became apparent that King Hussein intended these reforms to be no more than another cycle of "tactical liberalization," a long-standing political practice "to sustain rather than transform autocracies" in Arab states including Egypt, Jordan, Morocco, Algeria, and Kuwait.[30] Under both King Hussein and his successor, the Jordanian regime has endured "by adroitly wielding the twin survival strategies of

liberalization and deliberalization," expanding liberty and political space
when necessary "to shore up its legitimacy" and then "reversing the process when the opposition threatened to get too strong."[31]

Like his father, the young king expressed a rhetorical commitment to
democratic reform but put priority on regime survival and "strengthening the political base of the monarchy."[32] The Hashemite monarchy had
spent over half a century on the precarious front line of the Arab-Israeli
conflict, and the Palestinian refugee population had grown to probably
outnumber the indigenous Jordanian tribes.[33] Thus, King Abdullah
emphasized economic reform, including trade liberalization, rather than
a specific political agenda. In fact, in 2000, soon after his ascension to the
throne, the Israeli-Palestinian peace process collapsed, and in the face of
deteriorating regional security, the Jordanian regime clamped down politically. In June 2001, parliament was suspended for what would stretch to
two years while the king issued more than two hundred decrees, many
reversing previous gains in freedom of organization, demonstration, and
the press. Though parliament and elections were revived in 2003, it was
under an electoral system—introduced in 1993 "to curb the electoral success of Islamists"—that permitted each voter to choose only one candidate in multiseat districts and thus privileged personal ties and tribal
candidates over organized political parties, particularly the Islamic Action
Front (the party of the Muslim Brotherhood).[34] King Abdullah continued
to talk of political reform, creating a ministry of political development in
2003 and a national agenda in 2006 that, while again mainly focused on
economic reform, promised greater political and civil freedom. Yet, "real
power remains not with the cabinet or the parliament, but with the royal
court and the intelligence services."[35] Relations between the authoritarian state and the Islamists grew more confrontational, particularly after
the victory of Hamas in the January 2006 Palestinian elections, which
fanned fears in Jordan of a spillover effect.

As in Jordan, democratic hopes rose in Bahrain in 1999 when the
long-reigning emir died and his son, Sheikh Hamad bin Isa al-Khalifa,
assumed the throne, which his family has occupied for more than two
centuries. The forty-nine-year-old monarch (who named himself king as
part of a new social contract with his people) quickly loosened the rigid
political order, releasing all political prisoners, permitting the return of
exiles, eliminating emergency laws and courts, giving women the right to
vote, and holding parliamentary elections in 2002 for the first time in

twenty-seven years. Islamists boycotted those elections because of the creation of a more powerful upper house that was to be appointed by the king. But by 2006, they had determined to contest the elections and won a majority of seats; the Shiite Islamist group won all seventeen of the seats it campaigned for. That victory, however, defined the limits of the country's democratic reform. With the Shia making up at least 60 percent of the country's population of seven hundred thousand,[36] and with Shiite Islamists having called in the past for an end to the monarchy, the reigning Sunni Muslim al-Khalifa family could not countenance a genuine democratic breakthrough. When Bahraini Shiite democratic activists got the ingenious idea of using Google Earth to document the country's extreme inequality in land and wealth—revealing forty images of royal palaces and "vast tracts of empty land, while tens of thousands of mainly poor Shiites were squashed together in small dense areas"—it was too much for even an avowedly reformist monarchy, which reasserted greater control over civil society.[37]

In most of the rest of the Arab world as well, political openings closed and reform prospects fizzled. In Algeria, President Abdelaziz Bouteflika's pursuit of reconciliation with the Islamists following his election in 1999 wound down the civil war, significantly reducing terrorism and violence. The president also gradually reduced military control of politics and government while promoting a more competitive presidential election in 2004. (He nevertheless won in a landslide.) But the Islamist party, the FIS, remained excluded from politics, and as Bouteflika neared the end of his second term, rumors formed of a constitutional amendment to permit him to run again. It appears he constrained the military only "in order to increase his own freedom of action, not in order to democratize Algeria." Algeria increasingly resembles most other Arab states "that face the problem of excessive power concentrated in the hands of a single ruler."[38] In 2005, Syria freed hundreds of political prisoners and slightly relaxed political repression, but with international pressure bearing down on it over the assassination of Rafiq Hariri, the regime remained deeply authoritarian, ready to arrest and torture anyone who challenged its legitimacy. As President Zine el-Abidine Ben Ali headed toward his twentieth year in power in 2007, Tunisia remained only slightly less repressive than Syria's Baathist regime, and hardly more competitive. But with its liberal economic policies and strategic cooperation in the war on terror, the United States and Europe largely looked the other way.

BUSH'S IMPOSSIBLE STRADDLE

With democracy receding all over the Arab world while the United States strengthened its economic and security ties to Arab dictatorships, the Bush administration lost its remaining credibility on regional democracy. President George W. Bush was never more eloquent in his embrace of freedom and democracy than when he addressed a conference of democratic dissidents and activists from seventeen countries in Prague on June 5, 2007. Freedom, he insisted once again, is "the most powerful weapon in the struggle against extremism." Echoing the theme of his ground-breaking speech to the National Endowment for Democracy, Bush reiterated, "The policy of tolerating tyranny is a moral and strategic failure."[39] Yet, there was tyranny in much of the Arab world, creeping along with expanding American support in service of the war on terror.

After the speech, the Egyptian civil society leader and former political prisoner Saad Eddin Ibrahim told journalists, "I feel disappointed and betrayed by George Bush. He said that he is promoting democracy, but he has been manipulated by President Hosni Mubarak, who managed to frighten him with the threat of the Islamists."[40] In a private meeting, Ibrahim implored the Bush administration to condition U.S. aid on political reform and the release of political prisoners, including Ayman Nour. In fact, Bush had delivered a mixed message for Egypt and other friendly autocracies of the region, and they did not receive it any more amicably than did the dissidents. Praising Egypt, Saudi Arabia, and Pakistan for their "brave stands and strong actions to confront extremists, along with some steps to expand liberty and transparency," Bush then noted the "great distance" they still had to travel and vowed to continue "to press nations like these to open up their political systems." Egypt's foreign minister quickly shot back, expressing "astonishment and upset" over Bush's mild rebuke and declaring it "unacceptable interference."[41]

Citing the American experience with Korea and Taiwan during the Cold War, Bush confidently declared that "America can maintain a friendship and push a nation toward democracy at the same time." But Korea and Taiwan democratized only as the Cold War was ending—after nearly four decades of American friendship with their militaries and one-party dictatorships. The impossible straddle of Bush's Prague speech was painfully evident when, reaching for a sign of democratic progress in the Arab world, he "congratulate[d] the people of Yemen on their landmark presidential election." It was indeed something of a "landmark" when a president who had served continuously for twenty-eight years, and who had reversed his own pledge not to stand for office again in response to Soviet-style engineering of public appeals, was declared "reelected" with 78 percent of the vote. Perhaps it was something of a milestone as well when observers from the restrained EU mission declared the election to have had "important shortcomings," such as voter intimidation, underage voting, and violations of ballot secrecy.[42] It may also have been newsworthy when the opposition rejected the outcome of the election as illegal, alleging that the reelected president had ordered the brazen theft of 2 million votes from his principal opponent.[43] But was this the kind of "landmark" to be celebrated by a president of the United States in a speech that recommitted his country "to the advance of freedom and democracy"? What could the Yemeni people, cheated of the encouragement of a much closer election result, make of Bush's remarks when he insisted to dissidents everywhere, "We will always stand for your freedom"?

For the time being, the moment of democratic reform in the Arab world has passed. With the exception of a few countries—particularly Morocco—tentative (and probably never very sincere) democratization has been reversed, and opposition forces have been contained or crushed. Publics are sullen, alienated, and disillusioned. As Jafar al-Shayeb, a member of one of Saudi Arabia's powerless municipal councils, told the *New York Times* in 2007, "There is a state of depression and lack of trust, or faith, among the Arab masses in the regimes and little belief that these elections can lead to the change aspired to."[44] Moreover, as elections become again little more than a superficial legitimating ritual, Arab publics are staying at home.

In Egypt, the political opposition is in disarray and demoralized, not only by the speed and ruthlessness with which the regime has shut it down but by what it regards bitterly and justifiably as a betrayal by the United States. The Mubarak regime appears stable and secure, not a pharaoh tamed. However, stability has been purchased at the price of public alienation and the draining of the already shallow reservoir of the regime's legitimacy. One of Egypt's most astute social scientists, Amr Hamzawy, who is now a scholar at the Carnegie Endowment for International Peace in Washington, D.C., observes, "The regime risks its own stability by slamming the door in the face of a popular force that has grown increasingly committed to peaceful political opposition." That force, the Muslim Brotherhood, has become the only broadly viable political opposition in the country. While the Brotherhood reiterates its commitment to nonviolence and to democratic norms, in the face of severe repression, dissident members might return to violent methods, "as they did in the 1980s and 1990s, following similar blows. The assassination of Mubarak's predecessor, Anwar al-Sadat, is a stark reminder of the tragic repercussions of domestic unrest."[45] Ominously, the regime must confront this crisis of legitimacy alongside a succession struggle between the army and security apparatus and the party controlled by Mubarak's son, Gamal. If Gamal Mubarak is handed the office by his father, Egyptian analysts and activists fear that he would stand as a weak president, dependent on the security services and unable to contain their repression, much less liberalize anew.[46]

It helps stability to have a hereditary monarchy with some modicum of historic legitimacy rather than the kind of faux hereditary succession that Mubarak is poised to engineer. In Jordan, the succession of King Abdullah to the throne went smoothly enough to preserve the stability of the monarchy—but not to encourage democratic change. "Jordan's history shows that threatening regional scenarios undermine the reform agenda" by empowering the security apparatus and weakening advocates of democratic opening.[47] Wedged between the two most troubled and violent territories in the Middle East—Iraq and Palestine—the Jordanian state feels threatened and besieged. Since 2004, roughly a million Iraqis have fled to Jordan, a small country with only 6 million people, adding to the refugee strains of the Israeli-Palestinian conflict. In this context, the Jordanian regime's instinct is to clench its fist, and Europe and the United States have responded by deferring embarrassing political questions and pouring in more aid to the one remaining stable pillar between Israel and Iran. Since Jordan signed its historic peace treaty with Israel in 1994, the United States has provided about $225 million a year in annual economic aid, adding another $200 million per year in military support after the start of the Iraq War.[48] During the period, Jordan became the first Arab country to sign a free trade agreement with the United States. Europe, too, sees Jordan's authoritarian monarchy as a bulwark against regional instability and Islamic radicalism, and has made Jordan the second-largest recipient of EU assistance per capita after Palestine, with over a billion dollars in aid since 1997. As long as Jordan's neighborhood is in such turmoil and its moderation and stability are so prized by generous donors, democratic reform can merely remain a matter of vague rhetoric.

DEMOCRATIC PROSPECTS

The obstacle to democracy in the Middle East is not the culture, or the religion of Islam, or the society, but rather the regimes themselves and the region's distinctive geopolitics. Until the first region-wide "Arab Barometer" is available for study in 2009, a few, more limited public opinion surveys present a hopeful preliminary picture of the support for democracy in the Arab world.[49]

For example, at least 84 percent of people surveyed in Jordan and Palestine in 2006, in Iraq and Algeria in 2004, and in Egypt and Morocco between 2000 and 2002 agreed that "despite its problems, democracy is the best form of government." The proportions topped 90 percent in Jordan, Egypt, and Morocco.[50] And this belief in democracy cuts across demographic categories; according to the University of Michigan professor Mark Tessler, "there is almost no difference in the views of men and women, of better-educated and less-educated respondents, and of respondents of differing ages."[51] When asked in 2006 if democracy is a Western form of government, incompatible with Islam, two-thirds of those surveyed in Jordan and in Palestine disagreed.

To be sure, when Arab citizens say they support democracy, it is not necessarily secular democracy they have in mind. In each of the Arab countries surveyed, there is a fairly even division of opinion on whether Islam should play an important role in politics. In Jordan in 2006, the 85 percent who believe democracy is the best system split almost evenly between those who agree "men of religion should have influence in government decisions" and those who disagree. The 15 percent nondemocratic population is also split down the middle between religious and secular orientation. A virtually identical pattern was found in Iraq in 2004, with roughly similar patterns in Algeria and Palestine, as well. Supporters of democracy in these four societies more or less evenly divide between those who favor a secular democracy and those who favor an Islamic democracy (though it is not entirely clear what respondents mean by that preference). Tessler's statistical analysis of the recent Jordan survey shows that personal religiosity does not have much impact in shaping commitment to democracy; rather it is education that matters. And the most powerful predictor for a political Islamist orientation: a feeling of powerlessness. Political and economic problems, including low confidence in political institutions, are also associated with support for political Islam.[52]

Better and more democratic governance thus appears the best long-term strategy—and quite possibly the only one—for countering the growth of radical Islam.

Significantly, even as Arab authoritarian states have thrown the pendulum back to political closure, many elements of civil society—intellectuals, NGOs, dissident bloggers, and even moderate Islamist activists—have labored to keep democratic reform on the national agenda. The danger of the moment is that when the path of peaceful participation and dialogue (however limited and incremental) is closed, many Islamists—who constitute the best organized and most powerful opposition in almost every Arab country—might turn to violence, as they did in Algeria in 1992. States like Egypt, Jordan, and Saudi Arabia remain strong, resourceful, and proficient when it comes to repression. But as dissent is shut down and political reform is deferred for longer and longer, the legitimacy deficit becomes more acute, the young become more alienated and radicalized, and eventually the regime becomes more vulnerable to violent uprising in the wake of a performance failure, such as a sudden economic downturn or a miscalculated upsurge in brutal repression.

Arab authoritarian regimes will likely at some point revive political reform just enough to get by, renewing the cycles of "tactical liberalization" much like a pair of lungs, breathing in and out but never permanently expanding. A true shift in that stilted paradigm will not come until there is a transformation in the regional security context—a significant easing of the Israeli-Palestinian conflict, if not actual peace, and some measure of stabilization in Lebanon, Palestine itself, and most of all Iraq. Such broad improvement would provoke three changes: First, it would ease the deep fear of losing control that causes regimes to tighten their authoritarian grips. Second, it would remove a prominent excuse that regimes utilize to justify political stagnation and oppression to both local publics and external ones. And third, it would greatly diminish the strategic anxieties that cause the United States and Europe to back off from applying serious pressure for democratic reform.

It is not only in the Arab Middle East where democratic hopes have been crushed in the last few years. Nowhere in the Middle East has the repression of democratic hopes and movements been more vicious than in Iran. During the first few years of the two-term presidency of Mohammed Khatami (1997–2005), the Islamic Republic began to decompress. Political and civic pluralism widened, as "more than 200 independent newspapers and magazines were established representing a diverse array of viewpoints."[53] Internal debate and international exchanges accelerated, political pluralism increased, and the oppressive social restrictions of the Islamic Republic were loosened. But Khatami never held the predominant reins of power; those remained in the hands of unelected conservative theocrats, beginning with the supreme leader Ali Khameni and the Council of Guardians, which can veto legislation and disqualify candidates for office. Beginning with the 2000 elections, the hard-line clerical establishment, which controls the judiciary and the state security apparatus, struck back. It closed reformist newspapers and think tanks, vetoed political and economic reforms, and jailed hundreds of liberal journalists and student and civic activists (subjecting some to severe torture). Although Khatami was reelected in 2001, it was a hollow victory for a humbled president, leaving advocates of civil society deeply disillusioned. The reform movement retreated and fragmented. Hard-line elements swept the 2003 municipal elections and then won the 2004 parliamentary elections "after the Council of Guardians rejected the candidacies of most reformist politicians, including scores of incumbents."[54] Finally, in 2005, the regime reactionaries managed to maneuver and manipulate their stealth candidate, Mahmoud Ahmadinejad, into the presidency by disqualifying the most popular reform candidates. After attempting to rally the wider Muslim world with Holocaust denials and a vow to "wipe Israel off the map," Ahmadinejad proceeded to crack down on the modest political and social liberalization of the Khatami years.

In Iran, the suffocation of democratic aspirations has come with a unique twist. In contrast to the Arab world, where secular ruling establishments have lost political legitimacy and Islamist forces constitute the main alternative, it is the reactionary Islamists who constitute the corrupt and brutally oppressive ruling establishment, illegitimate and even despised in the hearts of most Iranians. And it is the disaffected majority—some of it purely secular, some of it privately religious but fatally disillusioned with the system of *Velayat Faqih* (the "guardianship of Islamic jurists")—that is liberal, prodemocratic, and thus even pro-American. In this respect, Iran has a unique advantage in establishing democracy in the short term: the necessary transition from Islamic utopianism (and before that Marxist utopianism) to liberal realism and skepticism has already been made by the bulk of intellectual and civil society. When the works being read in a country are authored by classical liberals like Isaiah Berlin, Karl Popper, and Hannah Arendt, the philosophical seeds of a democratic revolution are planted. The ideological transition is epitomized by the regime's most famous dissident, a "Revolutionary Guardsman turned investigative journalist,"[55] Akbar Ganji, whose eighty-day hunger strike in 2005, near the end of his six-year imprisonment, adopted the methods of Gandhian nonviolent resistance and posed a significant moral and political challenge to the regime. Ganji was willing to pay a price but was just as determined that the regime should also pay a price—which meant striking while the world was watching.[56]

Over the nearly three decades of the Islamic Republic, many other Iranians, most unknown to the West, have resisted the regime and paid dearly for it. In the midst of a consolidation of extreme conservative domination, it is easy to believe that their struggle has been in vain, but that is a highly questionable conclusion. Despite the boom in world oil prices, Ahmadinejad has so mismanaged the economy that the Iranian stock market has sharply declined in value during his presidency. "In a June 2006 open letter, 50 prominent Iranian economists accused the president of unsettling the investment climate, pursuing inflationary policies, opening the floodgate to imports and implementing misguided interventionist policies based on the faulty premise that there will be no end to oil money."[57] Officially, unemployment stood at 15 percent in 2007, but in urban areas it may have been double that level. Economic growth has been sluggish, unable to generate the many hundreds of thousands of jobs needed each year just to keep up with the staggeringly young population—two-thirds of which is under age thirty-five—that is trying to enter the workforce. Some 40 percent of the population is below the poverty line, and inflation is running in double digits, "outstripping wage increases."[58] The problems are deeply structural. The economy must struggle against the huge drag of "a bloated, inefficient state sector, over-reliance on the oil sector, and statist policies that create major distortions throughout,"[59] including massive subsidies of basic consumer goods that drain away investment from more productive purposes. The oil industry alone is in need of tens of billions of dollars each year in foreign investment that it cannot attract.

In many respects, the revolutionary regime in Iran resembles another revolutionary utopian regime that was breaking down from within during the 1980s: the Soviet Union. Belief in the ideology is gone. Corruption is rampant. The economy does not work and survives temporarily on natural resources, while massive subsidies rob future viability. The country is isolated from international capital flows. What is different in Iran is that the regime was never fully able to establish totalitarian control, and there remains considerable pluralism in various niches of society: "more than 8,000 NGOs continue to function; human rights lawyers are battling the state; select relatively independent media outlets are still in business,"[60] and over eighty thousand Iranian bloggers are daily challenging or debating the system.[61] Moreover, the conservative religious establishment and its repressive arms (such as the Revolutionary Guard and the paramilitary Basijis) are divided into complex factions as never before. While the regime seems strategically self-confident enough to defy the United States and the United Nations in seeking nuclear weapons, it runs great risks of further international sanction and isolation in doing so. And it faces serious dangers in its own strategic environment. With extensive Kurdish, Azeri, Arab, and other ethnic minorities—and Persians constituting barely half the population—the regime is vulnerable to serious destabilization should Iraq implode. As the Hoover Institution's Iranian American historian and democratic intellectual Abbas Milani argues, "The regime is tactically strong but strategically vulnerable," lacking—as the Soviet Union did—a long-term plan for its stabilization and renewal.[62] What the opposition lacks is leadership and organization, but some of that is poised to emerge from the battered but unbowed student and worker movements. The regime, in short, is brutal but fragile. If the United States avoids a military confrontation that would give the failing Islamic leadership a new political life, the profound contradictions are bound to catch up with it sooner or later.

Still, the best prospect for serious democratic reform in the Arab world today appears to lie in the country farthest away from its burning cauldrons, Morocco. Like Jordan and Bahrain, Morocco saw the succession to the throne in 1999 of a much younger and more politically modern new king following the death of his often severely repressive father, King Hassan II, who reigned for thirty-eight years. During the last decade of King Hassan's rule, constitutional and political reforms gave Morocco the most vibrant party system and the most meaningful parliament of any Arab monarchy, but real power remained a monopoly of the monarchy. The ascension of thirty-six-year-old King Mohammed VI ushered in a new era of political liberalization. King Hassan's feared interior minister was dismissed, thousands of political prisoners were released, and exiled opposition figures returned home. The 2002 parliamentary elections and 2003 municipal elections "were judged to be the most democratic since independence" was won from France in 1956.[63] Early in 2004, King Mohammed inaugurated the Equity and Reconciliation Commission to document human rights abuses under his father's regime and to compensate victims. The commission, which included former political prisoners, did not allow victims to identify their abusers, but in holding open hearings "officially recognizing state responsibility for human rights violations" and then paying compensation, the body charted a new path for human rights in the Arab world.[64] Later that year, with the king's support, Morocco reformed its personal status law to improve the social and family rights of women.

Today, "Morocco competes with Lebanon as the most open Arab country, while being [much] more stable."[65] There is more political pluralism in the electoral process, greater rights for women, more media freedom, and more space for criticism and initiative in civil society than in any other Arab country save for Lebanon (and in terms of electoral pluralism, Iraq). However, while reforms have liberalized political life and improved human rights, they have not altered the fundamental distribution of power. "A veritable shadow government of royal advisers keeps an eye on the operations of all ministries and government departments."[66] Mainstream party politicians and even many actors in civil society are constrained through the vast "informal system of clientelistic networks" that radiates down from the monarchy.[67] In this sense, Morocco is not much different from the typical Arab state. The power of the king is still unchecked; what he gives politically he can take away at any time. When the country was rocked by a series of suicide bombings killing forty-five people in Casablanca in May 2003, a harsh antiterror law was quickly adopted, "and thousands were immediately imprisoned and sentenced."[68]

If political liberalization is to extend beyond fragile improvements for human rights, women's rights, and civic and political space—to the actual democratization of power and thus the constitutional limitation of the monarchy—the initiative will have to come from below, most of all from the political parties.[69] But the traditional left and liberal parties, though they enjoy much stronger support than their kin elsewhere in the Arab world, are co-opted and wary of the larger public backing enjoyed by the Islamists.[70] Their tendency, as in Egypt, is to accept the role the authoritarian regime gives them rather than join Islamists in demands for democratic change. Genuine democratic reform thus requires "the emergence of independent political forces that the king can neither suppress nor co-opt."[71] That means the traditional secular parties must democratize their own internal structures and rejuvenate their stagnant leaderships, and the moderate Islamist party, the Justice and Development Party (or PJD), must join them rather than let itself be pulled into an alliance with the monarchy after it demonstrates its growing political support in elections.

Morocco highlights the common challenge of all Arab authoritarian regimes that carefully calibrate and periodically recalibrate the balance between liberalization and repression. Are these regimes, and the organized secular forces that have been granted varying degrees of status in them, willing to risk a redistribution of power that would inevitably mean a larger political role for Islamist forces? And will they ever summon the vision and self-confidence to negotiate with more moderate Islamists (those willing to commit to the democratic rules of the game) a new political dispensation? The September 2007 elections (which were considered reasonably free and fair) seemed to suggest that Islamists do not necessarily fill political openings, as the PJD scored very modest gains. But with a record low voter turnout of 37 percent (and with many voters spoiling their ballots in protest), the real lesson may be that voters want real power and real change.

There are a number of reasons why an enlightened ruling elite could be tempted to consider genuine democratic reform if the costs of resisting it were to rise considerably due to political pressure from below. For now, harder-line Islamists to the right of the PJD remain outside the system, limiting the hazards of opening up power. But poverty, inequality, and urban unemployment (at 20 percent) continue to breed disenchantment and could feed a deeper political radicalization. The modest scope of reform to date has failed to curb rampant corruption, which saps the country's development potential and its appeal to foreign investors. And Western aid and investment might pour much more effusively into an Arab country that was visibly moving toward democracy, transparency, and rule of law. The odds of such a transition in Morocco in the next few years are not good, but they are better than in any other Arab country. A transition scenario would be more likely if the United States and Europe were to facilitate the internal democratic "transformation of the major secular parties through pressure on their leaderships."[72] But more Western pressure is needed on the monarchy as well, and so is more open Western engagement with the PJD and other Islamists in the region who evince a commitment to democracy.

CROSSING THE RUBICON

For the United States and Europe, engaging Islamist parties and politicians is the toughest and riskiest step. It means granting them a measure of legitimacy and hence greater political credibility and electoral viability. Difficult determinations must be made as to which Islamist parties and groups are serious about democracy and which are posturing for tactical reasons.

Some of the major Islamist parties and movements of the Arab world show signs of serious movement toward pragmatism and tolerance. Since the mid-1990s, Egypt's Muslim Brotherhood—the oldest of the contemporary Islamist movements, dating back to 1928—has repeatedly revised its public doctrines, political strategies, and policy orientations. In the process, it has established, reaffirmed, or made more explicit its commitment to such core democratic principles as nonviolence, civic freedoms, popular sovereignty, separation of powers, political pluralism, free and fair elections as the only basis for the transfer of power, and the human rights of women and Copts, Egypt's Christian minority.[73] Even many fiercely secular opponents of the Mubarak regime, such as the liberal sociologist and civic activist Saad Eddin Ibrahim, perceive significant, if incomplete, democratic progression.[74] Jordan's Islamic Action Front has taken similar steps "toward an acceptance of the foundational aspects of democratic life."[75]

Yet, some of these Islamist movements, including the Muslim Brotherhood, remain ambiguous about their beliefs and intentions in a number of areas, such as the relative weight and imperative of the sharia (Islamic law), the rejection of violence against the state of Israel (and acceptance of its peace treaties with Egypt and Jordan), the extent of tolerance for non-Islamist options (that Islam may be "one solution . . . but not the only solution"), and the extent of commitment to individual liberties and the rights of women and religious minorities.[76] Islamist movements also need to clarify whether they are willing to accept pluralism among Muslims in interpreting Islam. Where, as with the Brotherhood in Egypt, Islamists are banned from establishing a political party and combine "missionary and political activities in one institutional structure," the ambiguity is more acute, as religious dogma hampers political pragmatism.[77] If Islamists want domestic and international secular support for their full incorporation into the political process, they will have to do more to clarify these gray areas. Egypt's Muslim Brotherhood, for example, must be willing to accept laws adopted through democratic procedures, even if they are deemed to violate the sharia. It must express its readiness to separate electoral and party activity from the religious movement, and to organize a new party (when allowed) by democratic and transparent means. The latter would necessitate a sweeping transformation of an organization that remains autocratically dominated by an unelected old guard. And it must commit more unambiguously to the universal and equal citizenship of Copts, the basic rights of women, the rights of individuals as codified in international conventions, and respect for the peace treaty with Israel.[78]

It is unlikely that continued evolution toward these liberal principles would be encouraged if Islamist movements were shunned by the West and isolated and oppressed by their own regimes. Rather, large swaths of the Islamist movements would draw the lesson that moderation is fruitless and that radical methods are their only hope. After studying and engaging nonviolent Islamist movements in a number of Arab countries, the Carnegie Endowment's scholars and partners find, "In all mainstream Islamist movements today, there are tensions between open-minded, often younger members who think the situation requires new tactics and the old guard," wedded to more rigid ideology and tactics. In many Arab countries, they argue, "the outcome of this struggle will determine the future of political reform."[79] If moderate Islamist parties like the PJD in Morocco and the still-unregistered Wasat Party (which split off from the Muslim Brotherhood) in Egypt are to prevail in their more patient, flexible, and democratic approach, they will need to be able to send clear signals to Islamic constituencies that moderation yields tangible gains in political inclusion and democratic empowerment.

To isolate Islamist parties and organizations means, in essence, to endorse the status quo of political stagnation in the Arab world—for there is no way that democratization can proceed in any Arab country today without finding some measure of accommodation with at least some substantial segment of political Islam. The goal must be to draw these parties into a process of democratic elections, democratic governance, opposition responsibilities, and pluralistic coexistence so that they are forced to respond to demands from their constituencies for real achievements in governance as opposed to mere ideology and rhetoric. When political parties have to assume responsibility for passing legislation, crafting compromises, creating jobs, and picking up the trash, it has a leavening effect. As it has elsewhere historically in the past two centuries, the practice of democracy, however tactical and insincere at first, could induce in the Arab world a process of "habituation," in which "politicians and citizens learn from the successful resolution of some issues to place their faith in the new rules and to apply them to new issues," widening the political trust, accommodation, and pragmatism that are ultimately necessary to sustain democracy.[80]

This does not require the relinquishment, particularly by the monarchies, of all levers of power at once. It is quite conceivable that Arab monarchies could pass through various stages of power sharing, retaining for a while some significant authority over national security as well as the kinds of informal power and checks of the Thai monarchy and military in the 1980s or the Turkish military over the past several decades. But with governments emerging out of democratically elected parliaments, rather than through rigged elections as in Egypt or out of royal choice as in Jordan and Morocco, genuine democratization could occur. Secular parties and social forces would be compelled to awake from their comfortable, co-opted stupor, formulate appealing policy platforms, and build grassroots political organizations that could challenge Islamist parties. Islamists would have to take responsibility for ruling—or opposing. At least in certain sectors and in certain cities, the practical burdens of governing and of forming legislative coalitions might well induce the development of Muslim democratic parties modeled after the Justice and Development Party (AKP) in Turkey or the Christian Democratic parties in Germany and Italy. It would be foolhardy to assume that the results would be as consistent with liberal democracy as in Western Europe or even Turkey under the AKP (whose long-term intentions are still questioned by many liberal Turks). And it remains to be seen whether even a few of the Arab world's Islamist parties (a diverse lot) can evolve, or have already evolved, from instrumentalists, using democracy "as a tool or tactic [to gain] the power to build an Islamic state," to "Muslim Democrats," who "view politics with a pragmatic eye" and "do not seek to enshrine Islam in politics."[81] So far, there is no clear sign of the emergence of a "Muslim Democrat" Party in the Arab world, as such parties have emerged in varying forms and degrees in Turkey, Pakistan, and Indonesia. But one cannot know what evolution Islamic-oriented parties are capable of until they are tested with some degree of power. In this respect, what happens to the PJD in Morocco may well have much wider implications in the region. Just as the repression of the FIS in Algeria created an ugly downward spiral in the Arab world, the inclusion of the PJD into a gradually democratizing Moroccan polity might eventually generate felicitous implications.

The plain fact is that Arab countries will not achieve democracy without Islamist participation, and possibly some period of Islamist leadership in governance. The challenge for these civil societies will be to constrain a democratically elected, Islamist-led government with effective constitutional checks and balances, so that Islamists, once elected, cannot barricade themselves in power. Such checks and balances cannot be constructed after the fact. To the extent that the capacity and independence of the judiciary, the parliament, the electoral commission, the audit agency, the central bank, and other institutions of horizontal accountability are firmly established and constitutionally embedded well before the gates of electoral competition are thrown wide open, the risks of democratization can be considerably reduced. In that event, what Islamist parties would be competing for is not the absolute control of Arab governments but properly constrained democratic power.

If an evolution from political Islam to Muslim democracy is to be possible, dialogue will be necessary—between the regimes and their oppositions, both secular and Islamist; between Islamists and secularists within Arab politics and civil society; and between the Islamists and the major Western governments, particularly the United States. For Islamists to gain or retain their seats at the table, they will have to commit to democratic principles and rules and clarify where they stand on secular freedoms. But the United States must also clarify where it stands, and whether it means it when it says—as George W. Bush did in his second inaugural address— "The United States will not ignore your oppression, or excuse your oppressors. When you stand for liberty, we will stand with you."[82]

PART THREE

THE PATH TO DEMOCRATIC RENEWAL

13

MAKING DEMOCRACIES WORK

Since 1974, democracy has struggled through several phases. After the tentative trend toward democracy in the late 1970s and early 1980s, the democratic transitions gathered momentum, reaching a crescendo with the collapse of communism in Eastern Europe and the former Soviet Union. By the early 1990s, even the poorest countries of postcolonial Africa—those then considered the least hospitable terrain for democracy—were joining the wave. There was a sense of euphoria about global democratic gains and prospects. If democracy had spread so far so fast, why could it not spread everywhere?

I shared this sense of joy over democratic breakthroughs and experienced on the ground the hope, resolve, and triumph with freedom's gains. Indeed, for more than two decades, I have argued for the open-ended possibilities of democracy—including the possibility, which I advance in this book—that the *whole world can become democratic*. However, it is not enough for the whole world to *become* democratic. The more consequential questions are, can those countries that become democracies remain democracies, and can they achieve a level of democracy that their people judge as worth having?

As I looked more carefully in the early 1990s at how the world's new democracies were actually performing, I encountered a worrisome development, which a number of other social scientists as well as civic organizations and human rights activists were noting as well. Many of the new democracies were performing very poorly and were in fact quite "illiberal," if they could be called democracies at all.[1] Yes, they had competitive elections, even real uncertainty about which party would win power, and even alternation in power, but for much of the population, democracy was a shallow or even invisible phenomenon. What many (or most) citizens actually experienced was a mix of distressed governance: abusive police forces, domineering local oligarchies, incompetent and indifferent state bureaucracies, corrupt and inaccessible judiciaries, and venal, ruling elites contemptuous of the rule of law and accountable to no one but themselves.[2] As a result, people—especially in the bottom strata of society, which in many new democracies comprised the majority—were citizens only in name. There were few meaningful channels of participation and voice open to them. There were elections, but they were contests between corrupt, clientelistic parties that served popular interests only in name. There were parliaments and local governments, but they did not represent or respond to broad constituencies. There was a constitution, but not constitutionalism—a commitment to the principles and restraints in that hallowed charter. There was democracy in a formal sense, but people were still not politically free. As a result, there was widespread public skepticism, even cynicism and disillusionment, toward "democracy."

As I observed in the first two chapters, there is good reason to question whether such a shallow rendition of democracy can legitimately be termed anything more than a *competitive authoritarian regime*. But whether a regime is competitive authoritarian or merely a badly governed, low-quality democracy, the challenge remains: For democratic structures to endure—and to be worthy of endurance—they must be more than a shell. They must have substance, quality, and meaning. They must, over time, hear people's voices, engage their participation, tolerate their protests, protect their freedoms, and respond to their needs.

In the coming decade, the fate of democracy will not be determined by the scope of its expansion to the remaining dictatorships of the world. Unfortunately, too many of these regimes have learned practical if ugly lessons on how to frustrate democratic change—and how to cooperate with one another in doing so. The odds of a great many of the autocracies in Asia, the former Soviet Union, and the Middle East becoming electoral democracies (not to mention liberal democracies) before 2015 are unfortunately small. Most are strong states with efficient and ruthless security apparatuses. They have learned the dangers of allowing more freedom for civil society and more space for dissent, not to mention more serious political opposition. They have watched as political liberalization has led—in Mexico, Senegal, Serbia, Georgia, Ukraine, Kenya, and elsewhere—to the "accident" of the ruling party being toppled from power. In most of the former Soviet Union—especially Belarus and Central Asia, and most likely Russia itself—and in most of the Arab and authoritarian Asian states, the best path toward democratic transition, through gradual liberalization, appears to be largely closed in the *near* term. Some of these regimes might collapse because of a sudden crisis or a split within the ruling ranks, but in the near term this might usher in a new brand of authoritarian rule rather than democracy.

Certainly, real prospects for democratic transitions in the next decade do exist. They reside in regional neighborhoods where democracy dominates or is substantially present (Latin America, South and Southeast Asia, and parts of Africa) and in regimes that are already somewhat open and competitive (Venezuela, Malaysia, Kyrgyzstan, Nigeria, and a number of other African regimes) or that are institutionally weak, internally divided, and crisis-ridden (Pakistan, Iran, and Zimbabwe). Among the Arab states, Morocco will remain the best placed to negotiate a path to democracy. And at this writing, Nepal is in the midst of a democratic transition, and Thailand's military regime seems likely to return power to civilian, elected rule within a year or two—albeit with a constitution less democratic than the one it toppled.

If recent history is any guide, the next decade will bring some surprises. Communism in Cuba might falter once Fidel Castro finally dies—or more likely, once the United States finally comes to its senses and lifts its self-defeating embargo of that island. Even in the context of a supremely strong and self-confident state, politics in Singapore might open up toward real competition once the founding ruler and "minister mentor," Lee Kuan Yew, passes from the scene. Smarter and better coordinated foreign aid might tempt or pressure many aid-dependent African countries to gamble on real democracy. But the surprises could well come from breakdowns of new democracies, accelerating the political undertow of the recent democratic recession.

Overall, then, it seems unlikely that the number of democracies in the world will increase significantly in the next decade. Neither is it likely—in the context of a continuing "global war on terror" and a deepening crisis in Iraq and the surrounding Middle East—that the United States and its democratic allies will use precious geopolitical leverage to promote democracy in troubled areas. Without such a forward-leaning approach, most of the countries with poor prospects for democratization will remain undemocratic.

Beyond the next decade, the prospects for renewed global expansion of democracy will depend primarily on three factors. One will be gradual economic development that lifts levels of education, information, and autonomous citizen power and organization. The second will be the gradual integration of countries into a global economy, society, and political order in which democracy remains the dominant value and the most attractive type of political system. These two conditions, obviously closely related, would produce rising pressures for democratization in Asia (particularly China and Vietnam), in Iran (if the regime does not collapse sooner), and in parts of the Arab world (if the region's colossal security pressures can be eased). For democracy to maintain its attraction and regain its momentum as a universal value, the established democracies of "the West"—most of all, the United States—must keep from losing their heads, and their freedoms, as they struggle against diffuse terrorist threats.

As for the third factor that will determine whether democracy booms again as it did in the 1980s and '90s: before democracy can spread farther, it must take deeper root where it has already sprouted. The new democracies that have come into being since 1974 must demonstrate that they can solve governance problems and meet citizens' expectations for freedom, justice, a better life, and a fairer society. If democracies do not work better to contain crime and corruption, generate economic growth, relieve economic inequality, and secure justice and freedoms, sooner or later, people will lose faith and embrace (or tolerate) other—nondemocratic—alternatives. The new democracies of recent decades must become consolidated, so that all levels of society are committed lastingly and unconditionally to democracy as the best form of government and come to believe in the norms of the democratic constitution. In other words, for democracies to endure, their leaders and citizens must internalize the spirit of democracy. If many new and unstable democracies do not last, the challenge before us will not be extending the democratic tide but instead managing the implosion of democracy, what Samuel Huntington would call the *third reverse wave*. It is a basic principle of any military or geopolitical campaign that at some point an advancing force or cause must consolidate its gains before it conquers more territory than it can possibly hold.

Related to this is a second reason why the near-term fate of democracy will mainly be determined in countries that have only become democratic in the last decade or two. To remain a global value and destination, democracy must be seen to be a viable model. It is still the case, as Huntington noted in documenting the *third wave,* that the most powerful demonstration effects are regional ones.[3] Is it plausible to imagine that China will democratize if democracy in Taiwan sinks deeper into political polarization and a crisis over national identity? Or to imagine that Vietnam (and eventually Laos, Cambodia, and Burma) will move toward democracy if it rots in Indonesia? What prospect does democracy have in the former Soviet world if it does not strengthen in Central and Eastern Europe? How will the blatantly authoritarian half of Africa democratize if the continent's emerging democracies, beginning with South Africa, cannot make democracy work? Can democracy remain viable in West Africa if Nigeria descends into military rule, political chaos, or—God forbid—state collapse?

To be sure, the gains for freedom in the world have been real and diffuse. But the celebration of democracy's triumph has been premature. Outside of the long-industrialized democracies, only a few countries have achieved a stable and liberal democracy of reasonably high quality. And astonishingly, as I have shown, even in many of these countries that we take for granted as democratic success stories—Poland, Hungary, Chile, Taiwan, Korea, South Africa, Ghana—there are real problems of governance and deep pockets of disaffection. If we take as our standard of democratic consolidation the presumption of *irreversibility*—that it is difficult to envisage, and indeed few citizens do envisage, the possibility of democracy breaking down—then we can probably declare the ten new EU entrants from the postcommunist world, along with Taiwan, Korea, Chile, Uruguay and arguably Mexico, Brazil, and Argentina, as newly consolidated democracies. But that is a small number from among the eighty or so post-1974 democracies in the world today.[4] And if we establish a higher bar for democratic consolidation, involving a broad, deep national commitment to democracy as the best form of government, then surprisingly few of the new democracies can be said to be truly secure.

A comparative list of the world's "at risk" democracies would have to count most of the twenty-two democracies with populations over one million in Latin America and the Caribbean; six of the ten Asian democracies (including the Philippines, Indonesia, Sri Lanka, and Bangladesh);

all of the non-EU post-Soviet democracies; and virtually all of the roughly twenty-three democracies in Africa, save for the oldest ones, Botswana and Mauritius. Any such list is inevitably judgmental and fuzzy at the borders, but by my count it amounts to more than fifty states. If we put aside industrialized democracies like Japan, the new European Union members, and the liberal democratic microstates of the Caribbean and Pacific islands, over three-quarters of the remaining democracies in the world can be seen as incomplete, insecure, and subject to reversal.[5] Three decades into the third wave of democratization, this is a sobering fact.

The most urgent democratic task for the next decade is to change this reality. To do so, we must understand the reasons for poor democratic performance and develop an agenda for reform.

WHY NEW DEMOCRACIES PERFORM POORLY

Why are many third-wave democracies weak and troubled? As we have seen in the preceding chapters, they have poor governance, which generates poor policy performance and disillusioned citizens. Some states, like Turkey and Brazil, have seen improving governance and development performance. Some, like South Africa and Indonesia, have historically stronger states that have helped them cope with the posttransition challenges. But most of the "at risk" democracies suffer from stagnating or simply bad governance. Some appear so trapped in patterns of corrupt, abusive, personalistic rule that it is hard to see how they can survive as democracies without reform.

The problem in these states, as well as most of those that are not democratic, is that bad governance is not an aberration or an illness to be cured. It is—as the economists Douglass North, John Wallis, and Barry Weingast trenchantly argue—a *natural state,* like the default position on a machine.[6] Historically, the natural tendency in human societies over ten thousand years of recorded history has not been to restrain power and submit it to the discipline of transparent laws and institutions and market competition. Rather, it has been to corner and monopolize power. Once political access is closed, power is used to restrict economic competition so as to generate rents that benefit the small minority of ruling elites over the broad bulk of the society. Such a "limited access order," or what I call a *predatory* system, can be stable if the ruling elites use some of the rents they collect to enforce and maintain political order, but it will not generate sustained economic development. Nor can it be compatible with a genuine democracy. In the long run, a stable and high-quality democracy needs to be embedded in an "open access order" featuring "systematic competition, entry, and mobility" in both the economic and political spheres.[7]

Open access can only be sustained in a corresponding culture and social structure, what the political scientist Robert Putnam calls the *civic community*.[8] In the model civic community, there is an abundance of social capital—"the trust, norms, and networks that can improve the efficiency of society by facilitating coordinated actions."[9] In a civic community, people trust one another, combine in many forms of association, and cooperate for larger, collective ends. Where they differ in beliefs and opinions, they mutually respect and tolerate their differences, and they feel some sense of attachment to the community or the nation that transcends their differences. Citizens see one another as political equals and believe in equality of opportunity, even though they recognize that perfect equality of outcomes can never be obtained. Relations among people are primarily horizontal: people come together as individuals with equal dignity, rights, and obligations; and this equality is embedded in the laws. Individuals are truly citizens; they have an interest in public issues and care about the welfare and progress of the community. In this sense, they are motivated at least to some degree by public-spiritedness. Like capitalism, the civic community is not fanciful, but consistent with the self-regarding impulses in human nature. Putnam writes:

> Citizens in the civic community are not required to be altruists. In the civic community, however, citizens pursue what Tocqueville termed "self-interest properly understood," that is, self-interest defined in the context of broader public needs, self-interest that is "enlightened" rather than "myopic," self-interest that is alive to the interests of others.[10]

They are "alive to the interests of others" in part because they are confident that most *other* citizens will behave in a similar way.

This confidence is not just rooted in a trusting civic culture. Citizens carry such confidence because there are strong, effective institutions of governance to induce and reward civic behavior. A culture of trust, cooperation, reciprocity, restraint, tolerance, and compromise cannot be sustained on a scale as large as the nation without supportive political institutions. People obey the law, pay their taxes, observe ethical standards, answer the call to jury duty, and otherwise serve the public good not *simply* because they are public-spirited but also because they believe others will be and because they know there is some penalty for failing to be. If it is somewhat discouraging to ponder that people would be less helpful toward one another without these enforcing institutions, there is also a hopeful corollary: just as the civic culture requires institutional support and nurturing, so a predatory culture of corruption and rent-seeking thrives in the absence of effective institutions and can be changed through the introduction of them.

The predatory society is the inverse of the civic community. First, there is no real community, no shared commitment to any common vision of the public good, and no respect for law. Behavior is cynical and opportunistic. Those who capture political power seek to monopolize it and the rents that flow from it. Thus, if there are competitive elections, these become a bloody zero-sum struggle where everything is at stake and no one can afford to lose. People ally with one another in the quest for power and privilege, but not as equals. Rather, relations are steeply hierarchical. Ordinary people are not truly citizens but rather clients of powerful patrons, who themselves serve as clients to more powerful patrons. Blatant inequalities in power and status cumulate into vertical chains of dependency and exploitation, secured by patronage and coercion. In a predatory society, officials feed on the state and the powerful prey on the weak. The rich extract wealth from the poor and deprive them of public goods. "Corruption is widely regarded as the norm," political participation is mobilized from above, civic engagement is meager, compromise is scarce, and "nearly everyone feels powerless, exploited, and unhappy."[11]

The masses of ordinary people at the bottom of a predatory society cannot cooperate with one another because they are trapped in fragmented, hierarchical networks and thus distrust one another. Very often, social fragmentation is reinforced by ethnic, linguistic, and other forms of identity cleavage that keeps the oppressed from collaborating and enables the privileged to rally ready political support. All too often, predatory elites mobilize ethnic tension or nationalism in order to direct public frustration and resentment away from their own exploitative behavior. Yet ethnic tensions and nationalist resentments have an independent origin, which is why elites often find such success when they inflame them. From Nigeria to the Congo, from Colombia to Kosovo, from Serbia to Sudan, ethnic violence, nationalist bloodletting, and civil war have been heavily mixed up with the corruption of cynical elites.

The predatory society cannot sustain democracy, for sustainable democracy requires constitutionalism, compromise, and respect for law. Neither can it generate sustainable economic growth, for that requires actors with financial capital to invest in productive activity. In the predatory society, people do not get rich through productive activity and honest risk taking; they get rich by manipulating power and privilege, by stealing from the state, by extracting from the weak, and by shirking the law. It is no wonder that predatory societies have weak, porous states that are prone to complete collapse, as has been Nigeria—one of the classic instances.

Political actors in the predatory society will use any means and break any rules in the quest for power and wealth. Politicians bribe electoral officials, beat up opposition campaigners, and assassinate opposing candidates. Presidents silence criticism and eliminate their opponents by legal manipulation, arrest, or murder. Ministers worry first about the monies they can collect and only second about whether the contracts they are signing have any value for the public. Legislators collect graft to vote for bills and to make or break governing coalitions. Military officers order weapons on the basis of how large the kickback will be. Soldiers and policemen extort rather than defend the public, and the line between the police and the criminals is a thin one, when it exists. The police do not enforce the law. Judges do not decide the law. Customs officials do not inspect the goods. Manufacturers do not produce, bankers do not invest, borrowers do not repay, and contracts do not get enforced. Every transaction is twisted to immediate advantage. Time horizons are extremely short because no one has confidence in the state and its future. Government warps into a criminal conspiracy, and organized crime penetrates politics and government.

I have painted an extreme portrait of the predatory society; the countries in trouble in the world fit this portrait to varying degrees. But those countries where order is decaying and the economy is stagnating are invariably much more predatory than civic. And the more predatory they are—the more rule is based on persons rather than laws and institutions—the more vulnerable democracy will be to corrosion.

OVERCOMING THE PREDATORY STATE

The triumph of democracy and the march to prosperity are largely a story of taming abuse of power, opening up access to political and economic markets, and binding the naturally predatory tendencies of rulers to impersonal, impartial rules and institutions. Several innovations are necessary in order to move a society from a state of predation and closure to one of openness and democracy.

First, horizontal relations of trust and cooperation must be constructed, ideally across ethnic and regional divides—to challenge elitist hierarchies and personal rule. This requires building a dense, vigorous civil society, with independent organizations, mass media, think tanks, and other networks that will generate social capital, foster civic norms, press public interests, raise citizen consciousness, break the bonds of clientelism, scrutinize government conduct, and lobby for good governance reforms.

Next, effective institutions of governance must be constructed to constrain the nearly unlimited discretion of rulers, to open their decisions and transactions to inspection, and to hold them accountable before the law, the constitution, and the public interest. This means building institutions of vertical and horizontal accountability. The premier institution of vertical accountability is a genuinely democratic election, in which citizens can evaluate the conduct of officials and replace those who do not perform. By this logic, state officials are not rulers to whom the people are subordinate; rather, they are agents of the people and must answer to them. Other effective agencies of vertical accountability include public hearings, citizen audits, and a freedom of information act. In complement, horizontal accountability invests some agencies of the state with the power and responsibility to monitor the conduct of other agencies, officials, or branches of government.[12] It requires "state agencies that are authorized and willing to oversee, control, redress, and/or sanction unlawful actions of other state agencies."[13] If horizontal instruments of accountability are to be effective, they must be independent of the government actors they are assigned to monitor, restrain, and if necessary, punish. These include judiciaries, parliamentary committees, public audits, ombudsmen, electoral commissions, and not least, countercorruption bodies. Where democracy functions inadequately, there are invariably weak and poorly performing agencies of horizontal accountability, and often tentative, compromised, and poorly resourced civil societies as well.

Third, poorly performing democracies need better, stronger, and more democratic institutions linking citizens not just to one another but also to the political process. Primarily, this means political parties, parliaments, and local governments. Of course, in all democracies, by definition, these institutions exist in a formal sense. But in shallow democracies, they constitute what the Carnegie Endowment scholar Thomas Carothers calls *feckless pluralism,* that is, political participation does not really amount to much except occasional voting because politics is so elite-dominated, corrupt, and unresponsive.[14] In such circumstances, the people are largely excluded from effective participation and representation of their interests. Power and resources are narrowly held, either by a dominant party— democratically in South Africa and Argentina, undemocratically in most of the former Soviet Union—or by multiple elite-based parties that either contest bitterly or, as they did in Venezuela before the Chávez revolution, collude but do not include. Here reform requires internal democratization of political parties by improving their transparency and accessibility and strengthening other representative bodies. External democratic assistance organizations, like those of the two U.S. political parties—the National Democratic Institute (NDI) and the International Republican Institute (IRI)—have been addressing the challenge of party building for two decades, but it has been hard to succeed in environments drenched in patron-client relations.[15]

Democratic bodies need to become valued and consolidated. Parliaments must grow more inclusive and effective. Often, it will help significantly if electoral systems and political institutions are redesigned, and constitutions amended, to decentralize power, manage ethnic and religious divisions, and generate incentives for accommodation.[16] Establishing civilian control over the military and intelligence agencies is essential, but often easier because of the competition among elites, and many new democracies have already made considerable progress on this front.[17]

In many badly performing democracies, there is the more general imperative of building the state: improving the technical skills, resources, professional standards, coherence, and organizational efficiency of the state so that it is better able to maintain security, establish authority, settle disputes, promulgate laws, collect taxes, enable markets, regulate commerce, manage the economy, develop infrastructure, and deliver services such as health, education, and water. A state must be able to perform these basic functions before it can effectively be democratic, as international actors have learned painfully when they have intervened to try to put failed states back together.[18] Well before the American-led invasions of Afghanistan and Iraq, or for that matter the international interventions in Bosnia and Kosovo, this lesson emerged from a comparison of democratic transitions in Latin America and postcommunist Europe in the 1970s through the early 1990s.[19] And as the political scientist Francis Fukuyama explains, a strong state does not necessarily mean a state that intervenes extensively in social and economic affairs. Rather, the ideal formula for democracy and development is a state that tackles some reasonably limited range of functions but performs them with high degrees of authority, capacity, and effectiveness.[20]

Finally, reforms must extend into the economic sphere, foremost with reforms generating a more open market economy in which it is possible to accumulate wealth through honest effort and initiative in the private sector—with the state playing a limited (and not primarily a productive) role. The wider the scope of state ownership of and control over economic life, the wider is the scope for rent seeking and control by abusive, predatory elites. "Legal and regulatory reforms that reduce administrative barriers to doing business serve to minimize incentives for corruption," while corporate governance programs to "inculcate values of [business] responsibility, transparency and accountability" can address the "supply side" of the corruption problem.[21] Strong guarantees of property rights, including the ability of small holders and informal sector workers to get title to their land and business property, set a broader institutional landscape that limits government corruption. Where state ownership is extensive, privatization may generate a more favorable context for democratic governance.

Yet, the privatization process can (and, in many cases, has) become a major outlet for corruption, which can seep into public life. This is why pure laissez-faire is hardly a formula for good governance and a good society. An effectively functioning market economy requires independent oversight of financial institutions, stock exchanges, and corporations for the same reasons that government itself must be monitored. Economic markets accumulate a variety of distortions that arise from inequities in power and information, and some degree of regulation—insulated from partisan political control—is necessary to level these inequalities, attenuate market failures, and ensure that private economic institutions operate within certain boundaries of fairness, responsibility, and transparency.

All of the above challenges must be met to some degree if a democracy is to work well (or even for very long at all). But there is a common, core problem in all badly governed democracies: pervasive corruption, cronyism, clientelism, and abuse of power. To change the way government works means changing the way politics and society work, changing the values and expectations of how people will behave when they acquire power and control over resources. That, in turn, requires sustained attention to how public officials utilize their offices. This is the fundamental challenge that *all* insecure democracies face.

CREATING HORIZONTAL ACCOUNTABILITY

Poorly performing democracies and even pseudodemocracies can point to their institutions of horizontal accountability—not just parliaments and judiciaries but anticorruption bodies and audit agencies—but in most cases, they are largely paper institutions. They do not work effectively to control corruption and tame abuses of power. To make a democracy effective, these institutions must be reformed and strengthened, restructured to fit together comprehensively, revitalized with more resources and authority, and insulated to ensure political independence and vigor.

Integrity and transparency in government are best achieved when state agencies of horizontal accountability interlock and overlap in a systemic fashion. Overlapping authority ensures that if one agency fails in its duty to expose, question, punish, and thus ultimately deter corrupt behavior, another may initiate the process. Interlocking authority allows different agencies to become reinforcing, so that, for example, an audit agency uncovers fraud, a countercorruption commission imposes civil penalties for it, the judiciary presses for criminal penalties, and an ombudsman stands by to investigate and report if any piece in the process breaks down or needs assistance. As Guillermo O'Donnell, who is in some ways the intellectual founder of the term and the field, argues, "Effective horizontal accountability is not the product of isolated agencies but of networks of agencies that include at their top—because that is where a constitutional legal system 'closes' by means of ultimate decisions—courts (including the highest ones) committed to such accountability."[22] Each overlapping and interlocking institution benefits from specific types of reforms to help sustain democracy.

THE LAW. Laws prohibiting bribery and misuse of public funds may be on the books but are underdeveloped and not taken seriously. Often, real reform means implementing or strengthening laws that bar conflicts of interest and requirements for public officials to make their own personal and family finances transparent. Actual corruption control requires that higher-level elected officials, political appointees, civil servants, military officers, and police officers declare their assets upon taking office, every year thereafter, and whenever their assets change in some significant, defined way. Declarations of assets should be filed with a countercorruption commission, but that is not enough, because without public inquiry and pressure, a co-opted or politically pliant commission may never investigate them. To ensure public confidence (and facilitate a complementary vertical accountability), asset declarations must be made publicly available for inspection by individuals, organizations, and the mass media. Ideally, the declarations of all top officeholders would be freely available for inspection on the Internet, enabling any knowledgeable party to call out undisclosed wealth.

Laws that give immunity to executive officials and members of the parliamentary body also need to be narrowed. It is one thing to give elected officials immunity against slander and other easily manipulated charges, but to give them sweeping immunity from criminal prosecution is to encourage abuse and even to invite criminals to run for office as a means of immunizing themselves from prosecution.

Beyond the sector of laws against violations of the public trust, effective rule of law requires a comprehensive and coherent legal code that is well documented and accessible to the public. Modernization of legal codes takes two forms: substantively, it revises, extends, prunes, and rationalizes the laws themselves, balancing the control of corruption and crime with the protection of civil liberties and property rights, and technically, it widens knowledge of the law and facilitates research on it by computerizing case administration procedures and legal codes and precedents.

FREEDOM OF INFORMATION. Malfeasance thrives in secrecy and obscurity. The more that government transactions and operations are transparent and visible, the more feasible it is to expose, deter, and contain corruption. For this reason, citizens must have the legal right to request and receive information on all functions and decisions of government that are not a matter of national security or an infringement on individual rights of privacy. In the fight against corruption, the public availability of information on government finance, procurement, and contracting is particularly important. Again, such information would ideally be posted on the Internet. In particular, all government procurement above a modest, defined level should be done through competitive bidding that is advertised on government Web sites.

ANTICORRUPTION BODIES. Control of corruption requires a specific body to scrutinize the conduct of public officials for signs of malfeasance. The body must have the authority not only to receive but also to monitor and verify the assets declarations of all high-level elected and appointed officials, including cabinet ministers, provincial governors, and members of parliament. In a large country like Nigeria, India, or Brazil, where significant power and resources reside at the state or provincial level, a counter-corruption commission must have offices and oversight at these lower levels of government. The commission must have the resources to annually investigate some significant percentage of officials' declarations on a random basis and the country's highest officials' declarations systematically.

Scrutiny must be comprehensive if it is to be effective and if the threat of detection is to be credible. Necessary staff include accountants, investigators, and lawyers trained in the ways that wealth is moved, accumulated, and hidden, along with computer specialists and other administrative support to back them. Not only does a countercorruption commission need a lot of well-trained staff, it needs to pay them enough to deter temptation and establish a high esprit de corps. There is no way to control corruption without spending money. Countercorruption bodies cannot succeed when there is a severe (and as often happens, deliberate) shortage of resources.[23]

Scrutiny, however, is not enough. If credible evidence of wrongdoing emerges, there must be the institutional means to try the suspected offender and impose punishment on the guilty. The single most crippling flaw in systems of corruption control is an inability to enforce this function free from interference by the highest levels of government. Since its creation in 2003, Nigeria's Economic and Financial Crimes Commission has enjoyed and utilized the power to bring charges for certain types of offenses, but because the body is appointed by the president, a strong suspicion has emerged that it is a weapon wielded against political opponents and restrained from punishing the president's allies. Critics may argue that trying public officials outside the normal judicial process undermines the rule of law. And in a democracy, the power to deny a person freedom through imprisonment should only be exercised through the judicial process. But it makes sense to enable a countercorruption commission to impose punishing civil penalties, including forfeiture of office and assets, through due process, even if the judicial system would be able to do this, and more.

OMBUDSMAN'S OFFICE. An ombudsman's office (which may go by diverse names, such as the office of the public protector, in South Africa) receives and investigates public complaints of abuses of office. Members of the public or the press should have a right—and indeed be encouraged—to bring evidence to the countercorruption commission if they believe a public official has misrepresented assets or abused power, but there needs to be a "redundant," overlapping channel available to the public in the case where the countercorruption commission does not seem to be doing its job or judges some abuse of power to lie outside its scope of authority. Members of the countercorruption commission should also know that they themselves could be exposed to public outcry if they fail to move aggressively on evidence of corruption.

The powers and functions of the office of the ombudsman have varied widely across democracies. In some countries, it is simply a mechanism to receive and investigate citizen complaints, while the Philippine constitution gives the ombudsman an explicit mandate to fight corruption through public assistance, prevention, investigation, and prosecution of suspect public officials.[24]

PUBLIC AUDITS. A dense, overlapping system of accountability requires that all major government bureaus, agencies, and ministries have their accounts regularly audited, and that they be open to inspection and evaluation of their performance more generally. To conduct these checks, each major government agency or bureau should have its own auditing office and inspector general. Periodic external audits are also essential. The government should have an office of the auditor general with the authority to conduct external audits on a periodic or random basis and responsibility for conducting an audit on any agency at any time when there is evidence of wrongdoing. One model is the U.S. Government Accountability Office (GAO), which is the investigative arm of, and is responsible to, the U.S. Congress, thus giving it substantial autonomy from executive-branch agencies. It "examines the use of public funds, evaluates federal programs and activities, and provides analyses, options, recommendations, and other assistance to help the Congress make effective oversight, policy, and funding decisions."[25]

PARLIAMENTARY OVERSIGHT COMMITTEES. Particularly in a presidential system with separation of governance powers, the national parliament or congress constitutes a general check upon executive power and thus represents a diffuse source of horizontal accountability. In the effort to combat corruption and secure good governance, however, oversight is more effectively performed by parliamentary committees that monitor and legislate on particular areas of government policy, such as health, public works, or defense. In many democracies, any parliamentary committee can investigate suspicions of waste, fraud, and abuse within the executive agencies under its jurisdiction. Some national legislatures go further, with standing committees to monitor the overall efficiency and integrity of government and to investigate allegations of wrongdoing. The Philippine senate has a standing Blue Ribbon Committee with broad authority to investigate corruption and other criminal behavior by government officials. During its fifty years of operation, the committee has probed many scandals, including the vast web of practices that ultimately forced President Joseph Estrada out of office in January 2001. Yet, it can do no more than recommend prosecution, and it suffers from a common deficiency among anticorruption bodies: "The lack of staff prevents the committee from following through and keeping track of cases once they have been reported out."[26]

THE JUDICIAL SYSTEM. Like the other agencies of horizontal accountability, the judiciary must have significant capacity and independence if it is to be effective in controlling corruption. There is much more to judicial capacity than modern court buildings with adequate means for communication, recording, and research. An effective judicial system requires well-trained, competent judges, clerks, prosecutors, investigators, and defense attorneys, and enough of them to keep caseloads to a level that is consistent with vigorous justice and due process. The courts need to streamline their administrative management and their capacity to track and process cases, both criminal and civil. All legal practitioners need the support of law libraries, computerized information systems, law schools, judicial training institutes, and professional bar associations. When they are independent and elicit broad participation from the legal community, bar associations can become powerful advocates for rule-of-law reforms and work to elevate professional norms and monitor the conduct of the legal community. A genuine rule of law also requires an extended network of legal assistance that can provide advice and counsel free of charge to those who need representation and cannot afford to pay for it.

ECONOMIC REGULATORY INSTITUTIONS. When corruption is endemic, it inevitably involves the banking system, and usually the stock market and other areas of the private economy, as well. Both for restrained, noninflationary macroeconomic management—a key foundation of good governance—and as a check upon corrupt practices in the banking sector, countries need central banks that are constitutionally and procedurally independent of political control. This reduces the possibility of reckless expansion of the money supply in order to cover large fiscal deficits (which can result from corruption). It also tends to produce better monitoring and regulation of private banks. Independent regulation of the stock market through a securities and exchange commission and of commerce can also help to preempt corrupt links between government and business.

THE ELECTORAL COMMISSION. If horizontal accountability depends in part on vertical accountability, it requires competitive elections that are fairly and neutrally administered and that take place at the times prescribed by the law and the constitution. Electoral administration consists of a daunting range of tasks, any of which may be compromised by fraud or ineptitude. These include registering voters; publishing and distributing voter lists; registering and qualifying parties and candidates; establishing and enforcing rules on campaigning and campaign finance; ensuring the security of campaigners, voters, and the polling stations; administering the polls during voting; counting the ballots; reporting, collating, and "announcing the results; investigating and adjudicating complaints; and certifying the results."[27] The range of tasks, many of them ongoing, necessitates a significant, professional, and permanent administration. The overriding imperative is that electoral administration not be subject to direction or manipulation by the incumbent officials or ruling party.

MAKING ACCOUNTABILITY WORK

The challenge is not simply to structure a system of horizontal accountability on paper, but to give it the authority, autonomy, and resources to do its job. The problems begin with the power to appoint. If a country cannot get high-quality, nonpartisan professionals into positions of horizontal accountability, all is lost. It should be underscored that this seemingly modest problem—who will appoint, if not guard, the guardians—is fundamental. Institutions that look promising in scope and design are often vitiated because it is the president (or prime minister) who appoints their leaders, and an executive who has fought his or her way to the top in even a partially corrupt (not to mention predatory) system is not going to enable serious mechanisms of accountability.

The 1991 Thai constitution sought to get around this problem by giving the power to appoint members of accountability agencies—such as the Constitutional Court and the countercorruption, election, audit, and human rights commissions—to a nonpartisan senate, whose members were elected for single six-year terms and were expressly forbidden to have any party membership or political appointment. The model foundered in 2001, when the Constitutional Court, in its controversial and tortuous 8–7 ruling, cleared the new and fabulously wealthy prime minister Thaksin Shinawatra of a finding that he had falsely declared his assets (which could have led to his dismissal from office).[28] The ruling was a huge blow to accountability in Thailand. Soon Thaksin gained control over the senate and the appointments process. And Thailand was far from being a purely predatory state.

Thus, officials of accountability agencies must be appointed, funded, and supervised in ways that cannot be subverted or suborned. Once independent appointments are made, officials must have significant tenure, removable only for established cause, and then by complex and difficult means. In the United States, the GAO's independence is supported by the relatively lengthy tenure of its head, the comptroller general, who serves a fixed fifteen-year term.[29]

The problem of neutrality has particularly vexed designs for electoral administration, one of the most sensitive of regulatory functions. In political systems with a tradition of corruption and abuse of power, and in which democratic norms are not deeply rooted, the electoral administration must have constitutional autonomy. There are a number of possible models. In Costa Rica, the Supreme Electoral Tribunal is virtually a fourth branch of government, whose members are elected to staggered six-year terms by a two-thirds vote of the Supreme Court. In India, the electoral commission's independence is protected by explicit constitutional mandate and by a powerful chairman who is appointed by the nonpartisan president. In other countries, independence is attained through supervision by a judicial body or by being made accountable to the parliament rather than the executive branch.[30] More generally, where there is some tradition of judicial independence at higher levels, it may make sense to vest the appointment and supervision of a number of horizontally accountable agencies with the constitutional court.

MOBILIZING CIVIL SOCIETY

The Thai experience shows that even elaborate and well-designed account-ability institutions are at risk of being conquered or subverted unless society has the will, the organization, and the resources to defend its institutions. Horizontal accountability needs to be stimulated and rein-forced by vertical pressures from civil society, as well as from outside (the subject of the next chapter).

As we saw in chapter 7, a vigorous civil society is vital to sustaining democracy. Civil society deepens and invigorates democracy by checking and reversing abuses of state power, recruiting and training new political leaders, developing new agendas for reform, and raising citizens' aware-ness of their rights and responsibilities. In addition, civil society can be a vital instrument for opening access and transcending a predatory state by breaking down the vertical bonds of clientelism and dependency, foster-ing horizontal forms of political participation and trust, generating new bonds of interest that cut across ethnic and local identities, and orga-nizing citizens to demand "more effective public service."[31] Thus, Robert Putnam was also right when he wrote, "Tocqueville was right: Demo-cratic government is strengthened, not weakened, when it faces a vigor-ous civil society."[32]

Three forms of societal accountability stand out:[33]

NONGOVERNMENTAL ORGANIZATIONS. A variety of civic organizations—bar associ-ations, women's organizations, student groups, religious bodies, think tanks, election monitoring and human rights groups, and other citizens' watchdog groups—may form coalitions to lobby for constitutional changes to improve governance while also monitoring the conduct of public officials. Transparency International (TI), with incipient or estab-lished chapters in more than ninety countries, has demonstrated the vital and creative role that international civil society can play in forming coali-tions with domestic constituencies for good governance and accountabil-ity. While not all of TI's national chapters are equally dedicated or effective, in many countries they represent the most focused civil society effort ever to monitor the conduct of government agencies and officials, to press for legal and institutional reforms to promote transparency and control corruption, and to raise public consciousness about the problems and costs of corruption. Each chapter pursues its own agenda, but they are all guided by a common operational philosophy, which includes focusing on long-term, systemic issues, avoiding the investigation of specific cases of corruption or the naming of corrupt officials, and seeking participation and cooperation from across the social spectrum in a strictly nonpartisan manner.[34] Both the international organization and national chapters have drawn extensive support from bilateral and multilateral aid donors, including the World Bank. Internationally, TI has also been a driving force behind the adoption of the Anti-Bribery Convention of the Organization for Economic Co-operation and Development (OECD).

A wide range of other NGOs, research centers, and social movements are monitoring government conduct, documenting abuses of human rights by the police and other officials, and "demanding information about the financial assets of public officials or denouncing electoral fraud or violations of environmental rights."[35] Independent democracy and public policy research institutes, like the Institute for Democracy in South Africa (IDASA), the Ghana Center for Democratic Development, a similarly named center in Nigeria, and dozens of others in the developing world[36] have a particularly important role to play because they have the expertise and resources to examine policies and budgets and to gather evidence from within their own countries. Since its founding in 1987, during the period of South Africa's transition, IDASA's policy research and advocacy have expanded to a breathtaking scope that makes it one of the largest, most multidimensional and effective pro-democracy organizations in the developing world. Today it tracks government budgets, spending, and service delivery; monitors the legislative process at both the national and provincial levels; surveys public opinion; periodically audits the quality of democracy; tracks the uses of money in South African politics; develops human rights training materials for schools and communities; grooms new leaders from the grass roots; conducts training, technical assistance, and workshops to improve local governance; promotes community dialogues; and campaigns for the "right to know" by developing legislation to promote access to information and protect whistle-blowers. Its programs also address judicial ethics and accountability, local government funding, government responses to the HIV/AIDS pandemic, and demands for transparency in a parliamentary scandal over abuse of travel vouchers. As its work becomes institutionalized in South Africa, IDASA is increasingly reaching out to build wider regional partnerships on issues such as governance, electoral administration, and police reform, and it also conducts election-monitoring and training activities in other African countries.[37]

AN INDEPENDENT MASS MEDIA. Transparency, virtually by definition, requires free and open flows of information. Without a free and pluralistic press, transparency is not possible. Pluralism entails market competition as well as diversity. The emergence of professional journalistic norms and standards is key to the growth of press freedom, vigor, and autonomy, which in turn may advance or accelerate democratization, as it did in Mexico.[38] Controlling corruption requires a press that is free from intimidation and restraint; a press that has the resources to investigate rumors and evidence of corruption; and a press that has the maturity, restraint, and professionalism to eschew loose and sensationalist charges based on any whisper of malfeasance. This latter point needs emphasis, because if the press is constantly accusing without credible evidence, it will discredit itself and the quest for accountability. For much of the developing and postcommunist world, it will take many years to develop the needed levels of pluralism, capacity, and responsibility, even where a climate of freedom exists.

Investigative reporting of corruption requires training and resources that few newspapers and magazines can afford. Yet it is increasingly becoming a field in itself, with an accumulation of lessons, tools, guides, clues, and standards, and a growing international network of cooperating organizations. The Philippine Center for Investigative Journalism trains journalists in this area and has published a comprehensive manual, *Investigating Corruption,* which distills a wealth of information on how to interview victims and eyewitnesses; catch wrongdoers in the act; look for procedural gaps and irregularities; map the structure of power and influence; trace money flows; determine who benefits in society; investigate the assets, lifestyles, conflicts of interest, and public behavior of public officials; and uncover their friends, relatives, and cronies.[39] The growing public disgust with corruption generates a strong market demand for such reporting, and the mass media need to develop the skills and tools to supply it.

A VIGILANT CITIZENRY. The last line of vertical defense is a vigilant, politically aware, and informed citizenry, concerned with public affairs and ready to utilize one or more of the overlapping mechanisms of accountability to report corruption and challenge abuses of power. Citizen reporting, including whistle-blowing by lower-level government and corporate officials, can be powerfully facilitated by laws that offer protections from dismissal and other retaliation and even incentives for reporting wrongdoing.

In addition, government can do much to facilitate citizen reporting of corrupt conduct by providing ready and confidential channels, particularly via the Internet. The GAO, for example, operates the "FraudNET to facilitate reporting of allegations of fraud, waste, abuse, or mismanagement of federal funds."[40] Anyone may report evidence of wrongdoing over the Internet, or by e-mail, fax, or postal mail. Citizens thus are able to augment the efforts of civil society organizations, the mass media, and political parties and accountability institutions.

New rules and organizations take time to develop capacity and authority. As Robert Putnam observes, "Those who build new institutions and those who would evaluate them need patience."[41] But before they can take root, they must take shape. Getting to the roots of corruption and bad governance requires comprehensive institutional reforms to open up access to information and power and to constrain the way that state power is exercised. Why should government officials—even if they are elected more or less democratically—*want* to accept these constraints?

Occasionally, political leaders come along who embrace the reform cause and even lead it, out of conviction and perhaps an enlightened view of the long-term bases of their success. The more old structures of domination have begun to dissolve under the pressure of popular mobilization or economic development, the greater the possibility for a leader—such as Ernesto Zedillo in Mexico or Fernando Henrique Cardoso in Brazil—to step forward and push the reform cause. But rulers rarely blaze the trail to reform when the political status quo leans heavily toward a predatory state that offers too many potent inducements to resist. In predatory-state contexts, reforms are spurred by complex coalitions of actors from below, in civil society, from within the state structures of accountability, and from outside, in the international community.

International actors can strengthen civil society actors, support their governance reform initiatives, improve the capacity of a wide range of horizontal accountability institutions, and press government leaders to accept painful reforms. But pressing successfully means having, and then effectively mobilizing, powerful leverage, as I explain in the next chapter.

14

PROMOTING DEMOCRACY EFFECTIVELY

Beyond its sheer scope, the most distinctive feature of the third wave of democratization has been the rise of a broad range of international efforts and initiatives to promote democracy. More than in any previous era, established democracies have pursued policies, pressed diplomacy, and built institutions and organizations to advance democracy elsewhere in the world. As we have seen in earlier chapters, these initiatives have paid significant dividends, helping to bring democracy to such diverse countries as Portugal, the Philippines, Poland, Chile, South Africa, Serbia, and Ukraine. In these cases and others, international efforts have helped tip the balance in favor of a democratic transition or at least accelerated the pace of transition and ensured that it would, for the most part, be peaceful. In many cases, assistance, often through small grants to grassroots organizations, has helped to till the soil of authoritarian stagnation and inspired democratic hopes and capacities, allowing democrats to prepare and mobilize for change when dictatorships fell into crisis. Ongoing political and economic aid efforts, both governmental and nongovernmental, have sought to create the foundations for successful democratic functioning as well as the economic reform and development that can help to consolidate public support for democracy. The expansion and refinement of democracy promotion and the growing international legitimacy of peaceful efforts to support local democratic initiatives are major reasons to be hopeful about the long-term future of democracy.

Yet, the authoritarian states that consider themselves as targeted for extinction orchestrated a pronounced backlash against democracy promotion. Since the invasion of Iraq in 2003, the public in many democracies, including the United States, has with growing intensity rejected the use of force to impose democracy elsewhere. This is true whether in Iraq (which is widely viewed as one such failed effort), the Middle East more generally, or other regions. Peaceful and especially multilateral efforts to foster and sustain democracy now run up against a brick wall of authoritarian resistance, at a time when global efforts to combat international terrorism seem to be taking precedence over concerns about democracy and human rights.

Moreover, foreign aid and other so-called international development assistance programs often do not take account of the underlying logic of politics—the incentives that lead officeholders to misuse aid, repress the opposition, rig elections, and barricade themselves in power. If the whole world is going to become democratic, these assistance efforts and their accompanying diplomacy must target the way politics itself works. We need a transformation in the way the rich, established democracies—the "donor countries"—relate to the less developed world.

Despite recent reversals, the democratic progress of the past three decades shows that there is no intrinsic economic, cultural, or religious obstacle to democracy and that democracy is becoming an increasingly universal value. But in order for the promise of a democratic world to be realized, the international community will need to do much more to generate the conditions that facilitate democratic development—and do it more wisely.

POLITICAL ASSISTANCE

Not every dimension of our approach internationally requires reinvention. As recounted in chapter 5, international efforts to support and strengthen democratic institutions have gained impressive scope, depth, and experience since the establishment of the National Endowment for Democracy (NED) in 1983.[1] From its initially modest efforts, NED has grown dramatically to over $80 million in annual congressional appropriations.[2] In addition, NED's four core institutes—the National Democratic Institute (NDI), the International Republican Institute (IRI), the Center for International Private Enterprise (CIPE), and the Solidarity Center—receive tens of millions of dollars each year in other government funding.[3] Counterpart organizations have emerged, such as Britain's Westminster Foundation, the Netherlands' Institute for Multiparty Democracy, and the Taiwan Foundation for Democracy.[4] In the summer of 2007, the Canadian parliament was encouraged by its foreign affairs committee to create a NED-style "arms-length Canada foundation" for supporting democratic development around the world.[5] Traditional aid donors are now providing much more extensive assistance—amounting to over one billion dollars a year each from the U.S. Agency for International Development (USAID), European aid agencies, and the United Nations Development Program (UNDP)—for democracy and governance reform (including civil society).

Democracy assistance programs vary in effectiveness and impact. Sometimes the impact is visible only later, when a moment of democratic opportunity arises and an array of democratic actors—including opposition parties, NGOs, professional associations, business groups, and trade unions—are able to take advantage of it because international assistance over the years has widened their support base and enhanced their organizational skills. Democratic assistance to state institutions sometimes has little impact because there is no political will to make use of it. As a result, parliaments and courts may have more modern buildings, advanced computer equipment, larger staffs, and better training, but still do not effectively stand up to executive branch abuses of democracy and human rights.

A few key principles can guide democracy assistance efforts. First and foremost is the need for *local* ownership, not government ownership. Assistance efforts must be grounded in the interests and needs of societal stakeholders, most of all the general public.[6] For democracy assistance to be legitimate, effective, and sustainable, it must respond to local priorities and initiatives rather than impose preconceived formulas from the outside. One reason for the NED's success is that it receives and funds proposals generated by organizations that are struggling to build, improve, or reform democracy in their various countries. These proposals, and the individuals and organizations who submit them, must be carefully vetted and periodically evaluated, given the opportunism and even charlatanism that seep into any field where funding becomes available. Further, democracy promoters need to formulate broad strategic goals, as the NED does every five years.[7] Potential grant recipients may consult with foundation program officers to identify comprehensible goals and feasible projects. They may also work with parties, business associations, or trade unions to develop a reform agenda. In the end, the best democracy work comes when the country's own stakeholders identify the imperatives and opportunities on the ground and craft programs in response.

Local ownership is necessary not only for financial grants but for the design of strategies for democratic change. Donors should involve individuals and organizations from the country when they target obstacles and priorities for democratic development. Such bottom-up assessments yield surprising and valuable insights. For example, based on Western experience, rule-of-law assistance programs instinctively tend to invest in courts. "Yet it is by no means clear that courts are the essence of a rule of law system in a country," according to Thomas Carothers, since "courts play a role late in the process."[8] The first question is, What laws are they enforcing? If the country's laws are undemocratic, a strong court system will do little to promote democracy. Further, in many societies traditional practices of dispute resolution hold more legitimacy and, in any case, are far more accessible. Police may be abusive, poorly trained, and poorly paid, but they are also a much more frequent point of contact between citizens and the state than are the courts. And then there is the underlying issue "that poorly performing judicial systems in many countries [serve] the interests of powerful actors."[9] Thus, a bottom-up assessment may point to the need to support other categories of rule-of-law reform—such as alternative dispute resolution mechanisms, traditional justice practices, civic education and empowerment, legal aid clinics, police training and monitoring, and human rights organizations—if anything significant and lasting is to be achieved.[10]

Second, effective aid to state institutions depends on the political will to use it *for* democracy. Aid to state agencies is a tricky business—and an expensive one. Formal state-to-state political assistance programs, particularly when they involve construction of buildings, purchases of equipment, and payroll for staff, are typically much more expensive than grants to civil society organizations. It does little good to train and equip judges, legislators, and countercorruption agents if they and the institutions they work in are not structurally independent. Before donor organizations spend millions of dollars, they have to analyze whether institutions have the independence, leadership, and will to advance democracy. In theory, this is part of what USAID's strategic assessment process of the political context means to achieve.[11]

A third principle is developing *realistic* expectations for what democracy assistance efforts can achieve, especially in the short run. Typically, democracy assistance has an incremental rather than a transformative effect. Where democracy is in place, assistance can absorb best practices from other countries and provide the resources to advocate and mobilize for additional reforms. In transitional or stalled democracies, it "can help actors keep some independent political and civic activity going and, over the long term, help build civic awareness and civic organizations at the local level." In highly authoritarian countries, it "may help democracy activists survive . . . and may increase the flow of political information not controlled by the government."[12] It is not practical to expect individual democracy aid projects to transform levels of freedom. But they can ensure that elections are better monitored and more transparent, that citizens know their rights and participate actively, that political parties become responsive to public concerns, and that legislative committees question and investigate executive branch actions more effectively—all worthwhile, and requiring a patient, long-term approach. Pressure to produce "showy," near-term results tends to generate simplistic formulas for counting people trained or extravagant claims that overlook subtle but real achievements.

Patience is also required in another sense. Donor organizations and their officers (who are often on fixed-term contracts or country assignments) are frequently under "pressure to spend money quickly."[13] This often leads to waste: splashy conferences, cushy tours for senior officials, big grants to just a few organizations that may not be in a position to deliver results. But it takes time to determine how funds can be spent effectively, from surveying a country to detect which programs are most needed to determining the most appropriate actors for developing and implementing a program priority. For example, political party assistance programs should move beyond their short-term focus on elections and campaigns, and even their traditional "fraternal" assistance to like-minded parties, and do more to address the challenge of building and reforming party organizations.[14]

The next principle involves the problem of *scale*. Democracy assistance programs at the level of 5, 10, or 20 million dollars annually may have a discernible impact in a small country, but they are a drop in the bucket for countries the size of China, Russia, Nigeria, or Indonesia. In large countries, democratic organizations and norms must be built up in dozens of provinces and hundreds of localities, well beyond the capital. No political assistance organization today is prepared to deliver on that kind of scale, even where, as in Indonesia, the political climate may be favorable. To make more headway there, let alone in China, Russia, and Nigeria, overall levels of funding for democracy assistance must be sizeably increased. Yet a massive burst of spending will not be enough unless it can be sustained over the long term. Often that means building institutions, crafting technologies, and developing practices that are scaled to a country's level of economic development. A simpler, lower-tech approach—for example, in the administration of elections—makes better sense if it will allow a country to operate and sustain democratic practices on its own for years to come.

Scaling projects for local sustainability does not mean, however, that donors are let off the hook on committing to longer engagements. For some years now, the aid industry, and particularly USAID, has been obsessed with the imperative of "graduation"—seeing aid recipients develop as quickly as possible to a point where they no longer need development assistance. This is a justifiable concern; no country should be lulled into an expectation of indeterminate dependency. Certainly middle-income countries like Thailand and Brazil (not to mention more developed countries like Malaysia, Romania, and Mexico) have reached the point where they no longer need conventional foreign aid to give them the basic means to grow out of poverty. Once a country reaches middle-income status, it can and should rely more on internal revenue generation and private capital markets. What it most needs from the international community is open trade and foreign investment to create jobs and stimulate economic growth. But even where there is much wealth in the economy, there may not be the resources or the tradition of philanthropy to support civic organizations pressing for democratic change. Organizations may desperately need external assistance to defend human rights, educate democratic citizens, build effective parties, and investigate and control corruption. Democracy promoters must be prepared to offer extensive training and exchange programs and to direct outright grants to organizations even in countries that would otherwise be too developed or too far past a democratic transition to qualify for conventional aid. The travails in the Philippines, Bangladesh, and Guatemala demonstrate that two decades after a democratic transition, enormous needs for institutional assistance remain.

Particularly in poor countries, there is a parallel need for *expanding and sustaining funding* among individual civil society organizations. Some critics suggest that NGOs tend to be too dependent on Western aid and too detached from their own societies.[15] But the fact that an NGO cannot raise its core funding in a poor country is hardly a reflection on its value to democratic development, or on its legitimacy and support in society. Where is such an organization supposed to get the funds to pay a professional staff, rent an office, purchase computers and cell phones, hire students to do research and polling, and deploy community organizers, if not from the international community? It cannot be expected to raise money from the state it is scrutinizing and holding accountable, or from a business community that may itself be politically captured or cautious, without becoming less effective as an agent of vertical accountability and reform. One of the strongest convictions I have formed in twenty-five years of studying civil society organizations in developing countries is that they need core organizational funding from external donors. Constant scrambling for specific project grants is too precarious. Thus, once an NGO accounts well for its international grants and demonstrates good performance in building democratic institutions and norms, it should become eligible for general support, ideally from multiple international donors. This would enable the organization to plan for the long term and develop a bottom-up reform agenda without growing dependent on any one country or funder—or of being perceived as such in local eyes.[16]

Just as civic organizations in a country must broaden their support, international donors must extend their *cooperation* and *networking*. While donors have been doing a somewhat better job of coordinating both individual country missions and international efforts, duplication still exists, decreasing the potential leverage that can be brought against recalcitrant or wavering governments. There is also a certain tendency toward competition among a country's donors for contacts and credit. Effective coordination often comes down to the particular mix of donor representatives and the amount of time they have had to work with one another. The growth of nongovernmental networks—including, as mentioned in chapter 5, NED-like democracy assistance organizations and the civil society organizations and networks drawn into the World Movement for Democracy—offers promise of better coordination.

This networking is not enough, however, to counter the gathering backlash against efforts to promote democracy. Authoritarian states like China, Russia, Egypt, Iran, and Uzbekistan are implementing an array of legal restrictions and extralegal measures to block, neutralize, criminalize, and disrupt the flow of democracy assistance. Increasingly, they are learning and borrowing from one another's efforts.[17] In these circumstances, *new methods* for supporting besieged democratic forces must evolve. Where the United States and other powerful democracies have leverage, they could condition their aid, trade, investment, and other ties on some measure of a state's tolerance for international assistance to civil society organizations and independent media. Western diplomats must take a principled, energetic stand, and the more they stand together, the more leverage they will have. Aid can also be channeled through neighboring countries, such as the cross-border efforts of NGOs in Poland, Slovakia, the Czech Republic, and Lithuania to aid Belarusian and Central Asian democrats. Whenever possible, democrats within a region should draw together to exchange techniques and strengthen networks, supporting those in more tenuous circumstances. More use can be made of new as well as old communication technologies—the Internet and satellite television, international radio broadcasting, and underground organizations like those that have aided dissident democrats in the former Soviet bloc.[18]

Finally, political assistance efforts have more impact when they are integrated into economic assistance efforts. Traditional development programs—literacy, HIV/AIDS treatment, health services for mothers and children, agricultural assistance—should include means for generating political participation and citizenship awareness. USAID and other donors are already seeking to do this. A national assistance strategy must weigh not only the purely political obstacles to democracy but also the social obstacles of poverty, economic inequality, and extremely hierarchical systems that treat citizens as peons or clients of powerful patrons. As we saw in chapter 4, higher levels of development and education provide a more fertile soil for democracy to take root. This requires a comprehensive agenda of policies and investments targeted to empower the poor and reduce extreme poverty.

CONDITIONING DEVELOPMENT ASSISTANCE

Democratic assistance of the types mentioned above can help to build the institutions, networks, capabilities, and values that make for democracy. But if democracy is to emerge and function decently, there must be some dedication to it on the part of the country's rulers. As I have argued throughout this book, a deep normative conviction that democracy is the best form of government is not necessary. That can emerge gradually, and may only really come with a generational turnover in the political elite.

However, even if the elites commit solely on the calculation of their own economic and political interests—that the costs of resisting democracy are greater than the costs of allowing it—it will open the door to transition.[19] Whatever the motivation, democrats can translate elite commitment into the political will for reform.

International efforts to facilitate democratic change must pay much greater attention to this question of the elites' incentives. What can induce authoritarian elites who have monopolized power for years, if not decades, to surrender it, or at least put it at risk in free and fair elections? What might persuade a dictatorship to begin a serious process of political liberalization, with the risk that it might eventually lead to its loss of power? Why might ruling elites, even democratically elected ones, who have grown fat feeding off the public trough decide to accept an independent judiciary, a serious countercorruption commission, and other potent structures of horizontal accountability? Rare in history is an enlightened authoritarian ruler. Usually, dictators yield power and scoundrels accept scrutiny because they judge that they have no better choice. One of the key levers that brings them to this painful reckoning is running out of the resources to sustain a ruling coalition and pay the coercive apparatus that keeps them in power.

Some regimes stay afloat on international rents from oil exports. It will take time for the Western democracies to engineer a revolution in energy use—through conservation and conversion to alternative energy sources—that can dramatically reduce oil prices. Yet doing so is vital to creating favorable conditions for democracy in the world's oil-dependent states.[20] Many of the remaining authoritarian regimes—including a number of elected authoritarians—are sustained, however, through foreign aid, which generates the resources to keep the state alive, pay the army, police, and bureaucrats, and to deliver just enough to the population to avoid widespread protests. For the developing countries that do not have large oil reserves, donors can do a great deal to change the interests and therefore the calculations of elites by conditioning aid on improvements in governance and then rewarding the better governments with higher levels of aid.

This conditionality—or more properly termed, *selectivity,* since countries are selected and rewarded *in advance* for demonstrating progress—is controversial. Many well-intentioned people believe the rich Western countries have a moral obligation to transfer wealth to the poor countries of the world, particularly to Africa. Some economists give intellectual foundation to this outrage by arguing that the biggest obstacle to development is a lack of resources.[21] The wealthy societies of the world do have an obligation to the world's poor. But the obligation is not to transfer money; it is to help lift suffering people out of degrading poverty and oppression. Aid is an instrument for fostering development and reducing poverty, nothing more, and where the instrument does not work, it must be reconsidered. As Steven Radelet, one of the most objective analysts of foreign aid policy, has observed, "Much aid is wasted on countries with governments that are not serious about development and cannot use it well."[22]

Unfortunately, the cause and effect relationship between governance and poverty has often been confused by this moral outrage. The Columbia University economist Jeffrey Sachs—the leading advocate for vastly increased aid—has it upside down when he argues, "Africa's governance is poor because Africa is poor." Africa is poor because its governance is rotten, and it will not truly develop until its governance improves. What good is done for a country's poor by dumping generous aid into the laps of a corrupt, repressive government? In such a case, the principal benefit of the aid is to salve the conscience of the West, leaving it to feel that it is not its fault if, as is common in the world's poor countries, half or more of the population lives in extreme poverty, earning under a dollar a day; a third or more of adults are illiterate; two in every five babies born will not live to the age of forty; and 10 percent will die before the age of one.[23] If, as the facts suggest, aid is actually making things worse by sustaining abusive governments, then it is the West's fault, and doubling aid uncritically and unconditionally will make it doubly so.

If the rich West is going to be effective at promoting democracy in the world's poor countries, it needs a radically new philosophy of aid and debt relief. Aid must become what it is now euphemistically labeled *development assistance,* and no longer be a guilt payment or the fuel for a massive industry of bureaucrats, for-profit corporations, and idealistic do-gooders who are too often not achieving much good in their results. Democratic change in the world's remaining corrupt dictatorships requires a radical manipulation of ruler incentives and a revolution in aid.

If they continue to provide aid on an unconditional basis, donor nations and organizations will merely cement the power of authoritarian rulers. But what principles should be followed? Many of the new directions needed in this revolution have already been set out in USAID's

2002 report, *Foreign Aid in the National Interest,* but they have only been partially implemented.[24] Here is a slightly revised agenda:

1. *Overall levels of foreign assistance must be linked clearly to a country's development performance,* and to demonstrations of political will for governance reforms. The historic pattern by which dictatorships received as much or more foreign aid than democracies must end.[25]

2. *Good performers must be tangibly rewarded.* When political leaders demonstrate respect for democratic procedures and freedoms and the will to implement reforms, they should benefit with increases in assistance, including debt relief, incentives for foreign investment, and trade liberalization.

3. *Governance performance must be judged by absolute standards, not by "grading on a curve."* If virtually all low-income countries lack the basic institutions to control corruption and foster transparency and a rule of law, then it does limited good to reward those that fall short less egregiously than others. It takes time to build a competent, functioning court system and state bureaucracy, but *every* government can create an independent countercorruption commission and electoral administration, and *every* parliament can pass laws giving citizens freedom of information and requiring that officials declare their assets. *Every* government can decide to tolerate an independent and critical press and a vigorous civil society. These require political will, not economic development or high state capacity.

4. *Rewards must be granted for demonstrated performance, not for promises that may be repeatedly made and broken.* The only way to exit from the chronic game of conditionality is to make increases in assistance contingent on what governments actually do, not what they say they will do.

5. *Rewards should be structured to lock into place the institutions, practices, and norms of good governance.* One obvious model is the European Union, with its detailed and rigorous conditions for entry into membership. As the United States seeks to enlarge free trade agreements with Mexico and Central America into a hemispheric Free Trade Agreement of the Americas, it should press for a requirement, similar to the European Union's, that all members must uphold democracy and human rights. Yet the EU does not do enough to monitor and demand good governance after accession. Free trade communities and transformative development assistance should be continually monitored, with aid

flows reduced or suspended for defections from good governance. When poor countries qualify for debt relief, the debt should not be forgiven in one fell swoop, but should be retired incrementally (for example, at 10 percent per year), as institutions and norms of accountability are developed.

6. *To the extent that commitment to democratic and good governance reforms is absent, assistance should be channeled through NGOs rather than state agencies.* In particular, where the political will for good governance is lacking, direct support for the general state budget should cease.[26] Leaders must learn that they will pay a heavy price for bad governance. Humanitarian and project-based assistance for public health, medical care, and nutrition should be delivered through NGOs, administered directly by donors, or at least intensively monitored.

7. *The principal aid donors must work closely together to coordinate pressure on bad, recalcitrant governments.* In most developing countries, U.S. aid constitutes a modest proportion of total foreign aid received. To change elite calculations, donors must impose common conditions for aid.

8. *Donors should use their voices and votes within the executive bodies of the World Bank and other multilateral development banks to shift assistance from bad governments to better, more democratic governments.* This requires that the nature and quality of a country's governance be considered when determining assistance levels.[27] Professional incentives for resident World Bank and other international development staff should be altered, so that officials are rewarded for considered decisions to withhold or suspend funding as much as for granting it.[28]

9. *Where committed reformers can be identified within the state, donors should work with them.* Donors should strengthen the hands of reform-oriented ministers, agency heads, and provincial governors not just by providing technical capacity and resources, but by helping them in the political struggle to "identify key winners and losers, develop coalition building and mobilization strategies, and design publicity campaigns."[29] Even in a corrupt state, one may find some honest officials in the judiciary, the legislature, accountability agencies, and executive departments who would like to do the right thing.

10. *Political assistance to reform governance, build democracy, and strengthen civil society should be significantly increased, and a greater proportion of development assistance should be invested in the democracy and governance sector.* A dollar invested in improving governance—making it more capable and efficient, more responsive to public needs, more subject

to public scrutiny and input, more honest, transparent, and accountable in the handling of public funds, and more respectful of the law—
will do more for economic development than a dollar spent in any
other sector. No other sector has so many multiplier effects. There is
certainly evidence, as noted in chapter 4, that increased levels of
democracy and governance assistance do generate improvements in
levels of freedom and democracy over time.[30] In intractable cases, generating demand for democracy through support for independent
organizations, interest groups, social movements, mass media, universities, and think tanks might be the main opportunity to advance
development.

11. *Donors should stand ready to increase significantly overall levels of develop-
    ment assistance, but only as governance improves.* This will enable more
    states to make use of aid for development.

For several decades, advocates have called for industrialized countries
to transfer at least 0.7 percent of their gross national incomes (GNI) annually in official development assistance, and the wealthy countries officially
committed themselves to this goal at the 1970 UN General Assembly.[31]
Most industrialized countries lag behind this target, particularly the
United States, which has provided between 0.1 and 0.2 percent of GNI in
aid. In 2006, the twenty-two members of the Organization for Economic
Cooperation and Development (OECD) fell "some $100 billion short,"[32]
giving only $104 billion (0.3 percent of collective GNI).[33] By this analysis,
the rich countries are only giving half or less of what they should.
Sachs estimates that if aid to developing countries (not including debt
relief and repayments) could be raised to half a percent of rich country
income, it could end extreme poverty in the world by 2025.[34] But what
is the point of dramatically increasing aid if it cannot be utilized *for*
development?

American foreign aid is slowly, partially moving in the direction of
greater selectivity and some other principles of aid reform, but much still
has to be done. At the 2005 summit of the Group of 8 industrialized powers (G8), the major donors pledged to double aid to Africa by 2010 as part
of a visionary commitment to "double the size of Africa's economy by
2015," to "lift tens of millions of people out of poverty every year," and to
dramatically improve public health, "save millions of lives a year," and
"bring about an end to conflict in Africa." But those pledges were predicated on African countries committing to heightened investments in

these efforts and to "good governance, democracy and transparency."[35] Two years later, neither side had gone very far toward fulfilling its part of the bargain, in part because there is no mechanism for independent monitoring and evaluation.

Only when countries put in place institutions to ensure accountability, transparency, and freedom will it be possible to effect the kind of sweeping "global compact to end poverty" that Sachs envisions. Then it would make sense to implement proposals to double aid (in net, real terms), to commit it for a longer time period (such as a decade), to enable "scaling up," and to make it more predictable (so as not to discourage or interrupt investment).[36]

AMERICA'S CENTRAL ROLE

In recent years, the George W. Bush administration has introduced the most far-reaching reforms in U.S. foreign aid policy since the passage of the Foreign Assistance Act in 1961. Aid has been increased by the largest amount in decades. While some of this aid has gone to American allies in the "global war on terrorism," such as Iraq and Pakistan, there have also been broad increases in aid and the initiation of programs, such as the President's Emergency Fund for AIDS Relief (PEPFAR). During its second term, the administration implemented an ambitious reform of aid flows, putting them under the direction of a single authority, a new director of foreign assistance with the dual role of administrator of USAID and deputy secretary of state. Yet these reforms remain too partial and weakly coordinated.

Conceptually, the administration's most important innovation was the establishment in January 2004 of the Millennium Challenge Account (MCA), an attempt to standardize "selectivity." MCA was designed to channel significant increases in development assistance to low- and lower-middle-income countries that would compete for the funds on the basis of three criteria: ruling justly (by providing freedom and a rule of law and by controlling corruption); investing in people (especially basic health and education); and promoting economic freedom. Sixteen publicly available indicators, drawn from independent agencies such as Freedom House, the World Bank, and the World Health Organization, are used to measure the criteria.[37] The result is a reasonably arms-length process of assessing candidate countries on their merits.[38]

As Steven Radelet observed, in its first few years, the MCA has met hurdles but has also made progress in pushing U.S. aid in this urgently needed direction. The level of effort has not met expectations. While the MCA aimed to disburse $5 billion of additional aid per year by 2007, in its first four years the *total* amount appropriated has been only a little over $6 billion, and for the 2008 fiscal year, the MCA has requested $3 billion, subject to congressional cutbacks. However, in focusing these new funds on a small number of countries "that have demonstrated a strong commitment to sound development policies," the MCA generates country grants that are large enough to make a real difference. Moreover, the MCA allows recipient countries to set their own priorities for how to use the assistance but requires broad societal consultation. In this new process, some of the ponderous bureaucracy of traditional aid is bypassed and recipient countries understand that they will be held accountable.[39]

Operationally, the MCA has begun to gather momentum, despite criticisms. Its selection process has been sufficiently transparent and credible to stimulate interest from other donors and incentives for aspiring recipients. In recipient countries, the Millennium Challenge Corporation (MCC), which administers the process, "has been on the forefront" of facilitating "broad participation" among government, civil society, and private sector representatives in "determining priorities and designing projects and programs." The aid is going primarily to very poor countries— seven of the thirteen countries to sign compacts with the MCC are in Africa, representing "over 60 percent of all MCC funding"—and the new aid aims to overcome some of the worst obstacles to equitable growth in Africa by raising agricultural productivity, developing rural communities, and building roads and other desperately needed infrastructure.[40]

Still, the MCA has conceptual and thus operational flaws: countries are graded on a curve, and political progress toward democracy and accountability constitutes just one of the three criteria.[41] As a result, the forty-one countries that, by mid-2007, had qualified for at least "threshold" assistance from the MCC included at least eight authoritarian regimes, and at least one, Uganda, that has seen alarming deterioration in governance.[42] Some of the democracies on this list (such as the Philippines and Senegal) have also been regressing to poorer governance, some (like Mozambique and Georgia) lie in a gray zone of limited political pluralism, and others (like Kenya, Albania, and the Kyrgyz Republic) have extensive corruption and weak horizontal accountability. Until these countries are held to absolute standards—a structurally independent judiciary, a free press, and a credible set of laws and autonomous agencies to monitor, control, and punish corruption—the MCA's great promise will not be realized.

Once countries are held to higher standards of governance, Congress should fully fund the program to its original aim of $5 billion annually. Even if it does so, the MCA will represent only a portion of a total U.S. foreign aid budget that is delivered by USAID and a bewildering maze of programs in the state, defense, agriculture, labor, and justice departments, the Treasury, and some dozen other agencies. The Bush administration has been pursuing overdue reform of the entire apparatus, but still "deeper reforms are necessary."[43] Executive action is not adequate. Congress must, as a full partner, comprehensively update the Foreign Assistance Act of 1961 and its welter of subsequent amendments, regulations, and earmarks, which have generated "33 different goals, 75 priority areas, and 247 directives" stretching over two thousand pages of legislation.[44] Far-reaching coordination is needed across the nearly twenty U.S. government agencies that provide foreign aid. By creating a new cabinet department of international development and reconstruction, the United States could much more effectively manage diverse programs and could also establish a prestigious lead institution that would be able to engage other donors in reform efforts. The department could build the long-term professional knowledge and resources—and the capacity for rapid deployment of civilian expertise—that will be needed in the coming decades to rebuild war-torn and failed states.[45] It could expand career development assistance staff to enable more direct management of grants, less reliance on for-profit corporations to deliver aid, more effective monitoring, and more intensive interactions with possible aid recipients in both government and civil society.[46]

With a revamped, more coherent strategy focused on promoting development and freedom, it should be possible to win public support for larger and sustained increases in U.S. foreign aid, especially if that aid is predicated on a country gathering the political will to make effective use of it. What is needed is intelligent "tough love," not open-ended commitments that amount to codependence when an authoritarian regime grows addicted to foreign aid.

FOREIGN POLICY FOR DEMOCRACY

Political and development assistance are only two of the many tools that the United States and other powerful democracies have at their disposal to promote and advance democracy around the world. As seen in chapters 5 and 6, foreign policy can bring to bear devices and incentives—such as military assistance, diplomacy, moral pressure, trade relations, foreign investment incentives, and societal and intelligence ties—for shaping the character and behavior of states. These can be deployed to induce authoritarian regimes to liberalize and to encourage incipient democratic regimes to respect constitutional norms.

In practice, foreign policy goals often conflict, and not infrequently authoritarian regimes have significant leverage against external forces, particularly if the regime is a major oil exporter or frontline state in the "global war on terrorism." Sadly, there has been something of a retreat to the logic of the Cold War, when the United States felt compelled to embrace authoritarian states in the struggle against communism. It is rather remarkable how similar the world can seem to that of three or four decades ago if we replace the word *communism* with *radical Islamic terrorism*. Even when—as in the case of Pervez Musharraf's regime in Pakistan and the monarchy in Saudi Arabia—it is not entirely clear which side of the struggle the regime is on, U.S. policy makers are spooked into granting massive military (and in the case of Pakistan, economic) assistance.[47] It will require smart minds and strong nerves to find the right balance between promoting freedom and fighting violent ideologies. Yet in the long run the two goals converge into one, and in the short run there are certain lessons from the Cold War that can serve us today.

A vigorous battle for democratic ideas must be waged. Diplomacy is not just about relations between states, it also links societies. International broadcasting can play a critical role in informing people of what is really happening in the world, stimulating honest and open debate, cultivating democratic principles and values, and giving democratic forces hope and inspiration. But to be credible, broadcasting for democracy, whether the Voice of America network or national programs like the Persian-language Radio Farda, must have the editorial independence to report the news objectively and offer differing opinions, even those critical of America. Nothing the United States can broadcast so powerfully conveys the democratic idea as its own willingness to air and tolerate criticism of its policies. In addition, donors should support the translation into multiple languages of philosophical and empirical works on democracy, including contemporary discussions. In the era of the Internet, classic works on democracy that are in the public domain should be made freely and extensively available.[48]

Societal linkages can ultimately generate political bonds. To win the battle of ideas, we must engage societies directly through a web of educational, economic, cultural, social, and scientific exchanges. Foreign students must again, and increasingly, be welcomed to American universities. Trade and investment should be used to proliferate these ties. While concessions must sometimes be held back to avoid rewarding and legitimizing particularly bad authoritarian regimes, the bias should be for opening closed societies and linking their citizens—including their businesspeople—to ours.

Candor about conflicting interests earns credibility. One reason the image of the United States has plummeted in the world is that Americans are seen as hypocrites—favoring democracy and the rule of law throughout the world so long as it does not in the least constrain how the United States acts in the world. America must show more respect for the law globally and, to quote the Declaration of Independence, "a decent respect for the opinions of mankind," including adhering to the UN Convention Against Torture, closing the legally unaccountable terrorist detention center at Guantánamo, and joining the International Criminal Court (ICC). Of course a superpower cannot only be guided by faith in democracy and the rule of law; it also has strategic interests to serve, sometimes requiring association with authoritarian regimes. But recognizing rather than pretending away conflicts buys broader credibility for American behavior. The U.S. government may need to pursue mutual security interests with autocrats like Musharraf in Pakistan and Hosni Mubarak in Egypt, but it doesn't have to call them democrats or praise them for vacuous reforms. Morton Halperin, a former director of policy planning in the State Department under Secretary Madeleine Albright, and his coauthors Joseph Siegle and Michael Weinstein have wisely proposed that when security considerations require the United States to give significant aid to an authoritarian government, the president should declare (and if necessary renew annually) a "security waiver" for the aid; draw the funds from national security—not development assistance—accounts; set a time limit on the special aid; and indicate political reforms that would improve relations.[49]

Democrats and defenders of human rights need the steadfast support of the international community. In every authoritarian country, ambassadors and visiting leaders from democratic countries should maintain a list of political prisoners and embattled dissidents and minorities, and they should press continually for their release or better treatment.[50] In Muslim countries, this list should include Islamists who commit to democratic norms, reject violent methods, and are not credibly charged with terrorist activity. "Words matter, and we can use them to denounce repression and support and inspire democratic forces."[51]

The democratic states of the world need to stand together to promote and defend democracy. The easy days of democratic enlargement in the 1990s are over. Authoritarianism is resurgent and newly resilient, and the challenges to extending and defending freedom are now more complex. Far-reaching, multilateral foreign policy can isolate and maximize pressure on recalcitrant authoritarian states, defend democracies threatened with coups, and boost the morale of embattled democrats. Like aid flows, diplomatic incentives to achieve or preserve democracy are always more effective when they are coordinated among the established democracies.

Finally, *a foreign policy for democracy must have a long time horizon, a comprehensive strategic vision, and a flexible set of tactics.* The whole world will not become democratic in a decade, or even two. The struggle to advance and consolidate freedom in the world is a generational task. It will require a sense of realism, a sense of optimism, a careful analysis of differing democratic prospects, and a careful assessment of differing tactics for engaging specific regimes. There must be unifying principles and overarching objectives, but every country is distinctive, and strategies to assist democratic development must be specific to the place and the time.

THE REGIONAL AND INTERNATIONAL CONTEXT

One promising trend has been the rise of democratic norms and initiatives within regional and international organizations, as we saw in chapter 6. But to combat democratic recession, regional actors will need to serve as the first line of promotion and defense.

In Africa, the long tradition of strict deference to state sovereignty is beginning to erode. It will take some time for the African Union (AU) to institutionalize procedures for the defense of democracy like those adopted by the Organization of American States (OAS). But for the first time since the birth of most modern African states in the 1960s and '70s, the AU is putting concerns about democracy and governance on the African agenda. Its principal instrument for doing so is the African Peer Review Mechanism (APRM) of the New Partnership for African Development (NEPAD).[52]

Created in 2003, the APRM serves as a means for realizing the AU's rhetorical commitment to good governance. It conducts voluntary self-assessments and "peer reviews" (by experts from within Africa chosen by Africans) in the areas of democracy and political governance, economic governance and management, corporate governance, and socioeconomic development. When it works well, an open, development-minded government welcomes the peer review process, extensively involves its civil society in the self-assessment process, and organizes a broad dialogue about its agenda for reform. More than any other African country so far, Ghana has embraced the spirit of the APRM, putting a different independent think tank in charge of each area of self-assessment and actively mobilizing the public through an educational campaign. Consequently, the resulting assessments were competent and thorough.[53]

Of course, Ghana was already a relatively liberal democracy, but now it has a road map for improvement and consolidation. In the few other countries where reviews have been done, the states have been more resistant to criticism and controlling of the process, as in South Africa, or appear less able and willing to respond to the issues raised in the peer reviews.[54] By 2007, roughly half the fifty-three AU member states had joined the APRM, with most of those still awaiting completion of their first assessments. Unless the process is reformed to ensure greater civil society participation,[55] to explicitly assess freedom of the mass media,[56] and to diminish governments' interference in the process, the reviews will not be as serious as Ghana's. Aid donors could make participation in the process a requirement for official development assistance, a shrewd way to improve governance since it would be Africans themselves, not the donors, doing the assessment.

Over several decades, the OAS has evolved a much more explicit regional approach to democracy, including its procedures for convening in the face of a suspension or overthrow of democracy. Now that the OAS has collectively responded to several military and executive coups, it is clear that its Resolution 1080 and Democratic Charter are not empty threats. But the means for response to incremental threats—like the steady desecration of democracy under Hugo Chávez—remain to be developed. One official in the OAS Department for Democratic and Political Affairs, Rubén Perina, proposes that the organization's secretary-general be authorized, "at the request *or not* of the government affected," to send a political observation mission to a country in democratic crisis or decay. The mission would be authorized not only to gather information and "put the opposing factions on notice that the international community was watching their behavior," but also to facilitate negotiations among the factions to resolve the crisis.[57]

Political observer missions are a useful step, but a more muscular capacity is needed. Sometimes the problem is not so much political polarization as it is the abuse of power by an elected president. OAS members need to summon both the means and the will to inform an offending government that it faces condemnation and suspension. More generally, democratic communities must develop stronger institutional capacities to detect and respond to limitations of voting rights, government subversion of free and fair elections, restrictions on the mass media, abuse of the judiciary, harassment of government critics, and the mobilization of violence against political opponents. After assessing whether an abuse is a onetime event or sustained antidemocratic campaign, regional neighbors and organizations should apply the appropriate pressure on those responsible. Democratic governments must be willing to use diplomacy, aid, trade, and suspension of membership in the regional organization to try to reverse democratic erosion. "Regional bodies should maintain a set of democratic indicators for a region" to guide the initiation of formal monitoring.[58]

A 2002 Council on Foreign Relations task force, chaired by former secretary of state Madeleine Albright and former Polish foreign minister Bronislaw Geremek, has championed more active and continuous monitoring of democratic performance, suggesting that the Community of Democracies (CD) create such a mechanism "to function on a permanent basis, and build up the institutional capacity to support it."[59] The task force proposed that CD monitoring be used "to help provide targeted assistance to stem erosions" of democracy; that the CD and regional organizations continue to recognize diplomatically any democratic governments deposed by coups; that the CD treat unconstitutional interruptions of democracy as crimes under domestic and international law; and that the CD members "adopt legislation to enable them to impose sanctions quickly, including targeted sanctions—such as asset seizures and visa denials—directed at coup plotters or elected officials engaging in autocoups."[60] The task force's recommendations were heavily focused on making the Community of Democracies a more potent body for the defense and advance of democracy. That is a worthy goal, but there is a long distance to travel.

Since its creation in 2000, the CD has mainly been a symbolic gathering of states. Many of the participating countries have been dubious democracies at best. Some authoritarian regimes—including Jordan, Morocco, Bahrain, Malaysia, Russia, and Venezuela—have participated fully, while others—such as Egypt, Algeria, Tunisia, and Singapore—have been invited to meetings as "observers."[61] While the convening group (a kind of steering committee) includes such major democracies as the United States, India, and Mexico, it lacks the participation of such key industrial democracies as Britain, Germany, France, and Japan.[62]

Meeting every two to three years, the CD has lacked the institutional means to develop, monitor, and enforce democratic standards and to coordinate more than a hundred member states.[63] Fortunately, the impending creation of a permanent secretariat, based in Poland, may partially fill this need. But most of all, the CD lacks backbone, as its broad membership drags the group down to the lowest common denominator of inaction. If the more committed democratic members are not able to draw the line by excluding authoritarian regimes and demanding serious collective action, the CD—so promising in conception as an alliance of democracies—will gradually fade into insignificance.

Precisely because the CD is so diluted, a group of foreign policy thinkers, gathered together in the Princeton Project, has recommended the establishment of a concert of democracies "to strengthen security cooperation among the world's liberal democracies." The group would provide a means to act—with military force if necessary—to defend liberty and protect human rights when other bodies, such as the UN Security Council, fail to move.[64] The Princeton Project suggests that the core of this new group would consist of the established democracies of NATO. However, with only a few exceptions—Australia, New Zealand, Japan, and perhaps South Korea—it is difficult to identify other democracies of any significant size or power that would agree to join a concert whose explicit purpose is to mobilize power outside the United Nations and established regional organizations and in defiance of traditional notions of sovereignty. The Princeton Project proposes expanding beyond NATO to include India, South Africa, Brazil, and Mexico, but all of these influential developing-country democracies (and others, such as Indonesia and Argentina) have long-standing reservations about the use of force in violation of sovereignty and about the exercise of force by the United States in particular. The better near-term prospect may lie in sharpening the CD by making its membership more selective and its institutions more robust, and in enhancing NATO's capacity to deploy military force rapidly and decisively in defense of democracy and human rights.[65]

Whenever possible, it is worth trying to make existing institutions work, or work better. One recently created institution with potential to advance the rule of law (and thus indirectly, democracy) is the International Criminal Court (ICC), the independent permanent court established by treaty in 2002 to try persons accused of genocide, crimes against humanity, and war crimes. The ICC's jurisdiction is limited to crimes committed on the territory or by a citizen of a state that has ratified its founding statute and those that have been referred by the UN Security Council or consented to its jurisdiction. While it may seem that punishing crimes against humanity will do little to advance or defend democracy, in order for democracy to be achieved the worst forms of abuse must be halted and a general, shared climate of respect for law must be inculcated and enforced. Anything that enhances legal accountability at the international level creates a more favorable environment for democracy—particularly when 104 countries have joined the institution.

Unfortunately, the United States stands as one of the few major democracies to reject the ICC's authority. Due to largely misplaced concerns that American soldiers could be subject to arbitrary prosecution, the United States is missing a significant opportunity to advance the global climate for freedom through the rule of law. It is not simply accountability for human rights crimes that is at stake. The mere threat of prosecution can help to rein in warlords and abusive states. The ICC can also promote the rule of law within countries, as its statute requires states to introduce constitutional safeguards against arbitrary rule and abuses.[66]

There is also the tantalizing prospect that the court could add to its jurisdiction a specific set of "crimes against democracy," involving "the use or threat of force to remove or replace a democratic government or to prevent the installation of a democratically elected government." Any such modification would have to first "identify an international right to democracy that is the subject of international regulation," but as I have argued in this book, existing international instruments provide that norm.[67] In time, the ICC could also advance the global rule of law by prosecuting crimes of massive predatory corruption that are not addressed by states because, for example, the president is the guilty party. The devastating humanitarian effects of such corruption and wanton misrule provide a compelling argument for its status as a crime against humanity.[68]

THE SPECIAL CHALLENGE OF THE MIDDLE EAST

As I suggested in chapter 12, a special strategy will be needed to promote freedom in the Arab Middle East as well as in Iran. Unfortunately, the mistakes of the Bush administration have compounded the difficulties in this most difficult region of the world for democracy. With Iraq burning, Palestine slipping into civil war, sectarianism aflame, and terrorism gaining, this is not a propitious moment for promoting democracy in the Middle East. The United States has a tall agenda just to regain some shred of credibility in the region. More effective, multilateral efforts to address the region's crises of instability are essential. But the United States must also demonstrate, with a sense of humility and realism, that it means it when it says it seeks freedom for *all* peoples, and that it is ready to live with the consequences.

One early imperative is a broader and more sustained dialogue among Americans, Europeans, and moderate Islamists of the Middle East. This should extend to all individuals and groups that publicly reject violence, denounce terrorism, and embrace democracy, even if they have as their goal a greater role for sharia in public life. In return for Islamist parties making a clear commitment to democracy, and to liberal principles including peaceful relations with Israel and equal rights for women and religious minorities, the United States and the European Union should press for those parties' rights to contest for power in free and fair elections. As a Council on Foreign Relations task force observed in 2005, the United States "should not allow Middle Eastern leaders to use national security as an excuse to suppress nonviolent Islamist organizations. Washington should support the political participation of any group or party committed to abide by the rules and norms of the democratic process."[69]

Next, the Western democracies need to facilitate strategies for political transition in the Arab world that will help to maximize the prospects for a "soft landing" from authoritarianism to democracy. Mechanisms of horizontal accountability need to be built up, from independent, secular courts to nonpartisan electoral administrations to countercorruption, public audit, and citizen complaint committees. To these might be added a semiautonomous national security council to ensure that an elected civilian government cannot politicize control of the military and police. While this would run some risk of undermining civilian control of the military, it might also reduce the risk to established elites of democratizing control of the government. Such a strategy might especially ease the transition in Arab monarchies, including Morocco, Jordan, Bahrain, Kuwait, and Qatar, because the appointment and supervision of the national security apparatus and agencies of horizontal accountability could remain with the monarchy for some time as a check on elected government. Another avenue is to help build secular, democratic political parties and movements that can better compete with Islamists; still another is to encourage Arab regimes and their oppositions, including more moderate Islamists, to negotiate political pacts that would provide for a transitional period of power sharing and certain guarantees (such as amnesties from prosecution) to protect the interests and assets of those being asked to surrender power. In the context of a gradual dialogue that fosters understanding and trust, some Arab leaders may come to see "extrication through a political deal" as "a much more attractive option than running the risk of being overthrown by a revolution."[70]

The democratic countries of the West need to do much more to engage and strengthen democratic actors in Arab civil society. Part of this involves assistance to NGOs, think tanks, women's and human rights groups, business chambers, and trade unions, but with so much suspicion of the U.S. government and its motives, this assistance needs to come as much as possible from nongovernmental channels, not the U.S. State Department or USAID. This suggests the wisdom of making the Bush administration's Middle East Partnership Initiative (MEPI) a nongovernmental organization, like NED.[71] A transatlantic partnership between the United States and the European Union would expand the credibility of these efforts and mitigate suspicion that it is an "American project."[72]

In general, Western democracies should foster more exchanges with the region and more opportunities for training and advanced study on the part of Arab and Iranian journalists, civil society leaders, businesspeople, legislators, and party leaders. In the enhanced security climate since September 11, 2001, obtaining visas for visits to and study in America is often a time-consuming and frustrating process, particularly for residents of the Middle East. The American government must invest more in the consular staff responsible for reviewing visa applications in order to allow more Middle Eastern professionals to study and train in the United States. And as it did during the Cold War (then with Russian and other Communist-bloc languages), the United States needs to invest in training more speakers of Arabic, Farsi, Turkish, Pashtu, Urdu, and other critical languages of the "Broader Middle East," while expanding foreign broadcasting in these languagues.

Many other creative ideas have been offered for promoting freedom in the region. Some of these, like the conditioning of aid and trade, overlap with the proposals I have offered above.[73] Alternatively, it can be argued that support for economic reform in the Middle East needs to be pursued since an independent business class can provide a much more favorable environment for democratizing.[74] By this logic, anything that can encourage Arab countries to make the reforms necessary for entry into the World Trade Organization (WTO) and for the attraction of foreign direct investment will likely have positive implications for democracy down the road. In addition, Europe and the United States must "work together to complete the full anchoring of a democratic, secular Turkey in the West,"[75] including support for Turkey's bid to enter the European Union and for continuing reforms under its successful Muslim democratic ruling party, Justice and Development. The United States should also support the creation of a security organization, modeled on the Organization for Security and Cooperation in Europe (OSCE), that could provide security guarantees among Middle Eastern states, reduce fears of aggression, and place human rights on the regional agenda.[76]

Finally, there is the vexing confrontation with Iran. Iran is the most dangerous country in the region, given its bid to acquire nuclear weapons and the vow of its zealous president, Mahmoud Ahmadinejad, to wipe Israel off the map. Yet, paradoxically, its population is the most receptive to democratic ideas. Simply isolating and sanctioning Iran (not to mention bombing it) is unlikely to bring about a change of regime. A better strategy would be to increase exchanges with Iranian civil society while offering the regime a broad bargain: the lifting of economic sanctions, the restoration of diplomatic relations with the United States, and the integration of Iran into international circles in exchange for the verifiable halt to Iran's nuclear enrichment program, the cessation of its support of terrorist groups, and the affirmation of basic human rights and the rights of its citizens to monitor those conditions. The more societies like Iran are opened, the better the chances of being able to encourage the political awareness, understanding of democratic values and institutions, and civic pluralism necessary for organic political change. To engage the Iranian people and encourage these processes, the United States needs an embassy in Tehran.[77]

LIBERATION TECHNOLOGY

The growth of technologies that empower individuals and nonstate actors is among the most hopeful dimensions in the struggle for human freedom and political participation. Cell phones, e-mail, and the Internet magnify the speed with which individuals can organize for social change, as well as the scale on which they can do so, creating what Thomas L. Friedman called "super-empowered individuals."[78] Unfortunately, what can empower civic activists for human rights can also empower terrorists. And authoritarian states are finding ways to control and obstruct the independent use of technology by citizens seeking greater freedom and democracy. Yet there is reason to believe that the net contribution of technology is and will be powerfully positive, and there are things that can be done to accelerate the spread of it.

The combination of mobile communication devices and "pervasive computing" (through inexpensive microprocessors embedded in every-day objects and environments) is enabling ordinary people to cooperate for social change and expand reformist networks as never before.[79] Cell phones with text messaging have been instrumental in facilitating protests against authoritarian rule and abuses of democracy, generating what technology guru Howard Rheingold calls "smart mobs," vast networks of individuals communicating rapidly and with little hierarchy or central direction to assemble or "swarm" into a certain location in order to protest. "On January 20, 2001, President Joseph Estrada of the Philippines became the first head of state in history to lose power to a smart mob," when first tens of thousands and then, within four days, more than a million Filipinos assembled at a historic protest site in Manila in response to messages reading "Go 2EDSA, Wear blck."[80] Text messaging along with e-mail helped to rapidly mobilize public support for the Orange Revolution in Ukraine, the Cedar Revolution in Lebanon (which drew more than a million demonstrators to demand the withdrawal of Syrian troops), the 2005 protests in Kuwait (demanding the right to vote for women), the 2007 student protests in Venezuela (against the closure of a major independent television station), and numerous student protests in Iran.[81] In Nigeria, the Network of Mobile Election Monitors used text messaging to gather reports of vote fraud in the 2007 elections that helped international observers gain a more convincing national picture of the rigging.[82]

In China, pervasive text messaging has been a key factor in the mushrooming of grassroots protests. "Now, one can use SMS [short message service, or text messaging] to organize a large-scale protest without asking governmental permission," says Xiao Qiang, a leading human rights advocate who directs the Chinese Internet Project at the University of California, Berkeley. "Today's Chinese youth have much more powerful communication tools in their hands."[83] In one recent case, an eruption of hundreds of thousands of cell phone text messages in Xiamen generated so much public protest over the construction of an environmentally hazardous chemical plant that the authorities suspended the project.[84] The technology is even seeping into the world's most brutally closed society, North Korea. An activist who works with North Korean refugees observes: "With radios, it takes many hours of airtime to convince North Koreans that there's something else out there. But with a cell phone, it can take one call to change someone's mind."[85] In the oil-rich Gulf states, text messaging allows civic activists and political opposition "to build unofficial membership lists, spread news about detained activists, encourage voter turnout, schedule meetings and rallies, and develop new issue campaigns—all while avoiding government-censored newspapers, television stations, and Web sites."[86]

Text messaging is often complemented, or preceded and then reinforced, by Internet blogging, which has become a revolutionary fourth dimension of the fourth estate. Virtually any citizen can become, in a sense, a columnist, journalist, or even television broadcaster. As protests against the construction of the chemical plant mounted in Xiamen, "citizen journalists carrying cell phones sent text messages to bloggers in . . . other cities, who then posted real-time reports for the entire country to see," thus magnifying the impact.[87] In Bahrain, bloggers used Google Earth during the 2006 parliamentary elections to expose the vast swaths of land held by the Sunni minority monarchy for its palaces, in contrast to the slums of the Shiite majority. Where authoritarianism is entrenched but contested, bloggers are now at the cutting edge of the challenge. Nowhere is this more the case than in Iran, which has an estimated seventy thousand to a hundred thousand bloggers, making Farsi one of the ten most popular languages on the Internet.[88] Globally, the blogosphere is growing at an exponential rate, increasing ninetyfold between 2003 and 2006—by which time, a hundred thousand new Web logs were being created *every day*.[89]

The speed of posting in relation to news, the lack of editorial filters and censorship, and the openness of access to any citizen makes blogging the most intrinsically democratic form of media ever established. Blogging embodies the democratic principles of open access and freedom of speech, but also the potential to raise political awareness and transform political values. As one Egyptian blogger told *Time* magazine in 2006—shortly before his arrest at a Cairo protest—he knew the risks but he had "developed a taste for freedom of speech and would not give [it] up so easily."[90] The dispersion of blogging to thousands or even tens of thousands in some countries makes the medium more difficult to monitor, censor, and suppress than newspapers or other traditional media. It is not only opening up traditionally closed societies but also deepening and invigorating democracy, widening the public discourse, and bringing new participants into the public sphere in established democracies like the United States and consolidating democracies like South Korea (one of the most Internet-intensive countries in the world).

Digital cameras combined with Internet sites like YouTube create new possibilities for exposing and challenging authoritarian abuse. Incidents of police brutality have been filmed on cell phone cameras and posted to YouTube and other sites, after which bloggers have called outraged public attention to them. In one famous incident, Malaysia's prime minister was pressured to call for an independent inquiry after it was publicly documented that a young woman had been forced by the police to do squats while naked.[91] When Radio Caracas Television was taken off the air by Venezuelan president Hugo Chávez in May 2007, it continued its broadcasts on YouTube.[92] It is precisely because of the revolutionary implications of this medium that authoritarian states like Iran and Saudi Arabia completely block access to the site.

Older communication technologies also retain great potential. In Serbia, independent radio was crucial in exposing the egregious blunders and abuses of Slobodan Milošević's rule, and then in reporting the vote fraud of 2000 and stimulating mass protests.[93] In Africa, radio is still the most important means of spreading information through nongovernmental channels. Community radio stations are educating people about politics and democracy, informing them about local issues, organizing them for change, and promoting peace and reconciliation.[94] Satellite television has also opened up possibilities for communication outside of government control. The impact has been especially powerful in the Arab world, where al-Jazeera and al-Arabiya not only increase the pluralism of news and information but also enable "ordinary Arabs [to] call in and voice their unedited grievances live before 30 million viewers."[95]

International actors can do a number of things to promote this "liberation technology." First, the established democracies must stand up for freedom of expression online and protest vigorously when citizens are arrested for stating their opinions and exposing government abuses, so long as their postings do not condone or incite violence. Increasingly, the blogosphere will be an arena where democratic dissidents must be defended and protected. The established democracies should condemn all laws that restrict Internet access and punish free expression.

Second, poor countries should be given assistance to expand their mobile phone networks. For the first time in history, millions of poor people in rural villages and urban slums, who may have little in the way of electricity or pipe-borne water, are gaining telephone access via mobile phones.[96] Whereas land lines have been prohibitively expensive, corruptly administered, and monopolized by the elite, now the less fortunate can skip a whole generation of technology and get a phone that not only helps them organize for politics and social change but also enables them to make appointments, receive orders, learn crop prices, and survey market conditions. The cell phone's potential as a tool for generating broad-based local democracy, development, and social capital is only beginning to be explored. Given how much cheaper cell phones (including those with a capacity to connect to the Internet) are than computers, the possibilities for leveling inequality are striking. Writes Google CEO Eric Schmitt: "Mobile phones are cheaper than PCs [personal computers], there are three times more of them, growing at twice the speed, and they increasingly have Internet access."[97]

Third, the established countries should put a higher priority on providing financial assistance, training, and technical support to community radio stations. As with NGOs, it is not realistic to expect that such endeavors will be financially sustainable (or in this case commercially profitable) on their own for some time to come. Where these radio stations and other alternative media perform a worthy and cost-effective service for democratic development, they should be supported financially for the long run.

Fourth, the technologically advanced countries, beginning with the United States, need to fight for freedom in this brave new world. A race is now under way between the technological advance of instruments of liberation and the technological advance of tools to control and suppress them. We need to ensure that liberation wins—even to the point of legally forbidding companies like Microsoft, Yahoo, and Cisco Systems from selling to China and other authoritarian states the tools to censor the Internet and to routinely monitor what people say to one another on it. The established democracies need to push the development and diffusion of technology that can outmaneuver authoritarian states' efforts to block democratic Web sites and disrupt civil society communications.

There is also a race within democracies, between technology to deepen democracy and technology to fight crime and terrorism. Efforts to surveil digital communications and record every move of the public through a profusion of cameras must be carefully monitored and assessed. The controversy over warrantless surveillance of Americans' international phone calls and digital communications by the U.S. National Security Agency (NSA) is one case in point. As Rheingold notes, the digital revolution is enabling people to gain new powers at the same time that they risk losing established freedoms, as both governments and companies relentlessly strip people of their privacy.[98] There are over 4 million public surveillance cameras in Britain (one for every fourteen people), and the government's information commissioner has validated fears that the country could "sleep-walk into a surveillance society."[99] It does little good to promote freedom abroad while it gradually slips away at home.

This of course underscores a broader theme. The United States and its fellow established democracies cannot be credible in promoting democracy abroad if it is deteriorating within their own borders. An imperative for promoting democracy effectively is to present a model of democratic quality, freedom, and vigilance that inspires respect and is worthy of emulation.

15

PHYSICIAN, HEAL THYSELF

During 2006, the Kettering Foundation, which specializes in strategies to strengthen democracy, gathered more than nine hundred "typical Americans" into a series of forums to discuss the state of politics in America.[1] The deliberations painted a picture of distress, disenchantment, and alienation among U.S. citizens. The participants were not simply saying the country was "on the wrong track," as happens when times become difficult, wars go badly, and presidential administrations deliver disappointing policy performance. More than this, they expressed low levels of confidence in the leaders of both political parties, anger at the disproportionate power of the special interests that dominate campaign giving, impatience with the polarization of political life, and a feeling that they were powerless to change things. Overwhelmingly, the participants said that elected officials "are more responsive to special interests and lobbyists" than to the public interest.[2]

Similarly, the forums exposed a decline in civil society and sense of civic responsibility, particularly in the willingness of ordinary citizens to join organizations, do volunteer work, and give to the community. Once the defining spirit of American democracy, which so struck Alexis de Tocqueville in the early nineteenth century, the inclination to associate and participate continues to wane, perhaps because alienation leads to detachment, perhaps because people are more politically passive when they have more diversions in consumption and entertainment. "Money talks," the foundation's report noted, and Americans believe "the average citizen has no voice and is unrepresented."[3] As the forums concluded, some of the participants became more hopeful about the possibilities for invigorating democracy in local communities but others "left feeling as cynical and dispirited as when they came in."[4]

The perspectives raised in the focus groups conform with the broad contours of public opinion data. Save for the blip of patriotic rallying after September 11, 2001, overall public trust in government has been declining since 2000, and only about a third of Americans in recent years "trust government in Washington to do what is right." This matches the prevailing level of trust during the Watergate period, down from three-quarters in the late 1950s and early 1960s and even from more than half of the public at the peak of the Vietnam War protests in the early 1970s.[5] Similar sharp declines in trust in government and in politicians have been evident in Europe as well.[6] Moreover, "fully 74 percent of [U.S.] voters in the 2006 exit polls single[d] out corruption and ethics issues as either 'very' (33 percent) or 'extremely' (41 percent) important"—more than did so for the Iraq war.[7] The Kettering Foundation concluded that "a national dialogue focused on public involvement about this deeply troubling issue might be the key to reducing the alienation, mistrust, and cynicism that are so widespread."[8] But while invigoration of democratic life through public dialogues is intrinsically good for democracy, it is hardly an end in itself. The participants in the forums were responding to deep-seated problems in the structure and performance of American democracy, problems that will not be repaired with talk alone. Yet many were also reluctant to sacrifice or change the system in any way. While some welcomed public financing of election campaigns as "a step in the right direction," others were adamantly opposed, especially if it were to involve higher taxes.[9]

Increasingly, Americans feel that there is something wrong with the way their democracy works—and with good reason. Although the United States remains one of the most liberal, institutionalized, and vigorous democracies in the world, it is also a democracy with serious and even growing problems of political corruption, influence peddling, abuse of liberties, decline of constitutionalism, and polarization of partisan politics. For the United States to be effective in promoting and inspiring democratic progress elsewhere in the world, it must be credible in its own practice of democracy. No country is a perfect democracy, but the United States must become a better democracy, and a reforming democracy, if its appeal to advance democracy is to resonate. It cannot continue to say, "Do as we say, not as we do."

CONTAINING CORRUPTION

I have argued in this book that controlling corruption is a key element in the struggle to build free and prosperous societies throughout the world. Without a reasonably honest government dedicated to generating public goods rather than private ones, development lags. If corruption and abuse of power are rampant in a democracy, citizens lose faith in it. Most political and economic development assistance programs work from the unstated assumption that these are problems of the developing and post-communist countries, not of the advanced industrial democracies. Indeed, most of the top-rated countries in controlling corruption are the wealthy democracies of North America, Europe, and Australia. Yet these countries vary in the extent to which they control (or at least are perceived to control) corruption, and some rank well behind others. American disenchantment with political corruption is far from groundless: in Transparency International's 2006 annual "Corruption Perceptions Index," the United States was tied (with Belgium and Chile) for twentieth place, ranking behind Hong Kong, Japan, and France, in controlling corruption.[10]

Many Americans (and most of those who promote democracy abroad) tend to think of overt corruption—criminal abuse of office for personal gain—as something rare in the United States. Certainly, it is not the norm; most public officials do not accept bribes or steal from the public trust. But every year, federal prosecutors charge more than a thousand individuals with corruption-related crimes.[11] Since 1986, the U.S. Justice Department has convicted an average of about 485 federal officials of corruption each year.[12] Most of these are not elected officials, but some have been prominent members of the U.S. Congress. In 2002, Representative Jim Traficant Jr., a Democrat from Ohio, was convicted of ten corruption-related felonies, including bribery, tax evasion, and racketeering.[13] Sentenced to eight years in prison, Traficant was subsequently expelled from the House of Representatives, the first member to be expelled since 1980; in November 2002, he ran—from his jail cell—for his old seat in Congress and received 15 percent of the vote as an unaffiliated independent.[14] Also in 2002, Democratic senator Robert Torricelli of New Jersey decided not to run for reelection after being implicated in a bribery and campaign finance scandal (though he was never formally charged with a crime).[15] In August 2005, the FBI videotaped Democratic representative William Jefferson of Louisiana accepting $100,000 in cash from an undercover operative as part of an ongoing corruption investigation. The cash was later found stuffed in frozen food containers in a freezer in Jefferson's home in Washington, D.C.[16] Despite the fact that two of Jefferson's associates pleaded guilty to corruption charges and implicated Jefferson in the scheme, Jefferson won reelection to the House in November 2006 and served in Congress as he prepared his legal defense. In November 2005, another representative, Randy "Duke" Cunningham, a seven-term Republican from California, and a former navy fighter pilot, resigned after pleading guilty to accepting $2.4 million in bribes and underreporting his income.[17] He was sentenced to more than eight years in prison and ordered to pay $1.8 million in restitution.[18] In January 2006, Republican businessman and lawyer Jack Abramoff pleaded guilty to three felonies connected to defrauding lobbying clients and corrupting public officials. In June 2006, fallout from the scandal led to the resignation of House Majority Leader Tom DeLay of Texas after two former aides pleaded guilty to related corruption charges; and, in October 2006, fellow Republican representative Bob Ney of Ohio pleaded guilty to similar charges.[19]

In the past decade, the Justice Department has also charged about one hundred state officials each year with public corruption crimes.[20] In the most infamous of these cases, former Democratic governor of Louisiana Edwin Edwards was convicted in federal court in May 2000 of seventeen counts of public corruption, involving a scheme to extort businesses seeking riverboat gambling licenses that allegedly netted the rogue governor more than $1 million.[21] In July 2004, Republican governor of Connecticut John Rowland resigned amid allegations that he accepted gifts and services from businesses seeking contracts with the state.[22] He pleaded guilty to federal corruption charges and was later sentenced to a year in prison.[23] In August 2005, Republican governor of Ohio Bob Taft was convicted of corruption charges stemming from his failure to disclose gifts and golf trips from lobbyists and businesses.[24] In April 2006, former Republican governor of Illinois George Ryan was found guilty on eighteen federal counts related to public corruption.[25] While Ryan served as governor from 1999 to 2003, he steered millions of dollars of state business to associates in return for cash and gifts for himself, his friends, and his family.[26] If these violations are the exception rather than, as in many emerging democracies, the norm, they should induce a bit more humility on the part of the United States when it preaches to the world about good governance.

The problem appears to be much worse in the European Union. As Carolyn Warner documents in her stunning book *The Best System Money Can Buy*, among the more established European democracies the processes of economic integration, privatization, decentralization, and intensified competition have provided new incentives and breeding grounds for bribery, kickbacks, and other forms of malfeasance, both to fund parties and campaigns and to enrich officeholders.[27] As a result, overt corruption, though skillfully hidden, is deeply entrenched in European politics and commerce:

> Fraud and corruption take a noticeable portion of the EU's annual budget, and major party-financing scandals within the states have led many to conclude that corruption has become the norm, not the exception, in Europe's democracies. Corrupt deals in Germany in the late 1990s and early 2000s have involved million of euros. . . . French firms have routinely paid kickbacks of 2–5 percent on public works contracts to political parties. France's privatized defense and engineering group, Thales . . . is . . . under investigation for bribing public officials in France, Greece, Argentina, and Cambodia . . . and for fraud against the European Union itself. After the launch of the Single Market, Dutch construction firms set up a racket on public procurement contracts, and evidence indicates that German industrial group Siemens spent more than EUR 420 million ($553 million) on bribes to win contracts overseas, at home, and in EU neighbors Greece and Italy between 1999 and 2006.[28]

Warner shows that corruption will not be restrained (in Europe or elsewhere) by simply trusting in the magic of the marketplace or by dispersing power and resources outside capitals, since corruption is typically worse at the local level. Oversight and enforcement mechanisms in the EU have thus far been weak and rife with political interference. Moreover, EU member nations have not found democratic ways to fund political campaigns or control their rapidly escalating costs. Illegal kickbacks provide a major means of funding for parties and campaigns, and there is little transparency in political funding. The tendency to abuse power and cut corners in order to accumulate wealth is present, more or less, in all societies, and is only effectively contained by strong, independent, and resourceful legal institutions. The fact is that the struggle against corruption is global, and no country or culture has a special purchase on morality.

REDUCING THE PURCHASE OF INFLUENCE

More subtle forms of corruption have become entrenched practice in the United States and have yielded only very slowly to demands for reform. Most of the funding that flows to U.S. parties and candidates complies with the letter of election law but is meant to peddle political influence, subverting the spirit of service to the public over private interests. In essence, corporate and other special interests are able to purchase public policy and legislation with campaign contributions. A common vehicle for this sale of influence is the legislative "earmark." These funds, also called "pork-barrel" spending, are specified for particular "projects, activities, or institutions not requested by the executive, or add-ons to requested funds which Congress directs for specific activities."[29] Some earmarked funds represent congressional efforts to push public policy causes, such as democracy in Burma or an emphasis on primary health care in foreign aid. But most of them benefit narrow economic or geographic interests and are assigned with little or no deliberation (or even awareness), often as the result of intensive lobbying.

The proliferation of earmarks is a sign of the deteriorating quality of democracy in the United States. From 1994 to 2006, the number of earmarks tripled overall and increased by a much wider margin in some sectors (for example, from 167 transportation earmarks in 1996 to more than 2,000 in 2005).[30] During this period, the cost of earmarks rose from under $800 million to over $3 billion in the Transportation Department budget, from under $3 billion to over $9 billion in the Pentagon budget, and from $2.5 billion to $9.5 billion in the appropriations bill for the Commerce, Justice, and State departments. In the latter case, the number of earmarks increased tenfold in a decade, and came to account for more than a fifth of all spending.[31] In a notorious case, in 2004 Republican senator Ted Stevens and Republican representative Don Young, both of Alaska, earmarked more than $200 million for the Gravina Island Access Bridge, which would connect Gravina Island (population fifty) to the Alaskan mainland even though the island was already served by a ferry that ran every five minutes. Critics dubbed the project "the bridge to nowhere."[32]

Other dubious examples include $1 million for Michigan's Waterfree Urinal Conservation Initiative (the company that makes the water-saving urinals is owned by a former cabinet undersecretary) and $400,000 for North Carolina's Sparta Teapot Museum (home to six thousand teapots).[33]

The explosive growth in earmarking has been accompanied by a similar growth in lobbying. In 2005, there were more than 34,750 registered lobbyists in Washington, D.C., more than double the number registered in 2000.[34] Spending on federal lobbying increased by nearly 60 percent between 1998 and 2005, to $2.28 billion.[35] "Pork-barrel spending has been reinforced by an army of lobbyists and firms that specialize in securing earmarks for clients, including private companies, government contractors, universities, cities, and state governments."[36] It is particularly troubling that earmarks allow legislators to funnel money to such clients without any competitive bid process, forfeiting both efficiency and fairness. A company or institution may receive funds simply because it is located in the district of a legislator who has been assigned to an appropriations committee or because it could afford to hire a lobbying firm.[37] Given the prodigious funding of political campaigns by lobbyists, much of the public now believes that government funding is for sale. During his tenure in the House, Republican Jerry Lewis of California reportedly earmarked hundreds of millions of federal dollars for clients of his close friend and former state senate colleague, lobbyist Bill Lowery. In turn, Lowery, the partners at his lobbying firm, and the firm's clients, provided 37 percent of the $1.3 million donated to Lewis's political action committee between 1999 and 2005.[38] Every earmark and campaign contribution was legal.[39] In the wake of the Duke Cunningham and other scandals, Democratic candidates attacked the Republican "culture of corruption" and won control of both chambers of Congress in November 2006. Earmark reform was widely discussed by both parties, and the newly elected Congress began to enact reforms, beginning with the public disclosure of earmark requests. The idea was that politicians would be reluctant to fund questionable projects if their names were publicly attached to the request. In January 2007 the House and Senate adopted new disclosure rules that require members of both chambers to submit written requests for earmarked appropriations, including the name and address of the intended funding recipient, the purpose, and a certification that the member and his or her spouse have no financial interest in the project; these requests will be made public for any bills sent to the floor for a full vote. The Senate also required that committees publish earmark requests on the Internet no later than forty-eight hours after receipt.[40]

Greater transparency is always an essential early step in any effort to control the peddling of influence. But it is rarely enough, and it will not be enough to rein in earmarking. Reform advocates have also set their sights on one of the sources of the problem—the booming lobbying industry. The Lobbying Disclosure Act of 1995 requires lobbyists to register with the House and Senate, and to file annual reports detailing clients and employers, issues lobbied, and estimated lobbying costs. However, enforcement of the lobbying rules is left to the understaffed offices of the clerk of the House and the secretary of the Senate, who refer alleged violations to the U.S. attorney for the District of Columbia.[41] In addition, the law includes loopholes for "grassroots" and "stealth" campaigns. Grassroots lobbying mobilizes the public to contact lawmakers about an issue, and, by targeting ordinary citizens rather than public officials, lobbyists are able to skirt disclosure laws but still influence lawmakers. Stealth lobbying efforts finance front groups that exist solely to obfuscate who is funding a lobbying activity, since only the front group is required to register and the actual donor remains anonymous.

Voter disgust with political scandals provided Congress the momentum necessary to pass several overdue lobbying and ethics reforms in January 2007. The new rules bar members of both chambers from accepting gifts, meals, or trips from lobbyists or the organizations that employ them, and from using borrowed corporate jets at discount rates. They also ban departing senators from negotiating with prospective new employers—such as lobbying firms and corporations or institutions with lobbying interests—until after their successors are elected and restrict senators from directly or indirectly lobbying the Senate for two years, a significant change since more than one-third of members retiring from Congress in 2005 immediately set up shop as lobbyists. Lobbyists are required to disclose fund-raising activities for senators, such as holding campaign fundraisers, soliciting campaign contributions, and soliciting donations from clients and friends and then presenting the stack of checks to candidates with a clear indication of their source, a practice known as "bundling."

While these new rules implement many of the reforms called for by government watchdog groups, they do not go nearly far enough. First, the architecture of enforcement must be overhauled to establish stronger horizontal accountability. With the 2007 legislation, lobbying, travel, gifts, and ethics rules and regulations fall under the oversight of four separate entities—the clerk of the House, the secretary of the Senate, the House Committee on Standards of Official Conduct, and the Senate Select Committee on Ethics—leading to confusion, inconsistency, and lax enforcement, especially when two of the bodies are made up of members of Congress who have obvious conflicts of interest. The group Public Citizen has proposed a single, comprehensive "independent ethics agency capable of acting as a strong watchdog" that would consist of full-time career officials who are not members of Congress.[42] The agency's budget would be approved only once every two years to protect it from political retaliation.

Second, the connections between lobbying, governance, and political campaigns need to be far more transparent. Public Citizen proposes prohibiting registered lobbyists from soliciting or arranging for campaign contributions to lawmakers and political parties; prohibiting privately sponsored travel for government officials and staff; and temporarily suspending access to congressional facilities for former representatives who become lobbyists.[43] Comprehensive steps are needed to improve the lobbying disclosure system, which has lagged behind the technological advances of the past decade. Public Citizen urges that lobbyists be required to 1) file electronically to help support the creation of a searchable, sortable, and downloadable public database; 2) file quarterly, as opposed to the current twice-yearly filing, to provide more timely information to the public, particularly in advance of elections; 3) disclose the frequency and subject of in-person meetings with legislators; and 4) disclose all previous federal employment.[44] Just as more transparency and better oversight help to control corruption in emerging democracies, they can clean up democracy in the United States.

Third, the revolving door between government, industry, and lobbying must be slowed. This now constitutes one of the most subtle, pervasive, and corrosive means by which policy influence is purchased. The "cooling off" period between government and lobbying jobs could be considerably lengthened, perhaps to four or five years, and the scope of prohibited activities could be widened to include indirect lobbying (such as strategizing and supervising the relevant work of other lobbyists). One reform group also suggests that officials be held to a binding "revolving door exit plan" that would set forth programs and projects on which the official would be banned from working after leaving office; the plans would be filed with the Office of Government Ethics and be available to the public.[45] At the level of state government, the distance to meaningful reform is much greater, as only half the states have laws restricting former legislators' abilities to work as lobbyists after leaving office, and many do not require legislators to disclose associations with lobbyists or the source and value of gifts and honorariums.[46]

Finally, it is time to upgrade the salaries and other compensation afforded to members of Congress and other elected and high appointed U.S. officials. While senators and representatives receive numerous benefits not figured in their annual salaries of $165,000, those salaries are now well exceeded by a large swath of their peers in business and the professions. Similarly, salaries of senior executive-branch officers declined in real value by 27 percent between 1970 and 2006.[47] Though no salary can ever be high enough to deter temptation completely, politicians' legitimate pay needs to be raised, and the setting of salaries should no longer be the duty of Congress. By forming a federal commission to set congressional and other high government salaries, Congress would be relieved of the political blame (and voter backlash) for aligning its salaries with its responsibilities, and executive-branch officers would no longer need to wrangle their salaries through the appropriations process. The problem is much more serious at the state level, where many legislatures are part-time and paid on a per-diem basis—which not only invites but literally requires parallel business or professional lives that may come into conflict with public duties.

Many citizens—angry with the corruption and insider dealing of American public life—will scream in protest at the thought of broad and significant raises in the pay of public officials. But it is the responsibility of independent and informed observers in the media, academia, and civil society to demonstrate the obvious point that, to a considerable extent, we get what we pay for in a democracy. If we are stingy with public pay and oversight commissions, the quality of democracy will suffer.

CAMPAIGN FINANCE

Few if any democracies in the contemporary world seem to have solved the problem of how to finance political parties and election campaigns— particularly in an era with insatiable needs for increasingly expensive television and radio advertising. In the United States, the problem is exacerbated by the Supreme Court's 1976 constitutional interpretation that any mandatory limit on campaign spending is a violation of the First Amendment guarantee of free speech.[48] Yet where there are draconian

limits on campaign spending, as in South Korea, there is also routine violation of the rules, and throughout both established and emerging
democracies, campaign finance laws are typically "honored in the
breach. . . . According to an expert employed by the French National
Assembly, 'the public statistics of party finances contained in official
accounts—in France as elsewhere—are works of fiction.' In Italy, honest
disclosure 'hardly ever happens.' In Japan, published accounts 'are just
the tip of the iceberg.'"[49] It is much better to have clear, realistic rules and
absolute transparency with robust enforcement than overly exacting or
complicated rules that produce widespread violations and cynicism
because they are not enforced. No single chapter can capture the com-
plexities of the campaign finance rules and debates in the United States,
but it is apparent that the system is broken and needs to be reformed.

Among the significant problems are the ability of so-called "soft
money" issue advocacy groups to spend unlimited amounts of money in
support of (or opposition to) a campaign so long as they are not too
explicit in their messages. Another is the ability of donors to amass influence through "bundling" contributions. The biggest problem, however, is
the sheer amount of cash needed, which compels elected officials to
mount permanent fund-raising campaigns for their next elections. The
cost of winning a House race has nearly doubled in the last twenty years,
to an average of more than $1 million in 2004, and the cost of a Sen-
ate seat has increased proportionately by almost as much (to well over
$7 million in 2004, and in some cases to well over $20 million).[50] While
there are provisions for partial public financing of presidential campaigns, the financial competition to run for office has so outstripped the
level of expenditures allowed under the federal matching funds plan that
most of the major candidates in both parties have chosen to forgo it.

The first and most achievable reform of campaign finance is full and
immediate transparency. All campaign-related spending by "soft money"
issue advocacy groups should be reported, with a clear indication of the
candidates being supported, no matter how indirectly. All candidates for
elective office at the federal and state level should be required—as candidates for president and the House of Representatives are—to file campaign finance reports electronically, within narrow windows of time.
Because Senate candidates are not required to file campaign finance
reports electronically, the final accounts do not become publicly available
for months after they are filed. In 2006, in highly contested Senate races
in Missouri, Montana, and Pennsylvania, reports detailing donations in

the closing weeks did not become public until after the election.[51] The Federal Election Commission (FEC) has urged changing the Senate filing requirements since 1997, but the reform has been resisted by senators.

There is also a need for a more independent, nonpartisan, muscular, and coherent oversight structure. Reformers like Republican John McCain and Democrat Russ Feingold argue that the FEC is plagued by an ineffectual structure, the politicization of the appointment of its commissioners, and congressional interference.[52] They would like to create in its place a Federal Election Administration with comprehensive authority to formulate, administer, and enforce policy regarding federal election laws. The administration would have the power to initiate enforcement actions, issue cease-and-desist orders, petition federal judges for temporary restraining orders and other preliminary injunctions, conduct audits, and administer disclosure.

The most ambitious reform—and the most difficult to achieve because it flies in the face of an industry that no politician wants to offend—is to lower the phenomenal cost of television and radio advertising. TV and radio ads are the biggest costs in national and statewide races, and providing candidates with free or reduced-cost airtime would significantly reduce the need for campaign cash. McCain, Feingold, and Democrat Dick Durbin introduced the "Our Democracy, Our Airwaves Act of 2003," which would provide qualified federal candidates and parties with vouchers for the purchase of television and radio advertising time.[53] The vouchers would be funded by a fee, proposed at 0.5 percent to 1 percent of gross annual revenues, on media companies for use of the broadcast spectrum. Candidates would qualify for vouchers by raising at least $25,000 in donations of $250 or less, agreeing to limit personal spending to a specified amount, and having at least one opponent who raises a specified amount. The bill did not make it out of committee, but its approach deserves to be resurrected. Or, more simply, candidates could simply be given free air time; "the United States stands out among the economically advanced democracies by its lack of any provision of free political broadcasts for political parties or candidates."[54]

An alternative strategy would be some form of partial or full public financing of campaigns for most federal and state offices. This approach is no longer so fanciful. Seven states (including New Mexico and New Jersey) have full public financing for at least some state offices, and three of them—Arizona, Connecticut, and Maine—provide full public financing for all statewide and legislative races.[55] Applied nationally, even a partial approach might offer candidates for Congress matching funds for all small contributions (for example, up to $250, the limit for matches in presidential primary elections) in primary elections for the party nomination and then a reasonable minimum floor of financing in general elections, which could be supplemented with any amount of smaller contributions (again, up to $250 or perhaps even $500). This would tackle the way in which campaigns foster the buying and selling of influence by allowing individuals to bundle stacks of maximum-size contributions from family, friends, and colleagues into huge campaign flows.

CHECKING POWER AND PROTECTING FREEDOM

Money is not the only area in which established democracies can falter, and accountability in governance must extend beyond these basic questions of corruption and influence. In the United States, nowhere is greater transparency and political accountability needed than in the executive branch, most especially the presidency. During the Bush administration, it has become routine to use arguments of "executive privilege" to block the testimony to Congress of presidential aides and cabinet officers whose performance or conduct is being evaluated or investigated. The claim of executive privilege may conform to a narrow and stilted reading of the Constitution's separation of powers, but it violates deep democratic principles of the rule of law, of oversight, and of political discourse and civil society.

Democracy cannot be robust when the executive branch overwhelms the others and concentrates excessive power in its own hands. The tendency toward what Gerhard Casper terms, going back to Max Weber, "caesarism"—in which the executive disdains parliament, circumvents established rules and procedures under guise of an "emergency," eclipses other autonomous sources of government power, and scorns "independent political minds" has been a recurrent problem in American democracy.[56] In fact, it is an intrinsic problem in presidential systems generally.[57] But it became a particular problem in the United States after September 11, 2001, as the Bush administration used the "global war on terror" to justify "claims of unreviewable powers to detain alleged noncitizen enemy combatants *ad infinitum*, to detain even citizens as enemy combatants, [and to round] up hundreds of aliens on immigration charges, holding them incommunicado, and proceeding against them in closed, essentially secret hearings," while a pliant Congress lent support.[58]

At the same time, the administration violated Americans' civil liberties by engaging in warrantless surveillance of international electronic communications of citizens outside the framework of the Foreign Intelligence Surveillance Act (FISA), claiming a sweeping and inherent ability of the president to defend the United States that trumps virtually all other restrictions. That is pure "caesarism." And when Congress passed legislation in August 2007 to grant the administration new legal authority for the surveillance, it did so in an astonishing rush, with virtually no debate or close scrutiny of the bill.

Renewing American democracy requires more vigorous assertion of legislative and judicial authority as coequal branches of government, in defense of basic constitutional principles. Fortunately, the courts have begun to do that. In 2006, in *Hamdan v. Rumsfeld*, the Supreme Court held that the Bush administration's plan for special military tribunals to try suspected terrorist detainees violated both the U.S. Uniform Code of Military Justice and the Geneva Conventions. That same year, a U.S. District Court found the warrantless surveillance program of the National Security Agency (NSA) illegal and unconstitutional. However, a federal appellate later reversed that decision, ruling that the plaintiffs lacked legal standing.[59] And hundreds of foreigners continue to be detained indefinitely at the U.S. naval base in Guantánamo Bay, where they have been (at least during the first few years) subjected to techniques widely considered to have crossed the line into torture. Such mistreatment of foreigners in American custody has done serious damage to America's standing in the world and its ability to promote freedom.[60]

As Freedom House eloquently notes in its new study on freedom in the United States, although American democracy remains remarkably free, pluralistic, and resilient in many respects, it must address longstanding injustices as well as new ones. These include persistent racial inequality and overcrowded and abusive prisons, resulting from a "jarring" fivefold increase in the rate of incarceration in the last quarter century. "Almost equally jolting is the statistic that a black man has a one in three chance of being imprisoned at some point during his lifetime"—almost six times the rate for a white man.[61]

The fourth estate must also more effectively play its historic role in scrutinizing and checking the exercise of executive power. This cannot be done when months pass with no systematic exchange between the president and the media, as has happened repeatedly in the Bush presidency. Pietro Nivola and William Galston of the Brookings Institution appeal for more regular presidential press conferences, with a goal of two per month on average, and a requirement that all licensed public media be required to carry them live, and to air much more public service broadcasting as well.[62]

ENHANCING PARTICIPATION

Given how much is at stake in national elections, it is surprising how few Americans turn out to the polls. Since 1948, no more than 65 percent of the eligible population has voted in a presidential election, and in four of the seven presidential elections since 1980, it has been under 55 percent.[63] In the midterm Congressional election years, it has been much worse, with only about two in five eligible voters turning out in 1998, 2002, and 2006.[64]

Whether we look at the percentage of the eligible population or the percentage of registered voters, voter turnout in the United States is dismal compared to other democracies. With an average turnout of about 48 percent of the voting-age population across all elections between 1945 and 2001, the United States ranks well behind not only all other industrialized democracies but even emerging democracies like India, Indonesia, Peru, and Romania. Among more than a hundred democracies and semi-democracies, only about ten have worse average voter turnout rates than the United States.[65]

In local elections, even fewer Americans vote—only about a third of eligible voters on average.[66] Voter turnout dwindles down to an appalling 10 percent or so of eligible voters in many state primary contests. For the 2006 state primaries, it averaged 15 percent, the lowest ever.[67] Under such circumstances, victory tends to go to the extremes—whichever political force can mobilize its hard-core ideological base.[68] For this reason, some American political scientists have endorsed the idea of mandatory voting, which in Australia (where it is most developed) has raised the turnout rate to over 95 percent.[69] Although the fine that Australians pay when they do not vote is modest, it is still hard to imagine the idea catching on in the United States, with its strong resistance to state compulsion.

However, there are other things that can be done to raise voter turnout, beginning with reforms to make it easier to register, and even to register at the polling booth on Election Day, which increases turnout especially among young adults. Nivola and Galston propose making Election Day a holiday and having local, state, and federal elections coincide

more, so that the electoral process is not so "fatiguing."[70] Digital technology can also play a role. At a minimum, it should be made possible, and
very soon, for every voter to type his or her address and zip code into a
computer search engine to find the local polling station. Down the road,
online voting may help to expand participation, though at a potentially
high cost—in my view, too high a cost, given the current state of technology—to the credibility of the election, because of the danger of computer
hacking to sabotage or to tilt the election.

Simply making elections more competitive will help increase turnout.
In addition to equalizing the field in campaign finance, presidential elections could be made fairer and more interesting for more voters if states
opted (as Maine and Nebraska already have) to give two of their electoral
college votes to the presidential candidate who wins the state overall and
then one vote to the winner of each congressional district. Such a shift,
which does not require a constitutional amendment, would likely result
in wider presidential campaigning, closer electoral college votes, and
higher voter involvement, interest, and turnout.[71] Big states like California and Texas would have to move simultaneously, however, or not at
all—for fear of unilaterally surrendering their impact.

The problem is not just with voting, however. Interest in politics and
citizen engagement in public life seem to be declining. The number of
candidates running for local offices dropped 15 percent nationally
between 1974 and 1994.[72] Seven California cities canceled elections in
2003 because of a lack of candidates.[73] The proportion of high school
seniors saying they "will probably work" or "have already worked" on a
political campaign declined from one-fifth in the mid-1970s to a tenth in
2001.[74] During the same quarter century, the proportion of high school
seniors interested in current events also eroded.[75] More worrisome still
are the indications of broader declines in civic engagement and the
underlying networks, norms, and patterns of trust and cooperation that
constitute our "social capital." In a pathbreaking work in 2000, the political scientist Robert Putnam presented a wealth of evidence showing substantial decline in America's stock of social capital, as reflected in such
diminishing practices as attending a public meeting on community or
school affairs, going regularly to church, and being a member of a union
or parent-teacher association. Metaphorically, he suggested that Americans
were "bowling alone" as opposed to gathering together in leagues. While
large-scale, professionally run organizations are booming, he (and others)
worry that they do not bring people together as much at the grassroots, in

face-to-face cooperation, and so do not foster the same patterns of trust and cooperation.[76] This is likely a major reason why Americans feel more cynical, powerless, and alienated from politics, since associational involvement and community participation give people more confidence in their ability to have an impact on public issues.[77]

The trends are deeply rooted and will not easily be reversed, but I believe the American Political Science Association's standing committee on civic education and engagement is correct when it observes that people are more likely to volunteer and become engaged if they are asked and given more opportunities. The panel notes positive trends of growth in the nonprofit sector and in volunteering to work with local social organizations, but new policies can stimulate these trends and better link them to active citizenship. One of the most promising steps would be a vastly expanded (but still voluntary) national service program targeted especially toward young Americans (both before and after college education), with multiple options ranging from traditional military service to postconflict reconstruction work abroad to local community service, teaching, and homeland security. Colleges and universities can also expand their innovative and often highly successful programs of service learning. The panel also suggests that the different forms of national service be tied to student aid and other public benefits, and this will require significant funding.[78] Some may balk at the cost, but the American public needs to be challenged to ask whether it can have the higher quality of democracy it wants without investing more in it.

Other innovative efforts are sorely needed to rekindle American civic interest and engagement. These can in part make creative use of new methods and technologies that bring citizens together to confer on public issues face-to-face and use the space of the Internet to diffuse political knowledge and promote debate. Stanford University professor of communications James Fishkin developed the deliberative poll as one avenue for fostering policy changes that reflect the public interest:

> A random, representative sample is first polled on the targeted issues. After this baseline poll, members of the sample are invited to gather at a single place for a weekend in order to discuss the issues. Carefully balanced briefing materials are sent to the participants and are also made publicly available. The participants engage in dialogue with competing experts and political leaders based on questions they develop in small group discussions with trained moderators. Parts of the weekend events

are broadcast on television, either live or in taped and edited form. After the deliberations, the sample is again asked the original questions. The resulting changes in opinion represent the conclusions the public would reach, if people had opportunity to become more informed and more engaged by the issues.[79]

Hosting such deliberative forums to assess local issues remains experimental and very labor intensive, which may limit its application to many regional and national issues. But more than twenty polling exercises around the world have, when combined with television coverage of the discussions, been associated with significant changes in public opinion. For example, a polling exercise dramatically increased Australians' awareness of the problems of the aboriginal population and support for reconciliation with it.

Political communities on the Internet have also been associated with a resurgence in U.S. political participation in some demographic groups since 2004, though it is not yet clear whether social-networking-based Web sites can provide the means for replacing the looser, geographically based communities whose loss Robert Putnam mourns. This is an important question in light of the charged partisan line that divides most of the highly trafficked political sites online, whether they are gathering politically engaged citizens in discussion or sharing news about the government and politicians.

BRIDGING THE PARTISAN DIVIDE

The polarization and rancor of party politics in the United States has also stifled the practice of democracy in recent years. Sharp differences between political parties are the stuff of a vibrant democracy, but when the gulf between parties becomes too intense and diffuse—pervading every issue—it can obstruct the search for pragmatic solutions to pressing policy problems and diminish public confidence in parties and politicians.

There are a number of worrisome signs. One is the declining incidence of "bipartisan" House districts, which vote for one of the two major parties for Congress but for the other party for president. In 1972, over 40 percent of congressional districts (192) split their votes this way; in 1996, the proportion declined to a quarter (110 districts), and in the 2004 and 2006 elections, it was around only 15 percent (59 and 69 districts).[80]

There is also the problem of the "vanishing marginals"—that is, seats in the U.S. House of Representatives that are reasonably open to capture by either of the two major parties.[81] With a few blips along the way, the percentage of these competitive seats has been steadily declining for a century, from about half at the turn of the twentieth century to about a quarter in the 1920s, a little over 20 percent in the 1940s through '60s, and only about 10 percent in recent elections.[82] Consequently, there is much less electoral turnover in the House than in the past. In the last thirty years, on average, less than 10 percent of seats shifted party control in each election compared with nearly a third of seats during the first half of the twentieth century. Such a stranglehold makes it increasingly difficult to displace legislative incumbents. Between 1946 and 1950, 87 percent of incumbents were reelected; that rate jumped to 94 percent between 1952 and 1980, then to 97 percent from 1982 until 2000, and then to 99 percent in 2002 and 2004. The rout of twenty-two Republican House incumbents in the 2006 election must be seen as an exceptional departure from this historical trend.

While the more pronounced partisanship of congressional districts can be traced to changing residential patterns, including the trend of voters sorting themselves along geographic as well as ideological lines, it is also driven by the massive advantage that comes with incumbency. That advantage has been boosted by incumbents' huge edge in fund-raising and progressively brazen "gerrymandering," the drawing of districts with often tortured boundaries to protect incumbents and heighten partisan benefit.[83] Particularly in populous states—where the way district boundaries are drawn has the most scope to swing seats to one party and to entrench incumbents—the process of gerrymandering has become more flagrant with the polarization of political life, the technological leaps in computer programming, and the increasing abundance of detailed census tract data that greatly enhances the ability to anticipate voter tendencies. In the first two statewide elections following a redistricting of California in 2001, not one of the eighty state assembly seats or the forty state senate seats changed party hands.

This has implications for the quality of democracy in three senses. First, political competition does more than pique interest in election results; it is itself an important value in democracy and a means for holding public officials accountable. When elected representatives come from districts so "safe" that it is virtually impossible for an opposing party to win, electoral accountability becomes a fiction. Second, voter enthusiasm and participation wanes when the outcome of an election appears predetermined. When your party always wins or loses the district in a landslide, why bother to vote? Finally, this diminished competition further polarizes politics and public policy. Districts that are competitive, with a more even balance between Republicans and Democrats, tend to have representatives with more moderate voting records than do safe districts.[84] The representatives must appeal (and remain accountable) to voters in the center in order to be reelected.

Partisan polarization is a more serious problem at the level of America's elite "political class"—including public officials, party activists and funders, and interest group leaders—than among the general voting public. But this does not make it less of a problem. The two major parties have come to represent in themselves a kind of tribal identity, in which red and blue displace black, brown, and white as the constituent elements of a national color divide. The structure of party primaries appears to be a central cause of this "disconnect" between the people and the political class. With voter turnout much lower in party primaries, it is the more ideologically committed activists who exercise vastly disproportionate influence over who gains the party's nomination. More and more polarizing nominees run for office, and officeholders hew to more ideological voting patterns once elected to fend off potential challengers in the next party primary.[85] In general elections, the bloc voting of most states in the electoral college gives a heavy geographic hue to the color divide, generating large regional swaths of solid Republican "red" states and Democratic "blue" states.

What can be done to diminish "partisan polemics" and incumbent entrenchment in American politics? Pietro Nivola and William Galston offer some intriguing ideas for depolarizing and rejuvenating American democracy. One of their simplest and most compelling recommendations would be for more states to move from "closed" to "partially open" primary elections, enabling not just registered members of a political party but unaffiliated, independent voters as well to weigh in on a party's nominees for public office (as is the case in some states, like New Hampshire).[86] Opening up primary elections to a wider range of voters (including independent voters, who generally hold more moderate positions) would attenuate the tendency of primaries to affirm ideologically "pure" candidates and positions.

Further, reform is urgently needed of the means by which congressional and state legislative districts are redrawn after each decennial census. As Nivola and Galston observe, "Precious few Western democracies draw up their parliamentary districts in so patently politicized a fashion as do the U.S. state legislatures."[87] The ideal solution is to remove the process from partisan politics and hand it to a nonpartisan commission (as four different states have done by a vote of their electorates in recent years). A study by the Institute for Government Studies at Berkeley found that shifting redistricting duties to an independent commission produces more competitive elections.[88] But why not go even further? Among established and emerging democracies, the United States is the glaring outlier in not having an independent, professional national electoral commission. American federalism will probably not allow a national electoral commission to do anything more than set standards for federal elections and identify best practices, but that is sorely needed in an era when many voters lack confidence in the integrity and security of the voting machines and procedures. A national standard could be used to guarantee voters, when electronic machines are used, some kind of paper record of their vote that can be verified on the spot and then placed in a ballot box as a final check on the count. And surely the United States can do better than the sorry spectacle of having a partisan elected official serve as the chief election official of a state (as is the case in Florida and California). That can only diminish confidence in the process when the chads start hanging or the voting machines malfunction. Some things in a democracy—like administering elections, and, for that matter, justice—are better left to nonelected professionals. Each state in the United States should have a career, nonpartisan official administering its elections.

Then there is the challenge of depolarizing Congress itself, or in the words of Nivola and Galston, restoring "a better balance between the competing values of majority rule and minority rights" within the two chambers.[89] They propose fuller involvement of the minority party in the House-Senate conference committees that reconcile different versions of bills; more restrained use of the Senate filibuster; and "a bipartisan pact" to cut back on the use of "closed rules" that forbid amendments to pending legislation, and thus make it *"harder* to form centrist coalitions."[90] Another of their laudable and long overdue innovations would shift the nomination of federal judges below the level of the Supreme Court to bipartisan commissions, allowing for an expedited Senate confirmation freed from much of its partisan grandstanding. Along with the designation of a single long (but not lifelong) term for Supreme Court justices, this reform of the confirmation process would help reduce the stakes in judicial politics, and so the polarization. It would, however, require a constitutional amendment, and Nivola and Galston thus wisely propose to affirm the filibuster as a legitimate method for blocking Supreme Court justices, thus mandating a sixty-vote supermajority and bipartisan support for all confirmed nominees.[91]

More generally, American democracy needs to move much more dramatically to depoliticize big and urgent issues that are prone to capture or obstruction by narrow interests. One possible model for how to proceed would be the Base Realignment and Closure (BRAC) process used by the Defense Department since 1989. Under this process, an independent, nine-member BRAC Commission of distinguished experts assesses the Pentagon's proposed changes to military bases (closures, reductions, and enlargements) through site visits and hearings. The president must either accept or reject the entire list, and if he accepts it, Congress has just forty-five days to enact a joint resolution to disapprove the entire list; if it fails to do so, the list is implemented. Stephen Flynn of the Council on Foreign Relations recommends this model to set priorities for repairing and modernizing the country's disintegrating physical infrastructure, which has long been the top target for earmarking. An "Infrastructure Resiliency Commission" of fifteen members appointed and approved through bipartisan congressional committees would "identify the investments that need to be made most urgently, regardless of which congressional district a project will reside in."[92]

These proposals for bipartisan (or nonpartisan) commissions—and in previous bipartisan commissions, for example, to investigate the September 11 attacks on the United States and to propose a new strategy for the U.S. presence in Iraq—carry three basic operational principles.[93] First, the commissions are evenly balanced in representation from both major parties, involving respected former members of Congress, governors, cabinet secretaries, and others. Second, because most or all of the serving members are retired from active political life, they have more room to consider the substantive issues, free of short-term political imperatives and constraints. And, third, the members are charged with searching for consensus. If, as in the case of the Iraq Study Group, their recommendations are controversial, then at least the representatives of the two parties are committed to jumping over the cliff hand-in-hand.

There is something undemocratic about entrusting the formation of big policy decisions to expert commissions, but the process is not less democratic than having nine unelected justices with lifetime tenure and no political accountability to anyone but themselves decide such basic questions as when a woman can have an abortion and where a child can go to school. Moreover, the commissions would not finally decide the issues on which they are tasked, but they could take some of the partisan sting and shameless maneuvering out of the debate by establishing a common, agreed-upon basis of facts and analysis, and then providing political cover for members of Congress to take painful policy steps that will offend key constituencies. On fundamental and difficult issues, such as restructuring Medicare or reducing carbon-based emissions, a bipartisan commission's consensus on basic principles could give members of Congress the courage and the political insulation to do what is right by claiming—honestly—that it was "the best reform we could get." In this way, American democracy might take a step back from the politics of partisan destruction and special interest obstruction.

There are other, far more radical, reforms that could further invigorate American democracy by changing the system for electing members of Congress and the president so as to diminish the shared monopoly of the Republicans and the Democrats. One method would be to move from the single-member-district, plurality method of election in favor of some form of proportional representation (PR), in which at least some congressional (and state legislative) seats would be elected from multimember districts. Particularly in larger states like California, Texas, and New York, this would make it possible for smaller parties (such as the Green Party, the Conservative Party, and the Libertarian Party) to win seats and would make elections more competitive (while also greatly diminishing the scope for gerrymandering). It would probably also accelerate the trends toward greater representation of women and ethnic and racial minorities in legislative bodies. The risk, however, would be that it would create even more divisive ideological battles, since Republicans and Democrats would have to defend against defections from their right and left flanks during the general elections.

Because PR tends to accentuate political differences and thus gives rise to multiple political parties, it fits better with a parliamentary system, where coalition government is much more natural than in presidential systems. The logic of presidentialism, in contrast, is aggregative, and it functions best with two principal political parties, so that the president has a reasonable chance of cooperation from, if not party control of, the congress. A more attractive and at least slightly more realistic option for the United States would be to shift to the alternative vote (AV), also known as the "instant run-off," which has been adopted in Australia for the legislature, in Ireland for the presidency, and in several developing countries, with generally positive results in moderating conflict.[94] Legislative districts could continue to be single-member—which also enables greater direct contact between individuals and their elected representatives. Under AV, however, voters are able to rank the candidates in order of preference. If no candidate wins a simple majority, the candidate with the lowest number of first-place votes is eliminated and each voter's second preference votes are redistributed, in an iterative process until a majority winner emerges. In this way, a centrist nonpartisan or third-party candidate might emerge the winner in a polarized contest, and, in any case, the field would be opened up to other contenders. The same logic would work especially well in a presidential election, making it conceivable that a third-party centrist could actually win the presidency, since people would not fear wasting their votes by defecting from one of the two major parties. With a moderate third-party candidate in the race, the Republican and Democratic nominees would have a strong incentive to appeal to centrist voters in order to win either their first- or second-preference votes.

Precisely because of their potential to break the shared monopoly of the two major parties—and the traditional patterns of influence selling and policy making that their closed system sustains—it is unlikely that such radical electoral reforms would be adopted nationally, though several local municipalities have begun to embrace AV.[95] Still, there is no telling what angry and determined voters might do if given the means to implement such changes through initiatives or referendums at the state level. It would certainly be interesting, and a tonic to American democracy, to see some states experimenting with AV to elect members of the state legislature as well as statewide offices such as governor, or even multi-member districts for local and state legislatures.

It is also time to question the size of the House of Representatives. Since 1910, the size of the lower house of Congress has been fixed at 435 members, but the population of the United States has more than tripled (from 91 million to about 300 million today). As a result, the number of Americans represented by each member of Congress has also tripled, from about 211,000 in 1910 to about 690,000 today.[96] This may be one reason—underappreciated in most commentaries—why people more and more feel disconnected from government. There is a simple solution: to increase the size of Congress, for the first time in a century. France has a parliament of about 550 members. There are almost 650 members in the British parliament, for a population barely a fifth the size of the United States; as a result, the number of people per parliamentary district in Britain is about what it was in the United States in 1850 (slightly under 100,000). To achieve such a ratio in the United States would require an impossibly sized House of 3,000 members, but a modest reform could increase the size of the House after the 2010 census by at least 100 members, with each member representing about 560,000 Americans. Such an expansion would have to be accompanied by dramatic reforms to depoliticize redistricting, so that the parties dominant at the state level would not seize upon the process to reward themselves unduly.

TOWARD A BETTER DEMOCRACY

It is one of the many ironies of political life that during the last quarter century the United States has led the way in promoting democracy globally while the quality of its own democracy has been deteriorating. More disturbing still has been the fact that, until recently, relatively little focused attention has been paid to it. While liberal democracy is stable and secure in the United States, it can again become a better democracy— freer, more participatory, more accountable, more competitive, more responsive. That will require some innovations to renew American political institutions and revive the founding spirit of American democracy, based on active citizenship and a healthy but not cynical skepticism of power.

No agenda of reform of American democracy can succeed from the top down. If American democracy is to be renewed and improved, it will have to come from the education and mobilization of the citizens themselves, who come to realize that corruption and abuse of power thrive amidst citizen detachment and that people get the quality of government they are willing to pay for. One should not underestimate the capacity of Americans to mobilize in this way, using both old forms of organization and new modes based on "liberation technology."

Yet, movements from below are often inspired by leaders who call forth our better instincts. In the face of great domestic and international challenges, it is not so difficult to imagine that Americans would respond again to the call of a president who bid them, as John F. Kennedy did on a cold January inauguration morning in 1961, to "ask not what your country can do for you—ask what you can do for your country." Neither is it impossible to imagine that such a new president might begin to restore American credibility in the world by reiterating, and then implementing, the next line of Kennedy's address: "My fellow citizens of the world: ask not what America will do for you, but what together we can do for the freedom of man."

APPENDIX

TABLE 1 THE FREEDOM HOUSE SCALE

Every year, Freedom House, an independent, nonprofit organization that monitors and promotes free-dom and democracy around the world, rates each state in the world on parallel seven-point scales of political rights and civil liberties. In each case, 1 represents most free and 7 least free. Below are some key elements of each scale.[a]

Political Rights

1. The extent to which political leaders and representatives are chosen in free and fair elections.
2. Fair electoral laws and framework.
3. The ability of alternative political parties to organize and contest.
4. The chance for opposition forces to make gains and eventually win power through elections.
5. The freedom of individuals to run for office and campaign.
6. Full political rights for cultural, religious, and other minorities.
7. The capacity of an elected government to exercise power free from military, religious, or other domination.
8. Accountability of government to the electorate in between elections.
9. A government free from pervasive corruption.

Civil Liberties

1. Freedom of expression and belief, including freedom of print, broadcast, and Internet-based media.
2. Freedom of religion.
3. Academic and intellectual freedom.
4. Freedom of assembly, demonstration, and open public discussion.
5. Freedom of organization, e.g., for NGOs, trade unions, and interest groups.
6. Independent judiciary and effective rule of law.
7. Protection from political terror, torture, and unjustified imprisonment.
8. Equal treatment of various segments of the population, including ethnic, religious, and sexual minorities.
9. Freedom to travel and establish residence.
10. Right to own property and establish private businesses.
11. Gender equality and personal social freedoms.
12. Equality of opportunity and absence of economic exploitation.

[a] For a detailed discussion of the Freedom House methodology and the coding schemes for these two scales, see Freedom House, *Freedom in the World, 2006* (New York: Freedom House, 2006), pp. 872–89, and the 2007 survey at Freedom House, *Freedom in the World Survey, 2007*, http://www.freedomhouse.org.

TABLE 2 THE GROWTH OF ELECTORAL DEMOCRACY, 1973–2006

Year	Number of democracies	Number of countries	Democracies as a percent of all countries	Percent of increase or decrease in number of democracies per year
1973	40	150	26.7	
1980	54	163	33.1	
1984	60	166	36.1	
1987	65	166	39.2	
1988	67	166	40.4	3.1
1990	76	165	46.1	
1991	91	183	49.7	19.7
1992	99	186	53.2	8.1
1993	108	190	56.8	8.3
1994	114	191	59.7	5.3
1995	117	191	61.3	2.6
1996	118	191	61.8	0.9
1997	117	191	61.3	−0.9
1998	117	191	61.3	0
1999	120	192	62.5	2.6
2000	119	192	62.0	−0.8
2001	120	192	62.5	0.8
2002	120	192	62.5	0
2003	115	192	59.8	−4.2
2004	117	192	60.9	1.7
2005	120	192	62.5	2.6
2006	121	194	62.6	0.8

Sources: Data from Freedom House, *Freedom in the World: The Annual Survey of Political Rights and Civil Liberties*, annual volumes. Figures for 1973 through 1988 reflect my own scoring of the number of democracies in the world at the end of each of those years. Figures for 1990 through 2006 are from the Freedom House survey for that year (published in the subsequent year), with the exception of the following reclassifications of countries that Freedom House considered democracies in these years but that I classify as nondemocracies: Russia 2000–3, Nigeria 2003–5, Venezuela 2004–6, and the Central African Republic in 2005–6. A few smaller countries rated as democracies by Freedom House could also be considered for reclassification.

TABLE 3 REGIME TYPES IN LEAST DEVELOPED STATES, 2006

The Human Development Index (HDI) is a composite index (ranging from 0 to 1) measuring three basic dimensions (which are equally weighted): a long and healthy life, knowledge/education, and a decent standard of living. Of the thirty-six countries with low Human Development, fifteen (42 percent) are democracies, and another have some degree of political competition and pluralism. Of the fifty-nine countries with low or low-medium Human Development, twenty-seven (47 percent) are democracies. It is the case, however, that about seven of these democracies are perhaps only ambiguously so (indicated by the ~ symbol in the table), because of doubts about the freedom and fairness of elections and of the overall political environment.

Country	2002 HDI score (rank)	Regime Type	Freedom House average score
Low HDI			
Sierra Leone	0.275 (177)	Democracy	3.5
Niger	0.277 (176)	Democracy	3
Burkina Faso	0.302 (175)	Authoritarian	4
Mali	0.326 (174)	Democracy	2
Burundi	0.339 (173)	Democracy	4
Guinea-Bissau	0.350 (172)	Authoritarian (competitive)	3.5
Mozambique	0.354 (171)	Democracy	3.5
Ethiopia	0.359 (170)	Authoritarian (competitive)	5
Central African Rep.	0.361 (169)	Authoritarian (FH democracy)	4.5
Congo, Dem Rep.	0.365 (168)	Authoritarian	6
Chad	0.379 (167)	Authoritarian	5.5
Angola	0.381 (166)	Authoritarian	5.5
Malawi	0.388 (165)	Democracy~	4
Zambia	0.389 (164)	Democracy~	4
Ivory Coast	0.399 (163)	Authoritarian	6
Tanzania	0.407 (162)	Authoritarian (competitive)	3.5
Benin	0.421 (161)	Democracy	2
Guinea	0.425 (160)	Authoritarian	5.5
Rwanda	0.431 (159)	Authoritarian	5.5
East Timor	0.436 (158)	Democracy	3
Senegal	0.437 (157)	Democracy	2.5
Eritrea	0.439 (156)	Authoritarian	6.5
Gambia	0.452 (155)	Authoritarian (competitive)	4.5
Djibouti	0.454 (154)	Authoritarian (competitive)	5
Haiti	0.463 (153)	Authoritarian	6.5
Mauritania	0.465 (152)	Authoritarian	5
Nigeria	0.466 (151)	Authoritarian (competitive)	4
Madagascar	0.469 (150)	Democracy	3
Yemen	0.482 (149)	Authoritarian (competitive)	5

Kenya	0.488 (148)	Democracy	3
Zimbabwe	0.491 (147)	Authoritarian	6.5
Uganda	0.493 (146)	Authoritarian (competitive)	4.5
Lesotho	0.493 (145)	Democracy	2.5
Congo	0.494 (144)	Authoritarian	5
Togo	0.495 (143)	Authoritarian	5.5
Pakistan	0.497 (142)	Authoritarian	5.5
Low-Medium HDI			
Cameroon	0.501 (141)	Authoritarian (competitive)	6
Nepal	0.504 (140)	Authoritarian	5.5
Sudan	0.505 (139)	Authoritarian	7
Bangladesh	0.509 (138)	Democracy~	4
Swaziland	0.519 (137)	Authoritarian	6
Comoros	0.530 (136)	Democracy~	4
Laos	0.534 (135)	Authoritarian	6.5
Bhutan	0.536 (134)	Authoritarian	5.5
Papua New Guinea	0.542 (133)	Democracy	3
Burma	0.551 (132)	Authoritarian	7
Ghana	0.568 (131)	Democracy	1.5
Cambodia	0.568 (130)	Authoritarian	5.5
Vanuatu	0.570 (129)	Democracy	2
Botswana	0.589 (128)	Democracy	2
India	0.595 (127)	Democracy	2.5
Namibia	0.607 (126)	Democracy	2.5
Morocco	0.620 (125)	Authoritarian (competitive)	4.5
Solomon Islands	0.624 (124)	Democracy	3
São Tomé & Principe	0.645 (123)	Democracy	2
Gabon	0.648 (122)	Authoritarian (competitive)	5
Guatemala	0.649 (121)	Democracy~	4
Egypt	0.653 (120)	Authoritarian	5.5
South Africa	0.666 (119)	Democracy	1.5

Sources: UNDP, *Human Development Report, 2004* (New York: UNDP, 2004), table 1, pp. 141–42, and Freedom House, *Freedom in the World, 2005: The Annual Survey of Political Rights and Civil Liberties* (New York: Freedom House, 2005), www.freedomhouse.org.

TABLE 4

DEMOCRACY AND FREEDOM BY REGION
(December 31, 2006)

Region	Number of countries	Number (percent) of democracies[a]	Number (percent) of liberal democracies Freedom House H score < 2.5	Average freedom score for region 1974	2002	2006
Western Europe and Anglophone states	28	28 (100)	28 (100)	1.58	1.04	1.02
Postcommunist Europe (Central European EU states and former Soviet Union)	28	18 (64)	11 (39)	6.50	3.39	3.16
Latin America and the Caribbean	33	31 (94)	18 (55)	3.81	2.49	2.28
Asia (East, Southeast, and South)	25	10 (40)	4 (16)	4.84	4.38	4.40
Pacific Islands	12	9 (75)	8 (67)	2.75	2.00	2.13
Africa (sub-Sahara)	48	23 (48)	8 (17)	5.51	4.33	4.24
Middle East–North Africa	19	2 (11)	1 (5)	5.15	5.53	5.10
Total	193	121 (63)	78 (40)	4.39	3.38	3.26
Arab and Muslim World Arab countries	16	0	0	5.59	5.81	5.40
Predominantly Muslim countries	43	7[b]	0	5.29	5.33	5.01

[a] The number of democracies as classified by Freedom House at the end of 2006, but excluding the Central African Republic.

[b] This group consists of Albania, Bangladesh, Indonesia, Mali, Niger, Senegal, and Turkey.

Source: Freedom House, *Freedom in the World Survey, 2007*, www.freedomhouse.org.

TABLE 5 **CLASSIFICATION OF REGIMES**
(December 31, 2006)

Freedom House ratings (1–7) of political rights and civil liberties are listed in parentheses.

Liberal democracy (Freedom House ratings 1.0–2.0)	Electoral democracy (Freedom House ratings >2.0, but classified as a democracy)	Competitive authoritarian	Electoral (hegemonic) authoritarian	Politically closed authoritarian
Western Europe and Anglophone states				
Australia (1,1)				
Canada (1,1)				
New Zealand (1,1)				
United States (1,1)				
Western Europe				
(24 states)				
Postcommunist Europe (Central European Union states and former Soviet Union)				
Czech Republic (1,1)	Serbia (3,2)	Bosnia-Herzegovina (3,3)	Azerbaijan (6,5)	Turkmenistan (7,7)
Hungary (1,1)	Ukraine (3,2)	Armenia (5,4)	Kazakhstan (6,5)	Uzbekistan (7,7)
Poland (1,1)	Albania (3,3)	Kyrgyzstan (5,4)	Russia (6,5)	
Slovakia (1,1)	Georgia (3,3)		Tajikistan (6,5)	
Slovenia (1,1)	Macedonia (3,3)		Belarus (7,6)	
Estonia (1,1)	Montenegro (3,3)			
Latvia (1,1)	Moldova (3,4)			
Lithuania (1,1)				
Bulgaria (1,2)				
Croatia (2,2)				
Romania (2,2)				
Latin America and the Caribbean				
Chile (1,1)	El Salvador (2,3)	Venezuela[c] (4,4)		Cuba (7,7)
Costa Rica (1,1)	Guyana (2,3)	Haiti[c] (4,5)		
Uruguay (1,1)	Jamaica (2,3)			
9 Caribbean states[a] with pop. <1 million	Mexico (2,3)			
Panama (1,2)	Peru (2,3)			
Argentina (2,2)	Bolivia (3,3)			
Brazil (2,2)	Colombia (3,3)			
Dominican Republic (2,2)	Ecuador (3,3)			
Suriname (2,2)	Honduras (3,3)			
Trinidad & Tobago (2,2)	Nicaragua (3,3)			
	Paraguay (3,3)			
	Guatemala (3,4)			

Asia (East, Southeast, and South)

Taiwan (2,1)	India (2,3)	Afghanistan (5,5)	Singapore (5,4)	Brunei (6,5)
Japan (1,2)	Indonesia (2,3)	Malaysia (4,4)	Cambodia (6,5)	Bhutan (6,5)
South Korea (1,2)	Philippines (3,3)	Nepal (5,4)	Maldives (6,5)	Vietnam (7,5)
Mongolia (2,2)	Sri Lanka (4,4)		Pakistan (6,5)	China (7,6)
	East Timor (3,4)		Thailand (7,4)	Laos (7,6)
	Bangladesh (4,4)			Burma (7,7)
				North Korea (7,7)

Pacific Islands

8 Pacific Island states[b]	Papua New Guinea (3,3)	Solomon Islands (4,3)	Fiji (6,4)
		Tonga[d] (5,3)	

Africa (sub-Sahara)

Cape Verde (1,1)	Lesotho (2,3)	Tanzania (4,3)	Burkina Faso (5,3)	Swaziland (7,5)
Mauritius (1,2)	Namibia (2,3)	Nigeria (4,4)	Mauritania (5,4)	Cote d'Ivoire (7,6)
Botswana (2,2)	Senegal (2,3)	Central African Republic[c] (5,4)	Angola (6,5)	Equatorial Guinea (7,6)
South Africa (2,2)	Kenya (3,3)	Gambia (5,4)	Congo, People Rep. (Brazzaville) (6,5)	Eritrea (7,6)
Ghana (1,2)	Niger (3,3)	Uganda (5,4)	Guinea (6,5)	Somalia (7,7)
Mali (2,2)	Seychelles (3,3)	Djibouti (5,5)	Rwanda (6,5)	Sudan (7,7)
São Tomé and Principe (2,2)	Comoros[c] (3,4)	Ethiopia (5,5)	Togo (6,5)	
Benin (2,2)	Liberia (3,4)	Congo, Dem Rep. (Zaire)[c] (5,6)	Cameroon (6,6)	
	Mozambique[c] (3,4)	Gabon (6,4)	Chad (6,6)[e]	
	Zambia[c] (3,4)		Zimbabwe (7,6)	
	Madagascar (4,3)			
	Malawi[c] (4,3)			
	Sierra Leone[c] (4,3)			
	Guinea-Bissau[c] (4,4)			
	Burundi[c] (4,5)			

Middle East-North Africa

Israel (1,2)	Turkey (3,3)	Jordan[d] (5,4)	Kuwait[d] (4,4)	Bahrain[df] (5,5)
		Lebanon (5,4)	Algeria (6,5)	Oman[d] (6,5)
		Morocco[d] (5,4)	Egypt (6,5)	Qatar[d] (6,5)
		Yemen (5,5)	Tunisia (6,5)	United Arab Emirates[d] (6,5)
		Iran (6,6)		Saudi Arabia[d] (7,6)
		Iraq (6,6)		Syria (7,6)
				Libya (7,7)

[a] Antigua and Barbuda, Bahamas, Barbados, Belize, Dominica, Grenada, St. Kitts & Nevis, St. Lucia, and St. Vincent & Grenadines.
[b] Kiribati, Marshall Islands, Micronesia, Nauru, Palau, Samoa, Tuvalu, and Vanuatu.
[c] Ambiguous case that was classified as a democracy by Freedom House at the end of 2006.
[d] Traditional monarchy.
[e] Technically a no-party regime, but with competitive and partially free elections.
[f] At the end of 2006, in transition to a more open and competitive political system.
Principal source: Freedom House, *Freedom in the World Survey, 2007*, www.freedomhouse.org.

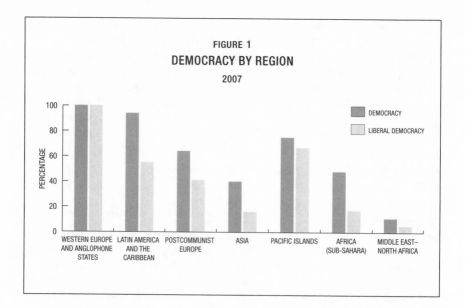

FIGURE 1
DEMOCRACY BY REGION
2007

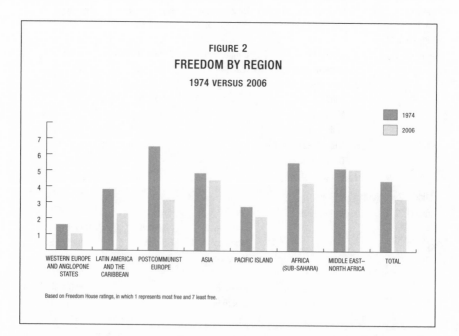

FIGURE 2
FREEDOM BY REGION
1974 VERSUS 2006

Based on Freedom House ratings, in which 1 represents most free and 7 least free.

NOTES

INTRODUCTION: AT THE DAWN OF THE DEMOCRATIC ERA

1. Samuel P. Huntington, *The Third Wave: Democratization in the Late Twentieth Century* (Norman: University of Oklahoma Press, 1991).

2. Juan J. Linz, *The Breakdown of Democratic Regimes: Crisis, Breakdown, and Reequilibration* (Baltimore: Johns Hopkins University Press, 1978), p. 18.

3. Karl Jackson, "The Philippines: The Search for a Suitable Democratic Solution, 1946–1986," in Larry Diamond, Juan J. Linz, and Seymour Martin Lipset, eds., *Democracy in Developing Countries: Asia* (Boulder, Colo.: Lynne Rienner, 1989), p. 242.

4. Ibid., p. 243.

5. Ergun Ozbudun, "Turkey: Crises, Interruptions, and Reequilibrations," in Diamond, Linz, and Lipset, *Democracy in Developing Countries: Asia*, p. 205.

6. Juan J. Linz and Alfred Stepan, eds., *The Breakdown of Democratic Regimes* (Baltimore: Johns Hopkins University Press, 1978).

7. Robert Dahl, *Polyarchy: Participation and Opposition* (New Haven, Conn.: Yale University Press, 1971), pp. 208–9.

8. Samuel P. Huntington, "Will More Countries Become Democratic?" *Political Science Quarterly* 99 (Summer 1984): 193–218.

9. Ibid., p. 218.

10. Seymour Martin Lipset, "Some Social Requisites of Democracy: Economic Development and Political Legitimacy," *American Political Science Review* 53, no. 1 (1959): 69–105.

11. Jeanne Kirkpatrick, "Dictatorships and Double Standards," *Commentary*, November 1979, 34–45.

12. Frank Tannenbaum, *Ten Keys to Latin America* (New York: Vintage, 1966), p. 144. In addition to this work, John A. Booth and Mitchell A. Seligson cite a host of similar expressions of cultural pessimism about the region. See their "Paths to Democracy and the Political Culture of Costa Rica, Mexico, and Nicaragua," in Larry Diamond, ed., *Political Culture and Democracy in Developing Countries* (Boulder, Colo.: Lynne Rienner, 1994), pp. 99–100.

13. Howard J. Wiarda, "Social Change and Political Developing in Latin America: Summary," in Wiarda, ed., *Politics and Social Change in Latin America: The Distinct Tradition*

(Amherst: University of Massachusetts Press, 1974), p. 274, and "The Dominican Republic: Mirror Legacies of Democracy and Authoritarianism," in Larry Diamond, Juan J. Linz, and Seymour Martin Lipset, eds., *Democracy in Developing Countries: Latin America* (Boulder, Colo.: Lynne Rienner, 1990), p. 423.

14. Lucian Pye, *Asian Power and Politics: The Cultural Dimensions of Authority* (Cambridge, Mass.: Harvard University Press, 1985), and Elie Kedourie, *Democracy and Arab Culture* (London: Frank Cass, 1994).

1. THE UNIVERSAL VALUE

1. Lee Kuan Yew, interviewed by Fareed Zakaria, "Culture Is Destiny: A Conversation with Lee Kuan Yew," *Foreign Affairs* 73 (March–April 1994): 111.

2. Transcript of interview on the PBS show *Commanding Heights*, conducted May 5, 2001, http://www.pbs.org/wgbh/commandingheights/shared/minitextlo/int_leekuanyew.html. Four years later, asked by the German magazine *Der Spiegel* why he had kept his "distance from Western style democracy," Lee replied: "I cannot run my system based on their rules. I have to amend it to fit my people's position. In multiracial societies, you don't vote in accordance with your economic interests and social interests, you vote in accordance with race and religion. Supposing I'd run their system here, Malays would vote for Muslims, Indians would vote for Indians, Chinese would vote for Chinese. I would have a constant clash in my Parliament which cannot be resolved because the Chinese majority would always overrule them. So I found a formula that changes that." *Der Spiegel* interview with Lee Kuan Yew, August 14, 2005, http://infoproc.blogspot.com/2005/08/lee-kuan-yew-interview.html.

3. Lucian Pye, *Asian Power and Politics: The Cultural Dimensions of Authority* (Cambridge, Mass.: Harvard University Press, 1985), p. vii; see also pp. 18–19, 22–29, 326–41.

4. Howard Wiarda, "The Dominican Republic: Mirror Legacies of Democracy and Authoritarianism," in Larry Diamond, Juan J. Linz, and Seymour Martin Lipset, eds., *Democracy in Developing Countries: Latin America* (Boulder, Colo.: Lynne Rienner, 1990), p. 450.

5. Quoted in Martin Kramer, "Islam vs. Democracy," *Commentary*, January 1993, p. 36. To be fair, Kramer saw the chief problem for democracy in the Middle East to reside not in Arab culture or Islam per se but in the rise of Islamic fundamentalism.

6. Elie Kedourie, *Democracy and Arab Culture* (Washington, D.C.: Washington Institute for Near East Policy, 1992), pp. 5–6. Kedourie was born and grew up in Baghdad, in an Iraqi Jewish family, before moving to England for higher education.

7. Ibid., pp. 6 and 103.

8. Samuel P. Huntington, *The Clash of Civilizations and the Remaking of World Order* (New York: Simon and Schuster, 1996), p. 309.

9. Ibid., p. 311.

10. Ibid., pp. 310 and 312.

11. Joseph Schumpeter, *Capitalism, Socialism, and Democracy*, 2nd ed. (New York: Harper, 1947), p. 269.

12. Larry Diamond and Leonardo Morlino, "The Quality of Democracy: An Overview," *Journal of Democracy* 15 (October 2004): 23. See also Guillermo O'Donnell, "Why the Rule of Law Matters," in idem, pp. 32–46.

13. See also Larry Diamond, *Developing Democracy: Toward Consolidation* (Baltimore: Johns Hopkins University Press, 1999), pp. 10–13. When a democracy meets all the institutional attributes of liberal democracy, it also satisfies "thick" conceptions of what a democracy should be. Some go further, however, and rate the degree of democracy in part according to the extent of political participation (including of women and minorities) and of commitment to democratic values. These dimensions may help to capture the overall quality of democracy, but when they are made equivalent in importance to free and fair elections in determining whether democracy exists at all, confusion can result, as it does with the new Economist Intelligence Unit's Index of Democracy, http://www.economist.com/media/pdf/DEMOCRACY_INDEX_2007_v3.pdf.

14. Diamond, *Developing Democracy*, pp. 15–16. There are many other pseudonyms for this species of regime, including *virtual democracies, electoral authoritarian* and *competitive authoritarian* regimes. See respectively Richard A. Joseph, "Africa, 1990–1997: From *Abertura* to Closure," *Journal of Democracy* 9 (April 1998): 3–17, Andreas Schedler, "Elections without Democracy: The Menu of Manipulation," and Steven Levitsky and Lucan A. Way, "Elections without Democracy: The Rise of Competitive Authoritarianism," in *Journal of Democracy* 13 (April 2002): 36–50 and 51–65.

15. Freedom House, *Freedom in the World 2000–2001: The Annual Survey of Political Rights and Civil Liberties* (New York: Freedom House, 2001), p. 121. See appendix, table 1, for a list of the elements monitored by Freedom House.

16. Levitsky and Way, "The Rise of Competitive Authoritarianism," p. 53.

17. Carolyn M. Warner, *The Best System Money Can Buy: Corruption in the European Union* (Ithaca, N.Y.: Cornell University Press, 2007).

18. This draws from Jorgen Elklit and Palle Svensson, "What Makes Elections Free and Fair?" *Journal of Democracy* 8 (July 1997): 32–46. See also the essays on electoral administration in Andreas Schedler, Larry Diamond, and Marc F. Plattner, eds., *The Self-Restraining State: Power and Accountability in New Democracies* (Boulder, Colo.: Lynne Rienner, 1999), pp. 75–142.

19. For a thoughtful critique of international election observing, see Thomas Carothers, "The Rise of Election Monitoring: The Observers Observed," *Journal of Democracy* 8 (July 1997): 16–31.

20. Miriam Kornblith, "The Referendum in Venezuela: Elections versus Democracy," *Journal of Democracy* 16 (January 2005): 136.

21. In counting the number of democracies from 1990 in appendix, table 2, I accept the classifications of Freedom House except when (as in the cases of Russia, Venezuela, and Nigeria in certain years), I find considerable evidence that they are wrong. I have also recoded the Central African Republic as a nondemocracy, as it is hard to see how any country with a 5 on political rights can really be a democracy. Some other recent Freedom House classifications of democracy, such as Malawi, Mozambique, and Comoros, are also highly questionable. In fact, Steven Levitsky and Lucan Way consider that a number of other countries classified by Freedom House as democracies—including Georgia, Albania, Moldova, Benin, Senegal, Zambia, and Kenya—are all *competitive authoritarian*. (See their forthcoming book, *Competitive Authoritarianism*). In the "gray zone," it is very hard to make a confident assessment of an ambiguous regime.

22. Seymour Martin Lipset, *Political Man* (Baltimore: Johns Hopkins University Press, 1981). The first edition of this book was published in 1960, and in fact Lipset's essay on this theme, "Some Social Requisites of Democracy," was published in the *American Political Science Review* in 1959.

23. Adam Przeworski, Michael E. Alvarez, José Antonio Cheibub, and Fernando Limongi, *Democracy and Development: Political Institutions and Well-Being in the World, 1950–1990* (Cambridge: Cambridge University Press, 2000), pp. 98–106.

24. Their poorest category was under $1,000 in 1985 purchasing power parity dollars, which is equivalent to $1,449 in year 2000 dollars. See ibid., pp. 92–103. Appendix, table 3, ranks the low and low-medium Human Development Index (HDI) alongside their prospects for democracy.

25. Amartya Sen, "Democracy as a Universal Value," in Larry Diamond and Marc F. Plattner, eds., *The Global Divergence of Democracies* (Baltimore: Johns Hopkins University Press, 2001), p. 13.

26. Ibid., p. 12.

27. Amartya Sen, "Human Rights and Asian Values," *New Republic*, July 14–21, 1997, p. 10 of 12, Internet version.

28. Amartya Sen, *Development as Freedom* (New York: Alfred A. Knopf, 1999), p. 235.

29. Kim Dae Jung, "Is Culture Destiny? The Myth of Asia's Anti-Democratic Values," *Foreign Affairs* 73 (November–December 1974): 191.

30. Hahm Chaibong, "The Ironies of Confucianism," *Journal of Democracy* 15 (July 2004): 102, 105.

31. Ibid., p. 106.

32. Amartya Sen, "Human Rights and Asian Values," p. 5.

33. Ibid., p. 8.

34. Abdou Filali-Ansary, "Muslims and Democracy," in Larry Diamond, Marc F. Plattner, and Daniel Brumberg, eds., *Islam and Democracy in the Middle East* (Baltimore: Johns Hopkins University Press, 2003), p. 198.

35. Ibid., p. 203.

36. Mark Tessler, "Do Islamic Orientations Influence Attitudes Toward Democracy in the Arab World? Evidence from Egypt, Jordan, Morocco, and Algeria," *International Journal of Comparative Sociology* 2 (Spring 2003): 233.

37. *The Arab Human Development Report, 2002* (New York: United Nations Development Program, 2002), p. 2.

38. Ibid, p. 114.

39. Kim Dae Jung, "Is Culture Destiny?" p. 190.

40. Sen, *Development as Freedom,* p. 247.

41. See http://www.worldvaluessurvey.org/.

42. Of course there is the huge challenge of translating questions across a vast number of languages to capture precisely the right nuance, but these comparative surveys work hard to check the reliability of translations.

43. The raw data and content of the survey may be found in Ronald Inglehart, Miguel Basáñez, Jaime Díez-Medrano, Loek Halman, and Ruud Luijkx, *Human Beliefs and Values: A Cross-Cultural Sourcebook Based on the 1999–2002 Values Surveys* (Buenos Aires: Siglo XXI Editores, 2004), questions E018, E114, and E123.

44. This question may seem similar to the first one in table 1.1, but it is actually more demanding, because it is not a simple yes/no question but allows two other potentially plausible options: "In some circumstances a non-democratic government can be preferable," or "For someone like me, it doesn't matter what kind of government we have." Wording varies slightly across regional barometers. This one is drawn from the Afrobarometer, http://www .afrobarometer.org/questionnaires/nig-R3Questionnaire-23aug05.pdf.

45. "Islam, Democracy, and Public Opinion in Africa," Afrobarometer Briefing Paper No. 3, September 2002, http://www.afrobarometer.org/papers/AfrobriefNo3.pdf.

46. Tessler, "Do Islamic Orientations Influence Attitudes Toward Democracy in the Arab World?" p. 240. See also Mark Tessler, "Islam and Democracy in the Middle East: The Impact of Religious Orientations on Attitudes toward Democracy in Four Arab Countries," *Comparative Politics* 34 (April 2002): 337–54.

47. Tessler, "Do Islamic Orientations Influence Attitudes Toward Democracy in the Arab World?" p. 245.

48. Richard Rose, "How Muslims View Democracy: Evidence from Central Asia," *Journal of Democracy* 13 (October 2002): 107.

49. Pippa Norris and Ronald Inglehart, "Islamic Culture and Democracy: Testing the 'Clash of Civilizations' Thesis," in Ronald Inglehart, ed., *Human Values and Social Change: Findings from Values Surveys* (Leiden, The Netherlands: Brill, 2003), pp. 30–31.

50. Yilmaz Esmer, "Is There an Islamic Civilization?" in Inglehart, *Human Values and Social Change,* p. 62.

51. Abdou Filali-Ansary, "The Sources of Enlightened Muslim Thought," in Diamond et al., *Islam and Democracy in the Middle East,* pp. 237–51.

52. Abdelwahab El-Affendi, "The Elusive Reformation," in Diamond et al., *Islam and Democracy in the Middle East,* p. 255.

53. Filali-Ansary, "Muslims and Democracy," p. 203.

54. Russell J. Dalton and Doh Chull Shin, "Democratic Aspirations and Social Moderniza-tion," in Dalton and Shin, eds., *Citizens, Democracy, and Markets around the Pacific Rim* (Oxford and New York: Oxford University Press, 2006), p. 83.

55. Ibid., p. 85.

56. Russell J. Dalton and Nhu-Ngoc T. Ong, "Authority Orientations and Democratic Atti-tudes: A Test of the 'Asian Values' Hypothesis," in Dalton and Shin, *Citizens, Democracy, and Markets around the Pacific Rim*, p. 101.

57. At the time of the first East Asia Barometer, when these questions were asked, the six democracies surveyed were Japan, Korea, Taiwan, the Philippines, Thailand, and Mongolia, but Thailand recently suffered a military coup, and Indonesia (among others) has been added to the second round of the survey, conducted in 2005 and 2006.

58. Doh Chull Shin and Jason Wells, "Challenge and Change in East Asia: Is Democracy the Only Game in Town?" *Journal of Democracy* 16 (April 2005): 95–96.

59. Diamond, *Developing Democracy*, pp. 188–90. Even as people in Taiwan have become weary of political deadlock and cynical about corruption, this commitment to liberal values has continued to deepen. Between the 2001 and 2005 surveys, the percentage who disagree that the government should decide what ideas are allowed to be discussed increased from 63 to 71 percent (continuing a trend from 1990 when it was only at about 50 percent), and those disagreeing that government leaders' decisions should be followed because they "are like the head of a family" increased from 63 to 71 percent.

60. Data are from the second round of the Asian Barometer.

61. Dalton and Shin, "Democratic Aspirations," pp. 87–88.

2. THE DEMOCRATIC BOOM

1. Samuel P. Huntington, *The Third Wave: Democratization in the Late Twentieth Century* (Norman: University of Oklahoma Press, 1991), p. 4.

2. Ibid.

3. Ibid., p. 5.

4. Ibid., p. 15.

5. Ibid., table 1.1, p. 26. My own count is twenty-eight.

6. For a gripping account of this important historical episode, and the larger story of how nonviolent civic action has ended oppression, secured rights, and established democracy, see Peter Ackerman and Jack DuVall, *A Force More Powerful: A Century of Nonviolent Conflict* (New York: Palgrave, 2000).

7. Michael McFaul, "The Fourth Wave of Democracy and Dictatorship: Noncooperative Transitions in the Postcommunist World," *World Politics* 54 (2002): 212–44. I consider the post-1989 democratic transitions part of the third wave because, following the framework of Huntington, there had not yet been a reverse wave ending the third wave, and in fact the entire period from 1974 to 1999 is one of continued democratic expansion.

8. Richard Joseph, "Africa: The Rebirth of Political Freedom," *Journal of Democracy* 2 (Fall 1991): 11–24.

9. Michael Bratton, "Second Elections in Africa," in Larry Diamond and Marc F. Plat-tner, eds., *Democratization in Africa* (Baltimore: Johns Hopkins University Press, 1999), pp. 18–33.

10. These movements, in fact, were influenced by the theory and examples of nonviolent civic action articulated in *A Force More Powerful* and advanced by the International Center for Nonviolent Conflict, http://www.nonviolent-conflict.org/.

11. Michael McFaul, "Transitions from Postcommunism," *Journal of Democracy* 16 (July 2005): 4.

12. Ibid., quotations from pp. 10, 11, and 13.

13. Huntington, *The Third Wave*, pp. 104–6.

14. There is an enormous literature on the "pacted" character of democratic transitions. In addition to Huntington, see, for example, Juan Linz, "Transitions to Democracy," *Washington Quarterly* 13 (1990); Guillermo O'Donnell and Philippe Schmitter, *Transitions from Authoritarian Rule: Tentative Conclusions about Uncertain Democracies* (Baltimore: Johns Hopkins University Press, 1986); and Terry Karl, "Petroleum and Political Pacts," in O'Donnell, Schmitter, and Laurence Whitehead, eds., *Transitions from Authoritarian Rule: Latin America* (Baltimore: Johns Hopkins University Press, 1986), pp. 196–219.

15. O'Donnell and Schmitter, *Transitions from Authoritarian Rule: Tentative Conclusions*, p. 19.

16. Larry Diamond, *Developing Democracy: Toward Consolidation* (Baltimore: Johns Hopkins University Press, 1999), pp. 232–39.

17. Huntington, *The Third Wave*, pp. 174–85.

18. Staffan Lindberg, "The Surprising Significance of African Elections," *Journal of Democracy* 17 (January 2006): 139–51, and *Democracy and Elections in Africa* (Baltimore: Johns Hopkins University Press, 2006).

19. For a comprehensive classification of all the world's regimes as of the end of 2006, see appendix, tables 4 and 5.

20. Empirically, I classify as *liberal* any democracy that scores a 1 or a 2 on each of the Freedom House seven-point scales of political rights and civil liberties. For more on Freedom House criteria, see appendix, table 1.

3. THE DEMOCRATIC RECESSION

1. All quotations in this paragraph and the one that follows are from Ahmed Rashid, "Pakistan's Coup: Planting the Seeds of Democracy?" *Current History*, December 1999, p. 409.

2. The following analytic account draws heavily from the following sources: Ameen Jan, "Pakistan on a Precipice," *Asian Survey* 34, no. 5 (1999): 699–719; Leo Rose and D. Hugh Evans, "Pakistan's Enduring Experiment," *Journal of Democracy* 8 (January 1997): 83–94; and U.S. Department of State, 1999 *Country Reports on Human Rights Practicies*, February 25, 2000, www.state.gov/www/global/human_rights/1999_hrp_report/pakistan.html.

3. Rose and Evans, "Pakistan's Enduring Experiment," p. 89.

4. Jan, "Pakistan on a Precipice," p. 702. The MQM was seen as a particularly serious threat because of its political dominance in the country's commercial capital, Karachi, which contains a mixture of all of Pakistan's ethnic groups.

5. United Nations Development Program, *Human Development Report, 2002* (New York: Oxford University Press, 2002), table 1, p. 151.

6. Ibid., table 2, p. 155, and World Bank, *Entering the 21st Century: World Development Report, 1999/2000* (Baltimore: Oxford University Press, 2000), tables 3 and 11, pp. 235 and 251.

7. Jan, "Pakistan on the Precipice," p. 708.

8. Adrian Karatnycky, "Liberty's Expansion in a Turbulent World: Thirty Years of the Survey of Freedom," in *Freedom in the World, 2003: The Annual Survey of Political Rights and Civil Liberties* (New York: Freedom House, 2003), p. 7.

9. Arch Puddington, "Freedom in the World, 2006: Middle East Progress Amid Global Gains," in *Freedom in the World, 2006: The Annual Survey of Political Rights and Civil Liberties* (New York: Freedom House, 2006), p. 3.

10. Adrian Karatnycky, "The 2001–2002 Freedom House Survey of Freedom: The Democracy Gap," in Freedom House, *Freedom in the World, 2001–2002: The Annual Survey of Political Rights and Civil Liberties* (New York: Freedom House, 2002), p. 7.

11. Arch Puddington, "The 2006 Freedom House Survey: The Pushback Against Democracy," *Journal of Democracy* 18 (April 2007): 119.

12. Michael McFaul, "What Went Wrong in Russia? The Perils of a Protracted Transition?" *Journal of Democracy* 10 (April 1999): 11. Not all analysts agreed that Russia was a democracy even under Yeltsin. For the Russian political scientist Lilia Shevtsova, that regime was a

"constitutional electoral autocracy" featuring "a constant conflict between a democratically elected and legitimated government and a leader whose powers are authoritarian in scope." "Russia under Putin: Can Electoral Autocracy Survive," *Journal of Democracy* 11 (July 2000): 37.

13. Ivan Krastev, "New Threats to Freedom: Democracy's 'Doubles,'" *Journal of Democracy* 17 (April 2006): 54.

14. Charles Fairbanks, "What Went Wrong in Russia? The Feudalization of the State," *Journal of Democracy* 10 (April 1999): 47–53.

15. Lilia Shevtsova, "Russian Democracy in Eclipse: The Limits of Bureaucratic Authoritarianism," *Journal of Democracy* 15 (July 2004): 68. Critics would later charge that Putin and his allies had staged the explosions to whip up support for the war in Chechnya. This had been one of the principal allegations of the assassinated Alexander Litvinenko, a former KGB and FSB operative who defected to Britain in 2000 after claiming he had been ordered to kill Boris Berezokvsky, the billionaire Russian oligarch who fell out with Putin.

16. Freedom House, *Freedom in the World, 2000–2001*, p. 446.

17. Michael McFaul, "Russia under Putin: One Step Forward, Two Steps Back," *Journal of Democracy* 11 (July 2000): 32.

18. Michael McFaul and Nikolai Petrov, "Russian Democracy in Eclipse: What the Elections Tell Us," *Journal of Democracy* 15 (July 2004): 24.

19. Freedom House, *Freedom in the World, 2005: The Annual Survey of Political Rights and Civil Liberties* (New York: Freedom House, 2005), p. 522.

20. Fred Weir, "Slain Russian Journalist Kept Eye on Chechnya," *Christian Science Monitor*, October 10, 2006, http://www.csmonitor.com/2006/1010/p04s02-woeu.html.

21. Alan Cowell, "London Riddle: A Russian Spy, A Lethal Dose," *New York Times*, November 25, 2006.

22. McFaul and Petrov, "Russian Democracy in Eclipse," pp. 21–22.

23. Freedom House, *Freedom in the World, 2005*, p. 520.

24. Ibid.

25. Kathryn Stoner-Weiss, "Russia: Authoritarianism without Authority," *Journal of Democracy* 17 (January 2006): 105.

26. Freedom House, *Freedom in the World, 2005*, p. 3.

27. Krastev, "Democracy's 'Doubles,'" p. 52.

28. The process of decline is documented and analyzed in a number of outstanding academic works, including Terry Lynn Karl, *The Paradox of Plenty: Oil Booms and Petro-States* (Berkeley: University of California Press, 1997), pp. 92–185; and Michael Coppedge: *Strong Parties and Lame Ducks: Presidential Partyarchy and Factionalism in Venezuela* (Stanford, Calif.: Stanford University Press, 1994), and "Explaining Democratic Deterioration in Venezuela through Nested Interference," in Frances Hagopian and Scott P. Mainwaring, eds., *The Third Wave of Democratization in Latin America: Advances and Setbacks* (New York: Cambridge University Press, 2005), pp. 289–316.

29. This was a reference to Simón Bolívar, the nineteenth-century leader of several South American wars of independence from Spanish rule.

30. Phil Gunson, "Chávez's Venezuela," *Current History* 105 (February 2006): 59. By shifting the country to a majoritarian electoral system, Chávez was able to win 93 percent of the seats in the constituent assembly with only 65 percent of the vote. Moreover, because of low turnout and opposition boycotts, his support in successive election victories never exceeded one-third. Michael Coppedge, "Popular Sovereignty versus Liberal Democracy," in Jorge I. Dominguez and Michael Shifter, eds., *Constructing Democratic Governance in Latin America*, 2nd ed. (Baltimore: Johns Hopkins University Press, 2003), p. 167; Javier Corrales and Michael Penfold, "Venezuela: Crowding Out the Opposition," *Journal of Democracy* 18 (April 2007): 101.

31. Freedom House, *Freedom in the World, 2006*, p. 786.

32. Jennifer McCoy, "The Referendum in Venezuela: One Act in an Unfinished Drama," *Journal of Democracy* 16 (January 2005): 113.

33. Miriam Kornblith, "The Referendum in Venezuela: Elections versus Democracy," *Journal of Democracy* 16 (January 2005): 134.

34. Ibid., p. 128. Among the many malpractices that Kornblith, who was a member of the electoral commission, details, were these two: "Thousands of voters had their polling stations changed without their consent and with little or no warning, and foreigners received citizenship and voter status without meeting the legal prerequisites" (p. 134).

35. Ibid., p. 130.

36. Corrales and Penfold, "Crowding Out the Opposition," p. 103.

37. McCoy, "One Act in an Unfinished Drama," p. 116.

38. Gunson, "Chávez's Venezuela," p. 60.

39. Freedom House, *Freedom in the World, 2006*, p. 786.

40. Gunson, "Chávez's Venezuela," p. 60.

41. Freedom House, *Freedom in the World, 2006*, pp. 786–87.

42. Gunson, "Chávez's Venezuela," p. 60.

43. Freedom House, *Freedom in the World, 2006*, p. 788.

44. Corrales and Penfold, "Crowding Out the Opposition," pp. 104–8.

45. Gunson, "Chávez's Venezuela," p. 60.

46. On the failure of the First Republic, see Larry Diamond, *Class, Ethnicity, and Democracy: The Failure of the First Nigerian Republic* (Syracuse, N.Y.: Syracuse University Press, and London: Macmillan, 1983). On the rigging of the 1983 elections, see Larry Diamond, "The 1983 General Elections," in Victor Ayeni and Kayode Soremekun, eds., *Nigeria's Second Republic* (Lagos, Nigeria: Daily Times Press, 1988).

47. Darren Kew, "The 2003 Elections: Hardly Credible, But Acceptable," in Robert I. Rotberg, ed., *Crafting the New Nigeria: Confronting the Challenges* (Boulder, Colo.: Lynne Rienner, 2004), p. 139.

48. Ibid., p. 148.

49. Ibid, p. 149.

50. Ibid., p. 162.

51. Ibid., p. 161.

52. Ibid.

53. Ibid., p. 164.

54. Ibid., p. 165.

55. Interview with Nigerian civil society activist, November 2006.

56. Richard L. Sklar, Ebere Onwudiwe, and Darren Kew, "Nigeria: Completing Obasanjo's Legacy," *Journal of Democracy* 17 (July 2006): 101, 106.

57. Lydia Polgreen, "Money and Violence Hobble Democracy in Nigeria," *New York Times*, November 24, 2006.

58. Sklar et al., "Completing Obasanjo's Legacy," p. 109.

59. http://africanpress.wordpress.com/2007/04/24/ and http://www.eueom-ng.org/.

60. Domestic Election Observation Group, "An Election Programmed to Fail: Preliminary Report on the Presidential and National Assembly Elections Held on Saturday, April 21, 2007," http://www.american.edu/ia/cdem/nigeria/report_070421.pdf.

61. Afrobarometer, "Performance and Legitimacy in Nigeria's New Democracy," Afrobarometer Briefing Paper no. 46, July 2006, http://www.afrobarometer.org/papers/AfrobriefNo46.pdf.

62. Michael Ross, "Does Oil Hinder Democracy?" *World Politics* 53 (April 2001): 356.

63. Of the countries where oil accounts for over half of exports, Norway is the only democracy. While some may protest at my omitting Norway from this list, oil accounts for only about 56 percent of export earnings and slightly more than 10 percent of the economy. Moreover, Norway did not emerge as a major oil exporter until the 1970s, after it had already consolidated an effective, liberal, democratic state. http://www.state.gov/r/pa/ei/bgn/ 3421.htm.

64. Karl, *Paradox of Plenty*.

65. Transparency International, "Corruption Perceptions Index 2006," http://www .transparency.org/policy_research/surveys_indices/cpi/2006. Most of the Gulf oil states have either no gap or are perceived to do slightly better in controlling corruption than would be expected by their rank in human development. This method is only meant to be a crude indicator, in part because of the well-known problems with any index of corruption based on reputations and perceptions. If per capita income were used instead of human development, the gap between ranks on development and controlling corruption would be even more striking.

66. Ross, "Does Oil Hinder Democracy?" p. 328.

67. Karl, *Paradox of Plenty*, p. 16.

68. Samuel P. Huntington, *The Third Wave: Democratization in the Late Twentieth Century* (Norman: University of Oklahoma Press, 1991), p. 65. On these political and sociological effects of oil dependence, see also Karl, *The Paradox of Plenty*, and Ross, "Does Oil Hinder Democracy?"

69. Ronald Inglehart and Christian Welzel, *Modernization, Cultural Change, and Democracy: The Human Development Sequence* (Cambridge: Cambridge University Press, 2005), p. 160.

70. Pasuk Phongpaichat and Chris Baker, "Challenge and Change in East Asia: 'Business Populism' in Thailand," *Journal of Democracy* 16 (April 2005): 61.

71. Ibid., p. 63.

72. Ibid.

73. Amy Kazmin, "Thailand's Thaksin to the Rescue," *Current History* 104 (March 2005): 112.

74. Pasuk and Baker, "Business Populism," p. 65.

75. Kazmin, "Thailand's Thaksin," p. 112.

76. Freedom House, *Freedom in the World, 2006*, p. 713.

77. Pasuk and Baker, "Business Populism," p. 66.

78. Kazmin, "Thailand's Thaksin," p. 111.

79. "Back to the Wall, Thaksin Hits Out," editorial, the *Nation*, July 2, 2006.

80. Thongchai Winichakul, "A Royalist Coup with Ulterior Motive," unpublished essay, September 21, 2006, University of Wisconsin–Madison, quoted with permission of the author.

81. See also Paul Handley, "What the Thai Coup Was Really About," *Asia Sentinel*, November 6, 2006, http://asiasentinel.com/index.php?option=com_content&task=view&id= 249& Itemid=31.

82. *Latinobarometro Report, 2005: 1995–2005, A Decade of Public Opinion*, Corporacion Latinobarometro, http://www.latinobarometro.org/uploads/media/2005_02.pdf.

83. Vitali Silitski, "Belarus: Learning from Defeat," *Journal of Democracy* 17 (October 2006): 139.

84. Ibid., pp. 140–41.

85. Ibid., p. 145.

86. Ivan Krastev, "Russia's Post-Orange Empire," *Open Democracy* 20 (October 2005), http://www.opendemocracy.net/democracy-europe_constitution/postorange_2947.jsp.

87. Carl Gershman and Michael Allen, "New Threats to Freedom: The Assault on Democracy Assistance," *Journal of Democracy* 17 (April 2006): 36–51.

88. Lionel Beehner, "The Rise of the Shanghai Cooperation Organization," Council on Foreign Relations Backgrounder, June 12, 2006, http://www.cfr.org/publication/10883/rise_ of_the_shanghai_cooperation_organization.html.

89. National Endowment for Democracy, "The Backlash against Democracy Assistance," report prepared for Senator Richard Lugar, chairman of the Senate Foreign Relations Committee, June 8, 2006, p. 7.

90. Krastev, "Russia's Post-Orange Empire."

91. National Endowment for Democracy, "The Backlash against Democracy Assistance," p. 7.

4. WHAT DRIVES DEMOCRACY: THE INTERNAL FACTORS

1. Three widely influential definitions of *legitimacy* along these lines are found in Seymour Martin Lipset, *Political Man: The Social Bases of Politics,* expanded ed. (Baltimore: Johns Hopkins University Press, 1981), p. 64; Juan J. Linz, *The Breakdown of Democratic Regimes: Crisis, Breakdown and Reequilibration* (Baltimore: Johns Hopkins University Press, 1978), pp. 16–18; and Robert A. Dahl, *Polyarchy: Participation and Opposition* (New Haven, Conn.: Yale University Press, 1971), pp. 129–31.

2. Guillermo O'Donnell and Philippe C. Schmitter, *Transitions from Authoritarian Rule: Tentative Conclusions about Uncertain Democracies* (Baltimore: Johns Hopkins University Press, 1986), p. 19.

3. See, for example, Dankwart A. Rustow, "Transitions to Democracy: Toward a Dynamic Model," *Comparative Politics* 2, no. 3 (April 1970): 337–63; Juan J. Linz, "Innovative Leadership in the Transition to Democracy and a New Democracy: The Case of Spain," presented to the conference on "Innovative Leadership and International Politics," Hebrew University, Jerusalem, June 8–10, 1987, and "Transitions to Democracy," *Washington Quarterly* 13, no. 3 (Summer 1990): 143–62; and for a perspective focusing more on elite structure, Michael Burton and John Higley, "Elite Settlements," *American Sociological Review* 52, no. 3 (June 1987): 295–307; and John Higley and Michael Burton, "The Elite Variable in Democratic Transitions and Breakdowns," *American Sociological Review* 54, no. 1 (February 1989): 17–32.

4. For a survey of how such legitimacy crises undermined these regimes, see Samuel P. Huntington, *The Third Wave: Democratization in the Late Twentieth Century* (Norman: University of Oklahoma Press, 1991), pp. 49–57.

5. Donald Emmerson, "Southeast Asia after the Crisis: A Tale of Three Countries," *Journal of Democracy* 10 (October 1999): 38.

6. UNDP, *Human Development Report, 2000* (New York: Oxford University Press, 2000), p. 184.

7. Emmerson, "A Tale of Three Countries," p. 39.

8. Ibid., p. 43.

9. World Bank, World Development Indicators Online, http://web.worldbank.org/ WBSITE/EXTERNAL/DATASTATISTICS/0,,contentMDK:20398986~menuPK:64133163~page PK:64133150~piPK:64133175~theSitePK:239419,00.html.

10. World Bank, *World Development Report, 1992* (Washington, D.C.: World Bank, 1992), table 1.

11. Larry Diamond, "Africa: The Second Wind of Change," *Times Literary Supplement,* July 2, 1993, reprinted in Peter Lewis, ed., *Africa: The Second Wind of Change* (Boulder, Colo.: Westview Press, 1998), p. 265.

12. Michael Bratton and Nicolas van de Walle, *Democratic Experiments in Africa: Regime Transitions in Comparative Perspective* (New York: Cambridge University Press, 1997), p. 1.

13. Ibid., pp. 1–2.

14. Hung-mao Tien, *The Great Transition: Political and Social Change in the Republic of China* (Stanford, Calif.: Hoover Institution Press, 1989), p. 27.

15. In 2004 dollars, the range is $2,700–$8,100. Between 1974 and 1989, sixteen of the twenty-one authoritarian regimes at this development level democratized or significantly liberalized, while five were already democratic. Huntington, *The Third Wave,* p. 62, table 2.1.

16. The figure of $13,000 and all others in this paragraph are in 2004 purchasing power parity (PPP) dollars. PPP adjusts for the possible distortion of exchange rates from the local currency to the U.S. dollar, and so enables a better comparison of dollar incomes in terms of what they can actually purchase in each country. "At the PPP rate, one international dollar has the same purchasing power domestic Gross National Income [of a given country] that the US dollar has over U.S. Gross National Income." World Bank, *World Development Report, 2007* (Washington D.C.: World Bank, 2006), p. 300. Spain's nominal GNP per capita in 1975 was $3,230, and most countries above $3,000 were already democracies. Huntington, *The Third Wave,* p. 62, table 2.1.

17. Tun-jen Cheng, "Democratizing the Quasi-Leninist Regime in Taiwan," *World Politics* 41 (July 1989): 481.

18. Ibid., p. 483. On the role of middle-class groups in fostering democratic transition in Taiwan and Korea, see also Hsin-Huang Michael Hsiao and Hagen Koo, "The Middle Classes and Democratization," in Larry Diamond, Marc F. Plattner, Yun-han Chu, and Hung-mao Tien, eds., *Consolidating the Third Wave Democracies: Themes and Perspectives* (Baltimore: Johns Hopkins University Press, 1997), pp. 312–33.

19. Seymour Martin Lipset, "Some Social Requisites of Democracy: Economic Development and Political Legitimacy," *American Political Science Review* 53 (March 1959): 69–105; Larry Diamond, "Economic Development and Democracy Reconsidered," in Gary Marks and Larry Diamond, eds., *Reexamining Democracy: Essays in Honor of Seymour Martin Lipset* (Newbury Park, Calif.: SAGE, 1992), pp. 93–139.

20. The three dimensions are weighted equally, but the formula for calculating scores is more complicated. For example, the per capita income measure is statistically adjusted to give less emphasis to very high levels of income (which also helps to correct for the distortions of the oil-rich countries). See UNDP, *Human Development Report, 2004* (New York: United Nations Development Program, 2004), pp. 258–59.

21. UNDP, *Human Development Report, 2006* (New York: United Nations Development Program, 2006), table 1, p. 283. Cuba is ranked 50 by the UNDP, but speciously, as the ranking is based on only two of the three indicators (health and education, not income). If the per capita income data were available, Cuba would rank well below 50, and I therefore exclude Cuba from the rankings here.

22. Diamond, "Economic Development and Democracy Reconsidered"; Henry S. Rowen, "The Tide Underneath the 'Third Wave,'" *Journal of Democracy* 6 (January 1995): 52–64.

23. Rowen, "The Tide Underneath the 'Third Wave,'" p. 55.

24. Carles Boix and Susan C. Stokes, "Endogenous Democratization," *World Politics* 55 (July 2003): 531. Ronald Inglehart and Christian Welzel reach a somewhat similar conclusion using 1950–90 data. *Modernization, Cultural Change and Democracy: The Human Development Sequence* (Cambridge: Cambridge University Press, 2005), p. 169. Both studies specifically reject the finding of Adam Przeworski and his colleagues that the likelihood of emergence of democracy is not related to the level of economic development. Adam Przeworski, Michael E. Alvarez, Jose Antonio Cheibub, and Fernando Limongi, *Democracy and Development: Political Institutions and Well-being in the World, 1950–1990* (Cambridge: Cambridge University Press, 2000).

25. Again, this per capita income figure (and all others in this chapter) are expressed in 2004 purchasing power parity dollars. Przeworski et al., *Democracy and Development*, p. 98.

26. Among cases of democratic breakdown in the third wave, the two richest cases were Russia in 2000, where the per capita income was about $8,600 (in 2004 purchasing power parity dollars), and Thailand in 2005, where it was about the same.

27. The eight relatively rich oil states (in order of development level) are Kuwait, Brunei, Bahrain, Qatar, United Arab Emirates, Oman, Russia, and Saudi Arabia.

28. Lipset, *Political Man*, p. 45. The book was originally published in 1960, and the chapter from which this quotation is drawn essentially reproduces his 1959 article, "Some Social Requisites of Democracy."

29. Carles Boix, *Democracy and Redistribution* (Cambridge: Cambridge University Press, 2003).

30. Huntington, *The Third Wave*, p. 67. This is not simply the result of economic development, however. In much of Latin America, the power of populist groups has often decreased precisely because of repression under authoritarian rule.

31. Daniel Lerner, *The Passing of Traditional Society: Modernizing the Middle East* (New York: Free Press, 1958).

32. The early studies establishing this correlation were Gabriel Almond and Sidney Verba, *The Civic Culture* (Princeton, N.J.: Princeton University Press, 1963), and Alex Inkeles,

"Participant Citizenship in Six Developing Countries," *American Political Science Review* 63 (1969): 1120–41. But these associations also emerge in most of the recent studies of attitudes and values toward democracy cited in chapter 1 as well as in the research associated with the World Values Survey. See Inglehart and Welzel, *Modernization, Cultural Change and Democracy*, and the sources they cite on p. 164.

33. Alex Inkeles and Larry J. Diamond, "Personal Development and National Development: A Cross-National Perspective," in Alexander Szalai and Frank M. Andrews, eds., *The Quality of Life: Comparative Studies* (London: Sage, 1980), pp. 73–109.

34. Ronald Inglehart, *The Silent Revolution* (Princeton, N.J.: Princeton University Press, 1977) and *Culture Shift in Advanced Industrial Societies* (Princeton, N.J.: Princeton University Press, 1990).

35. Inglehart and Welzel, *Modernization, Cultural Change and Democracy*, p. 54.

36. Ibid., pp. 58 and 76. The transition from traditional to secular values is associated with industrialization and thus represents a first phase of cultural shift.

37. Ibid., p. 150.

38. Ibid., pp. 123–24.

39. Ibid., p. 151. The correlation of self-expression values with "effective democracy" is .90, meaning that 80 percent of the variation in levels of effective democracy in the world can be explained by the extent of self-expression values in each society. Such a high correlation between two entirely independent phenomena (one, values; the other, political institutions) is virtually never seen in comparative political studies.

40. Ibid., p. 153.

41. Ibid., p. 209. See their chapter 8 for the evidence. They also find that there is no reverse effect, that is, the experience of democracy does not seem, in and of itself, to generate self-expression values to a significant degree.

42. Ibid., p. 152.

43. Ibid., p. 166.

44. O'Donnell and Schmitter, *Transitions from Authoritarian Rule*, p. 16.

45. Robert Barros, "The Left and Democracy: Recent Debates in Latin America," *Telos* 68 (1986): 49–70; Juan Linz and Alfred Stepan, "Political Crafting of Democratic Consolidation or Destruction: European and South American Comparisons," in Robert A. Pastor, ed., *Democracy in the Americas: Stopping the Pendulum* (New York: Holmes and Meier, 1989), p. 47.

46. O'Donnell and Schmitter, *Transitions from Authoritarian Rule*, p. 50.

47. Alexis de Tocqueville, *Democracy in America* (New York: Random House, 1945), first published in 1835.

48. Jyotirindra Das Gupta, "India: Democratic Becoming and Combined Development," in Larry Diamond, Juan J. Linz, and Seymour Martin Lipset, eds., *Democracy in Developing Countries: Asia* (Boulder, Colo.: Lynne Rienner, 1990), pp. 53–104; Richard Sisson, "Culture and Democratization in India," in Larry Diamond, ed., *Political Culture and Democracy in Developing Countries* (Boulder, Colo.: Lynne Rienners, 1993).

49. Christine M. Sadowski, "Autonomous Groups as Agents of Democratic Change in Communist and Post-Communist Eastern Europe," in Diamond, *Political Culture and Democracy*, pp. 163–95; S. Frederick Starr, "Soviet Union: A Civil Society," *Foreign Policy* 70 (Spring 1988): 26–41; Gail Lapidus, "State and Society: Toward the Emergence of Civil Society in the Soviet Union," in Seweryn Bialer, ed., *Politics, Society and Nationality: Inside Gorbachev's Russia* (Boulder, Colo.: Westview Press, 1989), pp. 121–47; Andrew Nathan, "Is China Ready for Democracy?" *Journal of Democracy* 1 (Spring 1990): 56; Minxin Pei, "Societal Takeover in China and the USSR," *Journal of Democracy* 3 (January 1992): 108–18. See also the essays by Robert Weller, Richard Madsen, and Merle Goldman and Ashley Esarey in Larry Diamond and Bruce Gilley, eds., *Political Change in China and the Taiwan Experience* (Boulder, Colo.: Lynne Rienners, 2008, forthcoming).

50. Thomas Gold, "Civil Society and Taiwan's Quest for Identity," paper presented to the Eighty-sixth Annual Meeting of the American Political Science Association, San Francisco, August 30–September 2, 1990.

51. O'Donnell and Schmitter, *Transitions from Authoritarian Rule*, pp. 48–56; Larry Diamond, "Introduction: Civil Society and the Struggle for Democracy," in Diamond, ed., *The Democratic Revolution: Struggles for Freedom and Pluralism in the Developing World* (New York: Freedom House, 1991), pp. 6–18; Clement Nwankwo, "The Civil Liberties Organization and the Struggle for Human Rights and Democracy in Nigeria," in Diamond, *The Democratic Revolution*, pp. 105–23; Larry Diamond, "Nigeria's Search for a New Political Order," *Journal of Democracy* 2 (Spring 1991): 54–69; and Gibson Kamau Kuria, "Confronting Dictatorship in Kenya," *Journal of Democracy* 2 (October 1991): 115–26.

52. Ruth Berins Collier and James Mahoney, "Adding Collective Actors to Collective Outcomes: Labor and Recent Democratization in South American and Southern Europe," *Comparative Politics* 29, no. 3 (1997): 287, 295.

53. Naomi Chazan, "The New Politics of Participation in Tropical Africa," *Comparative Politics* 14, no. 2 (1982): 169–89. See also the essays in John W. Harbeson, Donald Rothchild, and Naomi Chazan, eds., *Civil Society and the State in Africa* (Boulder, Colo.: Lynne Rienners, 1994).

54. Huntington, *The Third Wave*, pp. 73–85. On the Philippines, see also Carl H. Lande, "The Political Crisis," in John Bresnan, ed., *Crisis in the Philippines: The Marcos Era and Beyond* (Princeton, N.J.: Princeton University Press, 1986), pp. 118–22. In Kenya, politically outspoken Protestant and Catholic clergy took courageous stands, both individually and through ecumenical bodies like the National Council of Christian Churches (NCCK) and the Peace and Justice Commission, on behalf of democracy and human rights. In response, they suffered violent retribution from the state and ruling party. See Africa Watch, *Kenya: Taking Liberties* (New York: Human Rights Watch, 1991), pp. 217–36.

55. Michael McFaul, "Transitions from Postcommunism," *Journal of Democracy* 16 (July 2005): 5–19.

56. Felix B. Bautista, "The Philippine Alternative Press and the Toppling of a Dictator," pp. 145–66; Anthony Hazlitt Heard, "The Struggle for Free Expression in South Africa," pp. 167–79; and Ray Ekpu, "Nigeria's Embattled Fourth Estate," pp. 181–200, in Diamond, *The Democratic Revolution*.

5. WHAT DRIVES DEMOCRACY: THE EXTERNAL FACTORS

1. Edward R. McMahon and Scott H. Baker, *Piecing a Democratic Quilt: Regional Organizations and Universal Norms* (Bloomfield, Conn.: Kumarian Press, 2006), p. 134.

2. Samuel P. Huntington, "Democracy's Third Wave," *Journal of Democracy* 2 (Spring 1991): 2.

3. Samuel P. Huntington, *The Third Wave: Democratization in the Late Twentieth Century* (Norman: University of Oklahoma Press), 1991, p. 101.

4. Ibid., p. 103.

5. Laurence Whitehead, "Democracy and Decolonization: East-Central Europe," in Laurence Whitehead, ed., *The International Dimensions of Democratization: Europe and the Americas* (Oxford: Oxford University Press, 1996), p. 361.

6. Peter Gross and Vladimir Tismaneanu, "The End of Postcommunism in Romania," *Journal of Democracy* 16 (April 2005): 146.

7. *Sunday Concord* (Lagos, Nigeria), March 25, 1990.

8. Quoted in "The New Wind of Change," *Guardian Weekly* (London), September 23, 1990.

9. Ibid.

10. Claude Ake, "Rethinking African Democracy," *Journal of Democracy* 2 (January 1991): 36 (emphasis mine).

11. Quoted in Robert M. Press, "Africans Join Protests for Multiparty Rule," *Christian Science Monitor,* April 11, 1990.

12. Jonathan C. Randal, "In Africa, Unrest in One-Party States," *International Herald Tribune,* March 27, 1990.

13. Huntington, *The Third Wave,* p. 288.

14. Ibid., p. 102.

15. Ibid.

16. Tun-jen Cheng, "Democratizing the Quasi-Leninist Regime in Taiwan," *World Politics* 41 (July 1989): 483.

17. James Lee Ray, "The Global Origins of Transitions to (and From?) Democracy," paper presented to the Annual Meeting of the International Studies Association, Vancouver, March 20–23, 1991, pp. 13–15.

18. Steven Levitsky and Lucan A. Way, "International Linkage and Democratization," *Journal of Democracy* 16 (July 2005): 20–34.

19. Ibid., p. 24.

20. Ibid.

21. Cheng, "Democratizing the Quasi-Leninist Regime in Taiwan," p. 484.

22. On this effect in Chile late in Pinochet's rule, see George P. Shultz, *Turmoil and Triumph: My Years as Secretary of State* (New York: Charles Scribner's Sons, 1993), pp. 972 and 974.

23. Levitsky and Way, "International Linkage and Democratization," p. 22.

24. Robert G. Herman and Theodore J. Piccone, eds., *Defending Democracy: A Global Survey of Foreign Policy Trends, 1992–2002* (Washington, D.C.: Democracy Coalition Project, 2002), p. 214.

25. Ibid., p. 213.

26. Michael McFaul, "The American Strategy (or Lack Thereof) for Democracy Promotion," draft of May, 12, 2006, p. 11.

27. Kathryn Sikkink, "The Effectiveness of US Human Rights Policy, 1973–1980," in Whitehead, ed., *The International Dimensions of Democratization,* p. 94.

28. Jonathan Hartlyn, "The Dominican Republic: The Legacy of Intermittent Engagement," in Abraham F. Lowenthal, ed., *Exporting Democracy: The United States and Latin America: Case Studies* (Baltimore: Johns Hopkins University Press, 1991), p. 82. For a historical overview and analysis of this period, see Rosario Espinal and Jonathan Hartlyn, "The Dominican Republic: The Long and Difficult Struggle for Democracy," in Larry Diamond, Juan J. Linz, and Seymour Martin Lipset, eds., *Democracy in Developing Countries: Latin America,* 2nd ed. (Boulder, Colo.: Lynne Rienners, 1999).

29. Espinal and Hartlyn, "The Dominican Republic: The Long and Difficult Struggle for Democracy," p. 489.

30. Shultz, *Turmoil and Triumph,* pp. 608–42.

31. Huntington, *The Third Wave,* p. 95. On the U.S. efforts to induce and support democratic transition in Chile, see Thomas Carothers, *In the Name of Democracy* (Berkeley: University of California Press, 1991), pp. 150–63.

32. Shultz, *Turmoil and Triumph,* pp. 970–75.

33. J. Samuel Fitch, "Democracy, Human Rights and the Armed Forces in Latin America," in Jonathan Hartlyn, Lars Schoultz, and Augusto Varas, eds., *The United States and Latin America in the 1990s: Beyond the Cold War* (Chapel Hill: University of North Carolina Press, 1993), p. 203 (emphasis in the original).

34. Reagan struggled throughout his presidency between his passionate commitment to freedom and democracy and his strong emotional attachment to Cold War authoritarian allies like Marcos, the Chilean general Augusto Pinochet, and the Angolan insurgent Jonas Savimbi. Moreover, the first year and a half of Reagan's presidency, with Alexander Haig as secretary of state, charted a very different course, seeking to reverse Carter's human rights emphasis and refurbish relations with anticommunist authoritarian regimes in the Third World. See Tony

Smith, *America's Mission: The United States and the Worldwide Struggle for Democracy in the Twentieth Century* (Princeton, N.J.: Princeton University Press, 1994), pp. 286–90; and Carothers, *In the Name of Democracy*, pp. 118–27. Carothers provides a largely critical perspective of what the Reagan administration ultimately accomplished for democracy in Latin America; Smith, taking a global view, offers a more sympathetic assessment (pp. 297–307).

35. Robert A. Pastor, "Nicaragua's Choice: The Making of a Free Election," *Journal of Democracy* 1 (Summer 1990): 15.

36. Damjan de Krnjević-Mišković, "Serbia's Prudent Revolution," *Journal of Democracy* 12 (July 2001): 100, 103, and 104.

37. Both quotes from Pauline H. Baker, "South Africa's Future: A Turbulent Transition," *Journal of Democracy* 1 (Fall 1990): 8–9.

38. Joan M. Nelson with Stephanie J. Eglington, *Encouraging Democracy: What Role for Conditioned Aid?* (Washington, D.C.: Overseas Development Council, 1992), pp. 16–17, 32.

39. Larry Diamond, "Promoting Democracy in Africa," in John Harbeson and Donald Rothchild, eds., *Africa in World Politics*, 2nd. ed (Boulder, Colo.: Westview Press, 1995).

40. Joel Barkan, "Kenya: Lessons from a Flawed Election," *Journal of Democracy* 4 (July 1993): 91.

41. Quoted in ibid., from the World Bank, press release of the meeting of the Consultative Group for Kenya, Paris, November 26, 1991.

42. Githu Muigai, "Kenya's Opposition and the Crisis of Governance," *Issue* ("A Journal of Opinion" of the U.S. African Studies Association) 21, no. 1/2 (1993): 29.

43. Herman and Piccone, *Defending Democracy*, p. 215.

44. Levitsky and Way, "International Linkage and Democratization," p. 22. These principles are emphasized by Nelson and Eglington, *Encouraging Democracy*, who also stress the importance of a reform element within the regime (pp. 48–49). However, if aid dependence is extreme enough, as it is in much of Africa, and the donor community is sufficiently united (as with Kenya initially and Malawi), even a regime in which hard-liners predominate may have little choice but to concede to the pressure (or face financial collapse).

45. Morton H. Halperin and Kristen Lomasney, "Guaranteeing Democracy: A Review of the Record," *Journal of Democracy* 9 (April 1998): 145.

46. Guy Martin, "Francophone Africa in the Context of Franco-African Relations," in John W. Harbeson and Donald Rothchild, eds., *Africa in World Politics* (Boulder, Colo.: Westview Press, 1995), p. 180.

47. John R. Heilbrunn, "The Social Origins of National Conferences: A Comparison of Benin and Togo," *Journal of Modern African Studies* 31, no. 2 (June 1993): 277–99.

48. The United States, by contrast, suspended $14 million in aid following the election. *Africa Report*, March–April 1993, p. 62.

49. Martin, "Francophone Africa in the Context of Franco-African Relations," p.180.

50. In fact, until the early 1990s the combined spending of the four German foundations on assisting democratic associations, trade unions, media, and political institutions abroad equaled or exceeded that of all U.S. publicly funded institutions, including the U.S. Agency for International Development. For example, in 1988 about half of their total of $170 million in income from the German government was spent on these democracy-promoting activities ($85 million), exceeding by a factor of more than five the NED budget and nearly equaling estimated total U.S. democracy-promotion spending in 1989 of $100 million. Michael Pinto-Duschinsky, "Foreign Political Aid: The German Political Foundations and Their U.S. Counterparts," *International Affairs* 67, no. 1 (1991): 33–63.

51. Monica Jimenez de Barros, "Mobilizing for Democracy in Chile: The Crusade for Citizen Participation and Beyond," in Larry Diamond, ed., *The Democratic Revolution: Struggles for Freedom and Pluralism in the Developing World* (New York: Freedom House, 1992).

52. Michael McFaul, "Transitions from Postcommunism," *Journal of Democracy* 16 (July 2005): 12.

53. Krnjević-Mišković, "Serbia's Prudent Revolution," p. 103.

54. Taras Kuzio, "Ukraine's Orange Revolution: The Opposition's Road to Success," *Journal of Democracy* 16 (April 2005): 127.

55. *Election observing* is the term used to describe the work of international visitors who watch and assess the electoral process, typically for periods of no more than a few weeks in a country (though this may be spread out over periodic visits covering administrative preparations and the election campaign). *Election monitoring* denotes the work of much more numerous indigenous observers, organized and deployed by nonpartisan NGOs as well as the various political parties for a sustained period of time. A comprehensive effort will place at least one nonpartisan monitor (usually from a broad umbrella organization in civil society) at every polling site in the country on election day.

56. In June 1990, the thirty-four countries of the Conference on Security and Cooperation in Europe adopted a declaration institutionalizing a standing invitation for international actors to observe their elections. In December 1991, the UN General Assembly adopted a resolution endorsing the practice of international and domestic election observing. The National Democratic Institute for International Affairs (NDI) and the National Citizens Movement for Free Elections (NAMFREL), *Making Every Vote Count: Domestic Election Monitoring in Asia* (Washington, D.C.: NDI, 1996), p. 21.

57. Robert A. Pastor, "The Third Dimension of Accountability: The International Community in National Elections," in Andreas Schedler, Larry Diamond, and Marc F. Plattner, eds., *The Self-Restraining State: Power and Accountability in New Democracies* (Boulder, Colo.: Lynne Rienners, 1999), p. 128.

58. Thomas Carothers, "The Rise of Election Monitoring: The Observers Observed," *Journal of Democracy* 8 (July 1997): 17–31; and Neil Nevitte and Sergio Canton, "The Rise of Election Monitoring: The Role of Domestic Observers," *Journal of Democracy* 8 (July 1997): 47–61.

59. Larry Garber and Glenn Cowan, "The Virtues of Parallel Vote Tabulations," *Journal of Democracy* 4 (April 1993): 95–107. The quick count was pioneered by NAMFREL in the 1986 Philippine election, when its half-million volunteers covered about 70 percent of the country's ninety-five thousand polling sites, and has been used repeatedly since then in the country. NDI and NAMFREL, *Making Every Vote Count*, p. 39.

60. Pastor, "The Third Dimension of Accountability," p. 127; and Nevitte and Canton, "The Role of Domestic Observers," 47–61.

61. McFaul, "Transitions from Postcommunism," p. 10.

62. Mark R. Thompson and Philipp Kuntz, "Stolen Elections: The Case of the Serbian October," *Journal of Democracy* 15 (October 2004): 167.

63. Jennifer L. McCoy, Larry Garber, and Robert A. Pastor, "Making Peace by Observing and Mediating Elections," *Journal of Democracy* 2 (Fall 1991): 102–14. See also Joshua Muravchik, *Exporting Democracy: Fulfilling America's Destiny* (Washington, D.C.: AEI Press, 1991), pp. 208–10; Larry Garber and Eric Bjornlund, "Election Monitoring in Africa," in Festus Eribo, Oyeleye Oyediran, Mulatu Wubneh, and Leo Zonn, eds., *Window on Africa: Democratization and Media Exposure* (Greenville, N.C.: East Carolina University Center for International Programs, March 1993), pp. 28–50; Eric Bjornlund, Michael Bratton, and Clark Gibson, "Observing Multiparty Elections in Africa: Lessons from Zambia," *African Affairs* 91 (1992): 405–31.

64. Cited in Pastor, "The Third Dimension of Accountability," p. 134.

65. Carothers, "The Observers Observed," pp. 19 and 28.

66. This was no doubt in part because the organization's unmatched experience in election observing, and its early warning of serious flaws in preparations for the December 1992 voting, made it too great a risk to the Kenyan government. See National Democratic Institute of International Affairs, *1992: A Year in Review* (Washington, D.C., 1993), p. 8.

67. Barkan, "Kenya: Lessons from a Flawed Election."

68. Carothers, "The Observers Observed," pp. 25–26.

69. Press release of the OSCE International Election Observation Mission in Azerbaijan, November 7, 2005, http://www.osce.org/item/16887.html.

70. Leila Alieva, "Azerbaijan's Frustrating Elections," *Journal of Democracy* 17 (April 2006): 157.

71. See, for example, the second preliminary report of the EU Election Observation Mission to Nigeria, Abuja, April 22, 2003, http://ec.europa.eu/comm/external_relations/human_rights/eu_election_ass_observ/nigeria/2stat.htm, and the statement of the NDI Election Observer Delegation to Nigeria's April 19 presidential and gubernatorial elections, Abuja, April 21, 2003, http://www.ndi.org/worldwide/cewa/nigeria/statement_042103.asp.

72. See, for example, the NDI *1996 Annual Report* (Washington, D.C.: National Democratic Institute for International Affairs), and Nevitte and Canton, "The Role of Domestic Observers."

73. E. Gyimah-Boadi, "Ghana's Encouraging Elections: The Challenges Ahead," *Journal of Democracy* 8, no. 2 (April 1997): 88–89.

74. Thomas Carothers, *Confronting the Weakest Link: Aiding Political Parties in New Democracies* (Washington, D.C.: Carnegie Endowment for International Peace, 2006).

75. For examples, see the members of the Network of Democracy Research Institutes, http://www.wmd.org/ndri/ndri.html.

76. Larry Diamond, *Developing Democracy: Toward Consolidation* (Baltimore: Johns Hopkins University Press), chapter 6.

77. For the 2006 fiscal year, this included $1.48 billion for USAID democracy and governance programs, $80 million for NED, some portion of the $120 million for the Middle East Partnership Initiative (MEPI) (depending on how one classifies its diverse programs), and $48 million for the State Department's Human Rights and Democracy Fund. McFaul, "The American Strategy for Democracy Promotion."

78. Richard Youngs, ed., *Survey of European Democracy Promotion Policies, 2000–2006* (Madrid: FRIDE, 2006), p. 79.

79. Thomas Melia, "The Democracy Bureaucracy: The Infrastructure of American Democracy Promotion," paper prepared for the Princeton Project on National Security, September 2005, http://www.wws.princeton.edu/ppns/papers/democracy_bureaucracy.pdf.

80. Pippa Norris, private communication, June 19, 2006.

81. National Endowment for Democracy, *2005 Annual Report*, pp. 26–28, 75–78.

82. http://www.wmd.org/.

83. http://www.ned.org/grants/05programs/grants-asia05.html.

84. Thomas Carothers, *Aiding Democracy Abroad: The Learning Curve* (Washington, D.C.: Carnegie Endowment for International Peace, 1999), p. 307.

85. Ibid., p. 305.

86. Ibid., p. 308.

87. Marina Ottaway and Teresa Chung, "Debating Democracy Assistance: Toward a New Paradigm," *Journal of Democracy* 10 (October 1999): 102, 106, and 108.

88. Elizabeth Spiro Clark, "Debating Democracy Assistance: A Tune-Up, Not an Overhaul," *Journal of Democracy* 10 (October 1999): 114–18.

89. E. Gyimah-Boadi, "Debating Democracy Assistance: The Cost of Doing Nothing," *Journal of Democracy* 10 (October 1999): 121–22.

90. Carothers, *Aiding Democracy Abroad*, p. 311.

91. Ibid.

92. Steven E. Finkel, Aníbal Pérez-Liñán, and Mitchell Seligson, *Effects of U.S. Foreign Assistance on Democracy Building: Results of a Cross-National Quantitative Study*, final report to USAID, January 12, 2006, p. 83, http://www.usaid.gov/our_work/democracy_and_governance/publications/pdfs/impact_of_democracy_assistance.pdf.

93. UN Security Council Resolution 940, July 31, 1994, http://daccessdds.un.org/doc/UNDOC/GEN/N94/312/22/PDF/N9431222.pdf?OpenElement.

94. Pastor, "The Third Dimension of Accountability," p. 135.

6. WHAT DRIVES DEMOCRACY: THE REGIONAL INFLUENCE

1. This language was from the statement issued that night by the U.S. embassy in Asunción. Arturo Valenzuela, "The Coup That Didn't Happen," *Journal of Democracy* 8 (January 1997): 48.

2. Ibid, p. 53.

3. Quoted in Laurence Whitehead, "International Aspects of Democratization," in Guillermo O'Donnell, Philippe Schmitter, and Whitehead, eds., *Transitions from Authoritarian Rule: Comparative Perspectives* (Baltimore: Johns Hopkins University Press, 1986), p. 21.

4. Consolidated Version of the Treaty of the European Union, Articles 6 (1) and 49, Maastricht, February 7, 1992, http://europa.eu.int/eur-lex/en/treaties/dat/C_2002325EN .000501.html.

5. European Council in Copenhagen, "Conclusions of the Presidency," June 21–22, 1993, http://ue.eu.int/ueDocs/cms_Data/docs/pressdata/en/ec/72921.pdf.

6. Edward R. McMahon and Scott H. Baker, *Piecing a Democratic Quilt: Regional Organizations and Universal Norms* (Bloomfield, Conn.: Kumarian Press, 2006), pp. 40–41.

7. Jiri Pehe, "Consolidating Free Government in the New EU," *Journal of Democracy* 15 (January 2004): 36.

8. Jacques Rupnik, "Eastern Europe in the International Context," *Journal of Democracy* 11 (April 2000): 122.

9. Pehe, "Consolidating Free Government in the New EU," p. 39.

10. Ibid.

11. Ibid., p. 40.

12. Dan Bilefsky, "Romania and Bulgaria Celebrate Entry into European Union," *New York Times*, January 2, 2007.

13. Rupnik, "Eastern Europe in the International Context," p. 124; Pehe, "Consolidating Free Government in the New EU," p. 38; and Zoltan Barany, "NATO's Peaceful Advance," *Journal of Democracy* 15 (January 2004): 74.

14. McMahon and Baker, *Piecing a Democratic Quilt*, p. 47. On Turkey's political reforms, see also Freedom House, *Freedom in the World, 2006: The Annual Survey of Political Rights and Civil Liberties* (New York: Freedom House, 2006), pp. 730–33.

15. Alina Mungiu-Pippidi, "Europe Moves Eastward: Beyond the New Borders," *Journal of Democracy* 15 (January 2004): 55.

16. This is the conclusion of Jiri Pehe, "Consolidating Free Government in the New EU," p. 42, and many others.

17. McMahon and Baker, *Piecing a Democratic Quilt*, p. 78.

18. Barany, "NATO's Peaceful Advance," p. 75.

19. Conference on Security and Cooperation in Europe, Final Act, Helsinki, 1975, 1 (a) (I) and 1 (a) (VIII), pp. 2 and 4.

20. Democracy Coalition Project, "Defending Democracy: A Global Survey of Foreign Policy Trends, 1992–2002: Fact Sheets on Regional Organizations," www.demcoalition .org/pdf/Regional_Organizations.pdf.

21. McMahon and Baker, *Piecing a Democratic Quilt*, p. 70.

22. Bogotá Conference of American States, Charter of the Organization of American States, March 30–May 2, 1948. http://www.yale.edu/lawweb/avalon/decade/decad062.htm. Articles 9 and 15.

23. Charter of the Organization of American States, Article 2.

24. OAS General Assembly Resolution 1063, http://www.upd.oas.org/lab/Documents/ general_assembly/ag_res_1063_xx_O_90_eng.pdf.

25. Inter-American Democratic Charter, http://www.oas.org/charter/docs/resolution1_ en_p4.htm, Articles 1, 7, and 20.

26. Robert Pastor, "The Third Dimension of Accountability: The International Community in National Elections," in Andreas Schedler, Larry Diamond, and Marc F. Plattner, eds., *The Self-Restraining State* (Boulder, Colo.: Lynne Rienners, 1999), p. 125.

27. Tom Farer, "Collectively Defending Democracy in the Western Hemisphere: Introduction and Overview," in Tom Farer, ed., *Beyond Sovereignty: Collectively Defending Democracy in the Americas* (Baltimore: Johns Hopkins University Press, 1996), p. 19.

28. Francisco Villagrán de León, "Thwarting the Guatemalan Coup," *Journal of Democracy* 4 (October 1993): 124.

29. Andrew F. Cooper and Thomas Legler, "The OAS in Peru: A Model for the Future?" *Journal of Democracy* 12 (October 2001): 128, 129.

30. Ibid., p. 134.

31. Cynthia McClintock, "The OAS in Peru: Room for Improvement," *Journal of Democracy* 12 (October 2001): 139.

32. McMahon and Baker, *Piecing a Democratic Quilt*, p. 100.

33. The Organization of American States, "Supporting the Electoral Process," http://www.oas.org/main/main.asp?sLang=E&sLink=http://www.oas.org/key_issues/eng.

34. McMahon and Baker, *Piecing a Democratic Quilt*, p. 98.

35. Ibid., p. 101.

36. Constitutive Act of the African Union, Lomé, Togo, July 11, 2000, Articles 3 and 4, http://www.au2002.gov.za/docs/key_oau/au_act.htm.

37. African (Banjul) Charter on Human and Peoples' Rights, adopted June 27, 1981, Article 13, http://www1.umn.edu/humanrts/instree/z1afchar.htm.

38. Article 30 of the Constitutive Act.

39. Declaration on the Framework for an OAU Response to Unconstitutional Changes of Government, Lomé, July 12, 2000, http://www.africanreview.org/docs/govern/govchange.pdf.

40. McMahon and Baker, *Piecing a Democratic Quilt*, p. 134.

41. Ibid., p. 138; Freedom House, *Freedom in the World, 2006*, p. 716.

42. McMahon and Baker, *Piecing a Democratic Quilt*, p. 140.

43. Until 1949, Commonwealth members also swore allegiance to the British monarchy, but that ended in 1949 with the adoption of the "Nehru Formula," whereby the British monarchy remained the symbolic head of the Commonwealth but not necessarily of its individual members. McMahon and Baker, *Piecing a Democratic Quilt*, p 107.

44. The Declaration of Commonwealth Principles, 1971, Singapore, January 22, 1971, http://www.thecommonwealth.org/Internal/20723/32987/singapore_declaration_of_commonwealth_principles/.

45. Roland Rich, "Bringing Democracy into International Law," *Journal of Democracy* 12 (July 2001): 28.

46. McMahon and Baker, *Piecing a Democratic Quilt*, p. 124.

47. Ibid., pp. 125–26.

48. The Charter of the Arab League, March 22, 1945, Article II, http://www.middleeastnews.com/arabLeagueCharter.html.

49. Arab League Charter on Human Rights, adopted August 5, 1990, Article 4, http://www1.umn.edu/humanrts/instree/arabcharter.html.

50. McMahon and Baker, *Piecing a Democratic Quilt*, pp. 145–55.

51. John Burton, "Revolt Presents ASEAN with Its Greatest Challenge," *Financial Times*, September 30, 2007.

7. WHAT SUSTAINS DEMOCRACY

1. Jyotirindra Das Gupta, "India: Democratic Becoming and Developmental Transition," in Larry Diamond, Juan J. Linz, and Seymour Martin Lipset, eds., *Politics in Developing Countries: Comparing Experiences with Democracy* (Boulder, Colo.: Lynne Rienners, 1995), pp. 281–82. Indira Gandhi was no relation to the leader of the Indian independence movement, Mahatma Gandhi.

2. Jyotirindra Das Gupta, "A Season of Caesars: Emergency Regimes and Development Politics in Asia," *Asian Survey* 18, no. 4 (1978): 315–49.

3. Niraja Jayal, "Civil Society," in Sumit Ganguly, Larry Diamond, and Marc F. Plattner, eds., *The State of Indian Democracy* (Baltimore: Johns Hopkins University Press, 2007), p. 151.

4. Amartya Sen, *Development as Freedom* (New York: Alfred A. Knopf, 1999).

5. Sumit Ganguly, "India's Multiple Revolutions," *Journal of Democracy* 13 (January 2002): 42.

6. Alex Inkeles, "National Character and Modern Political Systems," in Francis L. K. Hsu, ed., *Psychological Anthropology: Approaches to Culture and Personality* (Homewood, Ill.: Doresey, 1961), pp. 195–98.

7. Sidney Hook, *Reason, Social Myth, and Democracy* (New York: Humanities, 1950), cited in Inkeles, "National Character," p. 196.

8. Richard Sisson, "Culture and Democratization in India," in Larry Diamond, ed., *Political Culture and Democracy in Developing Countries* (Boulder, Colo.: Lynne Rienner, 1993), p. 43.

9. Ashutosh Varshney, "India Defies the Odds: Why Democracy Survives," *Journal of Democracy* 9 (July 1998): 46.

10. Seymour Martin Lipset, "George Washington and the Founding of Democracy," *Journal of Democracy* 9 (October 1998): 24–38.

11. Ganguly, "India's Multiple Revolutions," p. 39.

12. Ibid., p. 46.

13. A useful guide to Gandhi's views on nonviolence and their significance can be found at http://www.mkgandhi.org/nonviolence/index.htm.

14. Das Gupta, "India," p. 273.

15. Jayal, "Civil Society," p. 147.

16. Sanjeev Khagram, *Dams and Development: Transnational Struggles for Water and Power* (Ithaca, N.Y.: Cornell University Press, 2004), p. 2.

17. Praveen Swami, "Breaking News: India's Media Revolution," in Ganguly, Diamond, and Plattner, *The State of Indian Democracy*, p. 180.

18. Sumit Ganguly, "Bangladesh and India," in Larry Diamond and Leonardo Morlino, eds., *Assessing the Quality of Democracy* (Baltimore: Johns Hopkins University Press, 2005), p. 169.

19. Swami, "Breaking News," p. 18.

20. Jayal, "Civil Society," p. 149.

21. Rob Jenkins, "India's Unlikey Democracy: Civil Society vs. Corruption," *Journal of Democracy* 18 (April 2007): 59.

22. Jayal, "Civil Society," p. 152.

23. Robert Putnam, *Making Democracy Work: Civic Traditions in Modern Italy* (Princeton, N.J.: Princeton University Press, 1993).

24. Jayal, "Civil Society," p. 158.

25. M. S. Gill, "India: Running the World's Biggest Elections," *Journal of Democracy* 9 (January 1998): 167.

26. E. Sridharan and Ashutosh Varshney, "Toward Moderate Pluralism; Political Parties in India," in Larry Diamond and Richard Gunther, eds., *Political Parties and Democracy* (Baltimore: Johns Hopkins University Press, 2001), p. 207.

27. James Manor, "India Defies the Odds: Making Federalism Work," *Journal of Democracy* 9 (July 1998): 22.

28. Sridharan and Varshney, "Toward Moderate Pluralism," p. 218.

29. Ibid., p. 214.

30. Donald Horowitz, *Ethnic Groups in Conflict* (Berkeley: University of California Press, 1985), pp. 598–628.

31. Alfred Stepan, "Federalism and Democracy: Beyond the U.S. Model," *Journal of Democracy* 10 (October 1999): 19–34.

32. Larry Diamond, *Developing Democracy: Toward Consolidation* (Baltimore: Johns Hopkins University Press, 1999), pp. 117–60.

33. Sridharan and Varshney, "Toward Moderate Pluralism," p. 208.

34. Sumit Ganguly, private communication to me, January 22, 2007.

35. Fortunately, the practice has fallen into abeyance.

36. Stepan, "Federalism and Democracy," pp. 23–25. As Stepan notes, if India had the minority vetoes and overrepresentation of states in a powerful legislative chamber that the United States does, the existing states would never have agreed to create these new states. So what has mattered for India has not just been federalism but its more flexible form.

37. Manor, "Making Federalism Work," p. 23.

38. Susanne Hoeber Rudolph and Lloyd I. Rudolph, "New Dimensions of Indian Democracy," *Journal of Democracy* 13 (January 2002): 54.

39. Sridharan and Varshney, "Toward Moderate Pluralism," pp. 209–10.

40. Sumit Ganguly, "Bangladesh and India," p. 174.

41. Guillermo O'Donnell, "Why the Rule of Law Matters," in Diamond and Morlino, *Assessing the Quality of Democracy*, pp. 3–17.

42. M. S. Gill, "India: Running the World's Biggest Elections," *Journal of Democracy* 9 (January 1998): 165–66.

43. Pratap Mehta, "India's Unlikely Democracy: The Rise of Judicial Sovereignty," *Journal of Democracy* 18 (April 2007): 73.

44. Ganguly, "India's Multiple Revolutions," p. 43.

45. Rudolph and Rudolph, "New Dimensions of Indian Democracy," p. 61.

46. Mehta, "India's Unlikely Democracy: The Rise of Judicial Sovereignty," p. 72.

47. Ibid.

48. Jenkins, "Anti-Corruption Activism and the Deepening of Democracy," p. 56.

49. Larry Diamond, Juan J. Linz, and Seymour Martin Lipset, "What Makes for Democracy?" in Diamond, Linz, and Lipset, *Politics in Developing Countries*, table 1.1, pp. 12–13.

50. Das Gupta, "India," p. 295. Statistical evidence also suggests that even moderate steady economic growth in poor countries can considerably reduce the chances of a democratic breakdown, as compared with a boom-bust type of performance. "Deaths of democracies follow a clear pattern: They are more likely when a country experiences an economic crisis and in most cases they are accompanied by one." Moreover, poor countries are particularly vulnerable to democratic breakdown in periods of declining national income. Adam Przeworksi, Michael E. Alvarez, José Antonio Cheibub, and Fernando Limongi, *Democracy and Development: Political Institutions and Well-Being in the World, 1950–1990* (Cambridge: Cambridge University Press, 2000), p. 111.

8. LATIN AMERICA'S UNEASY PROGRESS

1. Interview with Alejandro Toledo, Center for Advanced Study in the Behavioral Sciences, Stanford, February 8, 2007.

2. Cynthia McClintock, "An Unlikely Comeback in Peru," *Journal of Democracy* 17 (October 2006): 96.

3. These statistics (and others in this paragraph not otherwise referenced) can be found in *Peru on the Rise, 2001–2006: Economic and Social Report on Peru* (Lima: Government of Peru, 2006). For further documentation, see Marcelo M. Giugale, Vicente Fretes-Cibils, and John L. Newman, eds., *An Opportunity for a Different Peru: Prosperous, Equitable, and Governable* (Washington, D.C.: World Bank, 2007), introduction and chapter 1.

4. McClintock, "An Unlikely Comeback in Peru," p. 97.

5. One reason why poverty was not much reduced under Toledo is that "the growth spurt came in the wake of a sharp recession" under his predecessor, and thus first had to soak up excess capacity. Continued growth at that rate would reduce poverty more sharply, but deeper reductions require more targeted social policies and broader reforms of the state and the economy. Giugale et al., *An Opportunity for a Different Peru*, quoted from p. 45.

6. Freedom House, *Freedom in the World, 2006: The Annual Survey of Political Rights and Civil Liberties* (New York: Freedom House, 2006), p. 564.

7. McClintock, "An Unlikely Comeback in Peru," p. 98.

8. Ibid.

9. Polls placed his public approval rating upon leaving office in the range of 47 to 51 percent, and as high as 67 percent among the urban public. *La República* (Lima), July 27, 2006; *El Peruano*, July 1, 2006, and July 28, 2006.

10. Giugale, "A Synthesis," in Giugale et al., *An Opportunity for a Different Peru*, p. 1.

11. Interview with Alejandro Toledo, Center for Advanced Study in the Behavioral Sciences, Stanford, February 8, 2007.

12. Alejandro Toledo, "Democracy or Populism: Responding to the Crisis in Latin America," address to the New York Democracy Forum, April 18, 2007, www.ned.org.

13. Some observers, however, see Guatemala as still trapped in an electoral authoritarian state, given its continuing high level of violence and military impunity and autonomy.

14. Where voting is not obligatory, however, turnout has often been low: below 50 percent in the most recent elections in Guatemala, Honduras, El Salvador, and Colombia. I thank Charles Kenney for pointing this out.

15. Jorge Castañeda and Patricio Navia, "The Year of the Ballot," *Current History* 106 (February 2007): 51.

16. *Informe Latinobarómetro, 2006* (Santiago: Corporación Latinobarómetro, http://www.latinobarometro.org/uploads/media/2006_02.pdf), p. 72. These regional averages are not the average of all people living in Latin America but rather the average of the eighteen country percentages (not weighted by population). A new and different regional survey of Latin America, the Latin American Public Opinion Project (LAPOP, at http://www.vanderbilt.edu/lapop/), has recently found consistently higher levels of public support for democracy in the Americas. This may be because of a more systematic effort to capture rural respondents in proportion to their actual share of the population, and perhaps to other differences in sampling and implementation. The Latinobarometer figures may therefore be seen as low-end estimates, and possibly underestimates, of democratic support.

17. *Latinobarómetro Report, 2005: 1995–2005, A Decade of Public Opinion*, Corporacion Latinobarómetro, http://www.latinobarometro.org/uploads/media/2005_02.pdf., p. 51.

18. *Informe Latinobarómetro, 2006*, p. 65

19. *Latinobarómetro Report, 2005*, p. 52.

20. *Informe Latinobarómetro, 2006*, pp. 61–62.

21. *Latinobarómetro Report, 2005*, p. 14.

22. *Informe Latinobarómetro, 2006*, p. 66.

23. By contrast, 70 percent trust the church and radio. *Informe Latinobarómetro, 2006*, p. 30.

24. Ibid., p. 74.

25. By rating the level of democracy at least 6 on a scale of 1 to 10, with 10 being most democratic.

26. On the corruption and rule-of-law measures, see *Latinobarómetro Report, 2005*, pp. 23–30; on the evaluations of democracy and government performance, see *Informe Latinobarómetro, 2006*, pp. 63–80. The same data are used for the subsequent two groups of countries.

27. Ibid., p. 69.

28. Arturo Valenzuela and Lucía Dammert, "Problems of Success in Chile," *Journal of Democracy* 17 (October 2006): 65.

29. Anita Isaacs, "Guatemala," in Freedom House, *Countries at the Crossroads, 2006* (New York: Rowman and Littlefield, 2006), pp. 146–47.

30. On this trend in Brazil, see Frances Hagopian, in Larry Diamond and Leonardo Morlino, eds., *Assessing the Quality of Democracy* (Baltimore: Johns Hopkins University Press, 2005), pp. 123–62.

31. Ibid., p. 137, and World Bank, World Development Indicators, https://publications.worldbank.org/subscriptions/WDI/old-default.htm.

32. Matthew R. Cleary, "Explaining the Left's Resurgence," *Journal of Democracy* 17 (October 2006): 41.

33. David Holiday, "El Salvador's 'Model' Democracy," *Current History* 104 (February 2005): 77–82.

34. Donna Lee Van Cott, "Indigenous Peoples and Democratization in Latin America," *Journal of Democracy* 18 (October 2007): 127–41. Van Cott notes that reforms recognizing the cultural and social rights of indigenous peoples have gone the furthest in Colombia, Ecuador, Panama, and Venezuela, while making "modest" progress in Argentina, Bolivia, Brazil, Costa Rica, Guatemala, Honduras, Mexico, Nicaragua, Paraguay, and Peru. See also Van Cott, "Broadening Democracy: Latin America's Indigenous Peoples' Movements," *Current History* 103 (February 2004): 80–85.

35. Van Cott, "Indigenous Peoples and Democratization in Latin America," p. 135.

36. Human Rights Watch, *World Report, 2007*, http://hrw.org/englishwr2k7/docs/2007/01/11/chile14883.htm.

37. Human Rights Watch, *World Report, 2006* (New York: Human Rights Watch, 2006), p. 178.

38. J. Mark Ruhl, "Curbing Central America's Militaries," *Journal of Democracy* 15 (July 2004): 137–51. The quote is from p. 137.

39. Ana Arana, "How the Street Gangs Took Central America," *Foreign Affairs* 84 (May–June 2005): 98; Michael Shifter, "Latin America's Drug Problem," *Current History* 106 (February 2007): 62.

40. Paulo Sérgio Pinheiro, "The Rule of Law and the Underprivileged in Latin America," in Juan E. Méndes, Guillermo O'Donnell, and Paulo Sérgio Pinheiro, eds., *The (Un)Rule of Law and the Underprivileged in Latin America* (Notre Dame, Ind.: University of Notre Dame Press, 1999), pp. 1–5.

41. Paulo Sérgio Pinheiro, "Youth, Violence, and Democracy," *Current History* 106 (February 2007): 64.

42. Testimony of Adolfo A. Franco, assistant administrator, Bureau for Latin America and the Caribbean, United States Agency for International Development, before the Subcommittee on the Western Hemisphere, Committee on International Relations, U.S. House of Representatives, April 20, 2005, http://usinfo.state.gov/dhr/Archive/2005/Apr/21-965427.html.

43. Ibid.

44. Jens Glüsing, "The Mafia's Shadow Kingdom," *Spiegel Online*, May 22, 2006, http://www.spiegel.de/international/spiegel/0,1518,417450,00.html.

45. Arana, "How the Street Gangs Took Central America," p. 101.

46. Shifter, "Latin America's Drug Problem," p. 62.

47. "Mexican Official: Drug Gangs Still Strong," *Miami Herald*, February 16, 2007, http://www.miami.com/mld/miamiherald/news/world/americas/16710252.htm.

48. Glüsing, "The Mafia's Shadow Kingdom." See also Pinheiro, "Youth, Violence, and Democracy."

49. Arana, "How the Street Gangs Took Central America," p. 99.

50. Pinheiro, "Youth, Violence, and Democracy," p. 68.

51. In El Salvador, Venezuela, Guatemala, Honduras, and Argentina, crime is most often mentioned as the most important problem facing the country (and by large margins in the first three). In Mexico, Panama, and Paraguay, it is the second most mentioned problem. *Informe Latinobarómetro, 2006*, p. 41.

52. Danna Harman, "U.S. Steps Up Battle against Salvadoran MS-13," *USA Today*, February 23, 2005, http://www.usatoday.com/news/world/2005-02-23-gang-salvador_x.htm.

53. Freedom House, *Freedom in the World, 2006*, pp. 292–94.

54. More than 5,500 Guatemalans were murdered in 2005, a rate of over 43 murders per 100,000 population. According to FBI statistics, the U.S. rate that same year was 5.6.

http://www.fbi.gov/ucr/05cius/data/table_01.html. Recently the murder rate in Honduras was 154, more than twenty-five times the U.S. rate.

55. Mitchell A. Seligson, "Democracy on Ice: The Multiple Challenges of Guatemala's Peace Process," in Frances Hagopian and Scott P. Mainwaring, eds., *The Third Wave of Democratization in Latin America: Advances and Setbacks* (Cambridge: Cambridge University Press, 2005), p. 226. Seligson refers here to a study by Ted Robert Gurr.

56. Freedom House, *Freedom in the World, 2006*, p. 293.

57. Isaacs, "Guatemala," p. 151.

58. Human Rights Watch, *World Report, 2007*, http://hrw.org/englishwr2k7/docs/2007/01/11/guatem14861.htm.

59. Ibid.

60. Data are from the World Bank's World Development Indicators Online, generally from the period 2000–2003, https://publications.worldbank.org/subscriptions/WDI/old-default.htm.

61. Guillermo O'Donnell, "Polyarchies and the (Un)Rule of Law in Latin America: A Partial Conclusion," in Méndes, O'Donnell, and Pinheiro, *The (Un)Rule of Law and the Underprivileged in Latin America*, p. 323.

62. Isaacs, "Guatemala," p. 153.

63. Catherine Conaghan, "Ecuador's Gamble: Can Correa Govern," *Current History* 106 (February 2007): 81.

64. *Latinobarómetro Report, 2005*, pp. 65 and 74. Again, the "average" percentage is not an average of all people in Latin America but the average of the percentage figures for the different countries.

65. *Informe Latinobarómetro, 2006*, p. 50. That proportion was down from three-quarters during the period 2002 to 2005, showing the economic improvement in the region, but the continuing economic fragility of most families.

66. *Latinobarómetro Report, 2005*, p. 71.

67. *Informe Latinobarómetro, 2006*, pp. 35–39.

68. Shelley A. McConnell, "Nicaragua's Turning Point," *Current History* 106 (February 2007): 83–88.

69. Arturo Valenzuela, "Latin American Presidencies Interrupted," *Journal of Democracy* 15 (October 2004): 5–19.

70. Castañeda and Navia, "The Year of the Ballot," p. 51.

71. Freedom House, *Freedom in the World, 2006*, p. 42.

72. Valenzuela, "Latin American Presidencies Interrupted," pp. 14–18.

73. Interview with Alejandro Toledo, Center for Advanced Study in the Behavioral Sciences, Stanford, February 8, 2007.

9. THE POSTCOMMUNIST DIVIDE

1. I classify a political system as a *liberal democracy* if it scores either a 1 or a 2 on each of the Freedom House seven-point scales of political rights and civil liberties (see the appendix, table 1, for a description). Serious problems with the quality of democracy may nevertheless remain.

2. See the annual classifications by Freedom House in its annual *Freedom in the World* publications and at www.freedomhouse.org.

3. There is no consensus among observers as to whether Georgia is today a democracy. Like perhaps as many as twenty other countries in the world (including about a dozen in Africa), it stands somewhere in a gray zone between democracy and electoral authoritarianism. Freedom House classifies Georgia (and these other "gray zone" regimes) as democracies. I have my doubts, given the extent of concentration of power in President Saakashvili and what Freedom House itself refers to as "the absence of a credible opposition." *Freedom in the World, 2006: The Annual Survey of Political Rights and Civil Liberties* (New York: Freedom House, 2006),

p. 272. In their forthcoming book, *Competitive Authoritarianism,* Steven Levitsky and Lucan Way take a more rigorous stand, classifying as competitive authoritarian the regimes in Georgia, Albania, Moldova, and others often considered democracies. Lacking adequate information to render an authoritative dissenting assessment, I have generally accepted the Freedom House classifications of regimes, but not without doubts.

4. See the Web site of the European Union on enlargement, http://ec.europa.eu/ enlargement/key_documents/reports_nov_2006_en.htm.

5. The data that follow can be found in Richard Rose, "Insiders and Outsiders: New Europe Barometer, 2004," *Studies in Public Policy,* no. 404, Centre for the Study of Public Policy, University of Strathclyde, 2005. Similar differences between East European and post-Soviet states are apparent in earlier surveys conducted in the 1990s. See, for example, the 1995 data in Richard Rose and Christian Haerpfer, "New Democracies Barometer IV: A 10-Nation Survey, *Studies in Public Policy,* no. 262, Centre for the Study of Public Policy, University of Strathclyde, 1996.

6. Rose, "Insiders and Outsiders," pp. 17 and 19.

7. Richard Rose, "Diverging Paths of Post-Communist Countries: New Europe Barometer Trends Since 1991," *Studies in Public Policy,* no. 262, Centre for the Study of Public Policy, University of Aberdeen, 2006, p. 29.

8. Rose, "Insiders and Outsiders," p. 68, question D7.

9. The seven countries were the Czech Republic, Hungary, Poland, Slovakia, Slovenia, Romania, and Bulgaria. See Rose and Haerpfer, "New Democracies Barometer IV," pp. 21, 86.

10. The most striking difference is that the proportion of firm democrats in Poland, measured in this way, fell from 63 percent in 1995 to 50 percent in 2004.

11. In Poland, the electoral threshold for coalitions of parties is 8 percent, but only 5 percent for individual parties.

12. The Czech Republic is an exception here. Its principal left party, the Social Democratic Party, traces its roots back to 1878 and is a resurrection of the party of the same name during the interwar period of democracy in the Czechoslovak Republic, http://www.cssd.cz/ english-version. By contrast, the Communist Party in the Czech Republic, which won 13 percent in 2006, is only partially reformed and has been shunned until now as a coalition partner in government.

13. Freedom House, *Freedom in the World, 2006,* p. 574.

14. Alina Mungiu-Pippidi, "Poland and Romania," in Larry Diamond and Leonardo Morlino, eds., *Assessing the Quality of Democracy* (Baltimore: Johns Hopkins University Press, 2005), pp. 233–34.

15. Jacques Rupnik, "Populism in East-Central Europe," Institute for Human Sciences, Vienna Austria, IWM Post, no. 94, Fall 2006, http://www.iwm.at/index.php?option=com_content&task=view&id=496&Itemid=522.

16. Jacques Rupnik, "Popular Front: Eastern Europe's Turn Right," *New Republic,* February 19 and 26, 2007, p. 13.

17. Ibid.

18. Ibid.

19. Rupnik, "Populism in East-Central Europe."

20. Rupnik, "Popular Front," p. 13.

21. Anna Seleny, "Communism's Many Legacies in East-Central Europe," *Journal of Democracy* 18 (July 2007): 161–63.

22. Freedom House, *Freedom in the World, 2006,* p. 118.

23. Ferenc Gyurcsány, quoted in Pete Bell, "PM's Lies Spark Hungary Riots," *Sun,* September 19, 2006, http://www.thesun.co.uk/article/0,,2-2006430405,00.html; Judy Dempsey, "Night of Hungary Riots Fails to Win Resignation; Leader Who Admits Lying Defies Mob," *International Herald Tribune,* September 20, 2006; Christopher Condon, "Hungary Riots Mar Commemoration," *Financial Times,* October 23, 2006.

24. Judy Dempsey, "Hungary Coalition Stays the Austerity Course Despite Huge Protests," *New York Times,* March 11, 2007.

25. Alinga Mungiu-Pippidi, "Romania," in Jeanette Goehring, ed., *Nations in Transit, 2006* (New York: Freedom House, 2006), p. 480.

26. Ivan Krastev, Rashko Dorosiev, and Georgy Ganev, "Bulgaria," in Goehring, *Nations in Transit, 2006,* p. 195.

27. Rose, "Insiders and Outsiders," p. 21.

28. Ibid., p. 70.

29. Ibid., p. 64. Distrust in the president was everywhere much lower, averaging about a third. I excluded the levels for Belarus, which show much higher levels of trust, raising questions of whether some respondents felt free to answer as they really felt in the more blatantly authoritarian circumstances of Belarus.

30. Rupnik, "Popular Front," p. 13.

31. Statistical Yearbook of the Economic Commission for Europe, 2005, http://www.unece.org/stats/trends2005/Sources/120_Unemployment%20rate%20(%25).pdf.

32. Rose, "Insiders and Outsiders," pp. 41 and 43.

33. Rupnik, "Popular Front," p. 13.

34. Ibid., p. 14.

35. Oleksandr Sushko and Olena Prystayko, "Ukraine," in Goehring, *Nations in Transit, 2006,* pp. 677–81.

36. U.S. Department of State, *Country Reports on Human Rights Practices: 2006,* http://www.state.gov/g/drl/rls/hrrpt/2006/78846.htm.

37. Ghia Nodia, "Georgia," in Goehring, *Nations in Transit, 2006,* p. 258.

38. Ibid., pp. 273–77, and U.S. Department of State, *Country Reports on Human Rights Practices: 2006.*

39. "Constitutional Amendments Go into Force," *Georgia Online* magazine, January 10, 2007, http://www.civil.ge/eng/article.php?id=14425. The amendments also cut short the president's term by several months and extended the life of parliament by several months in order to make the two elections simultaneous, a constructive step in any system with substantial presidential power.

40. Nana Sumbadze, "Georgia Public Opinion Barometer, 2006," Institute for Policy Studies, Tblisi, http://ips.ge/barometrifin.pdf, pp. 15–18.

41. Michael McFaul, "Ten Years after the Soviet Breakup: A Mixed Record, an Uncertain Future," *Journal of Democracy* 12 (October 2001): 90–91.

42. Eric McGlinchey, "Autocrats, Islamists, and the Rise of Radicalism in Central Asia," *Current History* 104 (October 2005): 337.

43. Freedom House, *Freedom in the World, 2006,* p. 59.

44. U.S. Department of State, http://www.state.gov/g/drl/rls/hrrpt/2006/78821.htm.

45. Freedom House, *Freedom in the World, 2006,* p. 375.

46. Bhavna Dave, "Kazakhstan," in Goehring, *Nations in Transit 2006,* pp. 306–17.

47. Ibid., p. 310.

48. Ibid., p. 319.

49. C. J. Chivers, "Former Son-in-Law of Kazakh Leader Says He Was Framed," *New York Times,* July 6, 2007. At the time he assumed exile, Aliyev had just been dismissed as Kazakhstan's ambassador to Austria.

50. McGlinchey, "The Rise of Radicalism in Central Asia," p. 340.

51. Ibid., p. 338.

52. Freedom House, *Freedom in the World, 2006,* pp. 774–81.

53. "Uzbekistan: Human Rights Defenders under Siege," Human Rights Watch, December 9, 2006, http://hrw.org/english/docs/2006/12/09/uzbeki14799.htm.

54. Robert Freedman, "Uzbekistan," in Goehring, *Nations in Transit, 2006,* p. 691.

55. Ibid., p. 707.

56. McGlinchey, "The Rise of Radicalism in Central Asia," p. 340.

57. On corruption under Putin, see Marshall I. Goldman, "Political Graft: The Russian Way," *Current History* 105 (October 2005): 313–18.

58. Steven Lee Myers, "Kasparov, Building Opposition to Putin," *New York Times,* March 10, 2007.

59. McFaul, "A Mixed Record, an Uncertain Future," p. 91.

10. THE ASIAN EXCEPTION?

1. Transparency International, 2006 Corruption Perceptions Index, http://www .transparency.org/policy_research/surveys_indices/cpi/2006.

2. The PAP also won eighty-two of eighty-four seats in the 2001 parliamentary elections.

3. Cherian George, "Networked Autocracy: Consolidating Singapore's Political System," presented to the Workshop on Political Transitions and Political Change in Southeast Asia, August 27–29, 2006, p. 2.

4. Cherian George, "Calibrated Coercion and the Maintenance of Hegemony in Singapore." Working Paper Series 48, September 2005, Asia Research Institute, National University of Singapore. http://www.ari.nus.edu.sg/docs/wps/wps05_048.pdf.

5. Interview in Singapore, September 15, 2006.

6. Freedom House, *Freedom in the World, 2006: The Annual Survey of Political Rights and Civil Liberties* (New York: Freedom House, 2006), p. 635.

7. Cherian George, "Networked Autocracy," p. 4.

8. Chee Soon Juan, "Pressing for Openness in Singapore," *Journal of Democracy* 12 (April 2001): 165.

9. http://en.wikipedia.org/wiki/Tang_Liang_Hong.

10. Interview with Chee Soon Juan in Singapore, September 13, 2006.

11. Interview in Singapore, September 15, 2006.

12. Interview with Lee Kuan Yew, September 13, 2006.

13. Beng Huat Chua, "Communitarianism without Competitive Politics in Singapore," in Beng Huat Chua, ed., *Communitarian Politics in Asia* (New York: Routledge, 2004), pp. 78–99.

14. Garry Rodan, "Singapore 'Exceptionalism'? Authoritarian Rule and State Transformation," Working Paper no. 131, May 2006. Asia Research Center, Murdoch University, http://wwwarc.murdoch.edu.au/wp/wp131.pdf. See also Diane Mauzy and R. S. Milne, *Singapore Politics Under the People's Action Party* (New York: Routledge, 2002), and Suzaina Kadir, "Singapore: Engagement and Autonomy Within the Political Status Quo," in Muthiah Alagappa, *Civil Society and Political Change in Asia* (Stanford, Calif.: Stanford University Press, 2004), chapter 10.

15. IPS Post-election Survey Results, Institute of Policy Studies, Singapore, June 2006, http://www.ips.org.sg/ra/index_polgov.htm.

16. Chee Soon Juan, "Pressing for Openness in Singapore," p. 158.

17. Gillian Koh, Tan Ern Ser, and Jeanne Conceicao, "IPS Post-Election Survey 2006: Cluster Analysis of Political Orientation," Institute of Policy Studies, Singapore, June 2006, http://www.ips.org.sg/ra/index_polgov.htm.

18. Ken Kwek, "What the PAP Wants, What Voters Want: The Future of Singapore's Political System," speech to the Institute for Policy Studies, May 29, 2006, p. 12.

19. Freedom House, *Freedom in the World, 2006,* p. 667; and Chandra R. de Silva, "Sri Lanka in 2006," *Asian Survey* 47 (January–February 2007): 99–104.

20. Joseph Nevins, "Timor-Leste in 2006," *Asian Survey* 47 (January–February 2007): 163.

21. Pamela Constable, "A Wake-Up Call in Afghanistan," *Journal of Democracy* 18 (April 2007): 84–98.

22. David N. Gellner, "Nepal and Bhutan in 2006: A Year of Revolution," *Asian Survey* 47 (January–February 2007): 80–86.

23. Somini Sengupta, "Musharraf Finds Himself Weakened After Firing of Judge Stirs Anger in Pakistan," *New York Times,* March 25, 2007.

24. Doh Chull Shin and Jaechul Lee, "The Korea Democracy Barometer Surveys, 1997–2004," *Korea Observer* 37 (Summer 2006): 237–76.

25. The results from the second round of the Asian Barometer in these two countries were not available when this book went to press.

26. These and other data from the East Asia Barometer are from Yutzung Chang, Yun-han Chu, and Chong-min Park, "Struggling Democracies in East Asia: Through Citizens' Eyes," *Journal of Democracy* 18 (July 2007): 66–80. For more on the survey, see http://www.asianbarometer.org/newenglish/introduction/.

27. Only in Mongolia in 2006 did a majority fail to reject one option, a strong leader.

28. In Japan in 2003, 57 percent rejected all three options, but such dedicated democrats dwindled to 28 percent in Mongolia (from 44 percent in 2004) and stayed at just under 40 percent in the Philippines.

29. Again, all these figures are from 2004 surveys. Data are from the Asian Barometer.

30. Larry Diamond and Doh Chull Shin, "Introduction: Institutional Reform and Democratic Consolidation in Korea," in Diamond and Shin, *Institutional Reform and Democratic Consolidation in Korea* (Stanford, Calif.: Hoover Institution Press, 2000), pp. 5–18.

31. Yun-han Chu, "Taiwan's Year of Crisis," *Journal of Democracy* 16 (April 2005): 47.

32. Ibid., p. 49.

33. Ibid., p. 50.

34. Ibid., p. 51.

35. Yun-han Chu, "Taiwan in 2006: A Year of Political Turmoil," *Asian Survey* 47 (January–February 2007): 44.

36. Ibid., p. 45.

37. Ibid., p. 46.

38. Hahm Chaihark and Sung Ho Kim, "Constitutionalism on Trial in South Korea," *Journal of Democracy* 16 (April 2005): 28.

39. Freedom House, *Freedom in the World, 2006*, p. 660.

40. Norimitsu Onishi, "South Korean President Sags in Opinion Polls," *New York Times*, November 27, 2006.

41. John Lie and Myoungkyu Park, "South Korea in 2005: Economic Dynamism, Generational Conflicts, and Social Transformations," *Asian Survey* 46 (January–February 2006): 62.

42. Andrew Eungi Kim and John Lie, "South Korea in 2006: Nuclear Standoff, Trade Talks, and Population Trends," *Asian Survey* 47 (January–February 2007): 55.

43. Freedom House, *Freedom in the World, 2006*, p. 483, and Stephen Noerper, "Mongolia in 2006: Land of the Rising Khan," *Asian Survey* 47 (January–February 2007): 74–79.

44. Edward Aspinall, "Indonesia," in Freedom House, *Countries at the Crossroads, 2006* (New York: Freedom House, 2006), pp. 193–204.

45. R. William Liddle and Saiful Mujani, "Indonesia in 2005: A New Multiparty Presidential Democracy," *Asian Survey* 46 (January–February 2006): 132–39.

46. Ibid., p. 138.

47. Aspinall, "Indonesia," p. 190.

48. Ibid., p. 193.

49. Ibid., p. 191. While Indonesia has recently improved on Transparency International's "Corruption Perception Index," from a rank of 137 out of 158 countries in 2005 to a rank of 130 of 163 in 2006, this still means that Indonesia is about in the bottom 20 percent in controlling corruption. http://www.transparency.org/policy_research/surveys_indices/cpi/2006.

50. Ibid., pp. 195, 203.

51. For an even more hopeful assessment, see Damien Kingsbury, "Indonesia in 2006: Cautious Reform," *Asian Survey* 47 (January–February 2007): 161.

52. See, for example, John Sidel, *Capital, Coercion, and Crime: Bossism in the Philippines* (Stanford, Calif.: Stanford University Press, 2002), p. 1.

53. "Democracy as Showbiz," *Economist*, July 1, 2004, http://www.economist.com/research/backgrounders/displaystory.cfm?story_id=2876966.

54. Steven Rogers, "Philippine Politics and the Rule of Law," *Journal of Democracy* 15 (October 2004): 115.

55. Ibid., p. 117.

56. Ibid., p. 111.

57. Steven Rogers, "Philippines' Democracy in Turmoil," *Open Democracy,* August 16, 2005, http://www.opendemocracy.net/democracy-protest/philippines_2759.jsp, p. 2.

58. Rogers, "Philippine Politics and the Rule of Law," p. 111.

59. The constitution limits presidents to a single six-year term, but as she succeeded to the office in midterm, she was allowed to contest.

60. Rogers, "Philippines' Democracy in Turmoil," p. 3.

61. Rogers, "Philippine Politics and the Rule of Law," p. 113.

62. Freedom House, *Freedom in the World, 2006,* p. 569.

63. Ibid.

64. Rogers, "Philippines' Democracy in Turmoil," p. 3.

65. The debate over switching from a presidential to a parliamentary form of government in the Philippines has a long history in the post-Marcos era, and the move to parliamentary rule has its principled advocates in the Philippine and wider academic communities. Barred from running for reelection, President Macapagal-Arroyo seemed to have a far more instrumental agenda, however, and I agree with Steven Rogers that pervasive corruption and "the lack of established or ideologically differentiated political parties" would likely produce "endless rounds of political maneuvering" that would paralyze parliamentary government. "Philippine Politics and the Rule of Law," p. 120.

66. Some protests were held that day, but others were violently dispersed by state security personnel. The commandant of the marines was replaced two days later, and within a week the state of emergency was lifted, after much condemnation from civil society.

67. Sheila S. Coronel, "The Philippines in 2006: Democracy and Its Discontents," *Asian Survey* 47 (January–February 2007): 176.

68. Ibid., p. 175.

69. Ibid.

70. Between the 2001 and 2005 surveys of the East Asia Barometer, the belief that democracy is always preferable dropped from 64 to 51 percent; those saying democracy is suitable for the country dropped from 80 to 57 percent; satisfaction with democracy dropped from 54 to 39 percent; and the proportion rejecting the option of an authoritarian "strong leader" dropped from 70 to 59 percent.

71. Freedom House, *Freedom in the World, 2006,* p. 571.

72. Human Rights Watch Press Release, "Philippines: Climate of Fear Impedes Probe into Killings," September 28, 2006, http://hrw.org/english/docs/200609/29/philip14283 .htm.

73. "A Troublesome Priest," *Economist,* October 12, 2006, http://www.economist.com/ world/asia/displaystory.cfm?story_id=8031230.

74. Interview with Jose Luis Gascon, November 20, 2006, Stanford University.

75. Rogers, "Philippines' Democracy in Turmoil," p. 5.

76. Freedom House, *Freedom in the World, 2006,* p. 70.

77. In fact, in 2005 Bangladesh ranked dead last in Transparency International's annual Corruption Perceptions Index, surveying 159 countries.

78. Freedom House, *Freedom in the World, 2006,* p. 68.

79. International Crisis Group (ICG), "Bangladesh Today," *Asia Report* 121 (October 23, 2006): 3.

80. Freedom House, *Freedom in the World, 2006,* p. 69.

81. Ibid.

82. Eliza Griswold, "The Next Islamic Revolution?" *New York Times Magazine,* January 23, 2005.

83. "The Coup That Dare Not Speak Its Name," *Economist,* January 18, 2007.

84. C. Christine Fair and Sumit Ganguly, "Bangladesh on the Brink," *Wall Street Journal,* February 5, 2007.

85. National Democatic Institute, *NDI* Election Watch Bangladesh, February 11, 2007, http://www.accessdemocracy.org/library/2117_bd_watch4_021107.pdf, and Reuters, "Bangladesh Leader Says No Let-up in Anti-graft Fight," March 25, 2007, http://www.alertnet.org/thenews/newsdesk/DHA86010.htm.

86. ICG, "Bangladesh Today," p. ii.

87. Ibid., p. 7.

88. Minxin Pei, *China's Trapped Transition: The Limits of Developmental Autocracy* (Cambridge, Mass.: Harvard University Press, 2006), p. 50. The account that follows is drawn from Pei's book, pp. 50–57.

89. These are Pei's words. Ibid., p. 55.

90. Quoted in ibid.

91. Bruce Gilley, *China's Democratic Future: How It Will Happen and Where It Will Lead* (New York: Columbia University Press, 2004), p. 107.

92. Pei, *China's Trapped Transition*, p. 56.

93. Minxin Pei, "The Dark Side of China's Rise," *Foreign Policy* (March–April 2006): 40.

94. The estimate comes from U.S. Department of State, *Country Reports on Human Rights Practices, 2006,* March 6, 2007, section 1a, http://www.state.gov/g/drl/rls/hrrpt/2006/78771.htm.

95. Pei, *China's Trapped Transition*, p. 87. The latest figure on Internet use is from U.S. Department of State, *Country Reports on Human Rights Practices, 2006,* section 2a. The data on the estimated number of bloggers come from Tony Saich, "China in 2006: Focus on Social Development," *Asian Survey,* 47 (January–February 2007): 35.

96. Reporters without Borders, "Microsoft Censors Its Blog Tools," June 14, 2005, http://www.rsf.org/article.php3?id_article=14069.

97. Reporters without Borders, "Shareholders Ask Cisco Systems to Account for Its Activities in Repressive Countries," November 17, 2006, http://www.rsf.org/article.php3?id_article=19782.

98. Reporters without Borders, "China," http://www.rsf.org/article.php3?id_article=10749.

99. According to the UNDP, annual growth in per capita income averaged 8.4 percent between 1975 and 2004, and 8.9 percent between 1990 and 2004. United Nations Development Program, *Human Development Report, 2006,* http://hdr.undp.org/hdr2006/pdfs/report/HDR06-complete.pdf, table 14, p. 332.

100. According to UNDP statistics. Ying Ma, "China's Stubborn Anti-Democracy," *Policy Review* 141 (February–March 2007), http://www.hoover.org/publications/policyreview/5513661.html, p. 4 of online version.

101. Pei, *China's Trapped Transition,* p. 2.

102. UNDP, *Human Development Report, 2006,* pp. 324, 289.

103. Andrew Nathan, "China's Changing of the Guard: Authoritarian Resilience," *Journal of Democracy* 14 (January 2003): 6–17.

104. Dali Yang, "Can the Chinese Regime Adapt? Reforms and Institutional Adaptations," paper presented to the Conference on Democratization in Greater China, Center on Democracy, Development, and the Rule of Law, Stanford University, October 20–21, 2006, p. 3.

105. Wei Pan, "Toward a Consultative Rule of Law Regime in China," *Journal of Contemporary China* 12 (January 2003): 3–43. Also in Suisheng Zhao, ed., *Debating Political Reform in China: Rule of Law vs. Democratization* (Armonk, N.Y.: ME Sharpe, 2006), pp. 3–40.

106. Larry Diamond, "The Rule of Law as Transition to Democracy in China," *Journal of Contemporary China* 12 (May 2003): 319–31. Also in Zhao, *Debating Political Reform,* pp. 79–90.

107. Henry S. Rowen, "When Will the Chinese People Be Free?" *Journal of Democracy* 18 (July 2007). See also his original projections in "The Short March: China's Road to Democracy," *National Interest* 45 (Fall 1996): 61–70.

108. Gilley, *China's Democratic Future,* p. 69; Larry Diamond, *Developing Democracy: Toward Consolidation* (Baltimore: Johns Hopkins University Press, 1999), table 5.7, p. 189.

109. Yun-han Chu, "Political Value Change in Hong Kong, Taiwan, and China, 1993–2002," paper presented to the Conference on Democratization in Greater China, Center on Democracy, Development, and the Rule of Law, Stanford University, October 20–21, 2006.

110. Pei, *China's Trapped Transition,* p. 209.

111. Ibid., pp. 161–65. As in the United States and Europe, favored sectors for the mafia include real estate, transportation, and construction.

112. Ibid., pp. 189, 191–96. The party itself reported a total of eighty-seven thousand "mass incidents" in 2005, an increase of over 6 percent from the year before. Saich, "China in 2006," p. 35.

113. The figure rose to 90 percent in some cities. Saich, "China in 2006," p. 38.

114. Ibid., p. 39.

115. Pei, *China's Trapped Transition,* p. 208.

116. Ibid., pp. 210–12.

117. Gilley, *China's Democratic Future,* p. 33.

118. An Chen, "China's Changing of the Guard: The New Inequality," *Journal of Democracy* 14 (January 2003): 51–59.

119. Gilley, *China's Democratic Future,* pp. 62–94.

120. Ibid., p. 73.

121. Ying Ma, "China's Stubbon Anti-Democracy," p. 6.

122. Gilley, *China's Democratic Future,* p. 99.

123. "China's Sort of Congress," editorial, *New York Times,* March 15, 2007.

124. Pei, *China's Trapped Transition,* pp. 55–80.

125. Gilley, *China's Democratic Future,* p. 101.

126. Ibid., p. 38. The Gini coefficient of income inequality is now estimated at somewhere between 0.45 and 0.50 (on a scale where 0 is most equal and 1 is pure inequality). Saich, "China in 2006," p. 40. But Gilley cites some sources indicating that it may be as high as 0.60, making it one of the most unequal in the world. Saich cites official sources as reporting the urban-rural income gap at 3.22 to 1 in 2005.

127. Ying Ma, "China's Stubborn Anti-Democracy," p. 5 of online version.

128. Harry Harding, "Think Again: China," *Foreign Policy* 159 (March–April 2007).

129. Pei, *China's Trapped Transition,* pp. 175–76. The data on dams is from Gilley, *China's Democratic Future,* p. 103. In 1975, he reports, twin dams burst in Henan Province, killing an estimated three hundred thousand people. No catastrophe on anything approaching such a scale could be covered up today in China, even with the level of state control of the Internet and other media. For similar views anticipating that profound governance crises will cripple and probably bring down Communist Party rule in the next two decades, see Shaoguang Wang, "China's Changing of the Guard: The Problem of State Weakness," *Journal of Democracy* 14 (January 2003): 36–42, and Guogang Wu, "Why the Regime Is Decaying and Headed for Crisis," paper presented to the Conference on Democratization in Greater China, Center on Democracy, Development, and the Rule of Law, Stanford University, October 20–21, 2006. Both Wang and Wu are skeptical, however, that crisis generated by state decay will lead to democracy.

130. Pei, *China's Trapped Transition,* p. 170. See also Chen, "China's Changing of the Guard: The New Inequality."

131. Gilley, *China's Democratic Future,* p. 103.

132. Seth Faison, "In Beijing, a Roar of Silent Protestors," *New York Times,* April 27, 1999, http://partners.nytimes.com/library/world/asia/042799china-protest.html.

133. Richard Spencer, "Christianity Is China's New Social Revolution," *Telegraph,* July 30, 2005, http://www.telegraph.co.uk/news/main.jhtml?xml=/news/2005/07/30/wchina30.xml. See also Simon Elegant, "The War for China's Soul," Time, August 20, 2006, http://www.time.com/time/magazine/article/0,9171,1229123,00.html.

134. In fact, one of China's leading secular democratic intellectuals observed to me that without some kind of moral or religious faith, "we can only have democratic knowledge, not democratic culture."

135. Gilley, *China's Democratic Future*, p. 70.

136. I was stunned to witness this directly in 2002, when I gave a carefully worded lecture to the Central Party School in Beijing on how economic development would gradually generate demands for "more accountability of political leaders to the citizenry." To avoid making trouble for my hosts and sponsors, I omitted mention of the "*d* word"—*democracy*. But my remarks set off a storm of blunt debate among the resident teachers and researchers at the party school, with several insisting that the party had to introduce internal democracy. A crucial passage of my speech is reproduced in Gilley, *China's Democratic Future*, p. 65. Gilley provides evidence of the existence of a "freedom faction" within the party, p. 88.

137. Ibid., pp. 118–37. Quoted from p. 133.

11. AFRICA, OVERCOMING PERSONAL RULE

1. Peter Lewis, *Growing Apart: Oil, Politics, and Economic Change in Indonesia and Nigeria* (Ann Arbor: University of Michigan Press, 2007), p. 140.

2. Ibid., p. 155.

3. Larry Diamond, "Nigeria: The Uncivic Society and the Descent into Praetorianism," in Larry Diamond, Juan J. Linz, and Seymour Martin Lipset, eds., *Politics in Developing Countries: Comparing Experiences with Democracy* (Boulder, Colo.: Lynne Rienner, 1995), p. 437.

4. Quoted in ibid.

5. *Punch*, March 31, 1983.

6. Diamond, "Nigeria," pp. 439–40.

7. The circumstances of Abacha's death will probably remain a mystery forever. Many Nigerian political leaders and civic activists believe his military colleagues eliminated him to spare the country and the armed forces as an institution. The *Economist* reports that he "expired in the arms of two Indian prostitutes, possibly from an overdose of Viagra." "Big Men, Big Fraud, Big Trouble," *Economist* April 28, 2007, p. 55.

8. Ibid.

9. Specifically, the index is an average of the standardized scores (from 0 to 100) on life expectancy, the combination of the adult literacy rate and the gross ratio of school enrollments to age-relevant population, and the per capita gross domestic product in purchasing power parity dollars. United Nations Development Program, *Human Development Report, 2006: Beyond Scarcity; Power, Poverty, and the Global Water Crisis* (New York: Palgrave Macmillan, 2006), p. 276, and table 1, pp. 283–86.

10. Figures are from ibid., tables 1–7, pp. 283–308.

11. United Nations Peacekeeping, "List of Operations," http://www.un.org/Depts/dpko/list/list.pdf.

12. See the study and data set of James D. Fearon and David Laitin, "Ethnicity, Insurgency, and Civil War," *American Political Science Review* 97 (February 2003): 75–90. Using an inclusive but broadly accepted definition of *civil war* (at least a thousand deaths, at least one hundred on each side, from internal hostilities in which one side tries violently to change the state or its policies), they count thirty-six civil wars in twenty-two sub-Saharan African countries between 1960 and 2002. I am grateful to Jim Fearon for providing me their updated data.

13. United Nations High Commissioner for Refugees, *2005 Global Refugee Trends*, p. 3, http://www.unhcr.org/statistics/STATISTICS/4486ceb12.pdf.

14. Richard Posner, "Should the U.S. Provide Foreign Aid?" the Becker-Posner Blog, January 21, 2007, http://www.becker-posner-blog.com/archives/2007/01/should_the_unit.html.

15. Steven Radelet, "A Primer on Foreign Aid," Working Paper 92, Center for Global Development, July 2006, http://www.cgdev.org/content/publications/detail/8846, table 2, p. 21.

16. A number of African civil society activists, journalists, and academics have been

making these points about the destructive consequences of unconditional foreign aid. Among the most forceful has been Andrew Mwenda. See notes 23, 25, 33, and 35 below.

17. Michael Bratton and Nicolas van de Walle, *Democratic Experiments in Africa: Regime Transitions in Comparative Perspective* (Cambridge: Cambridge University Press, 1997), p. 62. For the closely related concept of "sultanism," see Houchang Chehabi and Juan J. Linz, eds., *Sultanistic Regimes* (Baltimore: Johns Hopkins University Press, 1998).

18. Bratton and van de Walle, *Democratic Experiments in Africa,* pp. 61–68; Robert H. Jackson and Carl G. Rosberg, *Personal Rule in Black Africa: Prince, Autocrat, Prophet, Tyrant* (Berkeley: University of California Press, 1982), pp. 38–42.

19. Human Rights Watch, "Chop Fine: The Human Rights Impact of Local Government Corruption and Mismanagement in Rivers State, Nigeria," January 2007, p. 1, http://hrw.org/reports/2007/nigeria0107/nigeria0107web.pdf.

20. Richard A. Joseph, *Democracy and Prebendal Politics in Nigeria: The Rise and Fall of the Second Republic* (Cambridge: Cambridge University Press, 1987), p. 6; see also pp. 55–68 for elaboration of the concept and its relationship to clientelism.

21. These themes are developed at length in ibid. Quoted from p. 8.

22. AFP, "Analysis: 'New Generation' of East African Leaders Falls from Western Grace," *Middle East Times,* January 9, 2006, http://www.metimes.com/storyview.php?StoryID=20060109-102257-6310r.

23. Andrew M. Mwenda, "Please Stop Helping Us," paper presented to the Novartis Foundation, August 12, 2006.

24. UNDP, *Human Development Report, 2006,* table 14, pp. 333–34.

25. As a percent of total national product (GDP), fiscal deficits exploded from 5 percent in 1995 to 16 percent in 2003. Andrew Mwenda, "Anatomy of a Predatory State: The Political Economy of Public Administration in Uganda," unpublished paper, 2006, p. 15.

26. Mwenda, "Please Stop Helping Us," p. 3, and UNDP, *Human Development Report, 2006,* pp. 285, 307.

27. Ibid., p. 4.

28. Ibid.

29. Andrew Mwenda, "Anatomy of a Predatory State."

30. Human Rights Watch, "Chop Fine," p. 4.

31. As summarized in "Big Men, Big Fraud, Big Trouble," *Economist* April 28, 2007, p. 56.

32. Human Rights Watch, "Chop Fine," p. 3.

33. Andrew Mwenda, "Background to the State in Africa," draft manuscript, p. 7. I am grateful to the author for sharing this with me.

34. Mwenda, "Please Stop Helping Us," p. 3.

35. Andrew Mwenda, "Personalizing Power in Uganda," *Journal of Democracy* 18 (July 2007): 23–37.

36. Freedom House, *Freedom in the World, 1991–1992* (New York: Freedom House, 1992), p. 313.

37. One World, "Malawi Guide," http://uk.oneworld.net/guides/malawi/development #Politics.

38. Freedom House, *Freedom in the World, 2006: The Annual Survey of Political Rights and Civil Liberties* (New York: Freedom House, 2006), pp. 440–41.

39. Daniel Posner and Daniel Young, "The Institutionalization of Political Power in Africa," *Journal of Democracy* 18 (July 2007): 126–40. The data in this paragraph are drawn from their article.

40. Ibid.

41. Michael Bratton, "The 'Alternation Effect' in Africa," *Journal of Democracy* 15 (October 2004): 147–58.

42. Staffan Lindberg, "The Surprising Significance of African Elections," *Journal of Democracy* 17 (January 2006): 139–51.

43. The evidence and arguments here are developed at greater length in Larry Diamond, *Developing Democracy: Toward Consolidation* (Baltimore: Johns Hopkins University Press), chap. 6.

44. Africa Democracy Forum, http://www.africandemocracyforum.org/.

45. Most of the data presented here from the Afrobarometer are available in the publications of the project, at http://www.afrobarometer.org/publications.html. See, in particular, "The Status of Democracy, 2005–2006: Findings from Afrobarometer Round 3 for 18 Countries," *Afrobarometer Briefing Paper* no. 40, June 2006. Some of the data have been provided directly by the project's executive director, Michael Bratton, and its associate director, Carolyn Logan, both at Michigan State University, and I thank them for their cooperation. Throughout this discussion, unless otherwise indicated, the average levels of opinion represent the average of the individual country percentages, not the overall average of all twenty-five thousand Africans surveyed.

46. Michael Bratton, "Formal Versus Informal Institutions in Africa," *Journal of Democracy* 18 (July 2007): 96–110.

47. Michael Bratton, Robert Mattes, and E. Gyimah-Boadi, *Public Opinion, Democracy, and Market Reform in Africa* (Cambridge: Cambridge University Press, 2005), pp. 69–70.

48. Bratton, "Formal Versus Informal Institutions," figure 2.

49. Ibid.

50. Bratton, Mattes, and Gyimah-Boadi, *Public Opinion, Democracy, and Market Reform*, pp. 272–77. These results are based on analysis of the first two rounds of surveys (around 2000 and 2002), not on the third round in 2005.

51. Bratton, "Formal Versus Informal Institutions," table 2.

52. Bratton, Mattes, and Gyimah-Boadi, *Public Opinion, Democracy, and Market Reform*, p. 277. In his recent analysis of the third-round data, Bratton finds education to be by far the strongest social factor shaping demand for democracy.

53. Andrew Feinstein, "South Africa's Democracy in Trouble," *Spiegel Online*, February 14, 2007, http://www.spiegel.de/international/0,1518,465912,00.html.

54. Robert Mattes, "South Africa: Democracy without the People," *Journal of Democracy* 13 (January 2002): 22–36.

55. Afrobarometer, "Where Is Africa Going? Views from Below," Working Paper no. 60, May 2006, pp. 16–23.

56. Afrobarometer, "Citizens and the State in Africa: New Results from Afrobarometer Round 3," Working Paper no. 61, May 2006, tables 1.2 and 2.1.

57. Freedom House, *Freedom in the World, 2006*, pp. 491, 493.

58. Rose Skelton, "Senegal's Rap Artists' Despair Over 2007 Elections," Voice of America, August 4, 2006, http://www.voanews.com/english/archive/2006-08/2006-08-04-voa32.cfm.

59. Officially, Wade was eighty-one in 2007, but there is speculation in Senegal that he is several years older.

60. Because of the danger of retaliation by the government, I am preserving the anonymity of the activist, a respected intellectual and civic leader whom I interviewed after the February 2007 presidential election.

61. Robert Pringle, "Democratization in Mali: Putting History to Work," *Peaceworks* no. 58, U.S. Institute of Peace, October 2006, http://www.usip.org/pubs/peaceworks/pwks58 .html.

12. CAN THE MIDDLE EAST DEMOCRATIZE?

1. Remarks by the president at the twentieth anniversary of the National Endowment for Democracy, U.S. Chamber of Commerce, Washington, D.C., November 6, 2003, http:// www.whitehouse.gov/news/releases/2003/11/print/20031106-3.html.

2. Freedom House, *Freedom in the World, 2006: The Annual Survey of Political Rights and Civil Liberties* (New York: Freedom House, 2006), p. 229.

3. This is part of a regional trend. In Syria, Bashar al-Assad was positioned to succeed his father, Hafez, and Muammar Qaddafi and Ali Abdullah Saleh are rumored to be grooming

their sons in Libya and Yemen respectively, in what people in the region are calling *jumlukiyas,* or Republican monarchies.

4. Freedom House, *Freedom in the World, 2006,* p. 230.

5. During the three decades from 1975 to 2004, Egypt received "over $50 billion in U.S. largesse." Charles Levinson, "$50 Billion Later, Taking Stock of U.S. Aid to Egypt," Christian Science Monitor, April 12, 2004, http://www.csmonitor.com/2004/0412/p07s01-wome.html.

6. "Egypt: Faces of a Crackdown," Human Rights Watch video, May 30, 2007, http://hrw.org/video/2007/egypt05/.

7. Freedom House, *Freedom in the World, 2006,* p. 409.

8. "Lebanese Officers Forced to Quit," BBC News, February 28, 2005, http://news.bbc.co.uk/2/hi/middle_east/4305927.stm.

9. Shadi Hamid, "Parting the Veil," *Democracy* 5 (Summer 2007): 40.

10. Freedom House, *Freedom in the World, 2006,* pp. 371–72.

11. Ibid., p. 5.

12. Adeed Dawisha and Larry Diamond, "Iraq's Year of Voting Dangerously," *Journal of Democracy* 17 (April 2006): 99–100. See also Larry Diamond, *Squandered Victory: The American Occupation and the Bungled Effort to Bring Democracy to Iraq* (New York: Owl Books, 2006 paperback edition), "Afterword," pp. 337–60.

13. Jason Campbell, Michael O'Hanlon, and Umy Unikewicz, "The State of Iraq," *New York Times,* March 18, 2007. Electricity production stood at 3,600 megawatts in February 2007, less than the prewar level, and much less than the 6,000 megawatts that had been the declared goal of the American occupation administrator, Ambassador L. Paul Bremer. Baghdad was receiving only a few hours of electricity per day.

14. "Iraq Poll 2007," BBC News, March 19, 2007, http://news.bbc.co.uk/2/shared/bsp/hi/pdfs/19_03_07_iraqpollnew.pdf.

15. This account was shared with me by the activist in question during the first half of 2007.

16. Fred Wehrey, "Saudi Arabia: Shi'a Pessimistic About Reform, but Seek Reconciliation," *Arab Reform Bulletin* 5 (June 2007): 2. http://www.carnegieendowment.org/publications/index.cfm?fa=view&id=1302&prog=zgp&proj=zdrl.

17. Amr Hamzawy, "Egypt, 2005–2007: Backsliding on Democratic Reform," presentation to the Center on Democracy, Development, and the Rule of Law, Stanford University, May 23, 2007.

18. William B. Qaundt, "Algeria's Uneasy Peace," in Larry Diamond, Marc F. Plattner, and Daniel Brumberg, eds., *Islam and Democracy in the Middle East* (Baltimore: Johns Hopkins University Press, 2003), p. 58.

19. Freedom House, *Freedom in the World, 2006,* pp. 26–27.

20. Omar Shakir, "Taming the Pharaoh: Political Accountability in Modern Egypt," unpublished senior honor's thesis, Stanford University, Center on Democracy, Development, and the Rule of Law, May 2007, p. 35.

21. Ibid., chap. 4.

22. The Egyptian Organization for Human Rights reported a voter turnout in the referendum of less than 5 percent. Amr Hamzawy, "Amending Democracy Out of Egypt's Constitution," *Washington Post,* April 2, 2007, http://www.carnegieendowment.org/publications/index.cfm?fa=view&id=19085&prog=zgp&proj=zdrl,zme.

23. Ibid.

24. Ibid.

25. "Egypt: Flawed Military Trials for Human Rights Leaders," Human Rights Watch, June 5, 2007, http://hrw.org/english/docs/2007/06/05/egypt16072.htm.

26. "Egypt: Muslim Brothers Arrested Ahead of Election," Human Rights Watch, May 30, 2007, http://hrw.org/english/docs/2007/05/30/egypt16018.htm.

27. "Egypt: Faces of a Crackdown," Human Rights Watch, video, May 30, 2007, http://hrw.org/video/2007/egypt05/.

28. Kamel Labidi, "Arab States: The Paradox of Press Freedom," *Arab Reform Bulletin* 5 (June 2007): 5.

29. Human Rights Watch, "Suspicious Sweeps: The General Intelligence Department and Jordan's Rule of Law Problem" (September 2006), http://hrw.org/reports/2006/jordan0906/.

30. Daniel Brumberg, "The Trap of Liberalized Autocracy," in Diamond, Plattner, and Brumberg, *Islam and Democracy in the Middle East,* p. 35.

31. Russell E. Lucas, "Deliberalization in Jordan," in Diamond, Plattner, and Brumberg, *Islam and Democracy in the Middle East,* pp. 99–100.

32. Julia Choucair, "Illusive Reform: Jordan's Stubbon Stability," Carnegie Papers no. 76, Democracy and Rule of Law Project, Carnegie Endowment for International Peace, December 2006, p. 8.

33. "According to a September 2002 official statement, Palestinians constitute 43 percent of the Jordanian population, but the more commonly cited estimate is 60 percent." Ibid., p. 5.

34. Ibid., p. 7.

35. Ibid., p. 10.

36. Vali Nasr puts the proportion of Shia in Bahrain at 75 percent. "When the Shiites Rise," *Foreign Affairs* 85 (July–August 2006): 65.

37. Faiza Saleh Ambah, "In Bahrain, Democratic Activists Regret Easing of U.S. Pressure," *Washington Post,* November 27, 2006, http://www.washingtonpost.com/wp-dyn/content/article/2006/11/26/AR2006112601135.html. Even before that incident, the Bahrain Center for Human Rights was shut down and its Web site was blocked when the center's director, Abdulhadi Khawajah, openly accused the prime minister of corruption.

38. Rachid Tiemçani, "Algeria: Bouteflika and Civil-Military Relations," *Arab Reform Bulletin* 5 (June 2007): 4–5. See also Freedom House, *Freedom in the World, 2006,* pp. 26–30.

39. "President Bush Visits Prague, Czech Republic, Discusses Freedom," Czernin Palace, Prague, June 5, 2007, White House press release, http://www.whitehouse.gov/news/releases/2007/06/print/20070605-8.html.

40. Robin Wright, "Bush Is Losing Credibility on Democracy, Activists Say," *Washington Post,* June 10, 2007, http://www.washingtonpost.com/wp-dyn/content/article/2007/06/09/AR2007060901469_pf.html.

41. Ibid.

42. Donna Abu-Nasr, "Yemeni Opposition Threatens Protest," Associated Press, September 22, 2006, http://www.washingtonpost.com/wp-dyn/content/article/2006/09/22/AR2006092200956.html?nav=hcmodule.

43. "Saleh Re-elected President of Yemen," Aljazeera.net, September 26, 2006, http://english.aljazeera.net/English/archive/archive?ArchiveId=36226.

44. Quoted in Michael Slackman, "Ballot Boxes? Yes. Actual Democracy? Tough Question," *New York Times,* June 7, 2006.

45. Amr Hamzawy, "Burying Democracy Further in Egypt," *Daily Star* (Beirut), March 16, 2007, http://www.carnegieendowment.org/publications/index.cfm?fa=view&id=19069&prog=zgp&proj=zdrl,zme.

46. Hamzawy, "Egypt, 2005–2007."

47. Choucair, "Illusive Reform: Jordan's Stubborn Stability," p. 12.

48. This came on top of a onetime special supplement of more than a billion dollars "to offset the effects of the war on Jordan's economy and bolster its security." Ibid., p. 17.

49. The Arab Barometer project is managed collectively by principal investigators Mark Tessler of the University of Michigan and Amaney Jamal of Princeton University and by five Arab country directors. I am grateful to Mark Tessler for providing me with some of the data from the 2006 surveys. The Web site for the project is http://www.arabbarometer.org/index1.html.

50. Mark Tessler and Eleanor Gao, "Gauging Arab Support for Democracy," *Journal of Democracy* 16 (July 2005): 83–97.

51. Ibid., p. 88.

52. Analysis provided to me by Mark Tessler.

53. Freedom House, *Freedom in the World, 2006,* p. 338.

54. Ibid. For more extended historical interpretation, see Ladan Bouramand, "Iran's Peculiar Election: The Role of Ideology," *Journal of Democracy* 16 (October 2005): 52–63.

55. Ibid., p. 55.

56. Interview with Akbar Ganji, September 8, 2006, Palo Alto, California.

57. International Crisis Group, "Iran: Ahmadi-Nejad's Tumultuous Presidency," Middle East Briefing no. 21, February 6, 2007, p. 8.

58. Bahman Baktiari, "Iran's Conservative Revival," *Current History* 106 (January 2007): 13, and "The World Factbook: Iran," U.S. Central Intelligence Agency, https://www.cia.gov/library/publications/the-world-factbook/geos/ir.html#Econ.

59. Ibid.

60. Michael McFaul, Abbas Milani, and Larry Diamond, "A Win-Win U.S. Strategy for Dealing with Iran," *Washington Quarterly* 30 (Winter 2006–7): 133.

61. Vali Nasr, "Iran's Peculiar Election: The Conservative Wave Rolls On," *Journal of Democracy* 16 (October 2005): 11.

62. Abbas Milani, "Whither Iran? Nukes, Kooks, or Democracy?" presentation to the Hoover Institution, Stanford University, June 5, 2007.

63. Freedom House, *Freedom in the World, 2006,* p. 488.

64. John Damis, Morocco, in Freedom House, *Countries at the Crossroads, 2006: A Survey of Democratic Governance* (New York: Rowman and Littlefield, 2006), p. 362.

65. Marina Ottaway and Meredith Riley, "Morocco: From Top-down Reform to Democratic Transition?" *Carnegie Papers,* Middle East Series, no. 71, September 2006, p. 18.

66. Ibid., p. 3.

67. Ibid., p. 10.

68. Freedom House, *Freedom in the World, 2006,* p. 487.

69. This is the central argument of Ottaway and Riley, "Morocco," pp. 10–17.

70. The two most important of these traditional secular parties have been the Socialist Union of Popular Forces (USFP) and the Istiqlal (Independence) Party, which have formed the nucleus of an alliance that has cooperated with the government in parliament and that has held the largest bloc of seats, though still a distinct minority. Ibid., pp. 6–9.

71. Ibid., p. 11.

72. Ibid., p. 19.

73. Emad El-Din Shahin, "Political Islam in Egypt," Centre for European Policy Studies Working Document no. 266, May 2007, p. 2, http://shop.ceps.eu/BookDetail.php?item_id=1495.

74. Ibrahim came to this conclusion through protracted (if somewhat complicated) interaction with the Islamists during his detention as a political prisoner of the Mubarak regime off and on between 2000 and 2002.

75. Hamid, "Parting the Veil," p. 43.

76. Carnegie Endowment for International Peace and the Herbert Quandt Stiftung, "Islamist Movements and the Democratic Process in the Arab World: Exploring the Gray Zones," *Carnegie Papers,* Middle East Series, no. 67, March 2006, p. 13.

77. Ibid., p. 7.

78. Amr Hamzawy, Marina Ottaway, and Nathan J. Brown, "What Islamists Need to Be Clear About: The Case of the Egyptian Muslim Brotherhood," *Policy Outlook,* Carnegie Endowment for International Peace, February 2007.

79. Carnegie Endowment and Stiftung, "Islamist Movements and the Democratic Process in the Arab World," p. 18.

80. Dankwart Rustow, "Transitions to Democracy: Toward a Dynamic Model," in Lisa Anderson, *Transitions to Democracy* (New York: Columbia University Press, 1999), p. 34. Originally published in *Comparative Politics* 2 (April 1970).

81. Vali Nasr, "The Rise of 'Muslim Democracy,'" *Journal of Democracy* 16 (April 2005): 13–14.

82. "President Sworn-in to Second Term," White House press release, January 20, 2005, http://www.whitehouse.gov/news/releases/2005/01/print/20050120-1.html.

13. MAKING DEMOCRACIES WORK

1. I first noted this trend in detail in Larry Diamond, "Democracy in Latin America: Degrees, Illusions, and Directions for Consolidation," in Tom Farer, ed., *Beyond Sovereignty: Collectively Defending Democracy in the Americas* (Baltimore: Johns Hopkins University Press, 1996). The phenomenon of dubious, shallow, and illiberal democracies first became widely apparent in Latin America, and it was Latin Americanists who first diagnosed it for a wider audience in the 1980s and '90s. See, for example, Terry Lynn Karl, "Imposing Consent? Electoralism versus Democratization in El Salvador," in Paul Drake and Eduardo Silva, eds., *Elections and Democratization in Latin America, 1980–1985* (San Diego: Center for Iberian and Latin American Studies, Center for U.S./Mexican Studies, University of California at San Diego, 1986), pp. 9–36; Terry Lynn Karl, "Dilemmas of Democratization in Latin America," *Comparative Politics* 23, no. 1 (1990): 14–15; Terry Lynn Karl, "The Hybrid Regimes of Central America," *Journal of Democracy* 6 (July 1995): 72–86; Guillermo O'Donnell, "On the State, Democratization and Some Conceptual Problems: A Latin American View with Glances at Some Postcommunist Countries," *World Development* 21, no. 8 (1993): 1355–69; and Guillermo O'Donnell, "Delegative Democracy," *Journal of Democracy* 5 (January 1994): 55–69.

2. I documented these trends more extensively in Larry Diamond, *Developing Democracy: Toward Consolidation* (Baltimore: Johns Hopkins University Press, 1999), pp. 43–63. The flaws of illiberal democracy also form a major theme in Fareed Zakaria, *The Future of Freedom: Illiberal Democracy at Home and Abroad* (New York: W. W. Norton, 2003).

3. Samuel P. Huntington, *The Third Wave: Democratization in the Late Twentieth Century* (Norman: University of Oklahoma Press, 1991), p. 105.

4. In addition to these "new" democracies, the pre-1974 Third World democracies of India, Costa Rica, and Botswana, as well as a dozen or so small island states, could be added to the list. On *irreversibility* as one of several possible understandings of democratic consolidation, see Andreas Schedler, "What Is Democratic Consolidation?" *Journal of Democracy* 9 (April 1998): 91–107.

5. My count includes the eight postcommunist democracies not yet admitted to the European Union; seventeen of twenty-two democracies in Latin America; Mongolia, Indonesia, the Philippines, Sri Lanka, East Timor, Papua New Guinea, and Bangladesh in Asia and Oceania; every African democracy except Botswana and Mauritius; and Turkey.

6. Douglass C. North, John Joseph Wallis, and Barry R. Weingast, "A Conceptual Framework for Interpreting Recorded Human History," National Bureau of Economic Research, Working Paper no. 12795, December 2006, http://www.nber.org/papers/w12795.

7. Ibid., p. 6.

8. Robert D. Putnam, *Making Democracy Work: Civic Traditions in Modern Italy* (Princeton, N.J.: Princeton University Press, 1993).

9. Ibid., p. 167.

10. Ibid., p. 88. The above discussion of the *civic community* draws primarily from pp. 87–90.

11. Ibid., p. 115.

12. Andreas Schedler, "Conceptualizing Accountability," in Andreas Schedler, Larry Diamond, and Marc F. Plattner, eds., *The Self-Restraining State: Power and Accountability in New Democracies* (Boulder, Colo.: Lynne Rienner, 1999), pp. 13–28.

13. Guillermo O'Donnell, "Horizontal Accountability in New Democracies," in Schedler, Diamond, and Plattner, *The Self-Restraining State*, p. 39.

14. Thomas Carothers, "The End of the Transition Paradigm," *Journal of Democracy* 13 (January 2002): 10–11.

15. For some of my earlier thoughts on the imperatives of building and structuring effective parties and representative institutions, including local and provincial governments, I refer the reader to Diamond, *Developing Democracy,* pp. 96–111 and 138–60.

16. This is another challenge that I do not have the space to address in this book, but I refer the reader to a vast and rich literature on the subject. See the many works cited on pp. 311–13 of *Developing Democracy* and more recently Larry Diamond and Marc F. Plattner, eds., *Electoral Systems and Democracy* (Baltimore: Johns Hopkins University Press, 2006).

17. Diamond, *Developing Democracy,* pp. 112–16; Larry Diamond and Marc F. Plattner, *Civil-Military Relations and Democracy* (Baltimore: Johns Hopkins University Press, 1996); and Steven C. Boraz and Thomas Bruneau, "Reforming Intelligence: Democracy and Effectiveness," *Journal of Democracy* 17 (July 2006): 28–42. See also the three country studies on intelligence reform that follow that article.

18. James Dobbins, Seth G. Jones, Keith Crane, and Beth Cole DeGrasse, *The Beginner's Guide to Nation-Building* (Santa Monica, Calif.: RAND, 2007); Francis Fukuyama, ed., *Nation-Building: Beyond Afghanistan and Iraq* (Baltimore: Johns Hopkins University Press, 2006); Larry Diamond, *Squandered Victory: The American Occupation and the Bungled Effort to Bring Democracy to Iraq* (New York: Times Books, 2005); and Larry Diamond, "Promoting Democracy in Post-Conflict and Failed States: Lessons and Challenges," *Taiwan Journal of Democracy* 2 (December 2006): 93–116.

19. Juan J. Linz and Alfred Stepan, *Problems of Democratic Transition and Consolidation: Southern Europe, South America, and Post-Communist Europe* (Baltimore: Johns Hopkins University Press, 1996), pp. 12 and 16–33.

20. Francis Fukuyama, *State-Building: Governance and World Order in the 21st Century* (Ithaca, N.Y.: Cornell University Press, 2004).

21. Center for International Private Enterprise, "Helping Build Democracy That Delivers," 2007, http://www.cipe.org/about/DemocracyDelivers07.pdf, p.4. As part of the National Endowment for Democracy, the center has played a leading role in funding and stimulating efforts to promote these reform programs.

22. O'Donnell, "Horizontal Accountability," p. 39.

23. Larry Diamond, "Political Corruption: Nigeria's Perennial Struggle," *Journal of Democracy* 2 (October 1991): 73–85.

24. Sheila S. Coronel and Lorna Kalaw-Tirol, eds., *Investigating Corruption: A Do-It-Yourself Guide* (Manila: Philippine Center for Investigative Journalism, 2002), pp. 257–64, quoted from p. 259.

25. "About GAO," U.S. Government Accountability Office, http://www.gao.gov/.

26. Coronel and Kalaw-Tirol, *Investigating Corruption,* p. 279.

27. Robert A. Pastor, "A Brief History of Electoral Commissions," in Schedler, Diamond, and Plattner, *The Self-Restraining State,* pp. 77–78.

28. Duncan McCargo, "Democracy under Stress in Thaksin's Thailand," *Journal of Democracy* 13 (October 2002): 112–26.

29. One indication of the stability and autonomy of the office, and of its separation from partisan politics, is that since the agency was created in 1921, there have only been seven comptrollers general.

30. Pastor, "A Brief History of Electoral Commissions," pp. 78–79.

31. The quote is from Putnam, *Making Democracy Work,* p. 182. For important insights along these lines, see Jonathan Fox, "The Difficult Transition from Clientelism to Citizenship: Lessons from Mexico," *World Politics* 46, no. 2 (1994): 151–84.

32. Putnam, *Making Democracy Work,* p. 182.

33. The term is drawn from Catalina Smulovitz and Enrique Peruzzotti, "Societal Accountability in Latin America," *Journal of Democracy* 11 (October 2000): 147–58.

34. "About Us," Transparency International, http://www.transparency.org/about_us.

35. Smulovitz and Peruzzotti, "Societal Accountability," p. 154.

36. See, for example, the profiles of more than fifty such institutes in the developing and postcommunist worlds that are part of the Network of Democracy Research Institutes, http://www.wmd.org/ndri/ndri.html.

37. This is documented at http://www.idasa.org.za/.

38. Chappell H. Lawson, *Building the Fourth Estate: Democratization and the Rise of a Free Press in Mexico* (Berkeley: University of California Press, 2002).

39. Coronel and Kalaw-Tirol, *Investigating Corruption*.

40. "FraudNet," U.S. Government Accountability Office, http://www.gao.gov/fraudnet/fraudnet.htm/.

41. Putnam, *Making Democracy Work*, p. 60.

14. PROMOTING DEMOCRACY EFFECTIVELY

1. The German Party foundations, or *stiftungen,* include the Konrad Adenauer Foundation, affiliated with the Christian Democratic Party; the Friedrich Ebert Foundation, affiliated with the Social Democratic Party; the Friedrich Naumann Foundation, affiliated with the centrist Free Democrats, the Hans Seidel Foundation, affiliated with the Christian Social Union (of Bavaria); and more recently the Heinrich Boll Foundation, affiliated with the Green Party.

2. Initially, NED's budget was well under $20 million annually.

3. These are respectively affiliated with the Democratic Party (www.ndi.org), the Republican Party (www.iri.org), the U.S. Chamber of Commerce (www.cipe.org), and the AFL-CIO (www.solidaritycenter.org).

4. Like NED, these are publicly funded but nongovernmental organizations.

5. "Advancing Canada's Role in International Support for Democratic Development," Report of the Standing Committee on Foreign Affairs and International Development, Kevin Sorenson, chair, July 2007, p. 6, http://cmte.parl.gc.ca/Content/HOC/committee/391/faae/reports/rp3066139/391_FAAE_Rpt08_PDF/391_FAAE_Rpt08-e.pdf.

6. Laure-Hélène Piron, "Time to Learn, Time to Act in Africa," in Thomas Carothers, ed., *Promoting the Rule of Law Abroad: In Search of Knowledge* (Washington, D.C.: Carnegie Endowment for International Peace, 2006), p. 275.

7. NED's latest strategy document (released in 2007) is available at http://www.ned.org/publications/documents/strategy2007.pdf. For the previous ones, see http://www.ned.org/publications/publications.html.

8. Thomas Carothers, "Promoting the Rule of Law Abroad: The Problem of Knowledge," in Thomas Carothers, *Critical Mission: Essays on Democracy Promotion* (Washington, D.C.: Carnegie Endowment for International Peace, 2004), pp. 136–37. This "narrow preoccupation with judicial reform" as rule of law reform is a central theme in the case studies and findings of Carothers, *Promoting the Rule of Law Abroad,* quoted from p. 330.

9. Ibid., p. 138.

10. In the late 1990s, the Democracy and Governance Office of USAID developed a comprehensive framework for "strategic assessment" of the democracy and governance assistance priorities in a given country. An important phase of that process is to identify the key actors in the state, the political system, and civil society, as well as their interests, resources, and alignments. Once a USAID assessment team identifies key advocates of democracy in politics, civil society, and (if they are there) the state, it is not clear how much they are actually consulted in the preparation of the country strategy. Probably this varies across USAID country missions, and over time, and any strategies must be approved by the U.S. embassy in the country, the central USAID office, and the U.S. State Department. Center for Democracy and Governance, USAID, "Conducting a DG Assessment: A Framework for Strategy Development," November 2000, http://www.usaid.gov/our_work/democracy_and_governancepublications/pdfs/pnach 305.pdf.

11. Center for Democracy and Governance, USAID, "Conducting a DG Assessment."

12. Thomas Carothers, *Aiding Democracy Abroad: The Learning Curve* (Washington, D.C.: Carnegie Endowment for International Peace, 1999), p. 308.

13. Piron, "Time to Learn, Time to Act in Africa," p. 295.

14. Thomas Carothers, *Confronting the Weakest Link: Aiding Political Parties in New Democracies* (Washington, D.C.: Carnegie Endowment for International Peace, 2006), p. 215.

15. See for example Marina Ottaway and Theresa Chung, "Debating Democracy Assistance: Toward a New Paradigm," *Journal of Democracy* 10 (October 1999): 99–113.

16. Laure-Hélène Piron writes of Nigerian rule of law and human rights organizations: "One of the most effective forms of assistance was that provided by the Ford Foundation, through substantial direct institutional grants rather than project support. This is a high-risk strategy given widespread financial misappropriation or simply poor accounting practices, but where it worked it delivered impressive results." "Time to Learn, Time to Act in Africa," p. 293. Piron is right to emphasize the problem and danger of corruption in civil society. NGOs must be held to the same principles of accountability, and monitored by donors, just as state recipients of aid are.

17. National Endowment for Democracy, "The Backlash against Democracy Assistance," report prepared for Richard G. Lugar, chairman, Committee on Foreign Relations, U.S. Senate, June 8, 2006, http://www.ned.org/publications/reports/backlash06.pdf, pp. 15–29.

18. Ibid., pp. 34–37.

19. This is the formulation that Robert Dahl has used to explain why ruling elites in Europe and elsewhere conceded to democracy. See his classic work, *Polyarchy: Participation and Opposition* (New Haven, Conn.: Yale University Press, 1971), pp. 14–16.

20. This is vital as well to dealing with the most important challenge facing human civilization, global warming.

21. The most forceful and eloquent advocate of this perspective is Jeffrey Sachs, *The End of Poverty: Economic Possibilities for Our Time* (New York: Penguin, 2005).

22. Steven Radelet, "Foreign Assistance Reforms: Successes, Failures, and Next Steps," Testimony for the Senate Foreign Relations Subcommittee on International Development, Foreign Assistance, Economic Affairs, and International Environmental Protection, June 12, 2007, p. 3, http://www.senate.gov/~foreign/testimony/2007/RadeletTestimony070612.pdf. Radelet is a Senior Fellow at the Center on Global Development, one of the best sources of independent analysis on aid and development policy, www.cgd.org.

23. United Nations Development Program (UNDP), *Human Development Report 2006: Beyond Scarcity: Power, Poverty and the Global Water Crisis* (New York: Palgrave Macmillan, 2006), pp. 286, 294, and 308.

24. USAID, *Foreign Aid in the National Interest: Promoting Freedom, Security, and Opportunity* (Washington, D.C.: USAID, 2002), http://www.usaid.gov/fani/. I was the principal author of chapter 1, "Promoting Democratic Governance," and most of the following recommendations are adapted from that chapter, pp. 50–51.

25. Between 1960 and 2001, democracies and autocracies received about the same levels of aid per capita in very poor countries but at somewhat higher levels of per capita development, autocracies actually got significantly more aid. Although it is generally assumed that things changed after the end of the Cold War, the period 1990 to 2001 saw autocracies getting more aid at every level of national income per capita. Morton H. Halperin, Joseph T. Siegle, and Michael W. Weinstein, *The Democracy Advantage: How Democracies Promote Prosperity and Peace* (New York: Routledge, 2005), pp. 154–55, tables 5.1 and 5.2.

26. As I have presented these proposals to various public policy and academic audiences over the past few years, this recommendation, more than any other, has occasioned passionate objections. My critics ask, Won't a cut-off of aid to deeply corrupt governments push them over the edge into state failure? Why should we punish the people of these states for the failings of their leaders? Honesty requires recognition of the risks in reducing and even terminating assistance to badly governed states. In the short term, things could get worse. But the historical record shows that deeply corrupt and abusive states gradually slide toward collapse, even with generous foreign aid (as has been the case with Liberia, Sierra Leone, Somalia, Zaire/DRC, and now Zimbabwe). Indeed, foreign aid is part of the structural problem, helping to sustain

irresponsible governments and providing a source of external rents for contending elites to want to capture. Given as well the high probability of diversion of the resources and the limited amount of total aid available in the world, the more humane and responsible course is to cease support for the worst governments while mobilizing international pressure for a fundamental change in governance that would enable the resumption of development assistance. For similar arguments, see Halperin, Siegle, and Weinstein, *The Democracy Advantage,* pp. 183–85.

27. The international financial institutions have historically been prohibited from taking such political considerations into account. Ibid., p. 157.

28. The volume of funds disbursed is a simple criterion that donors have relied on "to measure staff effectiveness," which creates perverse incentives to make "frequent and large-scale loans" even when governance is bad. Ibid., p. 167.

29. Derick W. Brinkerhoff, "Assessing Political Will for Anti-Corruption Efforts: An Analytic Framework," *Public Administration and Development* 20 (2000): 249.

30. Steven E. Finkel, Aníbal Pérez-Liñán, and Mitchell Seligson, "Effects of U.S. Foreign Assistance on Democracy Building: Results of a Cross-National Quantitative Study," final report to USAID, January 12, 2006, p. 83, http://www.usaid.gov/our_work/ democracy_and_governance/publications/pdfs/impact_of_democracy_assistance.pdf.

31. UN General Assembly Resolution 2626 (XXV), October 24, 1970, para. 43, http://www.un.org/documents/ga/res/25/ares25.htm. The only countries that met the 0.7 percent goal in their 2006 aid levels were "Sweden, Luxembourg, Norway, the Netherlands and Denmark." In 2006, the United States had the lowest level of aid as a percent of its national income (0.17 percent), but it was the biggest donor in absolute terms, "followed by the United Kingdom, Japan, France and Germany." OECD, "Development Aid from OECD Countries Fell 5.1% in 2006," April 3, 2007, http://www.oecd.org/document/17/ 0,2340,en_2649_201185_38341265_1_1_1,00.html.

32. Anup Shah, "US and Foreign Aid Assistance," Global Issues, April 8, 2007, http:// www.globalissues.org/TradeRelated/Debt/USAid.asp.

33. OECD, "Development Aid from OECD Countries Fell 5.1% in 2006," April 3, 2007, http://www.oecd.org/document/17/0,2340,en_2649_201185_38341265_1_1_1,00.html. This figure represented a 5 percent drop from 2005, but that was mainly due to the exceptionally high levels of debt relief to Iraq and Nigeria that year.

34. Sachs, *The End of Poverty,* pp. 298–99. More precisely, he estimates the needed effort at $135 billion to $195 billion (in 2003 dollars) annually for a decade, representing "about .44 to .54 percent of the rich-world GNP each year during the forthcoming decade" (p. 299). But since a significant slice of current aid levels is debt relief and some comes back in debt repayments, this would probably require a doubling of net aid flows.

35. Chair's summary, Gleneagles Summit of the Group of 8 (G8), July 8, 2005, http://www.g8.gov.uk/servlet/Front?pagename=OpenMarket/Xcelerate/ShowPage&c=Page&c id=1119518698846.

36. Sachs, *The End of Poverty,* pp. 276–77. He also wisely recommends that donors "harmonize" their plethora of aid flows so that poor countries can deal with a single set of coordinated donor expectations.

37. For a list and description of the sixteen indicators (plus two supplemental ones) and a discussion of the selection process, see http://www.mcc.gov/selection/indicators/index.php. All of the six "ruling justly" indicators, such as the Freedom House measures of political rights and civil liberties and the World Bank Institute measures of rule of law and control of corruption, have been discussed and utilized in this book. Investing in people is measured by such items as public expenditures on basic health and education, girls' primary school completion rates, and immunization rates, while economic freedom is manifested in such measures as regulatory quality and the number of days it takes to start a business.

38. This is the conclusion of Steven Radelet, "The Millennium Challenge Account in Africa: Promises vs. Progress," Testimony Before the House Committee on Foreign Affairs,

Subcommittee on Africa and Global Health, June 28, 2007, p. 3, http://foreignaffairs.house .gov/110/rad062807.htm. Some other assessments suggest that political judgments may enter in the final decisions, but only on the margins and for countries that qualify or nearly so.

39. Radelet, "The Millennium Challenge Account in Africa," pp. 2–3.

40. Ibid., p. 4.

41. Larry Diamond, "Promoting Real Reform in Africa," in E. Gyimah-Boadi, ed., *Democratic Reform in Africa: The Quality of Progress* (Boulder, Colo.: Lynne Rienner Publishers, 2004), pp. 287–88.

42. For the list of MCC-eligible countries, see http://www.mcc.gov/countries/index.php. Of the forty-one, only the Gambia has been suspended from eligibility. I take as democratic here the countries identified as such by Freedom House (see the appendix, table 5), but recall that some observers, such as Steven Levitsky and Lucan Way, consider a number of these regimes, like Mozambique, Niger, and Malawi, to be electoral authoritarian.

43. Radelet, "Foreign Assistance Reforms," p. 1.

44. Ibid., pp. 3–4. Earmarks are legislative directives requiring that specific amounts of money be spent for specific purposes, and thus reducing administrative flexibility and judgment. Radelet also recommends consolidating the foreign aid budget in one account and greatly strengthening monitoring and evaluation. I am not sure that it is realistic to incorporate purely military assistance into this integrated framework, but everything else in the way of assistance to states and countries should be possible. As Radelet notes, the Bush administration reform plan as of 2007 only brings 55 percent of U.S. aid flows under the management of the director of foreign assistance; 19 percent remains with the Pentagon and 26 percent with other agencies (p. 5).

45. I have spelled out this idea in Larry Diamond, "Promoting Democracy in Post-Conflict and Failed States: Lessons and Challenges," *Taiwan Journal of Democracy* 2 (December 2006): 113, and in Larry Diamond and Michael McFaul, "Seeding Liberal Democracy," in Will Marshall, ed., *With All Our Might: A Progressive Strategy for Defeating Jihadism and Defending Liberty* (Lanham, Md.: Rowman and Littlefield, 2006), p. 65. Radelet also recommends a new department of international development.

46. USAID saw a 35 percent decline in its professional staff from 1992 to 2000. Halperin, Siegle, and Weinstein, *The Democracy Advantage*, pp. 167–68.

47. Since the September 11, 2001, terrorist attacks on the United States, Pakistan has received almost $5 billion in Coalition Support Funds administered by the Pentagon, with almost no oversight or documentation on how the money is spent, and "Pakistan has become the no. 3 recipient of U.S. military training and assistance, trailing only longtime leaders Israel and Egypt"—even while Al Qaeda has, by all accounts, established a new safe haven on Pakistani territory. "Billions in Aid, with No Accountability," Center for Public Integrity, May 31, 2007, http://www.publicintegrity.org/MilitaryAid/report.aspx?aid=877.

48. Some high-priority languages in the struggle for democracy would obviously be Chinese, Russian, Arabic, and Farsi. It is important, however, that the translations be of high quality, and that coordinated efforts emerge to assess what has already been done. When I served with the Coalition Provisional Authority in Iraq in early 2004, I found different democracy groups translating the same classic works on democracy into Arabic, and some translation work was done with dubious quality control.

49. Halperin, Siegle, and Weinstein, *The Democracy Advantage*, pp. 193–95.

50. I am indebted to Michael McFaul for eloquently and repeatedly stressing this point (and many related ones in which we have collaborated) in his writing and speaking.

51. Diamond and McFaul, "Seeding Liberal Democracy," p. 59.

52. The NEPAD was established alongside the AU in 2001.

53. Steven Gruzd, "Africa's Trailblazer: Ghana and the APRM," South African Institute of International Affairs, 2006, p. 2, http://saiia.org.za/images/upload/Steve_APRM.pdf, pp. 3–5.

54. Herbert Ross "Act Now, or History Will Say SA Ruined Peer Review," *Sunday Times* (South Africa), May 30, 2007, http://www.sundaytimes.co.za/article.aspx?ID=474717; Zachary Ochieng, "African Leaders Turning Peer Review into a Farce," *East African* (Nairobi), April 10, 2007, http://allafrica.com/stories/printable/200704100335.html.

55. Ousmane Déme, "Between Hope and Scepticsism: Civil Society and the African Peer Review Mechanism," Partnership Africa Canada, October 2005, http://saiia.org.za/images/upload/Contents_ACADEMIC-CS%20and%20the%20APRM.pdf.

56. Raymond Louw, "Media, Cornerstone of Democracy, Left Out of APRM," *APRM Monitor*, no. 3, p.1, http://www.pacweb.org/e/images/stories/documents/aprm_monitor_3-web.pdf.

57. Rubén M. Perina, "The Role of the Organization of American States," in Morton H. Halperin and Mirna Galic, eds., *Protecting Democracy: International Responses* (Lanham, Md.: Lexington Books, 2005), pp. 154–55.

58. Esther Brimmer, "Vigilance: Recognizing the Erosion of Democracy," in ibid., pp. 233–58, quoted from p. 255.

59. "Report of the Independent Task Force on Threats to Democracy," Council on Foreign Relations, November 2002, in ibid., p. 180. (Also at http://www.cfr.org/publication.html?id=5180).

60. Ibid., quoted from pp. 180 and 185.

61. For the list of invited and participating countries at the 2005 meeting, see http://www.ccd21.org/Conferences/santiago/attendees.htm.

62. The current members of the convening group are Cape Verde, Chile, the Czech Republic, El Salvador, India, Italy, Mali, Mexico, Mongolia, Morocco, the Philippines, Poland, Portugal, South Africa, South Korea, and the United States.

63. The CD met in Warsaw in 2000, Seoul in 2002, Santiago in 2005, and was scheduled to meet in Bamako, Mali, in late 2007.

64. The Princeton Project, "Forging a World of Liberty under Law: U.S. National Security in the 21st Century. Final Report of the Princeton Project on National Security," http://www.wws.princeton.edu/ppns/report/FinalReport.pdf, pp. 25–26. G. John Ikenberry and Ann-Marie Slaughter were codirectors of the project and principal authors of the report.

65. One problem with NATO, as the Princeton Project notes (p. 27), is the ability of small member states to veto the collective use of force. A more serious problem, however, is the underinvestment of European states in their own military capacity and the means to deploy it rapidly, with robust rules of engagement. There are also other problems of military coordination. As a result, NATO's capacity to project force outside of Europe is limited, and its forces have not fought as effectively in Afghanistan as have the purely American military units.

66. The ICC can also take over cases that countries do not prosecute, heightening the incentive for the country to act. William Burke-White, "The International Criminal Court and the Future of Legal Accountability," *ISLA Journal of International and Comparative Law* 10 (2003): 203.

67. Brian D. Tittemore, "International Legal Recourse," in Halperin and Galic, eds., *Protecting Democracy*, pp. 266 and 280.

68. Ibid., pp. 282–90. Modification of the ICC's scope would likely have to wait until the court's statute becomes open to amendment in mid-2009, or could be achieved through the negotiation of a separate treaty.

69. *In Support of Arab Democracy: Why and How*, Report of the Independent Task Force, Council on Foreign Relations, 2005, p. 5. The task force was chaired by Madeleine K. Albright and Vin Weber, with Steven A. Cook as project director. I was a member.

70. Steven A. Cook, "Getting to Arab Democracy: The Promise of Pacts," *Journal of Democracy* 17 (January 2006): 68.

71. The Council on Foreign Relations Independent Task Force recommends transferring the bulk of MEPI's funding to an independent organization like NED; currently it comes under the U.S. State Department. *In Support of Arab Democracy*, p. 8.

72. This was one of a number of proposals put forward by a working group, on which I served, appointed by the German Marshall Fund to craft a transatlantic strategy for promoting democracy in the Middle East. See "Democracy and Human Development in the Broader Middle East: A Transatlantic Strategy for Partnership," Istanbul Paper no. 1, German Marshall Fund of the United States, June 25, 2004, http://www.gmfus.org/publications/article .cfm?id=47.

73. Ibid., p. 5; *In Support of Arab Democracy,* p. 8, supports conditioning of aid, not trade.

74. *In Support of Arab Democracy,* pp. 21–28.

75. Ronald D. Asmus, Larry Diamond, Mark Leonard, and Michael McFaul, "A Transatlantic Strategy to Promote Democracy in the Broader Middle East," *Washington Quarterly* 28 (Spring 2005): 16.

76. Michael McFaul, Abbas Milani, and Larry Diamond, "A Win-Win U.S. Strategy for Dealing with Iran," *Washington Quarterly* 30 (Winter 2006–7): 128.

77. Ibid., pp. 126–28.

78. Thomas L. Friedman, *The Lexus and the Olive Tree: Understanding Globalization* (New York: Anchor Books, 2000), p. 15.

79. For indications of how this is happening, see http://mobileactive.org.

80. Howard Rheingold, *Smart Mobs: The Next Social Revolution* (New York: Basic Books, 2003), p. 158.

81. Michael McFaul, "Transitions from Postcommunism," *Journal of Democracy* 16 (July 2005): 12; Cathy Hong, "New Political Tool: Text Messaging," *Christian Science Monitor,* June 30, 2005; Jose de Cordoba, "A Bid to Ease Chavez's Power Grip; Students Continue Protests in Venezuela; President Threatens Violence," *Wall Street Journal,* June 8, 2007.

82. "Monitoring Elections with SMS," http://www.smartmobs.com/2007/04/22/ monitoring-elections-with-sms/.

83. Quoted in Hong, "New Political Tool: Text Messaging."

84. Edward Cody, "Text Messages Giving Voice to Chinese," *Washington Post,* June 28, 2007.

85. Ibid.

86. Steve Coll, "In the Gulf, Dissidence Goes Digital; Text Messaging Is the New Tool of Political Underground," *Washington Post,* March 29, 2005.

87. Cody, "Text Messages Giving Voice to Chinese."

88. James F. Smith and Anne Barnard, "Iran Bloggers Test Regime's Tolerance," *Boston Globe,* December 18, 2006, http://www.boston.com/news/world/middleeast/articles/2006/12/ 18/iran_bloggers_test_regimes_tolerance/.

89. Technorati, "State of the Blogosphere, October 2006," http://technorati.com/ weblog/2006/11/161.html. By October 2006 there was an estimated 57 million blogs in the world.

90. Lindsay Wise, "Why Egypt Is Cracking Down on Bloggers," *Time,* June 1, 2006, http://www.time.com/time/world/article/0,8599,1199896,00.html.

91. "Malaysia Police Minister 'Sorry,'" BBC News, November 30, 2005, http://news .bbc.co.uk/2/hi/asia-pacific/4485360.stm.

92. "Silenced Venezuelan TV Station Moves to YouTube," CNN, June 3, 2007, http:// www.cnn.com/2007/WORLD/americas/05/31/venezuela.media/index.html.

93. McFaul, "Transitions from Postcommunism," p. 12.

94. See for example the Web site of the West Africa Democracy Radio, www.wadr.org.

95. Andrew Exum, "Internet Freedom in the Middle East: Challenges for U.S. Policy," PolicyWatch no. 1205, Washington Institute for Near East Policy, February 27, 2007, http:// www.washingtoninstitute.org/templateC05.php?CID=2574, p. 2.

96. The number of cell phone users in Africa has been exploding, from an estimated 63 million in 2003 to 155 million in 2006. Cellular coverage of African territory was only 10 percent in 1999 but rose to 60 percent in 2007 and is expected to rise to 85 percent by 2010. Brian J. Hesse, "A Continent Embraces the Cell Phone," *Current History* 106 (May 2007): 208.

97. Quoted in Hesse, "A Continent Embraces the Cell Phone," p. 211.

98. Rheingold, *Smart Mobs,* p. xiii.

99. "Britain Is 'Surveillance Society,'" BBC News, November 2, 2006, http://news.bbc .co.uk/2/hi/uk_news/6108496.stm.

15. PHYSICIAN, HEAL THYSELF

1. The forums were organized by the National Issues Forums (NIF) network. The participants were recruited to represent a cross-section of the population, but they were not selected through a scientifically random sample.

2. The Kettering Foundation, "Public Thinking About Democracy's Challenge: Reclaiming The Public's Role," November 13, 2006, p. 11, http://www.kettering.org/events/event _detail.aspx?catID=23&itemID=2595.

3. Ibid., p. 2.

4. Ibid.

5. The Gallup Poll, "Trust in Government," http://www.galluppoll.com/content/default .aspx?ci=5392.

6. Susan J. Pharr and Robert D. Putnam, eds., *Disaffected Democracies: What's Troubling the Trilateral Democracies?* (Princeton: Princeton University Press, 2000). See also Susan J. Pharr, Robert D. Putnam, and Russell J. Dalton, "Trouble in the Advanced Democracies? A Quarter-Century of Declining Confidence," *Journal of Democracy* 11 (April 2000): 5–25.

7. Pietro S. Nivola and William A. Galston, "Toward Depolarization," in Pietro S. Nivola and David W. Brady, eds., *Red and Blue Nation? Volume II: Consequences and Correction of America's Polarized Politics* (Washington, D.C.: Brookings Institution, 2008), p. 241, note 17.

8. The Kettering Foundation, "Democracy's Challenge," p. 2.

9. Ibid., p. 19.

10. Transparency International, "Corruption Perceptions Index 2006," http://www.trans parency.org/policy_research/surveys_indices/cpi/2006.

11. In 2005—the last year for which figures are available—federal prosecutors charged 1,163 individuals with corruption-related crimes, as compared with 1,000 in 2000 and 1,213 in 2004. "Report to Congress on the Activities and Operations of the Public Integrity Section for 2005," Public Integrity Section, Criminal Division, U.S. Department of Justice, p. 53, http:// www.usdoj.gov/criminal/pin.

12. Ibid. In 2005, the 390 federal officials were convicted.

13. Francis X. Clines, "Ohio Congressman Guilty in Bribes and Kickbacks," New York Times," April 12, 2002.

14. "Demo-Crank Locks Up Votes from Jail," *Australian,* November 7, 2002.

15. "Torricelli Drops Out of NJ Race," CNN.com, October 1, 2002, http://archives .cnn.com/2002/ALLPOLITICS/09/30/elec02.nj.s.torricelli.race/.

16. Jim Drinkard, "Democrats' Own Ethics Trouble 'Dulls the Message,'" *USA Today,* May 10, 2006.

17. John M. Broder, "Representative Quits, Pleading Guilty in Graft," *New York Times,* November 29, 2005.

18. Sonya Geis and Charles Babcock, "Former Lawmaker Gets Eight-Year Prison Term," *Washington Post,* March 5, 2006.

19. Walter F. Roche Jr. and Richard B. Schmitt, "Former Force on Capitol Hill Admits Fraud," *Los Angeles Times,* January 4, 2006.

20. "Report to Congress," p. 53.

21. Kevin Sack, "Former Louisiana Governor Guilty of Extortion on Casinos," *New York Times,* May 10, 2000.

22. Robert D. McFadden, "Downfall in Connecticut," *New York Times,* December 24, 2004.

23. Ibid.

24. Steve Eder and James Drew, "Taft Declared Guilty," *Toledo Blade*, August 18, 2005.

25. Monica Davey and John O'Neil, "Ex-Governor of Illinois Is Convicted on All Charges," *New York Times*, April 17, 2006.

26. Ibid.

27. Carolyn M. Warner, *The Best System Money Can Buy: Corruption in the European Union* (Ithaca, N.Y.: Cornell University Press, 2007).

28. Ibid., p. 14.

29. "Earmarks in Appropriation Acts," memorandum, Congressional Research Service, January 26, 2006, p. 2, http://www.fas.org/sgp/crs/misc/m012606.pdf. The government watchdog group Citizens Against Public Waste (CAPW) defines a pork-barrel project as having one of the following characteristics: 1) requested by only one chamber of Congress; 2) not specifically authorized; 3) not competitively awarded; 4) not requested by the president; 5) greatly exceeds the president's budget request or the previous year's funding; 6) not the subject of congressional hearings; or 7) serves only a local or private interest. Tom Finnigan, "All About Pork: The Abuse of Earmarks and the Needed Reforms," Citizens Against Public Waste, updated March 7, 2007, http://www.cagw.org/site/PageServer?pagename=reports_earmarks.

30. David Kirkpatrick, "In New Congress, Pork May Linger," *New York Times*, November 26, 2006.

31. "Earmarks in Appropriation Acts," pp. 10, 12, 41.

32. Timothy Egan, "Built with Steel, Perhaps, But Greased with Pork," *New York Times*, April 10, 2004.

33. Paul Chessler, "Teapot Museum Created Tempest," Carolina Journal Online, August 17, 2005, http://www.carolinajournal.com/exclusives/display_exclusive.html?id=2717.

34. Jeffrey Birnbaum, "The Road to Riches Is Called K Street," *Washington Post*, June 22, 2005.

35. Open Secrets, "Your Guide to the Money in U.S. Elections," http://www.open secrets.org.

36. Finnigan, "All About Pork."

37. As a result of the earmarking process, many universities have received earmarks for advanced research even though they do not have graduate studies programs in the relevant fields. Ken Silverstein, "The Great American Pork Barrel," *Harper's*, July 1, 2005, p. 31.

38. Jerry Kammer, "A Steady Flow of Financial Influence," *San Diego Union-Tribune*, December 23, 2005.

39. Ibid.

40. The publishing requirement, however, only applies to earmarks included in measures reported by the committee. These recent reforms are detailed in Citizens Against Government Waste, "Guide to Earmark Reform," January 26, 2007, http://www.cagw.org/site/PageServer?pagename=reports_earmarkguide.

41. The number of such referrals is not public information, but during a committee meeting in 2006, Senator Christopher Dodd, Democrat from Connecticut, noted that "since 2003 the [Senate] Office of Public Records has referred over 2,000 cases to the Department of Justice, and nothing's been heard from again." Senator Christopher Dodd, remarks during the hearing of the U.S. Senate Committee on Rules and Administration, February 8, 2006, http://cq.com/display.do?dockey=/cqonline/prod/data/docs/html/transcripts/congressional/109/congressionaltranscripts109-000002046780.html@committees&metapub=CQ-CONGTRANSCRIPTS&searchIndex=0&seqNum=1. The U.S. Justice Department, on the other hand, has reportedly claimed that it received around two hundred referrals between 2003 and 2005. R. Eric Peterson, "Lobbying Reform: Background and Legislative Proposals, 109th Congress," Congressional Research Service, March 23, 2006, p. 11, http://www.fas.org/sgp/crs/misc/RL33065.pdf.

42. Public Citizen, "Proposed Reforms Regarding the Disclosure and Regulation of Federal Lobbying," July 25, 2005, http://www.cleanupwashington.org/lobbying/page.cfm?pageid=49#influence.

43. Ibid.; and Revolving Door Working Group, "A Matter of Trust: How the Revolving Door Undermines Public Confidence in Government—And What to Do about It," October 2005, p. 46, http://www.revolvingdoor.info/docs/matter-of-trust_final-full.pdf. Half of retiring senior-level officials of the executive branch also became lobbyists.

44. Public Citizen, "Proposed Reforms." Lobbyists currently are only required to disclose federal jobs left in the two years prior to becoming a lobbyist.

45. Revolving Door Working Group, "A Matter of Trust," p. 57.

46. Center for Ethics in Government, National Conference of State Legislatures, http://www.ncsl.org/programs/ethics/e_revolving.htm.

47. Government Accountablity Office, "Human Capital: Trends in Executive and Judicial Pay," June 2006, p. 2, http://www.gao.gov/new.items/d06708.pdf.

48. *Buckley v. Valeo*, 424 U.S. 1, 39 (1976).

49. Michael Pinto-Duschinsky, "Financing Politics: A Global View," *Journal of Democracy* 13 (October 2002): 80.

50. Ibid.

51. Dan Morain, "Senators Move Donor Disclosures at a Snail's Pace,"*Los Angeles Times*, February 3, 2007.

52. Democracy21, "See No Bark, No Bite, No Point," May 2002, p. 5, http://www.democracy21.org/vertical/Sites/%7B3D66FAFE-2697-446F-BB39-85FBBBA57812%7D/uploads/%7BB4BE5C24-65EA-4910-974C-759644EC0901%7D.pdf.

53. Joseph E. Cantor, "Campaign Financing," Congressional Research Service, December 15, 2003, p. 4, http://fpc.state.gov/documents/organization/28105.pdf.

54. Pinto-Duschinsky, "Financing Politics: A Global View," pp. 74–75.

55. Public Campaign Action Fund, http://www.publicampaign.org/where.

56. Gerhard Casper, "Caesarism in Democratic Politics: Reflections on Max Weber," Robert G. Wesson Lecture, Freeman Spogli Institute for International Studies, Stanford University, March 13, 2007, http://iis-db.stanford.edu/evnts/4803/Caesarism_in_Democratic_Politics-FSI.pdf.

57. The classic statement of this is found in Juan J. Linz, "Presidential or Parliamentary Democracy? Does It Make a Difference?" in Juan J. Linz and Arturo Valenzuela, eds., *The Failure of Presidential Democracy: Comparative Perspectives* (Baltimore: Johns Hopkins University Press, 1994), pp. 3–87.

58. Casper, "Caesarism," p. 18.

59. I am one of the plaintiffs to that lawsuit against the surveillance program, which was filed by the American Civil Liberties Union.

60. See the introductory overview and chapter 3, "Civil Liberties," in Freedom House, *Today's American: How Free* (New York: Freedom House, forthcoming).

61. Ibid., overview, p. 7 of manuscript.

62. Nivola and Galston, "Toward Depolarization," pp. 256, 281–82.

63. Michael McDonald, "United States Election Project: Presidential Turnout Rates for Voting-Age Population (VAP) and Eligible Population (VEP)," http://elections.gmu.edu/turnout_rates_graph.htm. Even in the extremely closely fought and consequential 2004 presidential election, with massive turnout efforts by both parties, only 59 percent of eligible Americans voted—about the same as in the 1956 election, when Eisenhower coasted to an easy reelection.

64. The eligible population excludes the nearly 7 million Americans who are in prison, on probation, or convicted felons, as well as some 13 million adult noncitizens. Michael McDonald, "United States Election Project: 2006 Voting-Age and Voting-Eligible Population Estimates," http://elections.gmu.edu/Voter_Turnout_2006.htm.

65. Rafael López Pintor, Maria Gratschew, and Kate Sullivan, "Voter Turnout Rates from a Comparative Perspective," in International IDEA, *Voter Turnout Since 1945: A Global Report* (Stockholm: International IDEA, 2002), p. 84. The rankings of 169 political systems includes a

number of authoritarian regimes, but more than 100 democracies or near democracies rank ahead of the United States (which is ranked 138), and only about ten of the remaining 31 states have had mainly democratic elections during the period assessed.

66. This figure (34 percent) derives from a study of voter turnout between 1993 and 2000 in fifty-seven cities with populations between 25,000 and 1 million. U.S. Election Assistance Commission, "National Voter Turnout in Federal Elections," http://www.eac.gov/election_resources/htmlto5.htm.

67. In fact, the highest turnout for statewide midterm primaries in the last fifty years was only 33.5 percent, in 1966. Curtis Gans, "2006 Primary Turnout a Record Low," *American University News*, October 6, 2006.

68. Norman J. Ornstein, "Vote—Or Else," *New York Times*, August 10, 2006.

69. Ibid.; and Nivola and Galston, "Toward Depolarization," p. 271.

70. Nivola and Galston, "Toward Depolarization," pp. 252, 272.

71. This is the recommendation of a panel of political scientists drawn together by the American Political Science Association in 2002 to examine civic education and engagement. Stephen Macedo et al., *Democracy at Risk: How Political Choices Undermine Citizen Participation, and What We Can Do About It* (Washington, D.C.: Brookings Institution, 2005), p. 60.

72. Ibid., p. 66.

73. Michael Falcone, "Belmont Journal: What If They Had Elections and No One Ran?" *New York Times*, September 21, 2003.

74. Macedo et al., *Democracy at Risk*, p. 28.

75. Ibid., p. 30.

76. Robert D. Putnam, *Bowling Alone: The Collapse and Revival of American Community* (New York: Simon and Schuster, 2000). The transition from mass-membership organizations with more active citizen participation to professionally managed organizations with less engaged citizens is traced in Theda Skocpol, *Diminished Democracy: From Membership to Management in American Civic Life* (Norman: University of Oklahoma Press, 2003).

77. Macedo et al., *Democracy at Risk*, p. 120.

78. Ibid., p. 152.

79. James S. Fishkin, "Deliberative Polling®: Toward a Better-Informed Democracy," The Center for Deliberative Democracy, http://cdd.stanford.edu/polls/docs/summary/.

80. Nivola and Galston, "Toward Depolarization," p. 236.

81. This is indicated by the distribution of the congressional district vote for the two parties being within the range of 45 to 55 percent. See Thomas E. Mann, "Polarizing the House of Representatives: How Much Does Gerrymandering Matter?" in Pietro S. Nivola and David W. Brady, eds., *Red and Blue Nation? Characteristics and Causes of America's Polarized Politics* (Stanford, Calif.: Hoover Institution, and Washington, DC: Brookings Institution, 2006), p. 268.

82. Ibid., p. 269, figure 6.1.

83. Although the sizeable Republican losses in 2006 (thirty-one seats in all) suggests the possibility of renewed competitiveness within the current system, Democratic gains would likely have been larger in the absence of post-2000 census gerrymandering, and Democrats did best in 2006 in states like New York, Indiana, and Arizona where redistricting in 2002 was done on a bipartisan or nonpartisan basis. J. Gerald Hebert, "Gerrymandering Is Alive and Well: Why We Need Redistricting Reform," Campaign Legal Center Blog, December 20, 2006, http://www.clcblog.org/blog_item-99.html.

84. Mann, "Polarizing the House of Representatives," pp. 275–76.

85. Morris P. Fiorina and Matthew S. Levendusky, "Disconnected: The Political Class versus the People," in Nivola and Brady, eds., *Red and Blue Nation?*, pp. 49–71.

86. In completely open primary elections, any voter can opt to vote in any party's primary election. This permits Democrats to vote in the Republican rather than Democratic primary, and vice versa, thereby vitiating the entire idea of a party system. For this reason, I do not favor the completely open primary. Interestingly, Nivola and Galston report (p. 269) that

fully open primaries do not do as good a job as partially open primaries in electing House members who "reflect their district's median voter preferences."

87. Nivola and Galston, "Toward Depolarization," p. 263.

88. Lisa Vorderbrueggen, "Berkeley Analysis Backs Redistricting Changes," *Mercury News* (San Jose), February 24, 2007.

89. Nivola and Galston, "Toward Depolarization," p. 254.

90. Ibid., p. 274.

91. Ibid., pp. 258–59 of manuscript. Nivola and Galston propose a single, nonrenewable eighteen-year term for Supreme Court justices. Something in that range (or even twenty or twenty-five years) would diminish, at least somewhat, the stakes.

92. Stephen Flynn, *The Edge of Disaster* (New York: Random House, 2007), p. 112.

93. See *The 9/11 Commission Report: Final Report of the National Commission on Terrorist Attacks Upon the United States* (New York: W.W. Norton, 2004); and *The Iraq Study Group Report: The Way Forward—A New Approach* (New York: Vintage Books, 2006).

94. Benjamin Reilly, "Electoral Systems for Divided Societies," *Journal of Democracy* 13 (April 2002): 156–170; and Reilly, *Democracy in Divided Societies: Electoral Engineering for Conflict Management* (Cambridge, U.K.: Cambridge University Press, 2001).

95. In 2006, voters in Oakland, California; Minneapolis; Takoma Park, Maryland; and Pierce County, Washington, chose to adopt AV for some local elections beginning in 2008 and 2009.

96. Thirty-Thousand.org, "How Did the Size of the House Become Constrained at 435 Representatives?" http://www.thirty-thousand.org/pages/Why_435.htm. See also the accompanying Table B, http://www.thirty-thousand.org/documents/Apportionment_USCB_table_B.pdf.

ACKNOWLEDGMENTS

This book distills knowledge and insights I have gained in three decades of studying comparative democratic development. For its completion, I owe many more debts of gratitude than I can possibly acknowledge here. I would like to begin by expressing my appreciation to the institutions that have made my work on democracy possible. For twenty-two years, the Hoover Institution has been my professional and intellectual home and has given me the freedom and support to research democracy on a global basis. I express my deep gratitude to the Hoover Institution and its director for most of this period, John Raisian, for this extraordinary opportunity. Over the past five years, I have also drawn support and intellectual stimulation on these issues from Stanford's new Center on Democracy, Development, and the Rule of Law (CDDRL), where I coordinate the program on democracy. For this enriching experience, I thank the current and former directors of the center, Professors Michael McFaul and Stephen Krasner, and the Hewlett Foundation, whose generous support has made it possible for us to launch the center. I would also like to thank Coit D. ("Chip") Blacker, director of Stanford's Freeman Spogli Institute for International Studies (of which CDDRL is a part), and Stanford University provost John Etchemendy for the support they have given to the center and to my own work.

Above all, I am indebted to the National Endowment for Democracy (NED) for helping me to bridge the worlds of democratic theory and practice, and for introducing me to so many of the inspiring people and organizations struggling for democracy and liberty throughout the globe. My nearly twenty years of association with NED have given me an appreciation for the human dimensions of democratic change and for the roles of strategy, organization, innovation, and courage in the face of daunting risk. Through my participation in NED's international conferences, in editing its *Journal of Democracy,* and in codirecting for the past fifteen years its International Forum for Democratic Studies, I have come to know many of the activists who embody the spirit of democracy and are working, often against great odds, to build free societies. In particular, I am profoundly indebted to NED president Carl Gershman and to Vice President Marc F. Plattner, who has also been my coeditor of the *Journal of Democracy,* my codirector of the forum, and my most important intellectual partner in democratic studies. I would also like to thank the senior staff of the NED who have given so generously to me of their time and insights, especially Sally Blair, Nadia Diuk, Barbara Haig, Miriam Kornblith, Laith Kubba, David Lowe, Dave Peterson, and Abdulwahab Alkebsi (now with the Center for International Private Enterprise), as well as the presidents of three of the core institutes within the NED family, Kenneth Wollack of the National Democratic Institute, Lorne Craner of the International Republican Institute, and John Sullivan of the Center for International Private Enterprise. I am also deeply indebted—as is obvious to any reader of this book—to Freedom House for its work to assess the state of freedom around the world, and I thank in particular its vice president for research, Arch Puddington.

Several colleagues generously shared with me data and unpublished materials from their projects studying public opinion toward democracy. I would particularly like to thank Michael Bratton and Carolyn Logan of the Afrobarometer, Marta Lagos of the Latinobarometer, Mark Tessler and Amaney Jamal of the Arab Barometer, and my many associates in the Asian Barometer, especially Yun-han Chu, Doh Chull Shin, Andrew Nathan, and Robert Albritton. I would also like to thank the many people who generously allowed me to interview them for this book, often for several hours. Several of them have preferred to remain off the record because of their vulnerable situations at home, but I would particularly like to thank Alejandro Toledo, Saad Eddin Ibrahim, and Akbar Ganji.

At Stanford, I was fortunate to have a number of highly talented and motivated students helping me with my research. I am pleased to acknowledge here and thank for their outstanding research assistance the following Stanford undergraduates: Kevin Hsu (introduction and chapter 1), Robert Fuentes (chapter 8), Sebastian Burduja (chapter 9), Matthew Platkin and Chan-hong Yiu (chapter 10), Michael Wilkerson (chapters 11 and 14), and Omar Shakir (chapter 12). And I express my high regard and deep appreciation for the superb research support of two brilliant Stanford law students, Alexander Benard (chapters 5 and 6) and Ben Joseloff (chapter 15). I also thank the following students who have helped me research democratic efforts to utilize and authoritarian efforts to suppress what I call in this book "liberation technology": Galen Panger, Tucker Herbert, Ryan Delaney, Daniel Holleb, Sampath Jinadasa, and Aaron Qayumi. I owe a special debt of thanks to Galen Panger as well as Mark Lieber, who made me aware of the exceptional power and political potential of Internet-based communication technologies at a time when I was only dimly aware of YouTube and had never heard of Facebook.

Two of my most valued intellectual mentors, Alex Inkeles and Juan J. Linz, read most of the manuscript and offered numerous helpful comments and suggestions. I also thank for their reading and commentary on individual chapters and/or their more general encouragement and stimulation of this book project Abdulwahab Alkebsi, Edward Aspinall, Jamal Benomar, Sumit Ganguly, Carl Gershman, Bruce Gilley, Emmanuel Gyimah-Boadi, Jonathan Hartlyn, Charles Kenney, Miriam Kornblith, Nicholai Lidow, Cynthia McClintock, Andrew Mwenda, Marc F. Plattner, Rob Raznick, Henry Rowen, Emad El-Din Shahin, John Sullivan, and a number of my Stanford colleagues at CDDRL, particularly Michael McFaul, Gerhard Casper, Laura Cosovanu, Thomas Heller, Erik Jensen, Terry Karl, Stephen Krasner, Helen Stacey, and Kathryn Stoner-Weiss. Thanks also go to my sister, Linda Raznick—a gifted editor herself—for her perceptive and supportive feedback on many issues of substance and design. As with my previous book, *Squandered Victory*, my assistant at the Hoover Institution, Alice Carter, once again held together my professional life while I wrote this book and quickly helped me obtain information and publications—always with efficiency and good cheer. I have been extremely fortunate to have her intelligent and devoted assistance throughout this project.

I am very grateful to my editor at Times Books, Robin Dennis, for her creative and skillful efforts to refine, reorganize, and pare back an overly long manuscript, and again to Paul Golob, editorial director of Times Books, for his generous support and immensely wise counsel, particularly with regard to the title, structure, and overall concept of the book. I thank them both as well for their patience and graciousness during periods when teaching and other programmatic and personal obligations delayed the delivery of chapters. And I thank my agent, Scott Mendel, who first suggested that I turn my paper "Universal Democracy?" (published in *Policy Review* in June 2003) into a book. This book would have been completed some two or three years earlier if I had not received a call that autumn asking me to go to Iraq to advise on the political transition under American occupation, which ultimately drew me into the momentous debate over that debacle. Since the global democratic story is now rather different and less immediately promising than it was in 2003, I believe the delay has resulted in a better and more accurate account of global democratic prospects.

Finally, I note with sadness the recent passing of two individuals who would have wanted to read and help me celebrate this work. Seymour Martin Lipset—my teacher, friend, coauthor, and the most enduring intellectual influence on my work—passed away on December 31, 2006, after a long illness. My views about the transformative impact on democracy of socioeconomic development and the role of a moderate, tolerant, and pluralistic culture in making stable democracy possible owe more to him than any other single individual. As I was finishing this book in early August, my dear friend Beverly Canali died after a brief and sudden illness. During thirty-seven years of a very special friendship, Bev had been one of my strongest sources of personal support and one of my most enthusiastic readers. An ardent democrat and devoted citizen, she shared my passionate interest in American politics and my acute concern over its many signs of deterioration. I particularly regret that she was not able to read the final chapter of this book, which expresses not only the frustration but also the hope and ultimately the confidence we have shared in American democracy.

INDEX

Entries in *italics* refer to charts and tables.

ABOUT THE AUTHOR

LARRY DIAMOND is a senior fellow at the Hoover Institution at Stanford University. At Stanford, he serves as a professor by courtesy of political science and sociology and coordinates the democracy program of the new Center on Democracy, Development, and the Rule of Law. He is also codirector of the International Forum for Democratic Studies of the National Endowment for Democracy.

Diamond has lectured, taught, and conducted research in some twenty-five countries over the past thirty years. He has served as a consultant to the U.S. Agency for International Development (USAID). From January to April 2004, he was a senior adviser to the Coalition Provisional Authority in Baghdad.

Diamond is the author of four books, most recently *Squandered Victory: The American Occupation and the Bungled Effort to Bring Democracy to Iraq*. Among his two dozen edited books is the series *Democracy in Developing Countries,* with Juan Linz and Seymour Martin Lipset. He is the founding coeditor of the widely respected *Journal of Democracy.*

He lives in Stanford, California.